Delivering a Low-Carbon Electricity System

Meeting targets aimed at tackling the climate change challenge requires moving towards a low-carbon economy. These targets can only be met with major reductions in carbon emissions from the electricity sector.

Written by a team of leading academics and industry experts, *Delivering a Low-Carbon Electricity System* analyses the social, technological, economic and political issues that affect the attempt to create a low-carbon electricity sector and assesses the main instruments for achieving this aim. The book begins by looking at how low-carbon generation technologies might be added in sufficient quantity to the electricity system. Next, it examines how networks and the demand side can help to decarbonise the sector. It then highlights the role of innovation and discusses instruments for promoting technological progress. Finally, given the economic framework and technological possibilities, it presents a number of general and specific policy instruments and options for the future.

MICHAEL GRUBB is Chief Economist at the UK Carbon Trust and Senior Research Associate in the Faculty of Economics and the ESRC Electricity Policy Research Group (EPRG), University of Cambridge. He is also Visiting Professor of Climate Change and Energy Policy at Imperial College London.

TOORAJ JAMASB is Senior Research Associate in the Faculty of Economics and at the ESRC Electricity Policy Research Group (EPRG) at the University of Cambridge.

MICHAEL G. POLLITT is Reader in Business Economics at the Judge Business School and Assistant Director of the ESRC Electricity Policy Research Group (EPRG), University of Cambridge. He is also Fellow and Director of Studies in Economics and Management at Sidney Sussex College, Cambridge.

University of Cambridge
Department of Applied Economics
Occasional Papers 68
Delivering a Low-carbon Electricity System

Delivering a Low-Carbon Electricity System

Technologies, Economics and Policy

Michael Grubb

Tooraj Jamasb

Michael G. Pollitt

CAMBRIDGE
UNIVERSITY PRESS

CAMBRIDGE UNIVERSITY PRESS
Cambridge, New York, Melbourne, Madrid, Cape Town, Singapore,
São Paulo, Delhi

Cambridge University Press
The Edinburgh Building, Cambridge CB2 8RU, UK

Published in the United States of America by Cambridge University Press,
New York

www.cambridge.org
Information on this title: www.cambridge.org/9780521888844

First published 2008

Printed in the United Kingdom at the University Press, Cambridge

A catalogue record for this publication is available from the British Library

Library of Congress Cataloguing in Publication Data
Grubb, Michael.
Delivering a low carbon electricity system : technologies, economics,
and policy / Michael Grubb, Tooraj Jamasb, Michael G. Pollitt.
    p.   cm.
Includes bibliographical references and index.
ISBN 978-0-521-88884-4 (hardback)
1. Electric power production–Environmental aspects.   2. Air–Pollution–
Prevention.   3. Carbon dioxide mitigation.   4. Atmospheric
carbon dioxide–Environmental aspects.   5. Energy conservation.
6. Energy policy.   7. Electric utilities.   I. Jamasb, Tooraj.
II. Pollitt, Michael G.   III. Title.
TD195.E4G79   2008
333.793$'$2–dc22   2008013456

ISBN 978-0-521-88884-4 hardback

Contents

Contents   vii

Figures

Tables

Contributors

JONATHAN P. ATKINS is Senior Lecturer in Economics at the Business School, University of Hull.

GRAHAM AULT is Senior Lecturer in Electronic and Electrical Engineering in the Institute for Energy and Environment at Strathclyde University.

KESHAB BHATTARAI is Lecturer in Economics at the Business School, University of Hull.

JANUSZ BIALEK is Bert Whittington Chair of Electrical Engineering at the University of Edinburgh.

MARK BILTON is Doctoral Researcher at the Imperial Centre for Energy Policy and Technology, Imperial College London.

GRAEME BURT is Reader in Electrical Power Engineering in the Institute of Energy and Environment at Strathclyde University.

JIM CUST is Research Assistant in the Faculty of Economics at the University of Cambridge.

HANNAH DEVINE-WRIGHT is Research Associate in the School of Environment and Development at the University of Manchester.

PATRICK DEVINE-WRIGHT is Senior Lecturer in the Manchester Architecture Research Centre in the School of Environment and Development, University of Manchester.

IAN ELDERS is Senior Research Fellow in Electronic and Electrical Engineering in the Institute for Energy and Environment at Strathclyde University.

JON GIBBINS is Senior Lecturer in the Energy Technology for Sustainable Development Group, Mechanical Engineering Department, Imperial

College London, and Principal Investigator for the UK Carbon Capture and Storage Consortium.

RICHARD GREEN is Professor of Energy Economics and Director of the Institute for Energy Research and Policy, University of Birmingham.

MICHAEL GRUBB is Chief Economist at the UK Carbon Trust, Senior Research Associate at the Faculty of Economics, Cambridge University, and Visiting Professor (formerly Professor of Climate Change and Energy Policy) at Imperial College London.

NADINE HAJ-HASAN is Strategy Manager at the Carbon Trust.

SAM HOLLOWAY is Senior Geologist in the Sustainable and Renewable Energy Group at the British Geological Survey.

CHRIS HOPE is Reader in Modelling Policy at the Judge Business School at the University of Cambridge and was Advisor on the PAGE model to the Stern Review on the Economics of Climate Change.

TOORAJ JAMASB is Senior Research Associate in the Faculty of Economics and at the ESRC Electricity Policy Research Group at the University of Cambridge.

KIM KEATS-MARTINEZ is Associate Director of International Infrastructure Analysis at IPA Energy + Water Consulting.

DANIEL KIRSCHEN is Professor and Head of the Electrical Energy and Power Systems Research Group at the University of Manchester.

JONATHAN KÖHLER is Senior Research Associate at the Tyndall Centre and 4CMR (Cambridge Centre for Climate Change Mitigation Research) Department of Land Economy, University of Cambridge.

MATTHEW LEACH is Professor of Energy & Environmental Systems in the Centre for Environmental Strategy at the University of Surrey.

ALEXANDRA MARATOU is Research Assistant in the Faculty of Economics at the University of Cambridge.

JIM MCDONALD is Professor and Head of Department of Electronic and Electrical Engineering in the Institute of Energy and Environment at Strathclyde University.

KARSTEN NEUHOFF is Senior Research Associate at the Faculty of Economics, University of Cambridge.

DAVID NEWBERY is Professor of Applied Economics in the Faculty of Economics and Research Director of the ESRC Electricity Policy Research Group at the University of Cambridge.

WILLIAM J. NUTTALL is University Senior Lecturer in Technology Policy, a shared post of the Judge Business School and Cambridge University Engineering Department.

MICHAEL G. POLLITT is Reader in Business Economics at the Judge Business School, University of Cambridge and Fellow and Director of Studies in Economics and Management at Sidney Sussex College, Cambridge. He is also Assistant Director of the ESRC Electricity Policy Research Group.

CHARLOTTE RAMSAY is Research Associate in the Control and Power Group, Department of Electrical and Electronic Engineering, Imperial College London.

DAVID M. REINER is Lecturer in Technology Policy and Course Director of the MPhil in Technology Policy at Judge Business School, University of Cambridge.

FABIEN A. ROQUES is an economist in the Economic Analysis Division of the International Energy Agency.

GRAHAM SINDEN holds a public position with the Department for Business, Enterprise and Regulatory Reform's Renewables Advisory Board, and is Technical Manager at the UK Carbon Trust.

STEVEN SORRELL is Senior Fellow in the Sussex Energy Group at SPRU, University of Sussex.

STEPHEN TROTTER is Lecturer in Economics at the University of Hull.

RYAN TUMILTY is Research Assistant in Electronic and Electrical Engineering in the Institute for Energy and Environment at Strathclyde University.

PAUL TWOMEY is Jean Monnet Fellow at the Florence School of Regulation, European University Institute, Florence.

JAMES WILDE is Director of Insights at the Carbon Trust.

MILTON YAGO is Senior Lecturer in Economics and International Business at Leeds Metropolitan University.

Foreword

With its radical regulatory changes starting in the late 1980s, in many eyes the UK electricity system became a 'laboratory' for the world in new ways of running a power system. One consequence of being at the forefront of electricity liberalisation is that the UK needs to find innovative ways of meeting new challenges in ways that are consistent with its competitive electricity and gas markets. Twenty years after its initial market reforms, the UK system is facing a challenge which again may make it a focus of global attention: to decarbonise a largely fossil-fuel-based power system without compromising the sector's operational integrity and long-term sustainability, while improving security of supply and economic competitiveness.

At the beginning of this decade, the Engineering and Physics Research Council (EPSRC) formulated the Supergen research programme to prepare the analytic base for addressing this challenge. In addition to technology-specific research, Supergen FutureNet was established to investigate the system-wide issues associated with a low-carbon power system. The resulting programme emerged as a consortium of seven university groups around the UK, combining engineering, economic and social research expertise.

An important part of the consortium's work was to study how the transition to a new electricity system may come about. The work on 'System Evolution and Incentives', coordinated by the team at the University of Cambridge, drew on expertise across the consortium, and in particular the work on scenarios, and was linked to other Supergen consortia. This strand of research sought to combine the engineering insights into a view of the economic and policy implications of moving towards a low-carbon electricity system. In 2006, we published the first product of this work, *Future Electricity Technologies and Systems* (also from Cambridge University Press), assessing from a systems and economic perspective the technology options that can shape the future of the electricity sector towards 2050.

This second book represents the culmination of the research effort, by integrating the associated economic and social underpinnings, and assessing the policy dimensions of a low-carbon power system.

The first book concluded that there are many possible technological combinations that could deliver a low-carbon electricity system by mid-century. This book finds that important steps on the path can be made by 2020 at modest costs, and lays out the policy and societal choices that will have to be made to get us on such a path – and to sustain it. The first book found that, after a century of fossil-fuel-based power system development, a low-carbon system is technically possible: this book shows how it can be done.

Professor Sir John O'Reilly FREng
Vice-Chancellor, Cranfield University
Formerly Chief Executive, EPSRC

Professor Jim Skea OBE
Research Director
UK Energy Research Centre

Professor Tim Green
Professor of Electrical Power Engineering
Department of Electrical and Electronic Engineering
Imperial College London

Acknowledgements

The editors are very grateful to a large number of individuals without whom this book would not have been possible. We acknowledge the help and support of the UK Research Councils, the UK Carbon Trust and the Supergen community and especially the FutureNet consortium of universities researching Future Network Technologies for a sustainable energy policy for the UK. Together they have facilitated the collaboration of a wide range of individuals coming from different disciplines to communicate their expertise and views on the future of the electricity system and its place in meeting carbon emissions reduction targets.

We particularly wish to thank Shimon Awerbuch, Mark Barrett, Erik Britton, Paul Ekins, Tim Foxon, Rob Gross, Jason Hayman, Ben Jones, Alex Kemp, Gordon McKerron and Nils Røkke who, as external referees, have ensured the quality of the substance of this book. A special mention must be made of Jim Cust and Misato Sato, Research Assistants at the Cambridge Faculty of Economics and, above all, Alexandra Maratou and and Aoife Brophy, who successfully managed the entire process from inception to completion.

We are also grateful to David Newbery, Research Director of ESRC Electricity Policy Research Group, for his always useful insights and assistance throughout; Sean Holly, Research Director of the Faculty, as well as Chris Harrison and Philip Good at Cambridge University Press, for their support and work in preparing the book for publication. And last but not least we extend our sincere thanks to all the authors.

MICHAEL GRUBB
TOORAJ JAMASB
MICHAEL G. POLLITT

1 A low-carbon electricity sector for the UK: issues and options

Michael Grubb, Tooraj Jamasb and Michael G. Pollitt

1.1 Background

Tackling climate change will require reducing the rate of carbon dioxide (CO_2) emissions, ultimately down to levels that can stabilise its atmospheric concentration. This requires greatly reducing the carbon intensity of the economy. In most economies, most CO_2 emissions come from the production and use of energy, and the electricity sector accounts for a substantial portion of this (although the actual share of emissions varies across countries and depends on the extent of fossil-fuel-based generation in each country).

According to estimates by the International Energy Agency (IEA), taking government policies and measures enacted or adopted by mid-2006 into account, global primary energy demand is projected to increase by 53% from 11,204 to 17,095 Mtoe (million tonnes oil equivalent) between 2004 and 2030. Power generation accounts for 47% of the increase in global energy over this period, with its share of primary energy demand increasing from 37% in 2004 to 41% in 2030. World electricity demand is projected to grow at 2.6% per year on average, and to double by 2030; with developing countries – especially China and India – seeing the fastest growth in demand. As a result, the share of electricity in total final consumption grows from 16% in 2004 to 21% in 2030 (IEA, 2006, pp. 65–71).

Global energy-related CO_2 emissions will increase slightly faster than primary energy use, as the fuel mix becomes more carbon-intensive. The power sector contributes around half of the projected increase in emissions from 2004 to 2030 (IEA, 2006, p. 65). World CO_2 emissions from power plants are projected to increase by about two-thirds over the same period, at a rate of 2% per year. Power generation is currently responsible for 41% of global energy-related CO_2 emissions. This share is projected to rise to 44% in 2030, mainly due to the growing share of electricity in energy consumption and the strong reliance on coal in countries such as China, India and the USA (IEA, 2006, p. 144). At the

1

Table 1.1. *Energy- and electricity-related CO_2 emissions*

		1990	2004	2015	2030
Reference scenario (RS)	Total energy-related CO_2 emissions (Mt)	20,463	26,079	33,333	40,420
	of which related to power generation and heating plants	6,955	10,587	14,209	17,980
	Final consumption of electricity (Mtoe)	826	1,236	1,765	2,416
Alternative scenario (AS)*	Total energy-related CO_2 emissions (Mt)	20,463	26,079	31,586 (−5.24)	34,080 (−15.69)
	of which related to power generation and heating plants	6,955	10,587	13,203 (−7.08)	13,749 (−23.53)
	Final consumption of electricity (Mtoe)	826	1,236	1,682 (−4.7)	2,121 (−12.21)

* Figures in parentheses show percentage change AS vs. RS.
Source: Based on estimates by IEA (2006)

same time, currently 57% of greenhouse gas (GHG) emissions come from the combustion of fossil fuels in the power, transport, buildings and industry sectors, while agriculture and changes in land use (particularly deforestation, in a few major developing countries) produce 41% of emissions (Stern, 2007, p. 170).

A comparison between CO_2 emissions projections up to 2030 for two alternative scenarios considered by the IEA (2006) underlines the important role of the electricity sector in reducing global CO_2 emissions. Table 1.1 contrasts the projections for these scenarios. The *Reference* scenario takes into account those government policies and measures that were enacted or adopted by mid-2006. The *Alternative Policy* scenario analyses how the global energy market could evolve if countries were to adopt all of the policies related to energy security and energy-related emissions that they are currently considering. Comparing the two scenarios, Table 1.1 shows that power generation contributes almost two-thirds of avoided emissions globally (IEA, 2006, p. 190). Also, emissions related to power generation and heating plants decrease by a higher proportion than total energy-related emissions. In addition, emissions related to power generation and heating plants are cut by a higher fraction than total final consumption of electricity, indicating that policies can achieve a cleaner fuel mix in power generation as well as a more efficient use of electricity.

In late 2006, the publication of the influential report, *The Stern Review on the Economics of Climate Change*, made a strong case that the potential global social and economic consequences of climate change can be very significant. The report emphasised that the benefits of acting to mitigate CO_2 emissions early make economic sense and outweigh the potential costs of inaction. The report estimates the total costs of inaction towards climate change could ultimately result in impacts equivalent to at least 5% of global gross domestic product (GDP) each year, now and forever (on a 'balanced growth equivalent' basis). The costs could rise to 20% of GDP or higher if a wider range of risks and impacts are considered. In contrast, the costs of deep emissions reductions, if carried out globally and efficiently, could be limited to around 1% of global GDP each year. Whilst acknowledging many uncertainties in such quantifications, the Stern Review argued that some environmental resources cannot be substituted and that there might be immense risks inherent in exceeding certain thresholds, reinforcing the need to act to combat climate change (Stern, 2007).

Meeting the challenges of climate change requires a set of complex and multifaceted efforts across the economy and its main sectors. The specifics of the approach and measures adopted can be context-dependent and should take the specific circumstances of each economy and its main sectors into consideration. As noted, achieving the goal of a low-carbon economy and energy sector, globally and in most countries, is highly dependent on emissions reductions in the electricity sector. This book examines how the challenge can be addressed in the UK electricity sector.

1.2   The UK electricity sector and climate change

The UK accounts for only 2% of total global carbon emissions. However, the UK is one of the best-placed economies to demonstrate that ambitious climate change policy targets are achievable. Delivering a low-carbon electricity system is crucial for the UK in order to deliver a low-carbon economy and energy sector. Emissions from the UK electricity industry declined during the 1990s, partly as a result of the 'dash for gas', during which gas-fired electricity generation replaced coal-fired generation in the aftermath of the liberalisation of the sector. But the decline has halted in the past few years, and in 2005 power generation still accounted for almost one-third (31%) of total CO_2 emissions (DEFRA, 2007), whilst supplying approximately 17.5% of the UK's final energy consumption in 2005 (DTI, 2006c). Electricity demand, and its share of total energy consumption, continues to increase.

Climate change became part of the UK's policy debate in the 1980s. Since then the Government has committed to binding international agreements for reductions in GHG emissions as well as to voluntary national targets, with implications for the electricity sector (Table 1.2). The Labour Government pledged to achieve a 20% reduction in carbon emissions by 2010 and a 60% reduction by 2050. As part of the efforts to achieve its climate change goals, the target share of electricity generation from renewable energy sources is to increase to 20% by 2020.

In 2006/2007, the publication of several major official documents underlined the importance and challenges ahead of the UK energy sector. At the highest level, the overriding energy issues facing the UK are climate change and energy security. The *Energy Review*, published in 2006, highlighted the concerns about security of energy supplies in the light of the emerging increased energy dependence of the UK (DTI, 2006a). The report also reiterated the Government's commitment to the stated climate change targets through renewables and energy efficiency, while concluding that nuclear power could contribute towards achieving the energy policy goals.[1] This contrasted with a report by the Sustainable Development Commission (SDC) that emphasised the role of renewable energy and energy efficiency in reducing carbon emissions, and advised against relying on nuclear power (SDC, 2006).

The Stern Review argued that, even for the UK, the cost of adopting climate change measures now is far smaller than the potential economic costs of climate change (Stern, 2007). The review states that the potential regional impacts of climate change for the UK will include: (i) infrastructure damage from flooding and storms, (ii) water availability constraints and more regular occurrence of serious drought, (iii) a heatwave-related increase in mortality (in contrast with the reduced cold-related mortality rates and energy demand for heating attributed to milder winters), and (iv) an initial increase in agricultural productivity due to longer growing seasons and the carbon fertilisation effect, although this depends on adequate water and requires some changes to crops and sowing times (Stern, 2007, p. 128).

In November 2007, the Government's *Climate Change Bill* defined a framework for the UK to move towards a low-carbon economy. The Bill specifies legally binding CO_2 emissions targets of at least 26% by 2020 and 60% by 2050. The proposed targets will be achieved through a set of 5-year 'carbon budgets', specified at least 15 years in advance, with the

---

[1] The newly formed Department for Business, Enterprise and Regulatory Reform assumed the energy responsibilities of the former UK Department of Trade and Industry from the end of June 2007.

Table 1.2. *The UK's climate goals*

Year agreed	Gases covered	Target	Comments	Energy-sector-related proposals/commitments
1992 Framework Convention on Climate Change, Rio	CO_2 only	2000 emission no greater than 1990 emissions: voluntary agreement	Achieved very largely via electricity privatisation introduced by Conservative Government	• Commitment to promoting and cooperating in the development, application and diffusion, including transfer, of technologies, practices and processes that control, reduce or prevent anthropogenic emissions of greenhouse gases not controlled by the Montreal Protocol in all relevant sectors, including the energy sector
1997 Labour Manifesto	CO_2 only	2010 emissions 20% less than 1990 emissions	Language of commitment varies: December 2004 Government announced it was very unlikely to meet this target	• Emphasis on energy conservation – particularly by the promotion of home energy efficiency schemes • Commitment to an energy policy designed to promote cleaner, more efficient energy use and production, including a new and strong drive to develop renewable energy sources such as solar and wind energy, and combined heat and power • No economic case for the building of any new nuclear power stations
1997 Kyoto Protocol, agreed in EU 1998	Basket of six main greenhouse gases*	2008–2012 emissions 12.5% below 1990 emissions: mandatory under EU law	UK's share under the EU burden sharing agreement for the Kyoto Protocol	Each Party included in Annex I, committed to implementing and/or further elaborating policies such as: • Enhancement of energy efficiency in relevant sectors of the national economy • Research on, and promotion, development and increased use of, new and renewable forms of energy, of CO_2 sequestration technologies and of advanced and innovative environmentally sound technologies

Table 1.2. (cont.)

Year agreed	Gases covered	Target	Comments	Energy-sector-related proposals/commitments
2003 UK Energy White Paper	CO_2 only	~2050 emissions 60% less than in 1990 'with real progress by 2020': not mandatory	Commitment to be 'on a path towards' the target. Language of commitment varies from unilateral goal to conditional on other countries doing likewise	• Priority put into strengthening the contribution of energy efficiency and renewable energy sources • Aspiration to double renewables' share of electricity from 2010 target of 10% to 20% by 2020 • Commitment to review progress on Renewable Obligation in 2005/2006 and elaborate a strategy for the decade to 2020 • Increase in funding for renewables capital grants by £60 million within the period 2002/2003 and 2005/2006 • No specific proposals for building new nuclear, though it is mentioned explicitly that the possibility that it might be necessary at some point in the future is not ruled out • Commitment to competitive energy markets and use of market-based instruments to deliver wider energy policy goals • National Energy Research Centre to be established by the Research Councils
2006 UK Energy Review	• CO_2 directly • Basket of six main greenhouse gases* indirectly	Restatement of commitment to 60% reduction in carbon emissions by 2050 'with real progress by 2020'. EU ETS to remain central element of UK's emissions reductions		• Commitment to maintaining Obligation levels above the level of ROC-eligible renewable generation, to a maximum level of 20% of generation from renewable sources • Commitment to maintaining a household obligation on suppliers in some form until at least 2020. Consideration of moving in 2011 (once the third phase of the Energy Efficiency

	policy framework Strengthening the EU ETS and consideration of the inclusion of additional sectors and gases		Commitment expires) to a supplier obligation based on a tradable target set in terms of reducing absolute energy demand or carbon emissions from the household sector • Commitment to bringing forward proposals to improve the planning process for large-scale electricity generation • Commitment to clarifying position on new nuclear build
2007–08 Climate Change Bill	CO_2 only	Proposed legally binding targets for a 60% by 2050 and at least 26% by 2020 reduction in CO_2 emissions	The Bill introduces a clear, credible, long-term framework for the UK to achieve its goals of reducing CO_2 emissions	Details of further policies to ensure that the UK reduces its emissions and meets the long-term targets in the Bill are set out in the 2007 Energy White Paper (DTI, 2007). However, it is mentioned that: • Government's long-term aim is to build on the EU ETS by extending the application of the scheme to cover new sectors and gases • It is possible that in coming years Government may consider implementing upstream schemes to supplement the EU ETS, implementing schemes for emissions on downstream energy use and schemes to support cleaner technologies and fuels • Government is also likely to need to make improvements to existing schemes

* CO_2, CH_4, N_2O, HFCs, PFCs and SF_6
Source: Updated based on Pearce (2006)

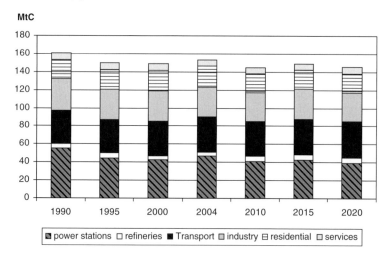

Figure 1.1. UK CO_2 emissions by source
Source: HM Government (2006) *Climate Change: The UK Programme 2006*

possibility of carbon borrowing across the periods (Climate Change Bill, 2007; Climate Change Bill, 2007; Climate Change Bill, 2008), and would establish an independent Committee to recommend future targets.

Figure 1.1 illustrates past CO_2 emissions and projections of future 'central' average emissions (average of projections produced by two central fossil fuel price scenarios: one somewhat favouring gas and the other somewhat favouring coal generation) by source. Emissions fall towards 2010, due to the assumption that the oil price will fall and lead to lower gas prices and increased use of gas in power generation, which more than offsets increased energy use driven by lower prices (because gas-fired generation is less CO_2-intensive than coal-fired generation). Moreover, the Climate Change Programme will also reduce CO_2 emissions. Between 2010 and 2015, emissions are projected to rise because of the expected closure of nuclear generation plants and growing energy use associated with economic growth outweighing the impact of existing measures. After 2015, emissions may fall again due to the expected closure of coal-fired stations and replacement by gas and renewable sources – if renewable energy targets are met and gas supplies are available at a reasonable cost.

With the existing policies, *excluding* the impacts of EU emissions trading, UK emissions of CO_2 in 2010 will be about 10.6% below the 1990 level. Although this projection, combined with emissions projections of greenhouse gases other than CO_2, indicates that the UK will meet its Kyoto commitment to reduce emissions of a basket of greenhouse gases, it is still about 9.4 percentage points short of the current self-imposed domestic goal of 20% by 2010. On the same basis, UK emissions of CO_2 in 2020 are projected to be about 9.2% below the 1990 level – and therefore even further away from the 26% target set in the Climate Change Bill (2007; 2008). The impact of the European Union Emission Trading Scheme (EU ETS) is considered separately; and certainly its inclusion moves UK emissions closer to the target. Taking the effect of the EU ETS into account, at a carbon price of €30/tCO_2, the UK's emissions will be 11.6–12.3% below 1990 levels by 2020, i.e. more than 15 percentage points short of the stated national goal. It is therefore clear that additional measures are needed in order to put the UK on the path towards this goal (DTI, 2006b). This highlights the scale of the challenge in making the transition to a low-carbon energy sector and economy in the UK.

The scenarios considered in DTI (2006b) reflect common assumptions about economic growth and policy measures, and explore the impact of different future fuel prices. The Supergen medium-term scenarios presented by Elders *et al.* in Chapter 14 of this volume offer a wider set of assumptions and demonstrate that a greater diversity of outcomes is possible, with most also showing lower emissions than the DTI's 'Central' scenario.[2]

Figure 1.2 shows the UK's historical and projected emissions by end-user group and is based on the estimates from the DTI (2006b). The business, transport and residential sectors already account for the bulk of the UK's CO_2 emissions and will continue to do so. While the breakdown by source in Figure 1.1 indicates the CO_2 reduction potential achievable through supply-side actions and interventions, the breakdown by end-user shown in Figure 1.2 shows the potential scope for CO_2 emission reductions through demand-side actions and interventions (e.g. energy efficiency).

Mitigation of GHGs will have implications for practically all the main sectors of the UK economy. Given that the electricity sector is a significant contributor to GHGs, it will be required to contribute to a high share of emission reductions. At the same time, the particular characteristics of the electricity sector require that a specific set of approaches, technologies and policies towards the overall climate change objectives should be developed.

Electricity is a technically homogeneous and non-storable product, and system reliability requires that supply and demand be matched

---

[2] The Supergen 2020 scenarios presented in Chapter 14, this volume, show lower emissions levels than the DTI's 'Central' scenario: 'A number of factors contribute to this. Most notably, the Supergen scenarios assume a greater output from nuclear generation, either as a result of new construction or of a more aggressive programme of life-extension to obtain carbon-reduction or investment-avoidance benefits. Renewable generation is also greater in all but the 'Economic Concern' scenario' (p. 388).

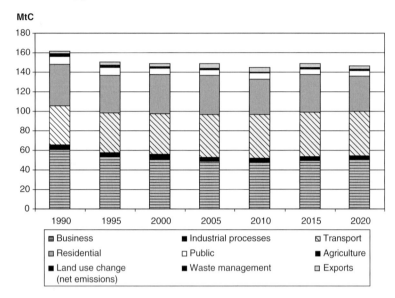

Figure 1.2. UK CO_2 emissions by end-user
Source: DTI (2006b)

simultaneously. At the same time, the electricity industry is highly capital-intensive, with a large proportion of the assets becoming sunk costs upon investment. As the existing assets in place need to be renewed, and demand continuously increases, the sector can experience investment cycles. The assets also, however, have long economic lives, with long-term implications for the composition of the sector.

The electricity system consists of the vertically connected and coordinated generation, transmission, distribution and supply activities. The generation stage comprises production and conversion of electric power from a number of technologies. Transmission involves long-distance transportation of electricity at high voltage. The distribution of low-voltage electricity through local networks requires overhead lines, cables, switchgear, transformers, control systems and meters to transfer electricity from the transmission system to customers' premises. Consumers comprise a large number of diverse end-users who utilise the electricity service through a range of plants, machinery and appliances. Finally, the supply function consists of the metering, billing and sale of electricity to end-users. The generation and supply activities are generally regarded as potentially competitive, while the transmission and distribution networks are characterised as natural monopolies.

At all the above-mentioned segments of the sector, technology, economics and policies can play a role in achieving a low-carbon electricity system. Low-carbon fossil fuel (high-efficiency gas and plants with carbon sequestration), renewable generation, and nuclear power sources could all contribute to reducing emissions. The transmission and distribution networks can contribute through large-scale connection of renewable sources, facilitating distributed and microgeneration technologies, and reduction of energy losses. The retail supply function can help achieve an active demand through, for example, real-time pricing and smart metering technologies. Finally, end-users have numerous opportunities for energy efficiency and energy-saving measures.

The climate change impact of emissions from the electricity sector can be viewed as a negative environmental external impact of the use of conventional fossil fuels. These have only just begun to be internalised with the advent of the EU Emission Trading Scheme (EU ETS) and, in some cases, established technologies will benefit from various direct and indirect subsidies. Also in the context of security of energy supply, there are negative externalities attributed to some conventional energy technologies, whereas most low-carbon options contribute to diversity and/or are domestically produced. Thus, while most carbon-free technologies are not cost-competitive in current energy markets, they carry various positive externalities that justify promotional policies.

The climate change debate in the electricity sector can be summarised as involving the following elements: (i) setting targets, which may include both emission and technology targets, (ii) incorporating the externalities of conventional and alternative generation sources into energy prices, (iii) accelerating energy efficiency improvements, (iv) supporting the use of alternative sources, and (vi) promoting development of new technologies for both supply and energy efficiency. An effective effort to achieve a low-carbon electricity system needs to carefully balance the closely interrelated technological, economic, and policy dimensions of climate change in the sector. The chapters in this book attempt to address important issues within these dimensions of mitigating climate change in the sector. The remainder of this chapter outlines those aspects of a comprehensive approach towards delivering a low-carbon electricity sector that are addressed in this book.

1.3 Technology assessment

Technological progress has a crucial role to play in achieving climate change goals. In the electricity sector, the most important barrier to the adoption of low-carbon generation sources is that most are relatively more costly than fossil-fuel-based sources and/or require further technical improvements. In the first book from the Supergen programme, Jamasb *et al.* (2006a) reviewed future electricity technologies and concluded that all the main components of low-carbon future electricity systems from generation, through network and storage, to end-use technologies, require cost reductions and technical progress.

In addition, liberalisation of the UK's electricity sector has replaced centrally planned investment with competitive markets and incentive-based regulation, where relative costs and reliability of technologies play a crucial role in technology selection. At the same time, both private and public research and development (R&D) spending declined following the liberalisation of the sector (Jamasb and Pollitt, 2005).

Jamasb *et al.* (2006b) stress that the future of electricity is likely to be characterised by a multitude of technological solutions. Indeed, the widening of future technological options should be an important part of energy technology policy. This is partly due to the inherent difficulty in identifying the most promising technologies and, in effect, picking the winners from a range of competing options. However, as discussed in Chapter 3 by Jamasb *et al.*, and in Chapter 16 by Reiner *et al.*, it is easier to broadly identify the UK's technological options in terms of short- and long-term resources, with a view to applying differentiated innovation promotion policies. Moreover, most sources of renewable technologies are subject to constraints on the extent to which they can individually contribute toward a future low-carbon electricity sector. Also, some of the effect of cost reduction in renewable technologies may be outweighed by increasing implementation costs. For example, the best sites for wind power may have already been developed or the opportunity cost of land for bioenergy may increase. In addition, the intermittent nature of some renewable sources requires that they be combined and backed up with other sources in order to maintain system reliability.

Low-carbon technologies also contribute towards diversity of energy sources and increased security of supply and therefore setting carbon emission reduction targets is an indirect way of promoting such technologies.

The challenges of reducing carbon emissions and ensuring security of supply are closely linked. Security of supply requires that we have good access to available fuel supplies, the infrastructure in place to transport them to centres of demand, and effective markets so that supply meets demand in the most efficient way. Many of the measures already described for tackling carbon emissions also contribute to the healthy diversity of energy sources that is necessary for meeting the energy security challenge (DTI, 2006a, *Energy Review*, p. 18).

Finally, the role of technology in reducing carbon emissions has an important international dimension. The resource requirements for effective R&D require that international collaboration be part of the efforts for technological change. In particular, cross-country collaboration in specific technology areas among countries with comparative advantage or shared interest can increase the effectiveness of R&D efforts (Jamasb *et al.*, 2006b). In addition, the positive spillover effects of technological progress can make a valuable contribution towards enabling developing countries to participate in climate change efforts.

The main vehicles of achieving technical change are through learning-by-research, through direct research and development (R&D), and learning-by-doing effects associated with capacity deployment. At the same time, it is important to promote technological progress where the scarce R&D funds yield the highest returns in terms of cost reductions. The Stern Review emphasised that the private sector plays the major role in R&D and technology diffusion, and that there is a need for closer collaboration between government and industry which will further stimulate the development of a broad portfolio of low-carbon technologies and reduce costs (Stern, 2007, p. 347).

Public support for the research, development and deployment of new technologies and industries to reduce emissions is vital. Carbon pricing alone is unlikely to reduce emissions on the scale and at the speed required, particularly with respect to new investment and innovation. This is because (i) future pricing policies of governments and international agreements cannot be 100 per cent credible, (ii) there are deep uncertainties and risks related to climate change and the development and deployment of the technologies to address it, and (iii) there can be major difficulties in financing innovation through capital markets for long-established reasons. Chapter 11 (Grubb and Newbery) discusses the challenges in establishing effective carbon pricing and securing the desired impacts on investment and innovation. On these grounds it is important that governments raise the level of support for R&D and demonstration projects, both in public research institutions and in the private sector, and that they support early-stage commercialisation investments in some sectors. Such policies should be complemented by tackling institutional and other non-market barriers to the deployment of new technologies. More specifically, the results from the Stern Review suggest that, in addition to a carbon price, deployment incentives for low-emission technologies should increase two to five times globally from current levels of around $34 billion p.a. and that global public energy R&D funding should double, to around $20 billion p.a., for the development of a diverse portfolio of technologies (Stern, 2007, p. 347).

The priorities of the UK's technology efforts must therefore be designed with regard to comparative cost and availability of its resource endowment. Chapter 3 of this volume (Jamasb *et al.*) focuses on the UK's technological issues and options. Some technologies have the potential to contribute toward climate change goals already in the medium term. These would primarily require suitable economic instruments, demonstration units, and lowering of institutional barriers. However, other technologies are in need of further progress through R&D efforts and can only make real contributions in the long run.

1.4   Economic analysis

Low-carbon supply technologies are generally more costly than the conventional fossil-fuel-based sources in the market.[3] Therefore, mitigation of carbon emissions through adoption of low-carbon solutions and development of new technologies involves significant investment. From both an economic efficiency and a public acceptance of policies and goals point of view, it is therefore crucial that the climate change objectives are achieved at the least possible cost, using efficient economic frameworks and instruments.

The economics of climate change is inherently complicated and involves some imprecise and subjective areas of economic analysis. An economic analysis of climate change requires identifying a measure of the social cost of carbon (DTI, 2006a). Hope and Newbery in Chapter 2, this volume, discuss the inherent uncertainties – and ethical and policy choices – that surround this, including uncertainty in issues such as the extent of climate change damages, distributional effects, and intergenerational considerations. One aim of internalising the social cost of carbon is to create a level playing field for low-carbon technologies in a market dominated by conventional fossil-fuel-based technologies. This also requires that fossil fuel subsidies are reduced or gradually phased out. In the context of the electricity sector, the chapter argues that, despite the uncertainties, the social cost of carbon is likely to be high enough to justify significant moves to decarbonise power sector investments.

---

[3] See Chapter 15 by Yago *et al.* for an example of generating cost inputs (fuel cost efficiency, operations and maintenance cost, capital cost and plant life) for several technologies.

The UK has been at the forefront of efforts to liberalise electricity systems, with the view that competitive forces would avoid many mistakes of the past and improve the efficiency of operation and investment. Despite this, Neuhoff and Twomey, in Chapter 10, argue that the market will not invest in the 'right' technologies from a public policy perspective for a number of reasons, of which inadequate carbon pricing is just one.

One of the other facets concerns the economics of technological progress and associated cost reductions. These can be promoted through R&D and the deployment of low-carbon technologies. Both types of measures are costly and require the efficient use and allocation of scarce resources between different technologies, depending on their level of maturity (Jamasb et al., 2006b). Jamasb and Köhler, in Chapter 12, discuss the relative economic effectiveness of learning-by-research and learning-by-doing rates in lowering costs, and argue that the importance of learning rates for technology analysis can be likened to that of discount rates in economic analysis of climate change. In addition, specific economic instruments are needed to promote R&D and support commercialisation of technologies through capacity deployment (see Chapter 13 by Grubb et al.).

1.5   Policy and political economy

The previous sections have highlighted the role and elements of sound technology assessment and economic analysis in achieving a low-carbon electricity system. However, technology and economic framework should ultimately translate into feasible policies that take into account the political economy realities. The scenario and economy–energy modelling approaches provide a useful platform for discussion of policy issues and actions under alternative futures and important contextual factors (see Chapter 14 by Elders et al. and Chapter 15 by Yago et al.).

However, due to political economy and practical considerations, the policies and instruments often deviate from optimal theoretical and analytical suggestions. For example, in sectors where companies compete on a least-cost basis – such as power generation – theoretical arguments generally favour the use of a carbon tax to curb carbon emissions. Yet emission cap-and-trade schemes have proved politically more feasible. In Chapter 11, Grubb and Newbery discuss aspects of climate change policies and instruments, including the use of price (carbon tax) versus quantity (tradable permits) controls. Based 'on simple economic arguments . . . there is a stronger case for a fixed, stable carbon price (via taxes or some other mechanism) than for fixed or stable quota allocations'. However, the merits of quantity controls are recognised and are mostly attributable to the relative practicalities of implementing emission cap-and-trade schemes, and their capacity to evolve over repeated rounds. Also, the case of the Climate Change Levy in the UK shows how political economy factors can reduce the economic efficiency of a carbon tax (Pearce, 2006). Grubb and Newbery argue that policy needs to evolve in more efficient directions from the current systems, rather than expecting an ideal taxation system for ideal markets.

Maintaining the appropriate balance between market mechanisms and intervention to achieve policy goals will remain a challenging task. Security of supply and diversity of resource mix considerations can result in the adoption of policies that are not cost-effective or economically efficient (see Chapter 4 by Roques). For example, the UK faces an increasing dependence on imported natural gas with associated security of supply implications. At the same time, it is not clear whether markets will adopt the most desirable technologies (see Chapter 10 by Neuhoff and Twomey). An energy policy aimed at enhancing security of supply and diversifying the electricity sector's resource mix can result in the adoption of polices favouring nuclear power – a carbon-free technology, or coal power – a carbon-intensive resource.

New generation technologies can increase the flexibility of the system; policy measures should be developed to take into account the preferences and enhance the role of a responsive demand side (see Chapter 5 by Sinden). The addition of new generation technologies needs to be backed by investments and regulation for active networks and removal of the barriers to developing them (Chapter 7, Pollitt and Bialek, and Chapter 6, Neuhoff *et al.*). This will be particularly useful for engaging the household, commercial and public segments of demand, which seem likely to increase their relative share of total consumption, as discussed in Chapter 8 by Bilton *et al.* and in Chapter 9 by Grubb, Wilde and Sorrell. The latter authors argue that the consumption of electricity in the commercial and public sectors has been a 'blind spot' in policy, and suggest that new instruments are required to tackle this effectively.

There are significant differences among the capital, operating, fuel and externality costs of various fossil-fuel-based and renewable generation technologies. However, in terms of total costs, the differences between the technologies tend to become smaller. Moreover, it is widely expected that technological progress will increasingly reduce the cost differences among the competing technologies (see, e.g. IPCC, 2007, pp. 60–62). The cost reduction trend will apply at the global level as well as in the UK. Technology policy and analysis can play an important role in improving the return from and the effectiveness of the process of technological progress. In the long run, however, as the cost differences among technologies will tend to decrease, emissions trading policies, network regulation, and market design instruments and incentives will play a greater role in the deployment and mix of technologies in competitive energy markets.

Governments' adoption of policies that entail the internalisation of the social cost of carbon will increase the market value of low-carbon technologies and underpin innovation in this direction. However, the use of a carbon price and instruments does not remove market failures in R&D and the need for learning-by-doing in low-carbon energy technologies (Chapter 10, Neuhoff and Twomey). Moreover, the value of the incentive depends upon uncertain future government policies to internalise carbon costs for very long-lived investments. Thus carbon pricing still needs to be complemented by other instruments (see Chapter 13, Grubb *et al.*).

Finally, due to the nature of the climate change phenomena, any mitigation strategy and framework must have a long-term perspective of policy issues, options and objectives. At the same time, the importance of public perception and acceptance in the context of energy policy issues, technology choice and the use of instruments is increasingly recognised (see Chapter 17 by Devine-Wright). In order to be effective, any climate change mitigation policy must itself be also politically as well as socially sustainable. It is therefore important to enhance our understanding of public acceptance and its determinants and how to incorporate these into climate change policy framework.

1.6   Overview of the chapters

Part I: The Fundamentals

Chapter 2 Calculating the social cost of carbon   Hope and Newbery discuss the central question of how to determine the appropriate price of carbon using the PAGE2002 model that was also used in the Stern Review. Calculating the social cost of carbon (SCC) is a non-trivial exercise that requires assumptions about future economic development, the range and likelihood of economic and social damage arising from climate change at future dates and the discount rate to apply to that damage. The debate over the choice of pure time preference, one of the major determinants of the discount rate, is critically examined, along with the weight to place on damage experienced by other countries in the distant future. A key conclusion of the PAGE2002 model is that the

SCC is not constant over time but is rising. It is also the case that the range of estimates for the SCC is wide, under plausible variations in assumptions. The SCC is sensitive to a number of factors; significantly including the equilibrium temperature rise for a doubling of CO_2 concentration, the pure rate of time preference, the non-economic impact, the inequality weighting parameter and the half-life of global warming. Within the model, the SCC appears surprisingly insensitive to the emissions scenario for reasons that are explained. The chapter points out that methane and SF_6 are also powerful GHGs whose impact can be estimated within the model. The chapter concludes by noting that a range of estimates of the SCC are plausible, but the factors behind the estimates need to be well understood.

Chapter 3 Technologies for a low-carbon electricity system: an assessment of the UK's issues and options   Jamasb *et al.* review the UK's technological issues and options in achieving a low-carbon electricity sector. The authors emphasise that the UK can potentially benefit from a range of renewable resources and that the resource base of low-carbon solutions is substantial. Consequently, the long-term future of the sector is likely to be characterised by technological diversity. However, the costs of these can be site-specific and the low-cost resource base is more limited. The chapter argues that it is important to distinguish between technologies that can contribute towards a low-carbon sector in the medium term and those that currently offer only long-term prospects.

The authors suggest that, while some low-carbon technologies can begin to make significant contributions to the resource mix of the sector in the medium term, some technologies can or may only be able to have an impact on the resource mix of the sector in the long run. The benefits of medium-term deployment of the latter technologies are likely to be mainly in terms of a learning-by-doing effect on their cost reduction rather than in the form of their energy contribution.

Chapter 4 The benefits of fuel mix diversity   Roques discusses the issues of resource mix in the UK electricity sector. The diversity of sources in UK power generation since the 1990 reform has increased mainly as a result of gas-fired CCGT (combined cycle gas turbine) generation. However, a continuation of the trend will lead to lower diversity. The chapter opens up the concept of diversity and what is meant by it. The chapter then discusses the macroeconomic impact and security of supply benefits of fuel mix diversification in the sector. The literature on quantification and valuation of diversity and relevant studies are also reviewed, pointing to the diversification value of non-fossil-fuel generation technologies.

Chapter 5 Variability and renewables   Sinden sheds new light on the important characteristics of renewable generation sources. The chapter differentiates between 'intermittency' a characteristic often attributed to renewable sources – and 'variability' as a better description of the nature of their generation pattern. Sinden argues that it is useful to note that renewable sources constitute a diverse set of technologies with varied and site-specific generation patterns. Sinden argues that these differences between the main renewable technologies amount to a smoothing effect on the production from renewables as a whole. The chapter concludes that, due to the smoothing effect, the required installed renewable capacity is, although growing with the level of penetration, lower than was generally anticipated.

Chapter 6 Implications of intermittency and transmission constraints for renewables deployment   Neuhoff *et al.* explore the impact of adding extra wind power to the UK electricity system using an investment planning model. They model the regional wind patterns and look at the addition of wind power to seven regions of Great Britain. They examine the impacts of transmission and new-build constraints within regions. Across the scenarios, with 20% and 40% of UK electricity produced by wind, a common result is that wind deployment is distributed across the country rather than focused in the North, where wind speeds are higher. This diversification reduces the volatility of total production and the impact of transmission constraints. If wind power is to contribute significantly to the UK energy mix, then the deployment policies that might be preferable are those that allow for such investment in various regions rather than focusing on the locations with the highest wind speeds. Such policies exhibit additional benefits where maximum build constraints are reduced. Undifferentiated support policies would create scarcity rents and additional costs to consumers, where public acceptance or planning processes constrain the maximum investment per region.

The simplified model – still ignoring various technical constraints that are investigated in ongoing Supergen work – suggests that the additional costs of providing 40% instead of 20% of UK electricity from wind power would be in the order of £6.5 billion. Costs could be significantly higher if the British Electricity Trading Arrangements do not evolve to make transmission more effective and flexible by internalising congestion management into the market design.

Part II: Incentives and the Demand Side: Demand-Side Management and System Requirements

Chapter 7 Electricity network investment and regulation for a low-carbon future Pollitt and Bialek discuss the requirements for network investment and regulation. They begin by reviewing the existing economic regulation of monopoly transmission and distribution networks in the UK, noting that recent price reviews have allowed for big increases in capital investment in both transmission and distribution. The requirement for significantly higher network investment seems certain as the capacity of distributed generation and large-scale renewables increases on the system. The authors make a number of significant suggestions for improvement to the current system of regulation. First, they suggest that the RPI-X system needs to be overhauled in favour of a simpler yardstick-based system which allows for more merchant transmission investments. Second, future regulation should involve more negotiated regulation involving agreements between network owners and purchasers of network services. This would be particularly advantageous for decisions on new network investments. Third, more extensive use needs to be made of locational pricing within the transmission and distribution system in order to facilitate the least-cost expansion of low-carbon generation, including micropower. Fourth, consideration needs to be given to ownership unbundling of distribution networks from retail supply. This would better facilitate the entry of distributed generation and the development of appropriate competition between grid and off-grid generation supply and demand-side management. Finally, there needs to be a significant increase in R&D expenditure in electricity networks supported by customer levies.

Chapter 8 Domestic electricity consumption and demand-side participation: opportunities and challenges for the UK power system Bilton *et al.* shift the focus on to the important, but complex, topic of demand participation in electricity, particularly concerning domestic users. The UK's electricity system, as in other countries, is predominantly supply-centric, leaving significant scope for demand participation. The chapter systematises the most widely used concepts associated with active demand and outlines the main types of action, benefits, measures, barriers and enabling conditions associated with these. The authors point to price-inelastic demand and lack of information as being among the main reasons that consumers in general, and the residential sector in particular, are not more active or responsive participants. The chapter then mainly focuses on the residential sector, which accounts for 27% of carbon emissions and 45% of peak demand in the UK. The authors emphasise the value of information and argue that the full potential of an active residential sector can only be achieved through a diverse set of measures. They stress that while most demand participation measures are of a long-term nature, the potential of short-term measures also needs to be utilised.

Chapter 9 Enhancing the efficient use of electricity in the business and public sectors   Grubb *et al.* examine the use of electricity in the business and public sectors and the potential policies to improve efficiency. Drawing upon analysis by the lead authors for the Carbon Trust, they emphasise that practical policy needs to start by identifying different types of user and establishing the principal barriers to efficient use in the different user groups. Their analysis points in particular to the less energy-intensive users – and, in particular, large commercial and public sector organisations – as a source of rapid growth in UK electricity consumption but also as having a large potential for cost-effective efficiency improvements. None of the existing policy instruments really address the core barriers for this group, which concern the internal structure of large organisations and the immateriality of most energy costs. This leads the authors to analyse a new instrument that could focus the attention of such large organisations on their electricity and associated indirect carbon emissions, estimating that this single measure could reduce UK CO_2 emissions by around 1%. The proposal has subsequently been taken up and developed by the UK Government as the *Carbon Reduction Commitment* in the UK's Energy White Paper (2007).

Part III: Investment, Price and Innovation

Chapter 10 Will the market choose the right technologies?   Neuhoff and Twomey examine the question of whether the market will choose the 'right' technologies. They outline the possible market failures in the electricity market with respect to long-term investments in generation capacity. They suggest that: (1) private investors do not have the right incentives to capture the social benefits of diversity, (ii) current electricity markets inefficiently penalise intermittent renewable generation, (iii) emissions markets do not reflect the social value of low-carbon investments, (iv) there are substantial regulatory barriers to investment, and (v) there may be learning benefits to renewable investments which cannot be captured by investors. They conclude by suggesting that nodal transmission and distribution pricing needs to be introduced, the EU ETS needs to be further reformed, and that appropriate learning subsidies need to be paid. They call for further research on the design of capacity payments, the incentivisation of optimal diversity, and the ending of retail competition to facilitate long-term contracting.

Chapter 11 Pricing carbon for electricity generation: national and international dimensions   Grubb and Newbery examine how carbon for electricity generation should be priced. They begin by suggesting that it is not clear what the correct price of carbon is (as noted in the chapter by Hope and Newbery), but that it spans the whole range of economically plausible prices. They then go on to discuss the theoretical merits of taxes versus quotas, concluding that theoretically a stable tax would best reflect the true social cost of emissions, which should not change with market conditions. They then evaluate the EU Emission Trading Scheme (EU ETS), where allowances for the emission of CO_2 are traded (EUAs). The price signals offered by the scheme in its first trading period have been very unsatisfactory, with high variability and the price trending downwards to very low levels as it became clear that governments had been much too generous in their initial allocation of quotas. What is needed is a stable investment environment for low-carbon generation investments. They discuss a number of policy options to achieve this: long period commitments on quotas; allowing unconstrained banking and borrowing of EUAs over multiple periods; long-term price declarations to be used in allocation auctions; government-issued contracts for differences on the future carbon price; or simply to issue low-carbon electricity contracts. The authors conclude with a discussion of the scope for international agreements on carbon emissions reduction. They argue that, imperfect though it is, the EU ETS is a good place to start to link up emerging trading regimes, and that quota systems have more of a chance of commanding international agreement, at least initially. However, any international climate change agreement will be difficult to establish.

Chapter 12 Learning curves for energy technology: a critical assessment   Jamasb and Köhler revisit learning curves and their application to energy technology and climate change policy analysis and modelling. The academic literature and official policy documents have, in recent years, embraced learning curves and applied the concept to technology analysis and forecasting cost reductions. The authors argue that learning curves have often been used or assumed uncritically in technology analysis, and draw parallels between the use of learning rates in energy technological progress and climate change modelling and that of discount rates in social cost–benefit analysis.

The chapter argues that care needs to be taken in applying learning curves – originally developed as an empirical tool to assess the effect of learning-by-doing in manufacturing – to analysis of innovation and technical change. Finally, the authors offer suggestions with regard to the extension of learning curves, e.g. by incorporating research and development (R&D) and diffusion effects into learning models, and other areas where learning curves may potentially be a useful tool in energy technology policy and analysis.

Chapter 13 Accelerating innovation and strategic deployment in UK electricity: applications to renewable energy Grubb *et al.* examine the nature of industrial innovation and the implications for policies aimed at developing industries based on low-carbon technology. Innovation is a complex process, in which technologies must traverse a long route from early ideas through demonstration and commercialisation, and then achieve cost reductions sufficient for them to attract investment in liberalised energy markets. Policies to promote such innovation are correspondingly complex, and also need to consider the potential UK contribution within a global context. With the global investment required in low-carbon innovation likely to run into hundreds of billions of dollars, this requires focusing efforts particularly on areas where the UK has a natural advantage and/or can make the greatest difference.

Offshore wind energy forms one of the UK's biggest low-carbon options and offers such an opportunity. The latter part of the chapter focuses upon policies for promoting renewable energy investment, and argues that the undifferentiated 'renewable energy obligation' is an inefficient mechanism that also results in almost all of the support going into the most established technology, namely onshore wind. The chapter discusses options for reform and presents quantified studies to 2020.

Part IV: Scenarios, Options and Public Attitudes

Chapter 14 Scenarios of the electricity industry in Great Britain in 2020: networks, generation and decarbonisation Elders *et al.* present a set of scenarios looking at the development of the electricity supply industry in the UK to 2020. They examine four scenarios on the basis of assumptions about the level of economic growth, environmental focus, technological growth and regulatory structure. These scenarios allow the share of renewable generation, the share of fossil fuel generation, and the level of CO_2 emissions from the sector to be estimated. Under their 'Environmental Awakening' scenario, economic growth continues at its current level, there is a stronger concern for the environment than there is now, and also strong technological growth and liberalised electricity markets with environmental intervention. By 2020 this gives rise to low demand growth for electricity, 25% renewable generation, and 43% lower emissions from the electricity sector than in 2005. Other scenarios show substantially higher levels of emissions than under this scenario but still well below the 2005 level. The discussion makes clear that, while it is possible to see substantial emissions reduction in the power sector by 2020, it will require significant incentives and regulatory support to bring about the component actions which lie behind the scenarios.

Chapter 15 Modelling the economic impact of low-carbon electricity   Yago *et al.* model the economic impact of low-carbon electricity behind the scenarios outlined in the previous chapter by Elders *et al.* They find that the average annual costs of electricity generation by 2020 vary between £35/MWh for their high-carbon base scenario to £51/MWh under the 'Environmental Awakening' scenario under moderately high gas prices; with a lower differential if gas prices are lower. On electricity prices, they find that, even with the higher gas prices, electricity prices under 'Environmental Awakening' are £11/MWh higher relative to a high-carbon baseline. They are also able to examine the profit impact on the generators, which varies considerably with the gas price assumption. The authors suggest that, while a significant rise in prices is to be anticipated under low-carbon scenarios, the price rise will only be of the order of 20%. While this will raise issues for fuel-poor households, existing schemes such as winter fuel payments could be adjusted to alleviate a significant part of the negative distributional consequences. Yago *et al.* point out that, if the electricity sector has to bear all of the economy-wide carbon reduction, or if other GHGs are not also targeted, the total cost of achieving a given reduction in equivalent GHG emissions will be much higher. Overall, they conclude that the cost of these scenarios is affordable at £2–3 billion per annum and the extra payment is equivalent to £40 per tonne of CO_2 saved.

Chapter 16 Bridging technologies: can clean fossil offer a bridge to a sustainable energy future in the UK?   Reiner *et al.* assess the role of carbon capture and sequestration technologies in achieving clean fossil-fuel-based electricity generation. The chapter outlines the main carbon capture technologies as well as issues associated with storage. There is considerable potential for carbon capture and storage (CCS) in enhanced oil recovery and power generation in the UK. Most of the technologies required for CCS already exist in some form, and storage capacity in the North Sea is abundant relative to current UK emissions. A major challenge is how to combine capture, transport and storage in an effective and cost-efficient manner in workable business models. Public acceptance will also play a role in adoption of the technology. While the public has limited knowledge of the option, the current perception of CCS is less favourable than that of renewables, although it is better than for nuclear power. The authors discuss the potential for CCS technology in the medium term in the UK in the light of the ageing coal and nuclear generation plants. They also discuss the implications of changes in coal, gas and carbon prices on the penetration of CCS technologies and assess the rapidly changing policy environment for CCS in the UK and internationally.

Chapter 17 Reconsidering public acceptance of renewable energy technologies: a critical review   Devine-Wright, in a survey of the literature, revisits the concept of public acceptance of renewable energy technologies. The chapter points to a lack of clarity and coherence in the literature, which uses a multitude of terms such as public perception, public opinion, public beliefs, public attitudes and public awareness. The chapter argues that, despite the importance of public acceptance as a major condition for the development of these technologies, our understanding of the factors and processes determining public acceptance is rather limited. It also outlines priority directions for future research in public acceptance, whilst noting that there are differences in public acceptance between different technologies and that awareness of the link between energy and global warming varies.

1.7   Conclusions and policy implications

The demand for electricity (and thus the associated CO_2 emissions) has grown inexorably worldwide with economic development. As we suggested earlier, this trend is expected to continue. However, it is incompatible with all we now know about climate change and the actions that we need to take.

In 1989 the UK began a sweeping reform of its power sector that helped to stimulate and inform moves towards radically reshaping the structure, market design and regulation of national electricity sectors in many different countries. One topic of intense debate was the likely impact of such liberalisation on the sector's environmental impacts, for example in relation to choice of generation technology and regulated investment in energy efficiency. In practice, in the decade following the liberalisation of its electricity system, the UK bucked the global trend, as its power-sector CO_2 emissions declined sharply. Since then, however, the decline has halted.

The analysis in this book, as brought together in Chapter 18, suggests that the trend towards a decarbonised power sector can be resumed and extended over the coming decades – but only if stronger policies are adopted to deepen the economic incentives, improve both public and corporate engagement with the issues, and accelerate innovation towards that goal. Thus a principal finding is that decarbonising electricity does not require a retreat to central planning, but it will require the stronger application of a range of government policies. These need to ensure not only that private investors face a real, credible and durable carbon price, but also that they can harness the full range of benefits arising from adopting and exploring better ways of both using and generating power, at different points in time and space over the UK system.

The UK is rich in energy options and can play a leading role in global moves to decarbonise power systems over the first half of this century. By adopting policies that create the right incentives in its liberalised power sector, the UK can demonstrate that low-carbon electricity futures are possible, affordable – and even desirable – to citizens and companies that engage in the challenges of building a low-carbon economy. If the UK rises to this challenge, it may again help to inspire and inform the new wave of power-sector innovation that climate science suggests is so desperately needed.

References

DEFRA (2007). *Estimated Emissions of Carbon Dioxide by IPCC Source Category, Type of Fuel and End User: 1970–2005*, e-Digest of Environmental Statistics, Department of Environment, Food and Rural Affairs, London. Available from www.defra.gov.uk/environment/statistics/airqual/index.htm

Climate Change Bill (2008). *Draft Climate Change Bill (amended)*, HL Bill 44, 18th March 2008, House of Lords, London.

(2007). *Climate Change Bill*, HL Bill 9, 14th November 2007, House of Lords, London.

DTI (2007). *Energy White Paper: Meeting the Energy Challenge*, Department of Trade and Industry, London.

(2006a). *Energy Review: The Energy Challenge*, Department of Trade and Industry, London.

(2006b). *UK Energy and CO_2 Emissions Projections: Updated Projections to 2020*, Department of Trade and Industry, London.

(2006c). *Digest of UK Energy Statistics 2006*, Department of Trade and Industry, London. Available from www.berr.gov.uk/energy/statistics/publications/dukes/page29812.html

(2003). *Energy White Paper: Our Energy Future – Creating a Low Carbon Economy*, Department of Trade and Industry, London.

HM Government (2006). *Climate Change: The UK Programme 2006*, SE/2006/43, HM Government, London.

IEA (2006). *World Energy Outlook 2006*, International Energy Agency, Paris.

IPCC (2007). *Intergovernmental Panel for Climate Change Fourth Assessment Report, Working Group III*, Chapter 4: Energy supply, Final Draft, Cambridge University Press.

Jamasb, T. and Pollitt, M. (2005). *Deregulation and R&D in network industries: the case of the electricity industry*, Cambridge Working Papers in Economics CWPE /0533/ Electricity Policy Research Group Working Paper EPRG 05/02, August, Faculty of Economics, University of Cambridge.

Jamasb, T., Nuttall, W., Pollitt, M. (2006a). *Future Electricity Technologies and Systems*, Cambridge University Press.

Jamasb, T., Nuttall, W.J., Pollitt, M. (2006b). *The Case for a New Energy Research, Development, and Promotion Policy for the UK*, Submission to State of Science Review on Public Policy in the Energy Context, Office of Science and Innovation, Foresight and Horizon Scanning Centre, Department of Trade and Industry, London.

Pearce, D. (2006). The political economy of an energy tax: the United Kingdom's climate change levy, *Energy Economics*, **28**, 149–158.

SDC (2006). *The Role of Nuclear Power in a Low Carbon Economy*, Sustainable Development Commission, London.

Stern, N. (2007). *The Economics of Climate Change: The Stern Review*, Cabinet Office – HM Treasury, Cambridge University Press.

United Nations (1992). *United Nations Framework Convention on Climate Change*, United Nations.

(1997). *Kyoto Protocol to the United Nations Framework Convention on Climate Change*, United Nations.

Part I

The Fundamentals

2   Calculating the social cost of carbon

Chris Hope and David Newbery

2.1   Introduction

Fossil fuel electricity generation accounted for 74% of total electricity in Great Britain in 2005, 62% in the OECD, and 66% in the world (in 2003). Burning fossil fuels releases carbon dioxide (CO_2) which, as the main greenhouse gas, is the major contributor to future climate change. Greenhouse gases (GHGs) are, in technical economic language, a global stock pollutant that is a non-excludable pure public bad. That is, emissions today add to the stock of atmospheric GHGs, which only decay slowly and which affect everyone, regardless of their location and the source of the emission, whether or not they are willing to pay to avoid the resulting cost. Unless properly priced, they will be released in excessive amounts. Carbon pricing would thus be a way of confronting those emitting GHGs with the social cost they impose. 'Companies that face a price for carbon will be incentivised to reduce their emissions, either through energy efficiency improvements, investing in new technology, or switching to the use of less carbon-intensive sources of energy' (*Energy Review*, DTI, 2006, p. 27).

Most technologies for delivering low- or zero-carbon electricity are not competitive at current electricity prices without either a carbon price or some other subsidy. Projections of how economies like the UK's might move towards a low-carbon configuration imply that over the next 40 years a large fraction of the least-cost decarbonisation could come from the electricity supply industry; so a proper carbon price for generation is critical. Carbon is currently priced within the European Emission Trading Scheme, but its future post-2012 is still in doubt. Generation investment has a lifetime of 20–60 years, and so its profitability will depend heavily on views about likely future electricity and carbon prices. This chapter assesses how carbon should be priced and, more fundamentally, how to assess the benefits of moving to a low-carbon economy, so that one can better judge whether the extra costs of low-carbon electricity are worthwhile.

The fundamental concept is the social cost of carbon, which measures the present discounted value of the additional social costs (or the marginal social damage) that an extra tonne of carbon released now would impose on current and future society. This immediately raises four questions:

- What is society and social value?
- How should we measure the social cost when it occurs?
- What rate of discount should we apply to these costs?
- How should we take account of the considerable uncertainty about the future damage and costs?

Climate scientists attempt to model the effects of releasing greenhouse gases over the next few decades on concentrations of these gases and the consequential impacts on climate by region, specifically temperature distributions over time and space, sea levels, storm frequency and other damaging impacts. In order to translate these impacts into costs that can be compared with the costs of reducing emissions, one needs an integrated assessment model (IAM) that estimates the economic impact of the climate impacts, and aggregates these impacts across regions and over time to give a present value that can be compared with the investment costs of mitigating climate change. The *Stern Review* (Stern, 2006) provides two ways of making this comparison – it computes the social cost of carbon released as GHGs and it estimates the damage done by climate change compared against a world in which GHG emissions had no adverse effects. The specific way in which it measures these damages is in terms of their 'balanced growth equivalent' (BGE); a concept that appropriately goes back to Mirrlees and Stern (1972).

Both concepts of the cost of climate change depend on science, economic modelling and ethics, as is made very clear in the *Stern Review* and explained below. This is not the place to discuss the climate science, but rather the economic modelling and especially the ethical assumptions needed to value impacts, which are critical to the magnitudes of damage measures and warrant some further discussion. The BGE has certainly hit the headlines with the dramatic claim that the impacts of climate change could be equivalent to 5–20% of world GDP, while the costs of mitigation might only be 1%, implying a large benefit–cost ratio for mitigation. However, it is not a particularly useful guide to policy, and is not further discussed here (rather elliptical details are provided in the *Stern Review*, 2006, Box 6.3, p. 161).

The figure of 5–20% is higher than many previous estimates for three sets of reasons.

1. Most previous estimations of costs used the results from the Third Assessment Report of IPCC, and Stern included more up-to-date

scientific evidence. The subsequently released Fourth Assessment Report of IPCC confirmed this approach.

2. Many cost estimates only considered direct economic impacts, but the *Stern Review* attempted to include all of the IPCC's five reasons for concern about projected climate change impacts (risks to unique and threatened ecosystems, risks from extreme climate events, distribution of impacts, aggregate impacts, and risks from future large-scale discontinuities) (IPCC, 2001a, p. 5).

3. The *Stern Review* used endogenous discounting and lower rates of pure time preference (0.1%) than many other authors.

As the *Stern Review* relies heavily on the PAGE2002 integrated assessment model (IAM), this is also a suitable place to provide a brief description of the model, and to illustrate the way in which the damage costs are derived, and their sensitivity to different ethical and statistical assumptions.

The *Stern Review* reviewed various IAMs before selecting the PAGE2002 model, and argued that

A model of the monetary cost of climate change ideally should provide:

- Cost simulations across the widest range of possible impacts, taking into account the risks of the more damaging impacts that new scientific evidence suggests are possible.
- A theoretical framework that is fit for the purpose of analysing changes to economies and societies that are large, uncertain, unevenly distributed and that occur over a very long period of time.

... The model we use – the PAGE2002 IAM – can take account of the range of risks by allowing outcomes to vary probabilistically across many model runs, with the probabilities calibrated to the latest scientific quantitative evidence on particular risks (Stern, 2006, p. 152, emphasis in original).

2.2   The PAGE2002 model

Integrated assessment models incorporate knowledge from more than one field of study, with the purpose of informing climate change policy. The first version of the PAGE (**P**olicy **A**nalysis of the **G**reenhouse **E**ffect) integrated assessment model was produced in 1991 for the European Commission. The latest version, and the one used in the *Stern Review*, was updated in 2002 to PAGE2002. It is able to include all of the IPCC's five reasons for concern about climate change, by virtue of its sectoral and regional structure, and its aggregation of impacts into a global net present value.The main structural changes to the earlier versions of PAGE incorporated in PAGE2002 are the introduction of a third greenhouse gas and, crucially for the *Stern Review*, the incorporation of possible future large-scale discontinuities into the impact calculations of the model. Default parameter values have also been updated to reflect changes since the IPCC Second Assessment Report in 1995. PAGE2002 contains equations that model:

- *Emissions of the primary greenhouse gases, CO_2 and methane*, including changes in natural emissions stimulated by the changing climate. PAGE2002 allows the explicit modelling of a third gas whose forcing is linear in concentration (which is the way in which various trace GHGs contribute to global warming), and models other greenhouse gases such as N_2O and (H)CFCs as a time-varying addition to background radiative forcing.
- *The greenhouse effect.* PAGE2002 keeps track of the accumulation of anthropogenic emissions of greenhouse gases in the atmosphere, and the increased radiative forcing that results, using a logarithmic relationship between concentration and forcing for CO_2, a square-root form for methane, and a linear form for the third gas (included to allow the social cost of trace gases to be estimated).
- *Cooling from sulphate aerosols.* The direct and indirect reductions in radiative forcing are separately modelled.
- *Regional temperature effects.* For the eight world regions in PAGE2002, the equilibrium and realised temperature changes are computed from the difference between greenhouse warming and regional sulphate aerosol cooling, and the slow response as excess heat is transferred from the atmosphere to land and ocean. Sulphate cooling is greatest in the more industrialised regions, and tends to decrease over time due to sulphur controls to prevent acid rain and negative health effects.
- *Non-linearity and transience in the damage caused by global warming.* Climatic change impacts in each analysis year are modelled as a polynomial function of the regional temperature increase in that year above a time-varying tolerable level of temperature change, $(T-T_{tol})^n$, where n is an uncertain input parameter normally in the range from 1 to 3. Impacts are aggregated over time using time-varying discount rates.
- *Regional economic growth tracking each region's GDP and GDP per capita over time.* Impacts are evaluated in terms of an annual percentage loss of GDP in each region, for a maximum of two sectors; defined in this application as economic impacts and non-economic (environmental and social) impacts.
- *Adaptation to climate change.* Investment in adaptive measures (e.g. the building of sea walls; development of drought-resistant crops) can increase the tolerable level of temperature change before economic

losses occur and also reduce the intensity of both non-economic and economic impacts.

- *The possibility of a future large-scale discontinuity.* This is modelled as a linearly increasing probability of a discontinuity that substantially reduces gross world product occurring as the global mean temperature rises above a threshold.

The PAGE2002 model (hereafter abbreviated to the PAGE model) uses relatively simple equations to capture complex climatic and economic phenomena. This is justified because the results approximate those of the most complex climate simulations, as shown by Hope (2006), and because all aspects of climate change are subject to profound uncertainty. The full set of equations and default parameter values in PAGE are included in Hope (2006). Most parameter values are taken directly from the IPCC Third Assessment Reports (IPCC, 2001a,b).

The outputs of PAGE include estimates of the impacts of climate change across the regions of the world and over time, how these impacts change if measures are taken to cut back the emissions of greenhouse gases or adapt to changes in climate, and what the costs of the abatement or adaptation measures might be.

To express the model results in terms of a single 'best guess' could be dangerously misleading. Instead, a range of possible outcomes should inform policy. PAGE builds up probability distributions of results by representing 31 key inputs to the social cost of carbon (SCC) calculations by probability distributions, making the characterisation of uncertainty the central focus, as recommended by Morgan and Dowlatabadi (1996). Figures 2.1 and 2.2 show the climate change impacts calculated by the PAGE model to 2200 on the IPCC's scenario A2 for the OECD, China, India (including the rest of South Asia), and the Rest of the World (ROW). The projections of GDP per capita in the A2 scenario at PPP (purchasing power parity) exchange rates are shown on a logarithmic scale so that lines of constant slope have a constant growth rate. Note the different vertical scales in the two graphs. In both figures the graph 'no CC' shows the evolution of per capita income assuming no climate change impacts, while the graphs labelled 'mean' show the evolution of per capita income under the mean climate change impact, and those marked 95% show the 95% worst case (i.e. 95% of possible paths have less severe impacts than this one).

Figure 2.2 shows the evolution of per capita income for India and the Rest of the World (ROW).[1] The ROW per capita income assuming no

---

[1] ROW is all countries other than OECD, India, and China

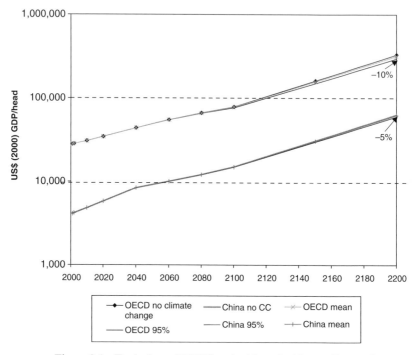

Figure 2.1. Evolution of GDP/head with and without climate change –
OECD and China

climate change (CC) grows on average at 1.5% p.a. reaching the dizzy
heights of $100,000 by 2200. The numbers at the right-hand side of
the graphs show the decrease in terminal GDP per head relative to the
'no climate change' impact. Thus for India the impact of climate
change in the 95% case causes a 69% fall compared to its level without
any climate change impact, i.e. there is a 5% chance that Indian
income in 2200 will be more than 69% below the 'no climate change'
reference path (although still over five times as rich as in 2001) and on
average it will be 27% below. For RoW, there is a 5% chance that
income in 2200 will be more than 40% below the 'no climate change'
reference path although still over 13 times richer than in 2001. Thus, in
both cases, these countries would still be considerably richer than now
even in the extreme case. In Figure 2.1 the percentage changes are too
small to see easily but the arrows show the 95% case – for OECD in
2200 the impact is only 10% of the 'no impact' level (and more than

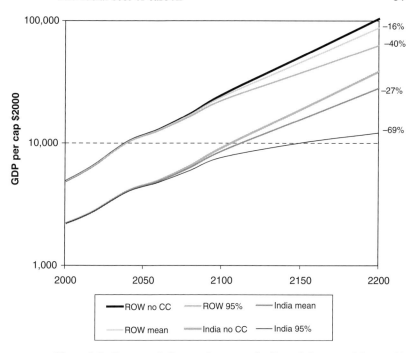

Figure 2.2. Impact of climate change on India and the rest of the world

ten times as rich as in 2001) and for China is only 5% (and over 14 times as rich).

The PAGE model provides only half of the story on climate change, for it captures the impacts of climate change across time and regions and, as we shall see below, values them to derive an estimate of the damage caused by climate change. Figure 2.2 shows that these impacts are delayed in time and concentrated on relatively poorer countries. Action to mitigate climate change will need to be taken in the near future and in countries that appear to be relatively sheltered from the full impact of climate change, as Figure 2.1 shows. The other half of the cost–benefit analysis is therefore to compare the costs of mitigation with the benefits of reducing the damage of climate change, and this chapter discusses some of the issues involved in making that balance. The critical element is to derive a price of carbon that will allow investors and consumers to make appropriate and decentralised decisions that collectively will deliver the right balance of mitigation and climate change.

As the *Stern Review* and other commentators have noted, the costs of mitigating climate change appear modest when compared with future decreases in income:

> In summary, analyses that take into account the full ranges of both impacts and possible outcomes – that is, that employ the basic economics of risk – suggest that Business as Usual (BAU) climate change will reduce welfare by an amount equivalent to a reduction in consumption per head of between 5 and 20%. ... *Resource cost estimates suggest that an upper bound for the expected annual cost of emissions reductions consistent with a trajectory leading to stabilisation at 550 ppm CO_2 is likely to be around 1% of GDP by 2050* (Stern, 2006, pp. x and xiii, emphasis in original).

While this suggests, but does not actually state, that the benefit–cost ratio of mitigation is highly attractive at between 5 and 20, the benefit estimates derive from a particular aggregation across countries and over long periods of time, while the costs will be incurred initially largely in developed countries such as the UK and in the next few decades. How this might be done is developed at greater length in Chapter 11 (Grubb and Newbery) where the choice of instruments is discussed. The rest of this chapter is directed to describing how the climate damage estimates are derived and how they can be translated into a carbon price.

2.3   Measuring the damage of greenhouse gas emissions

If we are to measure the damage of GHG emissions, we need to be able to value the impacts of the consequential climate changes. This is complicated for several reasons, but the idea is relatively straight-forward – what compensation (in money that can be used to buy other goods and services) would individuals require to make them as content with climate change as without? This immediately raises obvious problems – we are not sure what the physical consequences will be, and even if we were, we do not know how different future individuals would make the valuation (i.e. reveal what compensation would be just adequate), and (this is where the ethics comes in) how to balance these future monetary amounts needed to compensate future individuals (mostly as yet unborn) against expenditures by different people now to mitigate these impacts.

Nor can we leave the choice to the market, because, as noted above, GHGs are non-excludable public bads, and reducing GHG emissions is a pure public good (where 'pure' means non-excludable). Pure public goods require collective agreement on what action to take, and that involves balancing costs or payments now for future benefits to others, most of whom are not here to speak up for their shared common interest in our actions. We may be able to reach considerable agreement that we would like to pass on a better world (or at least not a worse world) to our descendants and those with whom we share an immediate gene pool.[2] We might therefore be willing to make some financial sacrifices now to benefit these descendants provided others (interested in their own relations) would do so as well in a collective agreement. The *Stern Review* goes considerably beyond this rather loose 'selfish gene' approach to take on board the full ethical content of a particular specification of classic utilitarian welfare economics. In doing so it follows a tradition of often controversial arguments for equity weighting in general, and a specific form of that weighting.[3]

Utilitarianism evaluates outcomes in terms of their consequences to individuals, while welfare economics assumes that these consequences can (to an operational extent) be measured in terms of consumption (or more broadly, well-being, which includes health, wealth and happiness to the extent that it can be measured by the same yardstick of money used to value material consumption). The ethics enters by supposing that consumption accruing to different individuals can be compared and aggregated using a social welfare function (SWF), $W(U^1(c_1), \ldots U^h(c_h) \ldots U^n(c_n))$, where c_h is the vector of consumption goods received by household h, and $U^h(\cdot)$ is a measure of utility of that household (which will typically depend on the number and age of household members and the internal distribution of goods between them).

The maintained assumption in the *Stern Review* (and the British Government's *The Green Book: Appraisal and Evaluation in Central Government* (HMT, 2003) and many of the references in footnote 5) is that the consumption bundle, c_h, can be measured by consumption expenditure per equivalent adult at market prices, c_h, and that the Social Welfare at some particular moment but including everyone on the planet takes the very specific additive form

$$W(U^1(c_1), \ldots U^h(c_h), \ldots U^n(c_n)) = \sum_{h=1}^{n} U^h(c_h) = \sum_{h=1}^{n} \frac{c_h^{1-v}}{1-v}, \quad v \neq 1,$$
$$= \sum_{h=1}^{n} \log c_h, \quad v = 1. \tag{2.1}$$

---

[2] Thus the famous British scientist, J.B.S. Haldane, is credited with saying that he would give his life to save more than two drowning brothers or more than eight drowning cousins, on the argument that if he were only concerned with passing on his genes to succeeding generations, as each brother shares half his genes and each cousin only one-eighth, in expected terms his genes would survive better provided the trades were sufficiently advantageous. It is thus not necessary (on the 'selfish gene' model at least) for everyone to have children to be concerned for future generations.

[3] See, e.g. Eyre *et al.* (1997), Fankhauser *et al.* (1997, 1998), Clarkson and Deyes (2002).

where v is Atkinson's (1970) coefficient of inequality aversion, analogous to the coefficient of relative risk aversion. One attraction of this iso-elastic form (v is the elasticity of marginal utility, which is constant)[4] is that it provides a single parameter to describe attitudes to inequality. Thus $v = 0$ corresponds to a complete disregard for inequality, where society is solely concerned with total consumption and not its distribution. Higher values of v attach increasing importance to redistributive goals. The social weight attached to consumption of person i is then $\beta_i = c_i^{-v}$. If, as in the *Stern Review* and the *Green Book*, one makes the further assumption that $v = 1$, the utility function is logarithmic, $U(c_h) = logc_h$ (sometimes referred to as the Nash–Bernouilli utility function). In that case, someone receiving half the average consumption level would count as twice as deserving in receiving an extra £1 in grant allocation as the average person – socially we would consider it as equally desirable to give £1 more to this poorer person as £2 more to the average. If $v = 2$, then the social weight of the poorer person would be $(1/2)^{-2} = $ four times as high as the average.

Where do these ethical ideas (and particular parameter values for the coefficient of inequality aversion, in this case $v = 1$) come from? One not very ethically convincing argument is that many perceptions (loudness of sounds, visual acuity, etc.) are logarithmic, so that a doubling of sound has an equal impact whether quiet or loud (and is measured in decibels, a logarithmic scale). If pain and pleasure are logarithmic, then perhaps the individual utility function should also be logarithmic. In the climate change debate, the ethical issue shows up sharply in whether to attach equity weights to future damages or not. Here, the two extremes are to count 1 dollar's worth of damage to a US citizen (per capita GDP $41,400 at purchasing power parity (PPP) in 2004) and someone in Bangladesh (per capita GDP $2,011 at PPP) as equal, or to weight them by the social marginal utility of consumption. If we take the Stern and *Green Book* weighting, then each person's gain or loss is given by the inverse of their consumption. On this basis, damage to the Bangladesh economy would be weighted nearly 21 times as heavily per citizen affected as damage to the US economy. If it so happened that damage to each were in proportion to their income, the effect would be to weight the damage as the same per head regardless of location in the world, which would have an appealing ethical simplicity.

As far as damage is concerned, a large part is likely to be the impact on human well-being, particularly the quality of life, where the approach of health economists of measuring benefits by quality-adjusted life years

---

[4] Stern uses the notation η for the elasticity of marginal utility.

(QALYs) gained, has immediate appeal. These are likely to be closely related to per capita GDP, so a Bangladeshi QALY might have a monetary value only 5% (at PPP exchange rates) of an American QALY. Weighting these by the inverse consumption per head would once again give an equal social weight to a Bangladeshi QALY as in the USA.[5] (Other elements of damage, e.g. to crops, property from flooding, hurricanes, etc, may also be roughly proportional to GDP, so this argument may extend more broadly.) Another way to appreciate the force of Stern's ethical assumption is that the social cost of reducing the consumption of a person in a rich country by 10% is valued equal to the social benefit of increasing the consumption of a person in a poor country by 10% now. Thus as the USA has 21 times the per capita consumption of Bangladesh (at Purchasing Power Parity exchange rates), incurring a cost of $21 in the USA to deliver a benefit of more than $1 in Bangladesh would register a net social gain on this calculus.

2.3.1   The social cost of carbon

The social cost of carbon (SCC) measures the present discounted value of the additional social costs (or the marginal social damage) that an extra tonne of carbon released now would impose on the current and future society. Other GHGs can be similarly valued and their social costs similarly expressed as a price per tonne. The PAGE model is set up to compute the social costs of carbon and other GHGs.

We noted above that estimating the SCC raises a number of related questions, including: What is social value and how should we measure the social cost when it occurs? In addition, we need to decide what rate of discount to apply to these future utility levels. A component of this discount rate, the rate of pure time preference, δ, measures the weight to attach to future levels of well-being solely because they are enjoyed later in time.[6] Some ethicists (notably Frank Ramsey, who developed the 'intertemporal theory of optimal investment') argued that to discount at any positive rate was solely because of a failure of imaginative sympathy, while others have argued that there is a non-zero risk of extinction of life as we know it (from asteroids, super volcanoes, or global nuclear war) and hence that $\delta > 0$. The number is critical when dealing with long time periods, as with climate change. The *Green Book* takes a value of

---

[5] The argument that lives lost in Bangladesh are no less valuable than those lost in the USA was persuasive in early debates, and is an attractive feature of the Nash–Bernouilli form.

[6] Stern uses the notation ρ for the rate of pure time preference.

$\delta = 1.5\%$, while the *Stern Review* takes the point estimate of $\delta = 0.1\%$. The implication of Stern's assumption that welfare is a logarithmic function of per capita consumption and that the rate of pure time preference is 0.1% is that the social cost of reducing the consumption of a person in any country by 10% (rich or poor) now is valued equal to the social benefit of increasing the consumption of a person in any country (rich or poor) by 11% in 100 years' time.[7] Thus if per capita consumption were to grow at 1.5% p.a. for 100 years, future generations would be 4.43 times richer than current generations, and $1 spent now would be more than compensated by avoiding a loss of $4.9 in 100 years, even though the future generations are much richer.

Finally, we need a method that can take account of the considerable uncertainty about the future damage and costs. This last point is handled by Stern's utilitarian ethics embodied in Eqn (2.1), combined with weighting each possible future outcome with a measure of its likelihood. The cost of a significantly adverse outcome is measured by the lower utility caused by a lower level of future consumption (or well-being) of agent h at time t in state of the world s: c^h_{ts}, while the weight to attach to state s is the probability of that state occurring, p_s. Putting this all together, the valuation of a trajectory of future levels of consumption is

$$W = \int_0^\infty \sum_{h=1}^{h=n} E \frac{(c^h_{ts})^{1-v}}{1-v} e^{-\delta t} dt, \qquad (2.2)$$

where δ is the rate of pure time preference, the sum is over all (equivalised for age) individuals, h, living at time t. E is the expectations operator, so that $E\,(c^h_{ts})^{1-v}$ is $\sum_s p_{ts}(c^h_{ts})^{1-v}$, where p_{ts} is the probability of state s occurring at date t. Taking account of the range of possible future levels of well-being profoundly affects the cost, as can be readily demonstrated. Suppose we follow Stern and take $v = 1$, so that the utility function is logarithmic. Suppose also that there is a 95% chance of consumption levels being 105, and a 5% chance of consumption being 5, so that the expected level of consumption is 100. However, the expected level of utility is 4.5, which is equivalent to a (certain) level of consumption of 90, and in terms of welfare risk has imposed a 10% reduction in the expected standard of living compared to the welfare associated with the expected point estimate of 100. If the two possible outcomes are 110 with $p = 90\%$ and 10 with $p = 10\%$, the loss of welfare

---

[7] $1.001^{100} = 1.105$ is the value of $1 invested at 0.1% for 100 years, so an increase of 10% now is as valuable as an increase of 11.05% in 100 years' time.

is 13.5%. Risk is costly in a way that can be quantified (once the utility function is specified).[8]

There is an obvious attraction in combining attitudes to risk and attitudes to inequality in the same utility function, and the coefficient of inequality aversion, v, in Eqns (2.1) and (2.2) is formally identical to Arrow's coefficient of relative risk aversion, which is often invoked to determine such critical parameters as the equity risk premium in discounting models, as discussed further below. They both relate to balancing the pain of suffering a loss or lower consumption level with the joy of a windfall gain or higher consumption level. Indeed, it is often argued that observing risky choices would allow us to infer the utility function, but most estimates suggest an implausibly high aversion to risk, measured by v.[9]

However, the concept of risk aversion attempts to describe a single person contemplating risky choices, where the person experiencing the gain or loss is the same as the one making the decision. Social risk aversion relates to social decisions (i.e. made by a policy maker) contemplating either good or bad outcomes for others affected by the decision. Inequality aversion is a further step in which decision makers contemplate actions which differentially affect the rich or poor, or, taking an even further step, contemplate transferring resources from the rich to the poor. Arguably, each extra step requires a somewhat stronger ethical position, or would require more discussion among the population affected. We come back to the issue of whether we are more likely to be concerned about outcomes to our potential genetically related descendants as we are about outcomes to future complete strangers and, more to the point, whether we need to be if each country collectively takes the appropriate supportive actions.

Finally, and this may be less obvious but is an immediate consequence of Eqn (2.2), attitudes to inequality (as well as the rate of pure time preference) affect the rate at which we discount the future. A simple example demonstrates this. Suppose that over long future periods of time we expect the rate of growth of per capita consumption to be g (which for Great Britain over the past half-century has averaged 2% p.a.). If we consider the person of average consumption at date t, $\bar{c}_t = \bar{c}_0 e^{gt}$, the

---

[8] $0.95^*\log_e(105) + 0.05^*\log_e(5) = 4.5$ and $\exp(4.5) = 90$. $0.9^*\log_e(110) + 0.1^*\log_e(10) = 4.46$ and $\exp(4.46) = 86.5$.

[9] There are many explanations, of which one of the more plausible is that hard-wiring in the brain has been selected to survive the kinds of risk encountered in the ancestral environments where humans evolved. Such instinctive responses are not necessarily well suited to more nuanced rational calculations of expected utility (Laland and Brown, 2002, p. 162).

associated weight to attach to marginal changes in well-being at date t is $\beta_t = \bar{c}_0^{-v} e^{-vgt}$ and the value now is $\beta_t e^{-\delta t} = (\bar{c}_0)^{-v} e^{-vgt} e^{-\delta t}$, which is falling at rate $i = \delta + vg$. This is the effective rate at which small changes in future standards of living (caused, for example, by the release of an extra Gigatonne of carbon now) should be discounted back to give a present value, essential to estimating the social cost of carbon. In social cost–benefit analysis it is known as the Consumption Rate of Interest (CRI), as it measures the trade-off between consumption now and consumption in the future. It should be contrasted with the Investment Rate of Interest (IRI), which relates the rate at which investible funds now generate re-investible profits in the future (and which might be distributed for consumption then). We shall return to the difference between them below.

If we think that high rates of growth, which lead to high future standards of living, should not therefore be given much weight, then this can be achieved by a higher discount rate, which might argue for a higher value for inequality aversion, v. In that case we automatically argue (in this particularly utilitarian framework) for a high weight to be placed on the poor now and less on adverse outcomes for future richer generations. Exploring the consequences of treating these various outcomes separately seems advisable.

The rate of pure time preference is a similarly powerful and contentious parameter that merits further discussion. For example, the *Stern Review* uses PAGE to project the world with and without climate impacts until 2200, and thereafter assumes that whatever damage climate change has done (as a percentage reduction in GDP below the 'no climate impact' reference) will continue thereafter. Thus, if in 2200 climate change has caused a 13.8% reduction in GDP relative to no climate change, then average per capita world GDP is assumed to continue to grow at 1.3% p.a. (with no further population growth) but 13.8% below the no-climate-change path. Yohe (2006) calculates that 55% of the present discounted value of the impact will occur after 2200 (when the model predictions cease) if the rate of pure time preference, δ, is 0.1%, but only 19% if the rate is 1% (and only 8% at 2%). A large part of the disagreement about the benefits of climate change mitigation arises from different views about this parameter (and about the 'right' way to discount the future more generally).

Perhaps the most persuasive argument for Stern's conclusions about the social cost of climate change, if not the logic of the argument, comes from Weitzman's (2007) review of the *Stern Review*. He notes that a not unreasonable consensus view on the rate of pure time preference, δ, might be 2%; of the elasticity of marginal utility, v, might be 2; and the rate of growth, g, might be 2%; suggesting a discount rate of 6%, leading to a valuation of damage 100 years hence only 1% as high as Stern's estimates. However, Weitzman notes that this fails to do justice to the possible variability of future growth rates, and that the correct discount rate when the rate of growth is variable is not the simple expectation of $\delta + vg$, because one should take discount factors into account, which gives a much lower average discount rate, considerably closer to the Stern value of 1.4%. The advantage of the PAGE model as used in the *Stern Review* is that, by applying the discount factor associated with each outcome and working with probability distributions of outcomes, as in Eqn (2.2), risk is correctly treated.

Weitzman also notes that the risk-free interest rate, the return to equity (risky) investment, the rate of growth and the variability of the rate of growth are closely related (using a similar logic to that used to derive the discount rate as $\delta + vg$). If the growth rate is normally distributed as $N(g, \sigma^2)$, then Weitzman shows that the equity risk premium (the difference between the risk-free rate and the return to equity) should be $v \sigma^2$. If the standard deviation of the growth rate, $\sigma = 2\%$, and the other parameters are taken as Weitzman's consensus values (which are all 2s), then the average return to equity would be 6% and the risk-free rate would be 5.9%. If climate damage is proportional to GDP, then the equity return is the correct discount rate, but the observed equity risk premium in the marketplace is closer to 5–6% than the 0.1% implied by the theory – hence the dual puzzles: the observed equity risk premium is apparently too high and/or the observed risk-free rate is too low.

Weitzman's resolution of these puzzles is to observe that observationally one cannot reject the hypothesis that the tails of the distribution of risky outcomes (growth rates, equity returns, etc.) are 'thicker' than the normal distribution, and over long periods of time, because the tails of the normal distribution fall off faster than a negative exponential, discounting makes extreme events carry little present weight. Fatter tails do not have this property and they can grow faster than any discount rate given a long enough period of time, meaning that future very uncertain events (such as extreme climate damage) can carry a far greater current weight than would be implied by simple equity discounting as illustrated above. Put another way, future climate damage may be perceived to be very costly today, not because our rate of pure time preference is very low, nor because our inequality aversion (or the elasticity of marginal utility) is rather low, nor because our growth predictions are rather cautious (Stern assumes $g = 1.3\%$), but because we attach greater subjective weight to a possibly extremely unlikely but very bad future outcome. Weitzman thus argues that Stern has the right answer (the damage may be five or more times as high as the cost of avoiding the damage) for the wrong reasons. Put in the context of the cost–benefit analysis of mitigating climate change, the high value of action now reflects the value of insurance against unlikely future disaster, where the probability and scale of that disaster are both unknown.

2.3.2   *Calculating the social cost of carbon using the PAGE model*

The PAGE model calculates the social cost of carbon (SCC) by finding the difference in the discounted economic cost of climate change impacts between two emission scenarios that are identical except for the emission of an extra 1 billion tonnes of carbon as CO_2 in 2001 for one of the scenarios. The difference in impacts is divided by 1 billion to obtain the SCC. The calculation is repeated with twice the difference in emissions to check that rounding errors for this small amount of extra emissions are not significant. The uncertainty in the SCC is captured by running the model 1,000 times, selecting different values for about 30 inputs from probability distributions. These probability distributions are triangular, and thus completely described by the minimum value, the value for the peak of the triangle, and the maximum value, expressed here as [minimum, most likely, maximum]. With wide enough ranges for the parameters, they can include the fat tails that have exercised people like Weitzman when attempting to reconcile rational responses to risk with observed behaviour, and this degree of uncertainty is a considerable improvement over simpler deterministic models.

The units in which damage is measured are, in the first instance, changes in GDP ($2,000 at PPP) by region and time. These are then equity-weighted, so that for region r at date t the total impact is the change in GDP multiplied by $\beta_{rt} = (c_{rt}/c_{Wt})^{-v}$, where c_{Wt} is average world per capita consumption at date t. The equity-weighted damage is then discounted at the time and regional varying consumption rate of interest $(\delta + vg_{rt})$, equivalent to multiplying β_{rt} by $(c_{rt}/c_{r0})^{-v}e^{-\delta t})$ and integrated over the period from now until 2200.[10] If eventually regions

---

[10] This is a rather hybrid approach to equity weighting, as Anthoff *et al.* (2006) argue. They propose using world average per capita consumption at date 0 as the numeraire, c_{W0}, so that the equity weight to apply for region r at date t is $\beta_{rt} = (c_{rt}/c_{W0})^{-v}$. This is then discounted by the rate of pure time preference, δ. If one chooses any other numeraire (e.g. EU per capita income, c_{EU0}) then the resulting SCC can be expressed relative to that numeraire by multiplying by $(c_{EU0}/c_{W0})^v$. This can make quite a difference. Thus, if $v = 1$ (the logarithmic and Stern case), as the world PPP income per head is $9,500 and the EU is $29,600, the result would need to be multiplied by 3.2 (see the CIA World Factbook, at https://www.cia.gov/cia/publications/factbook/rankorder/2004rank.html).

converge in their per capita growth rates, then there is a reasonably simple relationship between the unweighted cost of carbon, CC, and the equity-weighted SCC, SCC:

$$\frac{CC}{SCC} = \frac{Cov(D_r, Y_{r0})/Y_{W0} + D}{Cov(D_r, n_r) + D}, \tag{2.3}$$

where D_r is the present value of climate change damage in region r expressed each year as a fraction of region r's GDP of that year, and discounted at a suitable discount rate $(\delta + (v - 1)g)$, Y_{r0} is region r's GDP now, Y_{W0} is current world GDP, n_r is r's share of world population, and D is the average of the D_r values. If populous countries (those with high values of n_r) have higher than average damage impacts on future GDP, but smaller than average GDPs now, then $Cov(D_r, Y_{r0})$ will be negative and $Cov(D_r, n_r)$ will be positive, making the ratio less than 1 and hence making the unweighted cost of carbon less than the equity-weighted SCC.

Using scientific and economic inputs taken mainly from the IPCC's 2001 *Third Assessment Report*, and taking (as point estimates) the 2003 *Green Book* assumptions on the social rate of time preference $\delta = 1.5\%$, and $v = 1$ (the logarithmic case which is also the Stern assumption), the mean PAGE estimate for the SCC under the A2 scenario is $66/tC (tonne of carbon $= \$18/tCO_2$) emitted in 2001, in year 2000 dollars, with a 5–95% range of $13–185/tC ($3.5–50/tCO_2$). If the average rate of per capita growth until 2200 is 1.5%, this corresponds to a CRI of 3%. We see immediately just how broad the range of plausible estimates is, even with these fixed assumptions for discount rates and equity weights.

Allowing discount rates and equity weights to vary in PAGE gives slightly different results. With pure time preference rates, δ, of [1%, 2%, 3%] per year, and an equity weight parameter v of [0.5, 1.0, 1.5], the mean PAGE estimate for the SCC becomes $43/tC ($12/tCO_2$) emitted in 2001, with a 5–95% range of $10–130/tC ($3–35/tCO_2$). The figures are lower because the central value for the pure time preference rate, 2% per year, gives a slightly higher discount rate than the Treasury *Green Book*, and so the impacts that occur in the far future have less weight. The mean CRI would be 3.5% with a range from 1.75% to 5.25%.

Ignoring equity weighting altogether, but taking the discount rate as [2%, 3%, 4%], the mean SCC is $51/tC ($14/tCO_2$) with a range from $10 to $150/tC ($3–41/tCO_2$). Other authors have similarly explored the sensitivity of the SCC to equity weights. Clarkson and Deyes (2002) updated various estimates to 2001 and found that for Eyre *et al.* (1998), with no equity weighting, the SCC is $53/tC, $14/tCO_2$) at $\delta = 3\%$, which is very close to the PAGE mean estimate above for $\delta = [2\%, 3\%, 4\%]$ and not far from the mean value of \$66/tC (\$18/tCO$_2$) with equity weighting and a CRI of 3%.

The *Stern Review* takes point estimates $\delta = 0.1\%$, and $v = 1$ and, after updating PAGE to take account of more recent climate science that updates the IPCC 2001 models, arrives at a mean estimate of \$85/tCO$_2$ (\$312/tC). The difference between the *Stern Review* results and the estimates presented here is almost entirely due to the low value of δ; applying a value of $\delta = 0.1\%$ to the estimates in this chapter gives a mean SCC of \$330/tC (\$90/tCO$_2$), with a 5–95% range of \$65–870/tC (\$18–237/tCO$_2$).

The extreme sensitivity of the SCC (or the benefit–cost ratio of mitigating climate change) has been remarked on by other authors, including most recently Weitzman (2007), as discussed above. Cline (1992) argued for a very low discount rate and produced high damage estimates. Clarkson and Deyes (Table 2.1 in Clarkson and Deyes, 2002) cite Eyre *et al.*'s (1998) estimate for the equity-weighted SCC with $\delta = 1\%$ of \$244/tC (\$66/tCO$_2$) and, at $\delta = 3\%$, \$110 (\$30/tCO$_2$). Ackerman and Finlayson (2006) observed that the DICE model of Nordhaus and Boyer (2000), which fully recognises the seriousness of climate change, nevertheless found that 'the optimal carbon price is less than \$6 per ton in 1995 (\$1.6/tCO$_2$), and less than \$10 per ton in 2005 (\$3/tCO$_2$), rising very gradually to only \$140 per ton in 2195 (\$38/tCO$_2$)' (at \$1995). They demonstrate that 'a dramatically different policy recommendation results from just three plausible modifications to the model, involving the discount rate, the description of climate dynamics, and the benefits of moderate warming'. Combining all three effects and setting δ at zero increases the carbon price from \$6/tC to \$197/tC (\$54/tCO$_2$) rising at just over 0.5% p.a. to \$579/tC (\$159/tCO$_2$) in 2195.

The dramatic effect of apparently reasonable changes on the magnitude of the results may explain the disputes between climate scientists and economists over the past decade. Climate scientists effectively adopt very low discount rates when assessing future damages in a global system with very slow response times, while economists tend to discount future effects strongly, as the required rate of return for investments is typically rather high (8–15%). Once economists and climate scientists agree on how to treat the future and aggregate regional impacts, the disagreement almost entirely disappears.

The interim conclusion is that both the SCC (and the price) of carbon are very sensitive to a range of factors including the weights placed on future impacts and on impacts in other, poorer countries, and are therefore likely to be revised over time. Policy decisions therefore need to take account of this uncertainty, which typically means investing now to allow future decisions to be changed at lower cost, for example by enabling fossil-fired generation plant to be retrofitted with carbon capture. High values of the SCC can be defended either by assuming that we are willing to express significant social concern for distant future generations (low rate of pure time preference) or, in the spirit of Weitzman's review of the *Stern Review*, by assuming that the implied actions now, which are costly but not that costly (1–2% of GDP) should be considered as an insurance premium to avoid a possibly very low chance of very serious future damage. By definition, unpredictable events are impossible to model with any confidence, and the high SCC is warning us to take adequate steps now to reduce the risks of extreme, if unlikely, future disaster.

2.3.3   Growth of the SCC over time

Figure 2.3 shows how the PAGE estimates for the SCC vary with the date that the carbon dioxide is emitted. The values increase by about 2.4% per year; by 2060 the mean estimate has risen to $265/tC ($72/tCO$_2$). They

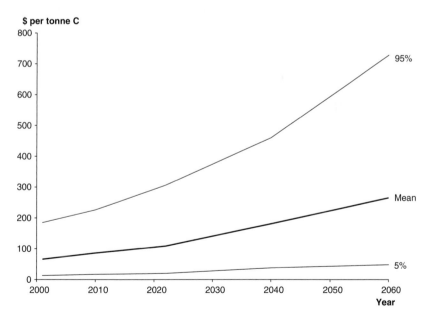

Figure 2.3. Social cost of carbon over time for $\delta = 1.5\%$ and $\nu = 1$

increase for the simple reason that, as we get closer to the time when we expect the most severe impacts of climate change to occur, then the extra impact from putting another tonne into the atmosphere gets higher.

2.3.4   *Invariance of the SCC with emission scenario*

All of these results assume that the extra tonne of carbon is emitted on top of an unconstrained emission path – scenario A2 from the IPCC *Special Report on Emission Scenarios* (SRES), shown in Figure 2.3. Under this scenario, PAGE projects the mean CO_2 concentration to be about 815 ppm by 2100 (1,140 ppm by 2150, 1,450 ppm by 2200), the mean temperature to be 4.1°C above pre-industrial by 2100, and the mean climate change impacts to be \$(2000)73 trillion, based on a time horizon of 2200 and discounted back to give a net present value. The probability distribution of impacts is shown in the first panel of Figure 2.5 (a small number of runs that gave impacts above \$200 trillion are not shown on the graph, but are included in the mean impacts of \$73 trillion).

If climate change is taken seriously, it is unlikely that emissions will be allowed to follow this unconstrained path. One constrained emission path that has been proposed aims to keep the atmospheric carbon dioxide concentration below 550 ppm, double the pre-industrial level, as also shown in Figure 2.4. Because of the stimulation of natural CO_2 included in PAGE, the scenario does not actually stabilise CO_2 concentrations at 550 ppm. Mean CO_2 concentration is about 594 ppm by 2100 (635 ppm by 2150, 670 ppm by 2200), mean temperature is 3.4°C above pre-industrial by 2100, and the mean NPV of climate change impacts is \$42 trillion (down from \$73 trillion in A2, mainly because of the big difference in temperature after 2100). The probability distribution of impacts from this scenario is shown in the second panel of Figure 2.5.

The social cost of carbon does not vary between the baseline A2 scenario and the '550 ppm' scenario; its mean value is \$(2000)43/tC under both scenarios, with a 5–95% range of \$10 to \$130/tC, reflecting several non-linearities in the chain of causality between emissions and discounted impacts that tend to offset each other. This finding is rather counter-intuitive and is a strong argument for using an integrated assessment model, as neither a scientific nor an economic model would be likely to pick it up.

The reason why this is true is not straightforward. It is caused by the interplay between the logarithmic relationship between radiative forcing (i.e. the global warming effect) and concentration (which will tend to make one extra tonne under the A2 scenario cause less impacts), the

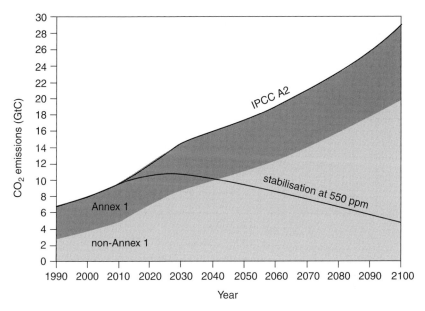

Figure 2.4. Evolution of emissions under IPCC A2 and to stabilise at 550 ppm   *Source:* IPCC and Stern (2006)

non-linear relationship of impacts to temperature (which will tend to make one extra tonne under the A2 scenario cause more impacts), and discounting (which will tend to make early impacts more costly than late impacts). This is shown in the four panels of Figure 2.6, in which the darker line represents the mean results from the A2 scenario, and the lighter one the mean results from the '550 ppm' scenario; each panel shows the mean effect of a billion extra tonnes of carbon emitted as CO_2 in 2001.

- *Forcing.* The first panel shows that 1 Gt extra C as CO_2 (1 Gt = billion tonnes) causes more extra forcing under the '550 ppm' scenario than under the A2 scenario. The extra forcing decays away over time both because the total CO_2 concentration rises and because most of the extra CO_2 eventually disappears from the atmosphere.
- *Temperature.* The second panel shows how this carries through into the extra temperature change from 1 Gt extra C as CO_2 emitted in 2001. The extra forcing takes time to have an effect on temperature, because of the thermal inertia of the Earth. The effect is still greater in the '550 ppm' scenario than in scenario A2, but the temperatures only really begin to diverge after 2060.

Distribution of total impacts, A2 scenario

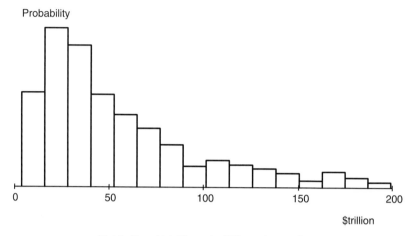

Distribution of total impacts, '550 ppm' scenario

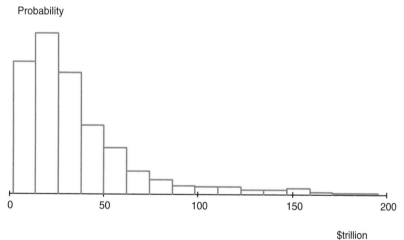

Figure 2.5. Probability distribution of climate change impacts from two scenarios
Source: PAGE2002 model runs

- *Undiscounted impacts.* The next panel shows how this carries through into the extra impacts. Up to about 2040 the extra temperature rise is very similar in the two scenarios, and the impacts anyway are small. From 2040 to 2100, the extra temperature rise in the A2 scenario causes slightly more extra impacts than the larger extra temperature rise in the '550 ppm' scenario, because it is superimposed upon a

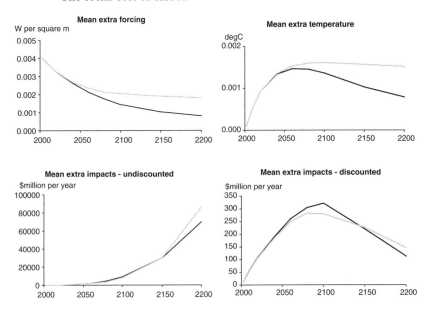

Figure 2.6. Mean effect of 1 Gt extra C as CO_2 on forcing, temperature, undiscounted impacts and discounted impacts by year
Source: PAGE2002 model runs

larger total temperature rise (a mean of 4.1°C above pre-industrial in 2100) in the A2 scenario than in the '550 ppm' scenario (a mean of 3.4°C above pre-industrial in 2100). By 2200, this relationship has reversed, and the larger extra temperature rise in the '550 ppm' scenario has the greater extra impact, mainly because even under the '550 ppm' scenario, global temperatures by 2200 are in the range where a large-scale discontinuity, such as the melting of the West Antarctic ice sheet, becomes a possibility.

- *Discounted impacts.* The final panel shows the extra impacts discounted back to the base year 2000. The peak contributions to the SCC come around the years 2080–2100. The SCC is found for each scenario by integrating the values under this curve, and dividing by 1 billion. The larger values for scenario A2 from 2040 to 2100 and for the '550 ppm' scenario in 2200 approximately cancel each other out.

This final panel also shows that a time horizon of 2200 is barely sufficient to capture all the contributions to the SCC with the discount rates used (a pure time preference rate with a mean value of 2% per year, and a range of 1–3% per year). Contributions to the SCC from beyond

2200, which are not captured in PAGE, would continue to be slightly higher for the '550 ppm' than the A2 scenario.

The SCC appears to be insensitive to the exact emissions scenario within quite a wide range. There has been some concern expressed about the accuracy of the emission scenarios from the IPCC *Special Report on Emission Scenarios* (SRES). All of the results from PAGE that use an unconstrained emission path are based upon scenario A2 from the SRES. What is the effect of making an extreme assumption about the inaccuracy of scenario A2, namely that global emissions of all green-house gases and sulphates in all future years are only half the values assumed in Scenario A2 from the SRES? The emissions of CO_2 that result are shown in Figure 2.7; note that they are below the year 2000 emissions until 2040.

How does this extreme assumption affect the concentration, radiative forcing, temperature and impacts in future years? Figure 2.8 shows the mean values from the PAGE model for these variables by date, expressed as a proportion of the mean values from running PAGE with the A2 scenario from the SRES. The emissions are at 50% of the A2 values throughout, as this is the assumption that we are making.

The concentration of CO_2 in the atmosphere is 88% of the A2 value in 2040, and stays above 66% of the A2 value all the way through to 2200. This is because past emissions stay in the atmosphere for many decades,

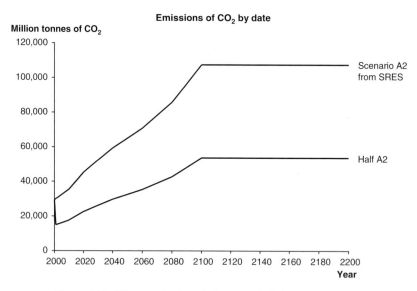

Figure 2.7. Time path of emissions modelled

Proportion of scenario A2

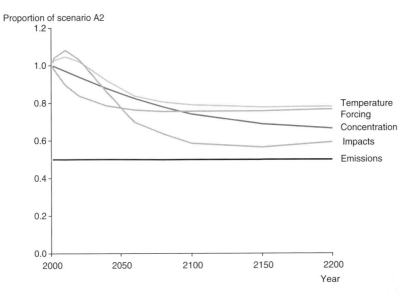

Figure 2.8. Impact of halving emissions relative to A2 scenario

and so it takes a long time for the lower future emissions to have an effect.

The radiative forcing from the greenhouse gases is 79% of the A2 value in 2040, and never drops below 75% of the A2 value. It is below the CO_2 concentration line for most of the next century because the radiative effects of the shorter-lived greenhouse gases such as methane disappear from the atmosphere much more quickly than CO_2.

The global mean temperature is actually higher than the A2 value until 2020, as the short-term influence of the lower sulphates outweighs the longer-term influence of the greenhouse gases. Sulphates cool the atmosphere, so if there are less of them, the global mean temperature will be higher. By 2040 the global mean temperature increase is 92% of the A2 value (1.34°C rather than 1.46°C above pre-industrial levels), and it never drops below 78% of the A2 value (6.15°C rather than 7.88°C in 2200).

The impacts of climate change are likewise higher than in the A2 scenario until 2020, and are 86% of the A2 value in 2040. By 2150 they have dropped to 56% of the A2 value, and by 2200 to 59% of the A2 value, as impacts are more than a linear function of temperature.

The net result of all this can be seen in the mean total impacts aggregated over time and discounted back to the present day, which are

Table 2.1. *Mean values of impacts and social cost of carbon, by scenario*

	A2 from SRES	Half A2
Total climate change impacts	$76 trillion	$45 trillion
Social cost of carbon	$43/tC ($12/tCO$_2$)	$43/tC ($12/tCO$_2$)

shown in Table 2.1. The mean value of $45 trillion is 59% of the A2 mean value of $76 trillion. Of more immediate policy relevance is the social cost of carbon, which is the benefit of reducing today's emissions of carbon by 1 tonne. As Table 2.1 shows, the mean value for the social cost of carbon is essentially identical to the A2 value.

2.4   Major influences on the social cost of carbon

If the emission path does not affect the SCC, what does? Figure 2.9 shows the major influences calculated by PAGE: the longer the line, the larger the influence. That the major influences divide into six scientific and seven economic parameters is another strong argument for the building of integrated assessment models such as PAGE. Models that are exclusively scientific, or exclusively economic, would omit parts of the climate change problem that still contain profound uncertainties.

The two top influences are the climate sensitivity, which is the temperature rise that would occur for a doubling of CO$_2$ concentration, and the pure time preference rate. The climate sensitivity is positively correlated with the SCC, so a rise leads to a higher SCC; the pure time preference rate is negatively correlated with the SCC, so a fall leads to a higher SCC, and so on. We can now see that it is not surprising that the *Stern Review* found such a high value for the mean social cost of carbon: their value for the second most important parameter, the pure time preference rate, was much lower, at 0.1% per year.

As an example of the changes that new scientific information can bring, the journal *Nature* has recently published a new likelihood-weighted probability distribution for the climate sensitivity, with a mean value of 3.6°C, and a 5–95% range of 2.4–5.4°C. Using these values for the climate sensitivity in PAGE, instead of the 1.5–5.0°C range given by the IPCC, increases the mean value of the SCC from $43 to $68 per tonne of carbon emitted in 2001, with a 5–95% range of $11–202.

Using the distribution from Stainforth *et al.* (2005), which has a most likely value of 3°C, and a long tail extending to high values over 8°C, increases the PAGE mean value of the SCC to $90 per tonne of carbon, with a 5–95% range of $10–220.

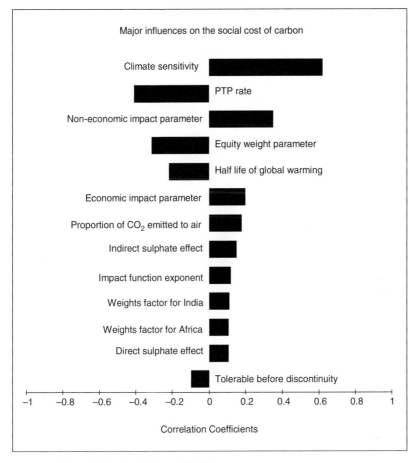

Figure 2.9. Sensitivity of SCC to parameters
Note: PTP = pure time preference.

2.5   Social cost of other greenhouse gases

The PAGE model includes a range of greenhouse gases, not just carbon dioxide, and can calculate the social cost of each of them. Using the original assumptions (point estimates $\delta = 1.5\%$ and $v = 1$, giving a SCC of \$66/tCO$_2$), the mean PAGE estimate for the social cost of methane is \$280 per tonne emitted in 2001, with a 5–95% range of \$80–750. The carbon equivalent of methane now is thus 4.24, i.e. 1 tonne of methane is 4.24/tC or 15.5/tCO$_2$. In the future, the social cost of methane increases faster than carbon dioxide, by 3.6% per year. This is because of the short atmospheric lifetime of methane; any extra methane emitted today will have disappeared from the atmosphere before the most severe climate change impacts occur, but emissions that occur later will not. The PAGE estimate for the social cost of SF_6 is \$800,000 per tonne emitted in 2001, with a 5–95% range of \$160,000–2,100,000, so 1 tonne $SF_6 = 12,121/tC = 44,444/tCO_2$.

It is interesting to compare these results with the other preferred method of global warming potentials (GWP). DEFRA (2006) explains the thinking behind them:

> To compare the relative climate effects of greenhouse gases, it is necessary to assess their contribution to changes in the net downward infra-red radiation flux at the tropopause (the top of the lower atmosphere) over a period of time. Ultimately the best way to do this is by comparing different emission scenarios in climate models, but a simple working method has been derived for use by Parties to the UNFCCC. This provides the relative contribution of a unit emission of each gas, relative to the effect of a unit emission of carbon dioxide integrated over a fixed time period. A 100-year time horizon has been chosen by the Convention in view of the relatively long time scale for addressing climate change. The factor is known as a global warming potential (GWP).

DEFRA (2006) lists the GWPs for methane and SF_6 as 21 and 23,900, respectively, in terms of CO_2. This means that 1 tonne of methane emitted to the atmosphere has 21 times the warming potential over 100 years as 1 tonne of CO_2. These figures are the 1995 GWP values. Whilst the global warming potentials have since been updated, the Kyoto Protocol states that 'global warming potentials used by Parties [to the Protocol] should be those provided by the Intergovernmental Panel on Climate Change in its Second Assessment Report' (DEFRA, 2006). More recent 100-year GWP values in the IPCC's *Third Assessment Report* (IPCC, 2001b) are 23 for methane and 22,200 for SF_6. Thus, compared to the present-day PAGE estimates, the GWP of methane is overstated and SF_6 significantly understated, illustrating the challenge for international political processes to update their processes as better methods become available.

2.6   Conclusions

What is the right price of carbon if we are to persuade countries to confront those releasing GHGs with a carbon price? Clearly the price should be the same for all countries to achieve a reduction in emissions at least cost; but equally clearly, the SCC with different countries taking their own standards of living as numeraire will all be different. Second, if consumption transfers to India (GDP/head of \$PPP 3,400) counts as 8.7 times as valuable now as consumption transfers to the EU (GDP/head of

$PPP 29,600), would it not be better to make such transfers now as well as over the next 150 years via GHG reductions? Third, if the marginal cost of avoiding damaging climate change is less than the estimate of the SCC, should not the price of carbon be set by the intersection of supply (of climate change mitigation) and demand (for damage avoidance, measured by the SCC)? The answer to this last question is that it certainly should be, but the PAGE model demonstrates that there is good reason to believe the carbon price for a tonne of CO_2 superimposed on an intertemporal optimal path of emissions will not be very different from the price for one superimposed on scenario A2 as calculated in this chapter.

This is related to another deep question in intertemporal welfare economics, for the implied Consumption Rate of Interest (CRI, which is what is being used to discount future carbon damage) in the *Stern Review* is of the order of 1.3–1.6% (per capita growth rate in the long run is about 1.3–1.5% plus the CRI so $i = \delta + vg$). The Investment Rate of Return (IRI) is certainly much higher than this, perhaps of the order of 5–8% (depending on the treatment of risk), and nuclear generation is likely to be cost-effective with a modest carbon price in this range. If IRI > CRI, which rate should be used for investing in climate change mitigation? The answer is that, if IRI > CRI, then there must be some constraint preventing the authorities who select projects (or guide such decisions) from raising the rate of investment to bring the two rates into equality. That is akin to asking why the price of carbon is not set to balance both the supply and the demand for mitigation.

Finally, as there is no global tax jurisdiction or emissions trading system setting a single carbon price to maximise global welfare, presumably the best we can do is to imagine a 'coalition of the willing' reaching an agreement on what price of carbon is in everyone's best interests. How does the SCC as computed relate to such a bargaining solution? For efficient climate change mitigation, the price of carbon should be the same everywhere, but the cash value of the damage done to each country will depend on its income level. Suppose that poorer countries have no higher electricity intensity (kWh/$GDP) than richer countries, and suppose that, at a carbon price, p, each country reduces its CO_2 emissions from electricity generation in the same proportion to total generation and hence to GDP, so that country i reduces emissions by μY_{i0} tonnes CO_2. The extra cost to each country will also probably be proportional to the amount of low-carbon electricity that displaces high-carbon electricity, and hence also proportional to its GDP, say $\kappa_i Y_{i0}$. The total global emissions reduction will thus be similarly proportional to global GDP, μY_{W0} and each country will benefit in PDV cash terms by $\mu Y_{WO} D_i Y_i$ where D_i is the ratio of the NPV of the damage that 1 tonne of CO_2 released now will do to current GDP in country i. The country-level benefit–cost ratio will be $\mu Y_{WO} D_i/\kappa_i$. Provided that D_i/κ_i does not increase with income, poorer countries should find such a uniform price as acceptable as richer countries. As poorer countries may have higher values of future damage to their GDP than richer countries, D_i may be higher in poorer countries, encouraging such countries to join a carbon-pricing club, but to the extent that they discount the future more heavily, D_i will be lower, making current sacrifices less attractive.

What this uniform price should be is less clear. Fortunately, we have argued above (and the model supports the algebraic claim) that the unweighted or cash value of the SCC, although less than the equity-weighted value using global per capita consumption as the numeraire, is not that different, and perhaps it is also closer to the price (path) of carbon that would ensure that the optimum climate change mitigation path is followed (optimal in balancing costs and benefits). At present these questions are not easily answered, and one must interpret any calculated *price* of carbon with caution.

Even if the SCC (with some suitable numeraire) provides some guidance for setting the carbon price (or determining the quantity of tradable permits to issue, adjusting quantities to drive the traded price towards the correct carbon price), the estimates from PAGE and other integrated assessment models are only as complete as the scientific and economic information that goes into the model. PAGE does make an attempt to cover all five reasons for concern about climate change identified by the IPCC, including a rudimentary treatment of large-scale discontinuities such as the melting of the West Antarctic ice sheet. It does not include the security implications of any large-scale migration caused by climate change. From an economic perspective it therefore only offers a lower bound to the damage cost, and policy that aims for the best guess rather than a 'scientifically' determined lower bound should take a higher social cost of carbon.

The main purpose of this chapter is not to promote any one estimate of the social cost of greenhouse gases. As we have shown, although the social cost of carbon is insensitive to the emission scenario on which an extra tonne of carbon is superimposed, it is influenced by many factors, which are still subject to great uncertainty, and the same is true of the social costs of other greenhouse gases.

Rather, we have tried to demonstrate that integrated assessment models such as PAGE can perform a useful service by taking the best information from the detailed scientific and economic research, and revealing its policy implications. They can also highlight just how much we still have to learn about the economic implications of climate change, and enable different views on economic and scientific parameters, such as discount rates, equity weights and climate sensitivity, to be rigorously explored. To quote from the *Stern Review*:

We would therefore point to numbers for the 'business as usual' social cost of carbon well above (perhaps a factor of three times) the Tol mean of $29/tCO$_2$ and the 'lower central' estimate of around $13/tCO$_2$ in the recent study for DEFRA (Watkiss et al., 2005) ... Nevertheless, we are keenly aware of the sensitivity of estimates to the assumptions that are made. Closer examination of this issue – and a narrowing of the range of estimates, if possible – is a high priority for research (Stern, 2006, p. 287).[11]

We have seen that the SCC is very sensitive to the treatment of impacts in the distant future (i.e. the discount rate), and the valuation of the more severe impacts on poorer regions (through the equity weights) as well as on the climate science. In addition, what is needed for policy purposes is a carbon price, which is not necessarily the same as the social cost of carbon. The relationship between the two concepts, and the design of a process to elicit a carbon price that can be widely (ideally globally) adhered to, is another and more practically pressing problem. The aim of this chapter has been to lay out the various factors that bear on these issues, which are taken up in Chapter 11 (Grubb and Newbery), which addresses the choice of instruments to guide the economy towards a low-carbon future.

References

Ackerman, F. and I.J. Finlayson (2006). *The Economics of Inaction on Climate Change: A Sensitivity Analysis*. mimeo, Medford, MA: Global Development and Environment Institute (GDAE), Tufts University.

Anthoff, D., C. Hepburn and R.S.J. Tol (2006). Equity weighting and the marginal damage costs of climate change. Hamburg, Germany [see http://ideas.repec.org/p/fem/femwpa/2007.43.html].

Atkinson, A.B. (1970). On the measurement of inequality. *Journal of Economic Theory*, 2, 244–263.

---

[11] Box 13.1 of the *Stern Review* summarises other estimates of the SCC, citing a study by Downing et al. (2005) for DEFRA, which observed that estimates in the literature range from £0–1000/tC (£0–273/tCO$_2$), and suggested a lower benchmark of £35/tC (£9.5 = $12.5/tCO$_2$) (all at 2000 prices). Tol's (2005) survey found a median value of $14/tC ($3.8/tCO$_2$) and the 95th percentile at $350/tC ($95/tCO$_2$), comparable to that of the *Stern Review* (Stern, 2006, p. 288). The IPCC has yet to publicly report on its latest findings, but has issued a Summary for Policymakers in which it says 'Peer-reviewed estimates of the social cost of carbon in 2005 average US$12 per tonne of CO$_2$, but the range from 100 estimates is large (−$3 to 95/tCO$_2$).'

Clarkson, R. and K. Deyes (2002). *Estimating the Social Cost of Carbon Emissions.* Government Economic Service Working Paper 140, London: HM Treasury and DEFRA [see www.hm-treasury.gov.uk/documents/taxation_work_and_welfare/taxation_and_the_environment/tax_env_GESWP140.cfm].

Cline, W.R. (1992). *The Economics of Global Warming.* Washington, DC: Institute for International Economics.

DEFRA (2006). *Climate Change: The UK Programme 2006.* London: HMSO [see CM6764 at www.defra.gov.uk/].

Downing, T.E., D. Anthoff, B. Butterfield, M. Ceronsky, M. Grubb, J. Guo, C. Hepburn, C. Hope, A. Hunt, A. Li, A. Markandya, S. Moss, A. Nyong, R.S.J. Tol and P. Watkiss (2005). *Scoping Uncertainty in the Social Cost of Carbon.* London: DEFRA.

DTI (2006). *Energy Review: The Energy Challenge.* London: Department of Trade and Industry.

Eyre, N., T. Downing, R. Hoekstra, K. Rennings and R.S.J. Tol (1998). *Global Warming Damages: Final Report of the ExternE Global Warming Sub-Task.* DGXII, Brussels, European Commission [see www.externe.info/ under Publications / ExternE Externalities of Energy Vol. 8: Global Warming].

Fankhauser, S., R. Tol and D.W. Pearce (1997). The aggregation of climate change damages: a welfare theoretic approach. *Environment and Resource Economics,* **10** (3), 249–266.

Fankhauser, S., R. Tol and D.W. Pearce (1998). Extensions and alternatives to climate change impact valuation: on the critique of IPCC Working Group III's impact estimates. *Environment and Development Economics,* **3,** 59–81.

Hope, C., (2006). The marginal impact of CO_2 from PAGE2002: an integrated assessment model incorporating the IPCC's five reasons for concern. *Integrated Assessment,* **6**(1), 19–56.

HMT (2003). *The Green Book: Appraisal and Evaluation in Central Government.* London: HM Treasury [see www.hm-treasury.gov.uk/economic_data_and_tools/greenbook/data_greenbook_index.cfm].

IPCC (2001a). *Climate Change 2001: Impacts, Adaptation and Vulnerability.* Contribution of Working Group II to the Third Assessment Report of the Intergovernmental Panel on Climate Change, Cambridge University Press.

    (2001b). *Climate Change 2001: The Scientific Basis.* Contribution of Working Group I to the Third Assessment Report of the Intergovernmental Panel on Climate Change, Cambridge University Press.

Laland, K.N. and G.R. Brown (2002). *Sense and Nonsense: Evolutionary Perspectives on Human Behaviour.* Oxford University Press.

Mirrlees, J.A. and N.H. Stern (1972). Fairly good plans. *Journal of Economic Theory,* **4**(2), 268–288.

Morgan, M.G. and H. Dowlatabadi (1996). Learning from integrated assessment of climate change. *Climatic Change,* **34**(3/4), 337–368.

Nordhaus, W.D. and J. Boyer (2000). *Warming the World: Economic Models of Global Warming.* Cambridge, MA: MIT Press.

Stainforth, D.A. *et al.* (2005). Uncertainty in predictions of the climate response to rising levels of greenhouse gases. *Nature,* **433,** 403–406.

Stern, N.H. (2006). *The Economics of Climate Change.* Cambridge University Press.

Tol, R.S.J. (2005). The marginal damage costs of carbon dioxide emissions: an assessment of the uncertainties. *Energy Policy*, **33**, 2064–2074.

Watkiss, P. *et al.* (2005). *The Social Cost of Carbon.* London: DEFRA.

Weitzman, M. (2007). The Stern Review of the Economics of Climate Change. draft book review for *Journal of Economic Literature.* mimeo, Cambridge, MA: Harvard University.

Yohe, G. (2006). Some thoughts on the damage estimates presented in the *Stern Review*. mimeo, Middletown, CT: Wesleyan University.

3 Technologies for a low-carbon electricity system: an assessment of the UK's issues and options

Tooraj Jamasb, William J. Nuttall, Michael G. Pollitt and Alexandra Maratou

3.1 Introduction

As noted in the first chapter of this book, the electricity sector is, both globally and in the UK, the single largest contributor to the emission of greenhouse gases (GHGs). Thus, it is to be expected that the sector will be called upon to carry a significant portion of the required reductions in emissions. This requires that low-carbon generation technologies be adopted. However, low-carbon generation technologies are currently either more costly than fossil-fuel-based sources and/or require further technical improvements. Most low-carbon technologies also contribute towards the diversity of energy sources and increased security of supply.

While the *Stern Review* recognises the role of the electricity sector and the importance of technological progress in achieving climate change goals, it does not provide a detailed assessment of the UK's technological context (Stern, 2007). This chapter addresses the main technological issues and options for the UK's electricity sector in achieving its international climate change commitments and the government's own policy goals.

The UK government has committed to challenging climate change and renewable energy objectives and policy targets. Most notably, the government has set out to reduce CO_2 emissions to at least 26% below 1990 levels by 2020, with a further aspiration of a 60% reduction in CO_2 emissions by 2050 (Climate Change Bill, 2008). This target is more stringent than the UK's legally binding commitment under the Kyoto Protocol to reduce emissions of a basket of six greenhouse gases by 12.5% below 1990 levels over the 2008–2012 period. Furthermore, the government aims to increase the share of electricity generation from renewable sources to 10.4% by 2010/2011, rising to 15.4% by 2015/2016 and 20% by 2020.

These targets have significant implications for the electricity sector in the UK, since electricity accounts for a significant part of total energy consumption – approximately 19% of final consumption in 2005 (DTI, 2006e), and total CO_2 emissions –approximately 31% of total CO_2 emissions in 2005 (DEFRA, 2007).

In parallel, the European Commission introduced a set of ambitious targets in January 2008. The proposed European Directive (COM/2008/0019) on the promotion of the use of energy from renewable sources sets overall EU targets of a 20% reduction in CO_2 emissions and a 20% share of renewable energies in energy consumption (i.e. electricity, heating/cooling and transport) by 2020. Member states will be required to adopt national targets in line with the overall renewable goal. The proposed national target by the Commission for the UK is a 15% share of energy from renewables by 2020. It is up to the UK to decide how the electricity sector will contribute to this target.

Achieving these ambitious targets has to take place within, and has implications for, the operating environment of some of the most established industries, including the energy sector itself. They also require a range of measures, arrangements and incentives. However, meeting these targets in practice has proved to be more difficult than was initially anticipated and it is evident that there are no obvious and readily available solutions to fully meet these targets in the short term.

Jamasb et al. (2006) discuss, in Future Electricity Technologies and Systems that, in future electricity systems, the range of technological possibilities and options from generation to networks and end-use will widen and that many of these will coexist. This also means that, for the foreseeable future, the conventional technologies will be an important part of the electricity system. Meeting ambitious policy targets is highly dependent on further technological progress and deployment of innovative solutions in the medium and long term. Technical progress will gradually reduce the cost differences between the technologies. As a result, factors other than cost of components, such as proximity to grid, local resource availability, and demand characteristics, as well as regulatory framework and policy, will increasingly play a role in the uptake of individual technologies. At the same time, it is important that the targets are achieved via cost-effective solutions. Therefore, there is also a need to assess the external cost of carbon and the cost of abatement in policy design.

However, the path leading to a future low-carbon electricity system is likely to be a gradual process that will evolve through different phases. At each phase, different issues will arise and specific technological options will become available that together would render certain types of measures and courses of action appropriate. In the short and medium term, the potential technological options will be at different stages of development. This chapter reviews the main technological issues and options facing the UK in achieving a low-carbon electricity sector.

As editors of *Future Electricity Technologies and Systems*, we acknowledged that the range of technologies discussed in that volume is not comprehensive and that technologies such as fusion, tidal and geothermal energy were omitted (Jamasb *et al.*, 2006, p. 20). In part, this is because those technologies are believed to be unlikely to achieve maturity by the mid-2030s and, as such, widespread deployment by 2050 is subject to significant uncertainty. In this chapter we deliberately broaden the discussion to include these somewhat more tentative technologies.

The next section of this chapter reviews the main categories and the development stage of the UK's main technological options for low-carbon electricity production. Section 3.3 reviews the cost and contribution potential of the technologies as evaluation criteria. Section 3.4 revisits the current R&D effort and the cost of low-carbon energy promotion policies in the UK with particular emphasis on the significance of liberalisation of the electricity sector as an important contextual factor. Section 3.5 presents an overall assessment of the technological options and conclusions.

3.2   Technological options and development stage

The resource mix of the UK electricity sector is currently more diverse than in any previous period. As more technologies gradually develop, the range of technological options will also widen, and the diversity of the available resource mix is likely to increase. Future progress towards a low-carbon electricity system is a function of the technologies available and their stage of development.

Major UK official documents reviewing the energy technology options identify a range of technologies that are in different stages of development (e.g. ICCEPT, 2003; ICCEPT and E4tech Consulting, 2003; House of Lords, 2004; House of Commons, 2005; National Audit Office, 2005). In any given period, there are some technological options that can contribute towards the goal of a low-carbon electricity system, while there are other technologies on the horizon that need time, resources and support to develop in the medium and longer term (Jamasb *et al.*, 2006). This section covers the main technologies mentioned in the *Stern Review*, i.e. onshore and offshore wind, wave and tidal, photovoltaic, carbon capture and storage, nuclear power, hydroelectric power, bioenergy, decentralised power generation including microgeneration, and combined heat and power. However, unlike that

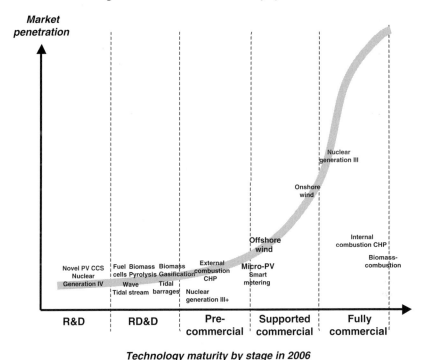

Figure 3.1. Technological options – maturity and market penetration
Source: IEA Energy R&D database

document, which simply lists some of the most prominent options for decarbonising electricity generation, this section delves deeper into discussing each option's stage of development.

Broadly, the UK's technological options can be classified into three groups comprising approximate periods on a progress timeline. Figure 3.1 shows the development stage of the electricity technologies considered in this chapter, based on their degree of maturity and market penetration. The axes of the figure are adopted from ICCEPT and E4tech Consulting (2003), but the actual technologies included and their position in the illustration can differ. The following development stages are considered, as described in ICCEPT and E4tech Consulting (2003, p. 19):

- *R&D* includes both 'blue skies' science and engineering/application-focused research.
- *RD&D* (research, development and demonstration) includes early prototypes and installed full-scale working devices – but only in single

units or small numbers, and still financed largely through R&D-related grants.

- *Pre-commercial* is the stage where multiple units of previously demonstration-stage technologies are installed for the first time, and/ or where the first few multiples of units move to much larger-scale installation for the first time.
- *Supported commercial* is the stage where, given generic support measures such as the UK Renewables Obligation, technologies are rolled out in substantial numbers and by commercially oriented companies.
- *Commercial* technologies can compete unsupported, within the broader regulatory framework.

As shown in Figure 3.1, at each development stage there are a few potential technological solutions on the horizon. Some of these technology types (such as wind, nuclear and biomass) consist of sub-categories, which can be at different stages of progress. An extended outline of the main technology types as well as their main sub-categories and stage of development is presented in Table 3.1. For the purpose of this chapter, we view these technologies in three broad categories.

The first category (moving from right to left in Figure 3.1) consists of technological options that are at the supported commercial and fully commercial stages of development and exhibit the highest levels of market penetration among low-carbon technologies. These technologies can begin to contribute to the resource mix of the sector in the short term. However, at present, the supported commercial technologies are generally only cost-competitive when their positive environmental externalities are taken into account. The main technologies in this broad group of technologies include onshore wind, nuclear generation III, and some forms of energy efficiency.

The UK has significant wind-power resources, which can be developed at varying costs. In recent years, wind-power development has, in response to government incentive schemes, increased and the trend is, given continued support, likely to continue. Nuclear power has emerged, in the first instance, as a replacement for plants planned for retirement, and subsequently as a policy option to achieve carbon emissions reduction targets. Under the current stated policy, nuclear projects will not receive subsidies and will need to be entirely privately financed. However, measures have been proposed to facilitate the planning and licensing process.

Energy efficiency consists of a rather wide range and large number of technologies in different applications and end-use sectors (see World Energy Council, 2004). These technologies cover the whole spectrum of

Table 3.1. *Stage of development for the main technological options in 2006*

Technology	Sub-category		Stage of development
Wind power	**Onshore**		Supported commercial (commercially viable under RO)
	Offshore		Pre-commercial
Photovoltaic electricity generation	**Off-grid systems** – 40% of the world market		Novel PV: RD&D
	1. Off-grid habitation		
	1a. Solar home system (SHS) on individual dwellings		
	1b. Solar system used to configure central village power plants		
	2. Off-grid industrial		
	Grid-connected systems are the fastest growing sector of the PV market – 60% of the world market		Conventional PV: Supported commercial
	1. Building integrated systems – over 95% of this sector worldwide		
	2. Large-scale plants – 5% worldwide		
Bioenergy: thermal processing of biomass	**Combustion**		Fully commercial
	Gasification		RD&D – commercial in niche markets
	Pyrolysis		RD&D – commercial in niche markets
	1. Fast pyrolysis – favours production of liquids		
	2. Carbonisation – favours production of charcoal		
	3. Gasification – favours production of gas		
Geothermal	**Natural hydrothermal**		International RD&D, but UK has few resources
	Geopressured systems		R&D
	Hot dry rock		R&D – Some prospects in SW England
	Magma		Speculative research plans
	Low-grade heat pumps		Supported commercial
Marine energy	**Wave energy**	**Wave shoreline**	RD&D
		Wave near shore (less that 20 miles to the coast)	RD&D
		Wave offshore	RD&D
	Tidal energy	**Tidal barrage**	RD&D stalled, but interest in the concept reviving
		Tidal stream	RD&D

Note geothermal energy depends on geothermal gradient and heat quality or grade. By 2000 more than 10GWe of capacity has already been installed in favourable international locations.

Table 3.1. (cont.)

Technology	Sub-category		Stage of development
CO₂ capture, transport and storage	**CO₂ capture**	Pre-combustion	Commercial – technology widely applied in fertiliser manufacturing and in hydrogen production
		Post-combustion	Commercial – separation of CO₂ in the natural gas processing industry
		Oxy-fuel	RD&D
	CO₂ transport	Pipeline	Commercial – in the USA, over 2,500 km of pipelines transport more than 40 Mt CO₂ per year
		Shipping	Commercial – analogous to shipping of liquefied petroleum gases, but is currently carried out on a small scale due to limited demand
	CO₂ storage	Deep underground (within aquifers, salt or fresh water layers)	Supported commercial – Statoil undertakes CO₂ capture and storage at the Sleipner field in the North Sea
		Abandoned gas and oil fields	Supported commercial
		Use of CO₂ for enhanced gas or oil recovery	Commercial (e.g. Weyburn project in Canada)
		Ocean storage	R&D
Nuclear energy	**Fission**	Generation II (e.g. existing BWRs, PWRs, CANDU, the Russian VVERs)	Commercial, but now superseded by Generation III designs
		Generation III – advanced reactors newly licensed or ready for licensing in the near future (e.g. AP600, AP1000, ABWR, EPR, VVER-640, ACR)	Evolutions of existing designs poised for commercial deployment
		Generation III+ (e.g. Pebble-bed modular reactor) and Generation IV advanced concepts subject to international R&D. Accelerator-driven systems – such as the 'Energy Amplifier' concept	Generation III+ technologies are moving from Development to Demonstration. Generation IV technologies are moving from Research to Development and Accelerator-driven systems are the subject of Research and Pre-research planning
	Fusion	ITER experimental research project now internationally funded for development in Cadarache France. Other fusion concepts such as Stellerators, Spherical tokamaks, Z-pinch and Inertial confinement subject to ongoing research	ITER at the Development R&D stage with plans for follow-up Demonstration most other concepts at the research stage

Miniaturisation	Fossil-fuel-fired microgenerators usually CHP units running on natural gas, LPG or liquid fuels	External combustion (Stirling) engines	Pre-commercial
		Internal combustion engines	Commercial
		Fuel cells	RD&D
		Rankine-cycle engines	R&D
		Steam cells	R&D
	Renewable microgenerators using	Solar power (photovoltaic solar cells)	Supported commercial
		Wind power	R&D
		Renewable fuels used in internal or external combustion engines, run as CHP or pure generators	R&D
Energy efficiency	**Industry**	Combustion technology	Energy efficiency technologies comprise a wide range and large number of technologies. Energy efficiency technologies are at different stages of technical progress. Some of the technologies are commercially available and can be easily implemented while others require more R&D, time and support to advance.
		Process intensification	
		Process control	
		Materials	
		Separation technologies	
		Alternative equipment	
		Waste heat recovery	
	Buildings	Heating	
		Ventilation	
		Cooling	
		Building fabric	
		Controls and energy management systems	
		Integrated building design	
	Appliances	Lighting and appliances	

Source: DEFRA (2005), Jamasb *et al.* (2006), Nuttall (2005), Tester *et al.* (2005)

development and maturity stages (and therefore the term 'energy efficiency' does not appear in one specific position in the diagram), more of which will gradually be developed and commercialised for adoption. The primary contribution of a more efficient use of energy is through reducing demand growth and energy intensity. As can be seen from Figure 3.1, internal combustion CHP and biomass combustion also fall within the first category. However, market penetration for these has not advanced as rapidly as technology maturity would imply for a successful option, as they face particular barriers to adoption.

The second category of technological options includes the solutions that are at demonstration and/or pre-commercial development stage. These technologies exhibit moderate levels of both technological maturity and market penetration. These technologies need to progress further in the medium term through a combination of R&D and adoption of incentive measures before their potential for becoming a significant share of the resource mix can be utilised. The technologies in this group include biomass gasification, offshore wind, external combustion combined heat and power (CHP), and carbon capture and sequestration (CCS).

A noteworthy aspect of the technologies in this category is that most of these are related to technology types that are at the supported or fully commercial stages of development. Therefore, progress in one of the branches of these technologies can also have a positive effect on progress in other areas of that technology. One exception, however, is the CCS technologies. Further progress in these technologies may also help conventional fossil fuel technologies maintain their significant shares of the resource mix in the electricity sector. Coal power (with higher thermal efficiency than currently) is the most likely first candidate, via CCS fitted to new plants, while gas power is also a possible candidate for CCS. In general, most component technologies of CCS are already commercial. The overall chain of CO_2 capture, transport and storage is, however, at the RD&D stage. Moreover, it should be noted that CCS reduces the thermal efficiency of the generation plants.

The third category of technologies consists of solutions that are at the research and development (R&D) and/or demonstration stage of development. Contribution of these technologies to a low-carbon electricity sector needs to achieve significant progress and is most probably only attainable in the long term. The main source of progress in this category is in basic research and demonstration, often with substantial public support. The technologies in this group include biomass pyrolysis, fuel cells, wave and tidal, nuclear generation III+ and generation IV, steam cells and photovoltaic power. A notable characteristic of this category is that it includes a wider range of options that are based on fundamentally different technologies from the second group. This signifies that the long-term potential for increased diversity of the resource mix of the sector is likely to be higher.

Much of the difficulty associated with commercialisation of new energy technologies lies not in an expectation of high costs, but rather in the uncertainty of cost predictions. For instance, the recent debate surrounding generation III nuclear new build occurs against a backdrop of a range of levelised cost estimates, some of which imply that nuclear power projects can be placed in the fully commercial category.

Fuller considerations of project risk and strategic options can be evaluated using real options analysis. Such analyses imply that some support in terms of underwriting risk or financial guarantees may be required if project completion is to be certain. The real options technique is well suited to addressing the challenges inherent in highly capital-intensive and somewhat uncertain new energy technologies. For example, the technique has been used to estimate optimal levels of public R&D support for keeping the roll-out options open while cost, information and attitudes to climate change still develop. The option value of waiting before implementing a capacity roll-out support programme can be high, given the current level of uncertainty about costs and the attitudes of other countries. Should a global technology consensus emerge, high levels of energy R&D will leave the country undertaking the R&D well placed to respond rapidly. Davis and Owen (2003) use a real options model to estimate the optimal level of annual federal renewable electricity R&D expenditure for the USA, viewing the federal R&D programme as an insurance policy for domestic energy security. The analogy to an insurance policy is inherent in the fact that an investment (in renewable electric R&D) is being made in order to insure against potential unfavourable future outcomes. However, in the case of R&D expenditures, there is no guarantee that the investment will pay off, since the outcome cannot be known in advance.

3.3   Evaluation criteria: cost and potential of technological options

As seen in the previous section, the UK's technological options are at different stages of progress. The main indicator of technological progress in economic terms is in the form of cost improvement. The main source of cost improvement, however, changes at different stages of the progress from basic R&D to market promotion and commercialisation (Figure 3.1, x-axis). Market penetration is, in turn, largely dependent on cost improvement of the technology. In this section we examine the UK's technological options further, using the cost and contribution potential of the technologies as assessment criteria. We choose to refer primarily to the latest available assessments offered in official publications, as these are produced by, and are intended for use in, policy discussions and decision-making.

Cost of technological options

Economic efficiency requires that policies must promote, and result in, cost-effective solutions. Long-term estimates of the cost of technologies indicate that the cost differences between these are expected to become smaller. As a result, the cost ranges of several technologies will overlap. As mentioned earlier, this will broaden the basis for a potentially more diverse resource base in the electricity sector. The diversity of sources, however, may still be more in the form of the number of technologies than in terms of their share of total energy demand.

At the same time, the cost of conventional electricity generation technologies in effect set important benchmarks against which cost performance of new technologies will be compared. Table 3.2 shows some recent estimates of the current cost of fossil-fuel-based electricity generation technologies with and without CCS technology as well as wind and nuclear power, as reported in the *Energy Review Report 2006* (DTI, 2006a).

Table 3.3 shows an example of the estimated costs of main technological options in 2020 and their trend towards 2050 (IEA, 2006). The cost estimates are reasonably consistent with the estimates outlined by Anderson (2006), which are based on interpretations from a large number of studies in the UK and abroad for the *Stern Review*. The cost estimates are the result of using 'learning curves' and 'engineering assessments'. The estimated costs for generation technologies include grid connection charges, but do not include additional locational charges – which can range from positive to negative. Additional system costs due to intermittency for renewables are not explicitly included, which are expected to be small at low levels of penetration. Indeed, the intermittency costs in Great Britain for a penetration level of intermittent generation of up to 20% of electricity demand are in the order of £5–8/MWh, made up of £2–3/MWh for short-run balancing costs and £3–5/MWh for the cost of maintaining a higher system margin, which is shared between all consumers. This would translate into a total of a 0.1–0.15p/kWh increase in electricity prices (UKERC, 2006). Higher levels of penetration are subject to much uncertainty and are considered elsewhere in this volume.

Table 3.2. *Example of estimated current costs of technologies*

Technology	Full sensitivities cost range* (p/kWh – 2005 prices)	Discount rate sensitivity (p/kWh – 2005 prices)	
		7% discount rate	12% discount rate
Gas			
Combined cycle gas turbine (CCGT)	2.47–5.51	3.28	3.58
CCGT with carbon capture and storage (CCS)	3.65–6.78	4.47	5.02
Coal			
Pulverised fuel (advanced super critical, ASC) with flue gas desulphurisation (FGD)	2.24–4.43	2.24	2.87
Pulverised fuel (ASC) with FGD and CCS	3.55–5.3	3.6	4.41
Integrated gasification combined cycle (IGCC)	2.53–4.8	2.53	3.23
IGCC with CCS	3.5–5.67	3.92	4.87
Retrofit coal plant based on pulverised fuel (ASC) with FGD and CCS	3.13–4.52	3.3	3.76
Nuclear energy			
Generation III (the analysis focuses on the light water reactor (LWR) design types)	3.04–4.37	3.09	4.21
Wind power			
Onshore wind	4.68–8.89	4.73	6.07
Offshore wind	5.62–13.3	6.99	9.26

*Up to 30 sensitivities, including ranges in the discount rate, capital cost, operations and maintenance costs, fuel prices, carbon prices, load factors, and interest rate margin for construction finance.
Source: Based on DTI (2006a).

Table 3.3. *Example of current and future costs of renewable technologies*

Technology		Cost (p/kWh 2004 prices)*		
		2005	2030	2050
Wind power	Onshore wind (5% LR)**	2.3–12.3	2.0–11.6	1.9–11.4
	Offshore wind (5% LR)	3.7–12.1	3.4–10.2	3.3–10.0
Biomass (5% LR)		1.7–5.7	1.7–5.3	1.6–5.2
Geothermal (5% LR)		1.8–5.4	16.7–4.8	1.6–4.7
Hydro	Large hydro (5% LR)	1.9–6.5	1.9–6.4	1.8–6.3
	Small hydro (5% LR)	3.1	2.9	2.7
Solar PV (18% LR)		9.9–30.1	3.9–18.1	<3.3–16.1
Solar thermal (5% LR)		5.8–12.8	4.8–10.6	<3.3–9.9
Tidal (5% LR)		6.8	5.2	5

* Converted from 2004 $US to 2004 £GB costs using a £1 = $1.8 exchange rate. Estimates are based on a 10% discount rate. Ranges reflect variation in investment cost and fuel price assumptions. The actual global range can be wider, as discount rates, investment cost and fuel price assumptions vary. Wind and solar include grid connection cost.
** LR = Assumed learning rate.
Source: IEA (2006)

The future costs of technologies are, as is often the case, reported in relatively wide ranges. This is partly due to uncertainty associated with costs of capital, operation and maintenance, fuel and installations. For example, the costs of offshore wind power and energy crops by 2020 are estimated at 2–3 and 2.5–4p/kWh, respectively. The cost estimates suggest that photovoltaics, fuel cells, wave and nuclear III+ generation will be at the demonstration or pre-commercial stage of progress.

A crucial area for achieving cost reduction by 2020 is CCS technologies. By this date, fossil-fuel-based generation still dominates the resource mix of the sector. At the same time, about 23,000MW of coal-fired generation capacity in the UK built between 1965 and 1975 will need to be replaced (IEA, 2006, p. 185). Coincidence of replacement of fossil-fuel-based plants with commercialisation of CCS can increase the cost-effectiveness and facilitate adoption of the technology. The costs of technologies will depend on R&D and the scale of roll-out, and hence, rather like the French vs. British nuclear experience, the more options that are picked the less learning by doing may occur. Also, many technologies are internationalised, and their cost in the UK will depend on roll-out rates elsewhere.

Moreover, it should be noted that, even in 2020, we are likely to observe significant 'within-technology' cost ranges. The cost of renewable technologies tends to be more sensitive to features of specific projects, such as siting, nature of demand and size, than conventional technologies. This may somewhat limit the availability and contribution potential of new low-cost renewable sources.

3.4   Carbon abatement costs and external costs

As the cost of technologies gradually declines, the cost of carbon abatement through renewable sources will also decrease. Table 3.4 shows an estimation of the cost of carbon abatement for the main technological options in 2020. The abatement costs refer to the cost of replacing emissions from combined cycle gas turbines (CCGTs). The uncertainty in the generation cost estimates is also reflected in the carbon abatement costs. To the extent that the cost of energy from alternative technologies can go below that of CCGTs, the abatement costs take negative numbers – i.e. they show net benefits.

As mentioned earlier, market promotion of low-carbon technologies may in some cases be justified, even before their economic costs are fully competitive. There are different external (environmental and social) costs associated with nearly every form of electricity generation technology. However, the levels of external costs are generally significantly higher for conventional fossil-fuel-based technologies. Table 3.5 shows the estimated external costs for some electricity generation technologies, as estimated by the ExernE project on the externalities of energy, which has been launched by the European Commission. The total carbon dioxide emissions in the UK amounted to 590 and 557 $MtCO_2$ in 1990 and 2005, respectively, while the emissions attributed to the electricity sector amounted to 204 and 175 $MtCO_2$ in 1990 and 2005, respectively (DEFRA, 2007).

Costs of the damage caused to health and environment by emissions of pollutants, as well as costs resulting from the impact of global warming attributable to emissions of greenhouse gases, are considered. The former category depends on the location of source and receptor points.

The magnitude of these cost estimates, and notably those concerning fossil-fuel-based technologies, indicates that their internalisation could bridge the generation cost gap between conventional and renewable technologies. This could be illustrated, for instance, for the case of CCGT and wind with reference to Tables 3.2 and 3.5: by adding the external costs, the current cost ranges for the two technologies amount to 3.15–6.19p/kWh for CCGT and 4.75–8.96p/kWh for onshore wind, resulting in increased overlap and therefore increased competition between the two technologies. As the relative costs of renewable resources decrease and their share of the resource mix rises, a relevant policy

Table 3.4. *An example of cost of carbon abatement estimates for alternative technologies*

	Carbon abatement cost £ per tonne of CO_2 equivalent in 2020 (2001 prices)*		Potential contribution to carbon emission reduction — GHG emissions in 1990 = 775 million tonnes of CO_2 equivalent; CO_2 emissions in 1990 = 592 million tonnes of CO_2		Potential for development specific to the UK
	Minimum	Maximum	2020 ($MtCO_2$)**	2050 ($MtCO_2$)	
Transport energy efficiency	Probably negative	Needs to be assessed in detail	51.33	110	International industry
Large CHP	−51.82	30.00	11	18.33	Strong
Micro-CHP	−171.82	−30.00	3.67	18.3	Significant, given UK gas dependence
Onshore wind	−21.82	13.64	3.67	18.3	International industry
Offshore wind	−8.18	40.91	29.33	>73.3***	Specific developments
Marine (wave and tidal)	19.09	122.73	small	>73.3***	Good prospects for UK-specific developments
Energy crops	19.09	54.55	11	36.7	International industry
Solar photovoltaics	141.82	340.91	<3.67	>73.3***	International industry
Nuclear	19.09	54.55	25.67	>73.3***	International industry
Carbon sequestration	21.82	76.36	small	>73.3***	Specific developments
Service sector energy efficiency	−70.91	13.64	14.67	36.7	Strong
Domestic energy efficiency	−81.82	13.64	55	110	Strong
Industrial energy efficiency	−21.82	8.18	33	91.7	Varied

* Based upon estimated cost ranges for 2020 (see PIU, 2002, Annex 6, p. 199).

** Approximate and taking into account practical constraints on build rates by 2020 for nuclear and offshore wind; that land use constraints limit the contribution from onshore wind; and assuming that the practicable potential for PV is constrained by the likelihood of continuing high cost in a 20-year time-frame.

*** A large proportion of electricity could be generated in this way by 2050, reducing emissions by at least 20 MtC (73.3 $MtCO_2$) compared with using gas. The potential increases substantially if electricity (or hydrogen made from it) is used to meet demands currently met from other sources, such as for transport. *Source:* Adapted from PIU (2002, p. 108)

Table 3.5. *External costs of current and advanced electricity systems, associated with emissions from the operation of power plants and with the rest of the energy chain*

Technology		External costs (p/kWh* in 2005 prices)		
		Total energy chain	Of which related to power plant operation	Related to greenhouse gas emissions
Coal	Lignite	3.97	3.86	1.588
	Hard coal	2.77	2.29	1.385
	Hard coal Pressurised fluidised bed combustion	1.23	1.06	1.033
Oil	Oil	3.28	2.77	1.476
	Oil combined cycle	1.06	0.75	0.678
Gas	Gas	1.06	0.79	0.832
	Gas combined cycle	0.68	0.51	0.558
Nuclear	Light water reactor	0.14	0	0.011
	Pressurised water reactor (centrifuge enrichment)	0.12	0	0.007
Hydro	Hydro-power (alpine)	0.03	0	0.005
Photovoltaic	PV panel (south Europe)	0.17	0	0.064
	PV panel integrated in roof (south Europe)	0.17	0	0.063
	Near future PV panel integrated in roof (south Europe)	0.14	0	0.043
Wind	Wind onshore 800kW	0.07	0	0.016
	Wind offshore 2MW	0.1	0	0.022
Cogeneration	Modern diesel unit using selective catalytic reduction, 200kWe	1.5	0.99	0.938
	Modern lambda=1 motor gas cogen. plant using three-way catalytic converter, 160kWe	0.99	0.68	0.807
	Modern gas cogen. plant without catalysts, 1MWe	0.99	0.75	0.752

*Figures converted from euro to sterling using the 2005 annual average exchange rate £1=€0.6837.   *Source:* Based on EU (2005, Figure 9, p. 35)

question is whether it is more appropriate to internalise the external cost of conventional resources or to continue to subsidise the renewable resources. This is an issue which later chapters in the book will address.

3.5   Contribution potential

There is considerable scope for carbon reduction from technically available and economically viable low-carbon resources in the UK. Table 3.6 shows the potential for electricity generation and carbon reduction from some technological options. As shown in the table, the potential onshore and offshore resources are both significant, although the prospects of contribution from the latter lie in the medium and long term. For the purpose of comparison, in 2005 the electricity production in the UK amounted to 409TWh (DTI, 2006e) while the CO_2 emissions from the sector were at 175 $MtCO_2$ (DEFRA, 2007).

Table 3.6 shows the contribution potential for several technologies in terms of technical and economic resources. The technical resource accrues from the total natural resource after technical factors (such as leaving areas of sea free for shipping or the preservation of environmentally sensitive regions) are taken into consideration, while the economic resource accrues from the technical one, after economic factors (for example increased cost of connection to the electricity network for offshore technologies) are considered.

However, although these technologies are low-carbon or carbon-free, in practice other environmental or economic concerns may constrain their contribution potential. For example, wind-power development can lead to wildlife and visual environmental concerns, while nuclear power is faced with siting, operational safety and waste management issues. Moreover, the intermittent nature of renewable energy means that these should be backed up by a sufficient conventional generation capacity. The required level of back-up, however, depends on the share of intermittent sources as well as their geographical and technological diversity (see Chapter 5 by Sinden).

It is important to note that some of the pressure towards resource diversification will be driven by resource constraints. For example, the amounts of suitable land for biomass or sites for wave and wind energy in the UK that can be developed economically are limited.

3.6   Technology push, market pull and context

As mentioned in the Introduction to this chapter, the objective of a low-carbon electricity sector and enhancement of the UK's technological

Table 3.6. *Contribution potential of technological options*

	Technology	Maximum capacity
Wind power	Onshore	50TWh/year of economic resource[1]
	Offshore	100TWh/year of economic resource[2]
Bioenergy: thermal processing of biomass	Forestry crops, dry agricultural residue, waste wood and woody energy crops	Current potential to supply 41TWh/year. In the future this could rise to c. 80TWh/year.[3]
Geothermal		Only one geothermal combined heat and power plant in operation in the UK, in Southampton – limited potential for further geothermal plants due to geological reasons.
		Ground-source heat pumps are becoming more popular, with an increasing number installed throughout the UK in homes, commercial buildings and for swimming pools (around 250 installed every year).
		It has been estimated that there are 1,550 large industrial sites in the UK where heat-pump systems could be installed, with an average size of 800kW of thermal power (or approximately 8TWh/year assuming 6,500 hours usage).[4]
Hydro	Large	4.648TWh generated in 2004 [6] – limited opportunities to increase large-scale hydroelectric in the UK, as most commercially attractive and environmentally acceptable sites have now been utilised.[4]
	Small	Technical potential of 10TWh per year.[4]
Photovoltaic electricity Generation		266TWh/year of technical potential for PV applied to all orientations. 37TWh per year of technical potential for BIPV in 2025.[5] 0.17TWh/year of economic potential in 2025 (limited to the possible rate of PV uptake in new buildings).[5]
Marine energy	**Wave energy** Shoreline	0.4TWh/year technical resource[6] 0.0TWh/year economic resource[6]
	Near shore (closer than 20 miles)	2.1TWh/year technical resource[6] 2.1TWh/year economic resource[6]
	Offshore	50TWh/year technical resource[6]
	Tidal energy Tidal barrages	50TWh/year[7] (not including current resource) 31TWh/year economic resource[6]
	Tidal streams	18TWh/year technical resource[8]

Table 3.6. (*cont.*)

Technology	Maximum capacity		
CO$_2$ capture, transport and storage[13]	256,100 MtCO$_2$ of estimated storage capacity in the North Sea.[9] This is sufficient for 1,000+ years of UK CO$_2$ production. The key determinant of annual capacity will therefore be injection rate, rather than reservoir size.		
Nuclear energy	Fission: 75.170 TWh(e) in 2005[10] Fusion: power plants are expected to operate at approximately 1.5GWe each. Fuel will be derived from lithium and deuterium from sea water. Both fuels have enormous abundance. One challenge could be helium availability. Helium is a required consumable for plant operations and is itself a finite resource[11]		
Energy efficiency	Potential carbon saving (MtCO$_2$) p.a. by:[12]		
	2010	2020	2050
• Industry	0.18	1.7	10.2
• Buildings	0.40	4.8	30.2
• Appliances	0.11	3.9	21.6

1 DTI (2005b); 2 DTI (2005a); 3 Paul Arwas Associates (2005); 4 www.dti.gov.uk; 5 ETSU (1999, p.141); 6 Jamasb *et al.* (2006); 7 www.dti. gov.uk; 8 Black and Veatch (2005); 9 Holloway (1996); 10 IEA (2006); 11 Clarke (2006); 12 DEFRA (2005). 13 There are 256,100 MtCO$_2$ of estimated storage capacity in the North Sea (Holloway, 1996). However, most of this (240,000 MtCO$_2$) is in the form of open saline aquifers, which is not the preferred option for storage. In contrast, closed aquifers have defined boundaries produced by geological folding or faulting, which considerably reduces the possibility for lateral movement and slow seepage of CO$_2$ into potable aquifers or to the surface (DTI, 2003a, p. 10). The rest, which is in the form of depleted oil or gas fields and closed saline aquifers, amount to 16,100 MtCO$_2$ of the estimated capacity. Given the UK's total electricity production (375TWh) and CO$_2$ emissions (174 MtCO$_2$) from the electricity sector, this would be equal to CO$_2$ emissions from generation of 34,698TWh (=16,100/(174/375)) to be stored in the closed saline aquifers of the North Sea or about 92 years (=16,100/174) of full CO$_2$ emissions abatement. Nonetheless, the main limitation is the rate at which it is possible to inject the CO$_2$. For example, the annual injection rate for the world's first large-scale storage project at the Sleipner Gas Field in the North Sea amounts to 1 MtCO$_2$.

options is dependent on achieving significant technological progress in the short and medium term. The main vehicles of technical change are R&D and market adoption, which are promoted by learning-by-research and learning-by-doing processes, respectively (see Jamasb, 2007). The notion of induced technological change implies that R&D and adoption can be supported through appropriate policies (see Chapter 12 by Jamasb and Kohler and Chapter 10 by Neuhoff and Twomey). In addition, liberalisation of the electricity sector has had profound effects on the context within which technological progress and diffusion is to take place. This section briefly reviews the current state of R&D and the specific features of market promotion in the UK related to particular technologies, and discusses the significance of liberalisation of the sector as a contextual factor.

Research and development

The public sector has traditionally played a major role in supporting and promoting energy R&D. This is mainly due to the occurrence of market failure associated with risk and uncertainty of success, appropriation of profits and spillovers, and the extent to which pre-commercial research should be regarded as a public good rather than a private commodity. As a result, the private discount rate of R&D investments can be higher than their social discount rate, leading to under-investment in R&D. New and emerging energy technologies are, in particular, prone to market failure and under-investment in R&D. However, the government's R&D spending on renewable energy and conservation technologies in the UK has shown a marked decline in the past 15 years (Figure 3.2).

As seen from the figure, nuclear research alone constituted a significant share of total energy R&D until its substantial decline beginning in the early 1980s. Another notable research area was energy conservation, which also began to decline in the early 1980s. Overall, the level of government energy R&D spending on low-carbon technologies in recent years has been at rather low levels. This includes technology areas such as wind and wave energy, where the UK has a comparative resource advantage. Much of the decline in R&D spend coincides with, and continues after, the liberalisation of the electricity sector based on privatisation and later competition. UK energy policy was dominated by such considerations aimed at improving the efficiency of the sector but to the relative neglect of the effect on energy research.

While it is difficult to say what the correct level of public R&D expenditure is, it is interesting to observe that the current level of expenditure on certain technologies, which are at early stages of development and which have significant potential in the UK, is very low. One

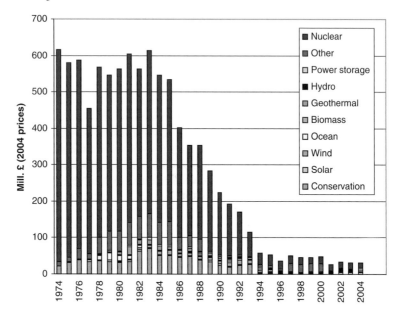

Figure 3.2. Public renewable energy R&D spending in the UK
Source: Format adapted from ICCEPT and E4tech Consulting (2003)

might expect that the amount and distribution of public R&D might reflect the latent potential for wave, solar and biomass deployment in the UK. It seems scarcely credible that the value of public R&D has declined in these areas from the levels of the late 1970s until now.

There are also strong indications that energy companies have reduced their R&D spending and that the new actors (e.g. independent power producers) are not involved in such activities. The decline in private R&D spending was matched by the concomitant decline in public support for energy R&D. While little is known about R&D spending among the equipment manufactures. This does not seem likely to have increased (Jamasb and Pollitt, 2005). In particular, R&D spending in the networks has declined. In 2003, the UK distribution network operators (DNOs) spent about 0.1% of their revenues on R&D (Mott McDonald, 2004).

While public R&D expenditure remains very low, capacity support mechanisms, such as feed-in tariffs and quota obligations with tradable permits for renewable energy, are increasingly expensive, although more careful design in their specifications could moderate these costs. It is important that the right balance and appropriate synergy between these two policy instruments is maintained. For example, within a given budget for public support, high levels of capacity support may reduce the scope for R&D expenditure. However, high levels of R&D without capacity support may result in little final benefit for society (and vice versa) and, ideally, funds towards capacity or R&D support should be allocated according to the return and relative effectiveness in reducing the cost of technologies. A further question for public R&D is how such funds are to be spent and whether the existing research infrastructure is fit for purpose. Private companies and universities may not be the most efficient recipients of public R&D. New laboratories, possibly drawing on experiences in other sectors (such as the National Physical Laboratory), including GOCO (government owned, contractor operated) private finance initiative-type arrangements, may be more appropriate to solving energy R&D problems which may be highly UK-specific in nature and which draw heavily on established knowledge in a range of fields (Wallard, 2001).

The UK is considering a significant expansion of energy laboratories. In 2007, it announced the establishment of an Energy Technologies Institute (ETI) to be funded to the level of £1 billion over 10 years, with half of the funding coming from the energy industry and half from the British government (DTI, 2006d). The ETI will not consider issues of nuclear fusion (handled by UKAEA Fusion) or nuclear fission. Fission research will be served by the creation of a National Nuclear Laboratory, based in large part on the research capacity of the now dismantled BNFL state-owned nuclear fuel cycle company.

Within the European Union, energy research policy, as part of energy policy, continues to be dominated by national rather than European concerns. European Union research policy therefore plays a relatively minor role in the matters of concern to this chapter. A recent report from the European Commission notes, for instance, on the impact of European energy research evaluation in the UK: 'the evaluation work does not impact much on overall resource allocation'. The report notes that: 'it is also difficult to assess institutional impacts, including those achieved from collaboration, and to disentangle the impacts of a range of factors' (European Commission, 2005, p. 25).

Government market promotion and support mechanisms

Turning to the market pull policies and arrangements in place to support the uptake and diffusion of renewable technologies, we find a mix of instruments. The main market promotion instrument is currently the Renewables Obligation (RO). The RO replaced the Non-Fossil Fuel Obligations (NFFO) arrangement, which applied in England and Wales,

Table 3.7. *Cost of non-fossil-fuel contracts*

Year	Cost of NFFO (m£)
1990/1991	6.1
1991/1992	11.7
1992/1993	28.9
1993/1994	68.1
1994/1995	96.4
1995/1996	94.5
1996/1997	112.8
1997/1998	126.5
1998/1999	127
1999/2000	56.4
2000/2001	64.9
2001/2002	54.7

Source: Adapted from Mitchell and Connor (2004, p. 1943)

while in Scotland and Northern Ireland, the Renewables Obligation (Scotland) and the Northern Ireland NFFO (NI-NFFO) applied. The England and Wales NFFO was originally conceived in response to the need to subsidise nuclear power, which remained in public ownership. It provided premium payments for electricity generated from nuclear (until the end of 1998) or renewables over a fixed period, with contracts being awarded to individual generators. Following the introduction of the Renewables Obligation, no new NFFO contracts were awarded. However, more than 400 NFFO projects are currently operational. Table 3.7 shows the cost associated with the NFFOs.

The Obligation is enforced by the Renewable Obligation Order, which was introduced in April 2002. It requires electricity suppliers to source an annually increasing proportion of their sales from renewables. The target was set at 6.7% for 2006/2007 rising to 15.4% by 2015/2016. In the 2006 *Energy Review*:

the Government commits to maintaining Renewable Obligation levels above the level of ROC-eligible renewable generation, to a maximum level of 20%. Increases in Obligation levels above 15.4% will not occur at pre-determined stages, as with existing announcements, but will follow a 'guaranteed headroom' model, where increases are contingent upon appropriate levels of growth in renewables generation (DTI, 2006a, p. 102).

Suppliers can meet their obligation by: (i) acquiring Renewable Obligation Certificates (ROCs) – one ROC is issued for each megawatt hour of renewable energy generated; (ii) paying a buy-out price (£33.24/MWh for 2006/2007); (iii) a combination of ROCs and paying a buy-out price.

ROCs can be acquired by building new renewable capacity and generating renewable energy or by purchasing ROCs from others. The share of obligations met by ROCs amounted to only 70% of the target level in 2004/2005 (Ofgem, 2006b).

A criticism of ROCs has been that it has only favoured the commercially attractive technologies and larger producers. Measures have been suggested to mitigate these effects (in contrast to NFFO). Two amendments for smaller generators (which includes PV and micro-generation) were proposed in 2006 – removing the sale and buy-back requirement, and allowing agents to act on their behalf and amalgamate output from different generating stations (DTI, 2006c). Furthermore, the Government is moving towards 'banding' – whereby emerging technologies are awarded more ROCs per MWh of electricity generated than other technologies (DTI, 2006a, p. 102).

However, the cost of RO is non-trivial and increasing. Between 2003 and 2006, estimated costs amounted to about £700 million per annum (Table 3.7). Moreover, by 2010 these are expected to reach £1 billion per annum. A further total of £1.6 billion is required to improve the transmission and distribution networks between 2003 and 2010. Some of this infrastructure cost relates to the renewal of ageing existing capacity, but some is needed to provide connection to new renewable resources. By 2015, the costs are expected to increase further to about £1.5 billion per annum. Meanwhile, the cost of CO_2 reductions through ROCs is estimated at £210–380 per tonne (House of Lords, 2004). However, the ROCS are not simply a technology-neutral tool to favour very-low-carbon electricity generation, as nuclear power is not eligible for the scheme. In addition, the European Union Emission Trading Scheme (EU ETS) arrangement also provides indirect support for renewable capacity. The importance of this is reflected in the *Energy Review*, according to which the government will 'set out the aim to strengthen the EU ETS post-2012 so that it provides a stable and transparent investment framework for business' (DTI, 2006a, p. 97).

In addition to market promotion through ROCs, there are a number of government grants and schemes in place. The grants are mostly aimed at providing support for capacity building but also for knowledge transfer in specific priority areas (Table 3.8). Furthermore, smaller amounts of support are also provided by the Climate Change Levy Exemption Certificate Income arrangement and European Union research funds, with the latter providing an indirect form of support for electricity generation from renewables.

Table 3.9 shows a detailed description of the support mechanisms for the main technologies. The UK is not alone in its emphasis on

Table 3.8. *Annual cost of supporting renewables between 2003 and 2006*

Income source	Average annual cost (£ million)	Who pays?
Renewable obligation certificate income	470	Consumer
Climate change levy exemption certificate income	30	Taxpayer
Government grants and other public support	180	Taxpayer
European Union research funding	20	Taxpayer (European)
Total	700	

Source: NAO (2005)

large-scale capacity deployment as a technology support mechanism. Other European countries such as Germany, Denmark and Spain have also adopted extensive market deployment schemes (Neuhoff and Sellers, 2005). It is clear from Table 3.9 that there is little consistency in the application of the various schemes to different technologies.

The emphasis on capacity deployment is sometimes justified on the grounds of industrial policy, suggesting that a domestic technological base can create employment and lead to becoming a producer and exporter of the equipment. The example of public support for development of a domestic wind power industry in Denmark, which subsequently became a successful export industry, is the most frequently used success case. However, there is reason to believe that this is an exception rather than the norm. The success of the Danish wind industry in export markets has greatly benefited from the willingness of other governments to subsidise wind-power generation. However, there may be some less-developed technologies where the Danish experience can be repeated. It is possible that the UK could be a significant global player in wave and CCS technologies and it has the potential to gain a global strategy advantage by significant early national deployment. However, in most of the other emerging low-carbon technologies, early mover technological advantages are unlikely due to the small size and unfavourable initial cost structure of the UK's resource. Thus strategic deployment on industrial policy grounds should be limited to a few well-chosen sectors. However, the UK's record in picking winners by industrial policy is pretty poor and this seems to be a weak basis on which to build a

Table 3.9. *Government market and other support mechanisms in 2006*

Technology	Market incentives/regulation	Government support Grants for capacity building	R&D and knowledge transfer
Wind power	Renewables Obligation (RO). Exempt from Climate Change Levy. Effective Non Fossil Fuel Obligation contracts.	DTI's Capital Grants Scheme – the scheme is now closed (offshore wind).	The Collaborative R&D Business Support Product of the Technology Programme (offshore wind). DTI and Scottish Executive's contribution to funding DOWNVInD, an innovative offshore wind power R&D project.
Photovoltaic electricity generation	Renewables Obligation (RO). Exempt from Climate Change Levy. VAT rates on the installation of solar panels have been reduced from 17.5% to 5%.	DTI's low-carbon buildings programme will provide grants for micro-PV.	The Collaborative R&D Business Support Product of the Technology Programme.
Bioenergy: thermal processing of biomass	Renewables Obligation (RO). Exempt from Climate Change Levy. Effective NFFO contracts.	The Energy Crops Scheme provides establishment grants (one-off payments). Prospective capital grant scheme for biomass boilers; further grants for biomass supply chains and commitment to consider using biomass heating in Government buildings as described in the action plan of 27 April 2006. Bioenergy Infrastructure Scheme; funding for 3 years from 2005/2006 a second application round is launched in 2006/2007.	The Collaborative R&D Business Support Product of the Technology Programme. Forum for Renewable Energy Development in Scotland Biomass Energy Group. Supergen Bioenergy Consortium. Prospective establishment of a new Biomass Energy Centre to provide expert information and advice. Forum for Renewable Energy Development in Scotland Biomass Energy Group.

Table 3.9. (cont.)

Technology		Market incentives/regulation	Government support Grants for capacity building	R&D and knowledge transfer
Marine energy	**Wave energy**	Renewables Obligation (RO). Exempt from Climate Change Levy. Effective Non-Fossil-Fuel Obligation contracts.	Wave and Tidal Stream Energy Demonstration Scheme (second application round open).	The Collaborative R&D Business Support Product of the Technology Programme. Supergen Marine Energy Research Consortium.
	Tidal energy	Renewables Obligation (RO). Exempt from Climate Change Levy.	Wave and Tidal Stream Energy Demonstration Scheme (second application round open).	The Collaborative R&D Business Support Product of the Technology Programme. Supergen Marine Energy Research Consortium.
CO$_2$ capture, transport and storage		CCS Regulation Task Force to identify the need for new regulation and any gaps in existing regulation. Clean Coal Task Group – joint industry/union/goverment advisory body.	North Sea Basin Task Force – agreement between Norway and the UK to include exploring development of commercial plant with CCS. EU Flagship Programme aims to have up to 12 large-scale demonstration projects operational by 2015 (Europe-wide).	The Cleaner Coal Technology Programme (direct financial support to R&D and technology transfer and export promotion). Establishment of the Carbon Capture & Storage Association; the group consists of 11 companies.
Nuclear energy		Major review of planning and safety licensing associated with Energy Review 2006. Planning measures will also affect renewables. Process for new nuclear build outlined in White Paper on nuclear power in January 2007.	UK Government and Conservative Opposition have both declared the new nuclear build should receive no public subsidy	Creation of the National Nuclear Laboratory. The Committee on Radioactive Waste Management (CORwM). KNOO (Keeping the Nuclear Option Open) Research Consortium.

Miniaturisation	A 5% VAT level applicable to most microgeneration technologies. Amendments to the Renewables Obligation Order to help small generators claim ROCs on annual, or monthly, basis Enabling micro-CHP to be used by suppliers as an 'innovative technology' to claim a 50% uplift in the 2nd phase (2005–2008) of the Energy Efficiency Commitment (EEC). Under the EEC, electricity/gas suppliers are required to achieve targets for improving household energy efficiency. Planning Policy Statement 22 established that local authorities may set targets for on-site renewable energy projects.	The DTI's low-carbon buildings programme will provide grants for microgeneration technologies; in Scotland, the Scottish Executive has provided support to the Scottish Community and Householder Renewables Initiative (SCHRI)	Funding specific research into issues facing the microgeneration industry under Workstream 4 (Microgeneration Solutions) of the Distributed Generation. Co-ordination Group (DGCG). Further research will be undertaken by the Electricity Networks Steering Group that succeeds the DGCG
Energy efficiency	Climate Change Levy and Climate Change Agreements (80% discount from the Climate Change Levy in return for meeting targets – in several cases, targets are expressed in terms of energy efficiency). Energy Efficiency Commitment (phase 2: 2005–2008) – an obligation on energy suppliers to encourage household energy efficiency. The Government is committed to maintaining a household obligation on suppliers in some form until at least 2020 '[and will consider]	The DTI's Low Carbon Buildings programme promotes a more holistic approach to reducing carbon from buildings by encouraging applicants to consider energy efficiency alongside microgeneration. Grants provided to households on certain benefits to improve their heating and energy efficiency. In England the scheme is known as Warm Front (previously called the Home Energy Efficiency Scheme), in Northern Ireland it is Warm Homes, in Scotland Warm Deal and in Wales	The Collaborative R&D Business Support Product of the Technology Programme (Support for technologies that provide better information to consumers, including through intelligent metering and enhanced energy bills). Market transformation Programme (MTP): its aim is to achieve sustainable improvements in the resource efficiency of products, systems and services. MTP collects information, builds evidence and works with industry and other

Table 3.9. (*cont.*)

Technology	Government support		
	Market incentives/regulation	Grants for capacity building	R&D and knowledge transfer
	moving after 2011 (post the third phase of the Energy Efficiency Commitment) to a supplier obligation based on tradable targets or caps for household energy demand or carbon emissions' (DTI, 2006a, p. 59). Mandatory energy labelling. Strengthened building regulations (part L of the Building Regulation for England and Wales, has been repeatedly tightened) and product standards. Fiscal instruments including reduced VAT rates on energy efficient materials and technologies. Mandatory energy efficiency requirements (boilers, domestic fridges/freezers and fluorescent lamp ballasts). Voluntary industry agreements with product manufacturers. Energy Star – A voluntary scheme that aims to promote energy-efficient office equipment.	it is the Home Energy Efficiency Scheme. Funding of the Carbon Trust and Energy Saving Trust to provide effective energy management to households, businesses and the public sector.	stakeholders to agree on action plans and measures to be implemented Raising awareness and encouraging personal action, including through the work of the Energy Saving Trust; the Carbon Trust; and the Climate Change Communications Initiative. Introduction of Home Information Packs in England and Wales from June 2007, which include energy performance certificates required for all buildings on change of occupation and in line with the EU's Energy Performance of Buildings Directive requirements.

deployment policy. Pitelis (1994) characterised British industrial policies from 1945 as 'mostly *ad hoc*, often *inconsistent* (both between themselves and with the theoretical framework supposedly informing them), *discontinuous*, and generally more *reactive* than proactive. British industrial policies were seen ... as attempted solutions to market failures' (Pitelis, 1994, p. 84). All these criticisms would seem to apply to any large-scale subsidy programme targeted at electricity generation technologies in the UK.

Barriers

Historically, the existing structure of national power industries involved centralised and increasingly larger generation plants connected through relatively passive networks. Some low-carbon generation technologies are smaller in scale, while others are based on decentralised solutions. These features and the intermittent nature of some resources require technical solutions such as back-up power and active network management to support their large-scale integration into the existing electricity systems. In addition, the specific features of new technologies mean that they face various regulatory, institutional and public perception barriers. The type and extent of the barriers can vary from one technology to another.

Table 3.10 shows the main types and relative strength of barriers to the extensive adoption of some of the main technological options for the UK. There is an increasing awareness that technology push and market pull mechanisms need to be supplemented with appropriate steps to reduce such barriers, and some such measures have been implemented. However, removal of barriers will also need to respond to changing circumstances as the different technologies progress (DTI, 2006b).

For wind-power and microgeneration, 'technical barriers' represent principally grid/network connection issues. In the case of wave energy, 'technical barriers' mainly reflect the early stage of development of the technology; while for nuclear energy they reflect the need for a publicly acceptable waste management solution. Technology choices will be shaped, in part, by socio-political factors. Large-scale adoption of thermal processing of biomass or carbon sequestration will need a workable business model, which is yet to be developed, while CO_2 transport dictates an infrastructure that is not yet available. Energy efficiency losses due to CO_2 capture and pressurisation determine, to a large extent, the cost of CO_2 capture (IEA, 2006 p. 204), and therefore R&D is also targeted towards improving that technical aspect. Regulatory barriers relevant to the development of large-scale renewable technologies

Table 3.10. *Type and degree of barriers faced by different technologies*

			Barriers		
Technology	Technical	Regulatory	Planning	Lack of standards	Public opposition/lack of awareness
Onshore wind	★	★	★★★		★★
Offshore wind	★★	★	★★★		★
Bioenergy: thermal processing of biomass	★	★	★★★		★
Wave energy	★★★	★	★★★		
CO_2 capture, transport and storage	★	★★★			★
Nuclear energy	★	★★	★★★		★★★
Miniaturisation (including PV)	★★	★★		★★★	★
Energy efficiency	★	★		★★★	★★★

★ = some barriers
★★ = moderate barriers
★★★ = significant barriers

mainly consist of the regulatory risk inherent in the Renewables' Obligation (investment exposed to potential reviews) and the lack of a long-term framework for positive, stable and predictable CO_2 prices. The establishment of credible long-term policy goals with regard to CO_2 emissions reduction is particularly critical to the development of CCS technologies. For the nuclear industry, regulation is performed by several agencies, which can risk a conflict of requirements for operators. Microgenerators face difficulty in acquiring ROCs and there have only been a few cases of microgenerators receiving payment for 'exported' electricity. Under the existing regulatory framework of full electricity metering competition, widespread adoption of smart credit meters by suppliers on their own initiative is unlikely. This is mainly due to the requirement in suppliers' licences that meters are subject to a visual inspection every two years, which reduces the benefits to suppliers associated with the ability to read the meter remotely. Furthermore, given the combination of the customer's ability to switch energy supplier and the lack of an absolute requirement on the new supplier to take on the previous supplier's meter, suppliers face the 'risk of stranding' of their investment (Ofgem, 2006a).

Existing planning and permitting procedures, which are usually lengthy and hence costly, appear to constitute a considerable barrier to the development of all large-scale technologies at or past the demonstration stage (wind power, thermal processing of biomass, wave power and nuclear energy). The lack of standards affects mainly the development of small-scale technologies that bring electricity generation closer to the consumption stage or influence the level of consumption itself, i.e. microgeneration and smart metering. Similarly, the absence of standardisation (either in the meter and/or the supporting communication methods and data flows) is likely to increase the risks to suppliers of new technology investment and cause potential technical difficulties related to technological incompatibilities when customers want to switch energy supplier.

Public opposition is a relevant barrier mainly to the development of nuclear power stations and, to some extent, onshore wind farms, while information campaigns raising awareness could help the take-up of small-scale technologies. It remains to be seen whether newly reduced opportunities for local planning objections will increase public opposition at the sites of proposed new nuclear power stations. It seems likely that after the *2006 Energy Review* legal planning processes will indeed be streamlined, but it remains unclear whether public demonstrations will be larger or smaller than those seen in the 1970s and 1980s. It also remains unclear whether such demonstrations would have the capacity to delay or derail nuclear power plant construction.

Finally, the lack of information about costs and benefits, along with absence of appropriate incentives and lack of motivation among consumers, comprise the main obstacles to the take-up of energy efficiency (DTI, 2006a, p. 12).

3.7   Conclusions

The UK government has committed itself to challenging targets for reducing carbon emissions levels, of which the electricity sector accounts for a significant amount. An important part of the drive to achieve this target is to increase the share of renewable energy sources. The key to achieving these objectives is technological progress and large-scale deployment. This chapter evaluates the UK's technological issues and options for achieving a low-carbon electricity sector in the medium and long term. A number of conclusions and policy implications may be drawn from our assessment.

As noted, the UK has only a few technology options between which choices need to be made in the short term, namely: energy efficiency, wind power and nuclear power. Due to a variety of constraints, these sources are, however, unlikely to be developed at sufficient scales to fully achieve a low-carbon electricity sector. In the medium term, more options such as offshore wind, advanced nuclear and microgeneration technologies are on the horizon, most of which may be regarded as more advanced and related branches of the short-term technological options. In addition, progress in CCS technology could maintain the dominant position of fossil-fuel-based technologies for the foreseeable future. In the long run, however, there is the potential for the most advanced branches of both existing and radically different technologies to collectively constitute a technology portfolio that can deliver the low-carbon electricity sector of the future.

Clearly, some technologies have a cost advantage over other options, at least in the medium term. However, in the long term, the cost differences between the options will gradually become smaller, although the extent of this is dependent on degrees of funding, diffusion and the inherent technical merits of different options.

As a result the importance of non-financial factors in the market uptake of technologies will increase. There is significant uncertainty with regard to the future cost of individual technologies. However, some aspects of certain technologies are likely to have particular advantages in terms of cost and economically exploitable resource base over other solutions. Nevertheless, the technological sector.

At the same time, conventional generation technologies will continue to be a major part of the future electricity system and may also benefit from technological progress. The role of conventional technologies is also likely to be extended to that of providing back-up power for the growing share of intermittent resources. The diversity of the resource mix will also require advanced technologies for managing more flexible electricity networks. At the same time, future technological progress will take place in the context of a liberalised sector.

The total cost of supporting renewable capacity deployment policies is set to increase for at least some time into the future. Therefore, it is important that the capacity deployment policies are consistent and technology-neutral – i.e. they should promote cost-effective development of low-carbon sources. It is also important that attention is paid to the implicit cost of carbon reduction, given emerging evidence on the actual damage costs of carbon.

At the same time, we pointed out that, while public sector support for energy R&D is important for the progress of renewable energy technologies, present-day spending levels are significantly lower than 1980s and 1990s levels, while some promising technologies remain at the earliest stages of development. The theoretical, rational and empirical evidence to support the current balance between capacity deployment and R&D is unclear and needs to be re-examined in the context of international developments. It is important to strengthen the domestic knowledge base and research capacity, with emphasis on collaborative research. Lessons of experience from public–private initiatives in recent years, including GOCO (government owned, contractor operated), can be useful. A strong domestic research base is a prerequisite for international cooperation and benefiting from knowledge transfer and spillovers, in particular in areas where the UK has a significant resource endowment and comparative advantage.

There are a number of non-financial barriers to the development of most renewable sources. Some of these barriers may be removed at relatively small cost in order to increase the economic efficiency outcome of policies and to create a level playing field for all technological options.

References

Anderson, D. (2006). *Costs and Finance of Abating Carbon Emissions in the Energy Sector*. Stern Review supporting documents. Available from www.hm-treasury.gov.uk/independent_reviews/stern_review_economics_climate_change/stern_review_supporting_documents.cfm

BERR (2008). *Meeting the energy challenge: a white paper on nuclear power*, London: Department of Business, Enterprise & Regulatory Reform. Available from www.berr.gov.uk/files/file43006.pdf

Black and Veatch (2005). *The UK Tidal Stream Resource and Tidal Stream Technology*. Report prepared for the Carbon Trust Marine Energy Challenge.

Clarke, R.H., Ward, N., Cai, Z., Glowacki, B.A. and Nuttall, W.J. (2006). *A Three Party Global Helium Resource Study*, in: *CryoPrague 2006: Proceedings of ICMC '06 and 9th Cryogenics Multiconference*, Vol. 2 (eds D. Evans, M. Lansky and V. Chrz), Prague: Icaris Ltd, pp. 215–218.

Climate Change Bill (2008). *Climate Change Bill (amended)*. HL Bill 44, 18th March 2008, House of Lords, London.

Davis, G.A. and Owen, B. (2003). Optimising the level of renewable electric R&D expenditures using real options analysis. *Energy Policy*, **31**, 1589–1608.

DEFRA (2005). *Assessment of Emerging Innovative Energy Efficient Technologies as Part of the Energy Efficiency Innovation Review*. Prepared for DEFRA by Future Energy Solutions, London: Department of Environment, Food and Rural Affairs.

(2007). Estimated emissions of carbon dioxide (CO_2) by IPCC source category, type of fuel and end user: 1970–2005. *e-Digest of Environmental Statistics*, January, London: Department of Environment, Food and Rural Affairs. Available from www.defra.gov.uk/environment/statistics/airqual/index.htm

DTI (2003). *Our Energy Future: Creating a Low Carbon Economy*. Energy White Paper No. 68, Cm5761, London: Department of Trade and Industry. Available from www.berr.gov.uk/files/file10719.pdf

(2005a). *Offshore Wind Energy: Wind Energy Fact Sheet 1.* London: Department of Trade and Industry. Available from www.berr.gov.uk/files/file17774.pdf

(2005b). *The UK Wind Resource: Wind Energy Fact Sheet 8.* London: Department of Trade and Industry. Available from www.berr.gov.uk/files/file17789.pdf

(2006a). *The Energy Challenge: Energy Review Report 2006.* London: Department of Trade and Industry.

(2006b). *Our Energy Challenge: Power from the People.* Microgeneration Strategy, URN 06/993, London: Department of Trade and Industry. Available from www.berr.gov.uk/files/file27575.pdf

(2006c). *Renewables Obligation Order 2006 – Final Decisions.* January, London: Department of Trade and Industry.

(2006d). *Energy Technologies Institute Prospectus.* September, London: Department of Trade and Industry.

(2006e). *Digest of UK Energy Statistics 2005.* London: Department of Trade and Industry. Available from www.berr.gov.uk/energy/statistics/

ETSU (1999). *New and Renewable Energy: Prospects for the 21st Century.* The Renewables Obligation Preliminary Consultation. Available from http://www.berr.gov.uk/files/file21097.pdf

EU (2005). *Externalities of Energy: Extension of Accounting Framework and Policy Applications* (ExternE-Pol). Final technical report. Available from www.externe.info/expoltec.pdf

European Commission (2005). *Assessing the Impact of Energy Research,* EUR21354. Available from http://ec.europa.eu/research/energy/pdf/erevia_en.pdf

Holloway, S. (1996). *The Underground Disposal of Carbon Dioxide.* Final Report of Joule II Project, CT92–0031, Keyworth: British Geological Survey.

House of Commons (2005). *Renewable Energy,* Sixth Report of Session 2005–06, HC 413. London: House of Commons, Public Accounts Committee. Available from www.publications.parliament.uk/pa/cm200506/cmselect/cmpubacc/413/413.pdf

House of Lords (2004). *Renewable Energy: Practicalities.* Fourth Report of Session 2003–04, London: House of Lords, Science and Technology Committee. Available from www.publications.parliament.uk/pa/ld200304/ldselect/ldsctech/126/126.pdf

ICCEPT [Imperial College London Centre for Energy Policy and Technology] (2003). *Innovation in Long Term Renewables Options in the UK: Overcoming Barriers and Systems Failures.* Final Report for the DTI Renewable Innovation Review, URN 03/1813, London: Department of Trade and Industry, available from www.berr.gov.uk/files/file22072.pdf

ICCEPT [Imperial College London Centre for Energy Policy and Technology] and E4tech Consulting (2003). *The UK Innovation Systems for New and Renewable Energy Technologies.* Final Report to the DTI Renewable Energy Development & Deployment Team, URN 03/1814, London: Department of Trade and Industry, available from www.berr.gov.uk/files/file22069.pdf

IEA (2006). *Energy Technology Perspectives: Scenarios & Strategies to 2050.* Paris: International Energy Agency.

Jamasb, T. (2007). Technical change theory and learning curves: patterns of progress in energy technologies. *Energy Journal,* **28**(3), 51–72.

Jamasb, T. and Pollitt, M. (2005). *Deregulation and R&D in Network Industries: The Case of the Electricity Sector.* Cambridge Working Papers in Economics CWPE 0533 / Electricity Policy Research Group Working Paper EPRG 05/ 02, August, Faculty of Economics, University of Cambridge.

Jamasb, T., Nuttall, W. and Pollitt, M. (eds) (2006). *Future Electricity Technologies and Systems.* Cambridge: Cambridge University Press.

Mitchell, C. and Connor, P. (2004). Renewable energy policy in the UK 1990–2003. *Energy Policy*, **32**, 1935–1947.

Mott Macdonald BPI (2004). *Innovation in Electricity Distribution Networks Final Report.* Brighton, UK: Mott Macdonald BPI.

National Audit Office (2005). *Renewable Energy.* HC 210 Session 2004–2005, 11 February, London: National Audit Office.

Neuhoff, K. and Sellers, R. (2006). Mainstreaming New Renewable Energy Technologies, Cambridge Working Papers in Economics CWPE 0624 / Electricity Policy Research Group Working Paper EPRG 06/06, March, Faculty of Economics, University of Cambridge.

Nuttall, W.J. (2005) *Nuclear Renaissance Technologies and Policies for the Future of Nuclear Power.* Boca Raton, FL: CRC Press (IOP).

Ofgem (2006a). *Domestic Metering Innovation.* Consultation Document 20/06, London: Office of Gas and Electricity Markets.

(2006b). *Renewables Obligation.* Third Annual Report, Ref: 35/06, London: Office of Gas and Electricity Markets.

Paul Arwas Associates (2005). *Biomass Sector Review.* Report prepared for the Carbon Trust, London: Carbon Trust.

Pitelis, C. (1994). Industrial strategy: for Britain, in Europe and the world. *Journal of Economic Studies*, **21** (5), 2–92.

PIU (2002). *The Energy Review.* Performance and Innovation Unit, London: Cabinet Office.

Stern, N. (2007). *The Economics of Climate Change: The Stern Review*, Cabinet Office – HM Treasury. Cambridge: Cambridge University Press.

Sustainable Development Commission (2005). *Wind Power in the UK: A Guide to the Key Issues Surrounding Onshore Wind Power Development in the UK.* London: Sustainable Development Commission. Available from www.sd-commission. org.uk/publications/downloads/Wind_Energy-NovRev2005.pdf

Tester, J.W., Drake, E.M., Driscoll, M.J., Golay, M.W. and Peters W.A. (2005). *Sustainable Energy: Choosing Among Options.* Cambridge, MA: MIT Press.

UKERC (2006). *The Costs and Impacts of Intermittency: An Assessment of the Evidence on the Costs and Impacts of Intermittent Generation of the British Electricity Network.* UK Energy Research Centre, 112.

Wallard, A. (2001). Successful contractorisation: the experience of the National Physical Laboratory, in: *Government Laboratories* (eds D. Cox *et al.*), Nato Science Series 4, Vol. 34, IOS Press.

World Energy Council (2004). *Energy End-Use Technologies for the 21st Century.* A Report by the World Energy Council, London: World Energy Council.

4   The benefits of fuel mix diversity

Fabien A. Roques

4.1   Introduction

The winter of 2005/2006 in Europe saw threats of gas supply disruptions and very high gas prices in some countries such as the UK, which revived concerns about energy security. The backdrop of such events is a general increase in fossil fuel prices over the last three years, which has rekindled interest in renewables and nuclear power generation as one of the potential solutions to diversifying the primary energy supply mix of oil- and gas-importing nations. While the 'dash for gas' that followed liberalisation in the UK has substantially increased the share of gas-fired power generation, the UK electricity system is today relatively diverse by historical standards. Should the preference for gas-fired power plants by investors continue, as is forecast, the UK electricity system would, however, become increasingly reliant on gas-fired generation.

The projected decrease in the UK's fuel mix diversity raises concerns with regard to both the security of supply and macroeconomic impacts of greater dependence on gas imports. The UK Government asserts in the 2003 *Energy White Paper* that it does not aim at controlling the primary fuel mix, as it considers that 'relying on imports need not be a problem in itself' (DTI, 2003).[1] However, some parliamentarians and energy experts insist that the Government should promote a strategic diversity of energy sources (Helm, 2002). The 2006 *Energy Review* raises the question as to whether the current market framework will reward diversity appropriately:

The Energy White Paper made clear that it is not the role of government to decide the fuel mix for generating electricity. Our policy is for the market to make these decisions within the right regulatory framework. But the White Paper

---

[1] The UK Government and Regulator actually have considerable influence on the fuel mix through their energy and environmental policies. Current subsidies and taxes meant to encourage the development of renewables (for instance, the Renewables Obligation Certificates (ROCs), the Climate Change Levy (CCL) and the UK and European Emissions Trading Schemes (ETS)) have an impact on the fuel mix. The government targets are that 10% of UK generating capacity be supplied by renewables by 2010, and 20% by 2020. Similarly, subsidies and taxes on fuels (coal or gas) have an impact on the relative competitiveness of generation technologies.

also said that diverse sources, fuel types, and trading routes should be promoted to avoid the UK being too reliant on too few international sources of oil and gas ... A major objective of this consultation is to ask what further steps, if any, the government should take to develop the market framework for delivering reliable energy supplies (DTI, 2006a).

This chapter explores the concept of diversity as applied to an electricity system. It argues that greater diversity generally enhances the robustness of an electricity system to fossil-fuel supply shocks, and hence yields macroeconomic and security of supply benefits. These are discussed in the light of the decreasing diversity of the UK electricity system. This chapter points out, however, that a diverse electricity system is not a necessary condition to guarantee security of supply. In addition, the concept of diversity as applied to an electricity system remains ill-defined: it is not clear *what* should be diversified, nor is it straightforward to quantify the *costs* and *benefits* of increased diversity. The different analytical approaches to *quantify* and *value* the diversity of an electricity system are then reviewed. While there have been many attempts to design diversity indicators which serve as useful proxies to quantify diversity, such indicators suffer from not taking into account the costs of increased diversity. More research is needed to identify the economic costs associated with greater diversity, as well as to weight the costs and benefits of increased diversity. This chapter discusses how new analytical tools borrowed from the financial literature can be used to trade off the costs and benefits of diversity. These include *static* valuation methods such as Portfolio theory, and *dynamic* valuation methods such as Real Options, which take into account the option value of diversity as a hedge against potential fossil fuel supply or price shocks.

4.2   Defining the diversity of the electricity system

The concept of diversity as applied to electricity generation is intuitively appealing at times when the resurgence of political tensions raises questions about the reliability of fossil fuel imports. However, the diversity of an electricity system remains ill-defined, both qualitatively and quantitatively (Roques, 2003; Stirling, 1998). The basic principle of diversity is straightforward – not putting all one's eggs in one basket. But this can apply to a wide range of characteristic features of the electricity system, including the mix of fuels used to generate electricity, plant technology and manufacturers, or plant operators. This chapter concentrates on fuel mix diversity, which appears to be the most important source of diversification in the electricity generation sector with regard to fuel import dependency and security of supply.

Greater fuel import dependency has different potential economic and security of supply consequences in the short and long term. A partial or complete sudden gas supply disruption would affect the UK economy differently depending on the length of the interruption. In addition, the potential benefits of fuel mix diversity hinge on the practical feasibility of fuel mix diversification. Most electricity infrastructure is long lived, such that, *in the short term*, a utility is limited to selecting power sources from its existing portfolio of generating facilities and third-party power purchases. *In the long term*, the utility would contemplate what fuels it would burn in new power plants or what fuels are contained in future power purchases. The following sections therefore examine the feasibility and potential benefits of greater fuel mix diversity under two different time-scales: in the short term, through improved system resilience to sudden supply disruptions; and in the long term, through a lower macroeconomic impact of high or volatile fossil fuel prices.

4.2.1   *Diversity and resilience to short-term supply shocks*

In the short term, a more diverse electricity generation system is likely to be less affected by fuel supply disruptions because of its greater ability to switch fuels. Fuel mix diversity is believed to provide a hedge against any shock that could render some fuel suddenly unavailable or extremely expensive. In particular, relying on imports for gas exposes countries such as the UK to any disruptive event either in the exporting countries or on the transit routes of the fuel. The diversity of the fuel mix is a multifaceted issue: not only does the primary choice of fuel matter, but also the geographical source of the fuel imports, as well as the transit routes of imports. Such considerations have a critical impact on the relationship between fuel mix diversity and security of supply. For instance, while most of the gas and coal burnt in British power stations is imported, gas and coal imports originate in different regions of the world. While coal can be bought on a global market, gas production and reserves are concentrated in a few regions – mainly Russia and North African countries for gas imported into the UK (IEA, 2006). Besides, while coal can be shipped easily, gas is mainly imported by pipelines through a few critical transit routes which are vulnerable to political instability or terrorist actions in the transit countries. From this perspective, the expected development of a global liquefied natural gas market (LNG) could greatly contribute to diversifying the transit supply risks associated with gas.

Energy price elasticities are generally much higher in the long term than in the short term, and vary largely by fuel and region. Price elasticities are particularly low for transport fuels, as few practical substitutes are yet available for oil-based fuels for cars and lorries. In a recent study, the International Energy Agency estimated that the weighted average crude oil price elasticity of total oil demand across all regions is −0.03 in the short term and −0.15 in the long term (IEA, 2006). Similarly, demand for electricity is highly price-inelastic, with estimates ranging from −0.01 to −0.14 in the long term and even lower in the short term (IEA, 2006). Different fuels – gas, coal and oil products – can provide non-electricity stationary services (such as fuel for heating boilers), so demand for these fuels in these sectors is generally more sensitive to changes in price, especially where multi-firing equipment is widespread. Power generators may also be able to switch more quickly to cheaper fuels if they have dual-firing capability or reserve capacity (see Section 4.3.3 for a discussion of the potential for gas demand reduction from gas-fired power generators in the UK).

Much debate remains, however, with regard to the link between energy dependency and security of supply. The threats to energy security are more subtle and varied than portrayed in the crude expression of concerns about import dependence (Grubb et al., 2006). Counter-arguments include the co-dependence of importers and exporters, and the nature of international markets as reasons not to worry about dependency-related threats. Bohi and Toman (1993) provide a detailed discussion of the conceptual arguments and empirical evidence related to the potential sources of market failure for energy security. There are many possible sources of interruption to supply: from unreliable political sources, from disruptions to transit routes and facilities, and even from the possibility of stalled European energy market liberalisation. Grubb et al. (2006) emphasise, for instance, that the major interruptions of the UK energy system in the past three decades have arisen from miners' strikes, domestic fuel blockades and occasional power cuts – not from foreign supply disruptions.

In short, diversity helps manage the risks that are associated with individual energy technologies or sources, but diversity is not a necessary characteristic of a secure system. For instance, the French electricity supply system, based on nuclear energy, is little diversified: there is a strong focus on one fuel, one technology and a small number of related designs. In some respects it is very secure, being robust to external political events and economic changes. In other respects it could be argued to be insecure to generic technical faults, terrorist threats or a serious nuclear accident. At the other extreme, the old UK coal-based system was also apparently secure, based on indigenous coal and a limited number of technologies. Because of its exposure to the action of trade unions, it was a non-diversified system, with a single vulnerability that turned out to be critical (Costello, 2005).

4.2.2   *Diversity reduces the macroeconomic sensitivity to oil and gas prices*

The growing share of gas-fired generation in most liberalised electricity markets raises concerns over the adverse macroeconomic effects of the decrease of fuel mix diversity and increase in imports for gas-importing countries. An important question is whether increasing reliance on gas-fired generation – hence greater gas import dependency for the UK – will increase the UK economy's sensitivity to the level and volatility of oil and gas prices. A related question lies in the role played by the link between oil and gas prices and its future evolution on the sensitivity of oil- and gas-importing countries to oil prices. The following paragraphs survey and put into perspective the relevant literature on the link between oil and gas prices and macroeconomic activity, as well as oil and gas price correlation.

For oil-importing countries, the immediate magnitude of the direct effect of a given oil-price increase on national income can be conceptualised as depending on the ratio of oil imports to gross domestic product (GDP) (IEA, 2006). This, in turn, is a function of the amount of oil consumed for a given level of national income (oil intensity) and the degree of dependence on imported oil (import dependency).[2] It also depends on the extent to which gas prices rise in response to an oil-price increase, the gas-intensity and gas-import dependency of the economy and the impact of higher prices on other forms of energy that compete with or, in the case of electricity, are generated from oil and gas. The impact of a given change in oil and gas prices on the economy is proportionally linked to the size of the shift in the terms of trade. That shift, in turn, depends on energy-import intensity. Levels of, and historical trends in, intensity vary between countries and regions. Some regions have seen a substantial decline in oil-import intensity since the 1980s, notably Europe and the Pacific region, while import intensity has risen in some developing countries, including China and India (IEA, 2006).

Figure 4.1 shows the evolution of UK energy demand intensity by type of primary fuel, indexed at 100 for all fuels in 1971. While the total primary energy supply (TPES) has decreased over the past three decades by about one-half, it has done so at different rates for the

---

[2] Oil import intensity (net oil imports/GDP) = import dependency (net oil imports/total oil use)*oil intensity ((total oil use/total energy use)*(total energy use/GDP)).

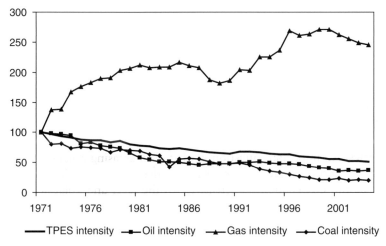

Figure 4.1. UK total primary energy supply intensity evolution by fuel, GDP at Purchasing Power Parity (PPP), index 100=1971
Source: IEA database

different primary fuels. The coal and, to a lesser extent, oil intensities of the UK economy have decreased relatively faster than the overall energy intensity of the UK economy (by 64% and 84%, respectively, since 1971). In contrast, the gas intensity of the UK economy has more than doubled since 1971, with a sharp rebound after 1990, increasing the sensitivity of the UK economy to potential gas supply disruptions or price increases.

As Awerbuch and Sauter (2006) note, a large body of academic literature suggests that oil price increases and volatility dampen macroeconomic growth by raising inflation and unemployment and depressing the value of financial and other assets in oil-consuming nations. The so-called 'oil–GDP relationship' has been statistically studied since the late 1940s (Greene and Tishchishyna, 2000; Awerbuch and Sauter, 2006).[3] The impact of oil price movements on economic growth depends largely upon the country considered. The quantitative relationship

---

[3] The IEA (2004) notes, however, that the negative correlation between oil prices and macroeconomic indicators seems to have substantially weakened over time. It gives three main reasons: first, the weight of oil and oil products in domestic production has dropped, so that terms of trade shifts are less important. Second, the wage formation process has become less responsive to fluctuations in oil prices. Third, heightened competition has helped to reduce the secondary impact on core inflation from changes in oil prices.

between oil price changes and economic activity and inflation can be broken down as follows (IEA, 2004):

- *Terms of trade effects.* The first, and principal, impact of oil price shifts on activity arises from changes in purchasing power between oil-importing and oil-exporting nations.
- *Effect on domestic prices and inflation.* Whether the increase in the price level translates into a shift in core inflation depends on the 'second round' effects – i.e. whether workers and/or enterprises are able to compensate for the income loss through higher wages and prices – which, in turn, depends on the monetary policy regime in place.
- *Domestic demand effects.* Since oil is an input into many goods, both consumers and producers would bear losses.
- *Supply-side implications: impact on output and employment.* The impact on output and employment is determined by the relative supply responses of labour and capital.
- *Longer-term outcomes.* The negative impact of an oil price rise on domestic demand and income will diminish over time as consumers and producers modify their behaviour. However, research indicates that there is an asymmetric effect, in so far as oil demand does not revert to its initial level as oil prices fall. In that case, the income losses experienced by energy importers may eventually be partly reversed. Where fluctuations in oil prices create uncertainty, there may be a reduction in trend investment activity, but it is less clear that the effects on profitability or capacity utilisation are asymmetric (Gately and Huntington, 2002; Awerbuch and Sauter, 2006).

While the mechanism by which oil prices affect economic performance is generally well understood, the precise dynamics and magnitude of these effects – especially the adjustments to the shift in the terms of trade – are very uncertain (IEA, 2006). Quantitative estimates of the overall macroeconomic damage caused to the economies of oil-importing countries by the oil-price shocks of 1973/1974, 1979/1980 and 1990/1991, as well as the gains from the 1986 price collapse, vary substantially. This is partly due to differences in the models used to examine the issue, reflecting the difficulty of capturing all the interacting effects. For the same reason, the results of models used to predict the impact of an increase in oil prices on GDP vary greatly.[4] The IEA (2006) estimates, as a rule of thumb, that the impact of a sustained $10 per barrel oil price increase would now cut average real GDP by around 0.3% in the OECD

---

[4] See, for example, Barrell and Pomerantz (2004), IMF (2005), Huntington (2005) and Hunt *et al.* (2001, 2002).

and by about 0.5% in non-OECD countries. Awerbuch and Sauter (2006) point out that the oil–GDP effect has significant ramifications for policies reducing fuel import dependency, such as increasing fuel mix diversity (for example, through greater use of renewable or nuclear energies) and demand-side energy efficiency and flexibility (for example, through greater fuel-switching possibilities). These policies mitigate exposure to fossil fuel risk and therefore help nations avoid costly economic losses; these arguments will be discussed further in Section 4.4.

Turning now to the impact of *gas price* level and volatility on the economy, it is important to note that the price of gas tends to be highly correlated with international oil prices. This is because of both explicit price indexation and inter-fuel competition at the burner tip. The European Commission (EC) Sector Inquiry investigated the indexation according to the region of the purchasing company (European Commission, 2005).[5] Figure 4.2 shows the indexation of long-term gas supply contracts depending on whether the buyer was from the UK, Western Europe or Eastern Europe.[6] Interestingly, the indexation present in long-term contracts for gas supply to continental Europe is very different from that found in the UK, where over 40% of the price volatility of gas under long-term contracts is determined by changes to the actual hub price of gas (usually the NBP or IPE prices). For Western Europe, changes in hub gas prices only account for around 5% of indexation. Conversely, the importance of heavy fuel oil and light fuel oil in determining the price level paid under long-term contracts is much higher in Western Europe (over 80% of indexation) and Eastern Europe (around 95% of indexation) than in the UK (around 30% of indexation).

Even in North America and Great Britain, where most contracts no longer include any formal links to oil prices, gas prices tend to move in line with oil prices because of fuel switching by industrial end-users and power plants (IEA, 2006). Opportunities for arbitrage with continental Europe, by LNG and, in the case of Great Britain, via the Bacton–Zeebrugge Interconnector, also tend to make oil and gas prices

---

[5] The results of the EU Inquiry are based on analysis of long-term purchase agreements (i.e. over 12 months) of 30 major producers and wholesalers of gas. The analysis is based on data for calendar year 2004 and indicates the average volume-weighted indexation found in the sample of over 500 long-term contracts, representing around 400 billion cubic metres of contracted gas. These contracts include those between companies exporting gas to Europe and major EU gas wholesalers, as well as contracts between different EU gas wholesalers.

[6] The Western Europe sample consists of long-term gas supply contracts to companies in Austria, Belgium, Denmark, France, Germany, Italy and the Netherlands. The Eastern Europe sample consists of long-term gas supply contracts to companies in the Czech Republic, Hungary, Poland, Slovakia and Slovenia.

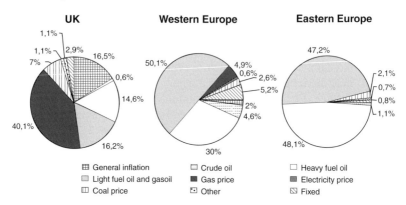

Figure 4.2. Indexation of long-term gas supply contracts by origin of the purchasing company
Source: European Commission (2005)

converge.[7] This explicit price indexation and inter-fuel competition results in wholesale gas prices reflecting the developments of the oil market, and in particular the market for oil derivatives such as heavy or light fuel oil. The EC Inquiry estimates that these account for around three-quarters of gas price volatility (European Commission, 2005). As a consequence, greater dependence on gas-fired power generation can be expected to amplify the sensitivity of a country's economy to oil and gas price fluctuations and shocks.

4.3   The diversity of the UK electricity system

The resurgence of political tensions has raised questions about the reliability of fossil fuel imports to the UK, and has revived interest in fuel mix diversification. This section reviews past and future trends and discusses the potential consequences for the UK of greater fuel import dependency.

---

[7] Term contracts – often covering very long terms of 20 or more years – account for well over 95% of bulk gas trade in continental Europe (almost 100% outside of Belgium and the Netherlands). Almost all of these contracts include oil-price indexation. In Britain, term contracts – which are generally much shorter in duration than in the rest of Europe – account for 90% of all bulk trade. In contrast to the rest of Europe, they almost always price the gas on the basis of spot or futures gas prices, usually at the Notional Balancing Point. None the less, a small number of contracts may have some limited degree of oil-price indexation (IEA, 2006).

4.3.1 A diverse fuel mix by historical standards

Since the liberalisation of the industry in 1989, the electricity production fuel mix in the UK has changed considerably, with the progressive replacement of coal-fired plants by gas-fired ones and, to a lesser extent, by switching from oil to gas. The emergence of gas-fired generation as the investors' favourite technology can partly be explained by improvements in gas-fired generation technology, as the thermal efficiency of combined cycle gas turbines (CCGTs) has reached 60% for modern plants.[8] But the rise of gas-fired generation technology is also due to its distinctive economics and financial features. CCGTs have attributes that make them particularly attractive to investors in liberalised markets. They have lower capital costs than any other type of base load plant – half as much as a coal plant, a quarter as much as a nuclear plant (Roques et al., 2006a, c). Construction time for a CCGT plant is 2–3 years; it takes at least twice as long to build a coal-fired or nuclear plant. As compared to other generation technologies, gas-fired power stations are modular and can be small scale; all of these features constituting critical advantages in liberalised markets.

So far, the replacement of coal-fired generators with gas-fired generators has increased diversity in the stock of generation capacity in Great Britain. Indeed, in 1990, nearly 80% of generation came from coal-fired generators. The UK now enjoys a healthy diversity in generation by historical standards, with coal, gas and nuclear all playing significant roles, as shown by Figure 4.3.

4.3.2 A likely decrease in diversity driven by gas-fired generation

There are concerns that, if the 'dash for gas' continues, the diversity of the future UK fuel mix may be reduced. Most of the new power plants built in the UK during the 1990s were CCGTs, and this trend is expected to continue in the next decade, despite the recent increase in gas prices, because of the favourable economics and operational features of CCGTs (DTI, 2006b). Much of the UK nuclear and coal generating capacity faces closure over the next two decades (in part because of the large Combustion Plant Directive aimed at reducing emissions in the European Union of substances such as sulphur dioxide). Based on UK Government projections (published in February 2006), Figure 4.4 illustrates likely changes in the UK generation mix (DTI, 2006b). Coal currently meets 32% of the UK's electricity requirements – this could

---

[8] See Colpier and Cornland (2002) for an analysis of the learning curve of CCGT plants.

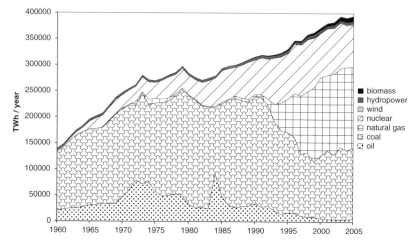

Figure 4.3. UK electricity output by fuel
Source: IEA database

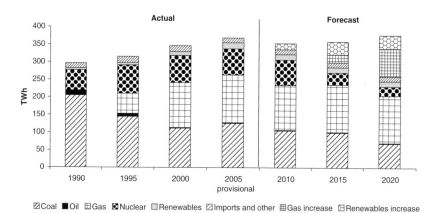

Figure 4.4. Fuel mix evolution forecasts
Source: DTI (2006d)

shrink perhaps to around 15–20% over the next 10–15 years. The share
of nuclear in generation might fall from its current level of around 19%
to 7% by 2020. By 2015, gas-fired generation is modelled to be producing 22TWh more than was produced in 2005, rising to an additional
80TWh in 2020. In contrast nuclear's contribution is expected to drop
from its peak of 90TWh in 1998 to 34TWh in 2015 and 26TWh

in 2020. It is assumed that eligible renewables will reach a market penetration of around 8% in 2010, although there is a great deal of uncertainty about the likely outcome. Penetration is assumed to reach 15% in 2015, remaining at the same absolute level of supply in 2020 (DTI, 2006b).

As a consequence of the increasing share of gas in electricity generation and the decrease in UK gas production, the UK will be increasingly relying on gas imports, and security of supply will become dependent on gas-exporting countries. National Grid's 2005 *Gas Transportation Ten Year Statement* forecasts an average increase in annual gas demand of 2.2% per annum through to 2014, with peak demand growing at the marginally lower rate of 2.1% per annum; and an import dependency of 46% by the end of the decade, rising to around 80% by 2014/2015 (NGT, 2005b). There will therefore be an increasing need for new gas supply sources as well as investment in infrastructure projects to meet both annual demand and the seasonal and daily swings in demand. There are a number of potential market options:

- Additional direct import connections from Norway, either to shore or via existing UK Continental Shelf (UKCS) infrastructure
- Liquefied natural gas (LNG) terminals to import gas from worldwide sources
- More interconnection with continental Europe to import gas from the Netherlands and beyond
- Pipeline upgrades to existing interconnectors to increase import capacity
- Additional investment in UKCS exploration and production
- Gas storage, both onshore and offshore, to provide additional seasonal and daily swing capacity.

This increasing import dependency has raised concerns over future security of fuel supplies, and over the ability of the current market framework to deliver the required large energy infrastructure investments (e.g. new interconnections, LNG terminals, and gas storage facilities). While there are promising signs that the required investments are forthcoming, tight gas supplies in the winter of 2005/2006 have put pressure on policy makers to revisit their commitment not to interfere with markets (DTI, 2006c). In particular, the loss of the unique large-scale gas storage facility in the UK in February 2006 (at Rough) shed light on the vulnerability of the UK gas supply system to sudden disruptions, and raised the issue as to whether the UK should finance some strategic gas storage capacity in addition to the existing and planned commercial storage facilities. The Rough storage facility had traditionally been able to back up supplies during the tougher winter months with a deliverability of 42 mcm/d over 74 days, but the outage on 16 February 2006 highlighted the fact that, compared with elsewhere in Europe, the UK has only minimal storage coverage. With 2005 capacity, the UK has only between 13 and 16 days of coverage compared with 76 days in Germany, 60 days in Italy, and 66 days in France.

The UK Government considers that the combined scale of the market's planned importation and storage projects indicates sufficient new infrastructure to create a margin of supply capability over demand in gas (DTI, 2006c). A number of major projects currently under development or construction are projected to substantially increase the UK's capacity for the import and storage of gas (DTI, 2006c, d).[9] These projects mean that, by 2010/2011, import projects should increase the capacity to import gas to the UK by approximately 100 bcm p.a. and the maximum daily deliverability is expected to be 300 mcm/d. New storage projects in the public domain are expected to double the UK's total storage capacity – an increase of approximately 2 bcm by 2008/2009. Were they all to go ahead, the capacity of existing import projects and those currently being considered could meet the annual shortfall in supplies from the UKCS well into the next decade. The secure supply of gas to the UK will, however, depend on the *timely* delivery of a sufficient proportion of these projects.

It is also important to emphasise that the availability of capacity does not guarantee the delivery of gas. Reliance on gas imports is not a new feature of the UK energy supply mix, as the UK imported over 25% of its gas requirement during the 1980s. However, the extent of previous dependence was not on the scale now anticipated (with net imports meeting perhaps one-third of UK annual gas demand by 2010 and four-fifths or more in 2020). Besides, in the 1980s gas was mainly imported from Norway, while the main producers in the future will be Russia, Algeria and the Middle East via LNG terminals. While this range of import sources and routes will contribute to gas supply diversity, the lack

---

[9] In addition to the projects scheduled for commissioning during winter 2006/07 (including the Humbly Grove storage facility, the Isle of Grain LNG import and storage facility, and increased interconnector import capacity), medium-term projects include the Langeled pipeline to bring gas to Great Britain from Norway, two new LNG import terminals at Milford Haven, and a new pipeline from the Netherlands. Further expansion to the Isle of Grain import facility and to the Belgium interconnector are also planned (DTI, 2006a).

of political stability of some of these countries might be a source of concern with regard to security of supply.

4.3.3 The impact of growing gas import dependency on security of supply

Turning now to the potential impact of a short- or medium-term gas supply disruption on the UK economy, it is important to note that almost all of the natural gas consumption increase since 1990 is due to the increased share of gas-fired generation in the power generation mix. Figure 4.1 showed that the gas intensity of the UK economy has greatly increased since the beginning of the 1990s. Figure 4.5 shows the evolution of the total UK gas demand intensity (TPES), and the evolution of the final consumption of the UK economy (TFC). The difference between the two corresponds to gas burnt in power stations to produce electricity and in other energy transformations. Figure 4.5 shows that most of the UK economy gas intensity increase since the 1990s can be attributed to the 'dash for gas' in power generation, which has nearly doubled the UK economy's gas intensity. This increase makes the UK economy more sensitive to gas price fluctuations and potential gas supply shocks.

Prior to the winter of 2005/2006, National Grid analysed the potential for gas-fired power stations to reduce gas demand in response to price signals in a severe winter (NGT, 2005a). The National Grid's analysis suggests that, if the market acted in such a way as to minimise CCGT gas consumption, this sector could make a significant contribution to the total level of demand-side response that would be required under severe conditions, while maintaining electricity security of supply (NGT, 2005b). A significant response from the electricity generating industry was observed during the winter of 2005/2006. However, the theoretical scope for fuel-switching behaviour and gas/power arbitrage often fails to be realised in practice, for a number of reasons, including: environmental constraints on substituting gas; the costs of maintaining back-up inventories and fuel-switching equipment, and of actually changing operations from base-running to alternatives and back; the often short duration of windows for profitable switching; and the conservatism of operational engineers.[10]

---

[10] Storage and delivery of back-up fuels create many problems for CCGT operators. A typical 700MW CCGT station requires around 3,000 tonnes of distillate fuel to operate at full output each day. Typically, CCGT plants are provided with around 3 days' storage, which would allow operation at full output for around 9 days operating

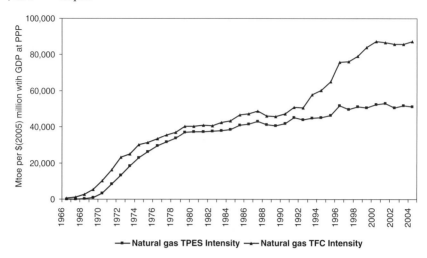

Figure 4.5. UK total primary energy supply and total final
consumption intensity evolution, GDP at PPP
Source: IEA database

A gas supply interruption to the industrial sector could cause
widespread commercial damage, depending on the extent of production lost in sectors upstream and downstream. ILEX (2006) studied
the impact of an interruption to the gas supply in the winter of 2005/
2006 on energy-intensive industry and those sectors of the UK economy that are directly upstream and downstream of it. Such a degree of
interruption would occur under emergency conditions – mandatory
interruption by the National Emergency Coordinator. It would also
require firm load-shedding, since the majority of energy-intensive users
are on firm rather than interruptible contracts. ILEX (2006) bases its
economic estimates on the loss of production resulting from a 3–6 week
emergency gas supply interruption to the energy-intensive industrial
sectors identified by DTI as the main potential providers of natural gas
demand reduction in the case of insufficient gas supply capacity to
meet overall demand. In the case in which the level of interruption is
limited to self-curtailment by industry (i.e. reductions in production by
industry in response to the price of gas), ILEX (2006) estimates that
the immediate economic consequence of this self-curtailment would be
a loss of GDP in 2006 of between 0.04% and 0.16%. Under the strong
assumption that gas supply would be fully interrupted for 6 weeks,

for the highest-priced eight hours each day. Even this requires 9,000 tonnes of fuel, or
14 storage tanks each 10 metres in diameter and 10 metres in height.

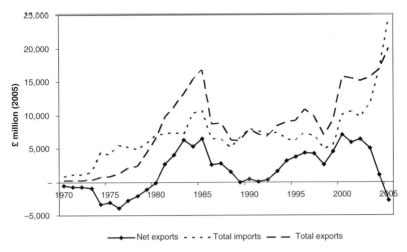

Figure 4.6. UK energy imports and exports value evolution
Source: DTI Statistics

all sectors would be forced to stop or severely curtail production, and their downstream consumers would be interrupted; the immediate effect on the economy would be a loss of between 0.18% and 0.81% of annual GDP.[11]

As is always the case with such attempts to estimate the economic impacts of a gas supply disruption, some of the assumptions and results of the study might be questioned. The study takes a short-term perspective, and isolates the industry sector without taking account of knock-on effects of the initial supply shocks on other sectors of the economy, and on dynamic adaptation impacts in the medium to long term. In the medium term, interruptions of production are likely to result in losses of market share, plant closures and job losses, which might worsen the production-loss-related GDP impact. On the other hand, the positive impact of a transfer of employment to other sectors of the economy, and of the rebound effect on subsequent years' GDP might partly compensate for the initial year's GDP losses.

Finally, another important aspect of the change of the gas supply pattern to the UK is the impact on the trade balance of greater energy imports. Figure 4.6 shows the evolution of the UK energy import and

---

[11] The lower end of the range assumes that all the energy-intensive industrial sectors, except the refining and water sectors, cease production, but that sectors directly upstream and downstream are unaffected, i.e. they can immediately find alternative suppliers/customers for their purchases/sales. The upper end of the range assumes that certain sectors upstream and downstream also cease production for 6 weeks.

export values over the past three decades. The UK became, in 2005, a net importer of energy in value, for the first time since 1980. While the value of the contribution of UK energy exports to the UK's trade balance has fluctuated over the past three decades, the sudden drop since 2000 of the contribution of energy exports to the UK trade balance has been more brutal than expected, and there will be some costs associated with the adjustments of the UK economy to this rapid change.

4.4   Quantifying and valuing the benefits of diversity

The multifaceted impact of decreasing generation mix diversity in the UK explains the difficulty in quantifying the costs and benefits associated with fuel mix diversity. In particular, it is difficult to estimate the value of diversity, as this would ideally require a detailed model of the energy sector integrated with a general equilibrium model of the economy. As discussed in Section 4.2.2, existing models used to quantify the 'oil–GDP' relationship sometimes give inconsistent results, as it is difficult to capture quantitatively the complexity of the relationships between the energy sector and the wider economy.

It is therefore important to advance research further in this area to provide a normative approach for policy makers. As pointed out by Costello (2005), care must indeed be taken that arguments in favour of diversity are not used opportunistically by those seeking (via political mechanisms) to protect particular firms and industries. This underlines the need to develop analytical tools to quantify the costs and benefits of increased fuel mix diversity. This section introduces various candidate indices that can be used to quantify fuel mix diversity, and then discusses how new analytical tools borrowed from the financial literature (such as Mean-Variance Portfolio theory and Real Options theory) can be used to value the costs and benefits of generation mix diversity.

4.4.1   *Quantifying fuel mix diversity*

Stirling (1994, 1998, 2001) pioneered research into the application of diversity concepts to the energy sector. Stirling argued that *uncertainty* and *ignorance*, rather than *risk*, dominate real electricity investment decisions, and conceptualises *diversification* as a response to these more intractable knowledge deficiencies. In addition to difficulties in definitively characterising or partitioning the possibilities, there is a prospect of unexpected outcomes, arising entirely outside the domain of prior possibilities.[12] Stirling (1998) shows that diversity can be considered from different angles, notably *variety* (the number of available options, categories, species), *balance* (the spread among options), and *disparity* (the nature and degree to which options are different from each other). Variety, balance and disparity constitute 'three necessary but individually insufficient conditions for diversity' (Stirling, 1998). Stirling, however, points out that inclusion of disparity remains cumbersome, as the concept of disparity differs from variety and balance in that it is inherently qualitative.

In a seminal contribution to mathematical ecology, Hill (1973) directly addressed the fundamental issue of the trade-off between variety and balance in the measurement of diversity. Based on the characterisation of diversity in terms of 'proportional abundance', Hill (1973) identifies and orders an entire family of possible quantitative measures of diversity. Each is subject to the same general form:

$$\Delta_a = \left(\sum_{i=1}^{I} (p_i^a) \right)^{1/(1-a)}, \quad a \neq 1,$$

$$= \sum_{i=1}^{I} -p_i \ln(p_i), \qquad a = 1.$$

where Δ_a specifies a particular index of diversity, p_i represents (in economic terms) the proportional representation of option i in the portfolio under scrutiny, and a is a parameter which effectively governs the relative weighting placed on variety and balance. The greater the value of the parameter a, the smaller the relative sensitivity of the resulting index to the presence of lower-contributing options.

For $a = 2$, the reciprocal of the function is referred to in ecology as the *Simpson diversity index* and in economics as the *Herfindahl-Hirschman concentration index*. Assuming that p_i is the market share of the ith firm or the proportion of generation met by one particular fuel source, then the Herfindahl-Hirschman concentration index is calculated according to $\Delta_2 = \sum_{i=1}^{I} p_i^2$. The Herfindahl-Hirschman index takes into account

---

[12] Stirling distinguishes three basic states of incertitude:

- Risk: 'a probability density function may meaningfully be defined for a range of possible outcomes'
- Uncertainty: 'there exists no basis for the assignment of probabilities'
- Ignorance: 'there exists no basis for the assignment of probabilities to outcomes, nor knowledge about many of the possible outcomes themselves'.

both the relative size and the distribution of each source, increasing as the number of firms falls and the disparity in the size of those firms increases.[13]

For $a = 1$, the result is the *Shannon-Wiener diversity index* (Stirling, 1998). Stirling asserts that the Shannon-Wiener diversity index is the most attractive simple index, reflecting both variety and balance in an even way. The reasons are that this index is insensitive to final ordering (changes of the base of logarithms do not change the rank orderings of different systems), and, it is additive in the case of a refining of the taxonomy (the index value for a system of options, which has been disaggregated according to a combined taxonomy, should be equal to the sum of the index values obtained for the same system classified under each taxonomy individually). The higher the value taken by the index, the more diverse is the system.

An intuitive rationale for the use of the Shannon–Wiener function as an index of electricity supply system security is to think of it as a measure of the probability that a hypothetical unit of electricity sampled from the system at random has been generated by any particular option. The more diverse the system, the greater will be the uncertainty over which option will have generated the next sampled unit of electricity. Jansen *et al.* (2004) elaborate on the Shannon–Wiener diversity index to design a macro-indicator for long-run energy supply security. Four long-term energy security indices are presented, allowing for an increasing number of long-term supply security aspects, and then applied to reference year 2030 for four long-term sustainability outlook scenarios. Aspects introduced in their indicators on a stepwise additional basis are successively:

- *Diversification of energy sources in energy supply.* This corresponds to the basic Shannon–Wiener diversity index.
- *Diversification of imports with respect to imported energy source.* This second indicator provides for an adjustment of the basic indicator for the net import dependency.
- *Long-term political stability in import regions.* The third additional adjustment to the indicator accounts for the level of long-term political stability in regions of origin, using the UNDP Human Development Indicator as the index for long-term socio-economic stability.
- *Allowance for resource depletion.* The fourth indicator allows for the level of resource depletion on an additional basis.

---

[13] The maximum value of the index is 10,000 in the case of a monopoly, falling towards zero as the market moves towards a situation of perfect competition.

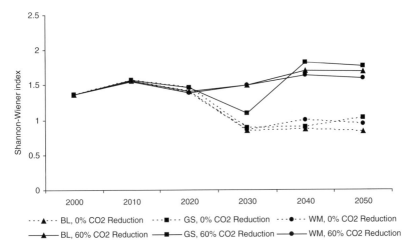

Figure 4.7. Shannon–Wiener index under UK DTI scenarios
Source: Grubb *et al.* (2006)

Grubb *et al.* (2006) use both Stirling's Shannon–Wiener diversity index
and the Herfindahl-Hirschman index to investigate the evolution of UK
fuel mix diversity according to the scenario work conducted by the
Future Energy Solutions (FES) consultancy for the DTI White Paper
analysis (DTI, 2003). The three reference scenarios hypothesised by the
DTI correspond to 'business as usual' ('Baseline'), high environmental
concern ('Global Sustainability'), and low environmental concern
('World Markets').[14] Figure 4.7 shows their results. Where no emissions
target is imposed, there is a decline in diversity in all three scenarios.
This decline is driven by an increase in the proportion of generation
accounted for by natural gas. The implication of this fall in diversity is an
increase in insecurity, as the electricity system becomes more exposed to
the dangers of relying on one fuel source. By contrast, under an emission
reduction target of 60% there is a substantial increase in diversity under
all three scenarios as the dominance of natural gas goes into decline.

---

[14] Further information on the assumptions underlying these scenarios is given in DTI
(2003b). In the Baseline scenario, the values of society and environmental policies
remain similar to today's. The Global Sustainability scenario is based on strong social
and ecological values, with collective environmental activity. In the World Markets
scenario, consumerist values predominate and environmental concerns are sidelined. In
both the Baseline and the Global Sustainability scenarios, GDP growth is projected at
2.25%, whilst in the World Markets scenario growth is 3.0%.

4.4.2   The weaknesses of concentration-based diversity indices

While Stirling's (1994, 1998, 2001) pioneering work on diversity indices greatly contributed to defining the diversity of an electricity system, it does not inform the question as to *how much* diversity is needed.[15] The extent to which diversity is to be pursued depends on the balance between the extra costs and the degree of risk reduction achieved. Fuel diversity should not be perceived as an end, but only as a means that has the capability to generate benefits less costly than other alternatives in achieving the same objectives. For example, financial instruments may have lower costs than fuel diversity, which can be viewed as a physical hedge in reducing price risk to a tolerable level. Fuel diversity may also create costs from the loss of scale economies associated with traditional generation technologies, and from owning and operating a portfolio of power sources that include several fuels and technologies, some of which may not have the lowest expected costs.

The diversity indices presented in the previous section do not exploit statistical information. Thinking about fuel mix diversity in terms of risk, e.g. price risk for fossil fuel supplies, one can make use of other analytical approaches using statistical data to identify the optimal degree of diversity of an electricity system, by trading off the degree of risk reduction achieved by diversifying away from gas-fired generation against the extra cost of doing so. As argued by Awerbuch and Berger (2003), such approaches rely on the assumption that, while these precise outcomes may never be perfectly repeated in the future, they at least provide a guide to the future.[16] The strength of such approaches rests on the presumption that the past is a reliable guide to the future. This is not to say that unexpected events will not happen – only that the effects of these events are already known from past experience (Awerbuch and Berger, 2003).

Fuel mix diversity provides a hedge against potential price shocks affecting one type of fuel, e.g. imported gas, or supply shocks due to physical disruption in the supply chain. Investing in generation technologies which help a country (or a utility) to mitigate its exposure to fossil fuel supply disruptions or price risks can be thought of as an *insurance*. Calculating the value associated with such insurance requires a different approach from the traditional static valuations of the 'least

---

[15] See also Western (1995) for a critique of Stirling's diversity index.

[16] While no particular random event may ever be precisely duplicated; nonetheless, historic variability is widely considered to be a useful indicator of future volatility (e.g. in the case of equity stocks).

cost option' on a stand-alone basis (see, e.g. Roques *et al.*, 2006a, for a critique of the traditional levelised cost methodology). Power generation investment valuations need to capture both the *portfolio effects* – the complementarity of one additional unit with the existing portfolio of plants of a country or utility – and the *option value effects* arising out of uncertainties in fossil fuel prices and volatility – e.g. the option value of operating renewables and nuclear plants in case gas prices increase. In other words, identifying the optimal degree of fuel mix diversity for a country or utility requires valuation approaches of power generation investments which trade off the risks and returns of increased diversification. The following sections introduce successively static (Value-at-Risk and Portfolio theory) and dynamic approaches (Real Options) to value the different benefits of fuel mix diversity.

4.4.3   Portfolio valuation approaches of diversity

The *Value-at-Risk* (VaR) approach had gained increasing popularity in banking and assets and liabilities management applications by the end of the 1990s.[17] The VaR approach calculates the maximum loss expected (or worst-case scenario) on an investment, over a given period and given a specified degree of confidence (Brealey and Myers, 2000). The VaR approach can be applied to any portfolio of assets and liabilities whose market values are available on a periodic basis. Typically, normal distributions are assumed, with values for price volatility based on past statistics. Using calculated parameter values for the whole portfolio, the maximum portfolio loss can be projected, provided that a specific unlikely event does not occur, for example a 5% chance of an adverse price movement within the next holding period. However, to implement it, the probability distribution of price changes for each portfolio instrument should be known, and the VaR approach depends critically on reasonable estimates of price volatility and correlations between financial assets, as well as the assumed distribution of price changes. Kleindorfer and Li (2005) provide a recent review of progress in the VaR theoretical literature, and apply it to characterise multi-period VaR-constrained portfolios of real and contractual assets in the power sector.

---

[17] VaR is based on the common-sense fact that, for investors, risk is about the odds of losing money. By assuming investors care about the odds of a big loss, VaR addresses one of the main issues with the traditional measure of risk: volatility. The main problem with volatility, indeed, is that it does not address the direction of an investment's movement: a stock can be volatile because it suddenly jumps higher. But investors are not distressed by gains.

Another probabilistic approach to valuing and optimising fuel mix diversity is Markowitz's *Mean-Variance Portfolio theory* (Markowitz, 1952).[18] Mean-Variance Portfolio theory (hereafter MVP) defines portfolio risk as *total risk* – the sum of random and systematic fluctuations – measured as the standard deviation of periodic historic returns.[19] An efficient (i.e. Pareto optimal) portfolio is one which has the smallest attainable portfolio risk for a given level of expected return (or the largest expected return for a given level of risk). The process for establishing an optimal (or efficient) portfolio generally uses historical measures for returns, risk (standard deviation), and the correlation coefficients between the different assets to be used in the portfolio. By computer processing the returns, risk (standard deviation of returns) and correlation coefficients data, it is possible to establish a number of portfolios for varying levels of return, each having the least amount of risk achievable from the asset classes included. These are known as optimal portfolios, which lie on the *efficient frontier*. Figure 4.8 shows the efficient frontier for a portfolio of two risky assets. For each portfolio on the efficient frontier:

- The expected portfolio holding period return (HPR) cannot be improved without increasing expected portfolio HPR risk.
- The expected portfolio HPR risk cannot be reduced without reducing expected portfolio HPR.

The investor then simply has to choose which level of risk is appropriate for their particular circumstances (or preferences) and allocate their portfolio accordingly. In other words, MVP theory does not prescribe a single optimal portfolio combination, but a range of efficient choices. Investors will choose a risk–return combination based on their own preferences and risk aversion.

Mean-Variance Portfolio (MVP) theory can be applied to generation assets to determine the optimal portfolio for a country or generation company. MVP theory makes assumptions on the assets considered and investors' behaviour (such as risk aversion), which are discussed in detail by Awerbuch and Berger (2003) and Roques *et al.* (2008) in the context

---

[18] See, e.g. Fabozzi *et al.* (2002) for a recent review of the developments of Portfolio theory.

[19] Modern Portfolio theory makes some assumptions about investors. It assumes that they dislike risk and like returns, will act rationally in making decisions, and make decisions based on maximising their return for the level of risk that is acceptable for them. When making asset allocation decisions based on asset classes, it is assumed that each asset class is diversified sufficiently to eliminate specific or non-market risk.

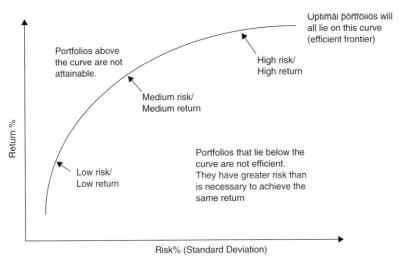

Figure 4.8. Efficient frontier for a portfolio of two risky assets

of investment in electricity markets. As Awerbuch and Berger (2003, p. 5) observe:

the important implication of portfolio-based analysis is that the relative value of generating assets must be determined not by evaluating alternative assets, but by evaluating alternative asset portfolios. Energy planning therefore needs to focus less on finding the single lowest cost alternative and more on developing efficient (i.e. optimal) generating portfolios.

Bar-Lev and Katz (1976) pioneered the application of MVP theory to fossil fuel procurement in the US electricity industry. They showed that the electric utilities were efficiently diversified, but that their portfolios were generally characterised by a relatively high rate of return and risk, which they interpreted as being a consequence of the 'cost-plus' regulatory regime, encouraging utilities to behave in a risky way. Humphreys and McClain (1998) used MVP theory to demonstrate how the energy mix in the USA could be chosen, given a national goal to reduce the risks to the domestic macroeconomy of unanticipated energy price shocks. They noted that the electric utility industry had moved towards more efficient points of production since the 1980s, and that the switch towards natural gas in the 1990s might have been driven by the desire for higher returns to energy investment in the industry. Awerbuch (2000) evaluated the US gas–coal generation mix and showed that adding wind, photovoltaics and other fixed-cost renewables to a portfolio of conventional generating assets serves to reduce overall portfolio cost and risk, even though their stand-alone generating costs may be higher. Awerbuch and Berger (2003) used MVP to identify the optimal European technology mix, considering not only fuel price risk but also O&M, as well as construction-period risks. They found that, compared with the EU-2000 generation mix, the projected EU-2010 mix exhibits a higher risk coupled with a higher return. Moreover, optimal EU-2010 would be likely to include higher shares of coal along with a higher share of wind.[20] Bazilian and Roques (forthcoming) provide on overview of state-of-the-art applications of MVP theory to optimise the power generation mix.

The general conclusion of the Portfolio theory applications to valuing diversity based on production costs and concentrating on fuel price uncertainty, i.e. taking a national or societal perspective, is that more diverse generation portfolios are, in general, associated with lower risks for the same returns. In particular, optimal portfolios contain a substantial share of fixed-cost (when considering only fuel price uncertainty) renewables and nuclear, whose costs have a low covariance with the production costs of fossil fuel technologies.

Roques *et al.* (2006b) applied Portfolio theory to identify optimal portfolios for electricity generators in the UK electricity market, concentrating on profit risk rather than production cost risk. In such a private investor perspective, electricity price risk (and in Europe CO_2 price risk) is also relevant for determining optimal portfolios, and in particular the covariance of electricity, fuel and CO_2 prices. Roques *et al.* (2008) concluded that, in the absence of long-term power purchase agreements, optimal portfolios for a private investor differ substantially from socially optimal portfolios, as there is little diversification value for a private investor in a portfolio of mixed technologies because of the high empirical correlation between electricity, gas and carbon prices. Moreover, Roques *et al.*'s (2008) results suggest that the current UK industry framework is unlikely to reward fuel mix diversification sufficiently to lead private investors' technology choices to be aligned with the socially optimal fuel mix, unless investors can find counterparties with complementary risk profiles to sign long-term power purchase agreements. These findings raise questions as to whether and how policy makers or regulators should modify the market framework, given the macroeconomic and security of supply benefits of a diverse fuel mix. Roques *et al.*'s (2008) results suggest, in particular, that alternative institutional risk allocation mechanisms (e.g. long-term power purchase contracts) might

---

[20] Note that this study does not account for the cost of CO_2 emission permits in the European Union Emission Trading Scheme.

render capital-intensive but fuel price risk-free technologies, such as nuclear power or renewables, more attractive to investors – and thereby provide power companies with stronger incentives for fuel mix diversification. This 'market failure', i.e. the diverging incentives for diversification from a private investor perspective and from a societal perspective, is discussed in more depth in Chapter 10 of this volume and in Bazilian and Roques (forthcoming).

4.4.4   Dynamic valuation approaches: the option value of diversity

Another concept borrowed from the finance literature, called *Real Option theory*, can be applied to supplement the information provided by static discounted cash flow analysis. In its simplest terms, Real Option theory says that, when the future is uncertain, it pays to have a broad range of options available and to maintain the flexibility to exercise those options. Real Option theory has highlighted the shortcomings of static valuation approaches for putting a value on the ability of a utility to dynamically react to changing market and other conditions. Specifically, static approaches can understate, if not ignore, *managerial flexibility*. Real Option valuation allows for adjustment of the *timing* of the investment decision. It is therefore particularly well suited to evaluating investments with uncertain payoffs and costs, as it can capture the option value contained in managerial flexibility in the face of future uncertain developments – if waiting is to have any value, there must be at least some degree of uncertainty about future costs or market conditions that is expected to be partially resolved during the waiting period; the greater the uncertainty that can be resolved, the more advantageous it is to wait, and thus the higher the option value will be. Real Option theory places explicit value on the ability of decision makers to be flexible and to learn (see, e.g. Dixit and Pindyck, 1994; Trigeorgis, 1996, for reference textbooks on Real Option theory).

Real Option theory can be applied to analyse the economics of renewable energy or nuclear power versus fossil fuel generation technologies when fuel prices and/or electricity prices are uncertain.[21] There are potentially two attributes of non-fossil-fuel technologies such as renewables and nuclear power generation that could improve their value to society or investors from a dynamic perspective. First, the production

---

[21] Quantifying the option value, however, requires restrictive assumptions on the stochastic behaviour of the electricity and natural gas market prices, and relying on data from relatively illiquid forward markets. See Frayer and Uludere (2001) for a description of the limits of applying Real Options analysis to power investments.

costs of such technologies are insensitive to both gas and carbon prices.[22] Therefore, rising gas prices and carbon trading or carbon taxes will make nuclear more competitive against CCGT and coal power. Second, investing in non-fossil-fuel technologies can be thought of as a hedge against the volatility and risk of gas and carbon prices for a country or a (large) generating company. The uncertainty over the evolution of gas and carbon prices implies that there is an option value associated with being able to choose between non-fossil-fuel generation technologies and fossil fuel technologies in the future. This 'hedging value' cannot be captured by the standard levelised cost approach, as it requires a dynamic model to capture the option value associated with the flexibility of waiting for more information on gas and carbon prices before making the best informed technology choice.

Real Option theory can therefore rationalise embarking upon a power-plant project that is not expected to be economic for a period of years but offers the possibility of benefits in the longer term. For instance, Murto and Nese (2002) compared natural gas-fired plant economics with biomass plants and showed that natural gas price uncertainty considerably improves the competitiveness of the biomass plant, when taking into account the option value associated with input cost uncertainty. Roques *et al.* (2006b) used a stochastic optimisation model to compute the option value to a company of the ability to choose between a nuclear and a gas-fired plant investment at successive moments in the future, when the company faces stochastic gas, carbon and electricity prices. Roques *et al.* (2006b) show that this option value depends sensitively on the degree of correlation between electricity, gas and carbon prices. They conclude that there is little private company value in retaining the option to choose between nuclear and CCGT technologies in the future in liberalised European electricity markets, which exhibit a strong correlation between electricity, gas and carbon prices.

Real Options analysis can also be applied to other benefits associated with a more diverse electricity generation system, as the value of real options is closely linked to the benefits of having more flexibility. The concept can apply to whether a utility should buy a new power plant or purchase power. An illustration of a failure to retain an option would be where a utility signs a long-term purchased power contract with rigid

---

[22] Nuclear fuel price have relatively little effect on electricity generation costs: a doubling of the uranium oxide price would increase the fuel cost for a Light Water Reactor by 30%, and the electricity cost by only about 7%, whereas doubling the gas price would add 70% to the price of electricity.

take and price provisions (Costello, 2005). If, subsequent to the signing of the contract, the market price of electricity plummets or expected load growth fails to materialise, or both, the utility could suffer large contractual liability. Real Option theory could also justify staggering the timing of capital expenditures for new generation facilities under uncertainty, committing to new construction in stages.[23] By waiting for new information, and in the meantime initiating the development of promising technologies (for example, on a pilot or demonstration basis), the utility would have more flexibility in adapting to the new conditions as they unfold. Options analysis also provides some insight into what actions and design features could improve the competitive position of a particular technology. For instance, some nuclear plant operators in the USA have applied to the NRC for early site permits. This is a low-cost option that will reduce the lead time for a nuclear plant when favourable market conditions occur.

Another interesting application of Real Option modelling concerns the valuation of the research, development, demonstration and deployment (RDDD) programmes of new power generation technologies. Cost–benefit analysis of such publicly funded programmes typically employs a deterministic forecast of the cost and performance of renewable and non-renewable fuels. For instance, Siddiqui et al. (2007) point out that the static valuation method of benefits of the US Renewable Energy RDDD suffers from three major deficiencies in that it ignores uncertainty in the cost of non-renewable energy, the possibility of adjustment to the RDDD effort commensurate with the evolving state of the world and the underlying technical risk associated with RDDD. Siddiqui et al. (2007) computed an estimate via a compound real option of the US RDDD programme in a future with uncertain non-renewable energy costs. They found that the total option value of renewable energies – between $36 billion and $104 billion (in 2002 US dollars) depending on gas price volatility and the share of gas- and coal-fired generation – is dominated by the value of existing renewable technologies, while the value of enhancements to renewable technologies from future RDDD is a modest 10% of the total, and the value of the abandonment option is insignificant. Davis and Owens (2003) used a more detailed Real Options approach to estimate the value of the USA's renewable electric technologies R&D programme in the face of

---

[23] Gollier et al. (2005) compare the benefit of a large nuclear power plant project, coming from increasing returns to scale, to the benefit of a modular sequence of smaller, modular, nuclear power plants on the same site. They show that, under price uncertainty only, the benefit of modularity is equivalent in terms of profitability to a reduction of the cost of electricity by one-thousandth of a euro per kWh.

uncertain fossil fuel prices. They found that a static discounted cash flow approach would yield a negative net present value, indicating that the US Renewable Energy R&D programme should be abandoned. In contrast, using a dynamic Real Options approach, the current value of expected future supply from renewable electric technologies, net of federal R&D expenditures, is $30.6 billion (in 2000 US dollars).[24] Of this value, 86% can be attributed to past R&D efforts, and 14% can be attributed to future federal R&D efforts, assuming continued federal R&D funding at $300 million per year – which is consistent with the 10% estimate of Siddiqui *et al.* (2007). The expected net option value of future renewable technologies R&D expenditures is $4.3 billion, of which 40% can be attributed to the value of optimal timing, and 60% to the insurance value. While these two models' estimates of renewable technologies option value are sensitive to the selected parameter values, which are subject to debate, Siddiqui *et al.*'s (2007) and Davis and Owens' (2003) results show that renewable technologies hold a significant amount of value that cannot be detected by using traditional static valuation techniques.

4.5   Conclusions

While the current UK electricity system is quite diverse by historical standards, there are concerns that, should the investors' preference for gas-fired plants continue, the UK power generation system's diversity would decrease, and the UK's gas import dependency would increase, with potential negative security of supply and macro-economic impacts. This chapter discussed the likely evolution of the UK generation mix, and the potential negative consequences in terms of security of supply and macro-economic resilience to oil and gas price movements. Greater diversity generally enhances the robustness of an electricity system to fossil fuel supply shocks, and hence yields macroeconomic benefits and security of supply benefits. However, while diversity can be seen as a desirable feature of an electricity system, it is not a necessary condition. Perhaps more importantly, it is not clear *what* should be diversified, and *how much* diversity is optimal. Because generation mix diversity is a multifaceted issue, it is indeed difficult to quantify the costs and benefits associated with greater fuel mix diversity.

---

[24] The model assumes a current ratio of renewables to non-renewables electricity generating costs of 1.29, and a 1–4% annual rate of decline of renewables generating costs, depending on the level of R&D funding. The cash flows of renewable and non-renewable technologies are discounted using the risk-free interest rate.

This chapter suggests that more research is needed to quantitatively assess the value of diversifying the electricity generation mix to provide a normative approach for policy makers. Care must indeed be taken that arguments in favour of diversity are not used opportunistically by those seeking to protect particular firms and industries. The last section of the chapter reviewed the weaknesses of the existing diversity indices. While there have been many attempts to design diversity indicators which serve as useful proxies to quantify diversity, such concentration indicators suffer from not taking into account the costs of increased diversity. More research is needed to identify the economic costs associated with greater diversity, as well as to weight the costs and benefits of increased diversity.

We also discussed how new analytical tools borrowed from the financial literature offer powerful analytical tools to value the costs and benefits of reducing some risks, and constitute a promising avenue for further research. These include *static* valuation methods such as Portfolio theory, and *dynamic* valuation methods, such as Real Options, which take into account the option value of diversity as a hedge against potential fossil fuel supply or price shocks. Findings of recent studies using such analytical approaches to value diversity were discussed, showing that non-fossil-fuel technologies have a significant 'hedging value' from a societal perspective *vis-à-vis* fuel and CO_2 price risks for the UK electricity system. Valuation approaches can therefore rationalise embarking upon a power-plant project that is not expected to be economic for a period of years but which offers the possibility of benefits in the longer term. Moreover, dynamic valuation approaches of diversity reveal that current static valuations of research, development, demonstration and deployment programmes for new power generation technologies may significantly understate the benefits of such programmes. Finally, contrasting the societal value of diversity with the results from studies quantifying the value of fuel mix diversity to private investors casts some doubt about whether the current UK market framework provides adequate diversification incentives.

Acknowledgements

The author would like to thank Shimon Awerbuch, Tooraj Jamasb, David Newbery, William Nuttall, Paul Twomey and the anonymous referees for their helpful comments. This chapter is dedicated to the memory of Shimon Awerbuch, who made a great contribution to the application of innovative valuation approaches from the financial literature to quantify the value of fuel mix diversity.

References

Awerbuch, S. (2000). Investing in photovoltaics: risk, accounting and the value of new Technology. *Energy Policy*, **28**, 1023–1035.

Awerbuch, S. and M. Berger (2003). *Energy Security and Diversity in the EU: A Mean-Variance Portfolio Approach*. IEA Research Paper, Paris. Available at: www.awerbuch.com/shimonpages/shimondocs/iea-portfolio.pdf

Awerbuch, S. and R. Sauter (2006). Exploiting the oil–GDP effect to support renewables deployment. *Energy Policy*, **34**, 2008–2819.

Bar-Lev, D. and S. Katz (1976). A portfolio approach to fossil fuel procurement in the electric utility industry. *Journal of Finance*, **31**(3), 933–947.

Barrell, R. and O. Pomerantz (2004). *Oil Prices and the World Economy*. London: NIESR.

Bazilian, M. and F. Roques (eds) (2008). Analytical methods for energy diversity and security – a tribute to Shimon Awerbuch. Elsevier: Energy Policy and Economics Series, forthcoming.

Bohi, D.R. and M.A. Toman (1993). Energy security: externalities and policies. *Energy Policy*, **21**, 1093–1109.

Brealey, R. and S. Myers (2000). *Principles of Corporate Finance*, 6th edition. Irwin: McGraw-Hill.

Colpier, U. and D. Cornland (2002). The economics of the combined cycle gas turbine: an experience curve analysis. *Energy Policy*, **30**, 309–316.

Costello, K. (2005). A perspective on fuel diversity. *Electricity Journal*, **18**(4), 28–47.

Davis, G. and Owens, B. (2003). Optimizing the level of renewable electric R&D expenditures using real options analysis. *Energy Policy*, **31**, 1589–1608.

Department of Trade and Industry (2003). *Energy White Paper: Our Energy Future – Creating a Low Carbon Economy*. Directorate-General for Energy and Transport, London.

(2006a). *United Kingdom. Energy Review: The Energy Challenge*. Available at: www.berr.gov.uk/energy/review/page31995.html

(2006b). *United Kingdom. UK Energy and CO₂ Emissions Projections*. Available at: www.berr.gov.uk/energy

(2006c). *United Kingdom. Second Annual Report to Parliament on the Security of Gas and Electricity Supply in Great Britain by the Secretary of State for Trade and Industry*. Available at: www.berr.gov.uk/energy

(2006d). *United Kingdom. Joint Energy Security of Supply Working Group (JESS) Sixth Report*. Available at: www.berr.gov.uk/energy/energy-reliability/security-supply/jess/index.html

Dixit, A. and R. Pindyck (1994). *Investment under Uncertainty*. Princeton University Press.

European Commission (2005). *Competition Directorate: Energy Sector Inquiry: Draft Preliminary Report*. Available at: http://ec.europa.eu/comm/competition/sectors/energy/inquiry/index.html

Fabozzi, F., F. Gupta and H. Markowitz (2002). The legacy of modern portfolio theory. *Journal of Investing*, Fall 2002, 7–22

Frayer, J. and N. Uludere (2001). What is it worth? Application of real options theory to the valuation of generation assets. *Electricity Journal*, **14**, 40–51.

Gately, D. and H.G. Huntington (2002). The asymmetric effects of changes in price and income on energy and oil demand. *Energy Journal*, 23(1), 19–55.

Gollier, C., D. Proult, F. Thais and G. Walgenwitz (2005). Choice of nuclear power investments under price uncertainty: valuing modularity. *Energy Economics*, 27(4), 667–685.

Greene, D. and N. Tishchishyna (2000). *Costs of Oil Dependence: A 2000 Update.* Prepared for Department of Energy, ORNL TM-2000/152.

Grubb, M., L. Butler and P. Twomey (2006). Diversity and security in UK electricity generation: the influence of low-carbon objectives. *Energy Policy*, 34, 4050–4062.

Helm, D. (2002). Energy policy: security of supply, sustainability and competition. *Energy Policy*, 30, 173–184.

Hill, M. (1973). Diversity and evenness: a unifying notation and its consequences. *Ecology*, 54(2), 427–432.

Humphreys, H. and K. McClain (1998). Reducing the impacts of energy price volatility through dynamic portfolio selection. *Energy Journal*, 19(3), 107–131.

Hunt, B., P. Lisard and D. Laxton (2001). *The Macroeconomic Effects of Higher Oil Prices.* IMF Working Paper, Washington, DC.

(2002). *The Macroeconomic Effects of Higher Oil Prices.* National Institute Economic Review 179, London: NIESR.

Huntington, H.G. (2005). *The Economic Consequences of Higher Crude Oil Prices.* EMF SR 9, Energy Modeling Forum, Stanford University, Palo Alto, CA.

ILEX Energy Consulting (2006). *Economic Implications of a Gas Supply Interruption to UK Industry.* Report to DTI.

International Energy Agency (IEA) (2004). *Analysis of the Impact of High Oil Prices on the Global Economy.* Economic Analysis Division Working Paper, OECD/IEA, Paris. Available at: www.iea.org/textbase/papers/2004/high_oil_prices.pdf

International Energy Agency (IEA) (2006). *World Energy Outlook.* Paris: OECD/IEA.

International Monetary Fund (IMF) (2005). *Oil Market Developments and Issues.* Washington, DC: Policy Development and Review Department.

Jansen, J., W. van Arkel and M. Boots (2004). *Designing Indicators of Long-term Energy Supply Security.* Energy Research Centre of the Netherlands (ECN) Report C-04-007.

Jansen, J., L. Beurskens and X. van Tilburg (2006). *Application of Portfolio Analysis to the Dutch Generating Mix.* Energy Research Centre of the Netherlands (ECN) Report C-05-100.

Kleindorfer, P. and L. Li (2005). Multi-period VaR-constrained portfolio optimisation with applications to the electric power sector. *Energy Journal*, 26(1),

Markowitz, H. (1952). Portfolio selection, *Journal of Finance*, 7(1), 77–91.

Murto, P. and Nese, G. (2002). *Input Price Risk and Optimal Timing of Energy Investment: Choice between Fossil- and Biofuels.* Working Paper No. 25/02, Institute for Research in Economics and Business Administration, Bergen.

National Grid Transco (2005a). *Winter Outlook 2005/2006.* Available at: www.ofgem.gov.uk

(2005b). *Gas Transportation Ten Year Statement 2005*. Available at: www.nationalgrid.com

Roques, F. (2003). *Security of Electricity Supplies*. UK Parliamentary Office of Science and Technology Report and Postnote 203, September 2003. Downloadable at: www.parliament.uk/post/pn203.pdf

Roques, F., D. Newbery and W. Nuttall (2006a). *Fuel-Mix Diversification Incentives in Liberalized Electricity Markets: A Mean-Variance Portfolio Theory Approach*. European Institute, Florence School of Regulation Working Paper, October 2006.

Roques, F., D. Newbery, W. Nuttall, R. de Neufville and S. Connors (2006b). Nuclear power: a hedge against uncertain gas and carbon prices? *Energy Journal*, **27**(4), 1–24.

Roques, F., D. Newbery and W. Nuttall (2008). Fuel mix diversification incentives in liberalised electricity markets: a mean-variance portfolio theory approach. *Energy Economics*, forthcoming.

Siddiqui, A.S., C. Marnay and R.H. Wiser (2007). Real options valuation of US federal renewable energy research, development, demonstration and deployment. *Energy Policy*, **35**, 265–279.

Stirling, A. (1994). Diversity and ignorance in electricity supply investment: addressing the solution rather than the problem. *Energy Policy*, **22**, 195–216.

(1998). *On the Economics and Analysis of Diversity*. SPRU Electronic Working Paper No. 28. Available at: www.sussex.ac.uk/spru/publications/imprint/sewps/sewp28/sewp28.html

(2001). Science and precaution in the appraisal of electricity supply options. *Journal of Hazardous Materials*, **86**, 55–75.

Trigeorgis, L. (1996). *Real Options: Managerial Flexibility and Strategy in Resource Allocation*. Cambridge, MA: MIT Press.

Western, R. (1995). Diversity and ignorance in electricity supply investment: a reply to Andrew Stirling. *Energy Policy*, **23**(1), 5–16.

5   Variability and renewables

Graham Sinden

5.1   Introduction

Electricity networks bring consumers and generators of electricity together, allowing demand to be matched by supply on a second-to-second basis. This balance is maintained while constant change is experienced by the network, with unexpected changes from forecast demand levels being met with sufficient generating capacity to ensure the reliable operation of the network, including the ability to cope with any unexpected shortfalls in available capacity.

The introduction of large-scale renewable electricity generation to a network has the potential to affect this balance, by delivering an electricity supply whose output can vary considerably over time. However, not all renewable generators exhibit this variability, and there are often different patterns of variability associated with different renewable resources.

This chapter commences with an overview of why variability is important in electricity networks, and how the variability of renewables should be seen in the context of the larger network to which they are connected. The variability characteristics of leading UK renewable electricity generators are discussed, presenting a view of the long-term patterns of variability that are associated with a range of resources. Not all renewables show the same patterns of variability, including a number of resources that do not differ significantly from existing thermal plant operating characteristics; the importance of scenarios that recognise this diversity in renewable generators is examined.

The chapter concludes with an assessment of three areas of particular interest regarding the role of renewables in electricity networks. These include the degree to which variable-output generating capacity can replace conventional thermal plant without affecting the long-term ability of the network to meet demand; the amount of thermal capacity required to ensure short-term balancing of the network; and the degree to which renewables alter the generation profile of the remaining thermal plant.

133

5.1.1   Terminology: variable or intermittent?

A term commonly applied to renewables is 'intermittency'; however, the use of this term runs the risk of being misleading about the characteristics of renewable resources. Intermittency, or having the property of being intermittent, implies that a generator is either operating or not operating. Under this definition, all generators exhibit some degree of intermittency; thermal plant will shut down for maintenance or due to mechanical failure, while renewable generators may cease generating due to lack of resource (e.g. low wind speeds). Indeed, a baseload thermal plant (such as nuclear) may be best described as an intermittent generator, as its production profiles tend to be presence/absence (Nordel, 2000). This terminology is not used here to detract from the performance of baseload generators, but rather to describe more accurately their pattern of electricity production. By contrast, the output characteristics of renewable resources such as wind, wave, tidal stream and solar resources are characterised by variation in output. Over time for example, variations in wind speed will (typically) result in variations in power output from wind turbines, and it is this variation in output over time that is of interest in terms of describing the resource, and assessing its contribution to electricity networks.

It should also be recognised that variable-output renewables represent a subset of renewable generating technologies. There are a wide range of renewable generating technologies, including electricity generating options such as landfill gas, co-firing of biomass, hydroelectric power and so on. These renewables do not exhibit variability in the same sense as resources such as wind power do, and as a result it would be inappropriate to group all renewables together under the label of variable. Given that these renewable resources exhibit properties more commonly identified with conventional thermal plant, it is appropriate to use the long-standing term 'dispatchable' to describe the availability and scheduling of both baseload and peak-load generators: that is, electricity production can be scheduled in advance, and dispatched as necessary. This is not inconsistent with the earlier discussion: the decision to describe an electricity generator as intermittent or variable is based on the typical pattern of electricity production, while the terms dispatchable and non-dispatchable relate to the ability to schedule power output from generators.

5.2   Balancing electricity demand and supply

The balance between supply and demand on electricity networks must be able to achieve both long-term certainty that there will be sufficient generating capacity to meet demand, and the short-term ability to ensure voltage and frequency stability. These long-term and short-term aspects of network reliability have been described as the static and dynamic requirements of reliability (Billinton, 1970), and are discussed below.

5.2.1   Static system reliability

The static or long-term reliability of an electricity network assesses the probability that there will be sufficient capacity available on the network to meet demand; this is commonly accomplished using a 'loss of load probability analysis', which determines the risk (probability) that some electricity demand will be forced to disconnect from the network because there is insufficient generating capacity available to meet demand (UKERC, 2006).

A central component of loss of load probability analysis is the representation of capacity availability as a probability distribution; while a given amount of generating capacity may physically exist, it may not be available due to operational factors such as scheduled maintenance or mechanical failure, with the operational availability of an individual generator given by an availability factor. By making some simplifying assumptions, such as all generating units being the same size, having the same availability factor, and periods of non-availability being independent between the different generators, the probability of a given level of generating capacity being available on the network forms a binomial distribution (often approximated by a normal distribution). Given this distribution of available capacity, the probability of expected demand exceeding available capacity can be determined. Alternatively, by specifying a given level of reliability that the network must achieve, the conventional capacity requirement needed to meet this reliability criterion can be determined for a given demand level.

The development of variable output renewables alters the probability with which a given level of generating capacity will be available. For conventional generators, an availability factor of 85% is commonly used (OECD, 2005), with the unit completely unavailable for the remaining 15% of the time. However, a simple presence/absence measure of renewable capacity availability is rarely adequate in describing the variability of renewable electricity generation. Instead, the availability of renewable resources such as wind power needs to reflect the underlying variability of the resource, as this variability determines the likely probability that a given capacity of wind power will be available.

By combining the probabilistic functions that represent both the conventional capacity and renewable capacity on the network, the true long-term reliability of the network can be assessed and compared against alternatives.

5.2.2   *Dynamic system reliability*

System reliability must also be assessed on a shorter time horizon, such that imbalances between supply and demand do not arise. Where the supply–demand balance is not maintained, imbalances (such as a sudden increase in demand or decrease in supply) are reflected in frequency fluctuations. To ensure that frequency returns to the required 50 Hz ± 1% (Strbac and Jenkins, 2001), changes to either electricity supply or demand occur. To accommodate unexpected fluctuations in both demand and supply, additional thermal reserve operates on the network, with the amount of reserve required being a function of the degree of uncertainty surrounding demand and supply.

Variance in demand arises from the difference between the forecast demand and the actual demand that is experienced by the network. As generating capacity is made ready to meet the forecast demand, any difference between the forecast demand and the actual demand will result in an imbalance between the available generating capacity and the demand to be met.

The ability to predict demand is improved by the aggregation and smoothing effects of the electricity network. Individual demand centres, such as a house or an office, can exhibit highly variable and erratic electricity demand patterns (Figure 5.1); however, the aggregation of millions of individual demand patterns by the network results in a smoothing of demand (Figure 5.2). By forecasting aggregate demand on the network, forecasters are relying on the natural smoothing of demand patterns that results from the network aggregating many poorly correlated loads together. The second benefit of this aggregation is that generators are required to meet the aggregate load profile (Figure 5.2), rather than undertaking the extremely difficult task of matching generation to individual demand changes (Figure 5.1).

Similar uncertainty arises on the supply side, where the actual availability of generators may not match the forecast availability (for example, due to mechanical failure). To compensate for the variations in both supply and demand, additional capacity is made available. This uncertainty surrounding future demand level and supply availability can be expressed in terms of the error (standard deviation) associated with the expectation of supply and demand, and is the sum of squares of the forecast error standard deviation and the supply error standard deviation, assuming that the errors are uncorrelated (Holttinen, 2003;

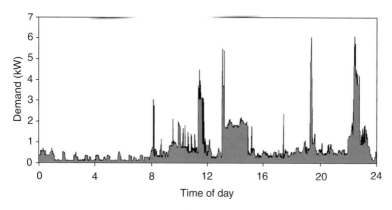

Figure 5.1. Electricity demand for a single dwelling, one day
Source: BG/Heriot-Watt University (2005)

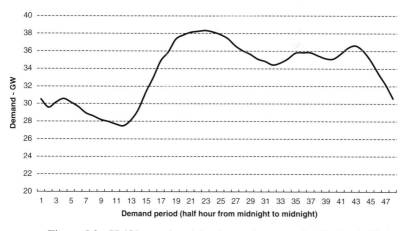

Figure 5.2. Half-hour electricity demand pattern for England, Wales and Scotland
Source: BMRS (2006)

Anderson, 2006). Historically, reserve capacity has been equal to ±3 standard deviations of the combined uncertainty in demand and supply (σ_t), plus an amount of reserve equal to the largest single generating unit connected to the system (UKERC, 2006). However, as the reserve associated with the largest conventional generator is independent of the presence of renewable electricity generators, the impact of including renewables on system reserve is seen only in the estimate of the combined uncertainty in supply and demand. Thus, in a system where σ_d is the standard deviation of changes in demand and σ_s is the standard deviation of supply, σ_t is the standard deviation of the combination of the uncertainty in supply and demand (Eqn 5.1).

$$\sigma_t^2 = \sigma_d^2 + \sigma_s^2 \qquad (5.1)$$

Renewables may increase the complexity of this relationship between supply and demand. This arises from the inherent variability in output of some renewable generators, particularly wind, wave, tidal and solar generators. The addition of these types of renewables to a network can increase the error (standard deviation) in supply, as there is less certainty surrounding future available capacity on the network. The degree of influence that the variability of renewables has on the existing network is dependent on both the size of the renewable generating capacity (in relation to the conventional plant) and the degree of variability in its electricity supply, such that:

$$\sigma_t^2 = \sigma_d^2 + (1 - p)\,\sigma_s^2 + p\,\sigma_r^2 \qquad (5.2)$$

where σ_r is the error (standard deviation) associated with electricity supplied from renewables and p is the proportion of energy being supplied by renewable generators. One outcome of Eqn 5.2 is that, at low levels of renewable penetration, the variability of the renewables will have very little effect on system variability. However, as the penetration of renewables increases (i.e. p gets larger), the greater is the impact that the variability of the renewables will have on overall system uncertainty. At significant levels of renewables penetration, small changes in the variability of the renewable electricity supply will have follow-on impacts on the amount of reserve capacity required to ensure the stable operation (balancing) of the network.

Non-variable renewables   Not all renewables impose additional variability on electricity networks. For example, co-firing of biomass in otherwise conventional coal-fired power stations results in a portion of the electricity being generated from a renewable source (the biomass); however, the overall electricity supply profile is identical to that of a coal-only power station. Even with those renewables that do provide variable output, there are significant differences in the characteristics of electricity generated from different renewable resources. While it is often convenient to consider 'renewables' as a single uniform method of electricity generation, large differences in the characteristics of renewables mean that they cannot be treated as a single generating type. For this reason it is important that σ_r represents the variability associated with the existing or future portfolio of renewables connected to a network, and not just a single renewable energy type or resource.

5.2.3   Diversification and renewable energy scenarios

Diversification within and between different renewable resources and locations can be an important strategy for reducing the variability in electricity from renewable portfolios. At an individual generator or site, fluctuations in hourly power output can be significant. However, in a similar manner to demand smoothing, the connection of a portfolio of renewable electricity generators to the electricity network has the potential to lower this variability considerably. For example, a diversified wind-power system in the UK would deliver electricity with around one-fifth the variability of that being delivered by individual wind-power sites.

The underlying reason for the smoothing effect of diversity is that changes in the availability of renewable resources are not perfectly correlated between different locations. For wind power, the correlation between power production patterns for paired locations in the UK is strongly related to the distance between the sites, with the similarity in output patterns decreasing with increasing separation of the sites (Figure 5.3): this relationship is similar to that shown by Giebel (2000) for 60 wind sites in Europe.

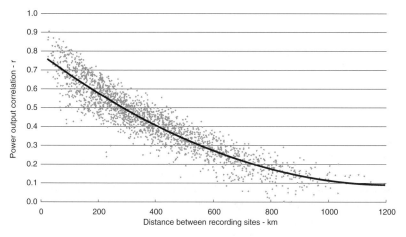

Figure 5.3. Relationship between wind output correlation and distance between wind sites; 2,800 pairs of wind sites, based on UK long-term average CF of 30%
Source: Sinden (2007)

There are two important implications of this relationship. First, for a geographically small area there is a physical limit as to how far apart different wind-power developments can be located – as a result, the power output from a country such as the Netherlands or Denmark would be expected to be more variable than that from a distributed UK wind system. Second, once the geographical limits of the region have been developed, all future developments will increasingly result in the average distance between sites decreasing. As correlation increases with lower separation between sites, this results in further sites having little effect in further smoothing patterns of variability. As a result, there is a minimum achievable variability in all regions where wind power is being developed.

The benefits of diversification are not confined to a single renewable resource; the development of different resources with different patterns of electricity generation will have a similar smoothing effect (Grubb, 1991). Indeed, this is a logical extension to managing variability once large-scale exploitation of a single resource has occurred, and thus the opportunity for further diversification within this resource is limited. For example, by including wave power alongside wind power on an electricity network, the variability of the total supply will be reduced (although the temporal availability of wave power is related to wind power, it is not perfectly correlated and, therefore, in combination with wind power it will act to smooth the aggregate output). Even the addition of tidal stream power, a resource with significant hourly variability, can reduce overall variability (providing the contribution from tidal stream power remains small compared with the contribution from wind and wave power).

5.2.4   Scenarios

As a result of this interaction between different renewable resources, the integration of renewables into electricity networks will be affected by the different types of renewables that are being developed. It is highly unlikely that all renewable electricity will be delivered by a single technology. Rather, a range of renewable resources are currently combining to deliver electricity in the UK. This mix of renewables will change over time; at present, renewable electricity generation in the UK is dominated by energy production from landfill gas together with other non-variable renewable output. However, this mix of renewables is unlikely to continue, with some scenarios for the UK suggesting that, by 2020, wind power will dominate renewable electricity production (Figure 5.4). Even under scenarios such as this, other renewable resources will continue to provide a significant level of generation.

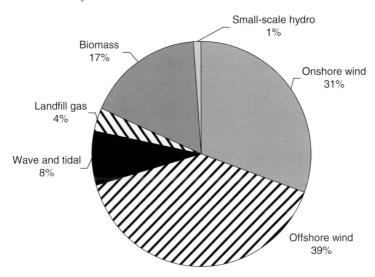

Figure 5.4. Contribution from different renewable resources in 2020,
delivering 20% of total UK electricity generation
Source: Mott MacDonald (2004)

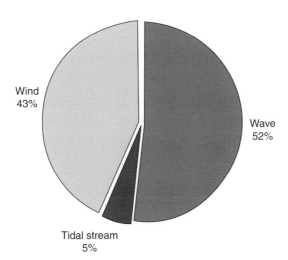

Figure 5.5. MEC scenario for 2020: contribution of wind, wave and
tidal stream power to a 20% renewable electricity scenario
Source: Sinden (2006)

It is possible to design scenarios that minimise the variability of a given renewables portfolio. By combining wind, wave and tidal stream resources, it has been demonstrated that the overall variability of the portfolio would be below that of any single renewable (Figure 5.5). The variability of this portfolio would decrease further with the replacement of a portion of the wind, wave and tidal stream capacity with non-varying renewable energy capacity.

5.3   Characteristics of renewables

There are a wide range of renewable electricity generation methods and concepts: this chapter focuses on four key resources; wind power, wave power, solar power and tidal stream power. The variability in electricity supply from renewable generators is both a resource-specific and site-specific characteristic of renewable electricity generation:

- *Different renewable resources* exhibit different patterns of electricity generation, and hence different types and degrees of variability.
- *Different locations* will show different electricity generation characteristics for the same renewable resource type.
- *Different technologies* will modify the electricity generation characteristics of renewable resources.

Another component of the characteristics of renewable resources is their availability in relation to electricity demand. Demand patterns are themselves location-specific, reflecting cultural, environmental and industrial aspects of different regions. For this reason, it is important that site-specific demand data is available to support specific analyses.

The variability of renewables changes depending on the time-scale over which output fluctuations are compared. For example, a high degree of persistence (or autocorrelation) in short-term wave power availability results in a low variability electricity supply when viewed at short time periods (1 hour). As the period over which generation is viewed increases, variability increases to a maximum, and then decreases again as the shorter-term variations are aggregated and smoothed by the longer time steps (Figure 5.6).

The characteristics described here are based on UK resources, and their interaction with current UK electricity demand patterns. Due to the site-specific nature of these resources, the characteristics described here may differ from those experienced in other locations. Furthermore, differing electricity demand patterns (for example, summer peak electricity demands) may alter the relationship between renewable resource availability and electricity demands in other locations.

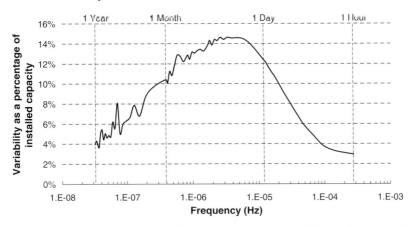

Figure 5.6. Variability of wave power output at different time periods
(deseasonalised at low frequencies)
Source: presentation based on a similar analysis for wind power by Twidell
(1987)

5.3.1   Seasonal variability

Wind, wave and solar resources in the UK show a distinctly seasonal
pattern of availability: wind and wave power are more available during
the winter months, while solar resources reach a maximum during the
summer months (Figures 5.7, 5.8 and 5.9). Tidal resources show very
little variability at the seasonal or monthly time scale, as the dominant
controls on tidal energy availability (planetary motion) occur at shorter
time-scales that are smoothed at the seasonal scale.

There is a strong similarity between the seasonal availability of wind
and wave power in the UK, and this does not occur by chance: waves
are formed by the friction of wind on the ocean surface, so for waves to
form it is necessary to have wind. However, this does not mean that
wind and waves are always present at the same time and location.
High-energy waves are formed by the action of wind over long distances (hundreds of kilometres); combined with the ability of waves to
efficiently travel great distances, this means that the waves arriving at
the shore may have been generated many hundreds or even thousands
of kilometres away, and may have been formed by winds that are not
present at the coast.

The similarity between the monthly availability of different renewable
resources can be expressed in terms of correlation of hourly energy
availability. The correlation between wind and wave energy availability

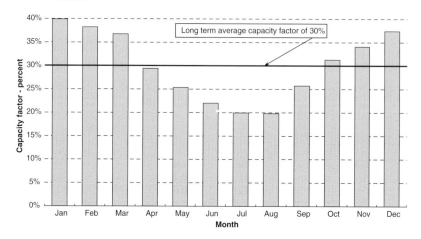

Figure 5.7. Seasonal variability in wind power availability, UK;
average monthly wind power capacity factor
Source: Sinden (2007)

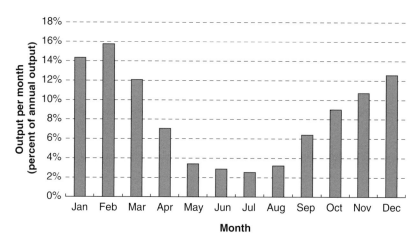

Figure 5.8. Seasonal variability in wave power availability,
North-west, UK
Source: Sinden (2005a)

in the UK is significant, but well below the perfect correlation that is
often assumed, while solar power availability is negatively correlated to
these resources, and tidal stream power is uncorrelated to either wind,
wave or tidal power availability (Table 5.1).

Table 5.1. *Correlation matrix for monthly wind, wave, tidal stream and solar power resource availability in the UK (values calculated using Spearman's rank correlation, as the underlying data is not normally distributed)*

	Correlation			
Resource type	Wind	Wave	Tidal	Solar
Wind	1.00			
Wave	0.86	1.00		
Tidal	0.01	0.10	1.00	
Solar	−0.53	−0.67	−0.01	1.00

Note: Correlation is partly dependent on the period over which it is calculated. Correlation at hourly resolution may differ significantly from the values shown here.

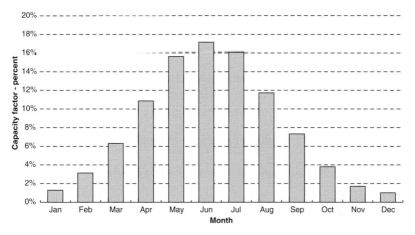

Figure 5.9. Seasonal variability in solar power availability, UK; average monthly solar PV capacity factor

5.3.2   Short-term variability

Short-term variability, particularly over time periods of 4 hours or less, is particularly important for the balancing of electricity networks (Milborrow, 2006). Fluctuations from hour to hour are a significant driver of the costs associated with balancing supply and demand on the electricity network, and the variability of renewables has the potential to increase this system error (Eqn 5.2).

Table 5.2. *Renewable resource variability (standard deviation of the difference in power output from one hour to the next, expressed as percentage of installed capacity). By comparison, hourly variability in demand is 3.1% (as a percentage of installed capacity)*

Resource type	Variability
Wind	3.2%
Wave	2.6%
Tidal	6–22%[1]
Solar	3.5%[2]

[1] The variability of the tidal stream resource is dependent on both site selection and the level of development at each site.
[2] This figure reflects hourly variability for all hours. For the solar resource, half of all hours will have a known and non-varying output (i.e. zero output overnight). The variability of the solar resource during generating hours is 5.0%.

There are considerable differences between the hour-ahead variability of different renewable resources (Table 5.2), with wave power showing the lowest variability of the resources discussed. The variability of solar power needs to be treated with caution, as the lack of output of solar overnight has the effect of lowering long-term variability. By assessing variability only during hours of generation, the variability of solar generated electricity rises.

5.3.3   Relationship with electricity demand

Over the long term, the variable output of some renewable resources can show a relationship with electricity demand; such relationships result from similarities in the long-term patterns of renewable resource availability and electricity demand levels. Examples of the relationship between resource availability and electricity demand are shown in Figure 5.10 (wind resource), Figure 5.11 (wave resource), Figure 5.12 (solar resource) and Figure 5.13 (tidal stream resource).

In the UK, the wind resource is more energetic during winter, broadly matching changes in electricity demand levels to result in higher average energy production from wind power at times of high electricity demand. For the results below (Figure 5.10), wind power has an average capacity factor of 28%; however, during the hours of high electricity demand (80–100 percentile demand hours) it averages around 35%, while during the lowest 20% of demand hours the average capacity factor of wind power is 16% (falling to around 10% during the very lowest of demand hours). A similar pattern of higher

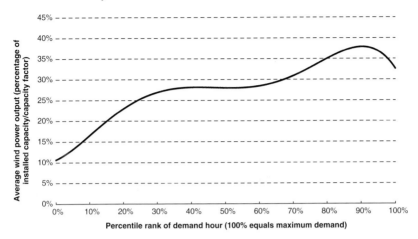

Figure 5.10. Long-term relationship between wind power availability
and electricity demand, UK
Source: Sinden (2005b)

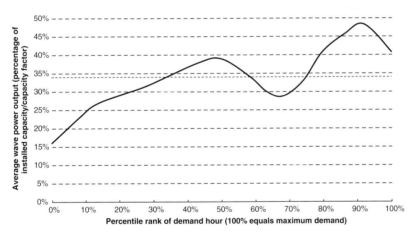

Figure 5.11. Long-term relationship between wave power availability
and electricity demand, UK
Source: After Sinden (2005a)

energy production during high demand hours, and lower production
during low demand hours, is observed for the relationship between
wave power and demand (Figure 5.11). By contrast, the UK solar
resource exhibits a more complex relationship with demand, where
the highest average contribution from solar PV would occur in the

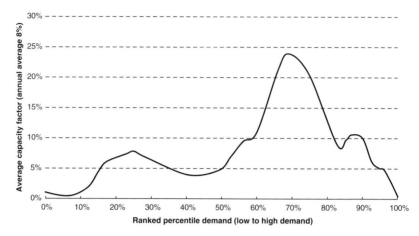

Figure 5.12. Long-term relationship between solar power availability and electricity demand, UK

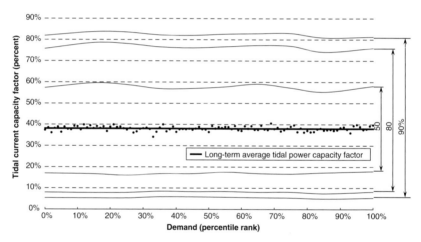

Figure 5.13. Long-term relationship between tidal power availability and electricity demand, UK

60–80 percentile demand range, with no contribution to demand at the very extremes of the demand range (Figure 5.12). This pattern again reflects the characteristics of the resource; minimum demand levels in the UK occur overnight in summer, while peak electricity demand occurs between 5 p.m. and 7 p.m. in winter: as both times are between sunset and sunrise, there is no contribution from solar PV. As a result, solar power in the UK is effective at providing energy to the UK electricity network (and therefore displacing fossil fuel use); however, it is unlikely to provide capacity on the network (meaning that there would be no net reduction in conventional capacity). These issues are discussed further in Section 5.4. Electricity generation from tidal stream power in the UK shows no relationship to demand (Figure 5.13), as there is virtually no correlation between the availability of the tidal stream resource (with availability varying in accordance with daily tides and the spring–neap tide cycle) and the pattern of electricity generation.

When considering the relationship between renewable resource availability and electricity demand levels, it is essential to obtain site-specific data for the system being investigated. For example, while the UK's solar resource provides little, if any, electricity generation at times of peak electricity demand, in other regions this relationship is reversed: Spain, California (USA) and Sydney (Australia) all experience a summertime peak in electricity demand, driven predominantly by the use of air-conditioners. Given that air-conditioners are typically run on hot, sunny days, it is highly likely that there would be a positive relationship between solar resource availability and peak electricity demand in these regions, resulting in solar displacing both energy and capacity on the electricity network.

5.3.4   Non-variable renewables

For electricity generated from the co-firing of biomass, the pattern of electricity production will be identical to that of the fossil fuel plant in which it is being burnt. From this perspective, the marginal increase in supply variability from co-fired biomass will be zero, while the actual variability (or intermittency) and relationship to demand will be the same as that of the conventional plant. For landfill gas, sewage sludge digestion, and other non-variable renewables where there is control over the availability of the fuel used to generate electricity, operational experience suggests that the reliability and availability of these generators is equal to or greater than that achieved by conventional thermal generation. As a result, the inclusion of non-variable renewables on electricity networks will decrease the variability of the renewables portfolio.

5.4   Impacts of variability on network operation

Electricity networks have evolved to accommodate the variability inherent in both forecasts of demand and forecasts of conventional (thermal) plant availability, ensuring that sufficient generating capacity is available

to provide the required security of supply level. The large-scale introduction of renewable generating capacity to existing electricity networks
does not fundamentally change this relationship; there will remain a
requirement for reliable electricity generation, and this will occur through
the provision of adequate thermal plant. This section considers the impact
of the variability that renewables introduce on the conventional capacity
requirement of the system, short-term balancing of the network, and
the impact of renewables on the generation profile to be met by the
remaining thermal plant.

5.4.1   *Offsetting thermal plant capacity*

Renewables will be able to offset thermal generating capacity where it
can be shown that the system with renewables will achieve an
equivalent security of supply standard to that of a conventional network. The capacity credit of conventional thermal plant is easily
determined, as 1GW of new generating capacity would be expected to
displace 1GW of existing capacity (assuming equivalent load factor and
availability at peak demand times). For variable output renewables,
this 1:1 relationship does not hold, due to their lower capacity factor.
More renewable capacity will therefore be required to deliver the same
amount of energy as the conventional capacity it is replacing, with the
actual amount dependent on the capacity factor of the renewable
capacity.

It is not just energy production that affects the ability of renewables to
offset conventional capacity; the variability of output may add uncertainty to the amount of capacity that can be expected to be delivered by
generators at any particular time (see Eqn 5.2). Were the variability of
the renewable generating capacity to result in low-renewables output
regularly occurring during times of peak electricity demand, then the
capacity value of the renewables plant would be undermined.

Concern has been expressed regarding the capacity credit of renewables, or the ability of renewables to reduce the amount of conventional
capacity required on the network while maintaining the same level of
security of supply. Some people have suggested that '100% back-up'
would be required for the installed wind capacity (Laughton, 2002; Fells
Associates, 2004), meaning that wind power would have no capacity
credit. However, the results of many other authors contradict this position; UKERC (2006) reviewed the results of 29 separate studies, all of
which identified a reduction in conventional capacity requirement due
to the introduction of renewables, while Giebel (2006) catalogued over
50 (mostly European) studies, which all conclude that wind power has a

capacity credit. Under a worst-case scenario, renewables would deliver energy to a network but not provide capacity on the network, due to the variability of output resulting in low generation during high-demand periods. The availability of solar energy in the UK provides a good example of such a relationship (Figure 5.12), as its availability during times of high electricity demand has been shown to be effectively zero, resulting in no offset of conventional capacity (UKERC, 2006). In such a situation, the thermal plant capacity requirement of the network would remain unchanged; however, the fuel costs associated with meeting demand would decrease due to substitution by the renewable energy plant. It is important to note that, even where renewables provide no capacity to the network, the thermal capacity requirement of the network cannot exceed that required prior to the development of the renewable generating capacity.

Loss of load probability modelling is commonly used to assess the reliability of electricity supply on networks. This statistical method determines the likelihood of demand being met, given the capacity and reliability of the plant available during times of peak electricity demand. Dale *et al.* (2004) provided a demonstration of the capacity credit of wind power in the UK context by evaluating an electricity system with a 70GW peak demand and 400TWh/year energy demand, which can be met by either 84GW of conventional capacity, or by 79GW of thermal plant and 26GW of wind capacity (with the wind capacity delivering 20% of annual energy demand). In this example, 26GW of wind capacity has displaced 5GW of thermal plant, while the overall system delivers the same level of security of supply, as determined from a loss of load probability analysis. This result is consistent with other reliable studies undertaken in the UK, as discussed by UKERC (2006).

A similarly sized network has been used to determine the capacity credit for a range of renewable resources in the UK (Table 5.3). This analysis demonstrates that the capacity credit of the UK's wind, wave and tidal stream is similar at the 20% penetration level, a result that reflects the long-term probability of renewable electricity from these resources being available at times of high demand. Sinden (2006) has also investigated the impact that diversifying the development of renewable energy resources in the manner suggested in Figure 5.5 would have if reducing the conventional capacity requirement of the network to 78GW – an improvement in the capacity credit of the renewable energy capacity of 20% over the wind-only result.

The capacity credit of renewables also varies with the amount of installed capacity relative to the size of the conventional network. At lower levels of penetration, the capacity credit of renewables rises in

Table 5.3. *Capacity credit for different variable renewables (assumes renewable capacity scaled to deliver 20% of annual energy demand)*

Renewable type	Capacity credit
Wind	5GW
Wave	5.5GW
Tidal	5GW

Note: The identified tidal stream resource in the UK (Black and Veatch, 2005) is equal to around 4% of UK energy demand. The figure for capacity credit of tidal stream resources given is based on a scaled-up development of tidal capacity which is unlikely to be available in the UK.

relative terms. For example, 10% wind power will deliver a capacity credit of around 25%, while a 20% wind penetration in the same network will achieve a capacity credit of approximately 20% (National Grid, 2004). Similar results have also been obtained by Grubb (1991) and Mott Macdonald (2004), while UKERC (2006) provides a comprehensive summary of similar studies.

5.4.2   Demand pattern to be met

Under a conventional electricity system, the pattern of generation is identical to the pattern of demand. However, the pattern of generation required from thermal plant connected to a network with a significant penetration of renewables will be modified. In some cases, this modification will be beneficial; for example an increase in renewables output during a period of increasing demand would remove the need for additional plant to be brought into operation. However, at another time an increase in demand may be accompanied by a reduction in renewables output, increasing the rate at which new thermal capacity would need to be brought onto the network.

A comparison has been carried out of the change in demand that would be experienced by thermal plant on electricity networks where no renewables were present, and where 20% wind power was present (Figure 5.14).

In this example, the introduction of wind power to the network has led to a small reduction in the number of hours with no appreciable change in thermal plant requirement, and a small increase in the number of hours where demand changes by ±3%. There is also an increase in the extreme 1-hour change in thermal capacity due to wind power; however, the frequency of this change is very low. The maximum reduction in

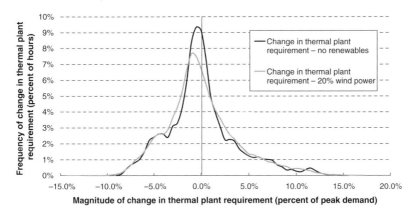

Figure 5.14. Frequency and magnitude of change in thermal plant requirement for a conventionally powered system, and a system with 20% wind power
Source: Based on historic UK electricity demand levels. Demand data modified to achieve an annual peak demand of 70GW

thermal plant requirement over 1 hour is equal to 9% of peak demand while, under the 20% wind scenario, this increases to 12.5%; however, changes above the 9% threshold occur on average in around 7 hours per year. The frequency with which the maximum increase in thermal plant seen on the conventional network is exceeded due to the presence of wind power is approximately 1 hour per year.

5.4.3   The cost of variability

Given that variable renewable generators can have an impact on the operation of existing electricity networks, the marginal cost of renewables can be measured in terms of the cost of generating electricity. This cost will be influenced by:

- *Capacity costs*: the cost of developing renewable generating capacity, and the avoided cost associated with reduced capacity requirements.
- *Fuel costs*: the costs associated with additional balancing requirements, and the avoided costs associated with lower use of thermal plant (and therefore lower CO_2 emissions costs).
- *Other costs*: including operation and maintenance, transmission, etc.

Importantly, the cost of renewable electricity generation is heavily dependent on the value of the fuel that it is displacing. At low fossil fuel prices, renewables tend to be at a cost disadvantage, as the benefits accrued through lower fuel costs are reduced; however, as fossil fuel prices rise (either directly or through surrogate measures such as carbon taxing or carbon trading), the value of the fuel displaced by renewables also rises.

A number of recent studies have addressed this issue in the UK (SCAR, 2002; Dale *et al.* 2004; The Carbon Trust and DTI, 2004; Anderson, 2006), with UKERC providing a thorough analysis of these and other cost estimates. Dale *et al.* (2004) identified generation costs (capital cost of both thermal and renewable capacity, plus operating and maintenance costs) as the single largest driver of system costs, with thermal-only generation on a network costing less than a network with 20% wind power. For fuel costs the opposite relationship is true: fuel costs for a 20% wind-power system are lower than those for a thermal (CCGT) system. Overall, the study found that a 20% wind-power scenario would increase generation costs by approximately 0.3p/kWh.

Dale *et al.* (2004) assumed a relatively low fuel cost of 22p/therm for gas, and did not include the cost of carbon associated with this fuel. As fluctuations in fuel price will affect the fuel cost comparison (but not the generating cost comparison), it is important to consider the sensitivity of these cost estimates to changes in fuel (gas) prices and the introduction of the European Union Emission Trading Scheme. Recent modelling that investigates these cost sensitivities suggests that a 20% wind-power scenario for the UK would be cost-neutral at a gas price of 40–45p/therm: in comparison, recent increases in fossil fuel prices have seen gas reach 45.2p/therm in the first quarter of 2006 (DTI, 2006).

5.5   Conclusions

Electricity networks have been designed to cope with variability, arising both from uncertainty in future demand levels and uncertainty in the availability of conventional generating capacity. The introduction of variable renewable electricity generation to such a system does not represent a fundamental departure from the traditional operation of the network; however, it does have the potential to affect the operation of the network. Variable renewables have the potential to reduce thermal capacity requirements on the network; however, the capacity credit will vary depending on the type of renewable resource.

Modelling of the costs of intermittency by a wide range of researchers and organisations suggests that the costs incurred through increased network balancing costs are modest, while under high fossil fuel prices they are offset by the value of the fuel saved.

Acknowledgements

The author acknowledges the support and assistance of the UK Met Office and the British Atmospheric Data Centre in providing the observed wind data used in this chapter. Thank you also to the Faculty of Economics at Cambridge University, and the Clarendon Fund Bursaries at Oxford University, for supporting this research.

References

Anderson, D. (2006). *Power System Reserves and Costs with Intermittent Generation*. UKERC 47. London: UER Centre.

BG/Heriot-Watt University (2005). *Electrical and Thermal Monitoring of Selected Dwellings*. Edinburgh: A. Peacock.

Billinton, R. (1970). *Power System Reliability Evaluation*. New York: Gordon and Breach, Science Publishers.

Black and Veatch (2005). *Phase II UK Tidal Stream Energy Resource Assessment*. London: The Carbon Trust.

BMRS (2006). *Initial Demand Turnout*. Balancing Mechanism Reporting Service, 10 July 2006. From www.bmreports.com

Dale, L., D. Milborrow, R. Stark and G. Strbac (2004). Total cost estimates for large-scale wind scenarios in the UK. *Energy Policy*, 32(17), 1949–1956.

DTI (2006). *Quarterly Energy Prices*. London: Department of Trade and Industry.

Fells Associates (2004). *Submission to the House of Lords Science and Technology Committee Enquiry into Renewable Energy*. HL Paper 126-II. House of Lords, London.

Giebel, G. (2000). *On the Benefits of Distributed Generation of Wind Energy in Europe*. Dissertation, Fachbereich Physik, Carl von Ossietzky Universität, Oldenburg, Germany.

(2006). *Wind Power has a Capacity Credit: a Catalogue of 50+ Supporting Studies*. Denmark: Risoe National Laboratory.

Grubb, M.J. (1991). The integration of renewable electricity sources. *Energy Policy*, 19(7), 670–688.

Holttinen, H. (2003). *Hourly Wind Power Variations and Their Impact on the Nordic Power System Operation*. Helsinki University of Technology, Finland: Department of Engineering Physics and Mathematics.

Laughton, M. (2002). Renewables and UK grid infrastructure. *Power in Europe*, 383(1), 9–11.

Milborrow, D. (2006). *Supply Variability and its Impact on Cost*. Oxford, UK: G. Sinden.

Mott MacDonald (2004). *Renewables Network Impact Study. Annex 4: Intermittency Literature Survey and Roadmap*. London: The Carbon Trust and the Department of Trade and Industry.

National Grid (2004). *Submission to Science and Technology Committee Hearings on Renewable Energy*. London: House of Lords, HM Government.

Nordel (2000). *Non-dispatchable Production in the Nordel System.* Nordel's Annual Meeting 2000. Denmark: Nordel's Grid Group.

OECD (2005). *Projected Costs of Generating Electricity.* Nuclear Energy Agency/International Energy Agency/Organisation for Economic Co-operation and Development. Paris: OECD.

SCAR (2002). *Quantifying the System Costs of Additional Renewables in 2020.* A report by Ilex Energy Consulting to the Department of Trade and Industry in association with Manchester Centre for Electrical Energy, UMIST, Manchester, UK.

Sinden, G. (2005a). *Variability of UK Marine Resources.* Oxford, UK: Environmental Change Institute, and London: The Carbon Trust.

(2005b). *Wind Power and the UK Wind Resource.* Oxford, UK: Environmental Change Institute.

(2006). *Diversified Renewable Energy Resources.* Oxford, UK: The Carbon Trust. Environmental Change Institute, and London: The Carbon Trust.

(2007). Characteristics of the UK wind resource: long-term patterns and relationship to electricity demand. *Energy Policy*, **35**(1), 112–127.

Strbac, G. and N. Jenkins (2001). *Network Security of the Future UK Electricity System: Report to PIU.* UMIST, Manchester, UK: Manchester Centre for Electrical Energy.

The Carbon Trust and DTI (2004). *Renewable Network Impacts Study.* London: The Carbon Trust.

Twidell, J. (1987). *Renewable Energy Resources.* London: English Language Book Society.

UKERC (2006). *The Costs and Impacts of Intermittency: An Assessment of the Evidence on the Costs and Impacts of Intermittent Generation of the British Electricity Network.* UK Energy Research Centre.

6 Implications of intermittency and transmission constraints for renewables deployment

Karsten Neuhoff, Jim Cust and Kim Keats-Martinez

6.1 Introduction

In order to meet its Kyoto objectives and accelerate the transition to a low-carbon economy, the UK has set itself the long-term target of cutting carbon emissions by 60% by 2050. One key aspect in the decarbonisation of the UK economy involves a move towards low-carbon electricity generation. Given increased emissions pressure from other sectors of the economy, most notably road transport and aviation, it is likely that more stringent cuts will be needed in the electricity sector. To push forward this structural adjustment, the UK government has set itself the target of providing 15% of electricity needs from renewable energy sources by 2015 and an aspirational target of 20% by 2020. Most renewable technologies are characterised by their intermittency and regional variation. In this chapter we explore the implications of the example of wind power, which is expected to provide a large proportion of renewable electricity over the coming years (see Chapter 14 by Elders *et al.*). We aim to understand some of the implications of this, or more ambitious targets, for the UK power system.

To structure the analysis, we use an investment planning model (IPM) that depicts the operation and evolution of the power system. Like any numerical model, our approach only allows us to provide meaningful insights relating to a limited set of questions. Therefore in this chapter we do not allow for the construction of technologies other than gas turbines and onshore wind turbines. We also assume that all market participants require the same real rate of return of 11% – and thus ignore potentially differing regulatory, technology and price risks between technologies. We list some cost estimates resulting from other models that complement our analysis. In order to explore the issues relating to a power system with high levels of wind energy, we model scenarios where 20% and 40% of total energy is delivered by wind power. We achieve these levels of investment by 2020 by choosing capital costs for wind power at which these targets are met.

A key question posed by the expansion of wind-powered electricity generation in the UK is one of location. This raises three important challenges.

1. The regions where the resource potential is greatest – Scotland, the north and south-west of England – have relatively low electricity demand. In contrast, the key load centres of central and south-eastern England have less wind resource (Grubb *et al.* 2006). We therefore model the capacity constraints on transmission lines between regions explicitly to see how they affect the optimal location of wind turbines and to what extent additional transmission capacity expansion is warranted.
2. Output of wind turbines is intermittent. However, the volatility of the aggregate output of wind turbines can be reduced if they are distributed over a larger area. As we are using hourly wind output data for each region, our model endogenously calculates the value of regional diversification.
3. Regional transmission constraints, scarcity of build sites, and socio-political tensions around new build make the large-scale deployment of wind turbines a challenge (Butler and Neuhoff, 2005; Devine-Wright, 2005). Thus we set regional build constraints and explore the cost reductions that can be achieved for the system if these constraints are relaxed. We can thus quantify the benefit of improving public acceptability or planning processes.

For this modelling we cooperated with ICF International to use their existing integrated planning model (Neuhoff *et al.* 2005) and database of the GB (Great Britain) power system. The model assumes perfect foresight and simultaneously optimises investment decisions in power stations and their subsequent operation. Thus it determines the volume and technology of investment in every 5-year period and the hourly dispatch of the system within that period. We expanded the model to capture the temporal and spatial characteristics of wind output using historical data for individual regions. Thus we can simulate the evolution of the GB electricity system with the gradual penetration of onshore wind power. We do not explicitly model the deployment of offshore wind power, due to limited data availability. We have verified the robustness of the approach and sensitivities to various input parameters in Neuhoff *et al.* (2005). Here we change the penetration of wind power by changing the assumptions about wind turbine construction and connection costs. This allows us to assess the impact and additional system costs of greater utilisation of the wind resource.

Our modelling work focuses on the impact of a variable energy source such as wind, as compared with more conventional generation technologies such as combined cycle gas turbines. As such, our work does not directly address other power engineering issues that may impose additional constraints that we cannot directly account for, such as fault ride through, system inertia and spinning reserve. Also, whilst ramping constraints are not included in our modelling work, we refer to separate modelling to estimate the additional impact (Strbac, 2002; Müsgens and Neuhoff, 2005; Gross et al., 2006). Our dataset uses onshore wind observations and, as such, cannot capture offshore planning decisions. Although currently offshore connection and construction costs are higher, cost reductions through learning-by-doing and the better offshore wind resource might compensate for these effects (L.E.K. Consulting, 2006). While the basic insights relating to locational choices and congestion management also apply to offshore wind, further modelling with the appropriate representation of offshore wind patterns is required in order to allow for quantitative insights.

Whilst our model does not impose grid connection charges within the regions, in two scenarios we increase the construction costs for wind turbines, which could reflect the impacts of increasing connection charges.

The modelling of optimal investment in new energy generation was first pursued in France during the 1950s (see Bessiere, 1970). Uncertainty was introduced in models relating to plant availability by Baleriaux et al. (1967). To cope with the increasing size of models, Bloom (1983) reformulated the problem to use a Generalized Benders decomposition, thus allowing for parallel processing. If we were to introduce additional detail in our simulations, we would probably have to follow this approach. In the recent literature, DeCarolis and Keith (2006) used 5 years of hourly demand and wind production patterns to calculate the optimal system configuration. This US model, however, is restricted to five production sites, one demand site, and only calculates a static long-term equilibrium that does not address the transition from today's energy system.

6.2 The model

The integrated planning model from ICF International is an investment planning model that uses a linear programming formulation to select investment options and to dispatch generating and load management

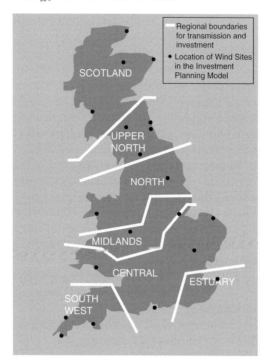

Figure 6.1. Wind measurement site location and regional boundaries

resources to meet overall electricity demand today and on an ongoing basis over the chosen planning horizon. We customised the model to more accurately represent wind power in the investment choices. The Xpress linear program solver from Dash Optimisation was used to find the optimal solution.[1]

We divided Great Britain (GB) into seven transmission-constrained regions as shown in Figure 6.1. The same approach is used by the National Grid in its *Seven Year Statement* (NGC, 2006). We refer to the GB regions using the following abbreviations: SCO – Scotland, UNO – Upper North, NOR – North, MID – Midlands, CEN – Central, SWE – South West and EST – Estuary. While the IPM could be used to model the transmission system at a more disaggregated level, we use this simplified representation, as we could not find a robust data representation at a lower level of aggregation.

Demand for electricity was assumed to grow from 363TWh in 2005 to 432TWh in 2020, with the peak growing from 60.7GW to 72.3GW over

[1] See www.dashoptimization.com/

Table 6.1. *Distribution of demand across dispatch regions*

	Scotland SCO	Upper North UNO	North NOR	Midlands MID	Central CEN	Estuary EST	South West SWE
Demand share	9.8%	5.3%	21.4%	13.3%	40.6%	5.2%	4.4%

the same time horizon. Both annual and peak demand were assumed to grow at the same rate; just under 1.5% per year up to 2010, falling to 1.0% for the following decade. The distribution of demand across the dispatch regions was kept constant, as shown in Table 6.1.

Our raw wind data is based upon observed hourly wind speed measurements taken at 24 different onshore sites around the UK in 1995 (UK Met Office and British Atmospheric Data Centre). It is generally accepted that wind speeds at a single location can be modelled as a Weibull distribution.[2] We attempted to fit a multidimensional Weibull distribution to our sample, but decided to use the actual data instead. Due to computational constraints, we used the wind speed data for a single day as representative for all seven days in a given week for all our weeks in the modelled year.

We used the wind data to model wind power output from a hypothetical array of wind turbines located in each of our seven geographical regions. As the wind speed measurements are for ground level, our data have been corrected according to power transform data for a Nordex N80 wind turbine (Nordex, 2004). To confirm that this sampling was not adding any bias, we used a bootstrapping approach, using wind data from different weekdays, and confirmed that the results were robust to different choices of wind input data (Neuhoff *et al.*, 2005).

Figure 6.2 illustrates the full wind load hours per region in each modelled year. The regions SCO and SWE have the highest wind load hours, yet relatively low demand profiles relative to the CEN, MID and EST regions. In turn, these high-demand regions have relatively poor wind resources. This feature presents challenges regarding the large-scale deployment of wind power in the UK, particularly in relation to transmission constraints and locational decisions.

For existing power stations we used the database developed by ICF International. Nuclear power stations retire as anticipated in the *Seven Year Statement* of NGT (2006). The closure of coal power stations, partially

---

[2] See www.windpower.org/en/tour/wres/weibull.htm

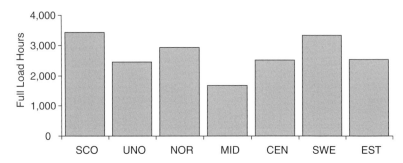

Figure 6.2. Wind power full load hours by region, relative to 8,760 hours per year

induced by the Large Combustion Plant Directive, is calculated in a separate model run and set as an exogenous decision in our calculations.

6.3   Model scenarios

The objective of our modelling was to investigate the impacts of, and challenges posed by, different penetration levels of wind power to 2020 in the GB electricity system. The level of wind power penetration can vary with either changes in fuel prices for conventional plants, CO_2 prices, changes in the capital cost of new wind power, or the application of constraints upon wind power. Table 6.2 shows the main assumptions for investment for new power stations, fuel costs and prices of CO_2 allowances. All figures are quoted in 2005 prices. Our model incorporates, in addition to wind turbines, two options to build conventional power stations. For baseload operation, we allow for the construction of new combined cycle gas turbines (CCGT). For investment in peaking capacity, open cycle gas turbines (OCGT) are modelled, as they offer the lowest capital costs.

With regard to wind turbines, we assume the same investment cost for both on- and off- shore wind turbine costs in all regions. Locations are only differentiated by availability of wind and their transmission links to other regions. Our investment costs are based on those utilised by the MARKAL modelling of DTI in the 2003 *Energy Review*.[3] However, we also allow for other scenarios. The first, labelled '20%' in Table 6.2, represents the cost profile for wind to achieve 20% of demand

---

[3] For fuel costs, current coal and natural gas prices are taken from *DTI Quarterly Energy Prices*, Table 3.2.1. Long-term coal and gas price assumptions are drawn from IEA (2005b). Capital costs decrease for onshore wind turbines and CCGTs are taken from MARKAL assumptions in modelling work for the 2003 DTI *Energy White Paper* (see Marsh *et al.*, 2002).

Table 6.2. *Baseline assumptions: wind costs are varied to reflect subsidies/taxes calibrated for target penetration*

	Investment costs					Fuel costs		EU ETS
	Gas		Wind					
	CCGT	OCGT	MARKAL reference	20%*	40%*	CCGT	Coal	CO$_2$
	(€/kW)					(€/MMBtu)	(€/t)	(€/tCO$_2$)
2005–2009	580	370	800	1,350	750	4.68	51.73	20
2010–2014	550	350	610	1,185	560	4.00	31.61	20
2015–2019	520	330	575	1,150	525	4.14	31.61	20
2020–2024	500	320	540	1,115	490	4.30	31.61	20

* *Note:* Investment cost assumptions in alternative wind penetration scenarios.

by 2020. In this case, costs are higher than the DTI reference case. A second alternative, based on achieving a 40% penetration for wind, assumes that investment costs are lower than the DTI reference case.

The costs of new power plants are assumed to fall, due to learning-by-doing effects. Learning-by-doing effects link the cost reductions to cumulative installed capacity. However, as we assume that the UK constitutes only a small fraction of the global market, we assume exogenous cost reductions at a rate of 2.5% per annum in the period 2005–2010 and 0.5% per annum thereafter.[4] We assume that the lifespan of the wind turbines is 25 years. The levelised cost of capital for all technologies and the modelling discount rate is set at a real discount rate of 11%. We also assume that demand-side response becomes available at €1,000/MWh. This is a simplified representation of the various different types of industrial (and in the future also residential) sector responses that we can envisage. As better data on these options become available, the model can easily be expanded to capture the different options with their specific contributions. For the time being, we do not restrict the maximum amount of demand-side response, as in all cases less than 1% of total demand is provided by demand-side response in any hour at any time.

The European Union Emission Trading Scheme (EU ETS) requires power stations to present CO$_2$ allowances for each tonne of CO$_2$ they are emitting. During the first two phases until 2012, power stations will have or will be allocated most of the allowances for free. However, they have the opportunity to sell these allowances in the secondary market.

[4] Coulomb and Neuhoff (2006).

Table 6.3. *Overview of scenarios*

Scenario	Contribution of wind to annual energy demand in 2020	Capital cost of wind required in 2005 (€/kW)	Details
M1 Base Case	20%	1,375	Wind achieves target of 20% of demand by 2020 using baseline assumptions with build limitations for Wind of 500MW per annum per region (except Scotland)
M2 Cheap Wind	40%	750	As with M1 but for 40% penetration
M3 Cheap Wind: Transmission expansion	40%	750	As with M2 but with 2GW transmission expansion to Scotland
M4 Base Case: No build constraint	20%	1,550	As with M1 but with no build constraint (and higher wind capital cost to fulfil 20% target)
M5 Cheap Wind: No build constraint	40%	1,350	As with M3 but with no build constraints
M6 Tailored build expansion	20%	1,375	As with M1 but with extended annual build constraint (+100MW) in one region in single time period

Hence we include the full (opportunity) costs of CO_2 allowances as variable costs. The price of CO_2 allowances is assumed to be exogenous and set at €20/tCO_2, which can be justified, for example, by the size of the UK power sector being small relative to the ETS scheme.

Table 6.3 summarises the key differences between the six scenarios investigated in this chapter. Only maximum build rates for wind turbines and investment costs for wind turbines vary between scenarios. Investment costs can change for any of the following three reasons:

1. With renewable support schemes, some of the investment costs are covered by the subsidy, reducing the investment costs that have to be covered by revenues from the energy market.
2. Grid connection costs for wind turbines can be higher, as they are potentially located further away from the grid and offer less economies of scale than large new power plants.
3. Uncertainty about the future cost evolution of wind turbines, especially for offshore applications, is high.

To reflect these factors, we increase the investment costs of wind turbines by a constant. We exclude any additional income derived from the Renewables Obligation.

We also impose a regional build constraint on new investment in wind turbines of 0.5GW per year. This is based upon the German experience.[5] We do not impose the build constraint in Scotland, where we consider land to be less scarce. This allows us to explore the impact of transmission constraints to Scotland and the viability of adjusting the transmission capacity (a key challenge in the GB system).

6.4   Model results

In this section we show the model results for the different assumptions and provide some interpretation of the implications.

6.4.1   Scenario M1: Base Case

The results of our Base Case run are shown in Figure 6.3 in terms of capacity additions across the period. This scenario is characterised by new investment in both wind and CCGTs. We do not observe any new investment in OCGTs in our scenarios. The high level of expansion in CCGT capacity is notable in the first 5-year period of our model run. This is driven by the relatively high CO_2 allowance price of €20/tCO_2 and gas prices that are based on long-term predictions of the IEA rather than current market prices, which are much higher. This is a conservative assumption, since higher gas prices would only increase the attractiveness of wind power.

Figure 6.4 illustrates the new investment picture characterised by CCGTs and wind turbines. Underlying this trend is an accompanying decline in coal-powered generation and exogenously set closure of existing coal power stations. We calculated the timing and volume of closures in separate model runs where the different provisions of the Large Combustion Plant Directive regarding SO_2 and NO_x emissions were explicitly modelled. In terms of new build, as we would expect – given the quality of the wind resource, investment is focused in the North, Scotland and the South West of England. The imposed build constraint for wind power of 0.5GW per year is binding in the Northern region in all periods. In addition we see it restricting additional investment in the South West in the 2005–2009 period and in the Central and Estuary regions in 2020–2024.

---

[5] See www.wind-energie.de

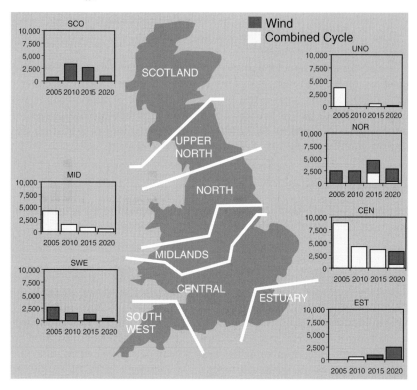

Figure 6.3. Spatial distribution of new wind investment (MW), Base Case (Scenario M1)

6.4.2   Scenario M2: cheap wind

In the second scenario we reduced the investment costs for wind power to achieve a penetration of 40% wind by 2020. We see a similar distribution of new gas-fired capacity early in the period to the Base Case. We also observe stronger wind investment, most notably in Scotland in the first period. Where our imposed build constraint is binding, this has been shown by an asterisk above the bars in Figure 6.5. This shows that the constraint is binding in most regions in most time periods.

Table 6.4 summarises the effect on total system costs. To achieve the higher wind penetration, we reduced the assumed total cost for wind turbines including grid connection from €1,375/kW to €750/kW in 2005. In the system cost comparison we corrected for this and added the subsidy costs (e.g. €625/kW in 2005) to total system cost. In this case a change from 20% to 40% wind power penetration results in discounted

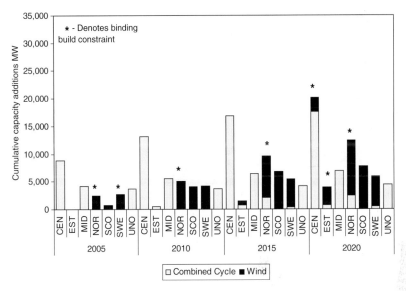

Figure 6.4. Cumulative capacity additions (MW), Base Case (Scenario M1)

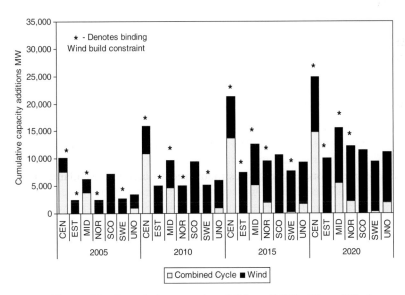

Figure 6.5. Cumulative capacity additions (MW), Cheap Wind (Scenario M2)

Table 6.4. *Increase in total system cost from Scenario M1 to Scenario M2*

Indicative years (in €million/5 years)	2005	2010	2015	2020	Total
Variable costs	−12	−36	−24	−23	
Fixed costs	0	0	0	0	
Fuel cost	−1,243	−1,468	−1,938	−2,321	
Capital repayments for simulated new build (with levelised costs of wind)	2,067	3,201	4,310	4,948	
CO_2 emissions valued at €20/t	−287	−368	−468	−500	**NPV**
Total	524	1,329	1,879	2,104	9,904

system costs rising by €9.9 billion. This represents roughly 7.5% of total discounted system costs and total sales volumes. This result is very much contingent on our assumptions about wind turbine plus grid connection costs. If these costs are lower, then the level of required subsidy and thus the increase in system costs are lower. But also the level of wind power penetration in the case without subsidy is higher.

Policy makers might choose to pursue policies that seem to increase total system costs for several   reasons. For example, because the assumed market price for carbon is below the damage costs or to support learning-by-doing in wind turbine construction to reduce future costs for UK customers and increase the use of renewables to reduce emissions abroad.

6.4.3   *Scenario M3: Cheap Wind with transmission expansion*

In this scenario we expand the commercially available transmission capacity from Scotland via Upper North, North, Midlands to Central by 2GW. We assume that this additional capacity is available from 2005. The simplification is intended to facilitate an intuitive understanding of the effect, rather than to reflect our best guess about the possible or desirable timing. The model simulates a sizeable increase in new investment in wind power in Scotland of 3.6GW in the period 2005–2009 (Figure 6.6).

The expansion in transmission capacity allows additional wind in Scotland to replace conventional gas generation elsewhere in the UK. As a consequence, we see overall emissions fall in response to the transmission upgrade by 230 million tCO_2 or 5% of total cumulative CO_2 emissions.

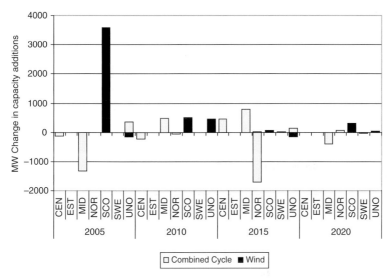

Figure 6.6. Change in investment in Scenario M3 relative to Scenario M2 with 2GW transmission expansion

This illustrates the potential benefit of efficient congestion management. Current GB trading arrangements largely ignore transmission constraints. This limits the connection of new generation in the North of the UK because transmission constraints would be violated if additional stations were to sell output at times when existing stations produce at large volumes. In an economically efficient solution, some conventional power stations reduce output during times of high wind output. Also, if times of high wind output coincide with low demand in the North, then some wind output can be spilled. These two effects together allow for the connection of 3.6GW extra wind generation capacity in Scotland; even so, the transmission capacity to the South increased by only 2GW.

However, in the absence of nodal or zonal pricing it is difficult to allocate transmission capacity in a sufficiently flexible way. As a result, the grid operator has incentives to be unnecessarily restrictive in connecting new generation capacity or requesting transmission upgrades.

Using the model, we are able to calculate the overall impact on total system costs of the transmission expansion. An expansion in the transmission line creates the opportunity for additional building of wind turbines in Scotland to take advantage of the resource potential, yet allows avoidance of additional gas turbine investment and the associated CO_2 allowance and fuel costs. Table 6.5 shows a breakdown of the

Table 6.5. *Additional system costs in Scenario M3 relative to Scenario M2 from increasing transmission capacity*

Indicative years (in €million)	2005	2010	2015	2020	Total
Variable costs	−4	−9	1	−1	
Fixed costs	0	0	0	0	
Fuel cost	−329	−339	−349	−400	
Capital repayments for simulated new build	213	283	258	273	
CO_2 emissions valued at €20/t	−84	−102	−89	−90	**NPV**
Total	−204	−168	−179	−218	−1,691

Table 6.6. *Cost estimates (€) for 2GW Scottish transmission expansion*

	Harmer 2GW (offshore)	Harmer HVDC (offshore)	Neuhoff (onshore)
200 km	€1,170m	€2,500m	
700 km	€2,500m	€3,400m	
Scottish link	<€2,500m	<€3,400m	€220–800m

Sources: Neuhoff (2001) and Harmer (2002)

system costs associated with the transmission capacity. Here we see an annual saving of about €0.2 billion, with an overall NPV of €1.7 billion – these savings do not include the cost of expanded transmission capacity. These are discussed below.

The estimated capital costs of transmission expansion vary between studies. The PB Power study (Harmer, 2002) puts the cost of a 2GW expansion of capacity based on 'point-to-point' transmission for Offshore Wind somewhere between €1,170 million (200 km) and €2,500 million (700 km). For a HVDC 'grid' concept scheme, the cost estimate rises to between €2,500 million and €3,400 million. Neuhoff (2001) surveyed the cost of a new interconnection to be between €190,000/km and €500,000/km with additional converter costs of around €57 million/GW. In the case of a new 2GW onshore transmission line from Scotland to Central England (approx. 600 km) the cost–benefit case for expansion alone may be sufficient justification for such an expansion. However, this analysis did not take into consideration environmental impacts of transmission expansions and the trade-offs between onshore and offshore transmission lines in the planning process.

6.4.4   Scenarios M4 and M5: Base Case and Cheap Wind with no wind build limit

In the previous scenarios we applied a maximum build constraint of 0.5GW per year for all regions except Scotland. In Scenarios M4 and M5 we remove the build constraints to see how investment patterns change. This shows how optimal policy needs to change if it takes public acceptability into consideration.

In order to see the impact of the removal of build constraints, we increased the capital costs for wind by 13% relative to the 20% and by 80% relative to the 40% wind penetration cases, so that we retained the same level of energy delivered from wind power.

Figures 6.7 and 6.8 summarise our results. First, the wind investment is shifted towards the North region, which enjoys one of the best resource potentials in the UK. In the Base Case with no limit, wind investment comes forward only in three regions as opposed to five of the total seven regions under the Base Case.

Second, the wind investment is delayed. In the Base Case with no limit, most wind power is built in the final time period. In the Cheap Wind case with no limit, the 20GW of wind in the first time period (Scenario M2) is shifted to the second period. As a result of the delayed

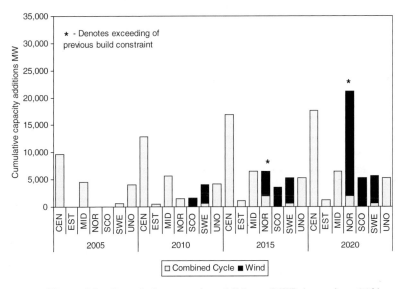

Figure 6.7. Cumulative capacity additions (MW) by region; 20% Wind with no build limit (Scenario M4)

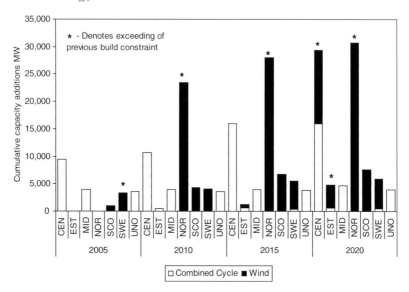

Figure 6.8. Cumulative capacity additions (MW) by region; 40% Wind with no build limit (Scenario M5)

investment in wind, the system faces a 20% increase in fuel costs of €565 million/year and additional CO_2 emissions of 330 million tonnes by the end of 2024.

These model runs illustrate the importance of considering, first, the maximum build rates, which are dictated by public acceptability and, second, the implied maximum penetration rates, which are dictated by resource availability. If these constraints are taken into consideration in the modelling, and therefore also in the policy design, then investment in wind power is spread more widely and deployment is started earlier in order to achieve the desired penetration.

Tables 6.7 and 6.8 illustrate the system cost effects for Scenarios M4 and M5, relative to their comparators; Scenarios M1 and M2 respectively. As shown in Table 6.7, the overall saving from having no regional build limitations has a net present value of almost €1 billion in 2005 of our model. This cost saving results largely from the decision to delay wind investment (Scenario M4), where no regional build limitation and no knowledge of future limits exist. The 20% wind target is achieved with significant amounts of wind being built in the final period, thus the deferred cost savings are notable (compared with the limited build case of Scenario M1). This picture is repeated to a greater extent in Table 6.8, where cost savings here (Scenario M5) are made up

Table 6.7. *System costs for Scenario M4 compared with Scenario M1: cost saving from relaxed planning constraint and 20% wind*

€million	2005–2009	2010–2014	2015–2019	2020–2024	Total
Variable costs	1	6	6	−7	
Fixed costs	0	0	0	0	
Fuel cost	565	670	651	−80	
Capital repayments for simulated new build	−734	−1,023	−991	−103	
CO_2 emissions valued at €20/t	141	181	170	−18	**NPV**
Total	−28	−166	−164	−208	−933

Table 6.8. *System costs for Scenario M5 compared with Scenario M2: cost saving from relaxed planning constraint and 40% wind*

€million	2005–2009	2010–2014	2015–2019	2020–2024	Total
Variable costs	17	15	19	19	
Fixed costs	0	0	0	0	
Fuel cost	1,350	9	303	−410	
Capital repayments for simulated new build	−1,068	−686	−1,135	−921	
CO_2 emissions valued at €20/t	323	−11	80	−99	**NPV**
Total	622	−674	−734	−1,411	−1,358

largely in deferred capital payments for the additional wind investment outlay in the limited build Scenario (M2).

6.4.5 Scenario M6: Tailored build expansion

An additional scenario was used to assess the marginal costs imposed on the system by maximum build constraints. These allow us to understand how much effort one might like to devote to increasing public acceptability in order to relax such a constraint. We therefore increased the maximum build constraint for an individual region and modelling period from 500MW per year to 600MW per year to see how this changes the discounted total system costs of supplying the electricity demand of UK customers. Figure 6.9 illustrates the change in investment pattern relative to the Base Case that results if the build constraint in the North is relaxed from 500MW to 600MW per year

Table 6.9. *System costs savings from increasing the build constraint by 100MW*

Impact of 100MW relaxed build constraint	Cost saving €million, 2005	Cost saving €million, start year
NOR 2010–2014	7.5 (2005)	12.7 (2010)
SWE 2010–2014	0	0
NOR 2015–2019	4.5 (2005)	12.9 (2015)
SWE 2015–2019	0	0

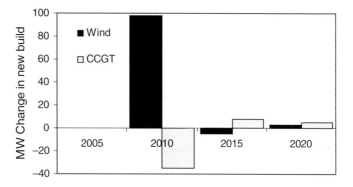

Figure 6.9. Capacity changes in North: Build expansion (Scenario M6) relative to the Base Case (Scenario M1)

for the period 2010–2014. This results in a shift of investment from gas-fired generation to wind.

Table 6.9 gives the reduction in the system costs if the maximum build constraint is relaxed in the North (NOR). A similar exercise was carried out for the South West (SWE) and the results are shown alongside. As the constraint is not binding in SWE, the relaxation does not have any impact. In contrast, the opportunity to build an additional 100MW of wind in the North during the period 2010–2019 creates system savings of about €250,000 per 2.5MW turbine. This would be about 10% of construction and grid connection costs of such a turbine.

6.4.6   Comparison of scenarios

In Table 6.10, we compare some of the scenarios. The additional costs in moving from a 20% to a 40% wind penetration scenario are €9.9 billion

discounted to 2005. If we divide this amount by the CO_2 savings calculated till 2025 then this extra cost amounts to €11/tCO_2 above
the €20/tCO_2 already internalised in the model. If 2GW of additional
interconnector capacity from Scotland to the South were available (for
free), then these costs would fall to €7–8/tCO_2.

This figure results if we assume that the net present cost of connecting
and operating wind power at the system is €1,350/kW while, for
example, the Markal model assumes the cost of building wind power is
€800/kW. Our model suggests that if the cost were €750/kW, then it
would be cost-optimal to operate the system with 40% energy delivered
from wind in 2020.

Table 6.10 also illustrates some implications from our modelling
approach. We keep the target wind generation by 2020 fixed across different scenarios by adjusting the investment costs for wind power.
Removing build constraints on the wind construction thus allows for a
later build of wind power, which increases emissions in the period to
2020. Under circumstances where CO_2 costs were higher by €12/tCO_2 in
the 20% scenario or by €4/tCO_2 in the 40% scenario, the building delay
would not be economic. While we argue above that it is unlikely that we
can remove all building constraints from the process of planning permission, grid connection and site availability, and thus need to accelerate
early build to achieve significant target levels, this analysis also shows that
earlier construction does not entail excessive costs. Note that all figures
are calculated relative to the high net present value costs of wind turbines
of €1,350/kW and fall in the scenarios with lower assumptions.

6.5   System costs

The previously described model runs could not capture all the dynamic
constraints of the power sector and the regional detail within the
transmission zones. We now refer to other studies that looked at the
corresponding costs. To allow for a comparison of capital and operational costs, we calculate the net present value of all costs involved,
again using our standard discount factor of 11% and time horizon of
25 years (note that this implies that an annual cost of €1 over 25 years
has a NPV of €9.35).

Table 6.11 gives the summary of the different cost components that
are not endogenously modelled. Estimates of investment costs can differ
significantly. While published list prices for turbines are available for
some countries, prices are typically negotiated bilaterally. Furthermore,
reported project and construction costs vary across countries, indicating
that similar differences might apply within countries.

Table 6.10. *Scenario comparison results*

Amount of Wind	Scenario	Models compared	NPV benefit to society at 20 Euro/tCO$_2$ (million 2005 €)	Cumulative change in CO$_2$ emissions by 2025 (Mt)	Change in CO$_2$ emissions in 2025 (Mt/year)	Corresponds to CO$_2$ price increase (€/t)
20%	Saving from lifting build constraint	M4/M1	900	75.5	−0.5	12
20%	Marginal saving from increasing build limit by 100MW	M6/M1	4.5 to 7.5	−2.8	−0.1	−2 to −3
40%	Extra costs of 40% wind over 20%	M2/M1	−9,900	−922.6	−25.8	11
40%	Saving from increasing Scottish interconnector capacity by 2GW*	M3/M2	1,200 to 1,500	−227	−4.4	−5 to −7
	Relative to 20% scenario*	M3/M1	−8700 to −8400	1149.6	−30.2	7 to 8
40%	Saving from lifting building constraint	M5/M2	1,400	329.9	−1.4	4

* *Note*: Excludes cost of interconnector.

Table 6.11. *Costs of wind that were not calculated endogenously*

Euro/KW	Markal	IEA (2005)	Strbac	UKERC	Mues 24h	Mues 4h
Investment cost (2005)	800	1000				
Response			48			
Synch reserve			51		47	24
Standing reserve			16	129		
start up			20		33	10
Distribution			28			

Source: Marsh *et al.* (2002), Strbac (2002), IEA (2005a), Müsgens and Neuhoff (2005), Gross *et al.* (2006)

Studies of system costs of integrating intermittent wind power into the system have recently been comprehensively reviewed by the UK Energy Research Centre (Gross *et al.* 2006). The additional costs of dealing with the more volatile and less deterministic pattern of wind were estimated to be in the order of £3/MWh of wind integrated in the UK system, which translates to €129/kW of wind installed, and are in line with studies for other countries. Strbac (2002) provides more detail, splitting up the costs into additional cost components for the provision of different system services. Although we present the figures averaged over four scenarios with 20% and 30% wind penetration, they all resulted in rather similar per kW costs. The aggregate figure is comfortably close to the best guess of UKERC (Gross *et al.*, 2006). Müsgens and Neuhoff (2005) modelled the costs that wind power adds to the German system. In the current market design, where the plant dispatch pattern is effectively fixed one day in advance, the costs of wind power are significantly higher than they would be if a more flexible operation of the system allowed for the use of forecasts updated 4 hours before actual dispatch.

The costs incurred for the expansion of the distribution network relate both to the direct grid connection and possible reinforcement of the regional distribution and transmission network. While most projects assessed by the IEA did include grid connection costs, they were not covered in the Markal model. Strbac calculated an average of €28/kW additional distribution costs. This might be on the low side, as local expansion of the transmission network might also be required, and in our model we only assessed inter-regional transmission capacity expansion.

6.6   Conclusions

The decarbonisation of the UK electricity system is likely to involve large shares of renewable electricity generation. We have developed a modelling approach that can capture the regional variation of wind output in the presence of transmission constraints and integrate this into an investment planning model. With surprisingly unchallenging cost assumptions, the system is able to deliver 20% or 40% of energy from wind output by 2020. We did not, however, model the regulatory, technology and price risk that investors perceive and that might increase the trigger prices for investments. Also, on-shore planning constraints might result in a shift towards use of off-shore wind, tidal and wave energy resources if the 40% target is to be achieved.

The approach did not explicitly represent technical constraints that affect operation, such as maximum ramp rates and minimum run constraints. Still, we referred to results from other models that are focused on the operation to represent related additional costs. We also ignored technical constraints, such as fault ride through capabilities or minimum system inertia. Nevertheless, we hope that the quantitative framework that this modelling approach provides can support electrical engineers in their further analysis of these constraints and in finding solutions to address them. So far we have not been able to estimate the costs and benefits that are related to, for example, improved power electronics.

Among the key constraints for the evolution of a system with large shares of renewables are planning constraints limiting the maximum build rates in UK regions; and also transmission between these regions. We used a rough number of maximum build rates, to illustrate the value that can be provided to the system if such constraints can be relaxed, and where this relaxation is most valuable.

While this work focused on the integration of intermittent generation using onshore wind patterns, future studies will be required in order to understand the diversification benefit that offshore wind farms can offer or that can be provided by other intermittent renewable energy sources such as marine power and photovoltaic resources.

References

Baleriaux, H., E. Jamoulle and F. Linard de Guertechin (1967). Simulation de l'exploitation d'un parc de machines thermiques de production d'electricite couple a des stations de Pompage. *Revue E edn SRBE*, **5**, 225–245.

Bessiere, F. (1970). The Investment 85 model of Electricite de France. *Management Science*, **17**(4), B192–B211.

Bloom, J.A. (1983). Solving an electricity generation expansion planning problem by Generalized Benders' decomposition. *Operations Research*, **31**(1), 84–100.

Butler, L. and K. Neuhoff (2005). *Comparison of Feed in Tariff, Quota and Auction Mechanisms to Support Wind Power Development.* Cambridge Working Papers in Economics CWPE 0503 / Electricity Policy Research Group Working Paper EP70. Faculty of Economics, University of Cambridge.

Coulomb, L. and K. Neuhoff (2006). *Learning Curves and Changing Product Attributes: the Case of Wind Turbines,* Cambridge Working Papers in Economics CWPE 0618 / Electricity Policy Research Group Working Paper EPRG 06/01 Faculty of Economics, University of Cambridge.

DeCarolis, J.F. and D.W. Keith (2006). The economics of large-scale wind power in a carbon constrained world. *Energy Policy,* **34**, 395–410.

Devine-Wright, P. (2005). Beyond NIMBYism: towards an integrated framework for understanding public perceptions of wind energy. *Wind Energy,* **8**(2), 125–139.

Gross, R., P. Heptonstall, D. Anderson, T. Green, M. Leach and J. Skea (2006). *The Costs and Impacts of Intermittency.* London: UKERC.

Grubb, M., L. Butler and P. Twomey (2006). Diversity and security in UK electricity generation: the influence of low-carbon objectives. *Energy Policy,* **34**(18), 4050–4062.

Harmer, K. (2002). *Concept Study: Western Offshore Transmission Grid.* PB Power. ETSU. February 2002.

IEA (2005a). *Projected Costs of Generating Electricity: 2005 Update.* IEA.

(2005b). *World Energy Outlook 2005: Middle East and North Africa Insights.* World Energy Outlook. Paris: IEA.

L.E.K. Consulting (2006). *Policy Framework for Renewables.* London: Carbon Trust.

Marsh, G., P. Taylor, H. Haydock, D. Anderson and M. Leach (2002). *Options for a Low Carbon Future.* London: AEA Technology/Imperial College Centre for Energy Policy and Technology.

Müsgens, F. and K. Neuhoff (2005). *Modelling Dynamic Constraints in Electricity Markets and the Costs of Uncertain Wind Output.* Cambridge Working Papers in Economics CWPE 06010 / Electricity Policy Research Group Working Paper EPRG 05/14, Faculty of Economics, University of Cambridge.

Neuhoff, K. (2001). Economic considerations for international electricity interconnection in northeast Asia. *Workshop on Power Grid Interconnection in Northeast Asia.* Beijing, China.

Neuhoff, K., J. Cust, L. Butler, K. Keats, H. Hoexter, A. Kreckzo, G. Sinden and A. Ehrenmann (2006). *Space and Time: Wind in an Investment Planning Model.* Cambridge Working Papers in Economics CWPE 0620 / Electricity Policy Research Group Working Paper EPRG 06/03, Faculty of Economics, University of Cambridge.

NGC (2006). *GB Seven Year Statement.* Available from: www.nationalgrid.com/uk/sys%5F06/

Nordex (2004). *Nordex Data in Wind Power and the UK Wind Resource.* Available from: www.eci.ox.ac.uk/publications/downloads/sinden05-dtiwindreport.pdf

Strbac, G. (2002). *Quantifying The System Costs of Additional Renewables in 2020.* DTI Report, Ilex Energy Consulting, Manchester.

Part II

Incentives and the Demand Side:
Demand-Side Management and System
Requirements

7 Electricity network investment and regulation for a low-carbon future

Michael G. Pollitt and Janusz Bialek

7.1 Introduction to the regulation of electricity networks in the UK

Around 30% of the current price of electricity relates to electricity distribution and transmission charges. In England and Wales, electricity transmission revenue in 2005/2006 totalled £1.2 billion (Ofgem, 2006a), while distribution revenue was around £3.1 billion (Ofgem, 2004a, p. 6). These charges are regulated by the electricity regulator Ofgem. In Northern Ireland, electricity transmission and distribution charges totalled around £0.2 billion in 2005/2006 (Viridian, 2006) and are regulated by the Northern Ireland Authority for Utility Regulation (NIAUR, formerly NIAER). There are 15 regulated distribution companies in the UK (though rather fewer independent owners) and three regulated transmission businesses in Great Britain (in Northern Ireland transmission and distribution are not separated out for regulation).

The introduction of large amounts of renewables (both large- and small-scale) and gas-fired microgeneration into the electricity system necessitates large amounts of new investment in these networks. Elders *et al.* (2006) identified the following technologies as being potentially important in future transmission and distribution networks: new power electronics, flexible AC transmission systems (FACTS), storage facilities (such as compressed air energy storage – CAES – and flywheel) and superconducting lines. There may be expenditure on DC transmission cables, which might be in the form of north–south undersea cables. Future networks will require more active management, as the intermittency of renewable energy requires increased network management to mitigate some of the effects (see DTI, 2006, pp. 210–211). The uncertainty of the timing, volume and location of new renewables also makes planning of network development more difficult than in the past and has implications for regulation.

Apart from the need for network investment due to the uptake of renewables, new investment is needed due to the ageing of the existing

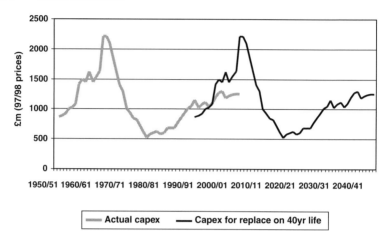

Figure 7.1. UK distribution gross capital expenditure
Source: Scottish Power

network. The current transmission and distribution network was con-structed mainly in the 1960s and 1970s and many assets are near the end of their design life (usually about 40 years) – see Figure 7.1. The advent of more sophisticated asset management, condition monitoring and life extension techniques means that the asset replacement can be delayed (i.e. the investment does not need to follow the lighter line in Figure 7.1), and the investment peak of the 1960s is unlikely to be repeated. In that context it is important that the asset replacement is not like-for-like but that the new assets enhance network security and maximise the uptake of renewables.

In the following sections we discuss the present system of economic regulation of networks in the UK and how this may need to adapt in order to facilitate significant volumes of renewable energy sources up to 2020 and beyond.

7.2   Transmission and distribution price control reviews

Currently, transmission and distribution charges are reviewed every 5 years. The last review of distribution charges in Great Britain was in 2004 for the period April 2005 to March 2010. At the end of 2006, the review of transmission charges in Great Britain was completed for the period April 2007 to March 2012. In Northern Ireland, transmission and distribution services are combined in one company. A review for the period April 2007 to March 2012 was completed in September 2006. These reviews determine the level of transmission and distribution charges. We briefly characterise the nature of these reviews.

Network price reviews follow a similar format (see Pollitt, 2005). Companies submit detailed business plans for the next 5 years, including projections of operating and capital expenditures. Capital expenditure plans detail load- and non-load-related investments and make specific reference to proposed major projects. Ofgem/NIAUR review these plans and make initial proposals for price revisions according to the RPI-X formula proposed by Littlechild in 1983 and in use in telecoms, gas, airports and water, as well as in electricity. The regulatory review includes efficiency studies of operating costs. These are of two types: 'bottom-up' – consultant estimates of cost categories; and 'top-down' – using efficiency methodologies such as corrected ordinary least squares. Capital expenditure plans are assessed using engineering consultancy audits of capital expenditure plans. Companies can then respond to the proposals which are then revised (once or twice) until a final proposals document is published. This final proposals document can be appealed against by one or more of the companies that it covers (the complaints go to the Competition Commission). The process of a price review takes around 18 months and is completed 4–5 months before the new prices are due to take effect.

The regulators are in a position where they decide what level of capital and operating expenditure is reasonable and also what the allowed rate of return should be on regulated assets. In distribution these three elements represent around one-third each of the total regulated revenue. Table 7.1 gives the revenue detail for one of the distribution companies (United Utilities) in the recent distribution price control review. The company receives discounted revenue (line 26) equal to the discounted value of its allowed costs (line 19) which include the 5-year movement in its discounted regulatory asset value (line 6). The discount rate is the weighted average cost of capital allowed by the regulator, and the discounting ensures that the company earns this return. Table 7.2 gives the revenue detail for National Grid Electricity Transmission (the largest transmission company in the UK) from the final proposals from the latest transmission price control review. The company receives discounted revenue (line 19) equal to the discounted value of its allowed costs (line 14). This discounted cost includes the 5-year movement in its net present value of regulated assets (line 6), and hence compensates the company for changes in its regulatory asset base.

Table 7.1. *Regulated revenue for a typical electricity distribution utility*

Price control calculations for United Utilities 2002/2003 prices

	2004/05 £m	2005/06 £m	2006/07 £m	2007/08 £m	2008/09 £m	2009/10 £m
RAV						
1 Opening asset value		920	964.3	1,002.50	1,034.70	1,060.80
2 Total capex		112.7	112.3	111.8	111.4	110.9
3 Depreciation		−68.5	−74.1	−79.7	85.3	−90.9
4 Closing asset value		964.3	1002.5	1034.7	1060.8	1080.9
5 Present value of opening /closing		920				825.2
6 Year movement in closing RAV						94.8
ALLOWED ITEMS						
7 Operating costs (excluding pensions)		67	64.7	63.1	61.7	60.2
8 Capital expenditure (excluding pensions)		103.5	103.1	102.6	102.2	101.7
9 Pensions allowance		16	16	16	16	16
10 Tax allowance		19.4	22	23.1	24.5	24.5
11 Capex incentive scheme		1.8	1	−0.6	−1.1	−0.5
12 Sliding scale additional income		1.6	1.7	1.8	1.8	1.9
13 Opex incentive /other adjustments		1.4	1.4	1.4		
14 Quality reward						
15 DP CR3 costs		1.5				
16 Total allowed items		212.3	209.3	207.5	205.1	203.8
17 Present value of allowed items		206.6	193.6	181.3	169.8	159.9
18 5-year movement in closing RAV						94.8

19 TOTAL PRESENT VALUE OVER 5 YEARS

REVENUE

20	Revenue index		1	1.011	1.013	1.022	1.024	
21	Discounted revenue index		0.973	0.932	0.885	0.846	0.803	
22	Price control revenue	205.2	220.9	223.2	223.7	225.8	226.1	
23	Excluded services revenue		5.8	5.8	5.8	5.8	5.8	
24	Total revenue		226.7	229	229.5	231.6	231.9	
25	Present value of total revenue		220.6	211.2	200.6	191.7	181.9	
26	TOTAL PRESENT VALUE OVER 5 YEARS							1006.1
27	PO based on the above Revenue (line 22)		7.6%					
28	PO for Innovation Funding Incentive (IFI)		0.4%					
29								
30	Total PO for comparison purposes		8.0					
31	X		0.0%					

Analysis of PC(%):

32	Include EHV	1.5%
33	Exclude metering	−1.3%
34	Change in Opex	−7.0%
35	Depreciation	7.8%
36	Return	2.7%
37	Rates	1.0%
38	Tax	5.0%
39	Other	−1.6%
40	Total	8.0%

Source: Ofgem (2004a, p. 127)

Table 7.2. *Regulated revenue for National Grid electricity*
(All prices are £m in 2004/2005 terms)

Licence = NGET TO		2006/07 £m	2007/08 £m	2008/09 £m	2009/10 £m	2010/11 £m	2011/12 £m
	Regulatory Asset Value (RAV)						
1	Opening asset value		5,415.6	5,634.2	5,761.3	5,931.6	6,187.4
2	Total capital expenditure		601.3	524.9	581.1	655.6	677.9
3	Depreciation		−382.7	−397.8	−410.9	−399.8	−416.1
4	Closing asset value		5,634.2	5,761.3	5,931.6	6,187.4	6,449.2
5	Present value of opening/closing RAV		5,415.6				5,041.1
6	5-year movements in PV of RAV						374.5
	Allowed items						
7	Operating costs (excluding pensions)		266.0	259.7	254.3	254.0	254.9
8	Capital expenditure		601.3	524.9	581.1	655.6	677.9
9	Pensions allowance		38.5	37.8	37.4	37.3	36.9
10	Tax allowance		101.1	105.6	110.4	110.2	108.1
11	Total of allowed items		1,006.9	928.1	983.2	1,057.1	1,077.7
12	Present value of allowed items		982.4	861.9	869.3	889.7	863.4
13	5-year movement in PV of RAV						374.5
14	Total present value over 5 years						4,841.3
	Revenue						
15	Revenue index		1.000	1.020	1.040	1.061	1.082
16	Discounted revenue index		0.976	0.947	0.920	0.893	0.867
17	Base price control revenue	924.9	985.5	1,005.2	1,025.3	1,045.8	1,066.7
18	Excluded service revenue	58.2	58.4	64.3	71.9	75.8	76.1
19	Total TO revenues	983.1	1,043.9	1,069.5	1,097.2	1,121.6	1,142.8
20	Present value of total revenue		1,018.5	993.3	970.0	943.9	915.6
21	Total present value over 5 years						4,841.3
22	IFI revenue forecast		3.9	4.0	4.1	4.2	4.3
23	Price control extension reconciliation		0.7	0.0	0.0	0.0	0.0
24	Total price control revenue		1,048.5	1,073.5	1,101.3	1,125.8	1,147.1

Source: Ofgem (2006a, p. 92)

Higher volumes of renewables embedded within distribution networks (load-related microgeneration and smaller-scale projects) and directly connected to transmission networks are already impacting on economic regulation of networks. The distribution price control identified a total capital expenditure requirement from 2005 to 2010 of £5.7 billion (an increase of 48% over the previous review period). This was during a period when the total renewables share on the system was only expected to grow by around 5% of total electrical energy. The growth of capital expenditure in electricity transmission is expected to be more substantial, growing by 125% over the previous price control period to £3.8 billion over 2007–2012 (Ofgem, 2006a, p. 9). The review also allows for adjustment mechanisms, which allow for more (or less) capital investment if connected generation capacity should be greater or less than the base line forecast (Ofgem, 2006a, b). In addition to this investment, an interim review had already allocated an additional £500 million of investment specifically to allow for extra renewable generation on the system (Ofgem, 2004c). These are significant sums of money and include only the beginnings of increased network investments to support large percentages of renewables on the system. Future reviews, as our opening discussion makes clear, seem destined to involve much bigger increases on the 2005 figures. Clearly, incentivising least-cost network support for renewables is a major issue, as is coping with the uncertainty in the development of network requirements in the face of different electricity futures (see Elders et al., 2006; Elders et al., Chapter 14, this volume).

Minimising the cost of network expansion and upgrade is a major issue for the regulators. The distribution price control review introduced a sliding-scale system for capital investment incentives. The incentives are outlined in Table 7.3. PB Power were the engineering consultants who reviewed the companies' capital expenditure plans. The higher the ratio of company base expenditure selected to PB Power's assessment, the weaker the incentive if the company actually delivered its investment below budget. Thus a company that selected as its base allowed revenue the lowest ratio of its cost to PB Power's estimate could keep 40% of any underspend, while the company that selected the highest ratio could only keep 20% of any underspend. Thus a company that estimated that it needed to spend £140 million, when PB Power estimated that only £100 million was required, would have a base target of £115 million. If it actually achieved £100 million, it would receive £100 million plus an incentive payment of £0.6 million. By contrast, a company that said it needed £100 million against PB Power's £100 million, and then actually achieved £100 million, would receive £100 million plus an incentive

Table 7.3. *Distribution price control capital expenditure incentive scheme*

DNO:PB Power Ratio	100	105	110	115	120	125	130	135	140
Efficiency Incentive	40%	38%	35%	33%	30%	28%	25%	23%	20%
Additional income	2.5	2.1	1.6	1.1	0.6	-0.1	-0.8	-1.6	-2.4
as pre-tax rate of return	0.200%	0.168%	0.130%	0.090%	0.046%	-0.004%	-0.062%	-0.124%	-0.192%
Rewards and penalties									
Allowed expenditure	105	106.25	107.5	108.75	110	111.25	112.5	113.75	115
Actual expenditure									
70	16.5	15.7	14.8	13.7	12.6	11.3	9.9	8.3	6.6
80	12.5	11.9	11.3	10.5	9.6	8.5	7.4	6.0	4.6
90	8.5	8.2	7.8	7.2	6.6	5.8	4.9	3.8	2.6
100	4.5	4.4	4.3	4.0	3.6	3.0	2.4	1.5	0.6
105	2.5	2.6	2.5	2.3	2.1	1.7	1.1	0.4	-0.4
110	0.5	0.7	0.8	0.7	0.6	0.3	-0.1	-0.7	-1.4
115	-1.5	-1.2	-1.0	-0.9	-0.9	-1.1	-1.4	-1.8	-2.4
120	-3.5	-3.1	-2.7	-2.5	-2.4	-2.5	-2.6	-3.0	-3.4
125	-5.5	-4.9	-4.5	-4.2	-3.9	-3.8	-3.9	-4.1	-4.4
130	-7.5	-6.8	-6.2	-5.8	-5.4	-5.2	-5.1	-5.2	-5.4
135	-9.5	-8.7	-8.0	-7.4	-6.9	-6.6	-6.4	-6.3	-6.4
140	-11.5	-10.6	-9.7	-9.0	-8.4	-8.0	-7.6	-7.5	-7.4

Source: Ofgem (2004a, p. 87)

payment of £4.5 million. This is a menu of contracts approach[1] to regulation which encourages companies to more correctly reveal the true estimated cost of capital investments. The transmission price control review has just implemented a similar scheme for its 2007–2012 control period (Ofgem, 2006a, pp. 96–106).

7.3   The regulation of congestion, losses, quality of supply, visual amenity and noise

Other aspects of economic regulation are also important as discussed below.

Transmission costs have two components: fixed and variable. The fixed component relates to the cost of the existing capacity of the grid. As most of the cost of the grid relates to sunk investments, the charges for access to it are also fixed and usually they are per capacity (i.e. per kW). In the UK, they are termed Transmission (or Distribution) Network Use of System charges. If a new generator wants to connect, then it has to pay additionally a one-off connection charge which covers the cost of the equipment used to connect the generator to the grid.

Actual transmission and distribution charges vary somewhat by location, load and type. They are paid by generators and suppliers. For suppliers, they are usually based on the MW load of the user during the system peak demand (so called triad charges), For generators, they are based on the declared net capacity of a plant. Distribution Network Use of System (DNUoS) charges vary by company area, while there are up to 21 transmission charging zones (different for demand and generation) in Great Britain. The Transmission Network Use of System (TNUoS) charges are levied per kW of capacity according to the imposed value to the system of generation/demand in those areas. Figure 7.2 shows the generation zones and charges in 2005/2006. These charges reflect the marginal increase in network flows caused by an increase in generation/demand at a particular node by 1MW. They are expressed in MW*km, i.e. they reflect the increase in a flow on a line multiplied by the length of the line. The marginal MW*km increases are multiplied by a notional cost of a particular line (the so-called expansion constant, which is different for different types of lines and rated voltages) and summed over all the lines. Due to the predominant north–south flows in the UK, generation in the South East receives a rebate, as it causes counterflows, i.e. the calculated marginal flows tend to be against the actual network flows. For example, a typical 1GW plant located in zone 21 (Peninsula) would receive a rebate

---

[1] See Baron (1989).

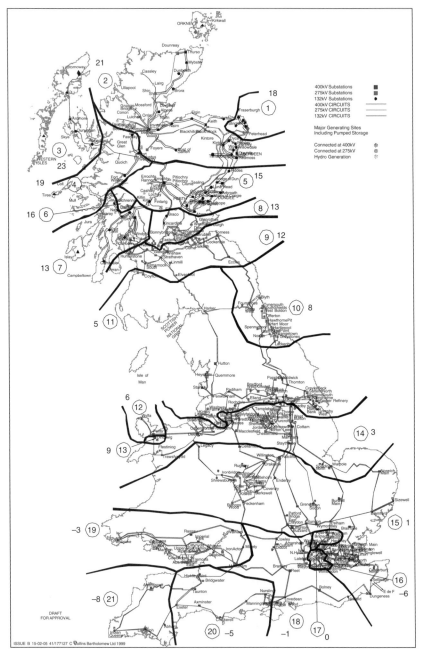

Figure 7.2. Transmission Network Use of System (TNUoS) zones and charges in GB in 2005/2006

Note: Zone numbers are circled, TNUoS charges in £/kW are the non-circled numbers. *Source:* National Grid (2005); map reproduced with the permission of Collins Bartholomew Ltd.

of £8 million a year. On the other hand, generation in the North and Scotland pays extra (see National Grid, 2006, p. 4), as the calculated marginal flows reinforce the actual network flows. Thus a similar 1GW power plant located in zone 2 (North Scotland) would have to pay £21 million a year. The supplier charges are designed such that there are no negative charges for suppliers (demand), as that would create perverse incentives to increase demand during system peak (triad charges).

It is recognised that high TNUoS charges could have a detrimental effect on renewable development in the North of Scotland, where considerable renewable resources (wind and marine) are located (see Chapter 3 by Jamasb *et al.* and Chapter 6 by Neuhoff *et al.*). Consequently, the Secretary of State can apply a dispensation in TNUoS charges in areas of high renewable energy potential up to 2024. Such a dispensation is undesirable in that it may encourage the location of generation in Scotland, which imposes inefficiently high costs on the system as a whole. However, the subsequent analysis performed for the Department of Trade and Industry (Bialek *et al.*, 2006) showed that introduction of a dispensation would not have a significant effect on reaching the Government's 2010 target. The main reason for this is that any shortfall in meeting the target would be mitigated by an increase in Renewable Obligation Certificate (ROC) price. Moreover, the North of Scotland enjoys a competitive advantage (even after inclusion of comparatively high TNUoS charges) over any other renewable technology with a significant remaining resource. At the time of writing (2007) no dispensation from high TNUoS charges has been applied.

Distribution charging follows a different pattern. Until recently, a renewable generator wishing to connect had to pay the 'deep connection' charge, i.e. the full cost of the necessary distribution network reinforcement. From 1 April 2005, a new electricity distribution charging framework came into force in the UK featuring a common connection charging boundary for demand and generation, the replacement of deep connection charging with a 'shallowish' charge, and the introduction of Generator Distribution Use of System (GDUoS) tariffs to supplement the costs that are not able to be recovered due to removal of the deep connection charge. The second party connecting to the distribution network within the first 5 years has to pay a proportion of the reinforcement cost. Ofgem has been working on the further development of GDUoS charges.[2] The objectives are cost-reflectivity, facilitation of

[2] See www.ofgem.gov.uk/Networks/ElecDist/Policy/DistChrgs/Documents1/11738-Ofgem %20GDUoS%20presentation.pdf

competition, predictability, simplicity and transparency. There are obvious tensions between some of these principles.

The variable transmission costs are the cost of transmission losses and congestion costs. Congestion costs are incurred when there is not enough transmission capacity in the system. In the UK, congestion usually occurs on the interconnector between Scotland and England. If that happens, the system operator (the National Grid) has to constrain-off a cheaper generation in Scotland and to constrain-on a more expensive generation in England. Congestion costs are currently (2007) recovered uniformly, i.e. non-locationally, from all the generators through Balancing Services Use of System (BSUoS) charges. BSUoS are uniform, i.e. everyone pays the same per MWh. TNUoS charges are not directly related to congestion although, as expected, there is correlation between the two due to the north–south pattern of flows. The reason for uniform, rather than more complicated locational charging for congestion (such as the nodal pricing practised in the PJM market in the USA) is that congestion costs are currently relatively small and would not warrant an expensive to set up and run pricing mechanism.

Power losses are proportional to approximately the square of a power flow in a line. Distribution losses consume about 5% of energy produced, while transmission losses consume about 2% (Ofgem website).[3] There are additional incentive schemes to reduce distribution network electrical losses through price review controls. In 2007 transmission losses are still paid for uniformly by all the users (generators and suppliers) despite numerous attempts to introduce locational charging for losses. Depending on the marginal generation connected to the system, reducing these losses could reduce emissions more or less proportionately to the energy saved. Analysis of a recent proposal for locational (zonal) charging for losses has shown that the energy loss savings from the scheme would be small, in the range of a few per cent of the losses incurred, while monetary transfers between generators and suppliers would be more than an order of magnitude higher (see Bialek *et al.*, 2004). If marginal charging for transmission losses was introduced, generators in the north and suppliers in the south would pay more, while generators in the south and suppliers in the north would pay less for transmission losses. Some generators in the south would even receive a rebate. Thus the overall pattern of charges would be to some extent similar to TNUoS charges.

[3] See www.ofgem.gov.uk/Networks/ElecDist/Documents1/Electricity%20Distribution% 20Units%20and%20Loss%20Percentages%20Summary.pdf and www.ofgem.gov.uk/ Licensing/ElecCodes/BSCode/Ias/Documents1/17073-3207.pdf

There are also incentives to improve network reliability in transmission and to reduce customer interruptions and minutes lost in distribution. In distribution, companies can typically be exposed to revenue adjustments of ±2% of review for over/underperformance against targets on reliability and quality of supply (see Giannakis *et al.*, 2005). There are also visual amenity and noise impacts of transformer substations and of overhead wires (see Ofgem, 2006a).

Ofgem has recently experimented with 'willingness to pay' surveys to establish whether companies should be allowed to recover more revenue in order to reduce the local environmental impact of electricity assets. More renewables create local amenity impacts within the distribution network or create the need for greater transmission capacity requirements to support long-distance power flows (particularly from Scotland to the South East). Household electricity meters currently form part of the regulatory asset base of distribution companies (though this has ended for new meters as of April 2007) and hence decisions about smart metering still need to be taken by Ofgem/NIAUR. Bilton *et al.* discuss this in Chapter 8.

7.4   Improvements to the current system of economic regulation

A key challenge for network regulation is that incentivising efficient investment in situations of uncertainty about the nature of demand growth is not very well understood. Network charges have fallen substantially in real terms since privatisation (by around 50% in distribution and 30% in transmission per unit of electricity). This has been the result of the strong incentive properties of the RPI-X system of regulation combined with pressure to reduce costs and prices via significantly positive values of X. However, network charges are now beginning to be driven by investment requirements. Over the period 2005–2010, continuing operating efficiency improvements did not fully cancel out the requirement for higher investment in electricity distribution, while the transmission review for 2007–2012 also involves significant price rises due to the substantial rise in capital investment. This has already led to calls for the system of regulation to be reviewed and reformed (see Pollitt, 2005). As the rest of this book suggests, there are ways that we can incentivise efficient investment in low-carbon generation which provide incentives for this to be added at least cost. However, network investment in the UK is still largely driven by a central planning type of system.

The requirement for large and increasing amounts of regulated investment in networks driven by uncertain renewables requires regulators to consider carefully the design of economic regulation and whether the current system is fit for purpose.

We suggest five areas which Ofgem needs to consider in future.

1. The current approach to RPI-X regulation needs to be updated.
2. The regulation of new investment needs to draw on emerging ideas for 'constructive' user engagement from other regulated sectors and other countries, incorporating more use of competitive tendering of network investments.
3. The issue of locational pricing signals both in transmission and distribution charges, drawing on nodal pricing concepts in use in the PJM market in the USA, should be examined.
4. Ownership unbundling of networks from retailing – as has happened in transmission – could be extended to distribution.
5. Innovation in networks needs to be encouraged, as is beginning to happen in distribution with the introduction of the Innovation Funding Incentive (IFI) and more recently for transmission.

7.4.1   Overhaul of RPI-X

The current system of price reviews makes a clear separation of the analysis of operating and capital efficiency. This made sense when companies had very similar mixes of capital and operating efficiency or where separability of capital and operating expenditure could be assumed. However, it has always been methodologically suspect (see Pollitt, 2005). In addition, loss incentive reduction schemes and quality of supply incentive schemes have been added on to the basic analysis of cost efficiency rather than incorporated into it. As Giannakis *et al.* (2005) have shown, this can lead to perverse results for operating efficiency analysis.

Rapid divergence in technology and investment between distribution company regions, caused by the increase in renewables, makes the current approaches to economic regulation increasingly open to challenge, as they have little underlying theoretical validity. Operating and capital expenditure trade-offs need to be encouraged, especially where extra operating expenditure can avoid large new capital investments and reduce total costs. Similarly, projects which significantly reduce operating expenditure for modest increases in capital cost need to be properly encouraged.

There is also the issue of proper risk allocation between customers and companies. RPI-X has the effect of reducing some of the risks to the customer (such as cost risk) but its actual operation, through submitted business plans and regular revisions, shifts much of the investment risk on to the customer. Proper risk allocation should occur. More explicit risk sharing needs to be considered such as occurs in US performance-based rate schemes (PBR), where companies share risk around a central target rate of return (see Joskow, 2005).

Other areas for attention are the length of the current review period. Longer review periods (7–10 years) would create a more stable environment for investment and innovation. Consideration should also be given to the ending of company-specific X factors based on detailed comparisons of own costs against other companies in a UK sample. This can lead to gaming between companies (Jamasb et al., 2004). A simpler 'yardstick' system based on average costs in the sector may yield better incentive properties and remains to be fully investigated (see Shleifer, 1985; Pollitt, 2005). These changes would be particularly useful for determining the revenue related to past investment.

Both Distributed Network Operators (DNOs) and the National Grid have monopolies over the commissioning and operating of new distribution and transmission links. The system of regulation guarantees them a fair rate of return on approved investments delivered to budget. Merchant (or competitive) transmission for some major upgrades may be an option, and the regulator should undertake a careful cost–benefit analysis of this if it is proposed. However, most scenarios imagine that such entirely new and potentially competitive capacity is rare (see Elders et al., 2006). However, it is possible that distinctly new links such as north–south DC cables could be proposed and built by third parties. Some links to Scottish Islands, the Netherlands and offshore generation may be built under this type of arrangement.

7.4.2 'Constructive' user engagement

Regulated network investments occur because of the absence of a competitive market for network services. However, there have been important developments in the creation of negotiated solutions to investments between buyers and sellers of network services. The most exciting development in the UK is that occurring in airport regulation. Airports exist in a rapidly expanding market, require substantial new investment, and are subject to significant demand uncertainty. BAA owns and operates London's Heathrow, Gatwick and Stansted Airports. These airports are regulated by the Civil Aviation Authority (CAA), which recommends prices following price reviews to the Competition Commission. Following widespread criticism of the last price review, the

CAA is pursuing a new approach to deciding its recommended charges (see CAA, 2004). This involves the CAA chairing negotiations between BAA and the airline users at each of the three London airports in order to negotiate a Price Control Business Plan (see CAA, 2005). This plan incorporates agreed investments to meet agreed growth targets and has the advantage of taking the regulator out of the process of deciding the appropriateness of investments. The CAA still has to approve the plan and continues to provide efficiency and other studies to inform the negotiations.

Such a plan to involve the users in determining how and when regulated investments should occur has been implemented for electricity transmission and sub-transmission in Argentina. Littlechild and Skerk (2004a, b) discussed the 'public contest method' for determining new transmission investments. This method involved users voting on new investment proposals. If 30% of the beneficiaries of an investment voted against it, it would not go ahead. If 30% of the beneficiaries voted in favour of a project and fewer than 30% against, it would be tendered and the cost shared out in proportion to the benefits (subject to a test that the system benefits exceeded the costs). Littlechild and Skerk found that this method was successfully adopted for a significant number of projects and that a controversial fourth transmission line into Buenos Aires was correctly delayed by this process. They also highlighted that the compulsory competitive tendering of the project and the use of the winning tender price in subsequent adjustments to the regulatory asset base of the transmission company led to multiple bidders and very competitive winning bids. Littlechild and Ponzano (2007) detailed a related user engagement process in Buenos Aires province (the area around the city) which led to the successful negotiation of a 10-year transmission plan (to run from 1999) between the transmission company and more than 200 local distribution companies. This paper strongly suggests the practicality of buyer–seller negotiations for the deciding of small investments (as part of a larger package).

Given the small number of retailers, distributors and transmission companies in the UK, such negotiated solutions to deciding transmission investments need to be considered seriously. The UK needs to move away from central planning of such investments and the control of longer-range planning of the system by the National Grid (who effectively controls it in the UK). Serious consideration needs to be given to the competitive tendering of transmission and large distribution investments wherever possible, as this makes regulation easier.

Both of these suggestions would greatly extend the role of the market in network investments.

7.4.3   Locational pricing

Generation and load investments impose different costs according to where exactly they occur in the electricity system. Locational price signals received by generation and loads should reflect this. In the UK, these locational signals are received through locationally differentiated transmission and distribution access charges. However, such signals can be provided via an independent system (or market) operator and be decoupled from charges imposed by transmission and distribution companies. The issue is whether there is sufficient geographical variation in the current charging systems to provide efficient market signals for the location of renewables and fossil microgeneration. In transmission there is a zonal system for TNUoS charges by kW (not kWh), with 21 zones in Great Britain. Within distribution networks there is currently no geographical differentiation of charges. A number of authors have argued for the superiority of a full nodal pricing system in the transmission system (e.g. Hogan, 1998). Under this system, widely referred to as Locational Marginal Pricing (LMP), charges for congestion and losses (as opposed to for capacity) are embedded within energy prices (per kWh) that vary at every significant node in the system. As noted above, no such charging exists in the UK. The best example of this in practice is the Pennsylvania–New Jersey–Maryland (PJM) market in the USA (now expanded to cover several other states). This market is the largest interconnected wholesale market in the world, with around 164GW of capacity by mid-2005. There are 3,000+ nodes in the system. These provide clear signals for new connection and avoid the averaging problem which exists in a zonal system. In PJM, energy prices are recalculated every 5 minutes from bids supplied by generators/suppliers. Nodal price differentials recover around 20% of the costs of transmission within PJM. Implementing a full PJM-type system would be very expensive and disruptive to the current system; however, a centrally administered system of LMP could be administered by the system operator (National Grid), who could calculate nodal energy prices from bids submitted to the current Balancing Market.

The current UK system of limited zonal pricing involves the averaging of capacity charges across zones and no locational variation in energy-related charges. This may be important in the context of renewables, where there are a number of potential sites where they could be built which may impose very different local power flows and require different patterns of system upgrades. Averaging was attractive in the early years of deregulation when there was a desire to improve competition and liquidity in the wholesale energy market by having a single energy price across the country. However, as energy markets build experience and market participants become better informed, this argument loses its force. In contrast to the current situation, where nodal marginal transmission losses do not vary much around the network (Bialek *et al.*, 2004), they may be higher in the future. In addition, some evidence shows that nodal pricing may actually mitigate market power relative to a zonal system (see Green, 2004) by magnifying the local demand response and hence making it less profitable. Other significant markets are moving towards nodal pricing, including the significant Texas market, which is the closest in terms of overall liberalisation to the UK globally (see Adib and Zarnikau, 2006). New Zealand is another market with significant experience of successful nodal pricing (see Bertram, 2006).

LMP or nodal pricing requires a detailed model of the system that it is applied to, capable of calculating the real-time locational prices. This model has to be commissioned and maintained by the system operator. It can be a non-trivial exercise and may have significant ongoing costs (high in PJM, low in New Zealand). Implementing such a system in the UK would require a major change and would be contentious. Any implementation scheme would need to be carefully evaluated. The UK currently enjoys a system which has low congestion costs relative to other systems (such as PJM). However, the most advanced electricity markets are moving in this direction, and large changes to the power flows in the network, coupled with the significant costs of upgrading individual lines, may make nodal pricing a sensible option.

Locational pricing is well understood in the context of transmission. However, in the context of distribution systems it may be just as important. Small-scale renewables connect directly to the distribution grid but may also be of more benefit or more cost in particular places. Jamasb *et al.* (2005) proposed that the UK should implement a form of locationally differentiated pricing within distribution networks, as this would properly signal the best places to build new capacity, especially at the ends of constrained distribution networks. It would be necessary to build detailed models to calculate location-varying prices, but the benefits would seem to outweigh the costs of doing this. At the level of distribution networks, zonal differentiation of Distribution Use of System charges may be a reasonable initial step which captures much of the benefit of locational signalling. Locational pricing within the distribution network might (in the future) facilitate the efficient connection of microgeneration and incentivise the installation of smart meters and automatic appliance control and battery equipment at the household level.

More finely differentiated locational prices serve the additional purpose of giving clear information to the regulator and to the users of the system as to the value of new transmission and distribution capacity, and form the basis of evaluating situations where lifting constraints would be worthwhile. They can also be used to collect some revenue which can be applied to finance new investments. In the past, large-scale generation investments, slow demand growth, and more predictability in the development of the system over the next price-control period made the lack of locational pricing signals a minor problem for the UK system. However, more disparate generation and demand growth makes it increasingly important to get locational signals right. Any change would require careful cost–benefit analysis and attention would be needed to examine the relative costs and benefits of alternative systems, some of which might offer less accurate price signals but be cheaper to implement.

7.4.4 Ownership unbundling

England and Wales provided the world's best example of effective unbundling of electricity transmission from the rest of the electricity system (see Jamasb and Pollitt, 2005, for a discussion of this in a European context). The creation of a separately owned National Grid company responsible for transmission and unable to invest in other parts of the electricity sector facilitated the development of a competitive generation market. This development occurred free from the discriminatory access to transmission problems that has plagued other markets which did not follow the UK model (in particular Germany). The regulation of the National Grid was made easier because it was a separate company and its regulated charges came down substantially as efficiency improved (see Newbery and Pollitt, 1997).

The experience in Scotland was rather different. Scottish Power and Scottish Hydro-Electric were privatised as bundled companies consisting of generation, transmission, distribution and retail assets. In 1991 residential prices were lower in Scotland than in England and Wales but now they are higher. An important explanation of this appears to be the failure to separate out the transmission function into a separately owned company (see Pollitt, 1999). This problem was recognised with the recent creation of an all-GB transmission system under the control of the National Grid. Although Scottish Power and Scottish Hydro still own the transmission assets, they are now independently operated by the

National Grid as the single GB-wide system operator. The result of this change appears to have been a relative lowering of prices in Scotland.[4]

The arguments for clear separation of transmission from the rest of the electricity system are based on the theory of vertical integration (see Tirole, 1988). Monopoly parts of the supply chain have an incentive to 'foreclose' on competitors by imposing unreasonable access conditions in related parts of the supply chain in favour of their own divisions in order to drive up margins in the competitive parts of the business. This is possible in practice because a monopoly transmission company controls the connection and dispatch of individual plants, and can be done by increasing connection costs or imposing expensive rules for dispatch on competitors' power plants. Distribution systems in the UK have traditionally been less prone to such foreclosure because they are passive rather than active networks. Tough non-discriminatory regulation and an initial lack of own generation seem to have been effective in preventing the exercise of serious market power in either generation or supply foreclosure. However, increases in embedded renewables mean that the distribution network is set to change to become more like a transmission network: actively managed two-way power flows with the potential for own generation projects to be favoured over rivals' projects.

Such transmission and distribution convergence (particularly at higher voltage levels in the distribution system) may mean that consideration should be given to ownership unbundling between distribution and the rest of the electricity system (i.e. retail (supply) and generation). This would have the additional advantage of encouraging competition between on- and off-grid electricity supply, as retailers would be separated completely from distribution owners, and would reduce the incentive to favour on-grid solutions. This was a scenario envisaged by Walt Patterson in his book *Transforming Electricity: The Coming Generation of Change* (1999). Such unbundling would eliminate the competitive advantage that DNOs currently have over other companies in locating distributed generation within their networks. One effect of such unbundling might be to increase the value of nodal pricing in distribution, as small-scale generation could not be added by the distribution company with superior grid information but only in response to clear non-discriminatory price signals. Arguments in favour of this would be strengthened by evidence that retail competition might be promoted by the separation of retailers from distribution. The evidence for this is limited in the UK, but it is the case that switching rates to non-former incumbents are

---

[4] *Source:* David Halldearn's (Ofgem) speech on '*British Electricity Trading and Transmission Arrangements*', 15 June 2006, available at http://www.iet.tv/search/index.html

highest in the regions where distribution companies are not integrated with any incumbent supply (see Ofgem, 2007).[5]

7.4.5 Innovation and RD&D expenditure

The high level of investment expenditure in networks required to support large-scale deployment of low-carbon technologies suggests that there is scope for significant technological progress in network technologies. However, RD&D expenditure continues to be very low in the UK electricity sector, suggesting limited scope for new innovation in the sector.

Jamasb and Pollitt (2005) note the collapse of UK energy RD&D following the liberalisation of the electricity sector and this is also a theme of Chapter 3 of this volume. By 2004 the amount of money spent by UK network companies on RD&D was very small (less than £4 million p.a. or less than 0.1% of revenue, see Ofgem, 2003, p. 8). The public-good aspect of RD&D is significant both in generation and in networks, given the large number of distribution and transmission companies in the UK and globally. RD&D activity also lacks critical mass (with no company having any significant in-house capability) and is not a strategic priority given the short-term and regulated nature of expenditure and profitability.

Ofgem have recently explicitly recognised this with the introduction of an Innovation Funding Incentive (IFI) (see Ofgem, 2004b). This scheme allows distributors to raise prices by up to 0.5% of revenue to fund research projects aimed at improving distribution network performance. The recent transmission price control review has extended this to transmission charges (Ofgem, 2006a, p. 66–67). The sums of money involved are small (in total for distribution and transmission they would be less than £25 million p.a.) but they may be significant in improving the rate of technical progress in UK networks at a time when capital expenditure is increasing significantly. Mott Macdonald BPI (2004) estimated benefits of the distribution IFI with a net present value of £386 million on consumer expenditure of £57 million.

7.5 Conclusions

Electricity transmission and distribution networks are a significant part of the total cost of electricity supply in the UK. Large amounts of low-carbon generation, particularly renewables, will necessitate increased

---

[5] The five non-integrated regions – Swalec, SWEB, Northern, Norweb and Yorkshire – have a weighted average switching rate of 51.3% against 46.5% for the other nine regions of GB in March 2007. See also Davies and Waddams Price (2007).

and currently uncertain investment in electricity networks. This is already beginning to occur in the latest transmission and distribution price control reviews. Although the system of network regulation to 2007 has successfully delivered more investment with lower prices, it is not clear that the current system of regulation is fit for purpose in a low-carbon electricity system.[6]

The importance of electricity infrastructure investment is recognised in the *Stern Review* (Stern, 2007). The Review recognises that electricity infrastructure services 'would change ... fundamentally' (p. 257) with a significant increase in low-carbon technologies – such as small-scale distributed generation and CHP – in the electricity system. The Review calls on regulators to 'innovate in response to the challenge of integrating these technologies to exploit their potential, and unlock the resultant opportunities that arise from shifting the generation mix away from centralised sources' (p. 421). The Review is necessarily silent on the details of what such a response might consist of; however, this chapter is an attempt to suggest some of the innovations in regulation that may be necessary.

We have recommended a review of the current practice of RPI-X setting. We suggest new thinking in the determination and regulation of required network investments, particularly the use of user engagement and competitive tendering. Consideration needs to be given to the locational signals inherent in current transmission and distribution pricing structures and whether these need to be changed. Ownership unbundling of distribution from the rest of the electricity system is an issue whose time will come and more thought must be given to the funding of increased RD&D in networks, given the increasing amounts of capital expenditure involved.

Acknowledgements

This work was supported by the ESRC Electricity Policy Research Group and the EPSRC Future Networks Consortium of Supergen.

References

Adib, P. and Zarnikau, J. (2006). Texas: the most robust competitive market in North America, in F.P. Sioshansi and W. Pfaffenberger (eds.), *Electricity Market Reform: An International Perspective*. Oxford: Elsevier, pp. 383–417.

---

[6] Indeed, Ofgem recently announced a comprehensive review of its approach to regulation. See speech by Alistair Buchanan, available at www.ofgem.gov.uk.

Baron, D.P. (1989). Design of regulatory mechanisms and institutions, Chapter 24 in R. Schmalensee and R.D. Willig (eds.), *Handbook of Industrial Organization*. Amsterdam: North-Holland.

Bertram, G. (2006). Restructuring of the New Zealand Electricity sector 1984–2005, in F.P. Sioshansi and W. Pfaffenberger (eds.), *Electricity Market Reform: An International Perspective*. Oxford: Elsevier, pp. 203–234.

Bialek, J., Hartley, M. and Topping, S. (2004). Average zonal transmission losses. *IEE Power Engineer*, **17**(5), 34–37.

Bialek, J.W., Zhou, Q., Bronsdon, C. and Connor, G. (2006). *Impact of GB Transmission Charging on Renewable Electricity Generation*. The 8th IEE International Conference on AC and DC Transmission ACDC 2006, March.

CAA (2004). *Airport Regulation: Looking to the Future, Learning from the Past*. London: Civil Aviation Authority.

   (2005). *Airport Regulation: The Process for Constructive Engagement*. London: Civil Aviation Authority.

Davies, S. and Waddams Price, C. (2007). Does ownership unbundling matter? Evidence from UK energy markets. *Intereconomics*, **42**(6), 301–305.

Department of Trade and Industry (2006). *The Energy Challenge: Energy Review Report 2006*. CM 6887. London: DTI.

Elders, I., Ault, G., Galloway, S., McDonald, J., Kohler, J., Leach, M. and Enteric, L. (2006). Electricity network scenarios for the United Kingdom in 2050, in T. Jamasb, W.J. Nuttall and M.G. Pollitt (eds.), *Future Electricity Technologies and Systems*. Cambridge: Cambridge University Press, pp. 24–79.

Giannakis, D., Jamasb, T. and Pollitt, M. (2005). Benchmarking and incentive regulation of quality of service: an application to UK electricity distribution utilities. *Energy Policy*, **33**(17), 2256–2271.

Green, R. (2004). *Electricity Transmission Pricing: How Much does it Cost to get it Wrong?*. CMI Electricity Project Working Paper No. 63.

Hogan, W.W. (1998). *Competitive Electricity Market Design: A Wholesale Primer*. Cambridge, MA: John F. Kennedy School of Government, Harvard University.

Jamasb, T. and Pollitt, M. (2005). Electricity market reform in the European Union: Review of progress toward liberalization and integration, *Energy Journal*. Special Issue on European Electricity Liberalisation, 11–42.

Jamasb, T., Nillesen, P. and Pollitt, M. (2004). Strategic behaviour under regulation benchmarking. *Energy Economics*, **26**(5), 825–843.

Jamasb, T., Neuhoff, K., Newbery, D. and Pollitt, M. (2005). *Long-term Framework for Electricity Distribution Access Charges*. Report prepared for and commissioned by Ofgem, Electricity Policy Research Group, Working Paper 05/07.

Joskow, P.L. (2005). *Incentive Regulation in Theory and Practice: Electricity Distribution and Transmission Networks*. Electricity Policy Research Group, Working Paper 05/11.

Littlechild, S.C. (1983). *The Regulation of British Telecommunications Profitability*. London: HMSO.

Littlechild, S.C. and Ponzano, E.A. (2007). *Transmission Expansion in Argentina 5: in the Regional Electricity Forum of Buenos Aires Province*. Electricity Policy Group Working Paper No. 0729.

Littlechild, S.C. and Skerk, C.J. (2004a). *Regulation of Transmission Expansion in Argentina. Part I: State Ownership, Reform and the Fourth Line*. CMI Electricity Project Working Paper No. 61.

Littlechild, S.C. and Skerk, C.J. (2004b). *Regulation of Transmission Expansion in Argentina. Part II: Developments since the Fourth Line*. CMI Electricity Project Working Paper No. 62.

Mott Macdonald BPI (2004). *Innovation in Electricity Distribution Networks: Final Report*. Brighton, UK: Mott Macdonald BPI.

National Grid (2005). *The Statement of Use of System Charges Effective from 01 April 2005*. London: National Grid.

(2006). *The Statement of Use of System Charges Effective from 01 April 2006*. London: National Grid.

Newbery, D.M.G. and Pollitt, M.G. (1997). Restructuring and privatisation of the CEGB: was it worth it? *Journal of Industrial Economics*, **45**(3), 269–304.

Ofgem (2003). *Innovation and Registered Power Zones: A Discussion Paper*. London: Ofgem.

(2004a). *Electricity Distribution Price Control Review: Final Proposals*. London: Ofgem.

(2004b). *Electricity Distribution Price Control Review, Appendix: Further details on the incentive schemes for distributed generation, innovation funding and registered power zones*. Ref.145b/04. London: Ofgem.

(2004c). *Transmission Investment for Renewable Generation*. 288/04. London: Ofgem.

(2006a). *Transmission Price Control: Final Proposals*. Ref.206/06. London: Ofgem.

(2006b). *Transmission Price Control Final Proposals: Appendices*. Ref.206a/06. London: Ofgem.

(2007). *Domestic Retail Market Report June 2007*. Ref.169/07. London: Ofgem.

Patterson, W. (1999). *Transforming Electricity: The Coming Generation of Change*. London: Earthscan.

Pollitt, M.G. (1999). *The Restructuring and Privatisation of the Electricity Supply Industry in Scotland*. Mimeo.

Pollitt, M. (2005). The role of efficiency estimates in regulatory price reviews: Ofgem's approach to benchmarking electricity networks. *Utilities Policy*, **13**(4), 279–288.

Shleifer, A. (1985). A theory of yardstick competition. *Rand Journal of Economics*, **16**, 319–327.

Stern, N. (2007). *The Economics of Climate Change: The Stern Review*. Cambridge, UK: Cambridge University Press.

Tirole, J. (1988). *The Theory of Industrial Organization*. Cambridge, MA: MIT Press.

Viridian (2006). *Viridian Annual Report and Accounts 05–06*. Belfast: Viridian.

8 Domestic electricity consumption and demand-side participation: opportunities and challenges for the UK power system

*Mark Bilton, Charlotte Ramsay, Matthew Leach,
Hannah Devine-Wright, Patrick Devine-Wright and
Daniel Kirschen*

8.1 Introduction

This chapter takes an overview of the state of demand-side activity in the UK today, and highlights some of the potential both for demand reduction and the development of innovative demand-side technology to help meet the future needs of a low-carbon electricity sector.

Until now, the UK power market has been driven predominantly by power generation on the supply side of the system, with less attention to customer demand. The system infrastructure reflects the same picture: flexible generators are used to match demand and keep the power system in balance through the ancillary services mechanism. Beyond the influence of their load in aggregate, the majority of consumers have no impact on either the power market or on the infrastructure that supplies them. If the demand side is to become a fully integrated actor in the electricity sector, a reappraisal of this supply-oriented focus is required. The sector must develop participatory and inclusive processes that recognise the extent of customer requirements, attitudes and knowledge (Devine-Wright and Devine-Wright, 2004).

Increasing pressure to improve end-user energy efficiency, reduce harmful emissions and decrease power consumption, along with changes in the scale and nature of power generation, are likely to stimulate a change in this *status quo*. Forthcoming European legislation on energy services and promotion of end-user energy efficiency[1] are promoting a new demand-side agenda in the UK. Energy efficiency already forms one

---

[1] The *European Directive on Energy Use in Buildings* (2002/91/EC) and the *Proposal for a Directive of the European Parliament and of the Council on Energy End-use Efficiency and Energy Services*, COM (2003) 739 final.

of the main pillars of UK energy policy (DTI, 2003). New developments are focusing on the importance of accurate information provision to facilitate electricity consumer activities (e.g. ECI, 2003; Ofgem, 2006) and increasingly on the facilitation of demand-side players of all sizes in the balancing (NGT, 2004) and ancillary services market (DTI, 2006; HMG, 2006).

To put the broader points in specific context, this chapter focuses predominantly on the residential sector, with a shorter commentary on industry. For further discussion of industry, see Price *et al.* (2006) and, for discussion of transport, see Vermeyen and Belmans (2006).

8.2   Defining demand-side activities

The possibilities for demand-side 'activities' are diverse and imply many different forms of interaction with, and outcomes for, customers, the electricity markets, the power system and the environment. In Figure 8.1 we propose a new framework to categorise these options, to try to bring together some of the differing terminology and definitions found in the literature.

Using this characterisation, demand-side activity can be separated into *static* and *dynamic* responses. Broadly, this defines the nature of the response: *static* activities (such as energy efficiency improvements and standards) are those that can be installed at any time and are not taken in response to a (time)-specific market signal or request from the system operator. Typically the duration of the action will be long term; for example, once installed, an energy-efficient appliance will save energy throughout its lifetime. *Dynamic* actions are those carried out in response to changing market or system conditions. They are made in response to short-term requirements and their impact is not usually felt beyond their duration (although the accumulated effect of many customers adopting dynamic actions may result in a sustained change in energy-use behaviour and market development).[2]

Both static and dynamic actions can be categorised further by considering the level of end-user involvement in the activity; this is defined as passive or active involvement. In the instance of *static* actions, passive involvement is exemplified through regulation, for example, through the

---

[2] The terms 'static' and 'dynamic' are used in a different way in economics, referring, for example, to short-term and long-term characteristics in models (where static is synonymous with short-term and dynamic with long-term). The use here is different, referring to the responsiveness of the action to conditions (with static actions characterised as long term, and dynamic as responsive in the short term).

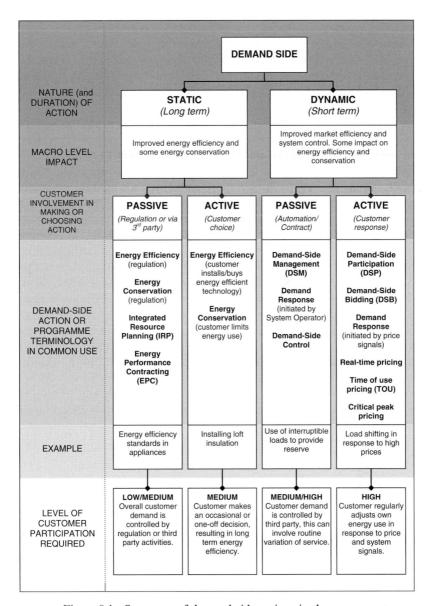

Figure 8.1. Summary of demand-side actions in the power sector

government setting minimum standards for electrical devices. It is this area of demand-side activity that has been most successful to date. Conversely, active involvement is driven by consumer choice; for example, the choice and purchase of an energy-efficient appliance. Considerable policy and programme activity has centred on this portion of demand-side activities, with the intent of changing behaviour and incentivising energy-efficient purchasing (HoL, 2005).

For a *dynamic* demand-side activity, a passive response is initiated or called for by those other than the end-user (e.g. system operators, energy suppliers, etc.). Most commonly, this is a scheduled or contracted demand-side activity that contributes towards system stability, balancing, or during network emergencies. It still requires end-user agreement, but the end-user does not decide when or how to make this kind of action. The primary challenge for this kind of activity is to recruit and maintain demand participants, and to ensure that they are motivated and able to take part in the programme (e.g. Gehring, 2002; PLMA, 2002). In contrast, the active response is one carried out by the end-user; for example, demand shifting in response to high prices. The end-user in this instance responds directly to information from the markets and networks and makes a decision to change usage patterns in response to these signals. A variety of mechanisms exist to facilitate this activity, from Time of Use pricing (IEA, 2005), to demand-side bidding in the energy markets (IEA, 2004). Market barriers to these activities arise from the current focus of most energy markets on the supply side, access issues, and a lack of information to demand-side actors which makes participation complex or uneconomic (IEA, 2003).

The impact of all these demand-side activities falls into two broad areas:

- Energy efficiency and emissions reductions (both *static* and *dynamic* activity).
- System operation and economic deployment of resources (*dynamic* activity).

These two outcomes are not mutually exclusive, but the drivers for action in each case can be quite different. System operation drivers are primarily based on maintaining security and quality of supply at lowest cost; demand actions here must be delivered within a short time frame and often with little advance warning, but the effect on the end-user's service through demand reduction can be recovered at a later point. Energy efficiency reductions are not time-critical in the short term, but the impact of the demand-side action is generally sustained, with no load recovery after the action is taken.

8.3   The current situation in the UK

8.3.1   Electricity consumption

To understand the potential for demand-side involvement in the power system, it is important to have an overview of the current statistics on energy consumption (see Figure 8.2). Although there have been steady improvements in energy efficiency, leading to continuous improvement in the energy intensity of the UK economy (right-hand axis of the figure shows energy intensity),[3] this is against a backdrop of steadily increasing absolute consumption from 1970 to the present decade (left-hand axis of the figure shows total electricity consumption for the UK). Forecasts for future consumption continue along this trajectory; baseline forecasts by the UK transmission system operator project an increase of 0.8% per annum for the short-term future (NGT, 2005).

By end-user, electricity consumption in the UK is dominated by three sectors: industry, residential users, and the commercial and public sector (combined), as illustrated in Figure 8.3. From 1970 up to 2003, the domestic and industrial sectors have increased their energy requirement by 50% and 36%, respectively. Most striking is the commercial and public services sector, with an increase of 152% over the same time-frame, reflecting the move towards a service-driven economy.

8.3.2   Static demand-side action: Energy efficiency and demand reduction programmes

Existing initiatives to curb the demand side and promote static demand responses (aimed at reducing consumption, improving energy efficiency and decreasing greenhouse gas emissions) have centred on the industrial sector, with the Climate Change Levy and the Emissions Trading Scheme being two of the most prominent policy instruments. These policies affect some of the larger organisations in the commercial sector, leaving a large percentage of smaller organisations (primarily SMEs)[4] unaffected. The residential sector has been addressed by initiatives such

---

[3] Measures of energy intensity by sector have been calculated using Gross Value Added (which contributes to the overall measure of Gross Domestic Product) for the industrial and service sectors, and by the number of households for the domestic sector. See the original source for more information (DTI, 2002).

[4] Small to medium-sized enterprises.

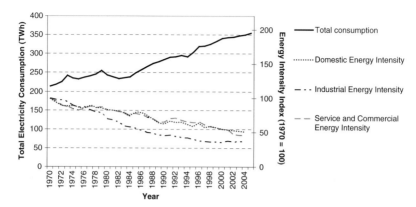

Figure 8.2. Total UK electricity consumption and sector energy intensity, 1970–2004
Source: IEA (1970–2003), DTI (2002, 2005)

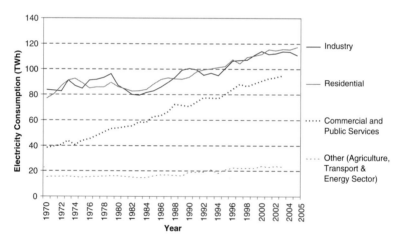

Figure 8.3. UK electricity consumption by sector, 1970–2005
Source: IEA (1970–2003), DTI (2005)

as the Energy Efficiency Commitment (EEC), carried out by energy suppliers, who (between 2005 and 2008) must demonstrate savings of 130TWh in their customer base, facilitated through the uptake of energy efficiency measures, again promoting static demand-side responses. For a full review of static demand-side actions see HoL (2005).

8.3.3 Dynamic demand-side action: System operation and market opportunities

At present, there is limited interaction between the demand side and the electricity markets or the operation of the power system. Mechanisms are in place for demand customers to participate in the wholesale and balancing markets; however, market reviews have shown that few demand-side customers take this opportunity. A review in 2002 revealed that only 0.15% of the bids and offers in the balancing market came from demand-side participants (Ofgem, 2002). Increased participation is seen amongst energy-intensive users who (in partnership with energy suppliers) have a strong incentive to avoid the highest transmission charge price periods during the year (the 'triad' periods) and shift their demand to lower price times. Many suppliers will offer triad management services and it has been estimated that this results in between 800 and 1,500MW of load shifting over these peak system price periods (DGCG, 2005a).

A similar situation is seen in the system operation roles, with a few large consumers having sufficient demand to offer ancillary services for system balancing and emergency control. As an example, large users on the demand side provide around 29% of the capacity (~600MW) for the standing reserve market (DGCG, 2005a). For smaller power consumers with electric storage heating, there is some use of radio teleswitching to shift loads to off-peak times. Apart from this initiative, there are few other opportunities for smaller consumers to participate in the market. For a comprehensive review of dynamic demand-side actions in the UK see DGCG (2005a).

8.3.4 Drivers for change

The factors driving interest in greater demand-side involvement stem from climate change and security of supply concerns and, to an extent, from market liberalisation initiatives. In particular, the climate change agenda has initiated many policies and programmes promoting low-carbon power generation. For example, the 2007 Energy White Paper aspires to the EU target of 20% of all electricity coming from renewable energy sources by 2020 systems, and to increasing the installed capacity of Combined Heat and Power (CHP) systems (DTI, 2007). Previous, lower targets were considered difficult of achieve (DEFRA, 2006) but whilst future capacity is uncertain, the UK is clearly set to see increased penetration of smaller-scale, decentralised renewable and intermittent generation.

At present, the continuous demand–supply balance for electricity is achieved through the functioning of the electricity markets, with balancing actions from the system operator over short time scales. Both of these processes are dominated by electricity generation and they rely on the presence of sufficient generation reserve and flexibility in the system to ensure that supply can match demand at all times. If the supply dominance of the market remains, the introduction of inflexible and intermittent sources of generation – including small CHP that is led by heat demand, and wind turbines reliant on the weather – will necessitate some increase in flexible and reliable (reserve) generation. Introduction of intermittent generation need not affect the reliability of the system but it will increase the overall system costs (UKERC, 2006).

Demand-side activity can help to address these issues and reduce the requirement for additional flexible generating plant. By using static and dynamic demand-side actions, overall consumption and emissions can be reduced and short-term load patterns can be adapted to match supply output better. Aggregation of similar loads offers potential for even the very small-scale residential consumer to participate in a more actively managed system that works with both supply and demand.

8.3.5   *Barriers to demand-side involvement*

Traditionally, the most important barriers to further involvement of the demand side are the perceived inelasticity of demand, and information asymmetry creating disempowered end-users unable to participate fully in a supply-centric market. Consolidation of the major electricity market actors into six overarching utilities has also restricted the emergence of more innovative market offerings that might engage with end-users and enable new routes to demand-side participation, particularly for smaller customers (DGCG, 2005b). For industrial users, where electricity bills make up a significant part of their overall costs, there has been greater incentive and opportunity to embrace energy efficiency and engage in offering dynamic demand-side services. But both the commercial and residential sectors, which account for 60% of UK electricity consumption, continue to be held back by these barriers (CT, 2005; HoL, 2005).

8.4   In context: the residential sector

The residential sector contributes around 27% (DEFRA, 2006) of the UK's carbon emissions, and notably 45% of the electricity demand peak. Other than building regulations, the only wide-reaching mechanism specifically aimed at residential emissions reductions is the Energy Efficiency Commitment (EEC) and, apart from some modest media campaigns, little has been done to foster personal responsibility for addressing climate change, which is considered a necessary precursor to pro-environmental, energy-related behaviour (Gardner and Stern, 2002).

The residential sector is distinct from the industrial and energy sectors in having no single identifiable target for efficiency improvements or demand reduction; rather, various emission reductions can be made, with a wide range of technologies and behavioural changes.

8.4.1   Drivers for change

As well as the macro-level drivers for change discussed earlier, the residential sector is affected by drivers related to the preferences and actions of individuals. Residential electricity demand is often considered to be relatively inelastic; however, anecdotal evidence suggests that recent rises in energy prices have stimulated sales of energy-efficient appliances to the detriment of less efficient equivalents:

The rising cost of electricity has led to a surge in demand for energy efficient washing machines, refrigerators and dishwashers, say retailers. The high-street store, Comet, says sales of the most energy efficient appliances have risen by 5% in recent weeks (Telegraph, 2006).

As this example shows, the provision of information in the form of energy efficiency labelling has provided a pathway for the adoption of static demand measures (albeit restricted to white goods). International experience has also shown that consumers will adjust their behaviour to dynamic price mechanisms, a notable mass market example being Florida's Gulf Power tariff, which has seen peak-load reductions of 42% (IEA, 2005). In Europe, France has a history of mass market domestic demand management: the 'Bleu' tariff uses a cutout relay to manage peak demand, and more recently the 'Tempo' tariff informs the user of the next day's price band.

The adoption of domestic microgeneration systems is also changing the *status quo;* this is one category of demand-side technology that has shown promising signs of public interest and acceptance. For example, recent surveys have shown that the adoption of microgeneration appears to have a positive effect on energy literacy, since when individuals are able to generate their own power and heat, they become more interested in their consumption of energy.

The advantage is that it makes you think about your energy use more. You value it more … You realise it's easier to save it than make it. That is especially true of the hot water panel, but also with the electricity too.

Male, Edinburgh, Photovoltaics and Solar Hot Water Panel (SDC, 2005)

This effect is enhanced by the installation of bidirectional metering devices that are required for microgenerating customers. Although currently relatively limited, this migration of metering technology is raising interest and expectations in respect of customer information, and offers a route to improved energy literacy.

When that red light is on we know we are exporting to the grid – so it's time to put the washing machine on or it's OK to boil the kettle. When that light is not on we make sure that everything is off – nothing is on standby because we know that it's probably really costing us.

Older couple, SW Lancashire, Wind Turbine (SDC, 2005)

8.4.2   *Barriers to change*

In the long term, within the context of the liberalised market, consumer choice must become a driver for change, but this is currently impeded by poor understanding of the causes and effects of climate change, low energy literacy, and barriers to market engagement.

Attitudes to climate change   Whilst climate change is clearly a driver at the policy level, it is not yet having a significant effect on energy consumption patterns in the home. This situation is in part due to a lack of understanding of climate change and the contribution made by residential activities. Individuals appear to be unaware of or understate their individual contribution and responsibility for climate change. A recent survey revealed that only 8% of the public attribute responsibility to individuals and families (Tyndall Centre, 2006). Paradoxically, when asked how the problem should be tackled, a majority suggest 'behavioural change' (Tyndall Centre, 2006).

Without any clear understanding in terms of an individual's contribution to climate change, the likelihood of behaviour change is diminished. This said, beneficial technology may be adopted for reasons other than climate change; for example, saving money or kudos. While in general the public is not knowingly engaged in carbon abatement, a small and growing minority is enthusiastically adopting new behaviour and available technologies.

Energy literacy   Looking beyond the need for the public to understand that their homes are a significant contributor to climate change, in order to engage with the problem, some knowledge of specific sources and abatement measures is required. In this context a lack of energy literacy also presents itself as a barrier to development of demand-side activities. Whilst improvements have been seen – for example with the labelling of white goods – on the whole, consumers are unaware of the relative impact of their various actions.

Although much existing research suggests a common lack of energy literacy held by residential energy consumers, it is also the case that social research using qualitative methods has shown that people have strong beliefs about energy generation, distribution and use issues – particularly concerning issues of responsibility for change. For example, a recent study conducted in two UK locations with contrasting salience of electricity supply infrastructure change (Beauly in Scotland, where significant upgrades are proposed to high voltage transmission lines, and Leicester in England, where no such changes have been proposed), showed that people were not uninterested in energy issues and held beliefs that were anchored in both personal experience and socially shared representations of electricity networks rather than 'factual', 'accurate', scientific or technical information (e.g. Kempton and Montgomery, 1982). The conclusion is that aiming to increase 'energy literacy' is not simply a matter of configuring appropriate incentives or increasing the amount of information available to domestic customers (often indicative of an 'information-deficit perspective') but of better understanding how personal experiences, beliefs and social factors such as social norms, issues of perceived equity, and attribution of responsibility influence energy behaviour.

This is illustrated in the following excerpt from a group discussion between several female Beauly residents (whose names have been changed to protect their anonymity).

ANNE: ... they can't reduce the amount of electricity that we need
            for the future
BETH: I agree ...
ANNE: I think they *have* to build nuclear power stations, it is an
            absolute necessity, it is essential if we are going to live the
            kind of life that we are used to
CLAIRE: but what is the alternative (to nuclear power stations)?
DEE: well the alternative is to use less, for a start
GERALDINE: yes
DEE: uh huh (in agreement)
FIONA: you'll never get that will you?

ANNE: the government has tried to teach us to switch off light bulbs
              and *yet* one plane taking off and the energy that it uses,
              there is a *massive* amount, and the *increasing* cars on the
              road, *increasing* planes in the air, and yet we're told to
              switch off light bulbs which is so *minimal*
CLAIRE: did you see in the paper yesterday? it was quoted, it was telling
              us lot to 'turn off the light bulbs' and it went round the
              country to the different government offices at 11 o'clock at
              night, they were all blazing with lights (laughs loudly)
ANNE: all blazing, so where does it start?

Information asymmetry and supply-side dominance   The UK's
supply-centric electricity sector has a long history of providing electricity
to residential consumers who have little notion of where the energy
comes from, or of its marginal price or emissions. This bias is reflected in
the EEC, where the responsibility to reduce residential emissions is
placed with the electricity supplier not the buyer.

If the UK population's understanding and attitude towards climate
change improves over time, this will not result in a more optimal use of
resources unless consumers become more energy literate and new
pathways to customer participation are created. Established information
asymmetries have created a situation where electricity suppliers and
generators have the ability to make decisions to reduce carbon emissions, but the consumer is less able to do so.

This market asymmetry manifests most clearly in the traditional
Ferraris electricity meter, which served its purpose in the era of the
centrally planned electricity system but is incongruous in today's world
of telecommunications and liberalised markets. The need to manually
read the Ferraris meter results in infrequent reading and estimated
billing. The flat tariff structure (all that is possible with the single
register) means there is no way to engage with the existing Time of Day
pricing mechanisms of the wholesale power markets and benefit from
the corresponding emission reduction possibilities.

The lack of information for consumers has a twofold effect; first it
sustains the low level of energy literacy, and second it reduces the ability
of the consumer to take appropriate action. Moreover, the lack of
dynamic market signals excludes the possibility of appliances to respond
to market conditions.

8.4.3   *Realising the value of residential demand-side activity*

If the value of the demand side is to be realised, any policy or infrastructure
must consider the current and potential future heterogeneity of the
sector, including, for example, microgeneration. Table 8.1 enumerates

Table 8.1. *Examples of existing and possible demand-side activity*

		MEASURE	BENEFITS TO CONSUMER	BARRIERS	ENABLING CONDITIONS
STATIC	PASSIVE	Average energy efficiency of white goods	Lower bills	Churn rate of stock	
		Average energy efficiency of other consumer devices	Lower bills	Lack of labelling and efficiency standards	
	ACTIVE	Installing loft Insulation	Lower bills, comfort	Inertia, cost, understanding	Knowledge, subsidy
		Installing cavity wall insulation	Lower bills, comfort	Inertia, cost, understanding quality concerns	Knowledge, subsidy, regulation of standards
		Fitting compact fluorescent lights	Lower bills, less maintenance	Inertia, cost, understanding quality concerns	Knowledge, subsidy, regulation of inefficient alternatives
		Buying A-rated appliances	Lower bills, less maintenance	Inertia, cost, understanding	Knowledge, subsidy, regulation of inefficient alternatives
		Remembering to turn off lights	Lower bills, less maintenance	Inertia, understanding	Knowledge
DYNAMIC	PASSIVE	Appliances defer activity to minimise cost of service.	Lower bills	Information and associated Infrastructure	Dynamic price data, or time/date-related tariffs
		Appliances defer activity to minimise carbon emissions.	Lower bills	Information and associated Infrastructure.	Dynamic emission data
		Home responds to request for DS service	Revenue, lower bills	Information and associated Infrastructure	Advanced metering with 'handshake'[*] capability
		Appliances wait until wind power is available	Lower bills	Information and associated Infrastructure	Advanced metering with 'handshake' capability
	ACTIVE	Individual chooses to defer demand activity.	Lower bills	Information and associated Infrastructure	Dynamic price data- or time-related tariffs. Advanced metering.
		Individual responds to request for service.	Revenue, lower bills	Information and associated Infrastructure	Advanced metering with 'handshake' capability

[*] 'Handshaking' refers to real-time service agreements where requests are broadcast and some demand-side participants respond with what they can offer.

some existing and potential demand-side measures using the static/dynamic – active/passive model introduced earlier.

Table 8.1 illustrates that the value of demand-side activities lies in a range of dynamic and static, active and passive approaches. Realising the full potential of residential demand-side activity is not likely to be achieved through one approach alone. To date, policies and programmes that promote demand-side interaction in the residential sector have focused primarily on static actions. This approach is consistent with the *status quo* of the supply-centric sector, which inhibits customer involvement in the electricity market and power system. To realise the full value of residential demand-side activity requires the adoption of dynamic actions; and that, in turn, involves a greater level of customer participation and the integration of customer-side technology into the wider power system.

This reveals a two-fold challenge for the sector.

- To recognise that the dynamic approach necessitates an evolution in both the technologies that provide domestic energy services (e.g. advanced meters, microgeneration, etc.), and the ways in which they interact with the wider system.
- To overcome some of the perceived and/or entrenched barriers to residential demand-side integration; and facilitate greater levels of customer participation in dynamic demand-side actions.

As Table 8.1 reveals, realising the value of this range of demand-side activity and facing these two challenges is in many instances tied up in the notion of information deficit and knowledge transfer. For the evolution of demand-side technologies, this is seen in the requirement for a greater level of detail and two-way information flows between customer-side technology and the wider system. Regarding the customer, this information challenge is rooted in the way in which information is acquired, the quality and quantity of information provided, and how, in the end, this information is processed by the domestic customer. Both of these issues are explored in more detail in later sections.

8.5   In context: industrial consumers

Lack of information is probably less of an issue among industrial consumers than with other classes of consumers. However, in an industrial setting, hard technical constraints may be faced, and financial considerations rather than enthusiasm determine the extent of the change in the pattern of consumption.

Like the other classes of consumers, industry finds it easier to implement static rather than dynamic actions. This is particularly true when the cost of electrical energy represents a substantial proportion of the overall production cost. It should be noted, however, that industrial processes that rely on electricity (such as variable speed drives and induction heating) can be much more energy efficient than processes that use other sources of energy. Some industries are therefore likely to increase their consumption of electrical energy while reducing their overall energy costs.

When considering the potential for a particular industrial consumer to take dynamic actions, it is useful to assume that this consumer has already optimised its static actions, i.e. that the amount of electrical energy it consumes is optimal, considering the average price of electricity and the revenue it earns from selling its production. This means that this consumer will not simply reduce its production if the price of electricity is significantly higher than average during parts of the day. Instead, it should try to reschedule its production to take advantage of lower prices at other times.

Rescheduling production without reducing total output is possible only if the industrial process can be adjusted to store the final product, an intermediate product, or a factor of production such as heat or cold that requires the consumption of electricity. If the final product can be stored, the overall production can be shifted from periods of high prices to periods of low prices. If only an intermediate product can be stored, only the upstream part of the process can be rescheduled. The ability to store something does not guarantee that rescheduling production to take advantage of periods of low electricity prices will reduce the overall production cost. Determining the optimal production schedule is a complex optimisation problem that must take into consideration a number of factors (Su, 2006):

- The profile of electricity prices over the optimisation horizon
- The profile of demand for the final product
- The storage capacity
- The production capacity
- The losses involved in the storage
- The cost of operating the industrial process at various levels of output
- The cost of restarting the process following an interruption
- All constraints (e.g. labour contracts) on the flexibility of the process.

Some industrial consumers may find it profitable to increase the storage capacity in their process to be able to take further advantage of spot variations in electricity prices. Determining the optimal storage capacity is an even more complex optimisation problem than the optimisation of the production schedule. This capacity optimisation problem must consider jointly the storage and production capacities because there is no point in increasing the storage capacity if there is not enough production capacity to fill it during periods of low electricity prices.

Consumers of electrical energy are generally risk averse and prefer to sign fixed-price contracts that shift the price risk to their supplier. Installing and using some form of storage capacity may be a more effective way to limit exposure to periods of very high prices.

8.6   New demand-side technologies and the data challenge

A situation in which there is more widespread use of dynamic demand-side measures requires augmentation of the power sector's existing information infrastructure. What information is required, by whom and when, depends on the specifics of particular tariffs and their associated demand-side effects.

In existing demand-side implementations, for example, Economy7 electric storage heating, all that is required with regard to infrastructure is two conventional meters and a time switch per participant. With such a tariff, the customer may choose to 'participate' through deferring their consumption, or may prefer to be 'managed' by automatic systems such as the teleswitch. Economy7 controlled by a teleswitch, although contributing to peak-load reductions reflects a very limited form of price responsiveness and, even then, only on the part of the supplier not the end-user. Improved demand-side integration primarily requires improved price information. Such information need not necessarily be real-time; for example, prices could be set every month, or every day, but better accuracy improves options for system optimisation.

For example, in the case of unexpected high demand, real-time prices or other signals could initiate a rapid demand response, which when aggregated could have significant value. Better still, if such demand responses could be confirmed as available before they are actioned, they would become a system balancing resource. The residential electricity contribution of 45% to the system peak suggests that there is significant potential value in such dynamic measures.

Clearly, such a scenario requires real-time bidirectional communications, since the requests for service require confirmation. The 'handshaking' required for such confirmation would involve information such as time, power abatement level, duration and price for service.

The need for different data types is also reflected in the anticipated need for some future coordination of microgeneration, given the challenges that a high-microgeneration scenario poses for the distribution networks. For example, back-feeding when local generation exceeds local demand raises power quality management and safety issues. To realise such options requires a bidirectional data flow between the domestic setting and supplier or third parties and, ideally, consumer appliances.

The extent to which options are available in the future rests heavily on the decisions made by sector actors in relation to 'smart metering'. First, the physical layer of the communication system will determine the speed of data transactions in either direction, which in turn determines the speed of demand responses. Second, the level of flexibility in data protocols will determine whether the right data can be communicated to facilitate novel demand-side measures.

The UK energy regulator Ofgem recently reviewed residential metering (Ofgem, 2006), and placed a conservative figure of 1% potential residential demand reduction from the deployment of smart metering. However, the scope of the review only considered the effect of short-term static-active measure such as 'remembering to turn off lights'. Residential metering trials have recently been announced by the government; however, small trials of a technology cannot gauge the wider effects of that technology upon other market players – for example, the impetus that the mass roll-out of smart meters might give to the development of smart appliances. The mere existence of these trials confirms that there is a bounded rationality about what a meter is and what it can facilitate (Devine-Wright and Devine-Wright, 2006).

The suggestion of a facilitating infrastructure (including meters) that can support a wide number of demand-side actions might appear to add an unnecessary level of complexity and risk, but this is not the case. There are many existing examples of infrastructure that facilitate, but do not prescribe, services or application-level technology – the internet and mobile phone networks being obvious examples. Both of these media have spawned a rich, unpredicted, service industry.

In summary, the full potential for demand-side measures will not be realised without widespread adoption of supportive infrastructure, the focus of which should be a generalised messaging system. Such a system needs some standards to be developed and to determine what data are universally required (for auditing and balancing) and what can be left open for innovation. How this information is reflected to the customer is for innovation and entrepreneurship to decide, and a likely future would see different tariffs, billing and information services per supplier.

8.6.1   *Enabling customer action through knowledge transfer*

A rich literature exists in applied psychology evaluating the effectiveness of information provision to promote energy conservation. This has indicated that providing information is most effective when it is:

- attention grabbing (Gardner and Stern, 2002)
- presented frequently or backed up by reminders (Stern, 1999)
- credible and easily validated by the recipient (Becker and Seligman, 1978; Stern, 1999)
- trustworthy (Craig and McCann, 1978)
- about a specific rather than general environmental issue (Gardner and Stern, 2002)
- specific or tailored to the individual (Dennis and Soderstrom, 1988)
- involves social comparison with people similar to the target audience (e.g. Winnet *et al.*, 1985)
- builds upon an existing commitment to act (Gardner and Stern, 2002)
- is delivered personally (Dennis and Soderstrom, 1988).

However, even the best-designed information campaigns usually only result in modest behaviour change – equivalent to a 10–20% reduction in the target behaviour (e.g. electricity consumption during peak-load periods) and this is only achieved because other factors shaping behaviour, such as financial cost or perceived inconvenience, are perceived to be weak (Stern, 1999).

The choice and format of information campaigns, and the design of appliances or electricity meters, can be influenced by the way in which the end-user is 'perceived' or represented by those involved in the design process. An 'information-deficit' model of public knowledge (e.g. Wynne and Irwin, 1996; Lutzenhiser *et al.*, 2001) can lead to a 'fit and forget' approach to energy demand technologies that is grounded in, and legitimised by, a perceived absence of knowledge, participation or 'care' on the part of the energy user.

This then sets up a self-fulfilling cycle where automated technologies, designed on the presumption of lack of interest or engagement, in turn set up and foster low levels of interest or engagement (Devine-Wright, 2007). Therefore, high levels of automation can decrease the likelihood that an individual actively participates or is willing to accept responsibility for the consequences of their actions. A maximal efficiency in technology approach may bring short-term efficiencies in terms of better coordination of appliance operation across a 24-hour period (in terms of load management), but it can also decrease the action competence of individuals using the appliance. It would therefore seem very important to ensure that even low levels of existing awareness are nurtured. This may be facilitated by the active inclusion in electrical technologies (e.g. meters, monitors, appliances) of both 'inefficiencies' and 'redundancies'. In the case of appliances, this may involve manual operation requirements of otherwise automatic systems, e.g. being required to turn air-conditioning units back on after they have been automatically switched off, or of including switches that permit the over-ride of otherwise optimally 'efficient' systems, in order that householders retain a sense of control of their own electrically powered environments.

8.7   Conclusions

Demand-side management is often characterised as comprising centralised, 'command and control', on/off type systems (perhaps because of the relatively successful 'Economy7' teleswitch being one of few examples in the UK), and demand-side participation is often characterised as causing inconvenience to the consumer.

Such stereotypes diminish the debate and reinforce the entrenched supply-centricity of the energy sector. In reality, electricity demand is governed by a complex variety of human behaviours and appliance types, and the harmful emissions caused by any given activity depend on its time, location and market forces, which in turn determine which supply plant is operating.

This suggests the need for a range of demand-side measures as opposed to a 'one size fits all' approach. However, many types of measure could be facilitated through improvements to the underlying infrastructure, allowing the provision of information flows, which in turn could be utilised by customers and their appliances, as well as suppliers and distributors and their system hardware.

Although there are ongoing efforts in this area by the UK government and energy regulator, there appear to be disconnects between the various policy actors. For example, the smart metering debate has not emphasised the common ground between the needs of distribution system operators and suppliers; rather, these groups appear to be taking parallel paths.

Without better coordination between market and policy-making actors, it is likely that a proliferation of different network standards may emerge, with risks to efficiency and economics:

- Metering technology might not be interoperable, requiring a meter change per supplier, asset stranding or supplier lock-in.
- Transaction costs associated with interfacing to disparate technologies could deter third parties from market involvement (for example, aggregation services).

- Proprietary systems may exclude consumers from using a mixture of microgeneration technology.
- Duplication of research and development costs.

In conclusion, there is a strong case for regulatory and policy action to bring about a power system, a policy framework, and end-user engagement whereby demand-side measures and microgeneration can fairly participate in the electricity market and system management. Moreover, the definition of such systems should necessarily involve potential actors that are not usually associated with the energy sector, for example internet, database and telecommunication experts.

If the above is achieved, there are significant opportunities in this arena for new market creation, system efficiency improvement, and ultimately for CO_2 emissions reduction.

Acknowledgements

This work was supported by the Demand Side Participation work-package of the Supergen Future Network Technologies Consortium (www.supergen-networks.org.uk). Supergen is funded by several research councils, led by the Engineering and Physical Sciences Research Council (EPSRC).

References

Becker, L. J. and Seligman, C. (1978). Reducing air conditioning waste by signalling it is cool outside. *Personality and Social Psychology*, **4**(3), 412–415.

Craig, C. S. and McCann, J. M. (1978). Assessing communication effects on energy consumption. *Journal of Consumer Research*, **5**, 82–88.

CT (2005). *The UK Climate Change Programme: Potential Evolution for Business and the Public Sector*. The Carbon Trust, London.

DEFRA (2006). *Climate Change. The UK Programme 2006*. Department for Environment, Food and Rural Affairs, London.

Dennis, M. L. and Soderstrom, E. J. (1988). Application of social psychological and evaluation research. *Evaluation and Program Planning*, **11**, 77–84.

Devine-Wright, P. (2007). Energy citizenship: psychological aspects of evolution in sustainable energy technologies. In J. Murphy (ed.), *Framing the Present, Shaping the Future: Contemporary Governance of Sustainable Technologies*. Earthscan, London, pp. 63–86.

Devine-Wright, H. and Devine-Wright P. (2004) From demand side management to demand side participation: tracing an environmental psychology of sustainable electricity evolution. *Journal of Applied Psychology*, **6**, 1343–1348.

Devine-Wright, H. and Devine-Wright, P. (2006). Prospects for smart metering in the United Kingdom. In T. Jamasb, W. Nuttall, M. Pollitt (eds), *Future*

Electricity Technologies and Systems. Cambridge University Press, Cambridge, pp.403–417.

DGCG (2005a). *A Scoping Study: Demand Side Measures on the UK Electrical System*. Distributed Generation Coordination Group (DGCG), Department of Trade and Industry (DTI), London.

(2005b). *An Investigation into the Development of Consolidation of Distributed Generation within the Wholesale Electricity Trading Arrangements*. Distributed Generation Coordination Group (DGCG), Department for Trade and Industry (DTI), London.

DTI (2002). *Energy Consumption in the United Kingdom*. Department for Trade and Industry (DTI), London, updated 2005.

(2003). *Energy White Paper: Our Energy Future: Creating a Low Carbon Economy*. The Stationary Office, Department for Trade and Industry, Department for Transport and Department for Environment, Food and Rural Affairs, London.

(2005). *Directory of United Kingdom Energy Statistics*. The Stationery Office, Department for Trade and Industry (DTI), London.

(2006). *Reducing the Cost of System Intermittency Using Demand Side Measures*. Department for Trade and Industry (DTI), London.

(2007). *Energy White Paper: Meeting the Energy Challenge*. The Stationery Office, Department for Trade and Industry, London.

ECI (2003). *The ALTENER Project: Consumer Choice and Carbon Consciousness for Electricity (4CE)*. Environmental Change Institute (ECI), Oxford, UK.

Gardner, G. T. and Stern, P. C. (2002). *Environmental Problems and Human Behavior* (2nd edn). Pearson Custom Publishing, Boston, MA.

Garmeson, K. (2002). *Energy Saving Trust: Desk Research to Inform the Energy Efficiency Marketing Strategy*. Kay Garmeson, London.

Gehring, K. L. (2002). Can yesterday's demand-side management lessons become tomorrow's market solutions? *The Electricity Journal*, **15**(5), 63–69.

Her Majesty's Government (2006). *Climate Change and Sustainable Energy Bill*. The Stationery Office, London.

HoL (2005). *Energy Efficiency Volume II, Evidence*. HL Paper 21-II, 2nd Report of Session 2005/2006. House of Lords, Science and Technology Committee. The Stationery Office, London.

IEA (1970–2003). *Energy Statistics of OECD Countries*. International Energy Agency (IEA), Paris.

(2003). *The Power to Choose: Demand Response in Liberalised Electricity Markets*. International Energy Agency (IEA) and OECD, Paris.

(2004). *A Practical Guide to Demand Side Bidding*. International Energy Agency Demand Side Management Program, International Energy Agency (IEA), Paris.

(2005). *Time of Use Pricing for Demand Management Delivery*. International Energy Agency Demand Side Management Programme, International Energy Agency (IEA), Paris.

Kempton, W. and Montgomery, L. (1982). Folk quantification of energy. *Energy*, **7**(10), 817–827.

Lutzenhiser, L., Harris, C. K. and Olsen, M. E. (2001). Energy, society and environment. In R. Dunlap and W. Michaelson (eds), *Handbook of Environmental Sociology*. Greenwood Press, Westport, CT, pp.222–271.

NGT (2004). *A Guide to Demand Turndown*. National Grid Transco (NGT), available from www.nationalgridinfo.co.uk

(2005). *Great Britain Seven Year Statement*. National Grid Transco (NGT).

Ofgem (2002). *The Review of the First Year of NETA: A Review Document*. Office of Gas and Electricity Markets (Ofgem), London.

(2006). *Metering Working Group Report*. Office of Gas and Electricity Markets (Ofgem), London.

PLMA (2002). *Demand Response: Design Principles for Creating Customer and Market Value*. Peak Load Management Alliance (PLMA), available from www.peaklma.com

Price L., Galitsky, C. and Worrell, E. (2006). End-use technologies – main drivers, and patterns of future demand: industry. Chapter 15 in T. Jamasb, W.J. Nuttall, M.G. Pollitt (eds), *Future Electricity Technologies and Systems*. Cambridge University Press, Cambridge.

SDC (2005). *Seeing the Light: the Impact of Micro-generation on the Way we Use Energy; Qualitative Research Findings*. The Hub Research Consultants, London.

Stern, P. C. (1999). Information, incentives, and proenvironmental consumer behavior. *Journal of Consumer Policy*, **22**, 461–478.

Su, C. L. (2006). *Optimal demand-side participation in spot electricity markets by industrial consumers*. PhD thesis, The University of Manchester.

Telegraph (2006). *The Daily Telegraph*, Monday 6 March.

Tyndall Centre (2006). *Public Perceptions of Nuclear Power, Climate Change and Energy Options in Britain*. Understanding Risk Working Paper 06–02. Centre for Environmental Risk, Norwich, UK.

UKERC (2006). *The Costs and Impacts of Intermittency: An Assessment of the Evidence on the Costs and Impacts of Intermittent Generation on the British Electricity Network*. UK Energy Research Centre, London.

Vermeyen, P. and Belmans, R. (2006). End-use technologies – main drivers, and patterns of future demand: transport. Chapter 16 in T. Jamasb, W.J. Nuttall, M.G. Pollitt (eds), *Future Electricity Technologies and Systems*. Cambridge University Press, Cambridge.

Winnet, R. A., Leckliter, I. N., Chinn, D., Stahl, B. and Love, S. (1985). Effects of television modelling on residential energy conservation. *Journal of Applied Behavior Analysis*, **18**, 33–44.

Wynne, B. and Irwin, P. (1996). *Misunderstanding Science? The Public Reconstruction of Science and Technology*. Cambridge University Press. Cambridge.

9 Enhancing the efficient use of electricity in the business and public sectors

Michael Grubb and James Wilde

(with contributions by Steven Sorrell)

9.1 Introduction

Almost all engineering assessments suggest that improving energy efficiency offers both the cheapest and the quickest route to electricity systems that are both more secure and lower in their environmental impacts. The predecessor to this volume (Jamasb *et al.*, 2006), in common with innumerable other studies, noted a wide array of technologies that appear to offer this potential; spanning buildings, industry and various 'system' technologies. The purpose of both this and the previous chapter is to address the question of what, realistically, can be done to encourage users to adopt more efficient technologies and practices.

Electricity use in the UK is divided roughly equally between the residential, industrial, and service (commercial and public) sectors; with the others (transport, agriculture and energy sector) comprising little over 5% together. The previous chapter focused upon electricity use in the domestic sector and the challenge of getting households more engaged in the opportunities for energy efficiency. This chapter addresses the business and public sector use of electricity.

Particular attention is paid to the *less* energy-intensive components, notably commercial and public sector services, for three reasons:

- As noted in Chapter 8, while industrial use of electricity has increased only slowly (by 36% over roughly the same number of years, i.e. 1970–2006), electricity use in commercial and public services has increased by 150% over the same period.
- The identified potential for cost-effective improvements is substantially greater in these sectors, as shown in Figure 9.1.
- In much of heavy industry, electricity costs are significant and the sector is consequently responsive to price signals, such as those that would be induced by carbon pricing, which is only weakly

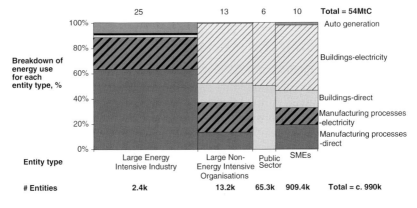

Source: Ecofys

Figure 9.1. UK business and public sector carbon emissions by energy and entity type (2002)

Note: For definition of entity type see text. Direct emissions are CO_2 emissions from gas, oil and coal consumption including those used for direct process conversion (e.g. in cement and steel). Electricity attributed at 1.43 tC/GWh. Building emissions include appliances, computers, etc.

Source: Carbon Trust (2005)

the case in the less energy-intensive sectors, for reasons outlined in this chapter.

Electricity demand in commercial and public services continues to grow in the UK, and DTI 2006 projections forecast and increase of approximately 10% from 2005 to 2020 (DTI, 2006b). It is, consequently, timely to focus on the question of what, if anything, can be done about this growing demand that threatens – just as much as the growth of transport – to wreck the UK's ambitious energy and environmental goals.

9.2   Overview of carbon emissions from business and public sector

Energy efficiency policies and programmes need to be founded on an understanding of the current and projected structure of energy demand. Of the UK's overall carbon emissions of ~150 MtC/year (excluding air transport and GHGs other than CO_2), ~54 MtC comes from the business and the public sector overall (including the attributed portion of power generation emissions).

More relevant than the generic split between 'industry' and 'services' is to segment these sectors into four categories based on the entity types that need to be engaged, and the principal types of use. Figure 9.1 indicates how UK CO_2 emissions from both direct fuels (solid areas) and electricity (hatched areas) are divided between four entity types (horizontal):

- *Large energy-intensive users*, which we have defined as sectors for which more than one-third of their emissions are covered by either the EU Emission Trading Scheme or the UK's Climate Change Agreements, both of which have been targeted at energy-intensive sectors (size cut-off applied of >50 employees in manufacturing sectors).
- *Large non-energy-intensive users*, which covers both low energy-intensive manufacturing and the larger service sector organisations (size cut-off applied of >50 employees in manufacturing sectors and >250 employees in service sectors).
- *Public sector*, covering all government estate including education, hospitals, local government, etc.
- *Small and medium-sized enterprises (SMEs)*, defined here as companies with <50 employees in manufacturing sectors or <250 employees in service sectors – almost 1 million legal entities in total.

As illustrated in Figure 9.1, the first category accounted for about 45% of the *total* business and public sector CO_2 emissions in 2002 – but barely a quarter of the *electricity-related* emissions. The energy-intensive sectors are dominated by activities such as steel and cement manufacturing that consume huge quantities of direct fuels. With the prime exception of aluminium smelting, electricity consumption is largely accounted for by far less energy-intensive operations.

Figure 9.1 also illustrates the split between emissions attributable to manufacturing process operations, and those associated with building occupancy, including heating, lighting, refrigeration and 'plug-in' loads such as computers. In the less energy-intensive sectors, electricity consumption accounted for about 70% of the total emissions; and electricity use in buildings-related uses, rather than manufacturing processes, accounted for at least two-thirds of this.

The complexity of tackling electricity use is indicated by the fact that these sectors comprise almost 1 million organisations. And yet, about half of the total use was accounted for by just 13,000 large companies – for example, supermarket and retail chains, financial service companies, etc. This is key to the proposal presented towards the end of the chapter for improving the efficiency with which they use electricity.

9.3   The technical and economic potential for carbon abatement

The abatement potential can be expected to vary by sector, and over time as capital stock replacement facilitates new opportunities. The Carbon Trust employed consultants ECOFYS to combine analysis from the ENUSIM model for manufacturing and the BRE model for buildings to establish the mitigation potential available by 2010 and 2020 (Carbon Trust, 2005). Figure 9.2 summarises the findings. This suggests that the potential emission reductions from the take-up of currently available more-efficient technologies by 2020 (allowing for stock turnover, etc.) would total around 25%, with more than half (15%) assessed as being 'cost-effective', i.e. financial rate of return >15%. Moreover, the cost-effective potential is largest in both the sector of highest electricity use (large non-energy-intensives, at 18%); and the activity that dominates this consumption (buildings-related consumption, with 22% cost-effective potential).

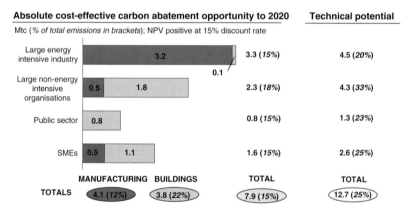

Figure 9.2. Carbon abatement opportunity by 2020: cost-effective (at 15% discount rate) and identified technical potentials by energy use and entity type

Note: Carbon-saving opportunity is based on detailed sector-level source data (ENUSIM and BRE abatement curves), providing a measure-by-measure breakdown of abatement opportunities using existing technologies and their cost implications (buildings figures based on opportunity in existing stock only). Cost-effective opportunity has positive net present value (NPV) at 15% discount rate; full technical potential includes all measures in abatement curves. Opportunity as stated does not allow for innovation and introduction of new technologies between now and 2020 (which would be expected to significantly increase the figures shown).

Source: Carbon Trust (2005)

Thus, really tackling the inefficiencies in how the business and public sectors use electricity could be expected to save up to 20% of their consumption – potentially at net economic benefit (note also that the sectors and activities with the greatest cost-effective potential are also those of most rapid projected growth). As discussed at the end of the chapter, the emission savings could, in practice, be even higher. Tackling climate change cost-effectively, in other words, means tackling the reasons why companies and other organisations apparently waste so much electricity, particularly in the buildings they occupy.

9.4   Drivers for, and barriers to, energy efficiency uptake

From a policy perspective, the key question is why the take-up of energy-efficient technologies is so slow when it appears so attractive. More fundamentally, the key to effective policy on energy efficiency is to understand in depth what factors drive, and what factors impede, changes in investment or other behaviour towards more energy-efficient choices.

The evidence around the inefficiencies in business energy use, and the barriers that explain this, is well documented (for a comprehensive analysis of energy inefficiencies in UK business, see Sorrell *et al.*, 2004). However, to date, most surveys have focused on listing barriers, rather than looking at their common roots and the relationship with what drives organisational change. From a business perspective, understanding what drives change is just as important as understanding the barriers. Our analysis sets these alongside each other and concludes that both barriers and drivers fall into four main categories, as summarised in Figure 9.3. Moreover, these can be ordered in a progression from the ideal of a perfectly optimising market with optimising agents to the messy reality of imperfect structures and decision-making in real organisations:

1. *Financial cost/benefit* expresses the simple trade-off between investment costs as a barrier, and energy cost savings as the driver.
2. *Hidden costs and co-benefits* are costs that may be real but are not expressed in financial terms (e.g. from transaction costs to imperfect substitutes) set against the intangible benefits that may also flow from adopting newer, better and lower-emitting equipment and practices.
3. *Split incentives and market failures* reflect all the ways in which contractual structures prevent a true alignment of costs and benefits; the most obvious example being the tenant–landlord split in rented buildings, and various misalignments in the corporate supply chain.

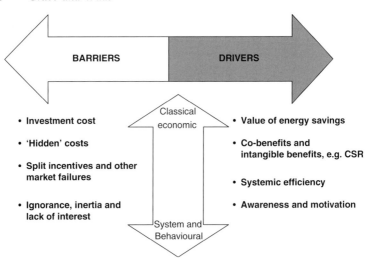

Figure 9.3. Barriers to, and drivers for, energy efficiency uptake
Source: Carbon Trust (2005)

4. *Organisational and behavioural realities* encompass all the ways in which organisations themselves fail to behave in a fully cost-optimising way due to limitations in information and organisational capacity, which leads to well-documented patterns of satisficing, inertia and rule-of-thumb approaches.

Figure 9.4 defines and summarises these categories more precisely, with examples and indications of some of the policy options that could be considered to leverage/overcome the drivers and barriers. We now discuss each in turn.

9.4.1   *Investment and returns: financial cost/benefit*

The first category is a straightforward financial calculation, in which the required additional investment is the main barrier and the financial value of reduced energy consumption is the main driver. This encapsulates the most simple view of corporate decision making, that it is a rational trade-off based purely on financial criteria. The associated policy levers are equally simple: increasing energy efficiency requires either reducing the up-front cost of more-efficient technologies, or increasing energy prices to the users.

The first question is thus whether prices are right – and, in particular, whether energy prices fully reflect environmental damage, systemic risks

Category	Definition	Examples	Policy options
Financial cost–benefit	Ratio of investment cost to value of energy savings	• More expensive but more efficient equipment	• Economic instruments that reduce equipment cost or finance cost, or increase energy prices • Direct legislative drivers on energy / emissions

Expanded cost–benefit (intangible, transaction and transition costs)	Cost or risk (real or perceived) of moving (or not moving) to more energy-efficient practices including managerial, information, risk and decision-making requirements, not captured above	• Costs and risks of change
		  - Incompatibility
		  - Performance risk
		  - Management time
		  - Other transaction costs
		• Exposure of not changing
		  - Higher emissions risk
		  - Equipment obsolescence
		  - Customer / employee pressure
			• Services providing information, technical support
			• Packaged energy service contracts
			• Standards requiring use of a particular technology/solution, e.g. product standards, etc. to avoid transaction costs

Market Misalignment (split incentives, system failures regulatory failures)	Market structure and constraints that prevent consistent trade-off between specific energy efficient investment and the societal energy saving benefits	• Landlord / tenant split • Regulatory failures, e.g. in electricity • First-mover costs and risks • Externally-imposed budget constraints	• Contractual or market organisation solutions to split incentives between organisations • Product standards Capital market solutions (e.g. public sector financing scheme) • Socialisation of first-mover costs
Behaviour and motivation (inertia, awareness, materiality)	Internal issues of firm behaviour linked to awareness, motivation and internal organisation	• Organisational failures (e.g. internal split incentives) • Inertia, rules of thumb • Tendency to ignore small opportunities	• Campaigns, sector learning networks • 'Attention raising' instruments, e.g. trading; CCAs with sector targets and 'cliff' incentives (tax exemption) • ECA lists and low interest loans available to equipment purchasers in organisations

Figure 9.4. Barrier–driver categories for uptake of energy efficiency and related policy options
Source: Carbon Trust (2005)

or other 'external' costs. Where they do not, there is a *prima facie* economic case for correcting this with economic instruments such as taxes and/or emission trading systems. Unfortunately, getting energy prices 'right' through such measures is politically difficult and faces huge uncertainties; and, in terms of energy efficiency, it may not even be addressing the most important driver–barrier across all sectors.

For energy-intensive sectors, in which energy is a major part of operating costs, the financial cost–benefit balance may well be a primary consideration. In most sectors, however, other factors are more important.

9.4.2 Hidden costs, intangible benefits: expanded cost–benefit

The second broad category is costs and benefits that are real but are not captured directly in financial flows. For example, if more-efficient equipment is newer but less reliable, or is harder to get serviced, that is a real cost to the user. If new light bulbs or motors do not fit in the old sockets or frames, that is a real – albeit transitional – cost. Also, if simply evaluating the options of more-efficient equipment or practices takes the time and attention of senior management, that is a real cost; the same is true of other potential 'transaction' costs of negotiating deals on more-efficient equipment.

Table 9.1. *Types of hidden cost*

Sub-category	Examples
General overhead costs of energy management	• costs of employing specialist people (e.g. energy manager) • costs of energy information systems (including: gathering of energy consumption data; maintaining sub-metering systems; analysing data and correcting for influencing factors; identifying faults; etc.) • cost of energy auditing
Costs involved in individual technology decisions	• cost of identifying opportunities; detailed investigation and design; formal investment appraisal • cost of formal procedures for seeking approval of capital expenditures • cost of specification and tendering for capital works to manufacturers and contractors • additional staff costs for maintenance • costs for replacement, early retirement, or retraining of staff • cost of disruptions and inconvenience
Loss of utility associated with energy-efficient choices	• problems with safety, noise, working conditions, service quality, etc. (e.g. lighting levels) • extra maintenance, lower reliability

Source: Sorrell *et al.* (2004)

Hidden costs come in a variety of forms (Table 9.1), but in many cases may be reduced through either policy intervention or organisational change. Also, hidden costs will be incurred for both energy efficient and inefficient choices (e.g. purchasing both energy efficient and inefficient motors), so what matters is the difference between the two. Some types of hidden cost may only be relevant when routines are changed (e.g. when a shift is made from purchasing standard to high-frequency fluorescent lighting) and may also decrease over time as the relevant knowledge becomes embedded within an organisation.

Most types of energy efficiency investment also have hidden benefits. For example, Lovins and Lovins (1997) used case studies to argue that better visual, acoustic and thermal comfort in well-designed, energy-efficient buildings can improve labour productivity by as much as 16%. Since labour costs in commercial buildings are typically 25 times greater than energy costs, the resulting cost savings can potentially dwarf those from reduced energy consumption. Similarly, Pye and McKane (1998) showed how the installation of energy-efficient motors reduced wear and tear, extended the lifetime of system components and achieved savings in capital and labour costs that exceeded the reduction in energy costs.

Benefits that are real, but less tangible than direct money savings, may also be important drivers. Benefits of more energy-efficient investment may include reduced exposure to future energy price volatility, or the 'corporate social responsibility' benefits associated with being seen to act responsibility in respect of environmental impacts; for example, in terms of 'green' consumers, 'ethical' financial institutions, or employee benefits.

Hidden costs and intangible benefits are complex and diverse, with correspondingly complex policy implications. Some forms of hidden costs may be inescapable and enduring. Others may be transitional, so that, if policy drives businesses to make more efficient purchases once, this becomes the least-cost default in subsequent decisions. Others still may be entirely policy-dependent; for example, if transaction costs are a principal barrier, an obvious solution is product standards that simply outlaw inefficient equipment – everyone then avoids the time and hassle of working out what bad purchases to avoid. Mandating clear information and labelling may be an intermediate solution, vastly reducing the cost to users of finding out about the energy performance of potential purchases.

Lack of adequate skills may similarly raise barriers. Organisations are often unwilling to take on the risks of installing new technology with which they are unfamiliar, particularly if they perceive any risk of compromising the running of core operations. Policy measures to overcome this barrier are likely to include services providing information or technical support, packaged energy contracts or, most bluntly, standards that mandate the use of a minimum energy performance.

Policies that create increased transparency and awareness can be used to leverage intangible benefits such as 'corporate social responsibility'. An example is a trading scheme linked to clear financial reporting guidelines, acting as an awareness-raising scheme that makes emissions reduction a compliance issue as much as an economic incentive for change.

9.4.3   Split incentives, system and regulatory failures: market misalignment

The third category of drivers and barriers lies where market structures prevent the benefits of an investment accruing to the organisation concerned. Conversely, the associated driver would be anything that helps 'external' benefits – i.e. benefits to society – accrue to those undertaking related actions.

The classic example of this barrier is the tenant–landlord split, which is particularly prevalent in commercial buildings. In the UK, only 10% of commercial property is occupied by the freeholder and 70% is multi-tenanted. Much of the stock is owned by institutional investors who treat the property purely as an asset, while management is outsourced to property consultants who pay little attention to energy efficiency (Wade *et al.*, 2003). Tenants may have little motivation to improve the performance of an asset they do not own, particularly if they have a short-term lease, while owners will be happy to pass on the energy costs to their tenants. In many cases, tenants will simply pay a fixed pro-rata share of the building's energy bill, which means that the savings generated by investment or behavioural changes by one tenant would accrue to all the other tenants as well, thereby diluting the incentive. The problem could be overcome through low-level sub-metering, but this could be costly and appears to be relatively rare.

There are many other examples of such split incentives. In most countries, electricity supply companies are responsible for the nature of meters installed in premises, but have no direct interest in (and may indeed lose out from) advanced metering that would enable their customers to better monitor and control their usage.

Supply chain structures may also promote inefficiencies. For example, a recent study revealed that a major contributor to energy consumption in potato crisp production – frying the potato – was driven mostly by the moisture content of the potato. However, because potatoes were bought on a weight basis, farmers were also using energy to artificially humidify the potatoes (Carbon Trust, 2006).

More generally, innovative investments and changed practices may generate large societal benefits through the learning acquired, but it may often be hard for a particular company to capture these wider benefits (Arrow, 1962). The majority may well hold back, waiting for someone else to pay for the 'field testing' that is a key part of establishing better technologies on a commercial scale. The hope of establishing a market leading position can be an important driver, but in general the result is persistent under-investment in innovative solutions.

A final, pervasive area of such failure is in capital availability – or the lack thereof – when it is imposed from outside. For example, budgetary constraints imposed on some public-sector organisations mean that they lack the capital to undertake even those investments that would yield net savings within just a couple of years.

Policy measures to overcome this barrier are likely to be contractual or market-organisation solutions to split incentives between organisations, standards, or explicit capital-market solutions; one example is the Salix fund established by the Carbon Trust to support public-sector energy efficiency investments. More often, however, 'lack of capital' for such investments reflects the fourth and final barrier – the realities of how most organisations actually behave in relation to non-core investment.

9.4.4 Inertia, awareness and materiality: organisational behaviour and motivation

The final area of barriers and drivers concerns the many ways in which organisational behaviour differs from the theoretical ideal of consistent, rational decision-making that maximises company profits.

This is generally reflected in a mix of 'internal split incentives' and simple payback criteria. From an economic point of view, energy efficiency investments should compete against alternative capital projects on a 'net present value' basis, i.e. with the stream of costs and benefits discounted by the relevant interest rate. However, energy efficiency is rarely core to a company's strategy; it may reduce costs, but even this may be modest compared with more radical measures such as staff reductions or relocation of production facilities.

Managers rarely have ring-fenced budgets dedicated to energy efficiency, and a lack of prioritisation at this level is also a significant barrier. As a result, even in organisations that may be sophisticated in core business evaluation, energy-related choices may be relegated to simple payback criteria, or even just taken on the basis of lowest first cost (Department of Energy, 1984; Sorrell et al., 2004). Given severe constraints on time and attention, the small reductions in costs available from energy efficiency investments are often downgraded and overlooked, despite the fact that such investments have frequently been shown to have a higher rate of return than large projects which receive more management attention (Ross, 1986).

Distrust of the energy savings may arise because monitoring requires the use of unfamiliar equipment – or because there is an inability to monitor savings, due to inadequate metering. This can lead to a risk-averse attitude amongst decision-makers. Because energy costs are often not material to many companies' competitive position, the incentives to sort out such organisational inefficiencies are minimal.

In many organisations, the person making the relevant decisions – for example, the engineer responsible for upgrading or replacing motor drives, or an IT equipment manager – may have no interest in the energy consumption of the product. Many items of equipment may be specified and procured by individuals who lack the knowledge, information and incentives to minimise operating costs, while constraints on staff time may inhibit the involvement of energy management staff. Similarly, maintenance staff may have a strong incentive to minimise capital costs and/or to get failed equipment working again as soon as possible, but may have no incentive to minimise running costs. This type of issue may also arise with building users, operators of process equipment, and designers and sub-contractors within construction projects.

If individual departments were accountable for their own energy costs, they could directly benefit from any savings from investment projects or housekeeping measures. But if cost savings are recouped elsewhere, this incentive is diluted. To introduce such accountability, it would be necessary to sub-meter and bill individual cost centres for their energy use – which would be associated with investment, staff and operational costs. The resulting incentives will be proportional to the importance of energy costs to the individual department and would only be effective if the department had the capacity to identify and initiate energy efficiency improvements. An alternative and preferable approach in many instances would be to place accountability for energy costs with the energy management staff, perhaps with individual posts made self-funding from the savings from energy efficiency improvements.

A striking example of the size of opportunities being routinely overlooked was BP's experience after deciding to address its own CO_2 emissions by reducing internal energy wastage – a programme which BP estimate ended up saving around £600 million per year in reducing the company's CO_2 emissions by around 10%. WBCSD (2002) has documented many such examples from a range of industries.

Few companies operate at such a scale, but the principle is the same. A troublesome issue for many economists is the implication that apparently well-managed and successful companies are overlooking such potential improvements in their economic – as well as energy – efficiency (Sutherland, 1994, 1996). In fact, this is not remotely a new suggestion in the management literature and is beginning to become mainstream in the economics literature as well. For example, the Nobel-prize-winning work of authors such as such as Stiglitz and Weiss (1981) in information economics and Kahneman and Tversky (2000) in behavioural economics can provide compelling explanations for this behaviour as well as pointing to some potential policy solutions (Sorrell et al., 2004). As an example, DeCanio (1993, 1994) has developed theories of firms as internal networks that, to cope with complexity, develop 'rules of thumb' that lead them to concentrate on their core business and miss other opportunities. In a similar manner, Howarth et al. (2000) have shown how modern 'theories of the firm' can explain why US businesses neglected energy-efficient lighting projects with an average annual rate of return of 45% and why targeted intervention – under the Green Lights Program – from the US Environmental Protection Agency enabled them to exploit such win–win opportunities:

> The decision-making level within the firm's hierarchy that maximises firm-wide profits for energy efficiency investments is where facilities management and production budgets are combined on the same ledger. This may be as high as the office of the chief financial officer. Without outside intervention, this level of the firm typically would not evaluate lighting retrofits or similar decisions. Such decisions would be left to appropriate divisions, where a negative decision likely would be reached. By focusing attention and providing credible data on products and services. Green Lights contributes to the resolution of this organisational failure (Howarth *et al.*, 2000, p. 483).

Whether and how such inefficiencies can be overcome is then a key challenge in climate change policy. The key issues with addressing this barrier revolve around lack of awareness, motivation and often indifference to taking action. The principal solutions, short of direct regulation, are twofold: to get help directly to energy decision-makers within firms – for example with technical or targeted financial assistance; and to use levers that raise awareness and motivate their senior managers to sort out the internal organisational failures that dominate this issue, not least in respect of how companies use energy in their buildings.

9.5   Mapping drivers and barriers onto emission sources

The drivers and barriers set out here do not apply uniformly across the different sectors, nor indeed the different types, of energy use. Figure 9.5, derived by aggregating the results of various market surveys, maps the relative importance of the different driver–barriers against the market segmentations introduced in Figure 9.1. This keeps the distinction between process-related and buildings-related energy use, because the same entities may treat these two differently and they may not even be subject to the same incentives: generally, an energy-intensive company may pay attention to the energy use in its process equipment, for which it is responsible, but still be relatively ignorant about the energy used by the buildings it occupies, which may indeed be rented and beyond the reach of the company to influence much.

Two main patterns emerge of importance for policy. In terms of energy use types, the evidence suggests that for *manufacturing energy use*, financial cost–benefit is a significant consideration but far from being

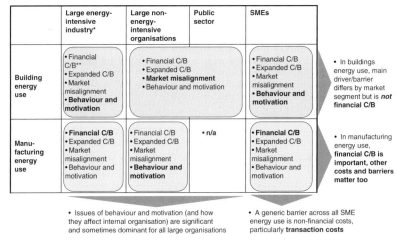

	Large energy-intensive industry*	Large non-energy-intensive organisations	Public sector	SMEs	
Building energy use	• Financial C/B** • Expanded C/B • Market misalignment • **Behaviour and motivation**	• Financial C/B • Expanded C/B • **Market misalignment** • Behaviour and motivation		• Financial C/B • Expanded C/B • Market misalignment • **Behaviour and motivation**	• In buildings energy use, main driver/barrier differs by market segment but is *not* financial C/B
Manu-facturing energy use	• **Financial C/B** • Expanded C/B • Market misalignment • Behaviour and motivation	• Financial C/B • Expanded C/B • Market misalignment • **Behaviour and motivation**	• n/a	• **Financial C/B** • Expanded C/B • Market misalignment • Behaviour and motivation	• In manufacturing energy use, **financial C/B is important, other costs and barriers matter too**

• Issues of behaviour and motivation (and how they affect internal organisation) are significant and sometimes dominant for all large organisations

• A generic barrier across all SME energy use is non-financial costs, particularly **transaction costs**

* Includes EU ETS and CCA sector companies with >50 employees

Figure 9.5. Mapping barrier–drivers against energy use and entity type
Source: Carbon Trust (2005)

the only one. Issues of expanded cost–benefit are also often important and take a variety of forms: on the cost side, the difficulty and potential cost of switching to new production methods and the transaction costs of evaluating new options; on the driver side, the fact that new more energy-efficient processes are often also more modern and have better production control technologies in many dimensions. In many cases, the idea that energy efficiency has to be traded off against other attributes is the reverse of reality, because newer technologies may embody better control technologies that improve production as well as energy performance – but switching to better processes may still not be easy.

In terms of the different market segments, the large energy-intensive industries pay the greatest attention to financial cost–benefit considerations – though even in this segment, the experience of Climate Change Agreements has shown considerable room for improvement. For SMEs, transaction costs, and the hidden costs of making demands on the time of over-pressed managers, are major factors, along with the lack of skills in many such companies to manage their energy. But issues of market misalignment and organisational structures dominate for the large non-energy-intensives and the public sector. Some typical insights into the realities, which illustrate these barriers in stark ways, are illustrated in Figure 9.6.

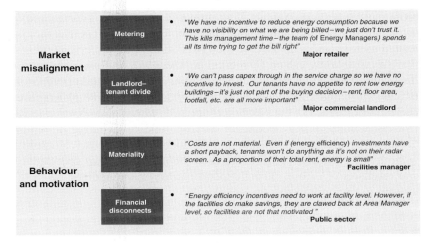

Figure 9.6. Key barriers to uptake of energy efficiency in non-domestic buildings: illustrations
Source: Carbon Trust (2005); participant at consultation workshops held in March and May 2005

9.6   Setting standards

In such circumstances, one appealing policy route is setting standards.

9.6.1   Building energy standards

The most obvious application is building energy performance standards. The UK's building stock has been notoriously inefficient and, driven largely by the growth of environmental concerns, standards were radically tightened in 2005. In the context of this book's study of UK electricity, however, building standards offer only a very limited contribution. They apply principally to new-build and major retrofits which, given the slow turnover in UK building stock, greatly limits their contribution to emission savings over the next couple of decades. Despite this, it is estimated that the new standards could save up to 3 MtC/year by 2020 (Carbon Trust, 2005). However, the major gains from building standards relate to *thermal* performance, which is primarily to do with direct fuels, not electricity.

The European Energy Performance in Buildings Directive (EPBD), which came into force in January 2006, greatly increases the range of buildings covered by requiring owners and occupiers of buildings over 1,000 m² floor area to generate energy performance certificates: both asset ratings and operational ratings. The latter will measure the (normalised)[1] actual energy consumption of a building, capturing most electricity-related uses. In buildings that are used to provide a public service, and are therefore frequently visited by the public, there will be a requirement to display the operational rating in a public place. Both asset and operational ratings will come with a list of recommendations on how to improve energy performance in the building concerned. This is an important lever that could make energy efficiency part of building purchase or rental decisions by increasing transparency of building energy use. However, without any particular obligations to act, the impact remains speculative, and estimates of carbon saving depend entirely upon assumed levels of take-up in response to this transparency.[2]

9.6.2   *Product standards and labelling*

Whilst building standards and the EPBD are particularly suited to the thermal performance of buildings – with the major savings likely to be in gas use – it is the products used by the non-energy-intensive sectors that dominate their electricity use. Some of the challenges for energy-consuming products are conceptually remarkably similar to those for buildings. The two dimensions of driving technical improvements, and informing users about options, can be addressed, respectively, through *product standards* and *labels and lists*:

- *Minimum standards* set compulsory standards to remove poor equipment from the marketplace, with the option to tighten standards over time. Simply removing the option of installing inefficient equipment can be particularly important in facilities management, where it is often easier to replace like-for-like rather than investigate more energy-efficient alternatives.

---

[1] To take account of deviations from standard usage patterns, the operational rating will need to be normalised before it can be compared with benchmark information.

[2] The analysis in Carbon Trust (2005) assumes 10% take-up rate for asset ratings and 15% for operational ratings. These estimates are based on the lower end of implementation rates observed in the site surveys conducted by the Carbon Trust across the commercial and public sectors. Finally, it was assumed that, if the implementation of cost-effective measures was made obligatory in asset ratings, an additional take-up of 1% p.a. could be achieved on an ongoing basis (i.e. 10% take-up from making cost-effective opportunities transparent and a 1% p.a. take-up from making implementation obligatory). On this basis, the total carbon savings would amount to over 1 MtC p.a. reduction by 2020, on top of the 3 MtC saving achievable through the UK building regulations described above. The Carbon Trust study noted also that savings could easily vary by a factor of 2, depending upon how governments chose to interpret and implement the EPBD Directive.

• *Labelling or the creation of preferred accredited technology listings* allows business consumers to differentiate products and create a market pull for better energy performance.

International experience Both approaches can be implemented in a number of different forms. For example, Japan and the USA have introduced variant forms of minimum standards that offer increased flexibility for manufacturers to improve standards over time.

Japan's Top Runner programme sets standards according to the energy efficiency level of the most efficient product available in a given category (this covers passenger cars and trucks, air-conditioners, heat pumps, fluorescent lights, refrigerators, TVs, videos, photocopiers, computers and hard-disk drives). Basing targets on best-in-class equipment dramatically improves the energy efficiency of products and stimulates technology development. For example, the Top Runner programme is expected to deliver a $\sim$60% reduction in the weighted average energy consumption of heat pumps by 2010. However, the Top Runner programme achieves this in a flexible way by setting a lower limit for the average efficiency of each manufacturer's total output, rather than imposing minimum energy performance standards for individual appliances. This gives more freedom to the manufacturer to adapt to the new regulation: they are free to keep higher-energy-consuming equipment on the market but they have to stimulate purchases of more energy efficient equipment in order to meet the sales-weighted average efficiency target.

The USA's Corporate Average Fuel Economy (CAFE) standards for passenger cars and light trucks adopted a similar approach to allow increased flexibility for manufacturers. The CAFE standards are applied on a fleet-wide basis for each manufacturer, i.e. the fuel economy ratings for a manufacturer's entire line of passenger cars must average above the standard set for fuel consumption. Manufacturers earn 'credits' for exceeding CAFE standards, and these credits can be used to offset fuel economy shortfalls in the three previous and/or three subsequent model years.

In the EU, most applications of energy efficiency standards and labels have been in the domestic sector, and are much less developed in commercial and business sector equipment, partly due to the diversity of these sectors.

Applications in the UK business and public sector The UK Government's Enhanced Capital Allowance scheme for energy-saving equipment, under which companies can claim 100% tax depreciation for expenditure on energy-efficient products, acts just as much as a driving force to improve the quality of goods that manufacturers bring to market. To qualify for a capital allowance, equipment must appear on the Energy Technology List (ETL). Currently, nearly 9,000 products from 15 technology groups have qualified to appear on the ETL. The qualification criteria for the ETL have impacted on the product development of many manufacturers, who value the seal of approval associated with qualification for a government financial incentive. Raising the ETL eligibility criteria is thus one means of improving the products brought to market, without going so far as to set obligatory standards.

There are a number of products used in non-domestic buildings where standards could be applicable, particularly in the areas of heating and lighting. Figure 9.7 shows five illustrative technologies that product standards could be applied to, selected from the detailed BRE abatement curves in conjunction with representatives from the Government's Market Transformation Programme who are tasked with improving the energy efficiency of products.

Figure 9.7 indicates that, for just the illustrative products selected, minimum standards introduced from today could save ~1.3 MtC/year by 2020 compared with current performance; the corresponding

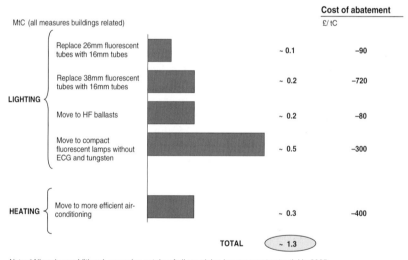

Note: *All savings additional, assuming uptake of all remaining improvement potential in 2005

Figure 9.7. Carbon savings by 2020 achievable from application of product standards in selected electricity-saving products
Source: Carbon Trust (2005)

reduction in electricity consumption would be about 10TWh/year. Allowing for realistic replacement cycles and the expected uptake of higher efficiency equipment that would have occurred in any case might halve the savings directly attributed to such standards.

Mandatory labelling would require manufacturers to explicitly label their products with energy efficiency performance data, audited by verification agencies. These data could also be used to compile and update the energy technology list (ETL), explicitly linking the labelling scheme to the system of Enhanced Capital Allowances for such equipment, to strengthen the business case for manufacturers to improve their energy efficiency standards. Clearly, however, labelling rather than standards would tend to lower uptake of the cost-effective opportunity.

There are other areas where product standards could offer significant efficiency gains. One of these is IT equipment, where product standards could focus on either the procurement of better quality equipment or on the more effective use of current stock, or both. Whilst any requirement to replace equipment inevitably carries a cost, changes in usage require minimal expenditure.

One potentially powerful, but simple, tool to change the way in which IT is used by businesses is to utilise existing power management capabilities that allow computers and monitors to enter low-power states when sitting idle. Nearly all machines now carry the facility but use is very low in practice, estimated at only 5%. Equipment is not always shipped with power management enabled, and even when it is, the facility is routinely disabled by the receiving IT department – who are, of course, not held accountable for the added costs and emissions involved.

Whilst not all PCs can be power managed (network connections must be kept open), there is no such restriction on monitors. In the US Energy Star programme, the 'Million Monitor Drive' initiative has successfully increased enablement rates to 60% amongst its target group of the Fortune 500 companies in the USA – far above the 5% utilisation in the UK. This has been achieved by actively targeting energy managers and guiding them to activate the appropriate settings over the telephone. Depending on the rate at which more-efficient technology comes into use, the savings from compulsory power management for monitors could be ∼0.1–0.2 MtC/year – perhaps representing 1 TWh/year of electricity consumption.

Product and building standards and labelling address two of the challenges in addressing energy use in non-intensive operations, but their impact may be impeded by the resistance of manufacturers, the bluntness of applying standards across differentiated products, the difficulty of continually ratcheting standards as technologies advance, and the fact that users may not respond to information when the costs are immaterial.[3] Delivering the full potential of energy efficiency requires attention to the third challenge outlined for the non-energy-intensive sectors: motivating the users to do better. This leads to the consideration of new instruments.

9.7   New instruments

Building and product standards would still not tackle the way companies operate their buildings and equipment. Currently, the only policy lever operating on this is the UK Climate Change Levy.[4] Widespread evidence, set out above, shows that this is a weak driver in the less energy-intensive sectors; if the commercial and public sector price elasticities are only around 0.1, even a 50% rise in energy bills would reduce energy use by only 5%.

Thus, much of the service sector, and in the longer term the less energy-intensive parts of CCA sectors, represent important gaps in present UK climate change policy, as illustrated schematically in Figure 9.8. Yet, many companies in these sectors have highly competent management structures that could be used to translate best practice in energy management across their operations nationwide. The challenge is to identify instruments that could leverage the attention of these companies to address the wastage in their energy use.

Several approaches can be considered. One is to adopt a 'baseline and credit' system that seeks to incentivise specific actions, rather than addressing emissions in their entirety. Rather than capping and recording overall emissions, these would give participants credits (or 'white certificates') for achieving savings relative to baselines, or for

---

[3] In addition, product standards may well overlap with incentives from other instruments, including prices, EPBD operational standards, ECA lists, etc. Product standards might ensure that some changes will occur more rapidly, but a significant proportion of the changes would be expected to be achieved in the longer term through other routes. One area where standards may well prove additional, even in the long term, is across the SME market, where transaction costs could otherwise inhibit the uptake of better-performing equipment and where trading schemes are unlikely to be introduced in the short term.

[4] Many of the somewhat more energy-intensive companies are covered by the Climate Change Agreements. Questions remain around the continuing effectiveness of the CCAs and their future. The CCAs have been a useful instrument, but it is unclear whether future rounds of target-setting negotiations should or will be considered after the current agreements expire, and many of the current CCA sectors may not be appropriate to move into the facility-based systems of the EU ETS, which is designed for large individual facilities and which anyway does not embody electricity at end-use.

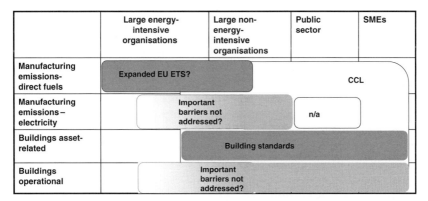

	Large energy-intensive organisations	Large non-energy-intensive organisations	Public sector	SMEs
Manufacturing emissions–direct fuels	Expanded EU ETS?			CCL
Manufacturing emissions–electricity		Important barriers not addressed?	n/a	
Buildings asset-related		Building standards		
Buildings operational		Important barriers not addressed?		

Figure 9.8. Key gaps in coverage of the UK Climate Change Programme
Source: Carbon Trust (2005)
Note: chart indicates the current coverage of policy instruments. The EU ETS and CCA focus only on energy-intensive sectors; the CCL is the only economic instrument acting upon the rest. Building standards do not capture manufacturing or operational emissions and the CCL does not address the key non-economic barriers; nor does the EU ETS address these barriers in respect of electricity-related emissions.

implementing specific energy-efficiency equipment or projects. Amongst large organisations, this would give companies credits for specific verified carbon-abatement projects, which could then be purchased by a set-aside government fund, or sold into trading systems through approved linkage mechanisms. This would target 'asset'-related abatement opportunities, associated with the purchase of more efficient equipment rather than behavioural measures, which are harder to monitor and verify. There is a total of ~2.1 MtC cost-effective 'asset-based' abatement opportunity in the buildings abatement curve. Large non-energy-intensive organisations and public sector buildings, the key target markets for such project certificates, make up about two-thirds of this opportunity (~1.4 MtC). If, by 2020, about 50% of the cost-effective asset-related measures are taken up (not 100% due to its voluntary nature and implementation complexities), this would deliver ~0.6 MtC/year. If the government were to purchase these carbon savings at a future EU ETS price of €30/tCO$_2$ (£70/tC), the total cost to government would be ~£40 million/year in 2020.

However, in addition to the limitations to 'asset-based' opportunities (when a significant proportion of abatement opportunities are associated with behavioural change) and their, voluntary nature, it may be hard to disentangle truly additional projects from those that would have happened anyway, regardless of the scheme. And, partly as a result, the cost-effectiveness is questionable: the government would effectively be paying for carbon savings that are already cost-effective, and obviously the larger projects are likely to generate larger energy bill savings, despite being more expensive for the fund to support. Also, the verification of such white certificates would need complex, costly up-front and ongoing monitoring of individual projects and devices. Pre-selecting a rigid pool of acceptable measures may make verification simpler, but would significantly reduce the potential carbon savings that such a scheme could generate. On this basis, other routes to addressing the large non-energy-intensive sectors seem more preferable, though project-based white certificates could play a role in relation to emissions that could not be captured under other approaches (e.g. some non-CO_2 greenhouse gas sources).

An apparently more forceful approach would be to shift the onus on to energy suppliers to limit their customers' energy consumption. The idea of placing a cap on allowable sales from energy suppliers has attracted considerable popular attention, but the exact nature of the proposal is often unclear. Figure 9.9 maps the specific options. An 'auctioned cap' is probably the only viable option. However, such approaches do not engage the user and it could end up with suppliers

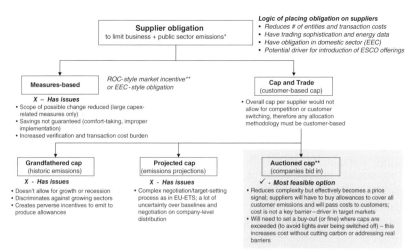

Note: * Target market non-energy-intensive sectors; **Revenues generated could be made available to business and public sector to fund energy-efficiency projects uptake of funds would be voluntary; uptake could be low if unsupported by a mandatory policy

Figure 9.9. Options for implementing a 'supplier cap'
Source: Carbon Trust (2005)

simply passing the costs of auctioned 'rights to sell' electricity through to customers – resulting in a far more complex version of the CCL that still fails to address the core behavioural and structural issues around the behaviour of large consumer companies.

9.8   The UK 'Carbon Reduction Commitment'

If you really want our companies to address energy and carbon, you have to get emissions into the financial reporting systems through which the company management structures work.

> Participant at CBI-hosted consultation with large non-energy-intensive sectors.

This analysis suggests that a different approach is required if the less energy-intensive sectors are to realise more fully their potential for improving energy efficiency. The most promising approach appears to be a mandatory trading scheme that caps direct and indirect emissions from large non-energy-intensive companies in the business and public sector – those that are currently outside the scope of the existing EU ETS and CCAs. Like the original pilot UK ETS – and unlike the EU ETS – it would include the 'embodied' emissions associated with their electricity consumption (which represent around 70% of the sector's emissions) but would otherwise be quite distinct, and simpler.

The defining features would be:

- A company-level trading scheme, in which companies must acquire allowances to cover their total emissions from sites across the country and may freely trade them between all other companies in the scheme.
- Both direct and electricity-related direct emissions would be included (electricity could be accounted at grid average carbon intensity, or supplier-specific intensities).
- Transaction costs would be minimised by:
  - Focusing the scheme on large companies (e.g. based on either energy consumption, turnover or employment threshold)
  - Basing the emissions on good metered energy bill data (possible selection criteria could include whether sites have half-hour electricity metering, which is only generally provided to sites with energy consumption above a specific threshold).
- Results to be published in company and public sector annual reports in consistent fashion: year on year total emissions, sales and purchases of allowances, etc.

The simplest implementation would auction all the allowances to avoid the complexities and administrative costs of company-specific negotiation.

From a purely economic perspective, the cost impact is very much like the Climate Change Levy. The key rationale lies in the analysis of the behavioural and organisational factors discussed above. The instrument requires companies to collect and aggregate information from their sites across the UK, to project the implied CO_2 emissions, and to be held transparently accountable for those emissions through the requirement to purchase allowances. This unavoidably puts the issue of carbon footprint and management – and associated costs – at Board level, rather than simply leaving hundreds of sites around the country to pay energy bills as a written-off incidental cost.

Figure 9.10 summarises the relative pros and cons of this cap-and-trade system for end-users in the business and public sector, compared to placing the cap on suppliers. The end-user scheme is preferred, fundamentally because it leads companies to look strategically at their

Criteria	Strengths of supplier cap	Strengths of end user cap
Relative expertise in recognising and implementing relevant 'on-the-ground' energy efficiency projects	• Not significant– low supplier familiarity with client processes and business situation, would incur costs of 'getting up to speed', which could be passed to the customer suppliers could strike deals with clients, though it would then be more direct to apply the obligation to the end-user	• Large organisations have dedicated energy managers-best placed to recognise / implement the right energy efficiency projects for their business
Relative action on genuine business barriers and drivers	• Not significant– regulatory only and would act to increase prices for end users where cost is not a significant barrier / driver for target market	• Compliance would enable internal energy managers to secure funding for energy efficiency projects on favourable terms • Enables companies to report carbon for CSR
Minimising regulatory overlap	• Not significant– double regulation of the same company on the same issue (generators and suppliers are vertically integrated) may not be desirable	• Double regulation of the same electron rather than regulating the same company twice on the same issue
Relative expertise in trading	• Places obligation on organisations with strongest experience of energy demand prediction and carbon trading • May be best placed to manage SME demand-side reduction where no in-house expertise exists	• Not significant - Trading expertise exists among some of the larger businesses - HH metering data exists, so minimal extra data capture cost would be incurred
Relative administrative burden	• Reduces government administration costs by placing burden on small no. of suppliers (<10) versus large no. of consumers (>10k) • Suppliers would incur admin costs and pass these through as customer price increases	• Projects are NPV +ve therefore financial benefits can offset internal admin costs, although government admin costs would be higher in this scenario • Use metered data and current financial reporting to keep it simple
Development of Third Party ESCOs	• This would encourage suppliers to develop ESCO abilities but could put up barriers to entry for third parties. If regulation / business case allows, third party ESCOs could play (competing more directly with suppliers)	• If regulation allows and a business case exists (customer demand + derisked margin), third party ESCOs would develop and the market could become more competitive–diverse

Figure 9.10. Relative pros and cons of end-user cap-and-trade (e.g. UK CRC) compared to supplier cap
Source: Carbon Trust (2005)

energy use and emissions footprint. It gets this information into the company's financial reporting and planning structures, then that feeds through in terms of incentives through operations nationwide. By doing so, it would greatly enhance the role, status and empowerment of energy managers to implement measures on a par with other investments that the company might consider.

The proposal, originally titled the UK Consumption-based Emissions Trading Scheme (UK CETS) has since been taken up by the government and was presented in the UK *Energy Review* (DTI, 2006a) as one of the two main options for tackling the growth of service sector CO_2 emissions (the other being mandatory reporting). Renamed the Carbon Reduction Commitment (CRC), it was then opened for formal consultation, that closed early in 2007. Following this, after refinement to define more carefully the target sectors taking account of transaction costs, it was adopted as probably the most significant new policy instrument in the UK *Energy White Paper* (DTI, 2007).

9.9   Potential impact of measures for energy efficiency

Obviously, the impact of individual policy instruments is complex, evolves over time, and also interacts with other instruments. Total impacts can only be plausibly assessed with models that capture many of these factors, including the overlaps between instruments. To test the potential impact of the various policy instruments discussed in this chapter (and some others), we applied a combination of the ENUSIM model for manufacturing energy use and the BRE model for the UK building stock. These models were run with a variety of policy packages out to 2020.[5] Figure 9.11 summarises the results from the package that had the highest impact by utilising the full range of policy instruments.

Prompt implementation of these instruments was assessed to reduce carbon emissions from business and public sector end-use by up to 5 MtC/year by 2010 and ~12.5 MtC/year by 2020 – about 10% and 20%, respectively, of projected emissions from these sectors – and turn projected growth into absolute decline, averaging about 1%/year. In 2020, ~9 MtC/year of this delivery comes from the existing instruments if they are implemented as fully as possible for the savings to be assured, whilst the net prize of broadening the package, primarily through use of

---

[5] For details of the range of packages and analysis, see Carbon Trust (2005).

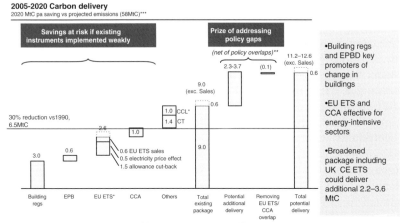

2005-2020 Carbon delivery
2020 MtC pa saving vs projected emissions (58MtC)***

Note: *EU ETS based on market price of (€30/tCO$_2$ in 2020 and 1%pa cut back, CCL at current strength; **Includes UK consumption-emissions trading scheme (CTS), net of overlap with CCL and CT (includes 0.5MtC from strengthened EPBD and 0.7MtC product standards – only additional to UK CE ETS in SMEs); ***Allowing for CCP delivery 2000–2005 (3MtC) Source: Ecofys

Figure 9.11. Carbon savings by instrument arising from a package of measures
Source: Carbon Trust (2005)

a downstream cap-and-trade system, adds an additional carbon saving of 2.2–3.6 MtC/year. The scenario assumes a carbon price by 2020 of €30/tCO$_2$ and doubling of the Climate Change Levy, but the impact of price on end-use behaviour is only part of the story. Indeed in terms of end-use impacts, the EU ETS only contributes around 2.6 MtC.[6] The majority of the savings can be delivered by technologies that are profitable at a 15% cost of capital, and are driven by other measures: efficient implementation thus offers the technical potential for net benefit to UK firms.

The lead instrument for large organisations would be the UK 'Carbon Reduction Commitment': the savings indicated arise from an assumption that its impact is sufficient to align company decision making on energy efficiency with typical sector rates of return, thus 'closing the gap' between the practical delivery of the other instruments and the identified economic potential, to give optimum investment at a 15% internal rate

---

[6] The modelling focused on energy use at a fixed electricity carbon intensity, and thus does not capture the fuel-switching impacts of the EU ETS on power generation, discussed elsewhere in this book. Sensitivity studies showed a negligible carbon benefit from changing the Climate Change Levy into a downstream carbon tax (i.e. aligning rates in proportion with carbon content), because the scope for fuel switching in these end-use sectors is actually very limited.

of return (IRR). Allowing for overlaps, the policy package that includes this delivers ~12.6 MtC/year savings by 2020 – over 20% of the total emissions from these sectors.

The modelling employed did not report the split in these savings between electricity and direct fuels savings. Clearly, for reasons articulated at the beginning of the chapter, more than half the total is due to savings attributed to reduced electricity consumption, at an assumed emissions intensity of 1.43 tC/kWh. This implies total electricity savings on the order of 50 TWh/year by 2020 – approaching 10% of *total* projected 'business as usual' electricity production by then. Clearly, enhancing energy efficiency in the business and public sectors is one of the most cost-effective, and rapid, ways of contributing both to emissions reduction, and security of supply.

References

Arrow, K. (1962). The economic implications of learning by doing. *Review of Economic Studies*, **99**, 155–173.

Carbon Trust (2005). *The UK Climate Change Programme: Potential Evolution for Business and the Public Sector*. CTC519, Carbon Trust, London. Available from: www.carbontrust.co.uk

(2006). *Carbon Footprints in the Supply Chain: The Next Step for Business*. CTC 616, Carbon Trust, London. Available from: www.carbontrust.co.uk

DeCanio, S. J. (1993). 'Barriers within firms to energy efficient investments, *Energy Policy*, **21**(9), 906–914.

(1994). Agency as control problems in US corporations: the case of energy efficient investment projects. *Journal of the Economics of Business*, **1**(1).

Department of Energy (1983). *Energy Conservation Investment in Industry: An Appraisal of the Opportunities and Barriers*. Prepared by Armitage Norton Consultants, Energy Paper No. 50, The Stationery Office, London.

DTI (2006a). *Energy Review: The Energy Challenge* Department of Trade and Industry, London.

(2006b). *UK Energy and CO2 Emissions Projections: updated projections to 2020*, Department of Trade and Industry, London.

(2007). *Energy White Paper: Meeting the Energy Challenge*. CM 7124, Department of Trade and Industry, London.

Howarth, R. B., B. M. Haddad and B. Paton (2000). The economics of energy efficiency: insights from voluntary participation programmes. *Energy Policy*, **28**(6–7), 477–486.

Jamasb, T., W. Nuttall and M. Pollitt (eds) (2006). *Future Electricity Technologies and Systems*. Cambridge University Press, Cambridge.

Kahneman, D. and A. Tversky (2000). *Choices, Values, and Frames*. Cambridge University Press, Cambridge.

Lovins, A. B. and L. H. Lovins (1997). *Climate: Making Sense and Making Money*. Rocky Mountain Institute, Old Snowmass, Colorado.

Pye, M. and A. McKane (1998). *Enhancing Shareholder Value: Making a More Compelling Energy Efficiency Case to Industry by Quantifying Non-energy Benefits.* Proceedings 1999 Summer Study on Energy Efficiency in Industry, Washington, DC.

Ross, M. (1986). The capital budgeting practices of 12 large manufacturing firms. *Financial Management*, **15**(4), 15–22.

Sorrell, S., J. Schleich, E. O'Malley and S. Scott (2004). *The Economics of Energy Efficiency: Barriers to Cost-Effective Investment.* Edward Elgar, Cheltenham, UK.

Stiglitz, J. E. and A. Weiss (1981). Credit rationing in markets with imperfect information. *American Economic Review*, **71**, 393–410.

Sutherland, R. J. (1994), 'Energy efficiency or the efficient use of energy resources?. *Energy Sources*, **16**, 257–268.

(1996). The economics of energy conservation policy. *Energy Policy*, **24**(4), 361–370.

Wade, J., J. Pett and L. Ramsay (2003). *Energy Efficiency in Commercial Offices: Assessing the Situation.* ACE, London.

WBCSD (2002). *Walking the Talk: The Business Case for Sustainable Development.* World Business Council on Sustainable Development.

Part III

Investment, Price and Innovation

10 Will the market choose the right technologies?

Karsten Neuhoff and Paul Twomey

10.1 Introduction

The experience of the last few years suggests that liberalised electricity markets can contribute to an efficient operation of the system, and most studies suggest that market incentives have reduced operational costs. However, it is still widely debated whether liberalised electricity markets create appropriate signals for investment. While many papers focus on the question of whether such investment will be induced at the 'right' time and volume, this chapter looks at the question of whether investors will choose the 'right' technologies. By the 'right' technologies we have in mind the following question: 'Does market-based investment lead to the socially optimal technology mix?'

This chapter does not argue that it is for the government to decide what the right technology mix is. Rather, it argues that for the market to choose the right technologies, market participants need to be made aware of the full costs and benefits created by their investment decisions. These include the social and environmental impacts of energy generation, the impact on technology improvements, and the risks created for an economy through exposure to foreign energy supplies. If some of these costs or benefits are not reflected in the decision process of investors, then this can bias the technology choice and might imply that the market will not choose the right technology.

The aim of this chapter is to identify some of the potential market failures and other barriers that inhibit an efficient market outcome. In doing so we address two particular concerns:

1. Can we rely on the market to develop technologies and make them available on a large scale?
2. Can we rely on the market to get the mix of commercially viable technologies right?

A particular focus of this chapter is on the role of renewable technologies. Using renewables on a large scale to replace fossil electricity generation offers two principal advantages. Environmentally, renewables offer a means to significantly reduce greenhouse gas emissions. This is a pressing priority, given the need to minimise the risks of climate change triggered by rapidly rising concentrations of greenhouse gases, caused in large part by the burning of fossil fuels. In addition, renewable energy sources can also help to diversify energy supplies in most countries. Reducing a country's dependence on energy imports reduces the exposure of the economy to international fuel price fluctuations and potential interruptions caused by political instability. While such fluctuations may be handled as normal business risks, energy price volatility has always been a significant issue in domestic affairs and geopolitics, which imposes social costs. In addition, most renewables are cleaner, thereby providing additional benefits to the environment and to human health.

Yet despite a variety of studies showing that renewables have a large technical potential, they only supply 3.75% of UK (DTI, 2005) and 13.5% of global energy demand (International Energy Agency, 2005a,b). Furthermore, nearly all of this is from established sources of hydropower and small-scale wood fuel and other biomass combustion, which are limited in their potential expansion. While the high cost of immature renewable technologies is obviously an important reason for their relatively small deployment, we also need to ensure that it is not market failures and other barriers that constrain their deployment.

The outline of this chapter is as follows. Section 10.1 examines the importance of diversity in the national portfolio and briefly characterises why it is beneficial. It then examines whether individual profit-motivated investment decisions deliver the socially optimal technology mix identified by macroeconomic studies. In Section 10.2 the issue of intermittency is examined and we investigate whether the current market design is creating a barrier to intermittent technologies. Section 10.3 examines whether environmental externalities have been properly internalised. There is a clear bias against clean technologies if this is not the case. Section 10.4 examines other marketplace and institutional biases against various technologies. Section 10.5 looks at whether new technologies can become cost-competitive, given the possibility of technological 'lock-out'. Section 10.6 concludes the chapter.

10.2   Do investors capture diversity benefits?

The recent debate on security of supply has highlighted how traditional energy planning, investing and pricing may not accurately reflect the social and economic risks that many societies run. Analysis indicates that it is socially desirable to diversify technology options when confronted with such supply uncertainties (Awerbuch *et al.*, 2006). Given that the value of diversity in reducing risk is not often discussed in the literature, this section briefly describes the source and measurement of this value before returning to the key question of whether the current market framework gives investors adequate incentives to capture the diversification benefits.[1]

The importance of diversity arises from the wide range of risks and uncertainties that power investors now face in liberalised electricity markets. While gas and coal technologies usually come out as the cheapest options using current cost figures, and nuclear proponents have access to figures that suggest that their technology is also cost-competitive at high CO_2 prices, this might not be the case for different fuel prices, CO_2 prices and other technology cost scenarios. Thus we need to represent the various risks and managerial options associated with different technologies.

The importance of considering both *costs* and *risks* can be illustrated using an example from financial management: investors do not dismiss government bonds as a potential investment just because they offer lower returns than corporate bonds. Rather, investors takes into account both the return and risk of the asset. Government bonds have lower risk than corporate bonds and, given that investors are typically risk-averse, this feature is to be valued. Furthermore, in the consideration of risk, a shrewd investor will not only consider the stand-alone risk of an asset (typically the volatility of an asset's return measured by a statistic such as the variance) but also how the risk of the asset is related to the risks of other assets held by the investor (the covariance). That is, the risk of an asset is evaluated in terms of the total investment portfolio. The same applies to generation technologies. Technology choices are not only based on expected costs but also on their impact on the overall risk profile of a generation portfolio. Some renewable technologies may be 'expensive' on a strict cost comparison with more traditional fossil technologies. They do, however, reduce the exposure to fuel prices and supply interruptions, and thus reduce the risk for a power system. This might, in turn, justify their inclusion in the generation portfolio.

In finance theory, a well-known methodology that is used to explore how investors can construct portfolios in order to optimise expected returns for a given level of risk is called mean-variance portfolio theory. Its application to the electricity sector has been pioneered by Shimon Awerbuch (Awerbuch and Berger, 2003; Awerbuch, 2004). The approach involves constructing an efficient frontier which contains those portfolio

---

[1] For a more in-depth discussion of the value of diversity from both a commercial and public perspective see Chapter 4 by Roques in this book.

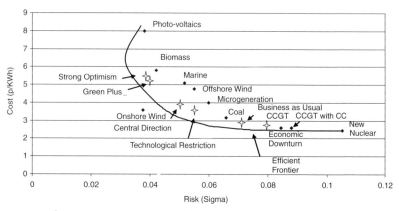

Figure 10.1. Illustrative cost–risk efficient frontier for UK electricity generation
Source: Twomey (2006)

mixes which have the maximum return (or minimum cost) for any given level of risk. While there are many types of risks, including risk of physical disruption, the focus here is on economic risk. This refers to the exposure to unexpected cost increases, in our cases for input fuels driven by unexpected international supply shortages or strategic output reductions by producers. The important conclusion from this type of analysis is that portfolios containing a diverse mix of technologies are usually preferable, from a societal perspective, over non-diverse portfolios. The basic intuition behind this result is simple – don't put all your eggs in one basket.

Figure 10.1 shows an indicative example of the risks and costs for various UK portfolio mixes from Twomey (2006). Figure 10.2 illustrates the portfolio mixes underlying three sample portfolios from the efficient frontier. Portfolio cost (including CO_2) is measured as pence/kWh. Risk is measured as the standard deviation of historic annual outlays for fuel, while operation and maintenance (O&M) and construction period outlays are primarily based on estimates by Awerbuch and Berger (2003). All these estimates are debatable; however, they illustrate the mainstream perspective that conventional generation technologies are cheaper than renewable sources.[2] The general

---

[2] This illustrative example also includes the debatable assumption that nuclear is relatively cheap and, on a stand-alone basis, risky. The latter is due to high capital construction risks. Following Awerbuch and Berger (2003) it has been assumed that construction-period cost risks are the same as a broadly diversified market portfolio, i.e. $\beta = 1$. However, from a portfolio perspective, nuclear has risk-reducing properties, due to its relatively low correlation with fossil fuel prices.

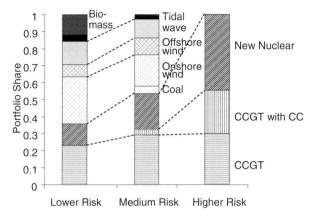

Figure 10.2.   Illustrative sample portfolio mixes from the UK efficient frontier
Source: Twomey (2006)

conclusion as to the benefits of diversity are robust to changes in these estimates.

Figure 10.1 shows the returns and costs of pure portfolios (100% in a single technology) as well as the efficient frontier. The latter illustrates the diversification effect – it is possible to achieve lower costs at lower risk by combining assets into mixed portfolios. For example, any portfolio on the efficient frontier located south-west of a pure (100%) portfolio outperforms such a portfolio in terms of having *both* lower cost and less risk. This is a rare example of a 'free lunch' in economics. The diagram also shows the cost–risk profiles of the scenarios developed by Ault *et al.* (2005).

Figure 10.2, which takes three illustrative portfolios from the efficient frontier, shows how renewables form an important part of these mixes, especially for the lower risk portfolios. It should be noted again that these are only illustrative graphs, where the share of any particular technology is sensitive to the initial assumptions. As renewables have low covariances with other generation technologies, they have a strong likelihood of being included in an efficient frontier portfolio, especially for small shares. The analysis does not determine what point along the frontier is optimal from a national perspective; however, it does indicate that lower economic risk (and thus greater security of supply) is almost uniformly associated with greater diversity and, in particular, the greater use of renewables.

This type of analysis is at a country level. Is the public-good value of a diverse fuel mix reflected in the costs and benefits that individual investors face and thus internalised in market prices? Under the strong assumptions of perfectly competitive markets, including a complete set of risk and futures markets, the resulting choices of decision-makers are efficient (see, e.g. Arrow and Hahn, 1971). These assumptions serve as a useful benchmark (Roques, 2006) but are, arguably, not always satisfied (Neuhoff and de Vries, 2004). This problem can arise from a lack of adequate financial or physical risk management products (low liquidity of futures and forward contracts), which may limit opportunities for appropriate hedging.

A particularly important institutional problem exists in the lack of long-term contracting possibilities for the output of investments with long payback periods. This is an important problem in the electricity sector, where different generation technologies produce a similar product. Typically, the price of electricity is determined in the market by marginal fossil fuel plant. In this case, electricity prices fluctuate in line with fossil fuel prices, and the market risk of technologies not using the marginal fuel is higher than fossil fuel generation, whose fuel costs are partly hedged via electricity prices. To allow generators to sign long-term contracts for their generation output, a counterparty is required. Consumers would need to sign contracts with generation companies for their expected electricity output for a number of years in advance. In the current model of competition between retail companies, the retail companies are the parties who would need to sign these contracts with the generation companies. The retail companies cannot carry the price risk involved in such contracts, so in turn, in their contracts with final customers, they would want to specify a termination period of an equal number of years, enforced with a cancellation payment.

However, regulators currently strive to reduce the barriers against switching by final customers in order to increase retail competition and reduce retail margins. If the switching of electricity contracts would take years, or would alternatively involve switching costs similar to those observed in the refinancing of bank loans, the struggle by regulators for retail competition would be made more difficult. Electricity suppliers may seek to encourage longer-term contracting with customers, and indeed in the UK longer-term domestic contracts are beginning to emerge (British Gas have offered 3-year contracts to domestic customers). This is, however, not yet long enough to cover the time-frames of investment projects or investment cycles. Thus we could consider re-introducing (or retaining) a franchise for domestic consumers. The franchisee signs long-term contracts, preferably using market-based instruments such as auctions, with generators on behalf of its customers. This would then provide the basis for a set of long-term contracts that feed all the way back to generators. Any decision to do this would have to be weighed against the benefits of retail competition. The fall-back option seems to be the reinforcement of a largely vertically integrated retail and generation sector in the UK, with better hedging possibilities than in the past, but less transparency and market liquidity.

Given the difficulties of finding credible counterparties for long-term hedging contracts, the best case for expecting commercially driven plant diversity is probably within the portfolios of large well-capitalised vertically integrated energy companies. Roques et al. (2005) attempted to measure the extent of such incentives. Using Monte-Carlo simulations they examined how the investment decision of a utility already operating four plants might be influenced by the risk–return complementarity of building a new plant (e.g. a nuclear plant complementing existing gas plants). For a gas-dominated utility facing uncertain gas, electricity and carbon prices, the diversification value was shown to be critically dependent on the degree of correlation between gas and electricity prices. In particular, when gas is highly correlated with electricity prices and carbon prices (as is typically the case), the diversity value of introducing nuclear is insignificant for the utility. The same would be true for renewables. This suggests that, unless more renewables lead, to changes in the degree to which the marginal price of electricity in the system depends on fossil fuel generation, more renewables do not offer any diversification benefits to utilities. This situation would change if long-term (take–or–pay) contracts for renewables pass the benefit of stable prices on to consumers.

10.3   Does the market design cope with intermittency?

An important market concern for renewable energy technologies is that wind, solar and wave output cannot be predicted with sufficient accuracy at the time of the liquid day-ahead market. By the time the prediction accuracy improves (about 4 hours before final production), most international electricity transmissions have been allocated and liquidity in energy markets is low. This is despite the fact that transmission flows can be adjusted within seconds, most power plants can be started and stopped, and all power plants can change their output within this time-frame.[3] Dual balancing prices, which penalise companies for being out of balance with contracted quantities, exaggerate the issue. As a result,

---

[3] This effect is enhanced if, in systems such as the English and Welsh NETA, renewables generators balance their output if they want to avoid high imbalance prices. As individual output is relatively more volatile than aggregate output, this results in higher levels of flexible plant that must be kept running, creating energy and capital costs.

the electricity system is operated inefficiently, and wind, solar and wave, selling their output in the general energy market, receive lower than justified prices. Electricity from intermittent sources will always be sold at a discount relative to firm output, but ineffective market design is likely to increase this discount. This increased discount represents the bias against intermittent generation sources.

In most countries, electricity generation companies have high market shares in their regional markets and can influence prices in day-ahead and intra-day markets. Currently, they sell most of their output on longer-term contracts and therefore profit little, and will typically refrain from, influencing short-term prices. With higher penetration by renewables, trade in the short-term market will increase. At times of low renewable output, conventional generation sells additional output in the short-term market. In the short term, demand is rather inelastic and therefore generators can exercise market power and sell electricity above cost. At times of high renewable output, conventional generation buys back energy sold on longer-term contracts. Once again, they are in a strong position and can buy below cost. The net result is that this market power will reduce the revenue of intermittent renewables below their fair value (Twomey and Neuhoff, 2005).

10.4   Have we internalised environmental externalities?

The failure to adequately 'internalise' environmental impacts in prices is another potential distortion that makes it difficult for clean energy technologies to make headway. Traditional environmental regulation sets emission limits and requires firms to invest in improved combustion or exhaust cleaning technology. Emissions below the limits also cause environmental damage, but firms are not exposed to these damage costs and will not include them in the energy price. Estimates for these damages, excluding the costs of global warming, range from an additional €8.7–25/MWh for modern coal power plants.[4] Most of this damage relates to human health problems. These unpriced externalities will obviously rise if some account is taken of CO_2 emissions and their contribution to climate change. Averaging over a large set of studies on the cost of climate change suggests that the CO_2 impact of electricity

---

[4] *Source: Externalities of Energy: A Project of the European Commission*, www.externe.info/. Roth and Ambs (2004) estimated externality costs of modern coal plants in $/MWh as NO_x 12.96, SO_2 1.68, PM 0.24, N_2O 0.15, upstream 2.57, land use 5.26, water-related 1.3 (best estimates quoted). All externalities are based on coal power plants, which have the highest emissions levels (apart from peaking oil plants) and are therefore most likely to set the marginal electricity price if externalities are priced.

produced by coal can be conservatively estimated at €10–23/MWh (Tol, 2003).[5] The true costs are likely to be higher, as current studies compare snapshots of future outcomes and ignore extreme weather events and the costs of changing infrastructure, agricultural practices and living patterns (Tol, 2003; Stern, 2006). The IPCC summarises existing modelling studies consistent with stabilisation at around 550 ppm CO_2-eq by 2100. Carbon prices will have to be in the range of 5 to 65 US $ / tCO_2 eq by 2030 (IPCC, 2007). However, more ambitious emission reductions – and higher carbon prices – will be required to avoid temperature increase above 2 degrees.

Cap-and-trade programmes aim to internalise the costs of SO_2, NO_x and, most prominently, CO_2, and might in the long run ensure that electricity prices reflect the true environmental costs. However, the current experience suggests that it does take some time to establish a stringent and effective emission trading scheme. This is because, in political negotiations, emission reduction targets, and therefore the scarcity price of emission certificates, are frequently set below the levels suggested by scientific evidence. Also, the experience with the first two phases of the European Emission Trading Scheme suggests that industry lobby groups are successful in securing large amounts of free allowance allocation to new fossil fuel power stations. This amounts to a subsidy for coal and gas power stations and discriminates against technologies that do not emit CO_2. Both effects distort technology choices (Keats-Martinez and Neuhoff, 2004). As a result of these political processes, electricity prices will only gradually come to reflect environmental externalities and provide the right incentives for investments in power generation. As Grubb and Newbery point out in Chapter 11 of this book, the EU ETS needs to be reformed such that it provides a less volatile price that reflects the true social cost of CO_2.

10.5 Other marketplace and institutional barriers

In addition to the above market design problems, which may result in costs or benefits of technologies not being fully internalised, there are a number of other issues, which may result in biases against certain generation technologies.

---

[5] Roth and Ambs (2004) estimated global warming externality costs of $26.38/MWh. ExternE (www.externe.info/) calculated a range of €3–111/MWh. Increasing the implied rate of time preference from 2% to 3% will reduce the weight on people in 100 years from 37% to 5% of today's population and thereby reduce the marginal cost of CO_2 emissions. Equity weighing of global population leads to a higher estimate of the marginal costs (Yohe, 2003).

For example, because liberalised electricity markets have been designed to replicate the historic operation of centralised power plants, their operations often discriminate against distributed generation. Solar PV installed on roofs, for example, can reduce peak loads on the distribution network in summer-peaking systems, and combined heat and power – whether gas or bioenergy – can do likewise in winter-peaking systems (Hoff and Cheney, 2000). Frequently, however, network tariffs do not reward this kind of system service (Alderfer *et al.*, 2000).

Market structure effects on the technology mix may also arise with vertically integrated companies. Such distortions will arise for such companies if the entry of renewable technologies takes market share from their conventional generation assets, or if it results in changes to the transmission system, which reduces the value of some of their existing assets (Alderfer *et al.*, 2000). Inexperienced or inert companies can also increase project costs for decentralised generation, and cause unnecessary delays, if they have not established procedures for interconnections or if they request technical assessments and insurance cover that are only appropriate for large central power plants. If the market share of a technology is at or below 1%, niche applications or specific regulatory provisions can dominate its economies even when they are economically competitive in a technology-to-technology comparison (Kammen, 2004). Regulatory intervention can reduce this effect or compensate initial investors for these costs. Jamasb *et al.* (2005) discuss how Ofgem could reform its system of distribution charges in order to provide the 'right' signals to distributed generation reflecting its local value to the electricity system.

A different set of questions relates to the regulatory and market risk of investment in electricity generation capacity. It is currently widely debated whether the risk might prevent timely investment in new generation capacity. Higher capital costs are one reason for investors to delay any investment until electricity prices rise. Capital costs are higher because future electricity prices are uncertain, increasing the risk that investors face. This risk could be eliminated by long-term contracts between final consumers, or consumer franchises, and the electricity generation companies. However, as already mentioned in the discussion of diversity, currently regulators prevent such long-term contracts in an attempt to foster retail competition. This exposes renewables investors to electricity price risk and induces them to charge a risk premium on their capital. The risk premium, increased by artificial regulatory constraints, affects capital-intensive technologies more than technologies with high fuel costs, and therefore biases against nuclear and renewables (Neuhoff and de Vries, 2004).

Regulators are concerned about the implications of investment risk because it could postpone investment, causing unpopular power

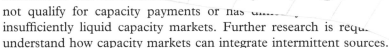

shortages. But instead of
typically implement finan
the bias against capital
reinforce the bias. Seve
ments or capacity ma
instruments can discrim
not qualify for capacity payments or has u........ ,
insufficiently liquid capacity markets. Further research is requ..
understand how capacity markets can integrate intermittent sources.

Furthermore, the short-term contracting in electricity markets can
reinforce cyclical investment patterns, as observed in oil-refining or in
the aluminium industry. This could create difficulties for producers of
renewable energy technologies. They have less production experience,
more problems in scaling-up production during boom periods, and will
capture less of the increased market size. Furthermore, focusing on rapid
upscaling of production is likely to divert focus from cost-efficiency,
thereby delaying technological learning. Market designs that support
long-term contracting might provide for more forward-looking information and could reduce the cyclical nature of the market.

Financial markets face difficulties in providing risk management
instruments for new renewable technologies.[6] There are at least two
reasons for this. First, historical actuarial data to assess risk is limited.[7]
Conventional technologies have never faced these difficulties because
they were already deployed before liberalisation. Historic records from
these times have allowed for risk assessment. A second disadvantage
faced by renewable energy projects is their small scale. This results in
disproportionately high transaction costs for risk management tools,
complex financing arrangements or export credit guarantees.[8]

The complex interactions between the public, administration, private sector and electricity system operators can also create non-marketplace barriers for new energy technologies. Administrative frameworks
were developed for existing technologies and are not yet tailored to the
needs of renewables. For example, while spatial planning traditionally
envisages specific zones for industrial development, local plans frequently have to be revised to allow for the location of wind or bioenergy
plants, thus creating uncertainty and costly delays for project

[6] For a detailed assessment see the United Nations Environment Programme (2004).
[7] See Sonntag-O'Brien and Usher (2004).
[8] Large institutions like the World Bank have little track record with the efficient
administration of small-scale projects (below $15 million). Beck and Martinot (2004)
argue that rural energisation and electrification policies should therefore start with small-
scale entrepreneurship.

developers.[9] The small scale of renewable energy projects multiplies the relative costs incurred through multiple administrative processes.

The successful deployment of wind turbines in Denmark is a result of long-term thinking, local community involvement, benefits to incumbent energy companies, public and private R&D support and government support.[10] Over time,[11] Denmark has developed domestic industries to design, finance, insure, manufacture, install and maintain renewables systems, using local equipment and labour.[12] This shows that industrial policies towards energy technologies can work, giving the population, industry and administration a chance to get used to a new technology and learn how to deal with its new characteristics.[13] Other countries may benefit from the knowledge acquired in leading countries but there is a question as to the extent to which the government needs to manage the 'institutional learning' process,[14] if a country is to see deployment of renewables before they are fully cost-competitive. This will remove non-marketplace barriers for subsequent use in competitive markets and accelerate their future growth.[15]

---

[9] Admire Rebus (2003) surveyed wind project planning phases in European countries. Average lead times are between 1.5 and 4.5 years. The principal administrative cause of delay is linked to spatial planning. The report lists general principles to allow competent authorities to simplify and clarify procedures.

[10] To achieve this objective, the Netherlands applies a transmission management in which a vision of the way forward is agreed with all stakeholders, and the government not only brings the parties together but also supports experiments to facilitate institutional and technological learning (Ministry of Economic Affairs, 2004; see also Kaplan, 1999). The IEA (2003) emphasises that stakeholders from all relevant groups need to be actively engaged in the programme, in some cases even in the design phase, and should contribute to case studies (Austrian Biomass Heating and Danish Labelling Scheme for Buildings).

[11] IEA (2003) points out that new technologies require major changes 'not just in routines and procedures familiar to many actors, but also in the models and concepts that underpin decisions. Basic ideas on 'How we do business around here' may have to be re-evaluated, for example in the shift from centralised to decentralised power generation.'

[12] See Sawin (2004).

[13] Duke *et al.* (2002) show that a wide variety of product quality constrains sales of PV modules for solar home systems in Kenya, as some customers refrain from purchases due to the associated performance uncertainty. Domestic product testing with public disclosure represents an inexpensive, low-risk strategy, but may prove inadequate. International certification with PVGAP (Geneva) or PowerMark (USA) exists, but seems to be insufficiently established in developing countries. PVPS (2003) reports that all PV models must qualify under IEC 61215.

[14] Institutional and organisational learning increases the capability of an organisation to act effectively(Espejo *et al.*, 1996). Users, insurers and the finance sector require data on realised project performances for evaluations (Sonntag-O'Brien and Usher, 2004).

[15] Dekimpe *et al.* (2000) use the mobile telecom industry to illustrate that the marketing paradigm of Rogers (1983), in which customer groups are classified in temporal segments from innovators and early adopters to laggards, also applies to the community of nations. This suggests that global partnerships could provide benefits if they manage to prevent delays in the deployment of profitable renewable technologies.

10.6   Do new technologies have the opportunity to become cost-competitive?

Even if some or all of the above market failures and barriers are removed, the problem of 'technology lock-out' may still result in the persistent under-deployment of new technologies. Here 'lock-out' refers to the historical path dependency of the development of a technology (Arthur, 1989; Kline, 2001; Unruh, 2002). An important implication is that if other barriers (as mentioned above) inhibit the development of a new technology, the removal of such barriers might not suffice to remove the 'lock-out' that has arisen from the barriers.

A particularly important source of lock-out is learning-by-doing, which can favour conventional, established technologies at the expense of innovative technologies. Figure 10.3 shows how new renewable technologies have consistently reduced their costs with increasing market experience.[16] The fact that the cost of new technologies falls with increasing deployment has been established in a large set of studies on energy technologies (Watanabe et al., 2001) and in other industry sectors (Isoard and Soria, 1997; IEA, 2003). Consequently, without large-scale applications, the cost of new technologies can stay high and investors will continue to use established technologies. As a result, new technologies can be 'locked out'.

The strength of technology lock-out varies across industries. In many consumer and information technology markets, the new services offered by new products dominate the higher costs; consumers buy what is new because it is different and appealing, and this surpasses any tendency to lock-out.

However, the energy sector exhibits three basic characteristics that result in a strong technology lock-out. First, new technologies produce the same basic product: electricity, in the case of most renewables. Hence, they have to compete mainly on price, making them immediately more vulnerable to lock-out. This is in sharp contrast to the IT, telecoms and other sectors, where product differentiation is a prime instrument of marketing and innovation, and the innovator can charge more for enhanced functionality or reduced size of a new device. Some high-value applications also exist for renewable energy technologies, but both the individual project size and the total market volume are probably too small to support significant learning-by-doing and research efforts. For example, photovoltaic cells are far more valuable in off-grid applications, but in 2002 this market segment contributed less than 10% to global PV sales (PVPS, 2003).

---

[16] For a more in-depth discussion of learning curves, see Chapter 12 by Jamasb and Köhler in this book.

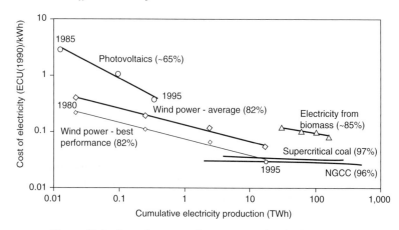

Figure 10.3. Learning-curve for energy technologies
Source: IEA (2000)

Second, perhaps because they involve transformation and delivery of large quantities of energy, the technologies and systems tend to involve large-scale engineering products that last decades. This greatly increases the scale and time horizon of financial investment, and multiplies the risks associated with innovation to the extent that private sector interest vanishes. It also means that new energy technologies compete with incumbents that have gained market experience over several decades and large quantities of global investment, often drawing on prior public R&D.

Third, both the above factors make it far harder for individual private firms to appropriate the full benefits of learning and R&D in the energy sector than in other sectors. Dasgupta and Stiglitz (1988) have shown in a model that oligopolistic firms might be prepared to incur initial losses by expanding their production if learning effects would reduce their future costs, thereby allowing for larger future market shares and profit margins. However, technology 'spillover' allows other companies to copy the initial learning at a fraction of the costs (Watanabe *et al.*, 2001; for a semiconductor example, see Irwin and Klenow, 1994). As more producers compete, the benefits of the invention are split among several producers, who share the market, and consumers, who pay lower prices (Duke and Kammen, 1999). This problem has been resolved in the pharmaceutical sector by granting patents for inventions, and companies spend 15% of their revenue on drug development. But the monopoly position granted by patent rights can result in inefficient markets and profit margins that might not be acceptable in the utility sector (e.g. in pharmaceuticals, profits can account for 30% of sales volume).

For at least two reasons it seems unlikely that patents will play a major role in promoting innovation and improvements of renewables. First, pharmaceutical patents protect a specific, distinct drug; it is far harder to define engineering patents in ways that cannot be circumvented over time. There is even the risk that enhancing intellectual property rights protection impedes innovation and the diffusion of new knowledge (Alic *et al.*, 2003). Second, renewable energy technologies consist of a large set of components and require the expertise of several companies to improve the system. A consortium will face difficulties in sharing the costs of 'learning investment', as it is difficult to negotiate and fix the allocation of future profits. Firms are therefore reluctant to invest for the benefit of consortium members (the hold-up problem). At the same time, the scale, expertise and time horizon of 'learning investment' tends to exceed the funds of individual companies and the patience of the venture capital markets.

Despite all these challenges to innovation in the energy sector, the oil extraction industry is relatively innovative. The example of deep-water oil drilling shows that government support was instrumental. Initially, costs were significantly higher than for onshore or shallow-water fields. Oil companies preferred to develop cheaper fields, as they had to sell output on a global oil market at a homogeneous price. Governments reduced extraction taxes to compensate private oil companies for the higher field development costs of deep-water oil fields. With improvements through market experience, costs for deep-water drilling fell and governments could reduce the scale of incentives.

10.7   Conclusions

We have set out to answer the question: 'Will the market choose the right technologies?' In the current market design, there are a number of reasons why the answer may be negative: investors are not benefiting from the diversity that their private sector choices offer for society; the current Emission Trading Scheme and other legislation need to evolve further to ensure that environmental externalities are fully considered in investment decisions; similarly, further work needs to be done on the support schemes for new energy technologies such that investors in these technologies are rewarded at the level of the benefits that society receives from their development. We also need to develop the market set-up to address various barriers for the efficient integration of intermittent generation technologies in power markets, and have to carefully monitor the future development of market power in short-term balancing markets. The latter might create significant biases against intermittent generation technologies through the difficulties they have in long-term forecasting of their output, and hence the difficulties in conducting long-term contracting.

Are these effects sufficiently large to justify actions by the regulator and government? While we do not quantify all the effects in this chapter, we suggest that the answer depends on the type of remedial actions taken. We examine six considerations here.

1. Measures that develop the market and institutional arrangements to avoid distortions need to be balanced against the transaction costs involved in their implementation. For example, a likely candidate over the coming years is an evolution of the electricity trading arrangement to a scheme that reflects transmission and distribution constraints in the marketplace (see Pollitt and Bialek, Chapter 7, this volume for more details on how this might work). Thus the network can be utilised more effectively, allowing for more connection of renewable generation while reducing the need for transmission expansion. This is of particular relevance for renewable technologies, as they tend to be in different locations from existing power stations and exhibit lower capacity factors. Thus an inefficient use of transmission capacity creates a disproportionate cost increase for renewables.

2. Measures to internalise environmental effects are economically uncontroversial. Emissions trading has illustrated a successful start to internalise CO_2 externalities, but also requires further evolution based on the experience from the first years, and more stringent targets and allocation methodologies to ensure that the full environmental costs are reflected in investment decisions.

3. With learning curve externalities, it is increasingly accepted that private sector investors in new energy technologies can only capture a fraction of the learning benefits that society draws from the use of these technologies. This suggests that enhancing the renewable energy support schemes and allowing these schemes to support multiple technologies is imminent.

4. In various countries, measures are being discussed that can compensate for market failures rather than removing them. For example, the use of capacity payments can provide additional investment incentives. They can compensate investors for higher capital costs from regulatory risk and the failure of market design to accommodate for long-term contracts with domestic consumer franchises to allow hedging of investment decisions. They can thus ensure the appropriate investment volume but create additional costs for consumers relative to a 'first best' market design. Capacity payments, as currently discussed, do not reduce the bias that higher capital costs introduce against renewable and high-efficiency technologies.

5. The question of how the benefits of diversity are reflected in the marketplace, and what measures could be used to better reflect them in private sector investment decisions, does warrant further theoretical research. In the absence of a consistent policy framework, we face the risk of *ad hoc* government decisions, such as the moratorium on gas in the late 1990s in the UK. These types of decisions are the least suitable in providing a stable investment environment for forward-looking investors in any technology.

6. A move from retail competition for domestic consumers towards consumer franchises would facilitate long-term contracting to support appropriate investment choices. This would involve a significant reversal of the trends foreseen in EU electricity directives and would need to be carefully evaluated against the other costs and benefits of retail competition. However, it might pick up momentum as investment requirements in the sector increase.

Our assessment suggests that we still have some ground to cover before the institutional and market framework we have put in place in the UK creates incentives for the right technology choice.

Acknowledgements

This chapter is dedicated to the memory of Shimon Awerbuch whose pioneering work in the application of portfolio theory to the energy sector has greatly enhanced our understanding of the value of diversity in energy portfolios.

References

Admire Rebus (2003). Renewable Electricity Market Development in the European Union, Final Report, www.ecn.nl/publications/default.aspx?nr=c03082

Alderfer R.B., Eldridge M.M., Starrs T.J. (2000). Making Connections: Case Studies of Interconnection Barriers and their Impacts on Distributed Power Projects, NREL/SR-200-28053.

Alic J.A., Mowery D.C., Rubin E.S. (2003). U.S. Technology and Innovation Policies: Lessons for Climate Change, Prepared for the Pew Center on Global Climate Change, Arlington, VA.

Arrow K.J., Hahn F.H. (1971). *General Competitive Analysis*, Holden Day, San Francisco, CA.

Arthur W.B. (1989). Competing technologies, increasing returns, and lock-in by historical events, *Economic Journal*, **99**(394), 116–131.

Ault, G., Elders, I., Galloway, S., McDonald, J., Leach, M., Lampaditou, E., Koehler, J. (2005). Electricity Network Scenarios for 2050, EPSRC/ SGFNT/TR/2005-001.

Awerbuch S. (2004). Portfolio-Based Electricity Generation Planning: Implications for Renewables and Energy Security, Report Prepared for REEEP Environment Policy Department Foreign and Commonwealth Office, London, and Division of Technology, Industry and Economics United Nations Environment Programme, Paris.

Awerbuch S., Berger M. (2003). Energy Security and Diversity in the EU: A Mean-Variance Portfolio Approach, IEA Report, No. EET/2003/03, Paris.

Awerbuch S., Stirling A. Jansen J. (2006). Portfolio and diversity analysis of energy technologies using full-spectrum uncertainty measures, in: D. Bodde and K. Leggio (eds.) *Understanding and Managing Business Risk in the Electric Sector, Topics in Global Energy Regulation, Finance and Policy*, Elsevier, Amsterdam.

Beck F., Martinot E. (2004). Renewable energy policies and barriers, in: *Encyclopedia of Energy*, Academic Press/Elsevier Science, San Diego, CA.

Dasgupta P., Stiglitz J. (1988). Learning-by-doing, market structure and industrial and trade policies, *Oxford Economic Papers*, **40**, 256–268.

Dekimpe M.G., Parker P.M., Sarvary M. (2000). Globalization: modeling technology adoption timing across countries, *Technology Forecasting and Social Change*, **63**, 25–42.

DTI (2005). Commodity Balances, available at www.berr.gov.uk

Duke, R., Kammen D.M. (1999). The economics of energy market transformation programs, *Energy Journal*, **20**(4), 15–64.

Duke, R.D., Jacobson, A., Kammen, D.M. (2002). Photovoltaic module quality in the Kenyan solar home systems market, *Energy Policy*, **30**, 477–499.

Espejo R., Schuhmann W., Schwaninger M., Bilello, U. (1996) *Organizational Transformation and Learning: A Cybernetic Approach to Management*, John Wiley & Sons, Chichester, UK.

Hoff, T., Cheney M. (2000). The potential for photovoltaics and other distributed resources in rural electric cooperatives, *Energy Journal*, **21**(3), 113–127.

International Energy Agency (2000). *Experience Curves for Technology Policy*, IEA, Paris.

(2003). *Creating Markets for Energy Technologies*, IEA, Paris.

(2005a). *Projected Costs of Generating Electricity*, 2005 Update, IEA, Paris.

(2005b). *World Energy Outlook 2005*, IEA, Paris.

IPCC, (2007). *Climate Change 2007: summary for policymakers*, Contribution of Working Group III to the Fourth Assessment of the Intergovernmental Panel on Climate Change, Cambridge University Press.

Irwin D., Klenow P. (1994). Learning-by-doing: spillovers in the semiconductor industry, *Journal of Political Economy*, **102**, 1200–1227.

Isoard S., Soria A. (1997). Learning Curves and Returns to Scale Dynamics: Evidence from the Emerging Renewable Energy Technologies, IPTS Working Paper Series WP 97/05.

Jamasb, T., Neuhoff K., Newbery D., Pollitt M. (2005). Long-term Framework for Electricity Distribution Access Charges, Report prepared for and commissioned by Ofgem, Cambridge Working Papers in Economics CWPE 0051/Electricity Policy Research Group Working Paper EPRG 05/07, November, Faculty of Economics, University of Cambridge.

Kammen, D.M. (2004). Renewable Energy Options for the Emerging Economy: Advances, Opportunities and Obstacles, Background paper for The

10–50 Solution: Technologies and Policies for a Low-Carbon Future, Pew Center and NECP Conference, Washington, DC.

Kaplan, A. (1999). Generating interest, generating power: commercializing photovoltaics in the utility sector, *Energy Policy*, **27**, 317–329.

Keats-Martinez K., Neuhoff K. (2004) Allocation of Carbon Emission Certificates in the Power Sector: How Generators Profit from Grandfathered Rights, Cambridge Working Papers in Economics 0444.

Kline D. (2001). Positive feedback, lock-in, and environmental policy, *Policy Science*, **34**, 95–107.

Ministry of Economic Affairs (2004). *Innovation in Energy Policy, Energy Transition: State of Affairs and the Way Ahead*, Ministry of Economic Affairs, The Netherlands.

Neuhoff, K., de Vries L. (2004). Insufficient incentives for investment in electricity generation, *Utilities Policy*, **4**, 253–268.

PVPS (Photovoltaic Power System Program) (2003). Trends in Photovoltaic Applications, Survey Report of selected IEA countries between 1992 and 2002, Report IEA-PVPS T1-12.

Rogers E.M. (1983). *Diffusion of Innovations*, The Free Press, New York.

Roques F. (2006). Technology choices and nuclear investment in liberalised electricity Markets, Presentation Ecole des Mines/CERNA 29 March 2006.

Roques F., Newbery D., Nuttall W., Connors W., de Neufville R. (2005). *Valuing Portfolio Diversification for a Utility: Application to a Nuclear Power Investment when Fuel, Electricity, and Carbon Prices are Uncertain*, Mimeo, Judge Institute of Management, University of Cambridge, UK.

Roth F.I., Ambs L.L. (2004). Incorporating externalities into a full cost approach to electric power generation life-cycle costing, *Energy*, **29**(12–15), 2125–2144.

Sawin J.L. (2004). Mainstreaming Renewable Energy in the 21st Century, Worldwatch Paper 169.

Sonntag-O'Brien V., Usher E. (2004). *Mobilising Finance for Renewable Energies*, International Conference for Renewable Energies, Bonn.

Stern N. (2006). The Stern Review on the Economics of Climate Change, www.hm-treasury.gov.uk/independent_reviews/stern_review_economics_climate_change/stern_review_report.cfm

Tol R. (2003). The Marginal Cost of Carbon Dioxide Emissions: An Assessment of the Uncertainties, Working Paper FNU 19.

Twomey P. (2006). *Renewable Energy Technologies and UK Electricity Generation: a Portfolio Theory Perspective*, IAEE International Conference, Potsdam, 2006.

Twomey P., Neuhoff K. (2005). *Market Power and Technological Bias: the case of electricity generation*, Cambridge Working Papers in Economics CWPE 0532/Electricity Policy Research Group Working Paper EPRG 05/01, August, Faculty of Economics, University of Cambridge.

United Nations Environment Program (2004) Financial Risk Management Tools for Renewable Energy Projects, www.uneptie.org/energy/act/fin/index.htm

Unruh G.C. (2002). Escaping carbon lock-in, *Energy Policy*, **30**, 317–325.

Watanabe C., Zhu B., Griffy-Brown C., Asgari B. (2001). Global technology spillover and its impact on industry's R&D strategies, *Technovation*, **21**, 281–291.

Yohe G.W. (2003). More trouble for cost–benefit analysis, *Climatic Change*, **56**(3), 235–244.

11 Pricing carbon for electricity generation: national and international dimensions

Michael Grubb and David Newbery

11.1 Introduction

The UK *Energy Review* states that

> The only way in which the international community will limit the rise in carbon emissions is if governments, industry and individuals take into account the costs associated with the emissions for which they are responsible ... A carbon price is essential for making lower carbon emissions a business imperative ... Establishing a price for carbon is best done internationally because climate change is a global problem requiring collective action (DTI, 2006, p. 27).

Policy to reduce emissions should be based on three essential elements: carbon pricing, technology policy, and removal of barriers to behavioural change (*Stern Review*, Stern, 2006).

The UK Government's approach to climate change is thus based on sound economics. Chapter 2 in this book, by discussing the 'social cost of carbon', has by implication discussed the level of carbon pricing that could be sought. This chapter addresses the *instruments* that might deliver such carbon pricing and the challenges in seeking to internationalise such instruments. Other chapters address instruments for energy efficiency and for innovation.

11.2 The social cost of carbon, carbon pricing and power sector mitigation

From an economic perspective, the most fundamental single step in climate policy is to establish a price for carbon. This should be informed by (but is not the same thing as) the social cost of carbon – the present discounted value of the additional social costs (or the marginal social damage) that an extra tonne of carbon released now would impose on the current and future society. As described in Chapter 2, the *Stern Review* uses the PAGE2002 model to calculate the likely damage caused by emitting an extra tonne of carbon and then to determine the resulting social cost of this damage, the social cost of carbon (SCC).

We emphasise again that this measure of damage is not just a prediction of the economic impact of climate change, but an ethical valuation of its significance to society. As Chapter 2 stressed, estimating the SCC is a multi-stage process.

The first two stages are to estimate the effect of greenhouse gases (GHGs) on temperature, and then the effects of this temperature rise on climate (regionally, seasonally, probability of extreme events, sea-level rises, etc.). After these two climate-science-driven steps, integrated assessment models (such as PAGE) attempt to estimate the regional impacts of this climate change on human well-being. If our economic modelling were as good as the climate science, we would then have a quantified description of the various economic effects, but over the long periods of time involved it would be foolish to claim any great degree of accuracy.

In addition to the cascade of uncertainties set out in Chapter 2, the result does depend on the rate of technical progress (which influences economic and emission growth rates, the capacity to adapt to climate change, and the cost of mitigation). A typical prediction of the rate of technical progress is to assume that it will continue as in the past century (when it has been historically most unusually high). We have little other idea of the nature of future technology and hence the future standards of living, but the rate of technical progress will be a key determinant.

The final step is to value these impacts when and where they occur and discount them to an equivalent present global aggregate. The valuation is one of the most controversial steps in the calculation. The PAGE model (like many other models) uses equity weighting, as discussed in Chapter 2. The preferred weights are inversely proportional to per capita consumption (often proxied by GDP/head at purchasing power parity, $PPP). This has the ethically agreeable implication that, if each country's value of a statistical life is proportional to GDP/head, then climate damage that involves loss of life or life expectancy when weighted with these equity weights treats a year of life lost in Bangladesh as equal to a year of life lost in the USA or the UK. Another way to appreciate the force of Stern's assumption is that the social cost of reducing the consumption of a person in a rich country by 10% is valued equal to the social benefit of increasing the consumption of a person in a poor country by 10% now. Therefore, as Western Europe has 25 times the per capita consumption of sub-Saharan Africa (at Purchasing Power Parity exchange rates), incurring a cost of $25 in Western Europe to deliver a benefit of more than $1 in SSA would deliver a net social gain on this calculus. The implications of this for the choice of policy instruments are discussed below.

The *Stern Review* adopts this approach, and also assumes a single view on the pure rate of time preference (PRTP, taken as 0.1% p.a.).

Given these, and updating the IPCC's 2001 *Third Assessment Report* to take account of stronger feedbacks and higher climate sensitivity, the *Stern Review* estimates the SCC as \$312/tC (= \$85/tCO$_2$, \$2006 prices) if we remain on the 'business as usual' (BAU) path (Stern, 2006, p. xvi, p. 287), although this estimate is given with considerable caution:

> We would therefore point to numbers for the 'business as usual' social cost of carbon well above (perhaps a factor of three times) the Tol mean of \$29/tCO$_2$ and the 'lower central' estimate of around \$13/tCO$_2$ in the recent study for DEFRA (Watkiss *et al.*, 2005) ... Nevertheless, we are keenly aware of the sensitivity of estimates to the assumptions that are made. Closer examination of this issue – and a narrowing of the range of estimates, if possible – is a high priority for research (Stern, 2006, p. 287).[1]

The PAGE estimates presented in Chapter 2 (Hope and Newbery) suggest a mean SCC of \$(2000)43/tC (\$11.7/tCO$_2$), for a range of possible baseline scenarios, with a 5–95% range of \$10–130/tC (\$2.7–35.5/tCO$_2$).[2] The central figure increases to \$90/tC (\$24.5/tCO$_2$) (5–95% range \$10–220/tC (\$2.7–60/tCO$_2$)) under updated estimates of climate sensitivity and other adjustments described in Chapter 2. These estimates assume equity weights centred on the inverse of per capita consumption, but with a range either side, and an average *consumption rate of interest* of 2±1%. If the rate of pure time preference is reduced (as in the *Stern Review*) to 0.1% – equivalent to setting a consumption rate of interest of about 1.5% – the model computes a mean SCC of \$330/tC (\$90/tCO$_2$) (5–95% range \$65–870/tC (\$17.7–237.3/tCO$_2$)); essentially the same as the Stern Review. Ignoring equity weighting altogether, but taking a consumption rate of interest of 3±1%, the SCC is \$51/tC (\$13.9/tCO$_2$) (5–95% range \$10–150/tC (\$2.7–40.9/tCO$_2$)). As such, it is comparable to those derived from other models using the same consumption rate of interest.

These estimates of the SCC and of the cost of climate change more generally, and the assumptions from which they flow, have attracted a great deal of economic discussion, as discussed in Chapter 2. High values of the SCC can be defended either by assuming that we are

---

[1] Box 13.1 of the *Stern Review* summarises other estimates of the SCC, citing a study by Downing *et al.* (2005) for DEFRA, which observed that estimates in the literature range from £0 to £1,000/tC (£0–272.7/tCO$_2$), and suggested a lower benchmark of £35/tC (\$12.5/tCO$_2$) (all at 2000 prices). Tol's (2005) survey found a median value of \$14/tC (\$3.8/tCO$_2$) and the 95th percentile at \$350/tC (\$95.5/tCO$_2$), comparable to that of the *Stern Review* (Stern, 2006, p. 288).

[2] As explained in Chapter 2, the baseline scenarios assume no effective climate change mitigation, although different possible evolutions of emissions, so that, eventually, damaging climate change will be unavoidable. In contrast, if we were to model a successful climate change mitigation strategy, then disaster would be averted and the SCC could be considerably lower.

willing to express significant social concern for distant future generations (low rate of pure time preference), or by assuming that the implied actions now, which are costly but not that costly (1–2% of GDP) should be considered as an insurance premium for a possibly very low (but essentially unknown) chance of very serious future damage. By definition, unpredictable events are impossible to model with any confidence, and the high SCC is warning us to take adequate steps now to reduce the risks of extreme, if unlikely, future disaster.

The SCC could be interpreted as the correct *price* to set for emissions of carbon if the world were to collectively agree to the associated system of equity weights and rate of pure time preference. Even then, as Chapter 2 indicates, the SCC depends on whose consumption is taken as numeraire. As reported, the numeraire (as in the *Stern Review*) is world average GDP/ head at $PPP, but the SCC would be much higher if EU GDP/head were the numeraire, and very much lower if sub-Saharan African GDP/head were used instead. The world average makes sense if there were a world government allocating resources for the benefit of all, but we are a long way from that situation. The PAGE SCC without equity weighting is rather more than half the equity-weighted value, and might represent a consensus view in which each country worries about the cash value of its own damage, but collectively recognises the public-good nature of mitigation. This is more likely if the costs of mitigation are proportional to GDP (as is likely in the electricity sector), since future damage is also likely to be proportional to GDP and, if anything, larger in poorer countries, encouraging their cooperation. On the insurance argument, though, the main point is that the price of carbon should be high enough to induce sufficient mitigation, regardless of the fine balancing of current cost for expected future gain.

To maximise global efficiency – and if international transfers (or allocations of carbon allowances) can address equity issues – the carbon price should be the same everywhere. Clearly, in practice, any such global price of carbon would have to emerge from negotiations, and would have to be a market price not an equity-weighted social value of the kind used in (typically national) social cost–benefit analysis (e.g. as in HMT, 2003). Given all the considerations noted above, it is hard to predict what price might emerge from such negotiations, and the range of potentially defensible outcomes is clearly very wide.

In terms of its implications for electricity policy, the most significant thing is that *the range of potentially defensible SCCs spans almost the entire range of possible relevance to the economics of power generation.* Chapter 3 summarises the implicit additional cost of the main low-carbon power sources available to the UK. The results are consistent with the IPCC conclusions that many large-scale options (e.g. nuclear, CCS, offshore wind and most biomass) would become economic at carbon prices in the range of $20–50/tCO$_2$ ($75–185/tC), if and as they were to be deployed at scale. The *Stern Review*'s estimate of SCC is comfortably above the upper end. The Tol mean is towards the lower part of this range. The PAGE results in Chapter 2 easily span the range and the 5–95% estimates go far beyond at both ends. In other words, plausibly defensible estimates of the SCC, applied as carbon prices, could imply anything ranging from a marginal additional cost insufficient to help most low-carbon power sources, to a huge carbon charge sufficient for such sources to unambiguously dominate power investment.

Given that investment decisions need to be made, and that neither further analysis nor global negotiations are likely to resolve the uncertainties quickly, a need for forward-looking judgement is inescapable. In this context, Figure 11.1 frames the cost–benefit economics of carbon pricing decisions. As prices increase roughly over the range indicated, there may be quite a rapid increase in the degree of abatement in

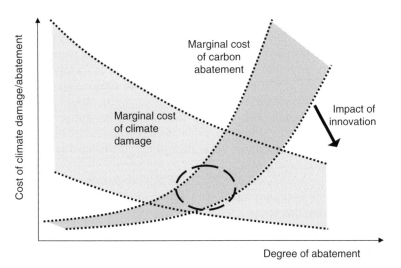

Figure 11.1. Plausible abatement marginal cost and benefit schedules
Note: The Figure illustrates schematically the cost–benefit trade-off in the face of uncertainty. The 'cost of climate damage' declines as the degree of abatement (*x*-axis) increases, but is highly uncertain (as indicated by the wide vertical range – that is, in fact, still very much narrower than suggested by the discussion of Impacts earlier in this chapter). The cost of abatement may be modest for small cuts, but both the cost and the uncertainty rise steeply for much more aggressive cutbacks. The dotted circle indicates that a rational trade-off would be to pursue abatement to a level just before these costs start to rise sharply, whilst innovation policies seek to generate new options to bring down the cost of deeper emission cuts.

response, particularly as investment decisions start to switch away from coal towards low-carbon sources. Above a certain price, however, most zero-carbon sources may be exhausted (or may be facing hard constraints on siting or rates of expansion), so additional abatement may be very limited, at costs that could anyway only be justified if the SCC were at the higher levels of estimation. In the context of such uncertainties, in other words, a rational mitigation goal would be for a price/quantity outcome somewhere around the 'point of inflexion' in the supply curve – in the circle indicated in Figure 11.1 that could minimise 'the cost of being wrong'. The circle itself spans a significant range. Where to aim is not just a matter of making a best estimate applicable – it also needs to consider the role that the UK wishes to take in the global process (discussed below), and the dynamic implications of the related decisions.

11.3   Taxes or quotas?

11.3.1   Theoretical fundamentals

A price for carbon can be established directly, either using a carbon tax or by setting a quantity limit and letting companies trade the resulting emission allowances. The EU approach is to issue EU Emission Allowances (EUA), each for 1 tonne of CO_2, while in the past, various countries, starting particularly in Scandinavia in the early 1990s, have imposed carbon taxes on fuels (with exemptions for internationally exposed industries). If there is complete information and no uncertainty, the efficient level could be achieved either by issuing the correct number of quotas or setting the pollution tax at the marginal damage cost at the efficient level. This equality of outcome breaks down under uncertainty or with asymmetric information. Weitzman (1974) started a lengthy debate by observing that, in the presence of uncertainty, quotas are only superior to taxes if the marginal benefit from abatement schedule (i.e. the marginal damage of emissions) is steeper than the marginal cost of abatement schedule. Figure 11.2 shows that, if the taxes and allowances are set on the basis of the expected marginal costs and benefits, but the correct marginal costs are higher than expected, then the deadweight or efficiency loss from incorrectly setting a permit at level Q rather than $Q^\star$ is considerably higher than incorrectly setting the tax or charge at t rather than $t^\star$.[3]

---

[3] Weitzman shows that the comparative advantage of prices over quantities is given by the formula $1/2$ *variance of MC* × *(slope of MC − slope of MB)/(slope of MC)²*, and is independent of the uncertainty in the position of the marginal benefit schedule, provided that policies are based on unbiased best estimates of the schedules. If that schedule is flat, then the formula simplifies to $1/2$ *variance of MC/(slope of MC)*.

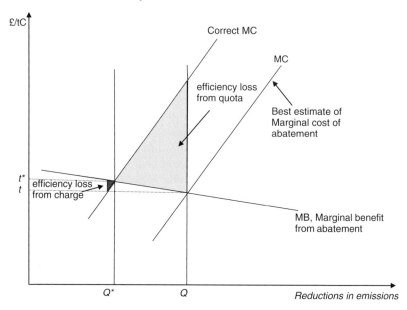

Figure 11.2. Relative efficiency of prices vs. quantities, as per
Weitzman (1974)

As already noted, GHG emissions contribute to an atmospheric stock
with a very slow rate of decay. The damage contributed by emissions
today is effectively the same as that contributed by the same amount of
emissions tomorrow, and so the marginal benefit of abatement is
essentially flat at each moment, while the marginal cost of abatement
rises rapidly beyond a certain point. The scale of the hazard of global
warming is very uncertain, as are the future costs of reducing carbon
intensity. All these are arguments for a stable global carbon price or tax.
As more information about the damage of global warming becomes
available, so the optimal tax can be adjusted (just as the allowed level of
emissions would have to be adjusted). The desirable stability of the
carbon price is not absolute, but only applies over (possibly quite long)
periods of time in which no significant new information arrives, as discussed below. In contrast, tradable quotas can give rise to volatile prices
over quite short periods of time, as illustrated for the European Union
Emission Trading Scheme (EU ETS) in the next section.

Hoel and Karp (2001) explore this question more carefully in a calibrated linear–quadratic dynamic model of global warming and confirm
Weitzman's insight robustly. Pizer (2002) demonstrates the same result

based on simulating a stochastic computable general equilibrium model while, as noted, the PAGE model discussed in Chapter 2 demonstrates the apparent insensitivity of the SCC (including the carbon price with no equity weighting) to the level of emissions on a 'business as usual' path. These simple economic arguments suggest that there is a stronger case for a fixed, stable carbon price (via taxes or some other mechanism) than for fixed or stable quota allocations, as long as the dominant determinants of emissions are to do with price more than with regulatory structure, and that the carbon price would be significant relative to other economic forces.

These generic economic considerations need to be tested against specific applications. The extent to which the likely characteristics of the cost and benefit schedules (Figure 11.1) may in themselves affect the Weitzman argument is unclear. The assumption that short-run mitigation has very little impact on long-run damages may not be true as far as some new power sector investments are concerned, such as the choice between a coal vs. nuclear or renewable plant that may last many decades. Moreover, whilst the *Stern Review* acknowledges the Weitzman argument for the short term, it also argues that increasing long-term risks make it desirable to aim at an equilibrium GHG concentration below 550 ppm (CO_2 equivalent). This is equivalent to specifying a stock of GHGs, or a quantity limit on the amount of fossil fuel that can be burned over the next 100–200 years. The argument for choosing this quantity target, loosely stated, is that mitigation costs are too high to aim at lower levels (e.g. 450 ppm), while overshooting 550 ppm runs a serious risk of irreversible and catastrophically expensive future outcomes. If so, then setting a quantity limit on the amount of carbon released appears prudent. Which is correct? The *Stern Review* leaves this open, noting that '*Establishing a carbon price, through tax, trading or regulation, is an essential foundation for climate-change policy*' (Stern, 2006, p. xviii, emphasis in original).

The two views can be reconciled by noting that the carbon price should be moderately stable over reasonable time periods (1–15 years if no new information about the costs of climate change materialises), but over longer periods of time the price will need to be adjusted to balance cumulative carbon emissions with absorptive capacity. Hepburn *et al.* (2006) discuss the relation between a longer-term target quantity and the need to stabilise the carbon price in the short to medium term.

The *Stern Review* proposes 550 ppm as a ceiling, but does not thereby conclude that the annual (or even decadal) emissions should necessarily be quantity controlled. Indeed, the Review points out that there are many trajectories consistent with meeting the eventual 550 ppm target, and that some will clearly be more expensive than others. Unfortunately, without knowing the rate at which cost-effective, low-carbon technologies will diffuse and improved technologies be developed, it is hard to choose between the possible paths. Faced with such uncertainty, and given that the SCC may be relatively insensitive to the choice of path, it makes more sense for the market, guided by the carbon price, to determine the least-cost path to the target.

11.3.2   *International and whole-economy approaches*

A carbon tax is an efficient instrument to the extent that energy price is a major determinant of the relevant decisions. Grubb (2007) argues that about half of the CO_2 emissions in industrialised countries arise from sectors which are economically 'well-behaved' in this sense. These comprise principally power generation and heavy industry, sectors in which coal is the principal source of emissions and the price of energy – and relative fuel prices – is the dominant determinant of emissions. However, buildings account for around one-third of CO_2 emissions (including the embodied emissions through their power consumption), and there is overwhelming empirical evidence that emissions from buildings and the appliances within them are determined far more by building codes and appliance standard regulations than by energy prices. This is due to a mix of contractual failure (the 'tenant–landlord' split), informational failures (consumer ignorance about the energy/emission characteristics of their purchases) and behavioural economic issues, particularly concerning economically trivial expenditures. These observations do not make price in these sectors irrelevant, but they do imply that an efficient response has to involve a range of measures in addition to carbon pricing.

Even in the economically 'well-behaved' sectors, there could be difficulties in determining the true 'additionality' of carbon taxes. Thus most countries levy heavy excise taxes on road fuel, which can be thought of as part of a system of road user charging, and could claim quite reasonably that some part of this fuel excise were a carbon tax and could be reduced to offset the agreed carbon tax (Newbery, 2006). Moreover, even under the clear carbon incentives of the EU ETS, its carbon effectiveness in some countries remains blunted by regulatory structures that prevent the pass-through of marginal carbon prices to final electricity prices (Sijm *et al.*, 2006). This points to fundamental difficulties in trying to define international mitigation policy through an agreement on carbon taxation. Such an agreement would not give an incentive for governments to fix market problems that increase emissions – indeed, by making carbon a source of revenue it could arguably do the opposite – and the real additionality of any such agreement could be almost impossible to define relative to existing tax and subsidy structures. Moreover, it touches on one of the most sensitive of all areas of domestic policy, namely sovereign authority to define the level and incidence of taxation. A stark illustration is the fate of the EU carbon tax. Despite the context of a successful completed Treaty of Maastricht, establishing the goal of a single market underpinned by the dilution of sovereign decision-making powers, the original EC proposal for a unified EU carbon tax was debated for 5 years after its proposal in 1990 before finally being buried in favour of a far looser structure of guidance and partial convergence in relation to existing petroleum taxes. Globally, there is simply no supranational authority to which countries would be willing to entrust power to set tax levels, and override national sovereignty to choose other or complementary instruments. Hence the focus of the Kyoto Protocol lies squarely on agreeing quantified goals for emission reductions, leaving the choice of implementation to national decision making. Allowance for trading between countries increases flexibility and encourages internationally efficient reductions, but without necessarily determining the same carbon price across all sectors of all participating economies. We discuss the challenges of international coordination further at the end of this chapter.

11.3.3   Tax vs. trading in domestic policy

The choice of tax vs. trading has more practical scope in terms of sovereign choice over the selection of domestic instruments. At this level there are additional differences between taxes and quotas that are important, although opposed. Pollution taxes raise revenue and allow other taxes to be reduced, thus reducing deadweight costs. The so-called 'double dividend' is discussed by Newbery (2005) and need not detain us here. Quotas could be auctioned to produce revenue, so this is not necessarily a critical difference. The more important difference is that quotas are normally allocated freely – not only to countries, but within countries to eligible firms under 'grandfather' clauses – in order to buy off opposition to their introduction. Again, this difference is not decisive, because countries could decide on a carbon price or tax, with each retaining its own tax proceeds (which has obvious attractions), subject to the problem of additionality mentioned above for the case of transport fuel excise taxes. One such example is the UK Climate Change Levy, which was imposed on industry but was compensated for by a reduction in the National Insurance Tax (a tax on labour) paid by those liable for the tax.

Nor is it immediately obvious whether quotas or taxes offer countries greater opportunities to renege on any international climate change agreement, as that will depend on the reliability of GHG monitoring and the sanctions available to other countries to punish any deviations. If, under the WTO, countries can impose border taxes to compensate for 'unfair subsidies' (i.e. a failure to properly charge for GHG emissions) and if these emissions can be observed, then tax floors may work. If countries use quota allocations to preferentially favour trade-exposed sectors, and are able to understate emissions from other sectors, then the agreement may come under greater pressure.

For some sectors, such as household energy consumption, a carbon tax would appear intrinsically simpler in part just because of the trans-actional complications of trading instruments (notwithstanding the need to address other issues surrounding buildings-related energy use). In sectors such as power generation, Weiztman-like arguments and the need for investment security favour a tax-like instrument. Such an application to industrial energy use, however, might exacerbate concerns about international competitiveness impacts. Indeed, an important final complication is that taxes, because they combine the function of a price incentive with large revenue transfers, are not only politically difficult but tend to be adapted heavily to reflect pre-existing circumstances. A study of Norway, Finland, Sweden and Denmark (Anderson, 2004) notes that, despite the strong common view in favour of carbon taxes since the early 1990s, the actual pattern of 'carbon' taxes to emerge varies radically between this group of four relatively closely aligned Scandinavian countries, in terms of level, coverage, derogations, etc.

In the EU, considerations of sovereignty, legal and institutional structures, and the inherent political difficulties of more visible large-scale revenue transfers embodied in a carbon tax, combined to make the EU ETS the only practical way to establish an EU-wide carbon price across the core power and industrial sectors.[4] Establishing a single carbon price across almost half the EU's total emissions, in theory, offers big efficiency gains that should not lightly be cast aside. Moreover, in principle, this need not stop each country auctioning off quotas (collecting the same revenue as a tax at the market-clearing price on that

---

[4] One might observe that allocating free EUAs for 95% of the power sector generated huge rent transfers from electricity consumers to generators, as they were able to include the EUA price in the variable cost of generation (as illustrated below), whereas a carbon tax would have allowed governments to reduce other taxes and so compensated consumers. Of course, auctioning the quotas would have had the same effect. Arguably the ETS was successfully launched because politicians (and consumer action groups) failed to appreciate the impact on electricity prices and the large rent transfers, while the electricity companies were aware of this.

level of emissions). In practice, the European ETS requires 90% of these quotas (during the Kyoto first period of 2008–2012) to be allocated or 'grandfathered'. If quotas are issued and are valid for a long time period and can be banked and borrowed (as with the USA's sulphur cap-and-trade system) the inter-temporal carbon price should be arbitraged, but this would not necessarily ensure that it remained constant even in present value over time (as the volatility of futures prices of storable commodities demonstrates). Nevertheless, the absence of a supra-national tax authority – and the establishment of the EU ETS – are not arguments against stabilising the price of carbon.

All this suggests that efficient climate policy may need a combination of price and non-price measures, set within the context of an inter-national agreement that gives incentives for governments to address the full set of inefficiencies in domestic price and regulatory structures that determine emissions. We return to this point below after considering the way in which the current EU Emission Trading Scheme works and how it may be improved.

11.4   The European Union Emission Trading Scheme

The European Union has agreed the EU Emission Trading Scheme (ETS) as its principal means of reducing emissions of the main green-house gas, carbon dioxide (CO_2). It started in 2005 with a three-year Phase I to 2007; Phase II runs from 2008–12 (the Kyoto Protocol first period); and subsequent phases will be designed after a wholesale review of its operation. It caps emissions from large central facilities, and in Phases I and II covers all power generators and six major industrial sectors which receive EU Emission Allowances (EUAs). After each calendar year, facilities must retire EUAs to match their actual verified emissions. Allowances can be freely tended across the EU-27 countries, and a carbon price emerges from the balance between EU-wide supply and demand. The Directive that established the scheme stipulated that Member States should give out at least 95% of allow-ances for free in Phase I and 90% in Phase II, with no constraints placed on allocated approaches thereafter.

11.4.1   EU ETS price trends and price pass-through

Figure 11.3 shows prices in the EU ETS for both first- and second-period delivery. Prices rose initially, as the European Commission sought to strengthen allocation plans, and stayed relatively high until Spring 2006, when detailed verified information about supply and

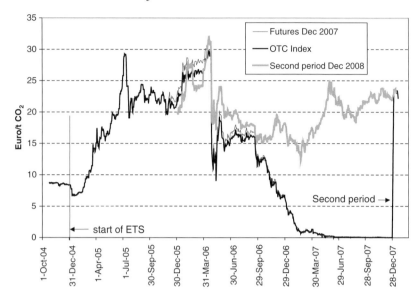

Figure 11.3. EUA price 25 October 2004–9 January 2008 (price of CO_2 in €/tonne)
Source: European Energy Exchange, Market Data

demand of EUAs became public.[5] The price of first-period EUAs, which expired at the end of Phase I and could not be carried forward subsequently crashed and dwindled close to zero, whilst an active forward trading market for Phase II allowances emerged, with prices in the range €15–25/tCO_2. The market for EUAs has clearly been volatile. Moreover, the price of EUAs can be expected to feed through to the wholesale price of electricity in a competitive market although, where final prices are regulated, the price could be held down to offset the windfall profits earned on the allocated EUAs.

Some evidence that the EUA price does indeed feed through to the wholesale price is provided by Figure 11.4, which shows the forward base year French and German electricity contract prices traded on the EEX, and the cost of the EUAs required for gas-fired or coal-fired generation.

---

[5] The European Commission published verified emissions data for 11,500 plants on 15 May 2006, suggesting that there was an excess of EUAs – either because of over-allocation or out-performance in emissions reduction – and this naturally caused prices to fall.

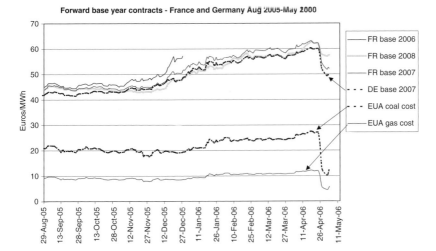

Figure 11.4. Response of forward electricity price to change in EUA price
Source: European Energy Exchange, Market Data

The May 2006 fall in the futures price of French baseload electricity (all generated by nuclear power) dropped by an amount better explained by the EUA gas cost than the EUA coal cost, even though the price in France is clearly set by the price in Germany (which has dominantly coal-fired base load electricity). We can investigate the link between electricity, gas and carbon prices by examining the 'clean spark spread' – that is, the price of electricity less the cost of gas needed in a combined cycle gas turbine (CCGT) of 50% efficiency and net of the cost of the EUAs required in such a plant. It measures the return to the capital cost of the plant (and any other non-fuel costs), and should tend towards the return needed to reward new investment, at least so long as CCGT remains an attractive investment choice.

Figure 11.5 graphs the clean spark spread in the UK, Germany and the Netherlands. The visual interpretation is that, after an initial period of adjustment, the gross profit margin has returned to where it had been, suggesting that most, if not all, of the EUA opportunity cost has been passed through into the wholesale price. Various authors have undertaken more careful econometric estimates of the extent to which EUA prices are passed through into electricity prices (IEA, 2007). Honka-tukia *et al.* (2006) estimated that 75–90% of EUA price changes were passed through to the Finnish Nord Pool day-ahead prices, even

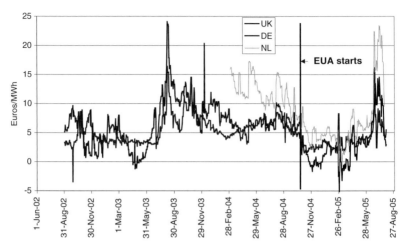

Figure 11.5. Gross profit of CCGT after paying for fuel and carbon (spark spread net of EUA)
Source: Platts, Energy Market Data

though the Nordic market is dominated by nuclear and hydroelectricity (but linked to the rest of Europe). In a sophisticated bootstrapping econometric exercise, Sijm *et al.* (2006) examined the impact of EUA price changes on the cost of generating from coal in Germany, finding complete pass-through for peak prices and 60–70% for off-peak prices (when interconnectors are less constrained and imports introduce competition from other fuels). In the Netherlands they found that 60–80% of the EUA price changes are passed through for peak hours for gas generation, and 70–80% passed through in off-peak hours for coal generation.[6]

Several consequences follow on from this unsurprising conclusion. The first is that the free allocation of EUAs to power generators constituted a large windfall gain, as they were compensated for the increase in the carbon cost of generation but could sell the electricity at a price inclusive of the carbon cost. For example, in Germany, the second-phase allocation of EUAs to the power sector will be €205 million p.a.,

[6] The impact of EUA price changes are roughly twice as high for coal, as it is more carbon-intensive. As Dutch electricity prices are higher than those of neighbouring countries, there may be less scope for passing cost increases through fully. Explaining spot electricity prices is particularly difficult, as they are affected by contract cover, market power, the extent of the market, i.e. whether interconnectors are constrained, and the supply–demand balance, so the match between theory and evidence is impressive.

which at a price of €20/tCO$_2$ amounts to a windfall gain of over €4 billion p.a. (and that is for just one of the 25 countries). There is therefore a strong case for not allocating the electricity supply industry (ESI) more than a very small number of EUAs in future periods. The second conclusion is less obvious, and provides an additional argument for stabilising the price of EUAs rather than allowing the price to be determined by supply and demand.

11.4.2   The impact of the EU ETS on the gas market

Under the current organisation of the ETS, the price of EUAs is determined by supply and demand, and both depend on the extent to which the ESI can substitute less-carbon-intensive fuels such as gas for more-carbon-intensive fuels such as coal through changes in the merit order. This is nicely illustrated in Figure 11.6, which shows the daily evolution of generation in Great Britain over a short period of time in which the UK gas price increased sharply.

As the cost of running gas-fired plant increased relative to coal, so the share of coal-fired generation increased sharply, increasing total emissions from the ESI, as coal is more carbon-intensive than gas. Thus as the price of gas increases, the price of EUAs increases, as the demand from coal-fired generation will increase the demand for EUAs. This will

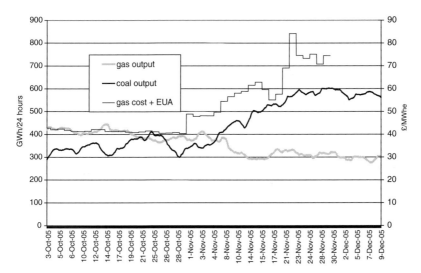

Figure 11.6. The impact of gas and carbon costs on the British merit order (weekday moving 24 hr average coal and gas generation)
Sources: European Energy Exchange, National Grid UK, Platts

raise the cost of burning coal instead of gas and reduce the extent to which electricity producers will switch from gas to coal in response to a gas price rise. The effect of fixing the *quantity* of EUAs, rather than their *price*, is that the elasticity of demand for gas will decrease (i.e. gas demand will become less sensitive to the price of gas because of the indirect effects on substitutes feeding through the EUA price change).

While the international market for coal is reasonably competitive, the same is not true for gas, particularly in Europe, which is heavily dependent on importing Russian gas from the monopoly supplier, Gazprom. In addition, gas producers and suppliers in the EU have more market power than the suppliers of other fuels, and are frequently vertically integrated into electricity generation. Ruhrgas, the dominant German gas company since its controversial merger with E.ON, has a dominant position in gas supply through its control of its gas pipeline network, and an incentive to raise the price of gas to raise electricity prices, and hence the profits of its merged partner, E.ON (Henriksson, 2005). The market power of gas suppliers depends on the elasticity of demand for gas – if the elasticity is high, so that demand falls sharply when prices increase, the dominant gas suppliers will have little market power. But, if the elasticity is low or reduced because of the ETS, then gas suppliers will have more market power, and a greater incentive to raise gas prices. There are therefore grounds for concern that the particular way in which climate change policy works in the EU, through pricing a fixed supply of EUAs, may amplify the existing market power in the gas market. The obvious solution is to cut the link between the demand for EUAs and their price by fixing or stabilising the price of the EUAs.

11.5   Stabilising the price of carbon and hybrid instruments

To recap, there are good economic arguments for fixing the price of carbon rather than fixing the total level of emissions in each period and allowing the market to determine the price. There are good political economy arguments for launching climate change policies through issuing tradable permits, as in the ETS (and most other market-oriented pollution abatement schemes). Various authors have argued that it may be possible to combine the best of both worlds through various hybrid approaches that are neither of the two extremes of Weitzman's (1974) 'prices *or* quantities'.[7] Thus, Pizer (2002) argues for an initial allocation of permits, followed by the issuing of additional permits at a fixed price. In the case of

---

[7] As Weitzman himself recognised when he added that 'The issue of prices vs. quantities has to be a 'second best' problem by its very nature simply because there is no good *a*

the ETS this could be done either by the European Commission (or some similar body) being prepared to buy and sell any number of EUAs at the fixed price, or by replacing the ETS by a fixed carbon tax per tonne of carbon burned. The former is likely to be politically more attractive than the latter, and can be made cash-positive or neutral to the EC by suitable reductions in the allocations of EUAs each year.

A similar proposal, termed the 'safety valve', was discussed by Jacoby and Ellerman (2004), while Hepburn (2006) surveyed the range of hybrid instruments, including price ceilings and floors, and penalties for failing to deliver permits (which effectively cap the price at the penalty level – the method used in the UK for Renewable Obligation Certificates). These alternative approaches to reducing or eliminating price volatility differ in the financial risks they place on the agency entrusted to stabilise the price. While there is little risk in capping the price (and penalties would generate extra income), the main problem is in providing a floor, as buying permits to support the price could be costly. Of course, if sufficiently few allowances are issued in the first place, this risk can be made arbitrarily small. If there is sufficient auctioning, one way of establishing a price floor would thus be for governments to set a minimum reserve price on auctions, so that additional allowances would not enter the market below this price (Hepburn et al., 2006). In the EU ETS, auctioning is not centralised but in Phase II. the total volume of auctions is dominated by the two biggest emitting countries, namely the UK (7%) and Germany (9%): if they agreed a minimum reserve price, this could help to set a floor price for the EU ETS overall. A more robust and inclusive approach would need to be developed for Phase III.

There remains one important issue that cannot be avoided. The social cost of carbon depends on ethical judgements, as noted above, as well as on economic and climate change forecasts, and is highly uncertain (as demonstrated by the width of the 5–95% confidence bands around the mean value). The Kyoto agreements and the ETS allocations were the outcome of a political bargaining process, albeit one influenced by ethics (particularly the contentious issue of the value of lives saved), as well as climate science. Any carbon price would probably have to be negotiated, perhaps on a better-informed basis than before (as a result of the remark-able impact of, and debates provoked by, the *Stern Review*, and the ever- greater confidence attached to the climate science). It seems most unlikely that any negotiation would agree anything like the Stern central value of $312/tC ($85.1/tCO$_2$), which would quadruple the price of burning coal, compared with figures around $70–180/tC ($19.1–49.1/tCO$_2$) at which EUAs have

priori reason for limiting attention to just these two particular signals' (Weitzman, 1974, p. 481).

traded. On the other hand, the ETS range sits comfortably with the PAGE equity-weighted estimates of Chapter 2. What then should be the target carbon price (or floor) that the EU should aim at, if we accept the desirability of stabilising the price, recognising the considerable uncertainty (and disagreements) about the right value?

One possible answer is to aim at the highest politically sustainable level, recognising that any political compromise is likely to fall short of the true SCC, but put in place an escalator that increases its value in real terms by, say, 2–3% p.a. (which is what should happen anyway, as Chapter 2 argued). This model of an escalating charge has been followed for setting the road fuel duty in the UK in the 1990s. It was also adopted as a way of adjusting the price of water towards a level that more closely reflected long-run marginal cost after privatisation in 1989. Prices were adjusted each year in line with the retail price index (RPI), *less* an efficiency factor, X, but *plus* a capital adjustment factor, K, hence $RPI - X + K$. The lower the agreed value, the more important that this should be stated as a floor, with possible upward revisions as new data or more political consensus (or a broader coverage of countries) emerges. If such a commitment could be made credible, it would do much to reduce investment risk. If any ceiling were set not too far above the floor, then the floor might be raised in response to sustained upward pressure on the ceiling, as with crawling peg exchange rates. If the price settled at the floor, then the fraction of EUAs to be auctioned rather than allocated should be increased (and more held back to support the floor).

11.6   Carbon price-investment security for the longer term

The current allocations under the Kyoto Protocol and the EU ETS end in 2012, injecting considerable uncertainty into subsequent commitments and prices. The DTI's *Energy Review* is very clear about the need for longer-term carbon price signals:

the Government is committed to there being a continuing carbon price signal which investors take into account when making decisions. This is particularly important given the scale of new investment required in UK electricity generation capacity. The EU ETS is here to stay beyond 2012 and will remain the key mechanism for providing this signal. The Government will continue to work with its international partners to strengthen the EU ETS to make it more effective. We will keep open the option of further measures to reinforce the operation of the EU ETS in the UK should this be necessary to provide greater certainty to investors (*Energy Review*, DTI, 2006, p. 157).

The *Energy Review* is, however, silent on how greater certainty could be provided. This section sets out *why* current instruments will not deliver an adequate investment response, and discusses the options for addressing this.[8]

11.6.1   Economic fundamentals: why the market may fail

Uncertainty is not new: investors face it all the time. There are, however, three things that make the low-carbon electricity issue fundamentally different:

1. The risk associated with carbon price is largely policy and political, i.e. a risk that private investors find particularly hard to judge and manage, and where alternative strategies include investing in lobbying, or just waiting for policy uncertainty to be resolved.
2. The time-scales of investment are very long, and there is a marked disjuncture between the time horizons of most corporate or equity investors (seeking a typical 10–15% rate of return for more speculative projects, though considerably lower for low-risk mainstream utility investments), and those of government (discount rates that reflect ethical bases for consistent intergenerational decision making, as in the *Stern Report* (of about 1.4%), and the UK Government *Green Book* rate of 3.5% – see Chapter 2). In itself, this would not necessarily matter (other investments are also long-lived but do not need special treatment), but it is the combination of long time scales *and* policy risk that is damaging.
3. While fossil fuel generation is at the margin in setting the electricity price, conventional generators will be largely hedged against both fuel and carbon price risk, as these will determine the price of electricity. Investors take comfort from the link between the marginal (fuel plus carbon) cost of generation and the electricity price, and are thus able to shift much of the input cost risk through to consumers, at least if they have a balanced portfolio of plant. Companies that specialise in renewables or nuclear power are exposed to an electricity price driven by the volatile marginal fuel cost and a possibly volatile carbon price, and so face more risk (Roques *et al.*, 2006). Thus *even with a fixed and guaranteed carbon price, the structure of electricity markets places the risk associated with uncertainties in the electricity price on low-carbon*

---

[8] The House of Commons (2006) report *New Nuclear? Examining the Issues* discusses the importance of and mechanisms for long-term carbon pricing at paras 179 *et seq.*

investors. Again, such risks are not necessarily indicative of market failure, but they may amplify the underlying problem of policy risk.

Other market actors   Consumers should be keen to hold shares in generation companies whose costs are independent of fuel and carbon prices, in order to hedge the electricity price risks they face. Similarly, suppliers (or even final consumers, as in Finland for nuclear power) may be willing to sign contracts for low-carbon electricity to hedge their exposure to electricity price risk. It has been suggested that insurance companies should be willing to finance low-carbon generation with electricity bonds (linked to the long-term purchase price contracted for the output of the power station) and issue these as part of a pension portfolio, offering insurance against the future cost of electricity. However, this would require pension funds to actively decide to make risky and possibly very illiquid investment decisions in new technologies – laying them open to charges of failing in their fiduciary duties to pensioners.

The most fundamental conclusion is that, without more stable long-term signals, investors will defer difficult decisions and are more likely to adopt the lowest-risk (to them) and most flexible investments. Fundamentally, this favours investment in combined cycle gas turbines: low cost, quick to build, and with the fuel and carbon risks passed on to customers. Sustained over the coming decades, such investments would not provide either a secure, or a very low-carbon, electricity system, although it may be preferable to investing in more expensive plant burning cheap coal.

The *Stern Review* is even more explicit than the *Energy Review* about the need for a credible long-term carbon price:

> In order to influence behaviour and investment decisions, investors and consumers must believe that the carbon price will be maintained into the future. This is particularly important for investments in long-lived capital stock (Stern, 2006, p. xix).

The *Review* is more specific about the design of instruments to achieve this goal, and its Chapter 15 considers these issues in depth, drawing out strong implications for the future design of the ETS, although without explicitly stating the need to stabilise the resulting carbon price (Stern, 2006, Box 15.3, p. 337).

11.6.2   *Policy options for longer-term investment security*

This chapter has argued that it is desirable to stabilise the price of carbon (around a steadily rising path) rather than limiting the *annual* level of emissions, and this objective also achieves the other desirable goal of delivering the desired low-carbon investments at least cost. There are several ways to establish longer-term, low-carbon incentives that could be considered in principle.

Option (a): Long-period commitments If Phase III EU ETS allocations could be agreed soon, and specified in a single period with a time scale covering investment time horizons, this would solve the problem. Neither is credible; it is debatable even whether the latter (much longer time periods of allocation) is desirable, since it would lock in an allocation, potentially for a couple of decades, whilst both the science and the politics of the issue are likely to develop far more rapidly.

Option (b): Allowing unconstrained banking and borrowing of EUAs over multiple periods Allowing extensive banking into, and borrowing from, future periods would, in theory, allow an intertemporal market to emerge with incentives and expectations feeding back to present prices. The most obvious way to bring some longer-term security is then to try and agree several rounds of quantity constraints in advance. A related approach is proposed for UK domestic policy on national emissions in the draft UK Climate Change Bill, which proposes 5-year budget periods defining allowed national emissions, which must be 'set at least three periods (i.e. for 15 years) ahead' (HMG, 2007). In themselves, such aggregate domestic quantity limits may be difficult for industry to translate into a future price, and in practice would leave the actual price in the power and industry sectors still contingent upon the EU ETS, not on the domestic targets.

The same approach could in principle be taken for the EU ETS itself; with full banking and borrowing this would be very similar to simply setting a longer commitment period, with the same fundamental trade-off. The difficulties of allocation and burden-sharing several periods ahead would be daunting at an EU level – and greater still at a global level.[9]

Pizer *et al.* (2002) set out in detail a fundamentally different approach to the problem. They show how defining appropriate long-term *price-based* rules for allocations in a sequential emissions trading system could be used to chart a long-term price path for quantity-based systems. The biggest difficulty lies in translating such theory into practice. It requires credibility of a governmental commitment to both a long-term target

---

[9] Indeed, in the Kyoto negotiations, the original US proposal did suggest negotiations on two commitment periods simultaneously, with banking and borrowing between them – a prospect that was rapidly dropped as the extreme difficulty of agreeing even on one became apparent (Grubb, 1999).

price and to sticking with the rules for translating that into allocations over many rounds. Thus it does not necessarily solve the fundamental problem of the reluctance of markets to speculate – and invest – around political risk. It may not remove the volatility associated with the appearance of important new information (of the kind that caused the EUA price drop in May 2006, as noted above) and additional measures, such as floors or caps, may be needed. It is governments that define the policy environment, and that are the best placed to bear the risks of changes in future policy directions, and they should therefore seek ways of bearing or underwriting those risks for investors.

Option (c): Long-term price declaration   A simpler, but less robust, route would be for governments to set out, perhaps in legislation, planned carbon prices further ahead than the specific instruments and allocations agreed at EU or international level. The issue again is one of credibility. This would be significantly enhanced if implementation of the EU ETS included mechanisms (such as minimum price auctions) that would enable direct implementation of a price floor – though this remains only a partial solution to the credibility problem. If governments are really serious about any price declaration, the obvious question is whether and how they should transmit that conviction to the private sector in legal form – through contracts that bind successive governments, as follows.

Option (d): Contract-for-difference (CfD) on the future carbon price (carbon contracts)   The fourth option would be for governments to issue a contract-for-difference (CfD) with investors on the future carbon price.[10] This could be a simple CfD in which the contract states a strike price of e.g. €15/tCO$_2$ (or €55/tC), and these are either sold or issued in proportion to declared net capacity of new zero-carbon generation. The holder would then be entitled to receive the strike price less the actual carbon price implicit in any UK-wide carbon instrument that applies to fossil generation (and if this price were above the strike price then the holder would be obligated to pay the amount by which the price were above the strike price).[11]

---

[10] See, for example, House of Commons (2006) at paras 179 *et seq.*

[11] This would require the Government to be quite explicit about the equivalent carbon value of any instrument that might replace the ETS, particularly if this took the form of a carbon tax (*not* an energy tax like the Climate Change Levy). If there were no such instrument that specifically charged electricity generators in proportion to the CO$_2$ emitted, then the price would be deemed to be zero.

An alternative would be to issue or sell a one-sided CfD with a floor price, say €10/tCO$_2$, with the issuer obligated to pay any shortfall below this floor price, but the holder would benefit from any upside. Another variant on this that has been explored by Ismer and Neuhoff (2006) is to issue 'put options' on the carbon price. These CfDs could be exercised either at particular dates (perhaps averaged over the previous year) or (particularly in the case of 'put options') over an extended period. Such instruments would provide a powerful commitment signal by the government (or the European Commission) to the continuation of the ETS or its successor, and would also help stabilise the future (and hence, with banking, the present) carbon price.

Option (e): Low-carbon electricity contracts   A way which is less direct from a carbon standpoint, but more direct in terms of electricity investment incentives, would be to sell a long-term CfD on the price of electricity from low- or zero-carbon generation. This would also provide a hedge against fuel price uncertainty. An obvious objection to this is that, if there is a demand for such instruments, the market should offer them and, as with government-financed strategic gas storage, such market interventions might distort the normal market and, worse, displace comparable, more efficiently designed instruments. The defence would be that there is a missing market for carbon and no obvious source of private supply, as the prime risk is political. If so, then the direct approach already described seems best suited to address that market failure. Nevertheless, the government may wish to consider such contracts as part of its commitment to alleviating pensioner fuel poverty, where such a contract may allow the future cost of dealing with such poverty to be lower, as it ought then to be possible to finance the capital-intensive generation at lower rates of interest (i.e. more indexed debt).

There are, of course, other options, some of which require cruder, direct intervention, such as direct government investment or subsidy for preferred low-carbon electricity sources. These face well-known and tested objections, and run counter to the entire thrust of UK energy policy over recent decades towards liberalisation and a declining direct role for the State in investment decisions, and so are unlikely to be contemplated and are not considered here. There is, however, one related set of issues that cannot be avoided, which is the need for appropriate investment in the UK electricity network in ways that would support low-carbon generation sources, and associated questions around the mandate and powers of Ofgem.

11.6.3   Preliminary conclusions

These options all have pros and cons. The first (option (a)) – although it seems to attract the most attention – risks ending up with an uneasy compromise that does not in fact deliver either objective: for example a 10-year fixed allocation for post-2012, finally agreed in, e.g. 2011, could be too long to give flexibility but still too short to help big investments. To the extent that option (b) still relies on future legislative decisions, rather than individual contractual commitments, it does not resolve perceptions of political risk. Option (c) also requires the market to have a high degree of faith in governmental promises and institutions.

Options (d) and (e) address this problem by setting the commitment in individual contracts – with the same status as any other government contractual obligation that can be matched by compensation clauses. Neither is equivalent to a 'whole economy' (or even 'whole sector') carbon price but, for the investing counterparties, they do ensure that the political risk is borne by the government, not the investors. By the same token, they may face the most resistance from governments reluctant to bind themselves to such future liabilities in the event of a weak carbon price. However, because the investment risk in this respect intrinsically arises because of uncertainty about future policy, *there is a compelling case that governments should bear these risks directly* in respect of long-term, low-carbon investments.

All the options raise issues of implementation, which are quite complex in the case of the two 'contracts' ideas that seek to give contractual force to long-term price goals. These consequently must rigorously define either additionality of carbon savings from individual projects (for option (d)), or qualifying generating sources (for option (e)). Defining the problem as being specifically to do with electricity investment may suggest that the electricity contracts route provides a more direct solution. However, it would be helpful to map the relative characteristics and questions around the two 'contract' options side by side, since many aspects might be shared, and might yet throw up fundamental difficulties.

As always, the difficulties of securing agreement on such measures increase the larger and more diverse the set of countries that need to reach agreement. Options (a) and (b) would clearly require international agreement amongst all those countries involved in the carbon pricing/trading scheme. In practice, option (c) would as well, if it is to have much credibility. Thus a further, and potentially decisive, feature of the two 'contract' options ((d) and (e)) is that any government, if it chose to do so, could establish long-term contracts-for-difference (CfD) for any facility sited in its territory. This would be a compelling statement of its own confidence in future carbon prices or, at least, its willingness to bear the risk of protecting domestic low-carbon investments against the possibility of failure of the international effort around more general carbon pricing instruments.

Such commitments would consequently lower the cost of delivering future lower-carbon technologies. The main downside is the risk of other countries free-riding, which suggests the importance of international 'sticks and carrots' for climate change commitment, to which we finally turn.

11.7   Evolution towards a global climate change agreement?

One tonne of GHG released anywhere has the same global impact regardless of its country of origin, but the damage caused by climate change varies across countries, and may be more serious in the tropics (at least as a share of GDP). Every country has an interest in solving this global problem, but not all are equally able or willing to contribute. The international problem is to devise policies that will make humanity better off, and which limit the incentives to opt out of such agreements; the latter probably implies, at minimum, structures which ultimately make each country better off participating than not.

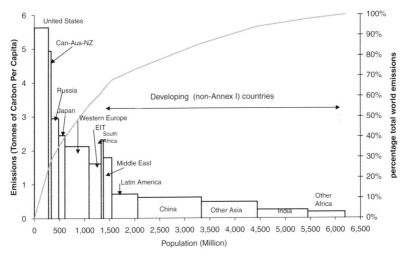

Figure 11.7. CO_2 emissions per head against population in 2000 (areas represent emissions)
Source: Energy Information Administration, International Energy Annual

Similarly, all countries will benefit from the development of cheaper low-carbon technologies that lower the total cost of addressing climate change, but their development will be costly. Chapter 12 discusses briefly the prospect for international cooperation to help to share this cost to encourage the most cost-effective research and deployment strategies to be followed, with those best placed to develop each technology encouraged to take the lead.

The objective of international negotiation is to maximise the extent (measured by GHG emissions) of international cooperation. Figure 11.7 shows emissions per head on the *y*-axis and population on the *x*-axis, so that the area of each rectangle is total emissions, with countries ranked by emissions per head (as well as showing the division between the industrialised countries, as defined in Annex I of the UNFCCC, and those classed as developing countries). China accounts for 16% of the world total emissions and the combination of the USA, the EU and China would account for over half of total emissions. If China were to be added to the Annex I countries, the coverage would be 78% of the total. The larger the share of global emissions covered by the cooperating nations, the lower the individual cost of achieving a given level of mitigation, and this provides an incentive for each country to encourage as many of the high emitters as possible to join the agreement. The first, and probably most important, step is ensure that public opinion and policy makers in the larger-emitting countries are made aware of the consequences of climate change, and the costs to their country and to others of failing to reach international agreement to address them. The next step is to select policy instruments that are politically feasible, sustainable and effective.

11.7.1   *International collaboration on carbon-based instruments*

On the face of it, it seems easier to negotiate over target emission reductions, and indeed that was the format for the Kyoto Protocol. The difficulty lies in the joint problem of agreeing the base allocation and the amount of reductions from that to be made. Developing countries argue on strong moral grounds that equal per capita entitlements are the only fair long-term basis, but the rich countries will never agree to the implied large carbon trade flows that this implies. To put this in context, at a carbon price of €50/tC (€13.6/tCO$_2$) and global emissions of 6 Gt of carbon per year,[12] the value of carbon allowances would be €300 billion p.a. Relatively small surpluses or deficits would lead to large transfers.

---

[12] Gt – gigatonnes, 1 Gt = 1,000 million tonnes.

This highlights a tension between different objectives. At one extreme, there is significant resistance in some countries (notably in North America) to *any* significant international financial transfer associated with climate change mitigation. At the opposite extreme, developing countries may seek to use international emissions trading as a vehicle for redressing wider perceived economic imbalances. It seems unclear why rich countries would agree to much bigger transfers through such an indirect route than, for example, in the context of the G8+ negotiations on debt relief. Nevertheless two arguments suggest the need for a compromise between these extremes. The first is simply that international transfers are inherent in an efficient trading-based solution to climate change: global efficiency requires richer countries to be able to spend money to reduce emissions wherever it is cheapest to do so. Second, the general principles agreed in the UNFCCC – and articulated more fully in the *Stern Report* – clearly imply that effective, equitable and efficient solutions require rich countries to assist poorer countries to abate.

Willingness to spend to these ends is already established: around 1 billion tonnes CO_2 emission reductions from developing country projects under Kyoto's Clean Development Mechanism were sold on international carbon markets during 2005 and 2006 (combined), at a total expenditure exceeding US$5 billion, mostly driven by compliance with the EU ETS (much of it in forward transactions, see PointCarbon 2007). The total projected demand of the EU-15 and Japan to meet their Kyoto obligations is about twice this, a little over 1 Gt CO_2 each over the Kyoto period. Their willingness to secure this is not in doubt (although governments may well be able to purchase more cheaply than the private-sector dominated trades in 2005/2006) – although this is not true for Canada.[13]

Various principles can be considered in negotiating the initial allocations that underpin such transfers. An equal proportional reduction from current levels has the advantage that the largest emitters make the largest initial contribution to solving the problem, but they are also the largest contributors to the problem in the first place. As countries become richer, their economic structure shifts away from energy-intensive manufacturing to less energy-intensive services, so their rate of

---

[13] Projections place the total EU deficit at about 1.1 Gt CO_2, and Japan at about 1.3 Gt CO_2, after taking account of all policies and official governmental procurement plans in place at present. Canada would require about 0.5 Gt CO_2 in total to comply with its Kyoto target, but the present government has indicated that it is unwilling to purchase international emission reductions. Since the government cannot raise a parliamentary majority to withdraw from the Kyoto Treaty and clearly has no intention of taking the drastic measures that would now be required to deliver the Kyoto target domestically, its current posture would place Canada in a position of almost unprecedented wilful non-compliance with international law to which it has acceded and ratified.

growth of emissions under 'business as usual' (BAU) is likely to be lower than for poorer countries poised to expand their manufacturing, power and transport sectors rapidly. The reductions might be better related to future predicted BAU levels than based on emissions at some past date (such as the UNFCCC/Kyoto choice of 1990), but the methodology for predicting future BAU levels will itself be the subject of argument and will, in practice, be constrained by the requirement that any likely international trade surpluses in carbon are modest in scale.

In theory, the alternative approach to an economically efficient solution would be to agree a carbon tax rate to apply to all GHG emissions, with each country keeping the revenue. This has both the pros and cons of avoiding international transfers. The simplest way to levy this would be as an excise tax on the carbon content of all fossil fuel, greatly simplifying the problem of identifying and taxing CO_2 emissions for each source (although other GHGs will also have to be dealt with). For the reasons set out under Option (b), this is unlikely to be effective or feasible as the *principal* focus of an international agreement, but it could still be considered for certain sectors with 'well-behaved' market conditions and minimal problems of defining tax additionality. The power sector, and other energy-intensive manufacturing sectors, could qualify. Because many of the latter produce internationally traded goods (and indeed electricity is increasingly traded internationally), such an approach would logically need to be complemented with a border tax on the carbon content of imported goods if they came from non-compliant countries. In principle, this could be compatible with WTO rules, in part on the grounds that countries not charging for the carbon damage would be providing unfair subsidies to their carbon-intensive exports (for a detailed discussion, see Brewer, 2003, 2004).

How do these alternatives compare as choices for international design? First, an explicit carbon tax may make border taxes simpler than tradable permits whose price fluctuates, although it would be possible to levy a carbon import tax equal to the deemed carbon content of best available technology multiplied by either the current carbon permit price or its average over some previous period. In addition, it would be much harder (or impossible) to justify border tax adjustments for the *marginal* (opportunity) costs in a trading scheme, as opposed to a full tax incurred from a carbon tax (Hepburn *et al.*, 2006).

Second, the textbook assumption that taxes and permits are equally efficient may not hold: on the one hand, international quota exchanges may offer the potential and temptation for large countries to exercise market power; whilst any tax agreement would be layered upon highly imperfect underlying energy market structures, including subsidies and areas of contractual failure.

Third, as discussed in Section 11.3.3, the evidence of political economy is that taxes are hard to adopt and almost always distorted compared with the ideal (though distortions in emissions trading systems are also possible; see Neuhoff *et al.*, 2006).

Fourth, as noted, some degree of international transfers may be essential to capture the low-cost options in developing countries. A tax-based agreement would thus need to be complemented by some explicit, probably centralised, international funding mechanism.

Finally, taxes generate revenue that can be used for, *inter alia*, supporting the development and deployment of low-carbon technologies (and reducing other more distorting taxes).

For that reason, though, taxes will be opposed by those on whom the taxes fall (i.e. everyone), while quotas can be granted in proportion to base use, and can compensate (or, as with the electricity supply industry in the EU ETS, overcompensate) emitters for the extra carbon charge. In theory, emitters could be given tax credits equal to the grandfathered permit allocations (Pezzy, 2003), and permit allocations could be progressively reduced with an increasing fraction being auctioned, so the differences in the redistributive properties of taxes and quotas can be exaggerated. From a political economy perspective, though, it is clearly much easier to introduce grandfathered tradable permits (as evidenced by the overwhelming preference for cap-and-trade systems to date).

A hybrid scheme might allow each country to allocate permits as they join the 'carbon abatement club' in any way they choose. The share freely allocated should decline over time on agreed schedules, with an increasing fraction auctioned. Once a sufficiently large part of the world is participating with a sufficiently high level of auctioning, it may be much easier to switch to an equivalent tax, and thereafter allowances would be traded in for the tax (i.e. fossil fuel sellers could either pay the carbon tax or surrender the appropriate number of allowances). This hybrid should also work internationally in that those liable to a tax in any country could discharge the liability with a permit from an eligible country (one in which the permit price were as high as the internationally agreed tax).

A major problem is that, for some countries, the implied tax on coal and even oil would be a high fraction of its cost, and probably much higher in some developing countries than in much richer countries. Thus the local cost of coal in India and China may be considerably below its price in rich countries, and so the carbon tax would be a higher proportion. If coal is \$60/mt imported into Europe, a carbon tax at the rate of \$40/mt of coal would give an import tax *rate* of 67% (although the tax would be levied per tC and as a share of the final delivered price the rate would be lower). If the domestic price of coal in India were only $30/mt, then the relative tax rate would be twice as high, at 133%.[14]

India is a test case, as most Indian states find it impossible to raise electricity prices to cost-reflective levels, and would probably find it even more politically difficult to pass through carbon taxes. Of course, the same argument would apply to permits if their price were allowed to be reflected in marginal electricity prices, as in most of the EU countries but, with regulated prices, free allocations would allow final electricity prices to be held down. Subsidies paid by carbon taxes could have a similar effect. If the local carbon tax were set using purchasing power exchange rates rather than market exchange rates, the result would lead to lower $ taxes for the same perceived carbon price, and this might allow an acceptable compromise. The broad conclusion, however, is that an international response based explicitly around carbon pricing is only likely to be achieved from a process that starts with emission cap-and-trade and evolves towards greater auctioning over time.

11.7.2   *International collaboration on longer-term instruments and enforcement*

Could international collaboration be extended to any of the options for longer-term carbon instruments discussed in the previous section? For the first option (long-period caps), the challenge is synonymous with that already discussed. For the second (pre-commitments on the use of banking and borrowing to secure target prices), the difficulties would be multiplied many times, and this clearly raises questions about the capacity of governments around the world to credibly commit their country to such a complex long-term carbon price management system. Declaring a long-term price objective is perhaps politically the most plausible, but carries the lowest credibility in terms of investment security. The complexity of international agreement on either of two contract-based options is also daunting, except to the extent that they address a more focused issue, namely relating to the specifics of power sector investments.

It is not entirely clear how much international agreement in respect of instruments for long-term investment security matters, however. If *some* countries successfully implement credible longer-term incentives, business will be comparing two regimes: one with a clear long-term incentive, in which low-carbon investments have been to a large degree

---

[14] The carbon tax needed to amount to $40/tonnes of coal might be $60/tC, depending on the carbon content of the coal.

'de-risked' through unilateral government commitments; the other with a short-term carbon control instrument only, with the likelihood that additional obligations will be agreed in the future but no security at all about their terms and nature. It is not at all obvious that business would prefer the latter: business itself might drive the pressure to underpin short-term commitments with longer-term certainty globally.

Finally, from an economic perspective, the greatest obstacles to securing any international agreement concern participation (willingness to accept a commitment) and enforcement (delivery of that commitment once written into an agreement). On the incentives, one issue is a potential linkage to the question of whether or not countries 'weight' a social cost of carbon, as discussed in Chapter 2. To the extent that SCC forms an operational part of policies (or commitments), if the degree of weight that countries attach to global SCC is linked to the breadth of participation, then large-emitting countries, in particular, have an incentive to participate because of the impact this would have on implementation in other countries.

The counter-argument is that leadership is essential in fashioning any international treaty, and that if all countries start with a low implied SCC weighting on the grounds of low international participation, then the international system may never make progress. For leadership to be effective, other countries would need to be reassured that the leaders have effectively committed their future abatement (or tax) policies, lest they believe that any additional abatement by new members would be countered by reduced abatement of the leaders. Ismer and Neuhoff (2006) show that 'put options' or one-sided contracts for differences on the price of carbon can commit a government to maintaining a minimum future price for carbon both internally (to its own low-carbon investors) and externally, to signal commitment to other countries. An explicit price element in a treaty may thus, paradoxically, assist with the challenge of ensuring compliance.

11.8   Conclusions

Addressing climate change efficiently requires that GHG emissions are properly priced, that relevant markets are not seriously distorted, and that low-carbon technologies are developed efficiently (see Chapter 13, which deals with technology support). These objectives require various interventions and international cooperation; the reach of carbon pricing in particular must expand to encompass all major emitters. These are daunting challenges. Table 11.1 summarises key characteristics of the different instrument choices as discussed in this chapter: not

Table 11.1. *Characteristics of different economic instruments at national and international levels*

National	Tax	Tradable quotas	Price contracts[1]	Quota offsets[2]
Political feasibility	*	***	**	***
Single-period efficiency	***	**	n/a	**
Outcome certainty[4]	*	***	*	**
Price stability	***	*	***	*
Long-term stability	**	*	***	*
Flexibility for learning[3]	**	***	*	**

International	Tax varied	Tax harmonised	No or indirect linkage[4]	Interchangeable	Long-term global contracts	International offsets (CDM/JI)
Ease of extending jurisdictions	**	*	***	**	*	***
Global single-period efficiency	**	***	*(*)[5]	***	n/a	**
International transfers	Not intrinsic: separate institutions would be needed		Possible through indirect linkages	Intrinsic determined by allocation	n/a	Intrinsic but constrained by additionality requirements[6]

Key: number of stars indicates the relative attractiveness of the different instruments in relation to the different criteria; n/a stands for not applicable.
Notes:

1. Contracts-for-difference on future prices of carbon and/or (for low-carbon sources) electricity prices.

2. Quota offsets in which projects earn 'emission reduction credits' that can be used in a quota scheme to comply with quotas or (in principle) offset against tax. Offset schemes in principle could also be directly state funded.

3. Flexibility to adapt over time. Quota and tax schemes also intrinsically generate different kinds of learning: quota schemes reveal the costs of given environmental goals; tax schemes, in principle, generate learning about the abatement response, though this is less easy to observe and separate from other factors than price observation in an emissions trading scheme.

4. Emissions trading schemes in different countries could be entirely isolated from each other, share an agreed platform in terms of contributing to negotiated national targets, or be linked indirectly through common recognition of some types of international offsets.

5. Global efficiency depends upon the degree of indirect linkage.

6. Additionality requirements are the requirement to demonstrate that emission credits reflect new and additional emission savings.

surprisingly, as in many complex policy choices, there are trade-offs to be made between competing objectives.

Given the immense political difficulty of establishing any carbon pricing system, the advent of the EU ETS – which ensures a uniform price of carbon across the major industrial emitting sectors for 27 countries – is a very big step forward. It nevertheless remains a highly imperfect and incomplete solution, for the reasons set out. Global efficiency requires a uniform carbon price across countries and over time (with a gentle increase in the price at a rate of perhaps 2–3% p.a.). The EU ETS alone scores badly on both counts. International linkages through the CDM offer only a partial contribution to the global objective, particularly in the absence of US participation, and hinge upon cross-border financial flows that might become unacceptable in scale if they are to seriously address, for example, the growth in Asian developing country emissions. Quota systems also yield unstable prices unless there are caps and floors, banking, and/or an agency charged with trading to stabilise the price. The current system of 5-year periods embodied in the Kyoto Protocol and the EU ETS offer flexibility to adapt, but at the cost of exacerbating the temporal problem, as its reliance on sequential negotiations yields inherent uncertainty about its future evolution.

Taxes do much better on the temporal dimension, but face the difficulties associated with imperfect markets, political resistance, and (particularly in the transport sector) establishing additionality of the instrument. Taxes may also be (even) harder to globalise.

A gradual transition from cap-and-trade schemes to carbon taxation, through increasing levels of auctioning over time, holds attractions that justify serious further work on the political–economic aspects. There are interesting hybrid schemes, such as auction releases with a commitment to a floor and ceiling price, that evolve in response to success or otherwise in limiting the cumulative emissions of GHGs, which could address some of these concerns. But, as ever, the main problem is designing a means of reaching international agreement to underpin a collective commitment to reducing these cumulative emissions. The *Stern Review* has signalled the seriousness of the task, and by placing high values on the social cost of carbon and the benefit–cost ratio of mitigation has endeavoured to convince the world that the problem is serious but worth collective action.

Finally, achieving an international climate change agreement with sufficient coverage will be an evolutionary process, combining a quest for instruments that command consensus support with an attempt to achieve efficiency in mitigating climate change. The first typically involves quantity instruments and targets to achieve satisfactory burden sharing, while the second requires markets to equilibrate prices across time and space. Designing the appropriate sequence of national and international instruments to achieve this is challenging.

In this sense the power sector, with its relative international homogeneity of production processes and international market for equipment, is probably better placed than many others to achieve these two objectives through careful design to achieve efficient, sustainable and credible instruments. As indicated in the introductory chapter (Chapter 1), power generation remains the single biggest source of CO_2 emissions globally, and is a prime driver of projected global emissions growth. If constructing a global regime to cover all sources proves too difficult, an agreement that builds out from and improves the EU ETS and other emerging trading initiatives, to establish a carbon price across the world's electricity systems, along the principles we have discussed, would still be a huge step forward.

Acknowledgements

The UK Research Council under project Supergen FutureNet supports this research.

References

Anderson, M.S. (2004). Vikings and virtues: a decade of CO_2 taxation, *Climate Policy*, 4(1): 13–24.

Brewer, T.L. (2003). The trade regime and the climate regime: institutional evolution and adaptation, *Climate Policy*, 3(4): 329–341.
   (2004) 'The WTO and Kyoto Protocol: interaction issues', *Climate Policy*, 4: 3–12.

Downing, T.E., Anthoff, D., Butterfield, B., Ceronsky, M., Grubb, M., Guo, J., Hepburn, C., Hope, C., Hunt, A., Li, A., Markandya, A., Moss, S., Nyong, A., Tol, R.S.J. and Watkiss, P. (2005). *Scoping Uncertainty in the Social Cost of Carbon*, London: DEFRA (www.defra.gov.uk/environment/climatechange/carboncost/sei-scc.htm)

DTI (2006). *The Energy Challenge: Energy Review Report 2006*, London: Department of Trade and Industry.

Grubb, M. (1999). *The Kyoto Protocol: a Guide and Assessment*, London: Earthscan
   (2007) 'Climate change impacts, energy, and development', *Proceedings of World Bank Annual Bank Conference on Development Economics*, Tokyo, 2006, Washington, DC: World Bank.

Henriksson, E. (2005). *Assessing the competitive effects of convergence mergers: the case of the gas-electricity industries*, Licentiate thesis / 2005:81 Lulea University of Technology, Sweden (http://epubl.ltu.se/1402-1757/2005/81/index-en.html)

Hepburn, C. (2006). Regulating by prices, quantities or both: an update and an overview, *Oxford Review of Economic Policy*, 22(2): 226–247.

Hepburn, C., Grubb, M., Neuhoff, K., Matthes, F. and Tse, M. (2006). Auctioning of EU ETS phase II allowances: how and why?, *Climate Policy*, 6(1): 137–160.

HMG (2007). *Draft Climate Change Bill*, CM 7040, London: HM Government.

HMT (2003). *The Green Book: Appraisal and Evaluation in Central Government* (www.hm-treasury.gov.uk/media/3/F/green_book_260907.pdf and annexes at http://www.hm-treasury.gov.uk/media/F/D/Green_Book2_03.pdf)

Hoel, M. and Karp, L. (2001). Taxes and quotas for a stock pollutant with multiplicative uncertainty', *Journal of Public Economics*, 83: 91–114.

Honkatukia, J., Mälkönen, V. and Perrels, A. (2006). *Impacts of the European Emissions Trade System on Finnish Wholesale Electricity Prices*, VATT-Discussion Papers, Helsinki.

House of Commons (2006). *New Nuclear? Examining the Issues*, London: House of Commons Trade and Industry Committee (www.parliament.uk/parlia mentary_committees/trade_and_industry/tisc_nuclearnewbuildreport.cfm)

IEA (2007). *CO₂ Allowance and Electricity Price Interaction: Impact on Industry's Electricity Purchasing Strategies in Europe*, OECD/IEA (www.iea.org/textbase/papers/2007/jr_price_interaction.pdf)

Ismer, R. and Neuhoff, K. (2006). *Commitments through Financial Options: A Way to Facilitate Compliance with Climate Change Obligations*, EPRG Working Paper (www.electricitypolicy.org.uk/pubs/wp/eprg0625.pdf)

Jacoby, H.D. and Ellerman, A.D. (2004). The safety valve and climate policy, *Energy Policy*, 32(4): 481–491.

Neuhoff, K., Keats, K. and Sato, M. (2006). Allocation, incentives and distortions: the impact of EU ETS emissions allowance allocations to the electricity sector, *Climate Policy*, 6(1): 73–91.

Newbery, D.M. (2005). Why tax energy? Towards a more rational policy, *Energy Journal*, 26(3): 1–39.

(2006). Response to DTI's *Energy Review*, Submission to the DTI *Energy Review* (www.electricitypolicy.org.uk/pubs/misc.html)

Pezzy, J.C.V. (2003). Emission taxes and tradeable permits: a comparison of views on long-run efficiency, *Environmental and Resource Economics*, 26: 329–342.

Pizer, W. (2002). Combining price and quantity controls to mitigate global climate change, *Journal of Public Economics*, 85(3): 409–434.

PointCarbon (2007). Carbon 2007: a new climate for carbon trading, K. Roine and H. Hasselknippe (eds) (www.pointcarbon.com)

Roques, F.A., Nuttall, W.J., Newbery, D.M., de Neufville, R. and Connors S. (2006). Nuclear power: a hedge against uncertain gas and carbon prices? *Energy Journal*, 27(4): 1–24.

Sijm, J., Neuhoff, K. and Chen, Y. (2006). *CO₂ Cost Pass Through and Windfall Profits in the Power Sector*, Cambridge University EPRG 0617 Working Paper.

Stern, N.H. (2006). *The Economics of Climate Change*, Cambridge: CUP.

Tol, R.S.J. (2005). The marginal damage costs of carbon dioxide emissions: an assessment of the uncertainties, *Energy Policy*, 33: 2064–2074.

Watkiss, P. et al. (2005). *The Social Cost of Carbon*, London: DEFRA.

Weitzman, M.L. (1974). Prices vs. quantities, *Review of Economic Studies*, 41(4): 477–491.

12 Learning curves for energy technologies: a critical assessment

Tooraj Jamasb and Jonathan Köhler

12.1 Introduction

One of the main drivers of current energy policy and research is the climate change issue. Climate science suggests that there is a need to drastically reduce greenhouse gas (GHG) emissions and one of the main sources of GHGs is the combustion of fossil fuels for electricity generation. This has, in turn, led to efforts to develop low-carbon technologies to reduce such emissions. The policy problem now is how to transform the electricity system to develop these new technologies and support their large-scale diffusion. Hence innovation and technical change are at the centre of the climate change and energy policy debate.

Technical change is a gradual process and evolves through different stages. A well-established account of this is Schumpeter's invention–innovation–diffusion paradigm (Schumpeter, 1934, 1942). Within this framework, invention refers to the generation of new knowledge and ideas. In the innovation stage, inventions are further developed and transformed into new products, while diffusion is the widespread adoption of the new products. Later, Solow (1957) attributed the unexplained element of productivity growth of the economy to technical change. At this time, the literature still viewed technical change as an exogenous factor to the economy.

In recent years, there have been considerable developments in macroeconomics and energy economics, both theoretical and empirical, on the theme of technical change. The focus of the literature has shifted to the role of economic factors on technical change (Thirtle and Ruttan, 1987). These changes have primarily been in the new macroeconomic endogenous growth literature and the application of the learning curve management literature to microeconomic analysis, including in the energy sector. As a consequence, there has been a transition in the climate change and energy literature, such that endogenous technical change (ETC) is now a major feature of many analyses (Köhler *et al.*, 2006).[1]

In the microeconomic context, learning curves emerged as an empirical method for analysis of the effect of learning on technical change. They measure technical change as the cost improvement of a product or technology as a result of learning. Learning as a distinct source of technical change was presented by Wright (1936) and Arrow (1962) and is often termed 'learning-by-doing'. The learning effect is measured in terms of reduction in the unit cost (or price) of a product as a function of experience gained from an increase in its cumulative capacity or output.

Early applications of learning curves, between the 1930s and the 1960s, were mainly production-orientated (Wright, 1936; Hirsh, 1952). In the 1970s and 1980s, they were also used in business management, strategy, and organisation studies (BCG, 1970; Argote and Epple, 1990).

The most common forms of learning curves measure improvement in the cost of a given technology from a power function of, for example, cumulative installed capacity or output (Eqn 12.1). The learning effect of cumulative capacity or output on cost improvement is then, generally, expressed as a learning rate measured in terms of percentage cost reduction for each doubling of the cumulative generation capacity or production (Eqn 12.2).

$$c = a^* Cap^\varepsilon \tag{12.1}$$

$$LR = 1 - 2^{-\varepsilon} \tag{12.2}$$

where: c = unit cost (£/kW or £/kWh); Cap = deployment (cumulative capacity or production, etc); ε = learning elasticity; and LR = technology learning rate.

Although the concept of a learning curve has been known for a long time, the pressing need for innovation in energy and environmental technology and policy analysis has been an important source of the recent interest for its application to this area. Since 1990, learning curves have attracted considerable interest for the purpose of technology and policy analysis, and in particular for application to energy technologies

---

[1] ETC, where technical progress is dependent upon variables and processes within the model, leads to possibilities for policy to induce technical change (ITC) by influencing these processes. If ETC is included, policy operates through the ETC mechanisms of the model to generate ITC that would not otherwise occur. This is in contrast to exogenous or autonomous technical change, often represented through the autonomous energy efficiency improvement (AEEI) in climate-economy models.

(Criqui *et al.*, 2000; IEA, 2000; McDonald and Schrattenholzer, 2001; Papineau, 2006).

Also, technology learning rates have been used in important official policy documents. For example, the UK Government's *Energy Review* (DTI, 2006) and in particular the *Stern Review on the Economics of Climate Change* (HM Treasury, 2006) have included assumptions regarding technology learning rates in their long-term cost projections. Learning rates are as important for technology analysis as discount rates are for cost–benefit analysis. However, moving from the application of learning curves to manufacturing and production activities and applying them instead to innovation and technological progress is a significant step that requires attention to the nature and determinants of innovation. It is, therefore, important to assess the potential and limitations of learning curves as an analytical tool in energy technology and policy analysis.

There is also significant interest in analysis of the potential and promise of new technologies: 'Which are likely to achieve most progress in terms of performance improvements and/or cost reductions?' with the objective of improving the efficiency of learning processes. Further, it is important to determine whether resources allocated to the promotion of technologies are better spent on research and development (R&D) or capacity promotion policies.

In this chapter we assess the current status of learning curves as applied to energy technologies, and discuss their strengths and weaknesses for energy policy analysis and modelling.

12.2   Learning curves and technical change

12.2.1   *Empirical evidence on learning rates of electricity technologies*

The literature on experience curves frequently summarises observations in terms of a single parameter – the 'learning rate'. Argote and Epple (1990) surveyed the literature in manufacturing, which goes as far back as studies by Wright (1936) on aircraft production in the 1930s and by Rapping (1965) on shipbuilding. Positive experience curves have been found both in manufacturing and service sectors. Recent contributions to this literature consider the learning processes that lead to experience curves, e.g. Thornton and Thompson (2001) for shipbuilding. Furthermore, the literature extends the idea to production processes, e. g. Jaber and Guiffrida (2004) for reductions in defects in current industries, and Hatch and Mowery (1998) for new industries such as semiconductors. Argote and Epple (1990) drew attention to the considerable variability in learning, not only across industries, but even within different plants of the same company. Variability is also observed in studies of international technology diffusion and its effects on growth in different countries (Keller, 2004). Dutton and Thomas (1984), quoted in Argote and Epple (1990), provided a frequency distribution of progress ratios (percentage cost reduction for a doubling of cumulative output) for 108 cases, with a range of 55% to 96% for the progress ratio and one case where the ratio is over 100%, i.e. where costs increase with cumulated output. The mode of this distribution is 81–82%, which has led to the common assumption of an 80% progress ratio, i.e. a 20% reduction in unit cost for each doubling of output.

A summary of surveyed literature quantifying experience curves in the energy sector is presented in Figure 12.1. The literature dates back to at least the early 1980s (Zimmerman, 1982; Joskow and Rose, 1985). The great majority of published learning rate estimates relate to electricity generation technologies. As illustrated in Figure 12.1, estimates associated with different technologies and time periods span a very wide range, from around 3% to over 35% cost reductions associated with each doubling of output capacity. Negative estimates have even been reported for technologies when they have been subject to costly regulatory restrictions over time (e.g. nuclear, and coal if flue gas desulphurisation costs are not separated), and for price-based (as opposed to cost-based) learning rates in some periods, reflecting aspects of market behaviour.

For many technologies, learning rates appear higher in the earlier stages. Thus early coal development (USA 1948–1969) showed rapid learning in contrast to later evidence (USA 1960–1980). Gas turbine data also suggest some evidence of learning depreciation (either kinked or smooth). However, wind energy has demonstrated a wide range of learning rates with no obvious pattern across locations or even time periods (early versus late development stages). Solar PV, in general, has enjoyed faster rates of learning than other renewable technologies. Grübler et al. (1999), IEA (2000) and McDonald and Schrattenholzer (2001) surveyed the evidence for energy technologies, showing that, in line with the more general results mentioned earlier, unit cost reductions of 20% associated with doubling of capacity have been typical for energy generation technologies, with the exception of nuclear power.

This learning rate literature has led, in some cases, to the use of a general 'rule of thumb' learning rate of 20%. This is a plausible proxy of the observed rates for many electricity generation technologies, but the evidence on the decline of learning rates over time suggests that it may

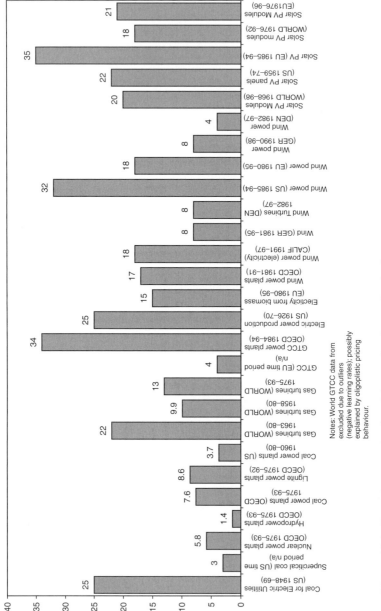

Figure 12.1. Learning rates in electricity production technologies
Sources: Köhler *et al.* (2006); adapted from McDonald and Schrattenholzer (2001)

err on the high side, if treated generically across these technologies as a constant in long-run modelling exercises. Indeed, the application of such learning rates has led to cost reductions so high that some studies have artificially imposed a 'floor price' to prevent technologies like wind energy from becoming absurdly cheap, which then changes the effective assumed average learning rate.

12.2.2 The implications of the adoption of learning curves

The incorporation of learning curves can significantly change the cost estimates of stabilisation and policy conclusions, compared with earlier models. Grubb et al. (2002) found that several (but not all) studies incorporating induced technical change suggest that it could make addressing climate change – including atmospheric stabilisation – quite cheap in the long run. Practically all estimates, including the results of the MARKAL modelling work (DTI, 2003), show that the effects would rise from a low level today to a range of 0–2% of world GDP by 2050 (Leach et al., 2005). In terms of GDP output lost, this represents a maximum cost of a loss of one year's growth in 2050, i.e. the modelled output in 2050 would not be reached until 2051, in a context in which GDP is likely to have risen by 200–300% in most economies by this date. Other recent surveys confirm these results (Azar and Dowlatabadi, 1999; Grübler et al., 1999), depending on the success of innovation in reducing the costs of low-carbon energy options.

However, the results depend on other features of the models besides the incorporation of learning curves (Barker et al., 2002). Grubb et al. (2006) and Edenhofer et al. (2006), considering the results of the Innovation Modelling Comparison Project (IMCP), find that, if major technological advances are projected to occur anyway in the base case, induced technical change (ITC) makes little difference to already 'modest' costs. If models have enough technological detail to allow substitution of higher by lower carbon options in supply, and responsiveness to the economic signals that enables the lower carbon supplies to 'break through' into markets on a large scale, this can lead to structurally different energy systems becoming established, with various economies of scale now applying to low-carbon instead of high-carbon systems. ETC can then have a large impact. However, overall the IMCP studies also emphasise that the global economic impact of stabilisation targets depends not just on technology, but also upon the nature of the assumed macroeconomic linkage between the energy sector and the rest of the economy. These can either ameliorate or exacerbate the costs incurred within the energy sector as a whole.

Edenhofer *et al.* (2006) found that the main economic mechanisms that drive ITC are:

- the level of ETC in the baseline
- 'first best' or 'second best' assumptions and model structure (CGE, optimal growth, macroeconometric, energy sector bottom-up)
- long-term investment decisions and assumptions about foresight
- prices of backstop and end-of-the-pipe technologies.

As Köhler *et al.* (2006) noted, an important assumption in an experience curve regards floor costs. The conventional experience curve is a declining exponential; hence in order to prevent costs from tending to zero in the long run, many models have to specify a 'floor cost' for each curve. In the long run, the process of switching to new technologies will tend towards a set of stable values for technology shares. These relative shares are determined by the relative floor price assumptions (as well as availability for non-backstop technologies), independent of learning rates. Thus, in the long run, a static equilibrium solution may emerge, even in these non-linear dynamic models.

Grubb *et al.* (2002) discussed the policy implications of these new results. Far more attention should be given to technical change, while induced technical change greatly broadens the scope of technology-related policies. Efficient responses may involve a wide mix of instruments targeted to spur market-based innovation in relevant sectors and broader mitigation policies including economic instruments. It may not be optimal to equalise marginal costs in each period because the returns of learning-by-doing will differ between sectors and technologies. Endogenous technical change usually increases the benefits of early action, which accelerates development of cheaper technologies. This is the opposite of the result from models with autonomous technical change, which can imply waiting for better technologies to arrive.

Numerical studies of CO_2 abatement imply that, for action taken at present, the benefits associated with endogenous technical change may be substantially larger than the direct Pigouvian benefits of CO_2 abatement. If climate change mitigation induces improved technologies in the industrialised nations, it is likely that these technologies will diffuse globally. This will result in a positive spillover that will offset the negative spillover usually hypothesised to result from the migration of polluting industries. Empirical data and analytic understanding are still extremely weak in this area. However, preliminary studies suggest that this effect may dominate over time, which will result in overall negative leakage (i.e. reductions in industrialised countries may also result in reduced emissions in the rest of the world) because of the enormous leverage potentially exerted by global technology diffusion over decades.

Grubb *et al.* (2006) argue that, to the extent that technological change is driven by learning-by-doing, it still does not necessarily follow that emission caps are the only or best way of stimulating this, particularly for some of the less advanced technologies. Such instruments do increase the general prospect of profiting from innovation in low-carbon technologies, but a far wider range of market-based policies may be required to stimulate the kind and degree of investment sought.

12.3   Theory-informed models of technology learning

While learning curves estimate the correlation between cumulative experience with a technology and falling costs, questions remain as to the causal links between experience and costs. Indeed, the literature on experience curves has little discussion on theoretical explanations, although the innovation literature thoroughly examines increasing returns in manufacturing evident from decreasing costs of production which are observed as an experience curve in a firm.

As noted, single-factor learning curve models exhibit shortcomings when applied to technology learning. These models can be improved upon by aligning them with basic features of technical change and innovation theory.

A typology of policies, consistent with the invention–innovation–diffusion paradigm, divides these into technology push and market pull policy measures. The aim of technology push is to promote the knowledge base of evolving and emerging technologies through R&D (learning-by-research effect). There are parallels between the process of technical change and R&D. Basic research broadly refers to the invention stage of a technology. Applied research and development activities are related to the innovation stage. Commercialisation refers to diffusion stage of technical change. The distinction is useful for the formulation of technology support policies. The relative importance of R&D in technical progress can vary in the different stages of development of a technology. The conventional view is that, at early stages of development, much of technical progress is likely to be achieved through R&D. As the technologies mature, the market mechanisms and commercial incentives play an increasingly important role in the further progress of technologies. However, R&D activities can be subject to three main types of market failure: namely, indivisibility, uncertainty and externalities (Ferguson and Ferguson, 1994).

Government support for R&D is generally regarded as more important at the basic research and development stage, where market failure is more likely to occur. Public support for early-stage R&D can therefore be characterised as a public good. Evidence suggests that a public-good view of government R&D support in energy technologies is stronger than in many other industries. For many sectors of the economy, broad public R&D combined with patent protection may be adequate to span the innovation chain. In pharmaceuticals, for example, the 'public good' (which is largely a private benefit) of better medicines is automatically matched by the large-scale purchase of better drugs by national health authorities, private health practices, or direct private purchase, while patenting of discrete, chemically unique drugs provides strong protection for the manufacturers. Thus the 'market pull' forces reach deep into the innovation chain. For the information technologies, product differentiation built on a strong base of publicly funded basic research provides a similarly strong combination. The way in which some of these basic principles of innovation plays out in practice varies radically between different sectors. Information technology and pharmaceuticals, for example, are both characterised by a high degree of innovation, with rapid technological change financed by private investment amounting typically to 10–20% of sector turnover (Neuhoff, 2005). This is in dramatic contrast with power generation, where a small number of fundamental technologies have dominated for almost a century and private sector RD&D has fallen sharply with the privatisation of energy industries to the point where it is under 0.4% of turnover (see Margolis and Kammen, 1999; Jamasb and Pollitt, 2005).

In turn, market pull measures are devised to promote technical change by creating demand and developing the markets for new technologies. As the technology matures, market pull policies will gradually become more effective in promoting technical progress. The experience gained in the process of manufacturing and operation of technologies through learning-by-doing is a source of technological progress. Growth in installed capacity remains limited until cost reduction and/or policies improve commercial viability. Commercial prospects and supportive policies encourage capacity expansion, all of which lead to further cost reduction. As the technology matures, the effects of R&D and capacity will decrease.

However, the above characterisation of the role of R&D versus capacity deployment at different stages of technical progress is yet to be firmly established by empirical evidence. At the same time, while model specification plays a crucial role in estimation of learning rates, this has rarely received formal treatment in the literature. Söderholm and Sundqvist (2003) is a notable exception in discussing econometric aspects of learning curves. It is important to study the relative importance of technology push and market pull factors and, in particular, their role in different stages of technological development (see Grübler *et al.*, 1999). This will not only enhance our understanding of the stages and process of technical changes but will also help to formulate better-informed and targeted technology policies.

Some recent studies have suggested that learning models should be extended to include learning-by-researching as R&D contributes to technical progress by enhancing the knowledge base. The effect of R&D on cost improvement can be accounted for in 'two-factor learning curves' that incorporate cumulative R&D spending, or alternatively the number of patents, as a proxy for the stock of knowledge. Two-factor learning curves were first proposed in Kouvariatakis *et al.* (2000), using cumulative R&D and cumulative production as drivers of technology cost improvement. Despite their relative advantages, however, there are few examples of application of two-factor learning models for technology analysis. Klassen *et al.* (2002) and Cory *et al.* (1999) applied two-factor learning curves to wind-power technology. Miketa and Schrattenholzer (2004) and Barreto and Kypreos (2004) have used two-factor learning curves in bottom-up optimisation models of energy technologies.

Inclusion of R&D in learning models adds a controllable or policy variable to the model and reduces the problem of omitted variables bias that would attribute some of the effect of cost reduction by R&D to capacity deployment instead (Söderholm and Sundqvist, 2003). In addition, learning rate estimations need to take into account endogeneity of capacity deployment on the unit cost of technology – i.e. diffusion results in unit cost reduction, which in turn encourages capacity promotion policies and market uptake. A simultaneous equations model with capacity and R&D as well as endogeneity of capacity on cost transforms single-factor models from partial empirical functions into learning–innovation–diffusion models that conform to the basic elements of the technical change process and the invention–innovation–diffusion paradigm.

Söderholm and Klassen (2003) used simultaneous learning and diffusion equations to estimate the effect of promotion policies for wind energy in the UK, Spain, Denmark and Germany. The study found a significant positive diffusion effect from cost reduction on cumulative capacity as well as the effect of the type of promotion policy on cost development of wind power. Jamasb (2007) used simultaneous equations for a set of electricity generation technologies at different stages of development. The results showed that single-factor learning curves overestimate the effect of learning-by-doing in general, and that of new and emerging technologies in particular (Table 12.1).

Table 12.1. *Learning-by-doing rates using single- and two-factor curves*

Technology	Learning-by-doing rate: Two-factor curves	Learning-by-doing rate: Single-factor curves
1 Pulverised fuel supercritical coal	3.75%	4.8%
2 Coal conventional technology	13.39%	15.1%
3 Lignite conventional technology	5.67%	7.8%
4 Combined cycle gas turbines (1980–1989)	2.20%	2.8%
Combined cycle gas turbines (1990–1998)	0.65%	3.3%
5 Large hydro	1.96%	2.9%
6 Combined heat and power	0.23%	2.1%
7 Small hydro	0.48%	2.8%
8 Waste to electricity	41.5%	57.9%
9 Nuclear light water reactor	37.6%	53.2%
10 Wind – onshore	13.1%	15.7%
11 Solar thermal power	2.2%	22.5%
12 Wind – offshore	1.0%	8.3%

Jamasb (2007) also indicates that R&D tends to be generally more effective in reducing the cost of technologies in different stages of development. Moreover, the paper reports significant diffusion effect for several of the technologies examined. Finally, the study finds a low substitution possibility between R&D and capacity for most of the technologies examined.

12.3.1 Limitations of learning curves

Despite their recent popularity and potential areas of application, there are important conceptual and practical limitations in the use of learning models for energy technology policy analysis. Although learning curves are used for forecasting technical change and policy analysis, they are essentially rooted in the historical development of technologies. Therefore, before learning curves may be used for predictive technology analysis, it is important to ensure that they reflect the main tenets of their past progress. It is particularly important to note that emerging technologies typically evolve through several stages of development. Therefore, from a theoretical point of view, the future development path of technologies is likely, and even expected, to be somewhat different from their progress in the past.

The above discussion touches upon the inherent difficulties in modelling and our limited understanding of the technology innovation process. As discussed, two-factor learning curves and incorporating endogeneity of cumulative capacity will go some way in improving the specification of learning models and aligning them more closely with basic features of innovation theory. In addition, there is the important issue of the lack of accurate and detailed data, e.g. in many instances in the form of relatively short time-series. In the long run, the quality and availability of suitable data may only be improved through allocation of resources and sustained coordinated international cooperation.

Applying experience curve data in modelling projections through the use of a single implied 'learning rate' is prone to the exaggeration of effects. The strongest reason for applying them in long-run modelling is not that these issues have been resolved, but rather that the evidence for *some* degree of experience-based cost reduction is overwhelming. Assuming a learning rate determined exogenously is problematic and there remains little consensus on the 'genuine' learning rate – only that zero, the implicit assumption in models that do not incorporate endogenous change, is a number that we can be most confident is wrong. Learning rates are therefore valid in economic analyses of technology, however they should be used with caution due to incomplete data (Köhler *et al.*, 2006).

12.4   Learning curves for a low-carbon electricity sector

The electricity sector accounts for a significant share of global carbon emissions. Therefore, achieving a low-carbon economy is highly dependent on significant emissions reductions in the sector. However, achieving this objective in the long term is only possible through innovation and developing new technological solutions. This section discusses specific issues in the use of learning curves as a tool in technology and innovation policy in the context of achieving a low-carbon electricity sector.

As low-carbon technologies are at early stages of development, they should ideally be analysed using suitable learning models that reflect the main factors that drive their progress, i.e. R&D capacity deployment. As discussed earlier, where possible, two-factor learning curves incorporating both capacity deployment and R&D should be used. Technical change can be promoted by combining capacity deployment and R&D according to their relative effectiveness at a given stage of development. Jamasb (2007) shows, while the relative importance of R&D in relation to capacity deployment or *vice versa* may be strong, the substitution possibility between these is generally small, and hence there is a need for using both but in proportion to their relative effectiveness in achieving technical progress.

Learning curves can help in the analysis of allocation of scarce resources for innovation. Jamasb *et al.* (2006) report that the UK spends substantial, and increasing, amounts of public funding to promote renewable energy sources and contrast this with the public energy R&D spend, which is only a fraction of the former. Learning curves could help in analyses of whether the funds earmarked for technology promotion are allocated in proportion to their relative effectiveness. At a more aggregate level, learning curves can also be used for allocation of innovation resources among alternative technologies. For example, from a technology policy view, it is useful to distinguish between technologies that can competitively contribute to the resource mix in the medium term versus long term and allocate innovative resources between these accordingly.

The role of individual countries in promoting a technology, whether through R&D or deployment, is rather limited. A related issue then is whether other countries will also engage in innovative activities and whether there is a high degree of spillover and transferability of learning across countries. Therefore, international collaboration based around common interest in specific technologies will be useful. Also, formal collaboration among countries reduces the incentive for free-riding and can increase the total level of effort.

Learning curves can also be used to estimate the total required investment in R&D and capacity support to bring the cost of a technology down to a given level. Where the time horizon for technical progress is long, using the present value of the required investment facilitates a comparison of alternative spending scenarios or across technologies. Despite their apparent usefulness, empirical analyses of required cumulative investments in learning are not yet common. One example of this type of analysis, Neuhoff (2005), measured the total required learning investments for solar photovoltaic technology. The results estimated the required learning investments in capacity for the 2005–2023 period under the base scenario at €20 billion. The study also showed the present value of benefits of cost reduction from the learning investments for the 2005–2040 period to be 15 times higher than the investments.

The estimates of required capacity deployment to reduce the costs of a technology through learning to a given level may need to be set against the technical potential and availability of resources. For example, if analysis implies that the required capacity deployment is too large and not feasible, then alternative approaches such as focusing on R&D or international collaboration can be considered. In addition, given the constraints for capacity expansion, it will be possible to estimate the time that each doubling of capacity is likely to take.

Where estimation of the learning potential of a specific technology may not be possible, analysis of comparable technologies may be used as a guide. Rubin *et al.* (2004) estimated the learning-by-doing rates of 11% for sulphur dioxide and 12% for nitrogen oxide control technologies. The study then used these estimates to assess the learning potential for carbon capture and sequestration (CCS) technology. These estimates were then fed into a large-scale model of the energy sector to calculate the estimated benefits of technical progress in CCS in reducing the cost of carbon mitigation for the energy system.

It is important to note that there is potentially a degree of interdependence among the projections for different technologies. Achieving the projected cost reductions by integrated large-scale models for several technologies simultaneously may, in practice, due to funding limits or technical constraints, not be possible.

12.5   Conclusions

The notion of learning curves was first introduced in the context of manufacturing industries in the 1930s. However, in recent years, the need for new energy and environmental technologies has been an important source of interest in their application to economic analysis of technology innovation and policy. In the climate economy literature, the incorporation of increasing returns to scale due to spillovers and learning are major recent innovations. The concepts of induced technical change and learning curves imply that the direction and rate of technical progress and the stages in the innovation process can be influenced. It then follows that policies can be devised to mitigate market failure for evolving and emerging technologies.

The fundamental policy lesson of the learning curve literature is that, while low-carbon technologies are more costly than the current dominant technologies, if there is investment in the new technologies, they will become cheaper more rapidly than the current technologies. The cheapest technology pathway in the medium to long term is, however, not clear in advance. The incorporation of learning curves can significantly change the estimates of costs of stabilisation and policy conclusions, compared with earlier models. Several (but not all) of the studies incorporating induced technical change suggest that it could make addressing climate change – including atmospheric stabilisation – quite cheap in the long run.

The use of learning rates for technology analysis in recent policy documents underlines the need for a critical assessment of the use of learning curves in technology analysis. The choice of learning models, or simply assumed learning rates, can have significant effects on the outcome of an analysis. The importance of learning rates for economic analysis of technology can be compared with that of discount rates in cost–benefit analysis. Therefore, the choice of learning models and rates, and the results of these, should be treated with care. Simple measures such as the use of alternative models or sensitivity analysis of results can be useful for this purpose.

In relation to the invention–innovation–diffusion paradigm, single-factor learning curves amount to leaving out the effect of R&D on technical change as well as the main aspect of technology diffusion – i.e. the effect of cost reduction on higher technology adoption. The effect of cumulative capacity on the unit cost of technology as in single-factor learning-by-doing models is only a secondary effect of technology diffusion. Therefore, single-factor learning curves are particularly unsuitable for analysis of technologies that are in the early stages of progress. A possible response to these shortcomings is to extend learning models to include R&D expenditures in addition to capital investment. This approach has only been undertaken in a few studies. There is also a lack of suitable data to estimate such learning models, especially for the new technologies.

There is a need for more research into the nature of the real effects and processes that learning curves tend to capture. As discussed earlier, whether (or the extent to which) learning curves capture the factors they appear to be measuring (i.e. learning-by-doing and learning-by-research), the effect on resulting policy recommendations can be as significant as choosing between a 'wait and see' approach versus extensive early actions to curb climate change.

There are several possible directions for future applications of learning models. Given the importance, though not well understood, of spillovers in technological development and diffusion, international R&D cooperation and collaboration can benefit innovation and increase the rate of technological progress. Learning models can be used to analyse the effect of international policy coordination and the pooling of R&D resources or capacity deployment initiatives in order to accelerate technical progress. Another possible area is to assess the potential for improvement in specific technology cost components.

The accuracy of the estimated learning rates remains a major issue. Cross-technology analysis can help to increase confidence in estimated learning rates. The literature also suggests that the application of learning curves to energy technologies is predominantly focused on electricity generation technologies. In principle, it is possible to apply learning curves to other important energy-related technologies. For example, the use of learning curves in the analysis of environmental and clean technologies has been very limited. Technological progress in these areas can have significant cost and qualitative implications for conventional generation technologies. Similarly, the application of learning curves to electricity networks and energy storage technologies is almost absent from the literature. A notable exception has been hydrogen-related studies.

Finally, learning curves may need to seek answers to a slightly different type of policy question. Instead of assessing the effect of a doubling of cumulative capacity or R&D on unit cost of a technology, it may sometimes be useful to ask short-term questions, such as how much of an increase in these measures can, for example, the next 5% or 10% cost reduction achieve and how long this may take. In addition to being more realistic than long-term predictions, such simple conversions of learning rates also have the benefit of allowing comparisons of required support for achieving a given percentage of cost reduction across different technologies.

References

Argot, L. and Epple, D. (1990). Learning curves in manufacturing, *Science*, New Series, **247**, 920–924.

Arrow, K.J. (1962). The economic implications of learning by doing, *Review of Economic Studies*, **29**, 155–173.

Azar, C. and Dowlatabadi, H. (1999). A review of technical change in assessment of climate policy, *Annual Review of Energy and the Environment*, **24**, 513–544.

Barker, T., Köhler, J. and Villena, M. (2002). The costs of greenhouse gas abatement: a meta-analysis of post-SRES mitigation scenarios, *Environmental Economics and Policy Studies*, **5**, 135–166.

Barreto, L. and Kypreos, S. (2004). Endogenizing R&D and market experience in the 'bottom-up' energy-systems ERIS model, *Technovation*, **24**, 615–629.

BCG (1970). *Perspectives on Experience*, Boston Consulting Group, Boston, MA.

Cory, K.S., Bernow, S., Dougherty, W., Kartha, S. and Williams, E. (1999). Analysis of Wind Turbine Cost Reductions: The Role of Research and Development and Cumulative Production, Paper presented at AWEA's WINDPOWER '99 Conference, Burlington, VT, 22 June.

Criqui, P., Martin, J.-M., Schrattenholzer, L., Kram, T., Soete, L. and Van Zon, A. (2000). Energy technology dynamics, *International Journal of Global Energy Issues*, **14**, 65–103.

DTI (2003). *Options for a Low Carbon Future*, Economics Paper No. 4, Department of Trade and Industry, London.

(2006). *The Energy Challenge: Energy Review*, Department of Trade and Industry, London.

Dutton, J.M. and Thomas, A. (1984). Treating progress functions as a managerial opportunity, *Academy of Management Review*, **9**, 235–247.

Edenhofer, O., Lessmann, K., Kemfert, C., Grubb, M. and Köhler, J. (2006). Induced technological change: exploring its implications for the economics of atmospheric stabilization: synthesis report from the innovation modeling comparison project models, *Energy Journal*, Special Issue, *Endogenous Technological Change and the Economics of Atmospheric Stabilization*, 57–107.

Ferguson, P.R. and Ferguson, G.J. (1994). *Industrial Economics: Issues and Perspectives* (2nd edn.), Macmillan, London.

Grubb, M., Köhler, J. and Anderson, D. (2002). Induced technical change in energy and environmental modeling: analytic approaches and policy implications, *Annual Review of Energy and Environment*, 27, 271–308.

Grubb, M., Carraro, C. and Schellnhuber, J. (2006). Technological change for atmospheric stabilization: introductory overview to the innovation modeling comparison project, *Energy Journal*, Special Issue, *Endogenous Technological Change and the Economics of Atmospheric Stabilization*, 1–16.

Grübler, A., Nakićenović, N. and Victor, D.G. (1999). Modeling technological change: implications for the global environment, *Annual Review of Energy and Environment*, 24, 545–569.

Hatch, N.W. and Mowery, D.C. (1998). Process innovation and learning by doing in semiconductor manufacturing, *Management Science*, 44, 1461–1477.

Hirsh, W.Z. (1952). Manufacturing progress functions, *Review of Economics and Statistics*, 34, 143–155.

HM Treasury (2006). *Stern Review on the Economics of Climate Change*, HM Treasury, London.

IEA (2000). *Experience Curves for Energy Technology Policy*, International Energy Agency, Paris.

Jaber M.Y. and Guiffrida, A.L. (2004). Learning curves for processes generating defects requiring reworks, *European Journal of Operational Research*, 159, 663–672.

Jamasb, T. (2007). Technical change theory and learning curves: patterns of progress in energy technologies, *Energy Journal*, 28, 45–65.

Jamasb, T. and Pollitt, M. (2005). *Deregulation and R&D in Network Industries: The Case of Electricity Sector*, Cambridge Working Papers in Economics CWPE 0533 / Electricity Policy Research Group Working Paper EPRG 05/02, Faculty of Economics, University of Cambridge.

Jamasb, T., Nuttall, W.J. and Pollitt, M. (2006). *The Case for a New Energy Research, Development, and Promotion Policy for the UK*, Submission to: State of Science Review on Public Policy in the Energy Context, Office of Science and Innovation, Foresight and Horizon Scanning Centre, Department of Trade and Industry, London.

Joskow, P.L. and Rose, N.L. (1985). The effects of technology change, experience, and environmental regulation on the construction cost of coal-burning generating units, *Rand Journal of Economics*, 16, 1–26.

Klassen, G., Miketa, A., Larsen, K. and Sundqvist, T. (2002). The Impact of R&D on Innovation for Wind Energy in Denmark, Germany, and the United Kingdom, Paper presented at the International Energy Workshop, Stanford University, Stanford, CA, 18–20 June.

Keller, W. (2004). International technology diffusion, *Journal of Economic Literature*, **42**, 752–782.

Köhler, J., Grubb, M., Popp, D. and Edenhofer, O. (2006). The transition to endogenous technical change in climate-economy models: a technical overview to the innovation modeling comparison project, *Energy Journal*, Special Issue, *Endogenous Technological Change and the Economics of Atmospheric Stabilization*, 17–55.

Kouvariatakis, N., Soria, A. and Isoard, S. (2000). Modeling energy technology dynamics: methodology for adaptive expectations models with learning by doing and learning by searching, *International Journal of Global Energy Issues*, **14**, 104–115.

Leach, M., Anderson, D., Taylor, P. and Marsh, G. (2005). *Options for a Low Carbon Future: Review of Modelling Activities and an Update*, Report for the DTI, Imperial College Centre for Energy Policy (ICEPT) and Technology and Future Energy Solutions (FES).

Margolis, M. and Kammen, D.M. (1999). Underinvestment: the energy technology and R&D policy challenge, *Science*, **285**, 690–692.

McDonald, A. and Schrattenholzer, L. (2001). Learning rates for energy technologies, *Energy Policy*, **29**, 255–261.

Miketa, A. and Schrattenholzer, L. (2004). Experiments with a methodology to model the role of R&D expenditures in energy technology learning processes: first results, *Energy Policy*, **32**, 1679–1692.

Neuhoff, K. (2005). Large-scale deployment of renewables for electricity generation, *Oxford Review of Economic Policy*, **21**, 66–110.

Papineau, M. (2006). An economic perspective on experience curves and dynamic economies in renewable energy technologies, *Energy Policy*, **34**, 422–432.

Rapping, L. (1965). Learning and World War II production functions, *Review of Economics and Statistics*, **47**, 81–86.

Rubin, E.S., Taylor, M.R., Yeh, S. and Hounshell, D.A. (2004). Learning curves for environmental technology and their importance for climate policy analysis, *Energy*, **29**, 1551–1559.

Schumpeter, J.A. (1934). *The Theory of Economic Development: An Inquiry into Profits, Capital, Credit, Interest, and the Business Cycle*, Harvard University Press, Cambridge, MA.

(1942). *Capitalism, Socialism, and Democracy*, Harper and Row, New York.

Solow, R. (1957). Technical change and the aggregate production function, *Review of Economics and Statistics*, **39**, 312–330.

Söderholm, P. and Klassen, G. (2003). *Wind Power in Europe: A Simultaneous Innovation–Diffusion Model*, Paper presented at the 12th Annual Conference of the European Association of Environmental and Resource Economists, Bilbao, Spain, 28–30 June.

Söderholm, P. and Sundqvist, T. (2003). *Learning Curve Analysis for Energy Technologies: Theoretical and Econometric Issues*, Paper presented at the International Energy Workshop (IEW), Laxenburg, Austria, 24–26 June.

Thirtle, C.G. and Ruttan, V.W. (1987). *The Role of Demand and Supply in the Genera-tion and Diffusion of Technical Change*, Harwood Academic Publishers, London.

Thornton, R.A. and Thompson, P. (2001). Learning from experience and learning from others: an exploration of learning and spillovers in wartime shipbuilding, *American Economic Review*, **91**, 1350–1368.

Wright, T.P. (1936). Factors Affecting the Cost of Airplanes, *Journal of Aeronautical Sciences*, Vol. **3**, No. 4, 122–128.

Zimmerman, M.B. (1982). Learning and commercialization of new energy technologies: the case of nuclear power, *Bell Journal of Economics*, **13**, 297–310.

13 Accelerating innovation and strategic deployment in UK electricity: applications to renewable energy

Michael Grubb, Nadine Haj-Hasan and David Newbery

13.1 Introduction: innovation processes in theory and experience

Accelerating innovation in low-carbon technologies is essential to solving the climate problem. The previous chapter explored the evidence around technology learning in the electricity sector. The policy issues that arise are how to bring about the scale of innovation required and how to efficiently accelerate 'mainstream' investment towards potential replacement low-carbon technologies. This chapter examines these issues in relation to UK power generation, particularly concerning renewable energy.

It has long been established and accepted that innovation processes are characterised by multiple market failures, of which the most extensive and widely acknowledged, compared with an idealised market, is the difficulty of innovators appropriating the full economic benefits of their efforts (i.e. there is spillover of learning and capabilities to others). In addition, there are many informational failures and associated risk asymmetries. All these form intellectual justifications for public funding of research and the patent system.

Additional barriers impede private-sector innovation in electricity where, as noted in earlier chapters, R&D intensities are extraordinarily low compared with more product-driven sectors. The incentives for power generation R&D are reduced further when the externalities associated with existing technologies are not priced. The incentives for innovation in networks, being largely regulated monopolies, are even lower, with less than one-thousandth of UK distribution company revenues (prior to 2004) going towards R&D (see Chapter 7 by Pollitt and Bialek). Accelerating innovation so as to decarbonise one of the least innovative sectors of the entire economy is a major policy challenge.

Extrapolation of this observation has tended to create a view that governments should solve the 'innovation problem' through public

R&D, taking technologies to the point at which 'the market' will automatically pick up the fruits and profit from them. Accumulated experience questions the effectiveness of this. As cited by Fri (2003), there has been a tendency to 'throw technology at social problems, and that has certainly been true of energy' with, at best, mixed results.[1] It is thus crucial to understand more deeply the innovation process, and the potential role of policy.

As discussed in previous chapters (see Chapters 3 and 12), innovation is a complex phenomenon which in reality encompasses both technology 'push' and 'pull' forces. The classification of energy-sector innovation in Grubb (2004) identifies at least six distinct stages to energy technology innovation in a market economy, as illustrated in, the upper section of Figure 13.1(a):

1. *Basic research and development.*
2. *Technology-specific research, development and demonstration plants.*
3. *Market demonstration and technology selection* – in which potential purchasers and users ('the market') can start to evaluate the options and back the most promising.
4. *Commercialisation* – either adoption of the technology by established firms, or the establishment of firms based around the technology.
5. *Market accumulation* – in which the use of the technology expands in scale, often through accumulation of niche, protected or subsidised markets.
6. *Diffusion on a large scale.*

This 'innovation chain' is not simply linear; there are overlaps and feedbacks. Each stage involves technology improvement and cost reduction, but the principal barriers and driving forces change across the different stages. 'Technology push' elements dominate early-stage research, whilst 'market pull' is increasingly important as technologies evolve along the chain. This classification matches that in Chapter 3 (see Figure 3.1), but with the 'pre-commercial' stage further subdivided into the need both for *market demonstration/selection* and *commercialisation* of the resulting choices as distinct steps.

From a finance and public policy perspective, it is useful to condense this innovation chain into three main stages (middle and lower sections

---

[1] 'Synthetic fuels, the breeder reactor, fusion power, most renewable technologies, and the persistence of the fuel cell option testify to this tendency. For the most part, however, these programmes have been either expensive failures or only slightly less expensive technological successes that serve limited markets' (Fri, 2003). Note, in qualification, that the level of funding involved in nuclear power dwarfed all funding to renewable technologies, and some renewables support (e.g. Danish wind power) did prove cost-effective.

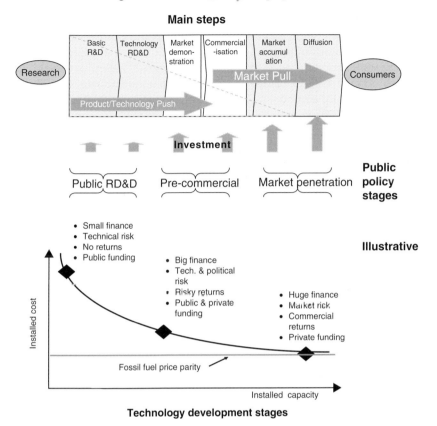

Figure 13.1. The innovation chain

of Figure 13.1). At one end are the new technology RD&D stages, where the main issues concern the funding and management of publicly financed technology RD&D. At the other end, what matters are policies and market structures that affect the economic returns to private investors. In the middle, challenges include the transition from publicly to privately financed operations.

Expanding public R&D is not, on its own, a satisfactory substitute for these later stages. The global decline of public-sector energy RD&D expenditure since the 1980s, charted in Chapter 3, was not only because the perceived oil crisis receded, but because several expensive forays into large-scale energy technologies failed to deliver commercial products (Cohen and Noll, 1991). There are many reasons for this – intrinsic obstacles to technologies successfully crossing from the stage of publicly funded demonstration to becoming a basis for commercially viable industries. This reflects the fact that, in the energy sector, technologies have not, in practice, easily migrated through the central stages of the innovation chain – the well-documented 'valley of death' in which RD&D fails to bridge the gap in either quantity or its linkage to commercially exploitable results (e.g. Foxon, 2003; Murphy and Edwards, 2003).[2]

The exceptions, moreover, are instructive. Combined cycle gas turbines (CCGTs) emerged commercially during the late 1980s. The underlying technology of gas turbines was established decades before, largely as a spin-off from military research. It was the combination of increased gas availability and the liberalisation of the power sector enabling new entrants, with higher discount rates, that resulted in the technology entering on a large scale. It is notable that the major innovation investment did not occur because governments *talked about* or *promised* liberalisation – but only once it happened, and companies could start turning real profits based on their initial forays with the technology. CCGTs also penetrated in rapidly growing developing country markets where power was needed urgently and gas was cost-effective. Other 'success' stories show a similar combination of 'technology push' support with strong 'market pull' that helped to finance a cycle of industrial learning investment (e.g. with the Danish wind R&D programmes feeding through capital supports into the Californian-subsidised renewable energy contracts).[3]

The innovation literature highlights other important findings. Innovation is a product of complex systems, in which feedbacks from the different stages of the innovation chain and the ability to learn from market experience are crucial (Shelton and Perlack, 1996). Also, major

---

[2] Note that the problem is particularly relevant in the power sector and in buildings; the oil sector is characterised by much higher innovation, not least because the huge rents in the sector can fund large risk-taking, whilst vehicles certainly involve product competition even if fuel consumption is generally a minor part of the competitive appeal. Note that many of the innovations to reduce pollution and improve efficiency were driven by industry-wide mandated standards, rather than by competition. Unfortunately, most of the oil sector's risk-taking is currently still in higher-carbon directions; and it is power generation and building energy use that remain the larger source of global CO_2 emissions.

[3] A study for the Carbon Trust (2003) estimated the total value of support measures by the Danish government since 1993 (to *c.* 2000) to be £1.3bn. This helped Danish companies to gain over 50% of market share, and 'annual revenues from this sector equate to some £2.7bn, with the vast majority of this revenue coming from export markets'. Denmark had supported wind energy since the early 1970s, but the total costs of these R&D and demonstration phases were probably modest compared with the value of capital grants and feed-in tariff supports since 1993.

innovations involve the co-evolution of technologies and the institutions that support them. Together, these factors tend to favour incumbents ('lock-in'), making it hard for new technologies to enter ('lock-out') (for a review, see Sandén and Azar, 2004). In this sense, the framework indicated by Figure 13.1 needs to be accompanied by broader perspectives on innovation processes in the accompanying systems and infrastructure.

The emergence of new power generation technologies at scale, therefore, requires a judicious combination of conditions that together encourage exploration, innovation and expanding investment in new ways of generating and distributing electricity. To tackle climate change, moreover, these need to be aligned in favour of low-carbon technologies – it is also important to discourage investment in new carbon-intensive facilities that could lock the system further into higher-emitting pathways.

Chapter 10 (Neuhoff and Twomey) summarised the various reasons why current markets will not deliver optimal investments – innovation included. Pricing carbon, discussed in Chapter 11 (Grubb and Newbery), starts to address the climate change dimension and will help to deter new carbon-intensive investments (depending to some degree on how quickly the protection for 'new entrants' is removed). However, the EU ETS neither provides a clear long-term signal sufficient to support innovation (or indeed other long-lived investments), nor does it address the many barriers in the innovation chain. Chapter 12 (Jamasb and Köhler) presents theory and evidence that technology costs can be brought down through a judicious combination of market expansion and supporting R&D. This chapter fills in the picture by considering specific innovation and capacity-building policies appropriate to UK electricity.

13.2   Economic fundamentals of low-carbon innovation

For innovation orientated towards a 'public good' such as climate change mitigation, clearly 'market pull' does not operate unless governments adopt policies that increase the market value of low-carbon technologies, most obviously through carbon taxes, cap-and-trade systems, or low-carbon obligations and contracts, as discussed in Chapter 11. Such emission control policies provide market-based incentives to underpin the diffusion of low-carbon technologies, and hence provide signals that innovation in this direction can ultimately expect some reward. Starting from carbon price considerations also sets some useful markers for innovation and capacity-building policies. The framing of Figure 13.2 helps to set some quantitative context.

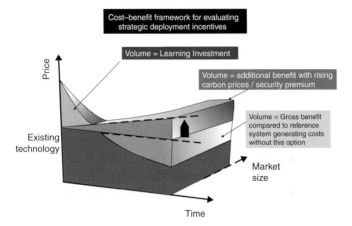

Figure 13.2. The economics of learning investments and the role of carbon pricing

Effective carbon price instruments should bring forward the date at which low-carbon technologies become economic, reduce the subsidy required, and increase the long-run returns to 'learning investments' in low-carbon technologies, relative to others. Carbon price instruments are therefore central to effective low-carbon innovation, as soon as technologies start to move towards the domain of private finance. As discussed in Chapter 2 (Hope and Newbery), the actual 'social cost of carbon' (SCC) is highly uncertain, but the conditions that lead to low SCC (notably a high discount rate) also imply a rapid increase. As a gross simplification, consider a scenario in which a given technology is saving 1 GtC (3.7 GtCO$_2$) by mid-century (corresponding to one of the 'Princeton Wedges'; see Pacala and Socolow, 2004). Even a relatively modest projection of carbon prices at, say, €50/tCO$_2$ by mid-century, indicates that the carbon-saving value of that technology wedge is approaching €200 billion *annually*. The cumulative discounted value of a truly successful low-carbon innovation – if it forms the basis for a major 'wedge' in these terms – may thus be measured in trillions of euros (or dollars), depending on the additional cost of the technology relative to the carbon price.[4] Even much smaller-scale contributions may be worth hundreds of billions of euros.

---

[4] The value is defined by the size of the 'wedge' between the new technology, and the cost of fossil fuels plus carbon costs. The social profitability of the investment will depend on the cumulative cost of deploying the technology.

From a global cost–benefit perspective, a few billion pounds of investment in learning that could generate emission savings worth some trillions sounds like a good investment. Unfortunately, many of the market failures that underpin the innovation process itself may also act to blunt the effectiveness of the carbon price as an incentive to orientate innovation investments in low-carbon directions. Moreover, the realisable value of the incentive depends upon uncertain future government policies to internalise carbon costs for very long-lived investments.

Thus, this theoretical construct may be of little practical value to an individual power company in the UK considering whether to risk billions of pounds of shareholder value. This illustration of the potential value of innovation does not mean that the investment will necessarily be forthcoming: it is, rather, a justification for targeted policy interventions that help socially beneficial technologies to traverse the technology 'valley of death', and accelerate the cost reductions arising from deployment.

Thus policies need to combine with R&D and a range of targeted supports to promote technology investment through different stages of the innovation chain. A case can be made that government has a key role at many stages, but its role changes radically along the innovation path and the appropriate extent of involvement, if any, may also vary greatly between different sectors.

13.3 Issues and dilemmas in 'front-end' support

Government finances basic and applied technology R&D, as well as underlying educational investment to train scientists and engineers. Typically, governments also fund some proof-of-concept demonstration, in order to lay a foundation of publicly available technology ideas for others to work with. To give companies any prospect of utilising these ideas in commercial products, governments need to define and enforce a basic regulatory structure which can reward innovators, most notably a functioning system of product patents that allows companies that invest in developing a unique product to be protected from copying by rivals for some defined period. In addition to rewarding innovators, market-side policies can act to sift out the best and guide the underlying research effort (Loiter and Norberg-Bohm, 1999).[5]

---

[5] 'Weak demand-side policies for wind energy risks wasting the expenditure of public resource on research programmes aimed at technological innovation. When these programme operate without the benefit of a market to test the results or provide guidance for future efforts, they are less likely to succeed (Loiter and Norberg-Bohm, 1999, p.85).

This chapter does not address the challenges of public R&D programme management directly. We note that, in the field of energy, as in some other sectors, the challenge of transferring knowledge and ideas from a publicly funded (often university) environment, into domains where the private sector understands and is willing to invest in the opportunities, may involve additional publicly funded activities, such as 'technology incubators' attached to universities that provide the management capacity required for university ideas to be comprehensible for a market assessment by private investment: this addresses a fundamental informational failure.

The Carbon Trust has also used public money for 'technology accelerators', which provide field-testing to a sceptical private-sector audience, again a role that addresses failures in information transfer and issues of credibility in the eyes of potential investors. In the classification of Grubb (2004) outlined in the Introduction, incubators and technology accelerators are both *market engagement programmes* that support new ideas to develop into viable businesses. The Carbon Trust's market engagement programmes now span at least a dozen technology areas, and typically cost a few million pounds each, depending obviously upon the inherent scale of the technology and its stage of development and commercialisation. This is a cost that can readily be borne through the Trust's direct State funding.

The equivalent processes for larger-scale power generation technologies, such as major offshore renewable technology developments or carbon capture and storage (CCS), are clearly on a bigger scale. These may benefit from the planned €1 billion UK Energy Technology Institute (ETI), which will be co-funded jointly by the UK government and a few major companies (see Chapter 16). The expenditures involved in either case remain quite trivial compared with the potential social option value of demonstrating feasibility and reliability, although the sums can be large compared with national R&D budgets. The IEA have estimated that demonstrating CCS as a viable option would require a programme of 'at least 10 full-scale integrated coal-fired power plants with CCS costing between US$500 million and $1,000 million each', over and above the cost of the power stations themselves (IEA, 2006). International cost-sharing mechanisms are clearly desirable for such expensive demonstrations as CCS. The UK *Energy White Paper* (DTI, 2007) confirmed commitment to £300 million funding for a CCS demonstration plant in the UK; some other planned demonstration facilities are summarised in Chapter 18.

The fact that several of the companies funding the ETI have benefited from windfall profits under the EU ETS, and recognise the need to plough some of that back into the technologies that could maintain their core operations in a carbon-constrained world, neatly captures the broader theme that innovation requires a mix of instruments, from R&D through to carbon pricing.

However, the conceptual case for a range of policies to help technologies span the 'innovation chain' does not answer key questions about which instruments are most effective and how, and to what, they should be applied. If governments understood all the technology options and could predict which would succeed, given the right kind of support, one could build a case that governments should focus public finance on supporting 'winners'. The inherent veil of ignorance surrounding the innovation process and its likely outcomes makes policy challenging. The risk of 'capture', in which governments become locked into subsidising industrial ventures on the basis of continuing promises of breakthroughs, is also high: the road of public support for big-ticket industrial R&D projects is littered with failures.

It is these factors that most sharply define challenges of where public expenditure should give way to the regulatory creation of low-carbon-technology markets, and where these, in turn, should give way to the general incentive of a robust and effective carbon-pricing instrument that does not differentiate between different technology categories.

13.4   Strategic deployment: aims and applications

The rest of the chapter considers policies to span the final stages in the innovation chain, namely incentives for increasing investment in technologies that are commercially available and which can contribute to strategic goals, but which are not yet fully cost-competitive. Such support can have multiple aims: to drive 'learning curve' cost reductions; to build up an industrial capacity which can both accelerate domestic deployment and capture a larger part of the value-chain of global deployment; to increase system diversity; and to reduce emissions in pursuit of domestic targets or in lieu of adequate environmental pricing.

Such deployment addresses the third and final phases of the innovation chain in the middle and lower sections of Figure 13.1, taking technologies from being 'commercially available' to being deployed at scale and being 'commercially competitive' without further support. Following Neuhoff (2005), we term this *strategic deployment*.

Because strategic deployment is concerned with moving technologies into the 'big league', it has the potential to be very expensive. The International Energy Agency estimate that US$10 trillion will be invested in the power sector globally out to 2030, divided more or less equally between industrialised and developing countries. The IEA 'Map' scenario (IEA, 2006), which returns global CO_2 emissions to 2005 levels by 2050 (and is consistent with trajectories towards stabilisation between 550 and 650 ppm CO_2eq) reflects the impact of switching investment from more to less carbon-intensive paths. Gross cumulative investments across renewables, nuclear and CCS are projected at $7.9 trillion. Of this, $4.5 trillion is offset directly by the reduced investment required in fossil fuel power plants, and most of the rest is offset by the reduced need for transmission and distribution investment arising from the increased energy efficiency.

The *net* additional cost for the Map scenario is 'only' $100 billion – about 1% additional to projected 'business as usual' power sector investment over the same period. However, this net amount is highly uncertain and conceals large changes in the temporal, geographical and technological profiles of expenditure, with much larger up-front expenditure associated with the low-carbon paths. Such numbers also conceal revenue transfers (e.g. associated with economic rents) and the costs of imperfect policy; for example, Yago *et al.* (Chapter 15) predict a low-carbon path to involve higher electricity prices equivalent to a consumer cost of £2–3 billion/year by 2020. The IEA studies collectively emphasise that the choice of path over the next few decades will have profound implications for the structure of capital stock, and its carbon intensity, well into the second half of this century and even beyond. The stakes are therefore high.

The UK's share of this total global power sector investment is trivially small. There is thus a need for some care in deciding whether and how to focus 'strategic deployment' incentives: there is a choice between seeking to develop a real industrial stake in a given technology area, and waiting for others to develop it and then importing the technology.

Against this backdrop, the main focus in the rest of this chapter is upon renewable technologies, principally wind and marine renewables. This is partly because wind energy is the principal 'new technology' that has the potential to contribute at scale to the UK's near-term (2015–2020) objectives, in terms of both environment and security of the UK power system. It is also because the UK has exceptional wind and marine resources, and the UK has the potential to secure a strong comparative advantage relative to many other countries in aspects of these technologies, through a combination of its exceptional resource base and existing industrial capabilities. This simplifies the issues compared to other technologies such as nuclear and CCS, where there is a strong global drive and extensive competing efforts, which raise additional complex policy issues about national comparative advantage.

For neither onshore nor offshore wind energy is the case entirely straightforward. Onshore wind energy has developed very rapidly globally, and the UK share of global capacity is modest; thus the contribution of UK deployment to learning-by-doing is likely to be small. In addition, the UK has already lost any significant stake in the wind turbine manufacturing industry, which is now dominated by Denmark, Germany and Spain. However, wind energy involves a significant range of local services, which potentially increases as the industry moves offshore: one of the first UK offshore windfarms, Scroby Sands, sourced about £40 million of the works from UK companies, i.e. almost half of the total contract value (Carbon Trust, 2006). This increases the scope for learning from strategic deployment in the UK, which could form a basis for recovering value from the UK investment if and as the industry expands internationally.

Moreover, although the UK's exceptional offshore wind resources appear of limited relevance globally, in the *near term* this has the advantage that UK deployment could dominate the global learning-by-doing investments, such that large-scale UK deployment could reduce costs from about 8p/kWh at present to under 5p/kWh in just a decade.[6] Yet, for the longer term, there are many areas with wind energy resources that are huge but remote from the major demand centres – including the US Midwest and western China. Experience with windfarms that are built for scale in remote locations where maintenance is expensive, and with efficient transmission and connection for large fluctuating power as key issues, could indeed turn out to be of high value globally. Support for strategic deployment of wind energy, formerly onshore but in the future focusing offshore, thus has a strong logic behind it over and above the direct emission savings.

---

[6] The central scenario in Carbon Trust (2006) projects that UK offshore wind energy capacity by 2015, based on extensive utilisation of Round 2 offshore project bids, could form about three-quarters of the global total. A learning rate of 15% per doubling of capacity has been applied, lower than the rate of 18% achieved in a similar stage of onshore wind development. While all UK capacity installations contribute to learning, only 20% of the projected overseas deployment was included for these purposes. Continued learning is expected in turbines for offshore applications, as well as the supporting infrastructure, in part because efforts are focused on larger machines than for smaller onshore clusters, due to higher access, maintenance and connection costs. With these (relatively conservative) assumptions, costs are projected to be in the range of 4.0–4.7p/kWh by 2020. For analysis and sources see Carbon Trust (2006); for general wind cost data and discussion on learning rates, including offshore, see Morthurst (2006). Recent data on estimated offshore wind energy costs from different sources, and from the four biggest existing offshore wind farms, are given in a UK ERC report (Gross et al., 2007, Table 4.2) which suggests that the Carbon Trust (and DTI) estimates were higher than the realised costs.

13.5   Strategic deployment: fundamental design choices

The first choice in design is whether to support *capacity* by subsidising construction costs, or to support *output* by subsiding revenues. The second choice is then whether to *differentiate* the support by kind of technology.

Capital subsidy   For technologies in the earlier stages of innovation, the dominant risk is construction cost and technological reliability. The most efficient support mechanism is then capital subsidy, to directly buy down the investment risk: in effect, because of the 'public-good' nature of improving reliability and knowledge about it, governments reduce the up-front risk. Grant funding for the less developed renewable energy sources is now well developed, with various BERR (formerly DTI) programmes in the UK operating at a scale of several hundred million pounds annually.

The principal design options surround how to determine the level of capital subsidy, and the allocation process. Determining grant levels in advance (e.g. per kW constructed) has the attraction of certainty and simplicity, and the drawback of risking significant over-subsidy – with the attendant problem also of extensive selection bureaucracy if many companies apply.

Auctioning the capital subsidy to bidders is, in principle, more efficient, but it faces the problem of the 'winner's curse' – the grants would tend to go to those with the most optimistic outlook, which also means they are the most likely to have underestimated the scale of the challenge, ending up with projects that may simply not be viable to bring to completion. Vickrey auctions (which result in a final price set at the second best bid) or other auction designs may reduce, if not eliminate, the problem. Requirements to deposit a bond to demonstrate serious commitment for winners might raise the expected cost of the subsidy required, but deliver a more timely commitment to invest, while ensuring that there is a sequence of auctions should encourage both learning about bidding, and learning about the improvements in expected cost forecasts. The early auctions under the non-fossil-fuel obligation (NFFO) (Mitchell, 1995) provide useful lessons, one of which is that the uncertainty of the auction outcome dissuaded bidders from engaging with local communities and smoothing the way to achieving planning approval. It would help if the government or planning body could agree in advance where visually intrusive renewables schemes (wind power, large dams, etc.) would be prohibited, and where they would be generally accepted. If these problems can be overcome, then auctions ought to be an attractive support mechanism, given recent developments in auction theory and practice (particularly with those 3-G auctions that were successful, such as that in the UK). Auctions should provide a way of eliciting information, competitive bids and successful deployment.

The other attraction of capital subsidy is that it removes the need for investors to predict future subsidy policy. The risk is that a subsidy per unit of self-declared capacity could distort choices (e.g. an oversized wind turbine with high peak but low average output). The solution might be to measure capacity as the actual output in one of the first few years after commissioning.[7]

Output (performance-based) subsidy   As technologies mature to basic reliability of operation, the focus shifts towards performance and efficiency and it becomes most efficient to subsidise output, so as to reward improved performance rather than just the construction of capital equipment. The scale of investment starts to rise dramatically as the technology starts to enter markets so that, in addition, political economy considerations affect policy choices. A capital subsidy requires a large payment up front, whereas an output subsidy is a smaller continuing subsidy (perhaps with the same or higher net present value) and, as such, puts off the pain of payment into the future, always a more palatable political choice. Moreover, it becomes more attractive to socialise the subsidy across consumers through electricity prices, rather than through general taxation.[8]

There are two broad instrumental approaches to output subsidies: predetermined prices, or explicit or implicit auctions. The former generally take the form of mandated feed-in tariffs for renewable energies. The UK's non-fossil-fuel obligation was an example of an auction approach. The development of the Renewable Obligation Certificates (ROC) market, from an economic perspective, represents an attempt to decentralise the auction process (market players are still, in effect, bidding in to the subsidy available to supply a given pre-specific capacity), but the introduction of a price cap on the system creates a hybrid instrument in which the 'auction price' is bounded.

---

[7] The first year may require some bedding down, and output may be hard to predict in that year, and hence risky.

[8] There may be several reasons why this is politically more attractive, including lower visibility, and the impact of trust factors that make the public more willing to pay higher electricity prices if they can see the money going directly to clean technologies rather than into government coffers. The NFFO mechanism generated an annual flow of revenue from consumer charges that could be used to finance either output or capital subsidies, as could auctioning EU emission allowances.

Specifically, the Renewables Obligation (RO) places a requirement on UK electricity suppliers to source a growing percentage of electricity from eligible renewable generation capacity. When introduced in 2000, it applied to to all renewable technologies equally, with subsidy flowing to different generating technologies on the basis of the number of MWh of electricity delivered, regardless of the cost of production. The Renewables Obligation targets renewables to contribute 15% of UK electricity generation by 2015, but with a 'price cap' set for the suppliers to pay £30 per MWh of shortfall if the target is not met. An unusual feature is that the revenue from this price cap mechanism is recycled back to holders of ROCs, and the value of this results in a trading price significantly above the actual cap price, increasing with the degree of shortfall.

The RO is thus ultimately funded by consumers through payment to suppliers in electricity bills and will cost consumers cumulatively *c.* £14 billion by 2020 and *c.* £18 billion by 2027 (in present-value terms), when the certificates expire.[9] The RO represents by far the largest part of financial support for renewable energy. There is a view amongst some in industry that the money that flows to developers from the RO is part subsidy and part payment for capacity additions; the latter can be viewed as a market correction cost as a result of the new trading arrangements in 2001 (which disadvantaged intermittent generators), though one reserved purely for renewable sources.[10]

In addition to funding received through the RO, generators of renewable energy presently receive a levy exemption certificate from the Climate Change Levy (CCL) for each MWh of renewable electricity produced, which at 0.43p/kWh provides an additional, albeit smaller, revenue stream from electricity suppliers.

The general argument for the ROC approach was the belief that the auction-type pressures it generated would make it much more efficient than fixed price tariffs. Empirically, there is now little doubt that it has stimulated the growth of renewable energy (if not as effectively as the feed-in mechanism in Germany) – to which economists might retort that any system can stimulate rapid growth if you throw enough money at it. But Butler and Neuhoff (2005) also question the supposed efficiency

---

[9] These data are from Carbon Trust (2006). See also the Introductory chapter. For comparison, the benefits from a successful offshore development programme indicated below are projected to be around £2bn/year in revenues by 2020.

[10] It might also be argued that the costs of balancing intermittent power have been exaggerated by the new balancing mechanism that replaced the former Electricity Pool, which makes the very short-term spot market illiquid and risky, particularly for small generating companies, and that therefore some additional compensation was required. It would, of course, be better to address such concerns directly.

benefits of ROC-type approaches, pointing out that feed-in tariffs maintain competitive pressures in the manufacturing industry, which is where innovation is most required, whilst reducing uncertainties and thereby financing costs for the project developers. In addition, the ROC approach transfers regulatory risk to the private sector, which accordingly prices that risk at a premium throughout the financial chain, thus 'leaking' a significant fraction of the subsidy away from actual project developers.[11]

Technology differentiation   The other aspect of this debate is that of technology differentiation. This issue – whether the support should be differentiated by technology – is often confused with that of the tariff vs. certificates debate, because feed-in tariffs have been traditionally differentiated, whilst certificates have generally been specified to cover all renewables as a single group. It is, however, a qualitatively different issue: one could have a uniform feed-in tariff, or a series of certificate markets differentiated by technology.

Until the most recent *White Paper* proposed reform (as outlined in the conclusions to this chapter), the Renewables Obligation offered undifferentiated supports to renewable electricity generation. Thus, it was designed to pull through the lowest-cost technologies sequentially, which has the effect of limiting the amount of support given to less mature technologies. In its first 5 years of operation (2001–2005), renewables penetration from eligible renewable sources increased from 1.5% in 2001 to *c.* 4% in 2005. However, this was dominated by onshore wind, and the original assumption that offshore wind investment would follow hard on its heels proved false. Offshore wind costs turned out to be higher than originally expected, due to higher steel and turbine prices and an increase in installation and construction costs as the industry has moved away from turnkey contracts.

A first round of bids for siting offshore wind energy projects resulted in a range of projects already operating or under construction (see Figure 13.3, left panel). However, these benefited from the previously lower turbine and construction prices, and many developers committed to build one offshore wind farm for strategic reasons and to gain onsite experience, and were therefore willing to invest in these projects at lower

---

[11] Power Purchase Agreement (PPA) providers (the electricity suppliers) demand a significant percentage of the ROC value (which can vary by technology) to compensate for the perceived political risk connected with the RO when providing long-term contracts. Financiers also discount the ROC value considerably when making their lending decisions, meaning that financing terms become less favourable for developers. Overall, there is a leakage of subsidy in the RO system away from developers.

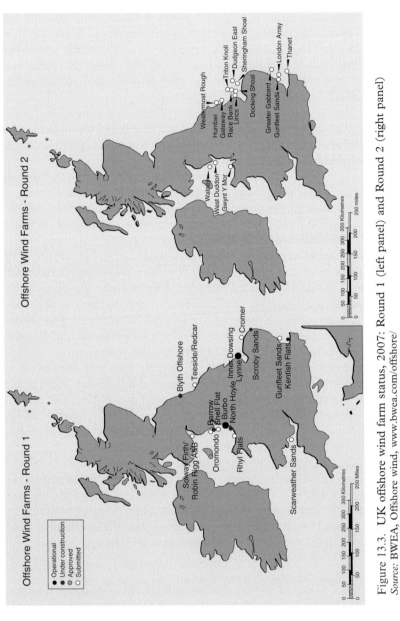

Figure 13.3. UK offshore wind farm status, 2007: Round 1 (left panel) and Round 2 (right panel)
Source: BWEA, Offshore wind, www.bwea.com/offshore/

rates of return. None of these conditions can be expected to apply going forward, and a much smaller fraction of the applications under Round 2 are as yet proceeding (Figure 13.3, right panel).

Not surprisingly, renewable energy finance under the RO has tended to flow to the most established and economically viable renewable technology available at scale, i.e. onshore wind. Before the next technology can be pulled through, there is a timing delay, as Renewable Obligation Certificate (ROC) prices have to rise to a high enough level to provide economic returns to an investor in the next technology (offshore wind) – a period characterised by the inefficiency of high returns for the lowest-cost technology (onshore). The larger the gap between the technology costs, the longer this delay can be expected to be.

At the same time, installation of onshore capacity is restricted by grid and planning constraints. The combination of these restrictions and the timing delay means that ROC prices remain high and the Renewables Obligation is unable to deliver capacity fast enough to close the projected UK supply gap.

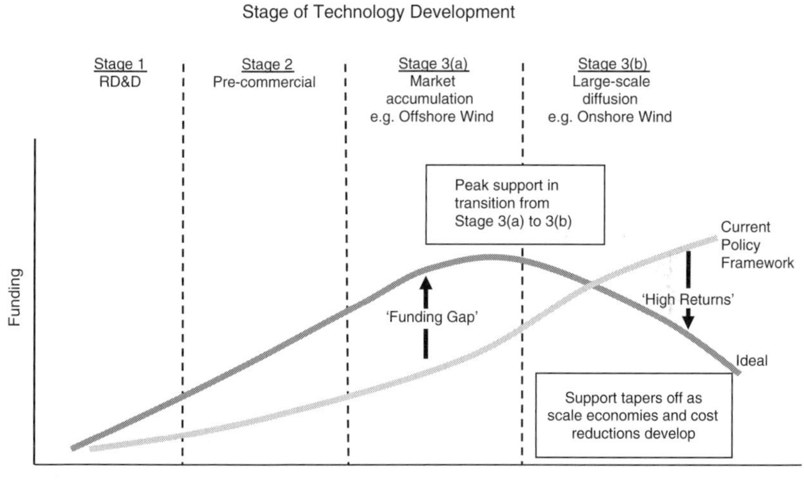

Stage of Technology Development

Stage 1
RD&D

Stage 2
Pre-commercial

Stage 3(a)
Market
accumulation
e.g. Offshore Wind

Stage 3(b)
Large-scale
diffusion
e.g. Onshore Wind

Peak support in
transition from
Stage 3(a) to 3(b)

Current
Policy
Framework

Funding

'Funding Gap'

'High Returns'

Ideal

Support tapers off as
scale economies and cost
reductions develop

Figure 13.4. Funding gaps and returns with undifferentiated renewable energy support mechanisms

Note: The figure illustrates qualitatively the trend in absolute scale of subsidy requirements (darker line) as a technology develops through the 'innovation chain' of Figure 13.1, and contrasts this with (lighter line) the scale of funding typically received through the Renewables Obligation, which is constant per unit output and thus channels most funding towards the most extensively deployed technology.

Source: Adapted from the L.E.K. analysis (Carbon Trust, 2006)

As a result, as depicted in Figure 13.4, high ROC prices are providing good profits to onshore developers, yet fail to provide sufficient subsidy to close the funding gap for offshore wind development – let alone technologies further back in the innovation process. All 'technology-blind' policy support options will have these characteristics by design: they reward the 'first past the post' within the broad category of the support mechanism, but do little to help the others.

Overall, the original Renewables Obligation policy suffers from inefficiencies, resulting in a cost of renewable energy to consumers that is higher than necessary given the current technology cost. In addition, a consensus has grown that undifferentiated supports do not solve the problem of innovation: they simply allow the 'first past the post' in any given category (in renewables markets that is generally wind energy) to reap large rewards, whilst leaving other, less well-established technologies foundering. A more efficient means of supporting innovation would close the funding gap for offshore wind and taper away support from onshore.

13.6   An analysis of options to 2020

The UK has established targets for renewable energy and CO_2 by 2020. Moreover, given the expected closure of old nuclear and coal plant, the UK faces the serious prospect of a 'capacity gap' during this period. Investment in renewable energy is needed. Diversity requires that different technologies be installed in meaningful amounts in parallel. This section outlines specific findings from a detailed study of various options for reforming renewable energy support schemes, conducted by L.E.K. Consulting with the Carbon Trust (Carbon Trust, 2006) as a contribution to the UK's *Energy Review* (DTI, 2006).

Modelling has confirmed that, under the Renewables Obligation as of 2006, almost all of the additional capacity for 2015 is likely to come from onshore wind, as the level of support for offshore wind is not sufficient to overcome unfavourable economics and begin to drive offshore wind projects' costs down the learning curve. ROC prices rise significantly (to £52/MWh in real terms by 2015) as renewables investment falls behind the 15% target. Onshore investments achieve very high rates of return, with internal rates of return of up to 15% – nearly twice the estimated real required rate of return of 7.75% for these projects. Offshore wind investment would not take place at scale until nearly 2020.[12]

---

[12] The investment case for offshore wind (as for all generation technologies) improves if the electricity price proves to be higher over the period of investment than current

Five options for developing or changing the RO system were selected for detailed analysis:

1. *'Stepped' fixed feed-in subsidy* (a 'renewables development premium'): replacing the RO with a form of fixed subsidy tailored to each technology, with different tariffs for onshore and offshore wind. Tariffs are set as a fixed premium on top of the wholesale electricity price and the levy exemption, and 'stepped' down for future projects with expected cost reduction. Two versions of the tariff were analysed: one that was designed to optimise delivery of renewable generation by 2015 and 2020 (termed the 'Base stepped feed-in tariff'); and the other to keep total funding levels (the present value of the cumulative subsidy) similar to that under the current RO (termed the 'No extra funding - stepped feed-in tariff')
2. *Top-up subsidy*: a capital grant for offshore wind on top of the RO.
3. *Fixed price ROC purchase agreements* by Government, providing a fixed subsidy for 2GW offshore wind capacity.
4. *A capping of the value of the ROC revenue recycling mechanism* at £5/ MWh, with the surplus funds being directed to offshore wind.
5. *Multiple/fractional ROCs*: varying the proportion of ROC value given to different technologies by providing a differential number of ROCs per MWh, now adopted as 'banded ROCs' (see Section 13.8).

The results are summarised in Figure 13.5 in terms of contributions and cumulative subsidies by 2015 and 2020. The numerical analysis assumes that the 15% Renewables Obligation is not increased beyond 2015, so that the additional time is 'catching up' to this, and also that offshore wind energy sites are restricted to those already approved under Rounds 1 and 2 of the UK's offshore development bids.

The 'stepped' fixed feed-in subsidy, with cumulative support of £15 billion by 2020, delivers the greatest amount of capacity: 8.8GW of additional wind capacity by 2015 and 11.7 GW by 2020, resulting in 13.2% and 14.9% of generation from renewable sources, respectively. It also has the lowest cumulative subsidy cost per cumulative MWh generated over the time frame, of £40/MWh.[13] It achieves this by

expectations. Using electricity price forecasts about 25% higher than in the base case leads to an additional 1.7 GW of wind by 2015 and 5.0 GW by 2020, as offshore wind projects clear investment hurdles. An increase in electricity prices of 50% from base case levels would lead to 5.6GW of wind being installed by 2015, with renewables achieving 14.7% of electricity generation by 2015.

[13] The subsidy cost per MWh is calculated by dividing cumulative subsidy by cumulative renewable generation. As a result, options that lead to capacity installation earlier rather than later tend to be more efficient on this measure given that such capacity will

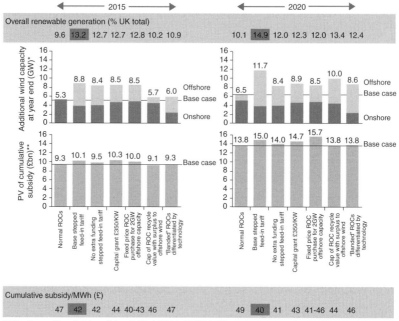

Figure 13.5. Renewable energy contributions and cumulative subsidies by 2015 and 2020 under a 15% RO target
Source: L.E.K. analysis (Carbon Trust, 2006, Figure 8)

driving greater offshore wind investment than other mechanisms through the use of differential support by technology and by providing increased funding certainty to developers, reducing risk and subsidy leakage. It also provides a mechanism for tapering support from technologies. If the total amount of support were to be restricted to the aggregate level under the existing RO, the 'stepped' fixed feed-in remains the most efficient in terms of the additional (subsidy) cost of delivered renewable energy at £41/MWh by 2020, and still delivers 8.4GW by 2015.[14] The efficiency of the 'stepped' fixed feed-in as

have been generating electricity for a longer period, albeit potentially at a higher initial capital cost.

[14] Investment costs are all appraised at a 15% rate of return, with electricity prices based on DTI projections before the gas (and power) price rises of 2005. Higher electricity prices – or assumed lower discount rates – would lower the scale of subsidy required for

compared to the current RO is perhaps best highlighted by the potential to deliver broadly the same amount of renewables capacity as projected under the current RO over the time-frame and still save c. £1 billion by 2020 and c. £3 billion by 2027 in present-value terms.

The top-up subsidy via capital grant also delivers significantly more capacity than the current RO, achieving 12.7% renewables contribution by 2015, as the capital subsidy supports early investment in offshore wind.[15] It involves a similar additional funding cost as the 'stepped' fixed feed-in subsidy at c. £1 billion by 2020[16] in present-value terms, but does not disrupt the RO mechanism; it is an example of a measure that has been used with the RO in the past (for example, Round 1 offshore wind capital grants). However, it would require pre-allocation of the capital funding. Capital grants also need to be carefully designed – the experience of Round 1 shows that making funds available by pre-allocation does not guarantee that investment in renewables will take place.

Government fixed-price purchase of 2GW of offshore wind ROCs produces similar capacity additions in the 2015 and 2020 time-frames as the top-up subsidy. It is also potentially one of the most efficient mechanisms in terms of cost per MWh of renewable electricity produced, depending on the view taken of the additional cost to Government arising from acting as guarantor under the fixed price purchase arrangements. The chief disadvantage of the proposal lies in this hidden cost, which requires Government to assume the risk (e.g. recycle shortfall, buyer credit default and working capital) involved in providing these long-term contracts for 2GW of offshore wind capacity. It is difficult to assess the price of this risk, but at a maximum it can be estimated by reference to the price the private sector attaches to this risk, which in this study is assumed to be reflected in the 30% discount to ROC prices.[17] Otherwise this approach provides minimal interference with the RO, though it does involve a specific government involvement in the 'market' choice.

The proposal to redistribute funds from the ROC price-capping mechanism (above £5/MWh) delivers little additional capacity over the

---

the same level of renewable energy investment. The data on total subsidy per MWh are undiscounted £ per undiscounted MWh delivered by 2020.

[15] The capital is used up early and does not support investment post-2015, so the percentage contribution actually declines a little after 2015, assuming continued growth in electricity demand. Note that the range of capacities projected in the Supergen scenarios set out in Chapter 14 is consistent with the model results in the Carbon Trust/L.E.K. modelling summarised here.

[16] Plus an additional c. £0.8 billion by 2027. Cost presented as monies spent, not committed, by a certain date.

[17] The private sector price of this risk assuming a 30% discount on ROCs represents a maximum cost of c. £1.9bn by 2020.

existing RO policy. This is because the surplus for redistribution from capping takes time to build up, in particular because, with grandfathering, only a small proportion of the renewables base is initially subject to the cap. However, it requires no extra funding and delivers rapid expansion of capacity after 2015 (although still falling short of the base 'stepped' fixed feed-in) as the capital raised is spent in later periods, by which time offshore wind economics have improved. However, because the capacity additions come so late in the time-frame examined, it is one of the least efficient mechanisms in terms of the cost per MWh of delivered renewable electricity, and the recycling raises the same issues as capital grants.

Finally, the base case of multiple/fractional ROCs does not deliver significant overall extra wind capacity in a 2015 time frame (10.9% of generation in 2015), assuming that no new money is applied. A significant amount of offshore wind (3.4GW) is delivered by 2015, but the targeting of funding towards offshore wind is (without extra funding) at the expense of onshore, leading to a much lower level of onshore development than in other options. While the support for new onshore and offshore wind projects can be adjusted by changing the relevant multiples (with corresponding effect on the installed capacity for each technology), this does not lead to a greater overall level of wind installation. Whichever fractions are used, a lower amount of new wind capacity is achieved than the options with additional funding in the 2015 time frame. Capacity additions by 2020 for this option are at a level similar to the top-up subsidy and government purchase of offshore ROCs. Overall efficiency, in terms of the cost per MWh of delivered capacity is low, due to diversion of funds from lower (onshore) to higher (early offshore) cost options.

Comparison and extensions The Carbon Trust study offers a more detailed comparison of the options. Overall, the underlying theme is that targeting and bringing forward support for more rapid development of offshore wind is a more efficient use of subsidy than allowing the original RO mechanism to run its course over a much longer time frame. In addition, all the options help drive offshore wind to a more cost-competitive position in 2020 than under the existing RO. However, driving offshore wind capacity quickly to meet the 2015 gap without overly compromising onshore returns involves extra funding, while options that require no extra funding or a less significant shift from the current RO do not deliver on 2015 capacity (although they deliver reasonable capacity by 2020). The other underlying theme is that the more efficient mechanisms require either greater up-front direct funding, or greater certainty and stability about the longer-term revenue streams associated with these inherently risky investments.

As indicated, this analysis was constrained by assuming the existing 15% renewables target, and restricting siting options to offshore applications from Rounds 1 and 2. Relaxing these constraints (with a 20% by 2020 renewables RO target) and adopting the most effective mechanisms generated up to another 9GW of installed capacity by 2020, with the contribution by 2020 coming very close to the 20% target.

13.7   Spanning the innovation chain in UK power generation

The key to a successful innovation strategy is to combine instruments appropriate to the different stages of innovation, discussed in the Introduction to this chapter, so as to build options that can then be brought down the cost curve through the cumulative impact of private-sector investment in response to government incentives. The broad structure, illustrated with respect to UK renewable energy generation, is indicated in Figure 13.6: a progression of instruments that starts with technology-specific R&D and then capital supports, and moves towards mechanisms that subsidise output as the technology develops and the industry grows.

The aim is to bring low-carbon technologies to the point where they compete purely on the basis of carbon advantage. This, however, is not an easy goal. A €15/tCO$_2$ carbon price adds about 1p/kWh to the cost of coal power generation.[18] For onshore wind energy, such a gap is within reach. For offshore wind energy, the projections above suggest that, even by 2020, and with up to £15 billion of cumulative subsidy invested, the industry is only likely to be competitive with conventional coal if carbon prices reliably exceed €25/tCO$_2$ or more (which is, interestingly, roughly the same amount as projected to be required to make carbon capture and storage economic, if development succeeds – see Chapter 15). Other options are further back still. Yet, at least such an investment in offshore wind deployment has a direct payoff in terms of generating substantial power that will help to close the 'capacity gap' and benefit UK energy security, in addition to helping deliver carbon targets.

It is the central span – the pre-commercial stage in the innovation chain of Figure 13.1 – that poses the greatest dilemmas for policy, and

---

[18] A modern coal plant may emit around 750 kgCO$_2$/MWh. The impact on actual cost comparisons may be softened, for example, if incumbents or new investments get significant free allocations.

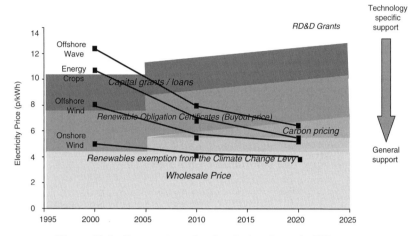

Figure 13.6. Progression of technologies through different support mechanisms

the greatest scope for policy error. In contrast to early-stage research, the scale of finance for major power generation at this stage typically moves from millions of pounds to tens of millions at project level – and from tens to hundreds of millions, or potentially billions, in terms of overall programme/investment commitments. Errors become much more costly and, because more money is at stake, the risk of 'capture' (as outlined earlier) increases. Also, because this is the stage at which resources start to focus on refining a given technology path, the wrong choice carries the risk of 'locking-out' ultimately superior but less developed ideas within a given category.

Because it is too expensive to support every plausible idea, there is greater need for strategic thinking in the choices made. There is thus a case for applying in the central part of the innovation chain similar logic to that suggested for strategic deployment programmes, seeking to 'build options' in areas of potential comparative advantage. Non-wind marine energy sources fall into this category, and typify the dilemmas: the UK has abundant resources and clear potential to establish a global lead, but it is unclear whether existing approaches offer enough 'learning-by-doing' promise to justify the costs of more extensive scale applications, relative to the need for continuing more fundamental R&D (Thorpe and Wallace, 2006).

An important dilemma for UK policy makers is that moving towards industrial support at scale does not sit easily with liberal economic philosophy, as it involves government funding decisions that discriminate between technology options with the aim of 'launching' industries, in ways reminiscent of 'industrial policy' in earlier decades – a strategy largely discredited in the eyes of many economists. Yet, there is no question that delivering a low-carbon electricity system will require new industries, above and beyond the current options, and that carbon pricing on its own is both inadequate, and indeed inefficient, for the reasons discussed in this and previous chapters in this section. The best that can be done is to learn from past mistakes and focus support more through performance incentives, in areas where there is a clear case of potential comparative advantage, rather than direct government backing for 'national' industries.

13.8   Recent policy developments and conclusions

After 5 years of relative stability since the introduction of the Renewable Obligation Certificates and the formation of the Carbon Trust, UK policy on innovation and renewable energy took big steps during 2006 and 2007. In 2006, the Chancellor announced the creation of the Energy Technologies Institute to support earlier-stage R&D – although its exact form, and even location and actual funding, remained unclear a year later. Also in 2006, the *Energy Review* announced the intent to ensure that the Renewable Obligation target remained above plausible deployment levels out to 2020, so as to ensure that the system stayed above the 'buy-out' price, giving investors the price security they had been seeking.

In the 2007 *White Paper*, the Government made an even bigger break, in announcing that the RO incentive would be 'banded' for different technology categories. Subject to further consultation, four Bands are proposed:

1. 0.25 ROC/MWh for established renewable technologies (including landfill gas, biomass co-firing)
2. 1 ROC/MWh for reference technologies (including onshore wind)
3. 1.5 ROC/MWh for 'post-demonstration' technologies (including offshore wind, dedicated biomass)
4. 2 ROC/MWh for emerging technologies (including wave, tidal stream, emerging conversion technologies such as anaerobic digestion and pyrolysis, solar PV and dedicated energy crop biomass).

The bands would remain fixed for a period – probably up to March 2013. Periodic reviews of the bands would be undertaken by an independent body. The *White Paper* confirmed also that, from 2015, increases in the RO target level will be on a 'headroom' basis – i.e. the target percentage of renewables will increase slightly in advance of the actually installed renewable capacity, up to a 20% target. These measures are anticipated to enable the UK to achieve a 15% renewable electricity contribution by 2015. Government projections suggest that, without further measures, the expansion slows thereafter.

There is considerable irony in these twin developments. The thought behind the original Renewables Obligation was that policy should create a single market-based, competitive incentive towards a targeted contribution from renewable energy, to secure least-cost delivery of the target (originally 10% by 2010 and later extended to 15% by 2015), but with a 'price cap' for economic protection in case meeting the target proved excessively expensive. At the time it was a bold move in UK policy. However, planning constraints, among other factors, made the target very hard to achieve, and recycling revenue from the cap mechanism back to renewable generators has meant that the RO price has always been above the buy-out price.

By now designing subsequent targets to be above deliverable quantities out to 2020, the buy-out price assumes the characteristic of a price floor; and the RO itself becomes much more like a feed-in tariff, but with the incentive added on top of wholesale power prices, and declining as the target is approached. In taking the second step of now banding the obligation, the system looks even more like a Continental feed-in tariff in terms of its main properties, but with far greater complexity. The evolution is testament to the fact that the Government did acknowledge and has sought to address the problems of the RO, whilst wishing to minimise changes; but there is a risk that the greater complexity of the system may itself now impede investment and lessen its efficiency.

Electricity, as explained, is a sector with exceptionally low private R&D investment, yet in which there is an urgent need to drive innovation in specific directions for the sake of long-term environmental considerations. Governments find it hard to adequately price environmental impacts, and markets find it even harder to judge the risks and potential rewards involved. Moreover, technologies are at diverse stages of development and also vary greatly in other characteristics, including the level of international competition. The barriers to 'socially optimal' R&D are manifold; the case for intervention is robust, but industrial innovation policy is complex and fraught with the risk of policy failure.

Some technology options inherently need to be considered in the international context, and the level of direct UK contribution to global development may be modest. For others – and offshore renewables are prime examples – the UK has both great resources and the potential to drive the global pace of innovation. The benefits of up-front investment are all the greater if, in the process of delivering on its environmental objectives, the UK can succeed in establishing a global lead in such sectors where it has a head start or natural potential advantage, as a springboard for global application. Yet the risks of failure – in either technology or policy – remain great.

Simultaneously building a carbon market that can lead to rising carbon prices over time enables a long-term goal in which the technologies can be weaned off these direct-support mechanisms to a context in which they are fully cost-competitive, given appropriate pricing of the 'external' factors – such as climate change and the contribution to domestic energy diversity and security. The faster that policy can adequately price these factors, the lower the costs and the risks of the associated mechanisms for accelerating innovation.

References

Butler, L. and Neuhoff, K. (2005). *Comparison of Feed in Tariff, Quota and Auction Mechanisms to Support Wind Power Development*, Cambridge Working Papers in Economics CWPE 0503, Department of Applied Economics, University of Cambridge.

Carbon Trust (2003). *Building Options for UK Renewable Energy*, CT/2003/08, Carbon Trust, London.

(2006). *Policy Frameworks for Renewables: Analysis on Policy Frameworks to Drive Future Investment in Near and Long-term Renewable Power in the UK*, A study funded by the Carbon Trust and carried out by L.E.K. Consulting in conjunction with the Carbon Trust, London.

Cohen, L.R. and Noll, R.G. (1991). *The Technology Pork Barrel*, Brookings Institution Press, Washington, DC.

DTI (2006). *The Energy Challenge: Energy Review Report 2006*, Department of Trade and Industry, London.

(2007). *Energy White Paper: Meeting the Energy Challenge*, CM 7124, Department of Trade and Industry, London.

Foxon, T.J. (2003). *Inducing Innovation for a Low-carbon Future: Drivers, Barriers and Policies*, A Report for the Carbon Trust, CT-2003–07, Carbon Trust, London.

Fri, R.W. (2003). The role of knowledge: technological innovation in the energy system, *Energy Journal*, 24(4), 51–74.

Gross, R., Heptonstall, P. and Blyth, W. (2007). *Investment in Electricity Generation: The Role of Costs, Incentives and Risks*, ICEPT/UK Energy Research Centre, London.

Grubb, M. (2004). Technology innovation and climate change policy: an overview of issues and options, *Keio Economic Studies*, 41(2), 103–132.

IEA (2006). *Energy Technology Perspectives: Scenarios and Strategies to 2050*, International Energy Agency, Paris.

Loiter, J.M. and Norberg-Bohm, V. (1999). Technology policy and renewable energy: public roles in the development of new technologies, *Energy Policy*, 27, 85–97.

Mitchell, C. (1995). Future support of renewable energy, *Energy Policy*, **23**(12), 1077–1091.

Morthurst, P.E. (2006). Wind power: status and perspectives, in: Jamasb, T., Nuttall, W. and Pollitt, M. (eds), *Future Electricity Technologies and Systems*, Cambridge University Press, Cambridge.

Murphy, L. and Edwards, P. (2003). *Bridging the Valley of Death: Transitioning from Public to Private Sector Financing*, National Renewable Energy Laboratory, Golden, CO.

Neuhoff, K. (2005). Large-scale Deployment of Renewables for Electricity Generation. *Oxford Review of Economic Policy*, **21**(1), 88–110.

Pacala, S. and Socolow, R. (2004). Stabilization wedges: solving the climate problem for the next 50 years with current technologies, *Science*, **305**, 968–972.

Perlack, R.B. and Shelton, R.D. (1996). *Government's Role in Energy Technology R&D: A Proposed Model for Strategic Guidance*, ORNL/TM-1321, Oak Ridge National Laboratory, Oak Ridge, TN.

Sandén, B.A. and Azar, C. (2004). Near-term technology policies for long-term climate targets: economy wide versus technology specific approaches, *Energy Policy*, **33**, 1557–1576.

Thorpe, T. and Wallace, R. (2006). Wave energy, in: Jamasb, T., Nuttall, W. and Pollitt, M. (eds), *Future Electricity Technologies and Systems*, Cambridge University Press, Cambridge, 155–176.

Part IV

Scenarios, Options and Public Attitudes

14 Scenarios of the electricity industry in Great Britain in 2020: networks, generation and decarbonisation

Ian Elders, Graham Ault, Graeme Burt,
Ryan Tumilty, Jim McDonald and Jonathan Köhler

14.1 Introduction

This chapter presents a set of scenarios for the development of the electricity supply industry in Great Britain in the years to 2020. These scenarios illustrate the varied sets of background circumstances which may influence the industry over the coming years – including political and regulatory factors, the strength of the economy, and the level to which environmentally driven restrictions and opportunities influence policy and investment decisions. The scenarios are intended to provide a set of plausible future situations in the electricity industry within which future measures for the development of renewable and low-carbon generation, and the corresponding developments to the network can be discussed. Recent thinking (Bows *et al.*, 2006; Stern, 2006) emphasises the key role of the electricity industry in managing overall national CO_2 emissions, and the need for early action if challenging targets are to be met.

Previous work by the authors (Elders *et al.*, 2006) has resulted in a set of six scenarios illustrating possible developments in the electricity industry in the period up to 2050. While such scenarios are valuable in gauging the long-term direction of the electricity industry and its economic and environmental consequences, shorter-range scenarios are useful in assessing the steps necessary to arrive at these long-range destinations, and to determine their relationship to current trends, policies and targets.

In this chapter, a set of medium-range scenarios focused on the year 2020 is developed and described. These scenarios are designed to be consistent both with the current state of the electricity supply industry in Great Britain, and with the achievement of the ultimate electricity generation, supply and utilisation infrastructure and patterns described in each of the 2050 scenarios. The consequences of these scenarios in terms of the emissions of carbon dioxide are evaluated and compared with other predictions.

Table 14.1. *Installed generation capacity in 2004*

Plant type	Capacity (GW)
Fossil-fuelled steam*	31.1
CCGT	24.6
Nuclear	11.8
OCGT and diesel	1.4
Renewables	3.1
Total	**72**

* Including coal, oil, dual-fuel and gas-burning steam plant.
Source: DTI (2005)

Table 14.2. *Ageing generation plant in 2020*

Plant type	Capacity > 40 years old (GW)	Capacity > 45 years old (GW)
Fossil-fuelled steam	27.2	24.9
CCGT	0	0
Nuclear	4.8	2.4
OCGT and diesel*	0.5	0.4
Renewables	1.1	1.1
Total	**33.6**	**28.8**

* Only transmission-connected OCGT and diesel plant, with a 2004 capacity of 1.1GW is included.
Source: National Grid (2005)

14.2   Current demand and generation

In 2004, the total volume of electricity supplied via the electricity network in Great Britain was approximately 355TWh (DTI, 2005; National Grid, 2005). Forty per cent of this energy was supplied by gas-fired generating units, 33% from coal, 19% from nuclear, and the remaining 8% from other sources including imports and renewables. The peak demand met by the transmission system was approximately 60GW.

Installed plant capacities in 2004 are shown in Table 14.1. A significant volume of this plant, and particularly the steam units, will be relatively old by 2020. Table 14.2 shows the capacity of transmission-connected plant which will have reached 40 and 45 years of age by that point.

While generating plant lifetimes are ultimately dependent on the actual condition of the plant, its market performance and regulatory compliance, 40 and 45 years have been used here to illustrate typical plant lifetimes, and the effect of limited life extension on the generation portfolio in Great Britain. It should be noted that the renewable capacity shown in Table 14.2 consists of hydro-generation; subject to the condition of major civil engineering works such as dams and aqueducts, it is expected that this plant would be life-extended indefinitely.

14.3   Forecasts and predictions

14.3.1   Short- and medium-term forecasts and scenarios

A detailed short-range forecast of the development of the British electricity system focusing in particular on the transmission system is produced annually by the transmission system operator, National Grid, in the form of its *Seven Year Statement* (National Grid, 2005). This document provides forecasts of the level of annual electricity demand to be supplied via the transmission system as well as the peak demand to be met. A range of forecasts is made – some on the basis of models and data provided by National Grid, while others are based on data supplied by distribution companies and large industrial customers. The range of forecasts considers factors such as variations in economic growth, energy efficiency, and the extent to which demand is satisfied from generation connected to distribution networks. The 2005 *Seven Year Statement* presents forecasts extending to 2012. At the end of this period, the range of peak demand forecasts is 56–71 GW, with a 'base estimate' of 65 GW. The high and low values of energy supplied by the transmission network in 2011/2012 are 410 TWh and 330 TWh, respectively, with a base estimate of 375 TWh.

The *Seven Year Statement* also provides a list of new generation projects with which arrangements have been made leading to formal connection to the transmission network – small-scale distributed generation is not listed. While not all of these developments will proceed to construction and commissioning, they provide an indication of the generation technologies which are currently of interest to developers. The projects listed in the 2005 *Seven Year Statement* are summarised in Table 14.3. It should be noted that this does not represent all the generation likely to be constructed up to 2012; lead times for construction of many generator types are significantly less than 7 years while, on the other hand, some of the planned developments will not proceed to construction. However, it can be seen that there is a strong

Table 14.3. *New generation projects listed in National Grid* Seven Year Statement

Plant type	Capacity (GW)
CCGT	8.8
Hydro	0.1
Wind	4.4
Total	**13.3**

Source: National Grid (2005)

focus on CCGT as the currently preferred form of conventional generation, with wind as the renewable energy source of choice for developers.

Another forecast of the future of the electricity industry has been produced as part of the Updated Energy Projections (UEP) exercise conducted by the UK Government's Department of Trade and Industry (DTI, 2006). The latest results of this work forecast the demand for electricity, the mixture of fuel sources used by generators and the resulting emissions of carbon dioxide. The results are based on a number of assumptions – for example, the rate of growth in output of renewable generators, and that economic growth over the period will be close to the long-term average.

Four scenarios, considering different future trends in fossil fuel price, are considered by the DTI, with more detailed discussion of two central-price cases which consider the effect of prices favouring coal or gas-fuelled generators. In these scenarios, electricity demand is forecast to be in the range 375–380TWh/year in 2020. Gas-fired generation accounts for between 53% and 60% of this total, while coal-fired generation produces 15–20% of electricity. Renewable generation production is 53TWh/year. Carbon dioxide emissions from electricity production in 2020 are in the range 135–160 $MtCO_2$/year over the range of the four scenarios.

14.3.2 Long-term scenarios

A number of bodies have produced long-term scenarios of the UK's energy use or electricity industry, generally considering the year 2050. The Royal Commission on Environmental Pollution (2000) proposed a set of four scenarios as an illustration of mechanisms by which a reduction of 60% in the UK's emissions of carbon dioxide could be achieved by 2050. These scenarios consider UK energy use in its entirety, including transport and heat demand, as well as electricity, and show the effects of different combinations of demand reduction, renewables, nuclear generation and carbon capture and storage. These scenarios were further analysed in terms of their effect on the British generation portfolio by the Tyndall Centre for Climate Change Research (Watson, 2003). This analysis showed that, under the RCEP scenarios (and to achieve the carbon emission reduction targets set out), renewable energy could be required to meet the majority of the UK's electricity demand by 2050.

Another set of scenarios was produced for the UK Department of Trade and Industry (Marsh et al., 2003) to investigate methods by which carbon dioxide emissions from the energy sector could be reduced, the effects on energy prices and demand, and the costs of carbon abatement. Three basic scenarios, delineated by economic and social factors, were proposed, and the effects of these scenarios and variations on them were evaluated using an energy system model.

The scenarios already mentioned in this section were drawn upon by the authors in proposing a set of long-term scenarios (Elders et al., 2006), which were focused more closely on the electricity industry to support the work of the Supergen Future Network Technologies Consortium. These scenarios (for the year 2050) specifically consider developments in electricity generation and end-use, and in transmission and distribution, together with issues of markets and regulation. These scenarios were characterised in terms of four key parameters: (i) the level of economic growth, (ii) the rate of technical advancement, (iii) the level of environmental concern in society, and (iv) the degree of central regulation and intervention in the industry. The scenarios are summarised in Table 14.4. These 2050 scenarios were used as the basis of the scenarios focusing on 2020 which are described in this chapter.

14.4   Identification of 2020 scenarios

As noted previously, an important aim in identifying a set of 2020 electricity industry scenarios was to achieve consistency both with the current situation and with the set of 2050 scenarios previously developed. In order to achieve this objective, consideration was given both to the likely trend in demand for electricity under each of the 2050 scenarios, and the technology mix which is anticipated. The effect of the underlying driving factors in each 2050 scenario is also taken into account in identifying a set of intermediate points (2020) in the development of each long-term scenario.

Table 14.4. *Summary of Supergen 2050 electricity industry scenarios*

2050 Scenario	Economic growth	Environmental focus	Technological growth	Regulatory structure	2050 Electricity demand (TWh)	Renewable-generated electricity (%)
Strong optimism	More than recently	Stronger	Revolutionary	Liberalised	600	50
Business as usual	Same as recently	As at present	Evolutionary	Liberalised	540	30
Economic downturn	Less than recently	Weaker	Evolutionary	Liberalised	275	10–20
Green plus	Same as recently	Much stronger	Revolutionary	Liberalised	390	80
Technological restriction	More than recently	Stronger	Evolutionary	Liberalised	680	40
Central direction	Same as recently	Stronger	Evolutionary	Interventionist	430	50–60

In considering the growth in demand for electricity, it was recognised that demand is likely to change gradually from its historic growth rate rather than making an abrupt transition directly towards the 2050 figure. In all cases, therefore, it is expected that electricity demand will have grown from today's value by 2020, although to different degrees in different scenarios. Beyond 2020, some scenarios will show continued growth in electricity use, while in others it will remain constant or decline. Considering both the final 2050 electricity demands shown in Table 14.4, and the description of the development in demand from the present day to 2050 in each scenario, it was found that they could be divided into two groups. In one, comprising the 'Green plus' and 'Economic downturn' scenarios, electricity demand grows relatively modestly to 2020 as a result of environmental or economic pressures; in the remaining four scenarios the rate of electricity demand growth over the period is only slightly slower than today's.

The technologies which were identified as being important to each of the 2050 scenarios were categorised into three groups according to their likelihood of being available for commercial deployment in 2020:

1. *Mature technologies* which are currently seeing large-scale deployment, but which might see incremental improvements in scale or efficiency by 2020.
2. *Developing technologies* which are currently seeing pilot or prototype use, but which might be expected to be available for deployment on a commercial scale by 2020.
3. *New technologies* which are at an earlier stage of development and may not have demonstrated their capability to achieve commercial viability and make a significant impact by 2020. Some of these technologies may achieve deployment in a commercial environment by 2020 in the form of pilot plants.

The rate at which individual technologies progress through these stages of development and the level of deployment which is achieved by 2020 will be dependent on the level of research and investment funding which is available to them, and the degree to which there is an economic, engineering or policy demand for the particular characteristics offered by the technology. Therefore, for each combination of technology and 2050 scenario, the level of deployment called for by the scenario was tabulated, together with an estimate of the likely progress towards that goal in 2020.

A further consideration in relation to technology mix is the influence of the current fleet of generation and network plant. While it is reasonable to assume that the vast majority of current plant will have been replaced or at least substantially refurbished by 2050, this assumption cannot be made for 2020 scenarios. The rate at which existing plant is taken out of service will depend both on its age and condition, and on drivers present in the scenario which will promote either life extension or early retirement. For example, scenarios in which there are strong economic constraints on new investment will promote the life extension of existing power stations or network facilities in preference to investment in new plant with corresponding new network extensions. Tables 14.1 and 14.2 provide some guidance on which categories of generating station are most likely to be candidates for replacement by 2020.

As a result of this analysis, four groups of medium-term equivalents of the 2050 scenarios were identified. As already mentioned, two of these addressed cases – the 2050 'Economic downturn' and 'Green plus' scenarios – in which electricity demand grows slowly. In these two cases, significant differences in the technology mix and degree of network development are apparent by 2020. Therefore, separate 2020 scenarios, labelled 'Economic concern' and 'Environmental awakening' are proposed to correspond to these 2050 scenarios.

In the remaining four 'higher demand growth' situations, two reasonably similar sets of circumstances could be discerned. In one ('Strong optimism'), strong economic growth leads to significant industry-led deployment of existing and developing technologies to meet – and to some extent limit – a growth in demand for energy services. In the other ('Technological restriction'), economic growth is not matched by an accompanying maturing and availability of power technologies. Public perceptions of environmental responsibility become an increasing factor in the thinking of industry players. Beyond 2020 these two cases diverge in the level to which more advanced technologies are successfully brought to market and deployed. The situation in 2020 is represented by a scenario labelled 'Strong growth'.

In the second pair of 'high-growth' situations ('Business as usual' and 'Central direction'), the influence of government and regulatory authorities is important in guiding and supporting technological innovation and environmental initiatives. Economically driven growth in demand for energy services is less of an influence in these situations, and there is less focus on measures to restrict growth in demand for electricity, attention being turned instead to issues such as energy and supply security, and the continued development of promising renewable technologies. These cases diverge after 2020 as the strength of central intervention increases in one case and relaxes in the other. The situation in 2020 is represented by a scenario labelled 'Supportive

Table 14.5. *Summary of Supergen 2020 electricity industry scenarios*

2020 Scenario	Economic growth	Environmental focus	Technological growth	Regulatory structure
Strong growth	Increased	Slightly stronger	Strong	Liberalised
Economic concern	Reduced	Reducing	Weak	Liberalised
Environmental awakening	Current level	Stronger	Strong with environmental focus	Largely liberalised with some environmental intervention
Supportive regulation	Current level	As at present	Moderate with central support	Mildly interventionist

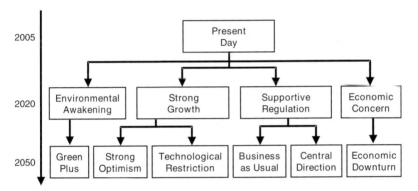

Figure 14.1. Relationship between 2020 and 2050 electricity industry scenarios

regulation'. Figure 14.1 shows the relationship between the four 2020 scenarios and the six 2050 scenarios. Table 14.5 characterises the four 2020 scenarios in terms of the four key parameters used to describe the 2050 scenarios.

Having identified the broad scope of each of the four 2020 scenarios listed in Table 14.5, the more detailed descriptions presented in the following sections were developed by evaluating the likely extent of deployment of each of the important renewable and non-renewable generation technologies in each scenario. In order to do so, the expected state of readiness for deployment of each technology, as qualified by the level of technological growth in the scenario, the ultimate deployment of the technology in 2050, and the effect of the other key parameters listed in Table 14.5 were considered. This process yielded the expected

Table 14.6. *Assumed generation load factor capabilities*

Generation technology	Load factor (%)
Onshore wind (Sinden, 2007)	27
Offshore wind (de Noord *et al.*, 2004; IEA, 2005)	42
Marine[*]	42
Biomass	>80
Hydro (DTI, 2005) [†]	30
Microgeneration (Watson, 2004)	28
Nuclear (DTI, 2005) [‡]	70
Large gas-fired units	>80
Coal	>80

[*] Marine generation technology is assumed to have similar characteristics to offshore wind.

[†] Load factor of GB hydro-generation is dependent on local rainfall; in recent years this has varied between 23% and 38%.

[‡] The load factor of nuclear plant has been reduced in comparison to recent performance (DTI, 2005) to reflect increased maintenance and inspection requirements of aging power stations. Where a scenario sees new nuclear construction, the load factor is increased.

installed capacity of each technology tabulated in the descriptions of the four 2020 scenarios. In determining their energy outputs, the generation technologies used were assumed to be capable of achieving the load factors shown in Table 14.6.

It has been assumed that the biomass and large fossil-fuelled generators will see their output reduced to match electricity demand and that they will also be used to compensate for intermittency in other generation sources; therefore these generators will not achieve the load factor of which they are technically capable. The geographical distribution of generation was determined by comparison with the 2050 scenarios.

Having determined the GB generation portfolio for each of the 2020 scenarios, a similar process was used to identify the readiness for deployment of the network technologies regarded as being important in the 2050 scenarios, and the extent to which they might augment or displace present-day technologies. The geographical distribution of generation in each scenario was used to determine the expected extent and location of network congestion; technologies which might be deployed to alleviate it were selected on the basis of their expected state of development, and the influence of the key parameters of each scenario, as listed in Table 14.4.

In each case, the main generation and network technologies and their locations are illustrated graphically using the following key:

14.4.1   Strong growth

The 'Strong growth' scenario envisions a future in which buoyant economic growth is supported by strong research and development investment in electricity network and generation technology. These factors result in an electricity industry of increasing technical sophistication, in which long-term growth in demand for energy services is addressed through a combination of continuing investment in network infrastructure and strong promotion of load management measures such as energy efficiency and demand-side participation. Figure 14.2 shows the location of important generation technologies and developments of transmission and distribution networks.

Under this scenario, demand for electricity continues to grow year-on-year at a rate which reduces slightly from that of the present day, so that by 2020 the annual demand for electricity is approximately 415TWh. Peak demand for electricity grows at a similar rate to overall demand, increasing to around 66GW by 2020. Demand-side management (DSM) is beginning to be applied to manage the increased demand on distribution networks as a means of avoiding significant network reinforcement. Smart metering is becoming increasingly widely adopted in all demand customer groups to underpin DSM and also support the integration of microgeneration.

There is continued investment in renewable energy, with wind generation having the largest installed renewable generation capacity. Of this, onshore wind dominates, with 10GW of installed capacity in Scotland, Wales and northern and south-west England. Increasing concern over the visual impact of onshore wind is, however, fuelling a transition to offshore developments, and large offshore windfarms are being planned. By 2020, around 2GW of offshore wind capacity has been developed, mainly located around the coast of southern England to avoid congestion in the electricity network.

Biomass is the second largest renewable generator in terms of installed capacity. By 2020, 7GW of biomass generation is in operation, divided between energy-crop-fuelled systems in rural areas and refuse-burning plants in towns and cities. Small plants of up to 20MW tend to be usual, in order to minimise the impact of the plants and associated transport infrastructure on the local area. These generators are usually connected to distribution networks.

Wave and tidal stream generation together account for 2GW of installed capacity, and there is 2GW of hydro-generation, almost all of which currently exists. Taken together, renewable energy accounts for around 20% of electricity generated in Great Britain in 2020.

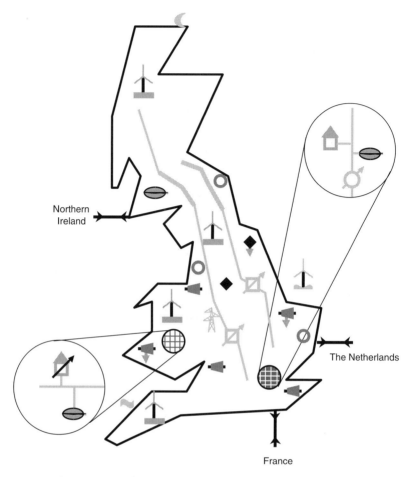

Figure 14.2. Generation and network technologies in 2020 'Strong growth' scenario

Non-renewable generation is dominated by natural gas-fired units, mainly in the form of combined cycle gas turbines (CCGTs), but with some combined heat and power (CHP) and a small but growing proportion of micro-CHP. To meet the growth in demand for electricity, some existing coal and nuclear units have been life extended, but by 2020 are being replaced by new-build gas- and coal-fired units. One or two of these stations, including integrated gasification combined cycle (IGCC)-based clean-coal plant are generating commercially while participating in a carbon capture and storage (CCS) scheme. Following a

Key to figures 14.2–14.5

⊕	Local rural network	⬆	Offshore wind	☾	Tidal generation
⊕	Local urban network	⬆	Onshore wind	⬮	Biomass
▬	Interconnector	◀	CCGT	∿	Wave generation
⚡	Overhead AC transmission	◀	CCGT with carbon capture	⌂	CHP
⚡	Overhead DC transmission	◆	Coal generation	▨	FACTS
▪	Underground AC transmission	◆	Coal with carbon capture	◌	Microgrid
⬗	Demand-side participation	○	Nuclear	▮	Energy storage

protracted planning process, new nuclear capacity is under construction, but has not yet begun operation.

The increase in demand for electricity, particularly at the time of peak load, is placing increased strain on transmission and distribution networks. Power electronic compensation and flow control devices are extensively deployed at transmission level to make maximum use of existing capacity, and there has been some upgrading of circuits within existing transmission corridors to increase their capabilities without significant additional environmental impact. Notably, the interconnector circuits between Scotland and England have been upgraded to operate at higher voltages in order to accommodate increased power transfers from renewable generation. Additionally, electricity imports from Europe have increased through the construction of a second interconnector.

There have been increases in small-scale generation connected to local distribution networks, including small-scale wind and biomass plants, together with gas-fuelled microturbine-based CHP systems, of which 3GW of capacity has been installed. At the same time, average and peak loads on these networks have increased as a result of the general increase in demand for electricity. As a result, power flows in these networks are significantly more variable in 2020 than in 2006, and a variety of methods of responding to these pressures are being investigated. In networks with significant concentrations of non-intermittent generation, such as biomass, microgrid technology is being trialled with the objective of increasing the reliability of electricity supply, while in areas where intermittent generation is more common, local market structures – sometimes incorporating demand-side participation – are being examined.

Table 14.7. *Generation technologies and electricity production in the 'Strong growth' scenario*

Generation technology	Installed capacity (GW)	Electricity production (%)
Offshore and onshore wind	12	7.5
Marine generation	2	1.8
Biomass	7	9.5
Hydro	2	1.3
Microgeneration	3	1.8
Nuclear	8	12
Large gas-fired units	44	55
Coal	9	11

14.4.2   Economic concern

The 'Economic concern' scenario envisages a future in which the economy enters a period of moderate decline, perhaps because of unfavourable conditions in the wider global economy. Concern over the economy tends to replace environmental issues in the public consciousness; therefore, pressure to achieve targets on emissions and thus deployment of renewables tends to reduce in this scenario. The availability of finance for investment in the electricity network and for research into generation and network technologies is restricted. Research and development tends to be concentrated on efforts to reduce the cost and improve the efficiency of generation and networks without substantial investment costs. Figure 14.3 shows the location of important generation technologies and developments of the transmission and distribution networks.

Demand for electricity is depressed by the economic situation in this scenario. There is less inclination on the part of the public to buy new electricity-consuming devices and appliances, and lack of growth in the industrial and commercial sectors also restricts electricity demand. There is interest in reducing expenditure on energy through the deployment of low-cost energy efficiency measures; expenditure on more expensive initiatives and devices is regarded as poor value under the tighter financial situation. By 2020, demand for electricity has risen only modestly to 360TWh/year, with the rate of increase declining to zero as 2020 is approached. There is some industrial and commercial interest in demand-side management schemes as a cost-saving measure to reduce the purchase of expensive peak energy. Peak demand for electricity is restricted to a level similar to that in 2006, at 60GW.

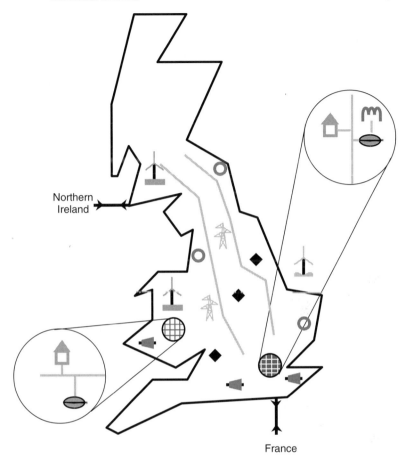

Figure 14.3. Generation and network technologies in 2020 'Economic concern' scenario

Renewable generation continues to develop in this scenario, but the deployment of intermittent generation such as wind and marine devices becomes increasingly restricted by network constraints, which are considered uneconomic to alleviate. Onshore wind capacity has reached 7GW by 2020, with a few hundred megawatts of pilot offshore wind capacity having been installed. Wind accounts for slightly more than 5% of the electricity produced in Great Britain. Few new wind generation schemes are in prospect, and results from the offshore pilots indicate that the extra costs over onshore schemes and their susceptibility to network constraints will make them commercially unattractive. No wave or tidal generation is installed in this scenario.

Biomass develops reasonably strongly in this scenario, as its less intermittent and more controllable nature is seen to offer improved prospects for efficiently exploiting electricity network capacity. In urban areas, waste-fuelled generation is integrated into local heating schemes associated with new building developments, while in rural areas, small combustion-based systems are fuelled by energy crops grown in the surrounding area. By 2020, 7GW of biomass capacity has been installed, supporting almost 10% of British electricity consumption.

Large generation dominates in this scenario, supplying almost 85% of all electricity produced in Great Britain. Existing coal and nuclear stations have been life extended in order to postpone investment in replacement capacity. Some new capacity has been constructed, being a mixture of CCGT and coal-fired steam plant. Investors increasingly prefer coal over gas in order to reduce their exposure to continuing uncertainty over future gas prices. New stations tend to re-use existing sites in order to avoid investment in transmission network extension. While some existing nuclear stations remain in operation through life extension, construction of new nuclear capacity has been frustrated by high costs and uncertainty over the financial risks of such projects.

Transmission and distribution networks remain largely unchanged from today under this scenario. Existing plant is life extended, often through the application of condition monitoring technology, and is replaced either like-for-like or with more cost-effective modern equivalent plant tailored to the demands actually placed on it (rather than being driven by any possible future requirements). The capabilities of the transmission system become an important factor influencing the location of new generation. At distribution level, networks remain largely passive, and there is a focus on postponing or avoiding major investment to an even greater level than for transmission networks. Generation connected to distribution networks is mainly confined to biomass-fuelled plants of a few megawatts in rural areas, whose location is influenced by the topology of the network as much as the location of the biomass resource. Small-scale wind generation is generally discouraged on the grounds that its intermittent output cannot be accommodated by distribution networks without investment to avoid power quality problems. Micro-CHP technology does not develop to the point of being economically attractive to individual households or businesses, and existing systems are replaced by heat-only boilers as a result of their greater simplicity, better efficiency, and withdrawal of support by micro-CHP manufacturers.

Table 14.8. *Generation technologies and electricity production in the 'Economic concern' scenario*

Generation technology	Installed capacity (GW)	Electricity production (%)
Offshore and onshore wind	8	5.4
Marine generation	0	0
Biomass	7	9.8
Hydro	2	1.5
Microgeneration	0	0
Nuclear	7	14
Large gas-fired units	36	50
Coal	13	19

14.4.3 Environmental awakening

The 'Environmental awakening' scenario considers a future in which the impact on the environment of the electricity industry, including generation, networks and end-use, is a matter of increasingly important and popular concern. This awareness has its foundation in the heightened public awareness of climate change and the environment evident in 2006. Figure 14.4 shows the location of important generation technologies and developments of transmission and distribution networks for this scenario.

By 2020, in this scenario, electricity demand will have reached a peak, and is beginning a gradual, but steady, decline as a result of the take-up of energy efficiency measures promoted by the increased public environmental consciousness. Advanced approaches to energy management in buildings and a growing number of smart meters for all customer classes are evidence of the concern for efficient use of electrical energy. The decline in energy consumption extends into the 2030s, by which time the use of fossil-fuelled CHP systems for space and water heating begins to give way to the use of renewably generated electricity in devices such as ground source heat pumps. Under this scenario, electricity demand in 2020 is 360TWh/year. Participation in demand-side management schemes by commercial and industrial customers results in the demand for electricity being less variable with time of day, and the annual peak demand is also comparable to 2006 at 60GW.

There is strong investment in new renewable generation capacity such that renewables account for almost one-third of the generation portfolio measured by plant capacity. Onshore wind generation has the largest share of renewable capacity, with rapid installation of relatively large

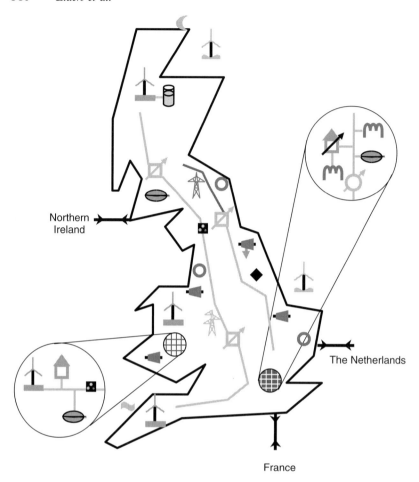

Figure 14.4. Generation and network technologies in 2020
'Environmental awakening' scenario

developments giving a total capacity of about 12GW by 2020. Important
concentrations of onshore wind are found in Scotland, Wales and north
and south-west England. However, increasing resistance to the visual
impact of onshore wind turbines, and negative perceptions of their effect
on the local environment, result in the maximum size of developments
falling from a peak of 500MW to 100MW or less in 2020, and a reduction
in their rate of construction as suitable sites become scarce. By 2020,
most onshore wind development is taking place in community-scale

schemes connected to local distribution networks. Large-scale wind generation focus has switched to offshore developments. By 2020, 3GW of offshore wind generation capacity is in operation, with considerably more in planning and development. Initial development has focused on relatively sheltered sites around the north-east of Scotland and the south-east of England, but developments are in prospect in other, more challenging, areas. Taken together, onshore and offshore wind generation accounts for over 10% of electrical energy production in 2020.

By 2020, the 'Environmental awakening' scenario foresees that marine energy sources, in the form of wave and tidal-stream devices, are achieving commercial success, with exploitation of tidal energy around the northern coast of Scotland and wave energy in south-western England. About 2.5GW of capacity has been installed, in developments of tens of megawatts each.

Biomass generation develops strongly in this scenario, in the form of relatively large generating units connected to higher-voltage distribution networks or lower-voltage parts of the transmission system. Refuse-fuelled urban plants participate in local CHP schemes. Almost 10GW of biomass plant is in operation. In total, renewables account for about 28% of electricity production in Great Britain.

Large generation plant is dominated by gas-fuelled units, mainly in the form of CCGT, but with some gas-fired CHP units. Existing nuclear capacity is life extended and retained for as long as possible in recognition of its low-carbon credentials and to allow the build-up of renewable capacity in preference to investment in fossil-fuelled replacements. No new construction of nuclear capacity is in prospect though, and the remaining nuclear stations are approaching their decommissioning dates. Coal-fired generation capacity is declining rapidly, with plants which survive the Large Combustion Plant Directive being rendered uneconomic by high carbon prices and reducing emissions allocations under international programmes. Carbon capture and storage have seen initial application to commercial-scale plants fuelled by gas and coal, but reservations over the long-term bulk transport and storage of carbon dioxide are being expressed on environmental and safety grounds.

The electricity network is experiencing progressively increased pressure as a result of the growth in renewable generation in more remote areas. Some extension of the transmission network into these areas has been undertaken to permit connection of renewable generators, but there is significant pressure to reduce the environmental impact of electricity networks in general, and thus general network reinforcement has not been possible. HVDC (high-voltage direct current) technology has, however, been introduced to one of the inter-connector routes between Scotland and England as a first step towards an offshore interconnector intended to accommodate the output of wind, wave and tidal generation which is in prospect. Undergrounding of sections of network as they fall due for refurbishment is an increasing trend.

Power-electronic-based flow management and control devices have been extensively deployed to maximise utilisation of the existing net-work, while prototype bulk energy storage devices have been integrated into one or two of the most recent renewable energy projects in Scotland to improve their market performance and access to the network.

Local distribution networks have seen a large increase in the volume of generation connected to them. As discussed above, smaller-scale wind and biomass plants are an element of this growth, but another important influence is the rapid development of domestic micro-CHP plants using gas-fuelled microturbine technology. Some models on the market include a small amount of battery-based energy storage to improve the proportion of domestic load they can support. Small-scale power electronic compensation and control systems are increas-ingly deployed in distribution networks. Various new approaches to network management, particularly at distribution voltages, are employed to manage the progressively more active nature of the power networks. Constraining of renewable generation is viewed as a cost-effective means of achieving large-scale integration of these energy sources.

Table 14.9. *Generation technologies and electricity production in the 'Environmental awakening' scenario*

Generation technology	Installed capacity (GW)	Electricity production (%)
Offshore and onshore wind	15	11
Marine generation	2.5	2.6
Biomass	9	13
Hydro	2	1.5
Microgeneration	6	4.1
Nuclear	7	12
Large gas-fired units	35	49
Coal	4.5	6.8

14.4.4   Supportive regulation

The 'Supportive regulation' scenario describes a future in which the government and regulatory authorities exert a gradually increasing influence over the development of the electricity industry. This development is brought about by increasing public concern over issues such as energy security, and strategic planning issues associated with power generation and network infrastructure. Figure 14.5 shows the location of important generation technologies and developments of transmission and distribution networks under this scenario.

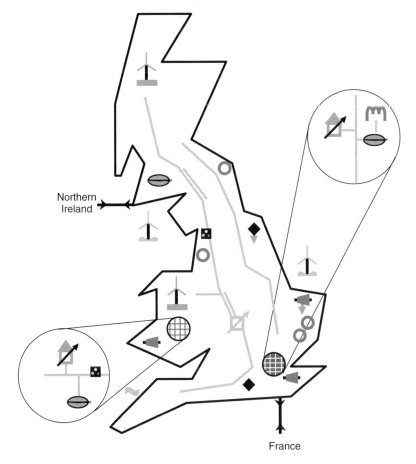

Figure 14.5. Generation and network technologies in 2020 'Supportive regulation' scenario

In this scenario, the demand for electricity continues to grow relatively strongly and reaches approximately 415TWh/year by 2020. This growth is restricted, to some extent, by government-sponsored energy efficiency initiatives, but a more important central influence on demand is government promotion of demand-side participation (DSP). DSP schemes are seen as providing increased security of supply in response to growing peak demand at a lower cost and environmental impact than increased generation capacity and network expansion. As a result, while peak demand continues to rise beyond current levels, it is restricted to about 63GW in 2020.

The deployment and development of low- and zero-carbon generation technologies is supported by government and regulatory authorities, both through research and development funding to improve the technology, and through favourable market arrangements and incentives for qualifying generation developments. Wind power is a beneficiary of these arrangements such that, by 2020, 9GW of generation capacity has been installed. Of this, almost 90% is in the form of relatively large onshore developments whose location is increasingly driven by central and regional government policies on suitable areas for development. Somewhat over 1GW of offshore wind capacity has been installed, initially in areas such as the south-east of England and the Irish Sea, but research into the development of deeper-water sites is benefiting from government support to the extent of larger-scale developments at the advanced planning stage.

Marine generation has also benefited from central support so that, by 2020, 2GW of wave and tidal-stream capacity has been installed. Initial deployment has been focused on two main geographical areas, with wave generation along the Atlantic coast of south-west England and tidal developments on the north coast of Scotland.

Biomass has been a beneficiary of government policy, with increasing incentives for the production of energy crops being provided through agricultural subsidy. 8GW of mainly small-scale biomass generation has been installed, with a limited quantity of urban waste-fuelled generation participating in local heating and cogeneration schemes associated with industrial and commercial developments. Taken together, renewables account for a little over 20% of electricity production in 2020.

Increasing pressure for diversity of energy sources influences government policy in relation to large generation. The most notable consequence is the resumed construction of nuclear generation. The first one or two of a planned fleet of new nuclear power stations have been recently commissioned in 2020, while existing stations have been kept in operation for as long as possible through life extension. Nuclear output in 2020 is similar to today's, accounting for 19% of the electricity produced. Coal-fuelled generation is another beneficiary of the increased focus on diversity, with new power stations being constructed to replace older, less efficient plant. New coal-fired plant is a mix of relatively traditional steam units, and newer technology such as IGCC. Large gas-fuelled generation using combined cycle technology remains the largest single source of electricity both by installed capacity and electricity produced, supporting about half of the annual electricity demand. Government incentives for the development of pilot carbon capture and storage schemes are being taken up, with about 5% of gas and advanced coal generation participating.

Network development has focused on maintaining supply reliability (mainly through ageing asset renewal programmes) and the connection of renewable developments in designated areas of Great Britain. Transmission network reinforcement has focused on improving the capacity of existing corridors through increases in the capacity of plant as it falls due for replacement or refurbishment, and deployment of power-electronic-based devices to influence patterns of power flow and manage voltage levels in steady state and transiently. Network extensions have been planned in concert with policies for the development of renewable generation resources in Scotland, Wales and south-west England.

Distribution networks have been affected by increases in the amount of generation connected to them. At the same time, there is increased regulatory pressure to maintain and improve the quality and reliability of electricity supply. Wind generation developments mainly influence higher distribution voltages (e.g. 33kV to 132kV), while biomass is con-centrated more in the middle range of voltages (e.g. 11kV to 33kV). Biomass generation tends to be controlled to balance local peaks in electricity demand, a task which is also the goal of government incentives for industry and large commercial electricity users to participate in demand-side control programmes. Neither domestic-scale DSP nor micro-CHP are encouraged by central policy, and thus see minimal deployment.

Volatility of output from wind generation connected to distribution networks is absorbed in part by DSP programmes, but there remains an increased level of variation in power transferred between the distribution system and the transmission network. Improvements to control systems at the interface between transmission and distribution are necessary to avoid power quality problems. Reliability of the local electricity supply is improved by increased undergrounding of lower-voltage distribution networks.

Table 14.10. *Generation technologies and electricity production in the 'Supportive regulation' scenario*

Generation technology	Installed capacity (GW)	Electricity production (%)
Offshore and onshore wind	10	6
Marine generation	2	1.8
Biomass	8	11
Hydro	2	1.3
Microgeneration	0.25	0.15
Nuclear	13	19
Large gas-fired units	38	45
Coal	12	15

14.5   Carbon dioxide emissions

In order to assess the extent of decarbonisation of the electricity industry under each of the 2020 scenarios, it is necessary to convert the levels of energy production for each of the generation technologies appearing in the scenarios into emissions of carbon dioxide. In this process, a number of simplifying assumptions are made; the effects of these are discussed below.

A single value of carbon dioxide emissions per unit of electricity generated is assigned to each generation technology. These values are based on those of the current state of the art in each technology or recent plant discussed in the literature. It is expected that the poorer efficiency of old plant which remains in service in 2020 will be balanced to some degree by improvements in plant technology over that period, so that generators which are constructed between now and 2020 will emit less carbon dioxide per unit of electricity generated than is assumed in the results presented here. Furthermore, no account is taken of plant inefficiency brought about by the requirement to provide reserve capacity to cater for unplanned generation shortfalls caused by unreliability of generators or intermittency associated with wind and wave generation. The volume of generation reserve required is dependent on issues including the geographical diversity of renewable generation, the reliability of new and old generators, the availability of rapid demand-side response, and the extent to which reserve can be provided by inexpensive, fast-starting generators provided specifically for peak and reserve use. The rates of carbon dioxide emissions assumed for each generating technology are listed in Table 14.11.

Table 14.11. *Carbon dioxide emissions by generation technology*

Technology	CO_2 emissions (g/kWh)
Wind	0
Marine generation	0
Biomass[*] (Howard and Olszak, 2004)	360
Hydro	0
Microgeneration[†] (Bozzolo *et al.*, 2003), (Newborough, 2004)	200
Nuclear	0
Large gas-fired units – CCGT (Spath and Mann, 2000)	370
Coal (Dettmer, 2005)	800

[*] Biomass generators fuelled with specifically grown energy crops are assumed to produce no net carbon dioxide emissions: 50% of biomass generation is assumed to be fuelled by municipal waste with the net emissions shown.
[†] We assume that carbon dioxide emissions from microgeneration – which is relatively inefficient in electrical terms – can be offset against those from heating boilers which would otherwise be installed. Thus, the figure given corresponds to the increase in emissions in comparison with a modern boiler of equal heat output.

The resulting carbon dioxide emissions in each scenario are shown in Table 14.12. Table 14.12 also shows, for comparison purposes, emissions calculated for the generation mix of the Central (favouring gas) scenario described by the DTI (2006) using the emission figures given above, together with the estimate of 2005 emissions from the same source.

By comparison, the calculated emissions for the DTI Central scenario are around 5% below those stated by the DTI, illustrating the effects of the assumptions made in the analysis.

The Supergen 2020 scenarios all have emissions below those of the DTI Central scenario. A number of factors contribute to this. Most notably, the Supergen scenarios assume a greater output from nuclear generation, either as a result of new construction or of a more aggressive programme of life extension to obtain carbon-reduction or investment-avoidance benefits. Renewable generation is also greater in all but the 'Economic concern' scenario. These increases in output from nuclear and renewables are counterbalanced by reductions in gas-fuelled generation in all Supergen scenarios, and in coal-fired generation in all but the 'Economic concern' scenario. However, notwithstanding these differences, it is notable that in the 'Strong growth' scenario, which most closely resembles the DTI Central scenario in its background assumptions, the calculated emissions differ from those calculated for the DTI scenario by 6%.

Table 14.12. *Carbon dioxide emissions from electricity generation by scenario*

2020 Scenario	Carbon dioxide emissions $(MtCO_2/year)$
Strong growth	124
Economic concern	127
Environmental awakening	89
Supportive regulation	121
DTI Central[*]	132
2005 estimate	169

[*] No separate figure for biomass or waste-fuelled generation is given: 15% of renewable generation is assumed to be generated from municipal waste.

In comparison to the estimated level of CO_2 emissions in 2005 (DTI, 2006), the four Supergen scenarios show reductions ranging from 25% in the 'Economic concern' scenario to 47% in the 'Environmental awakening' scenario. These reductions stem from the increase in renewable generation seen in all scenarios and the replacement of older, less efficient, fossil-fuelled power stations with modern plant, with an increased proportion of gas-fired generation.

14.6   Generation costs

While it is not the intention of this chapter to conduct a detailed analysis of the effects of each of the 2020 scenarios on the costs of individual generation technologies and of the electricity they produce, some qualitative indications of these factors can nevertheless be derived from the descriptions and generation mixes presented above.

Some types of generation likely to be represented in the GB portfolio in 2020 – for example, marine technologies and offshore wind – are currently at an early stage of deployment, with correspondingly high investment and energy costs. These costs can be expected to decline, according to the learning or experience curve theory (Köhler *et al.*, 2006; Jamasb and Köhler, Chapter 12, this volume). However, as noted in recent analysis (Carbon Trust, 2006b), the extent of cost reduction achievable by 2020 is dependent on both the current cost level of the ultimately 'successful' generation technology in each category and the learning rate associated with the build-up of installed generation. The former factor gives particular uncertainty in the field of marine generation, where a number of competing technologies exist which might ultimately go forward to large-scale commercial deployment.

Another factor affecting the rate at which costs of new generation technologies are likely to reduce is the improvement in expertise resulting from the increased deployment of such generators internationally. While it is beyond the scope of this chapter to develop global power supply scenarios, it is reasonable to expect that the key drivers of each 2020 scenario presented here will also be reflected to a degree in wider world attitudes and policy directions. Thus, in those scenarios with significant investment in deployment of renewable generation technologies, the effect will be supported by research and development, and construction of new generation capacity internationally.

More conventional technologies, such as CCGT and nuclear generation, are unlikely to see very significant cost reductions as a consequence of further increasing installed capacity, although incremental improvements leading to modest reductions in capital and operational cost are still likely to be achieved. However, for CCGT generation in particular, these will probably be offset in most, if not all, scenarios by increases in fuel cost resulting from increasing international demand for gas. However, important learning-related cost reductions in associated low-carbon technologies, such as carbon capture and storage, and clean coal technologies such as IGCC, are likely as a result of increasing deployment both in Great Britain and abroad.

In the 'Strong growth' scenario, there is significant development of renewable technologies, supported by a strong research and development activity. There is a shift away from onshore wind developments to offshore, supported by biomass generation development, and marine energy starts to see wide deployment. These changes imply that the costs of these technologies will fall both as a consequence of increases in the installed capacity, which permit progressive improvements in technology, and also as a result of effective investment in research to secure strong learning rates. Fossil-fuelled generation remains a very significant electricity source in this scenario, with continued investment increasing the proportion of capacity composed of CCGT; however, and as discussed above, a buoyant international economy might be expected to drive up global demand for gas. Therefore, as demand for electricity continues to grow, electricity prices may rise, to the extent that offshore wind is clearly competitive with fossil-fuelled generation by 2020, and marine generation is either attaining competitiveness, or is soon expected to do so.

By contrast, the 'Economic concern' scenario sees a slightly more restrained growth in renewable technology. Importantly, however, growth is concentrated in more established technologies, with onshore wind being more strongly developed in comparison with offshore wind and marine technologies. Biomass-fuelled generation sees growth as a result of its increased predictability and flexibility of location in comparison to intermittent and offshore technologies; costs here are thus reduced as experience is gained. In general, though, the cost of electricity from renewables does not fall as rapidly as in other scenarios, since there is less scope for experience-based improvement in the relatively mature technologies deployed. Fossil-fuelled generation investment is divided between CCGT and coal-fired capacity. An emphasis on low-risk, low-cost developments means that the scope for incremental improvement is limited, but increases in fuel costs are restricted by the low rate of increase in demand for electricity, and lower international growth in demand for gas than in other scenarios.

The 'Environmental awakening' scenario sees the largest deployment of renewable generation, with significant growth in all of the technologies considered. In particular, the rate of investment in wind generation continues to grow strongly, while marine generation increases have begun to see large-scale deployment. These developments are likely to result in significant reduction in the cost of renewable electricity, as experience in the design, deployment and operation of these technologies is accumulated. While the cost of renewable energy from developments being brought into use in 2020 will have fallen to the extent of being at, or close to, competitiveness with existing technologies such as CCGT, significant expenditure on support for earlier schemes, and on research and development, will be necessary in order to develop experience and expertise. As discussed earlier, significant reductions in the cost of established technologies such as CCGT are unlikely. However, the increasing international demand for fuel, together with increases in emissions costs driven by environmental concerns, are likely to drive up costs of electricity from such sources, increasing the competitiveness of renewables. Carbon capture and storage technology will see reductions in cost as experience is gained internationally but, even with increasing emission costs, are likely to require significant financial support in 2020.

Finally, the 'Supportive regulation' scenario shows a broadly similar pattern of renewable and conventional generation to the 'Strong growth' scenario, but with a slightly lower development of offshore wind, and increased investment in coal-fired generation at the expense of growth in CCGT capacity. As a result, offshore wind costs are likely to remain somewhat higher in this scenario, although the cost of onshore wind may be reduced through streamlining of the planning process and concentration of resources into specific geographical areas. As before, the significant deployment of marine generation is expected to drive cost reduction as experience is gained. Increased diversity in generation

Table 14.13. *Renewable generation capacity in Supergen 2020 scenarios*

Scenario	Wind (GW)	Marine (GW)	Hydro (GW)	Biomass (GW)	Total renewables (GW)
Strong growth	12	2	2	7	25
Economic concern	8	0	2	7	17
Environmental awakening	15	2.5	2	9	28.5
Supportive regulation	10	2	2	8	22

Table 14.14. *Summary of 2020 Supergen scenarios*

Scenario	Average annual demand growth (%)	Renewable electricity production (%)	Fossil-fuelled electricity production (%)	CO_2 emissions (MtCO$_2$/year)
2005 (DTI, 2006)		4	72	169
Strong growth	1.0	20	66	124
Economic concern	0.2	17	70	127
Environmental awakening	0.2	28	56	89
Supportive regulation	1.0	20	61	121

is likely to reduce the extent to which electricity prices are susceptible to growth in international demand for particular fuels such as gas, but worldwide growth in energy use may well lead to an increase in fuel costs for conventional generation in general, further increasing the competitiveness of renewables.

14.7 Conclusions and summary

This chapter described a set of four scenarios of the electricity industry in Great Britain in 2020, which are summarised in Tables 14.13 and 14.14.

Comparison of Table 14.13 with recent studies of the effectiveness of existing and possible future renewables incentivisation measures (Carbon Trust, 2006a, 2006b) suggests that the ranges of 2020 wind and marine generation capacities envisaged by the scenarios described in this chapter are consistent with other recent projections.

These scenarios have a diverse range of outcomes in terms of the generation mix and level of demand for electricity but, as can be seen from Table 14.14, they all exhibit a significant reduction in the carbon dioxide emissions from electricity production, and offer the prospect of reductions in the costs of investing in renewable electricity generation capacity. As might be expected, given the shorter time scale over which they develop, the scenarios described here show a much narrower range of outcomes than the 2050 Supergen scenarios. Nonetheless, they illustrate the range of future situations which might arise given their underlying assumptions. It is clear that, if substantial decarbonisation of the British electricity industry is to be achieved, considerable and sustained effort and investment will be required in the coming years.

References

Bozzolo, M., M. Brandani, A. Traverso and A.F. Massardo (2003). Thermo-economic analysis of gas turbine plants with fuel decarbonization and carbon dioxide sequestration, *Journal of Engineering for Gas Turbines and Power*, **125**(4): 947–953.

Bows, A., S. Mander, R. Starkey, M. Bleda and K. Anderson (2006). *Living Within a Carbon Budget*, Report for Friends of the Earth and the Co-operative Bank, Manchester: Tyndall Centre.

Carbon Trust (2006a). *Policy Frameworks for Renewables*, London: The Carbon Trust.

(2006b). *Future Marine Energy*, London: The Carbon Trust.

Dettmer, R. (2005). The right stuff? *IEE Review*, **51**(3): 44–48.

de Noord, M., L.W.M. Beurskens and H.J. de Vries (2004). *Potentials and Costs for Renewable Electricity Generation: A Data Overview*, Report ECN-C-03-006, Petten: Energy Research Centre of the Netherlands.

DTI (2005). *Digest of United Kingdom Energy Statistics 2005*, London: Department of Trade and Industry.

(2006). *UK Energy and CO_2 Emissions Projections: Updated Projections to 2020*, London: Department of Trade and Industry.

Elders, I., G. Ault, S. Galloway, J. McDonald, M. Leach, E. Lampaditou and J. Köhler (2006). Electricity network scenarios for the United Kingdom in 2050, in T. Jamasb, W.J. Nuttall and M.G. Pollitt (eds), *Future Electricity Technologies and Systems*, Cambridge: Cambridge University Press.

Howard, B. and C. Olszak (2004). *Fuelling Landscape Repair: A Bioenergy Industry as a Sustainable Land-use and Energy Option for Australia*, Barton, ACT: Rural Industries Research and Development Corporation.

IEA (2005). *Offshore Wind Experiences*, Paris: International Energy Agency.

Köhler, J., M. Grubb, D. Popp and O. Edenhofer (2006). The transition to endogenous technical change in climate–economy models: a technical overview to the innovation modeling comparison project, *Energy Journal*, Special Issue, *Endogenous Technological Change and the Economics of Atmospheric Stabilization*, 17–55.

Marsh, G., P. Taylor, D. Anderson, M. Leach and R. Gross (2003). *Options for a Low Carbon Future – Phase 2*, Harwell: AEA Technology, available from www.berr.gov.uk/files/file21349.pdf

National Grid (2005). *GB Seven Year Statement*, Warwick, UK: National Grid Company.

Newborough, M. (2004). Assessing the benefits of implementing micro-CHP systems in the UK. *Proceedings of the Institution of Mechanical Engineers Part A: Journal of Power and Energy*, **218**(4): 203–218.

Royal Commission on Environmental Pollution (2000). *Energy: The Changing Climate*, London: Her Majesty's Stationery Office.

Sinden, G. (2007). Characteristics of the UK wind resource: long-term patterns and relationship to electricity demand, *Energy Policy*, **35**(1): 112–127.

Spath, P.L. and M.K. Mann (2000). *Life Cycle Assessment of a Natural Gas Combined-Cycle Power Generation System*, Report NREL/TP-570-27715, Golden, CO: National Renewable Energy Laboratory.

Stern, N. (2006). *The Stern Review: The Economics of Climate Change*, London: HM Treasury.

Watson, J. (2003). *UK Electricity Scenarios for 2050*, Working Paper 41, Brighton: Tyndall Centre for Climate Change Research.

(2004). Co-provision in sustainable energy systems: the case of micro-generation, *Energy Policy*, **32**(17): 1981–1990.

15 Modelling the economic impact of low-carbon electricity

Milton Yago, Jonathan P. Atkins, Keshab Bhattarai, Richard Green and Stephen Trotter

15.1   Introduction

Most of the chapters in this book discuss the ways in which the electricity sector can reduce carbon emissions. In many countries, including the UK, the electricity industry is at the forefront of the move towards a low-carbon world. The industry is a major source of emissions when it burns fossil fuel to generate power, contributing about 30% of total emissions in the UK (DTI, 2006), 40% in Germany, and more than 50% of carbon emissions in Denmark. These emissions come from a limited number of point sources, which makes government intervention easier than for sectors such as transport, where there are many mobile sources. The sector has a relatively high potential for reducing emissions; by switching to lower-carbon fuels (gas instead of coal) in the short term, and building low-carbon power stations in the longer term. The sector is not directly exposed to significant international competition, and so environmental regulations do not put employment or profits in the sector directly at risk. At the same time, however, electricity is a vital input to other sectors of the economy, and rising electricity prices could increase costs for firms that are exposed to international competition. This chapter discusses the impact of higher electricity prices, driven by low-carbon policies, on the wider economy.

In the next section, we outline the model that we have used to predict prices for the four low-carbon Supergen scenarios for 2020, and for a high-carbon alternative. Fossil fuel prices are a key input, and we use the Department of Trade and Industry's 'Central case' predictions for all the scenarios, while recognising that some scenarios might be associated with different fuel prices. In Section 15.3, we estimate the impact on fuel and investment costs of moving to a low-carbon electricity system. Section 15.4 uses a model of wholesale pricing to predict the industry revenues in each scenario, and Section 15.5 estimates its profits. We find that prices are higher in the low-carbon scenario, although profits may be lower unless generators are given a significant number of carbon permits free of charge. In Section 15.6, we assess the impact of the higher prices on consumers and on firms. Section 15.7 calculates the cost of cutting carbon emissions in the electricity industry, and briefly discusses some other models of the overall welfare impact of cutting carbon emissions. Most of these consider economy-wide policies, but we mention one recent study that illustrates the additional cost imposed by narrowly focused policies and those that are poorly designed for the task of cutting carbon emissions. Section 15.8 concludes.

15.2   Modelling the electricity industry

The starting point for any analysis of the macroeconomic effects of moving to a low-carbon electricity system has to be that this will increase the direct cost of power. The size of this increase depends on a number of factors, including the technologies deployed, the extent of the shift, and the level of fossil fuel prices. The level of fossil fuel prices will not affect the cost of most low-carbon technologies (with the exception of those using carbon capture and storage after burning fossil fuels), but does affect the cost differential with conventional generation. Chapter 3 of this volume discusses the likely cost premium of various technologies, showing that it is likely to be substantial. Over time, however, the premium is likely to fall as a result of endogenous technical change (learning-by-doing), as discussed in Chapter 12.

The reference to 'direct' cost in the previous paragraph is an important caveat, as the costs in question are those directly incurred by the generator (including decommissioning costs for nuclear power), and excluding the cost of carbon emissions. The rationale for moving to a low-carbon system is that, once we include the cost of carbon, the overall cost of a low-carbon system will be lower than that of the present system. Policy measures such as emissions trading or a carbon tax will be required, however, to internalise carbon costs. Having adopted these measures, the cost of a low-carbon system becomes lower than that of a high-carbon system. The measured cost of either, however, will be higher than before the costs of carbon were included and, in this sense, the cost of power will rise.

The higher cost of electricity will be accompanied by higher selling prices. This will be a consequence of the way in which companies are given incentives to move to a low-carbon system. The UK currently uses emissions trading and support for renewable generation through a system of tradable green certificates as its main instruments in this area. The Renewables Obligation can be expected to increase electricity prices by an amount equal to the buy-out price (£33.24/MWh for 2006/2007) multiplied by the target proportion of power (6.7% for 2006/2007). The effects of the European Union Emission Trading Scheme (EU ETS) on electricity prices are more complex (Green, 2005 ; Neuhoff *et al.*, 2006), but the overall impact will also be to raise the market price of power. The overall rise in prices could well be greater than the average effect on costs, even if generators had to buy all of their permits from the government. At present, almost all permits are given away, and the ETS has led to a significant increase in generators' profits.

We can assess the impact of these policies in 2020, comparing the four Supergen scenarios described in Chapter 14 with a High-carbon scenario. Each of the Supergen scenarios assumes a significant amount of new investment in low-carbon electricity – nuclear power, wind power, biomass, marine power or microgeneration – while our High-carbon scenario assumes that practically all investment to 2020 is in CCGT (combined cycle gas turbine) stations, as over the previous decade. In total, 33GW of new CCGT capacity is added, while the older nuclear and coal-fired stations retire.

The demand for electricity in our High-carbon scenario is 435TWh. This represents annual growth of 1.4% from 2005. Two of the Supergen scenarios ('Economic concern' and 'Environmental awakening') assume practically no growth in electricity consumption, and a 2020 demand of 360TWh, and the others ('Strong growth' and 'Supportive regulation') assume demand growth of 1.1% a year. This is the same rate that the National Grid uses in its Central case in the 2006 *Seven Year Statement* (National Grid, 2006), giving a demand of 415TWh in 2020. Our High-carbon scenario thus has a demand approximately 5% above that in the higher Supergen scenarios. Moving ahead, we will find that the price of electricity in the High-carbon scenario would be approximately 10–20% below that in the Supergen scenarios, and this additional demand is consistent with an elasticity of -0.3, which is the figure used by Ofgem in regulatory impact appraisals.

Electricity prices are modelled using the techniques described by Green (2008). This is a strategic model, in which generators offer power to the wholesale market according to a supply function equilibrium. Its key features are that prices are close to marginal costs when output levels are low, but can rise well above marginal costs at peak times, depending on how concentrated the industry is, how much spare generating capacity exists and how responsive consumer demand is to wholesale prices. The industry is modelled as if it contains six symmetrical generators owning conventional capacity. This approximates to the current structure, and assumes that significant increases or decreases in concentration are unlikely.

The other key input to the model is the level of marginal costs, which depends on technology, fuel and carbon prices. We take the prices from

Table 15.1. *Generating cost inputs*

	Fuel cost/ efficiency	Operations and maintenance cost	Capital cost ($£$/kW)	Plant life (years)
Combined cycle gas turbine (CCGT)	58%[a]	$£$7/kW-year + $£$2/MWh[a]	440[a]	35[a]
Coal(without CCS)	44.9%[a]	$£$24/kW-year + $£$2/MWh[a]	900[a]	50[a]
Nuclear	$£$5/MWh[a]	$£$57/kW-year[a]	1,407[a]	40[a]
Biomass	$£$27/MWh[e]	$£$45/kW-year[e]	1,485[e]	25[c]
Marine	Nil	$£$42/kW-year[e]	1,060[e]	15[c]
Wind – onshore	Nil	$£$44/kW-year[a]	819[a]	20[a]
Wind – offshore	Nil	$£$46/kW-year[a]	1,532[a]	20[a]
Microgeneration	80%[d]	$£$90/kW-year[b]	1,000[b]	15[b]

Sources: [a]DTI (2006); [b]Energy Saving Trust (2005); [c]Enviros (2005); [d]Newborough (2004); [e]Scottish Energy Environment Foundation (2005)

the *Energy Review* (DTI, 2006), using both of its Central cases. The Central case favourable to coal (a higher gas price) is used with a carbon price of $£$17/tCO$_2$ (the DTI's own combination), whereas the case favourable to gas (a lower gas price) has a lower carbon price of $£$12/tCO$_2$. This is on the assumption that, if the price of gas is high, the price of carbon has to be high as well in order to discourage coal-fired generation. A lower gas price allows a lower carbon price. At the end of 2006, the price of 1 tonne of CO$_2$ was €6.48 (or $£$4.30), although prices for the second stage of the ETS were higher, at €18.25 ($£$12.15) per tonne (Powernext, 2007).

We took our technological data mainly from the *Energy Review* and other recent reports to government. Where two figures were given by a source, we used the mid-point. Where figures were given for several years, we used estimates for 2010 or 2015 (where available), reflecting the fact that much of the capacity installed by 2020 will be several years old by that date. The fuel cost for nuclear includes the DTI's estimate of $£$1/MWh for reprocessing and decommissioning costs. For microgeneration, we take the cost of a Stirling engine micro-CHP unit, over and above the costs of the gas-fired boiler that the household would otherwise install. The basic input parameters are given in Table 15.1.

Table 15.2 gives the forecast energy prices for two of the DTI fuel price scenarios. We use the same fuel price scenarios for all of our Supergen scenarios, to focus comparisons on the additional cost of moving towards a low-carbon electricity system. However, those scenarios might well be associated with different levels of fuel prices. For example,

Table 15.2. *Forecast energy input prices for 2020*

DTI fuel price scenario	Central pro-coal	Central pro-gas
Price of coal (£/MWh)	4.00	4.00
Price of gas (£/MWh)	12.45	9.70
Price of CO_2 (£/t)	17.00	12.00

Note: Prices are in real (2006) terms.

high fossil fuel prices might be one factor contributing to the slow growth seen in the 'Economic concern' scenario, while growth in the 'Strong growth' scenario might be boosted by low fuel prices. The very different demand levels assumed in the scenarios are affected by differences in incomes, attitudes, investment in energy efficiency and in the underlying fuel prices. The differences in electricity prices that are directly due to the different plant mixes within the Supergen scenarios will have a relatively minor contribution.

15.3   The pattern of costs: investment and fuel costs

Practically all sources of low-carbon power involve higher investment costs than the standard alternative of building combined cycle gas turbines (CCGT). The low-carbon technologies generally have lower running costs, however. This implies that a move to a low-carbon electricity system will also change the balance of the industry's costs, and will require a significant increase in investment.

Table 15.3 gives estimates of the amount of investment in the electricity industry that will be required by 2020, in each of the five scenarios. The figures for generation draw on the scenario capacities and the cost data in Table 15.1. This table also gives estimates of the additional investment in transmission and distribution that will be needed to connect renewable and microgeneration in each scenario, compared to a system based on large transmission-connected stations, no further from the main load centres than the (mostly coal-fired) stations they replace.

The cost of transmission will rise because most of the best sites for renewable generation are remote from consumers, in Scotland and the north of England, and the grid will need significant reinforcement before these can be used on a large scale. The *Energy Review* (DTI, 2006, Table E1) lists a number of these schemes, with an average cost of £145–175 per kW connected. Applying this cost to the additional renewable generation predicted in our scenarios implies extra investment of between £1 billion ('Economic concern') and £2.4 billion

Table 15.3. *Investment needs for the electricity industry to 2020 (£billion)*

	Gross investment in generation	Additional investment in networks	Total
Strong growth	33	4.6	38
Economic concern	20	1.9	22
Environmental awakening	36	6.8	43
Supportive regulation	31	2.7	34
High-carbon	15	–	15

('Environmental awakening') will be required by 2020. (This is based on wind and marine power, the types that will need to be in remote areas.)

Similarly, the distribution networks will need additional investment. Ofgem (2004, p.43) cites a figure of £82 of additional network investment per kW of distributed generation, and applying this to all the renewable investment in our scenarios gives a total of £1 billion to £2 billion Microgeneration also poses challenges for the distribution networks if consumers start to export electricity, and the Energy Saving Trust (2005) estimates that resolving these challenges could cost £2.5 billion.

The High-carbon scenario needs investment in generation averaging £1 billion a year to 2020, replacing coal-fired stations retired under the EU's Large Combustion Plant Directive, and allowing for load growth. In the 'Economic concern' scenario, investment is almost double this amount, despite a much lower level of demand growth. With a high level of demand growth under 'Strong growth', and a move towards a low-carbon system, the investment requirements are almost three times as great as with the High-carbon scenario. The greatest investment needs come in the 'Environmental awakening' scenario, with significant investment in renewable and distributed generation. In this scenario, demand growth is kept down by investments in energy efficiency. These are not included in Table 15.3, but will add to the overall investment needs of providing energy services in a low-carbon system. Given that gross fixed capital formation (GFCF) in the UK in 2005 was £195 billion, the investment required for a low-carbon electricity system should be easily affordable.

While investment costs will be higher in the low-carbon scenarios, operating costs should be lower. Table 15.4 combines these costs with the higher of the two gas prices used in this chapter, adopting the 10% discount rate used in the *Energy Review*. Two entries are made for the High-carbon scenario, the first with no price on carbon, as assumed

Table 15.4. *Annual costs for electricity generation in 2020 (£ billion – higher gas price)*

	Fuel	Carbon	O&M	Capital	Total	£/MWh
Strong growth	6.6	2.4	3.2	7.6	19.8	48
Economic concern	5.7	2.5	2.3	6.1	16.6	46
Environmental awakening	5.7	2.0	3.2	7.7	18.5	51
Supportive regulation	6.1	2.4	3.0	7.9	19.4	47
High-carbon (no CO_2 price)	7.3	0.0	2.2	5.8	15.3	35
High-carbon (£17/tCO_2)	7.3	2.8	2.2	5.8	18.1	42

Note: O&M stands for operating and maintenance costs.

within the scenario, and the second with the same price (£17/tCO_2) as the other scenarios. The cost per MWh is given in the final column.

Table 15.4 suggests that the scenarios are actually quite close together in terms of their non-capital costs. The High-carbon scenario has the highest fuel cost, but it is only £1.6 billion higher than the fuel cost in the two scenarios with much lower generation, 'Economic concern' and 'Environmental awakening'. Similarly, the cost of carbon emissions, valued at £17/tCO_2, is only slightly higher in the High-carbon scenario than in the others. The High-carbon scenario actually has lower operating and maintenance costs than the others, due to the relatively high costs assigned to most renewable generators compared to CCGT stations. Figures for the total cost are given, but the cost per MWh may allow a better comparison, given the different output levels across the scenarios. The highest cost comes in the 'Environmental awakening' scenario, while the other three Supergen scenarios have similar costs per MWh generated. The lowest cost, if carbon is valued at £17 per tonne, comes from the High-carbon scenario, suggesting that a higher carbon price would be required to make the investment in low-carbon electricity worthwhile. Table 15.5 repeats these calculations for the lower gas price (and related carbon price), with similar results.

15.4   Predicted electricity prices

While the previous section has set out the electricity industry's costs, consumers will be affected by changes in its prices. Our model calculates the revenues that the generators will receive in a (reasonably competitive) wholesale market. Since these are based on marginal costs, plus a margin reflecting the elasticity of demand, number of firms, and level of spare capacity, they may well exceed the industry's average costs, and do

Table 15.5. *Annual costs for electricity generation in 2020*
(£ billion – lower gas price)

	Fuel	Carbon	O&M	Capital	Total	£/MWh
Strong growth	5.8	1.5	3.2	7.6	18.1	43
Economic concern	5.2	1.6	2.3	6.1	15.2	42
Environmental awakening	5.0	1.3	3.2	7.7	17.2	47
Supportive regulation	5.5	1.5	3.0	7.9	18.0	43
High-carbon (no CO_2 price)	6.0	0.0	2.2	5.8	14.0	32
High-carbon (£12/tCO_2)	6.0	2.0	2.2	5.8	16.0	37

Note: O&M stands for operating and maintenance costs.

Table 15.6. *Forecast electricity revenues for 2020*

Wholesale electricity revenues (£/MWh)	DTI fuel price scenario		Demand (TWh)
	Central pro-coal	Central pro-gas	
Strong growth	51	45	415
Economic concern	49	43	360
Environmental awakening	52	46	360
Supportive regulation	49	43	415
High-carbon (CO_2 price is zero)	40	35	435

Note: Prices are in real (2006) terms.

so in this study. The difference can be described as supernormal profits, those in excess of the industry's cost of capital. The figures in Table 15.6 combine the revenues from the wholesale market proper, and those from the Renewables Obligation, effectively representing demand-weighted prices. The Obligation is set at 18% in three of the scenarios, but is raised to 30% of demand in the 'Environmental awakening' scenario, and kept at 5% in the High-carbon scenario. Most renewable generators are unable to cover their costs from wholesale revenues alone, and the expanded Obligation is needed for consistency with the high level of renewable capacity in the 'Environmental awakening' scenario. Similarly, an Obligation level above 5% would deliver too much money to the renewables sector in the High-carbon scenario, since this is assumed not to expand beyond its 2006 level.

Given the fuel price assumptions, the overall revenue per MWh is fairly similar across the four Supergen scenarios – this reflects the fact that wholesale prices will generally be set by CCGT stations at most times in the year in these scenarios. The Supergen scenarios also have much higher prices than the High-carbon scenario, by £9–12/MWh with the higher gas price (pro-coal), and £8–11/MWh with the lower gas price. Part of this is due to the higher level of the Renewables Obligation – an extra £4/MWh (or £8/MWh in 'Environmental awakening'). The rest comes from including the marginal cost of carbon in the marginal cost of generation. This can change the merit order (making coal-fired stations less competitive), and will tend to raise the wholesale price. With a reasonably competitive market structure and inelastic demand, the increase in price will be almost as great as the increase in marginal cost.

It is possible to calculate the average cost of carbon by multiplying the industry's total emissions by the price of a permit and dividing this by its output. This gives an average cost of £5/MWh with high prices for gas and carbon, and a cost of £3/MWh with low gas and carbon prices. For the 'Economic concern' scenario, with more investment in new coal-fired plant, the average costs are £6/MWh and £4/MWh, respectively. This implies that the generators' revenues, taken as a whole, will have risen by more than the cost of carbon, even if by 2020 they have to buy all of the permits that they need. If the generators continue to receive a significant number of permits free of charge, as with the first two phases of the ETS, the scheme will raise the profits of both fossil-fuelled and low-carbon generators. Such generous allocations would also be likely to reduce the incentives to invest in low-carbon capacity, making it harder to reduce emissions (Grubb and Neuhoff, 2006; Neuhoff *et al.*, 2006).

The price impact faced by consumers will depend on how much of the increase in wholesale prices is passed on to them, and how the industry's other costs will change as a result of the move towards a low-carbon system. Industrial and commercial power prices follow wholesale prices quite closely, and it is also safe to assume that these cost increases will be fully passed on to domestic consumers by 2020.

The higher costs of transmission and distribution have been discussed above. Additional transmission investment of £2.4 billion (the highest figure, for the 'Environmental awakening' scenario) would raise the regulated revenues for transmission by £100 million a year, counting depreciation charges, a return on the investment, and the cost of operating the additional assets. This is appreciable in terms of the £1.2 billion a year transmission business, but would not have a significant impact on electricity consumers – the extra cost in the scenarios varies between £0.1/MWh and £0.3/MWh. The annualised cost of additional investment in distribution would have a price impact of between £0.1/MWh and £0.5/MWh.

Table 15.7. *Annual profits for electricity generation in 2020* (£ billion – higher gas price)

	Revenues	Capital	Pure profit	Carbon
Strong growth	21.1	7.6	1.3	2.4
Economic concern	17.6	6.1	0.9	2.5
Environmental awakening	18.6	7.7	0.1	2.0
Supportive regulation	20.2	7.9	0.8	2.4
High-carbon (no CO$_2$ price)	17.3	5.8	2.0	0.0

Adding the price impacts on generation, transmission and distribution, we obtain an overall increase, assuming high gas prices, of between £9/MWh ('Economic concern' and 'Supportive regulation') and £13/MWh ('Environmental awakening'). With low gas prices, there is an increase of between £8/MWh ('Economic concern' and 'Supportive regulation') and £11/MWh ('Environmental awakening'). These should be seen in the context of average electricity prices of £33/MWh for industrial customers and £67/MWh for domestic consumers in 2004, the year before the Emission Trading Scheme started, when gas prices were at levels close to the lower of the two cases considered here (source: DTI, 2005, Table 1.7). In 2005, with higher gas prices (albeit still below the higher level considered here), industrial prices averaged £50/MWh and domestic prices £82/MWh.

15.5   Profits in the electricity industry

Given these predicted revenues, we can also derive the transfers from consumers to the industry in the different scenarios. Table 15.7 shows that the amount paid by consumers will rise by between £3 billion and £4 billion, comparing the two high-demand, low-carbon scenarios with the High-carbon scenario, and by up to £1 billion in the lower-demand scenarios. Much of these increases are taken up by higher costs, particularly capital costs, and the industry's pure profit – its returns over and above the 10% cost of capital assumed – is lower in all of the low-carbon scenarios. The final column shows the value of the emissions permits that the generators will need to buy in each scenario. If all of these were given away, then the generators would (collectively) more than regain the amount of profits that they make in the High-carbon scenario.

Table 15.8 repeats this analysis for the low gas price case, with very similar results. Overall, it is clear that the adoption of low-carbon policies will involve a significant transfer away from electricity consumers,

Table 15.8. *Annual profits for electricity generation in 2020*
(£ billion – lower gas price)

	Revenues	Capital	Pure profit	Carbon
Strong growth	18.9	7.6	0.7	1.5
Economic concern	15.6	6.1	0.5	1.6
Environmental awakening	16.7	7.7	−0.5	1.3
Supportive regulation	18.0	7.9	0.0	1.5
High-carbon (no CO$_2$ price)	15.4	5.8	1.4	0.0

Table 15.9. *Annual profits for power stations in 2020 (£/kW)*

	Higher gas price			Lower gas price		
	Coal	Gas	Nuclear	Coal	Gas	Nuclear
Strong growth	26	43	35	11	48	−8
Economic concern	13	30	22	−1	36	−21
Environmental awakening	6	24	15	−10	28	−29
Supportive regulation	12	29	21	−3	35	−22
High-carbon (no CO$_2$ price)	73	33	−14	40	36	−47

to either generators (if permits are given away) or the government (if they are auctioned).

We can also assess the profits made by different kinds of generator, and this is done in Table 15.9. Nuclear stations are unprofitable in the High-carbon scenario, but make a profit in all but one of the low-carbon scenarios, earning more when the gas price is high. Coal-fired stations are much less profitable in the low-carbon scenarios (these figures assume that they have to buy all their emission permits), and make losses when the gas price is low. The profits of a CCGT station are much less sensitive to the price of gas, since the wholesale power price is highly correlated with it. They are highest in the 'Strong growth' scenario, in which the overall level of capacity is slightly lower, relative to demand, than in the other scenarios, producing higher prices.

15.6   The impacts of higher electricity prices

The analysis above suggests that the price of electricity for industrial customers could increase by 20–35% by 2020 as a result of moving towards a low-carbon system, compared with a high-carbon alternative. For domestic customers, the increase could be between 11% and 20%. What impact would such price increases have?

For most consumers, spending on electricity (and gas) forms a very small proportion of their expenditure. Domestic customers spent £10.1 billion on electricity in 2005, compared to total consumers' expenditure of £760 billion. Electricity and gas together made up just 2.5% of consumers' expenditure in that year, and only 2.0% in 2004. An increase of 20% in the share (which ignores the impact of higher prices on demand) would raise even the higher figure to just 3.0%. While consumption of some other products (or savings) would have to fall to make room for an increase in spending on energy, the macroeconomic impacts would be small.

For a minority of consumers, however, fuel bills are a real source of concern. Fuel poverty can be defined as the inability to reach an acceptable standard of comfort without spending an excessive proportion of one's income. This is usually due to one or more of various factors, including low income, poor-quality housing which is difficult to heat and badly insulated, and/or high need, typically caused by old age, poor health, or both. For practical purposes, it is easier to monitor expenditure fuel poverty, which is based on the number of households that actually spend more than a given percentage of their income on fuel, power and light, usually 10%. This measure excludes those who are forced by other priorities to keep their fuel spending below the threshold and therefore fail to achieve an acceptable standard of comfort, but avoids the task of estimating what level of spending would be needed to achieve this standard. One of the government's four goals of energy policy is to ensure that every home is adequately and affordably heated, which can be seen as aiming to eliminate fuel poverty.

The number of UK households in fuel poverty had been steadily falling from the mid-1990s to 2003, helped by rising incomes and benefits, and falling energy prices. More recently, this trend was sharply reversed as fuel prices started to increase again. Wrigley (2006) estimated that the increase from 2003 to 2006 raised the number of households in expenditure fuel poverty from 1.5 million to nearly 2.5 million. Increasing electricity prices associated with low-carbon policies would push another 250,000 households into fuel poverty. For these households, the move to a low-carbon electricity system brings severe consequences. However, Wrigley also found that a 5% across-the-board reduction in consumption, due to energy efficiency measures, would reduce fuel poverty by around 250,000 households, and a 20% reduction would lift nearly

1 million households out of fuel poverty. Targeted benefits, such as the government's Winter Fuel Payments, could also reduce the number of households in fuel poverty, although such schemes almost inevitably involve either means-testing (with its disadvantages) or payments to those who may not need them.

What about the impact on industry? Once again, it will vary from sector to sector, depending on how important electricity is as an input, and how exposed the sector is to international competition. It is possible to use input–output analysis to see how a rise in electricity costs would feed through to the average cost of production in different industrial sectors. The analysis cannot distinguish between average and marginal cost, and ignores the possibility of substituting away from a more expensive input (which might mean an increase in the demand for labour, and hence employment and wages). The structure of the input–output tables will also affect the results. First, some very electricity-intensive products may be hidden within broader industry classifications. Since the impact of a cost change will be likely to rise more than proportionately to the change, this will lead us to underestimate the overall impacts. Second, electricity sold by Centrica (British Gas) is counted as an output of the gas distribution sector rather than as part of the electricity industry, while sales of gas by (predominantly) electricity companies are included in the electricity sector. This means that it is no longer possible to unambiguously identify the electricity-intensity of different industrial sectors.

Despite these shortcomings, the analysis can still give a reasonable picture of the impact of higher electricity prices. For most sectors, a 30% (initial) increase in electricity prices leads to a cost increase of less than 1%, using the 2000 input–output tables for the UK. Excluding the gas and electricity sectors themselves, less than one-tenth of the economy, measured by the gross value of its output, suffers a cost increase of more than 1%. The sectors affected include some parts of the textiles and engineering industries, and much of the chemicals industry. Sectors suffering from a cost increase of more than 2% include the rest of the chemicals industry (industrial dyes and gases, and inorganic chemicals), metals (iron and steel, non-ferrous metals, and metal castings) and pulp and paper. In terms of gross output, these make up 1.2% of the economy. Only the cement sector suffers an average cost increase of more than 3%. The impact on marginal costs, however, will typically be larger than the impact on average costs.

The *Stern Review* (Stern, 2007, Chapter 11) contains a broader analysis which reveals the carbon intensity of production in different sectors, and models the effects of a tax of £70/tC (£19/tCO$_2$) in terms of final consumer prices.[1] The overall impact is to raise the latter by just over 1%, assuming full cost pass-through (Stern, 2007, p.254). Not surprisingly, however, the effect is far from even: at one end of the scale, 48 industries out of 123 would face a rise in variable costs of less than 0.5%, whereas at the other end the rise for six industries would be 5% or more (and two of those – gas supply and distribution, and refined petroleum – exceed 20%).

Assuming that higher costs are passed through into retail prices, there will be substitution effects. Within the domestic economy, there will be a shift towards the purchase of goods and services which embody less electricity in their production, and towards those that use less power after purchase. From the point of view of the macroeconomy, however, the more important effects are likely to come from international trade, particularly if some countries do not adopt low-carbon policies. Electricity-intensive industries in the UK will lose comparative advantage relative to those based in countries where emissions are free, and the UK's net exports in these industries should decline. The *Stern Review* argues that these effects are likely to be limited, as 'only a small number of the worst affected sectors have internationally mobile plant and processes' (p.253). Moreover, trade diversion and relocation are less likely if firms expect that initially low-tax countries will come into line sooner or later; firms' decisions in this area are made for 'decades of production' (p.261). Even if there is some trade diversion, whether it leads to an overall decline in the UK's trade balance depends on the behaviour of the exchange rate, and the response of trade flows to changes in this. In a frictionless world, the exchange rate would adjust to clear the trade balance, and other sectors would become more competitive, offsetting the losses elsewhere in the economy. With frictions, either in the exchange rate markets or in the speed at which resources can move between sectors, the loss of competitiveness in some industries leads to a greater loss of welfare. Border tax adjustments that raise the cost of imports from countries that do not put a price (or tax) on carbon might offset this, however, and could be coupled with tax rebates on exports to such countries. Ismer and Neuhoff (2004) proposed a method of setting such adjustments that they believe would be allowed under World Trade Organisation rules and would be a feasible way of minimising any loss of competitiveness.

---

[1] 1 tonne of carbon can make 44/12 tonnes of CO_2 so a tax of £70/tC is equivalent to £19/ tCO_2. Both measures – tC and tCO_2 – are used in the literature. Stern's figure is close to the carbon price we use in the high gas price scenarios, and about 50% above the figure we use with our lower gas price.

Table 15.10. *Emissions reductions and costs in 2020, relative to High-carbon scenario*

	Higher gas price			Lower gas price		
	CO_2 saved (Mt)	Extra cost		CO_2 saved (Mt)	Extra cost	
		(£bn)	(£/MWh)		(£bn)	(£/MWh)
Strong growth	48	2.2	6	60	2.6	7
Economic concern	34	−1.1	4	49	−0.4	5
Environmental awakening	73	1.3	10	81	1.9	11
Supportive regulation	43	1.7	5	58	2.4	7

The impact on company profits depends on whether the cost increases are passed through into prices. For companies directly participating in the EU ETS, the increase in marginal costs is likely to be greater than the increase in average costs, at least as long as most permits are given away without charge. Smale *et al.* (2006) used Cournot models of several industries to suggest that most of the sectors directly participating in the EU ETS would be able to pass through much of their marginal cost increases, and would thus raise their profits, despite losing market share to imports. The aluminium sector, in contrast, is outside the ETS, implying that it will suffer from higher electricity prices (unless protected by existing long-term contracts) and does not gain from a free allocation of permits (unless generating power for its own use). Smale *et al.* (2006) predict that this could lead to aluminium plants in the EU closing as a result of the ETS. Sato *et al.* (2007) considered the vulnerability of a wider range of sectors, within and outside the ETS, comparing the amount of value at risk and the share of imports from outside the EU. Again, while many firms have little value at risk, the sums at stake for the most energy-intensive sectors are large.

15.7   Electricity emissions reductions in context

How much lower will emissions of carbon dioxide be in the Supergen scenarios, compared with the High-carbon scenario? Table 15.10 shows that emissions will be between 40 million and 60 million tonnes lower in the two scenarios with higher electricity demands ('Strong growth' and 'Supportive regulation'). Dividing the additional cost (taken from Tables 15.4 and 15.5, but excluding the cost of carbon) by the reduction in emissions, we get an average cost of just over £40 per tonne of CO_2 avoided. We obtain a higher reduction in the 'Environmental awakening' scenario, of 70–80 million tonnes, and an apparently lower cost. This is a potentially misleading comparison, however, as the amount of electricity being produced is also much lower – the cost increase per MWh is greater in this scenario. If investments in energy efficiency allow consumers to receive the same level of energy services from a lower amount of electricity, then it would be appropriate to compare the total cost of providing these high-carbon and low-carbon energy services. A comprehensive comparison would have to include the cost of the investments in energy efficiency. The low demand level in the 'Economic concern' scenario, however, stems from poor economic performance, and so the reduced cost of generating electricity is because fewer energy services are being provided. The cost per MWh of electricity rises by almost as much as in the two high-demand scenarios. Having a badly performing economy is not a good way to reduce carbon emissions.

So far we have considered individual effects of moving towards a low-carbon electricity sector. In reality, these effects will be interlinked, and there will be others we have not yet considered, for example those stemming from the changes in the electricity industry's input demands. With lower fuel consumption in the low-carbon scenarios, imports will be lower (given that the UK will be a net importer of fuel well before 2020). Higher investment in the electricity sector may crowd out investment elsewhere in the economy, although if there are unemployed resources it may act as a stimulus and increase output. If carbon permits are auctioned, the government will obtain revenue that it could use to cut distorting taxes. This will generally be the better option from the point of view of overall welfare, although if the permits are given away, this will boost generators' profits and hence the welfare of their shareholders. To assess these wider impacts, a more comprehensive model is needed, and it is to these that we now turn.

To identify the full impacts of climate policy, it is necessary to look at the whole economy, and preferably the whole world, given the scale of the problem and the importance of trade effects. While estimates of the cost of emissions reductions vary between models, for reasons explained by Barker *et al.* (2006), most models imply that the cost should be easily affordable. The median cost of cutting carbon emissions by 40% to 60% from their baseline predictions for the second half of this century is a reduction in Gross World Product of around 1% (Barker *et al.*, 2002, Figure 16).

Most of these models study the impact of reducing carbon emissions across the economy as a whole. This should be the most efficient way of doing so, even if some sectors may be expected to play a dominant role at particular times. For example, energy efficiency measures should be the most cost-effective way of reducing emissions over the next couple of decades, while the shift to low-carbon electricity would then take over in the middle decades of the century (IPCC, 2007, section 11.6). A recent series of studies takes this holistic approach further, looking at the scope to reduce emissions of other greenhouse gases (see Weyant *et al.*, 2006). Since significant reductions in emissions of some of these gases, such as methane, can be made at relatively low cost, and they typically have a much greater greenhouse effect than CO_2, it is hardly surprising that policies that curb the emissions of all greenhouse gases can deliver a given climate impact at a lower cost than those dealing with CO_2 alone.

However, it is also worth examining the cost of a partial policy, and this is done by Pizer *et al.* (2006). They modelled the cost of reducing US emissions with a carbon tax applied first to the whole economy, then to industry, transport and the electricity sector (78% of emissions) and, finally, to transport and electricity alone (53% of emissions). The carbon tax required to achieve a given total reduction rises more than proportionately as its coverage falls, implying that the marginal cost of reductions within a sector increases non-linearly with the reductions required. A tax of $19/ton of carbon would be sufficient for a 5% cut in emissions if applied to the whole economy, but this would rise to $53/ton, nearly three times as much, if it only applied to half the country's emissions. Interestingly, the welfare cost of exempting residential and commercial buildings from the carbon tax is very low,[2] but the cost of cutting emissions through a tax applied to electricity and transport alone is more than twice that of a broad-based policy: 0.038% of GDP against 0.016%.

Pizer *et al.* (2006) also considered two sector-specific policies, having carefully constructed a model that can simulate the responses to these policies within a general equilibrium framework. One of these is a renewable portfolio standard, requiring generators to produce a given proportion of their output from renewable sources, and the other is an increase in vehicle efficiency. The modelled cost of achieving a 5% reduction in emissions through these two policies is five times as great as with a carbon tax applied to electricity and transport alone, and more than ten times as great as with an economy-wide tax. In the USA, renewable generators tend to displace gas- rather than coal-fired generation, which minimises their impact on emissions, and raises the cost per ton of carbon saved. The quantitative result may well be country-specific, but the general lesson is that narrowly focused policies are an

---

[2] Pizer *et al.* (2006) argued that this is due to the interaction of a carbon tax with other distorting taxes on commercial buildings (p.158) – these are overtaxed, in general, and exempting them from the carbon tax makes the overall tax burden across sectors more equal, reducing distortions.

expensive way of creating a low-carbon economy. The electricity sector can make a significant contribution to the task of reducing carbon emissions, but should not be asked to make all the cuts that we will need.

15.8   Conclusions

We have presented estimates for the cost of generating electricity, based on the four low-carbon Supergen scenarios for 2020, and on a High-carbon alternative. We show that the cost of power rises significantly as we cut emissions, but that these costs should be affordable for most people and most firms in the UK. We also need to consider the alternative – the *Stern Review* (2007) shows that the cost of climate change could be very large.

We have found that UK electricity sector emissions in the low-carbon scenarios can be 30–80 million tonnes of CO_2 lower than in the High-carbon scenario, or from 5% to 14% of 2004 emissions. The direct cost increase in the scenarios with comparable levels of electricity generation is around £2–3 billion, equivalent to an average cost of just over £10 per tonne of reduced emissions. Compared to the UK's GDP of £1,224 billion in 2005, this direct cost is small. Other studies, which include macroeconomic effects (likely to raise the cost) and an economy-wide approach (likely to reduce it) produce a range of results. Analyses of these results have shown that policy decisions can significantly affect the cost of stabilising emissions, but that this cost is still very uncertain, and that choices made by modellers have systematic impacts on their estimates. However, the median estimate implies that the cost of action over the first half of this century would be of the order of 1% of Gross World Product. Comparing that to the likely costs of climate change, the conclusion in terms of cost–benefit analysis is thus very clear: the costs of early action seem low.

Acknowledgements

This work was supported by the Supergen Future Network Technologies Consortium. We would like to thank three anonymous referees and (particularly) the editors for very helpful comments.

References

Barker, T., J. Kohler and M. Villena (2002). Costs of greenhouse gas abatement: meta-analysis of post-SRES mitigation scenarios, *Environmental Economics and Policy Studies*, 5, 135–166.

Barker, T., M.S. Qureshi and J. Köhler (2006). *The Costs of Greenhouse Gas Mitigation with Induced Technological Change: A Meta-Analysis of Estimates in the Literature*, Report prepared for the HM Treasury Stern Review, 4CMR, Cambridge Centre for Climate Change Mitigation Research, University of Cambridge.

DTI [Department of Trade and Industry] (2005). *Digest of United Kingdom Energy Statistics 2005*, London: The Stationery Office.

[Department of Trade and Industry] (2006). *The Energy Challenge: Energy Review Report 2006*, Cm 6887, London, The Stationery Office.

Energy Saving Trust (2005). *Potential for Microgeneration: Study and Analysis*, London: Energy Saving Trust.

Enviros (2005). *The Costs of Supplying Renewable Energy*, Report to the Department of Trade and Industry, available from www.berr.gov.uk/files/file21118.pdf

Green, R.J. (2005). Electricity and markets, *Oxford Review of Economic Policy*, **21**(1), 67–87.

(2008) Carbon Tax or Carbon Permits: The Impact on Generators' Risks, Energy Journal, **29**(3), 67–87.

Grubb, M. and K. Neuhoff (2006). Allocation and competitiveness in the EU emissions trading scheme: policy overview, *Climate Policy*, **6**(1), 5–28.

IPCC (2007). *Climate Change 2007: Mitigation of Climate Change – Contribution of Working Group III to the Fourth Assessment Report of the Intergovernmental Panel on Climate Change*, Cambridge: Cambridge University Press.

Ismer, R. and K. Neuhoff (2004). *Border Tax Adjustments: A Feasible Way to Address Nonparticipation in Emission Trading*, Cambridge Working Papers in Economics CWPE 0409 and CMI EP 36.

National Grid (2006). *2006 Great Britain Seven Year Statement*, Coventry: National Grid.

Neuhoff, K., K. Keats-Martinez and M. Sato (2006). Allocation, incentives and distortions: the impact of EU ETS emissions allowance allocations to the electricity sector, *Climate Policy*, **6**(1), 71–89.

Newborough M. (2004). Assessing the benefits of implementing micro-CHP systems in the UK, *Proceedings of the I MECH E: Part A, Journal of Power and Energy*, **218**(4), 203–218.

Ofgem (2004). *Electricity Distribution Price Control Review: Final Proposals*, Publication 265/04, London: Office of Gas and Electricity Markets.

Pizer, W., D. Burtraw, W. Harrington, R. Newell and J. Sanchirico (2006). Modeling economy-wide vs sectoral climate policies using combined aggregate-sectoral models, *Energy Journal*, **27**(3), 135–168.

Powernext (2007). *Tendances Carbone: Bulletin mensuel du marché européen du CO_2*, 11, Paris: Powernext.

Sato, M., M. Grubb, J. Cust, K. Chan, A. Korppoo and P. Ceppi (2007). Cambridge Working Papers in Economics CWPE 0712 / *Differentiation and Dynamics of Competitiveness Impacts from the EU ETS*, Electricity Policy Research Group Working Paper EPRG 07/04, Faculty of Economics, University of Cambridge.

Scottish Energy Environment Foundation (2005). *Impact of GB Transmission Charging on Renewable Electricity Generation*, Report to the Department of Trade and Industry, available from www.berr.gov.uk/files/file30158.pdf

Smale, R., M. Hartley, C. Hepburn, J. Ward and M.J. Grubb (2006). The impact of CO_2 emissions trading on firm profits and market prices, *Climate Policy*, **6**(1), 29–46.

Stern, N. (2007). *The Economics of Climate Change: The Stern Review*, Cambridge: Cambridge University Press.

Weyant, J.P., F.C. de la Chesnaye and G.J. Blanford (2006). Overview of EMF-21: multigas mitigation and climate policy, *Energy Journal*, Special Issue on Multi-Greenhouse Gas Mitigation, **27**, 1–32.

Wrigley, J. (2006). *Fuel Poverty in the UK and the Impact of the 2006 Energy Review* MSc Dissertation, Department of Economics, University of Birmingham.

16 Bridging technologies: can carbon capture and storage offer a bridge to a sustainable energy future in the UK?

David M. Reiner, Jon Gibbins and Sam Holloway

16.1 Introduction

In just over a decade, the idea of removing the link between carbon dioxide and fossil fuels by capturing and then storing the CO_2 has moved from being an untried concept of interest to a handful of researchers to being the subject of significant attention from leading governments, industrial organisations and a number of environmental NGOs. The first major scientific meeting on the subject, held in Amsterdam in 1992, attracted some 250 scientists and engineers from 20 countries, many of whom had never met before. The eighth such gathering held in Trondheim, Norway, in 2006 attracted 950 participants from over 40 countries, including not just a greatly expanded scientific community, but large numbers of government officials and energy industry executives.

Røkke (2006) writing for an earlier book in this series, *Future Electricity Technologies and Systems*, offered a technology overview of carbon capture and storage (CCS). Even in the short intervening time since that chapter was prepared, there has been a remarkable surge in activity on the technology, and especially on the policy fronts. Extending this earlier work, we adopt a specific focus on the UK context. Finally, we also are able to offer different disciplinary perspectives drawn from geology, engineering and political science.

Large energy companies such as Shell (van der Veer, 2006) and BP (2005) have begun to invest in carbon CCS technologies, major electric utilities have drawn up plans for plants with capture, and the G-8 leaders at the Gleneagles summit in 2005 have highlighted the critical importance of developing CCS for meeting the challenge of climate change (G8, 2005). An important *Special Report by the Intergovernmental Panel on Climate Change* (IPCC) on the subject in late 2005 synthesised knowledge on all aspects of CCS, including the science, engineering and economics underlying different capture technologies, transport and storage options (IPCC, 2005). The issue is now being considered as part of the international negotiations over climate change under the Kyoto Protocol. CCS is also being developed by non-Kyoto participants, the USA and Australia[1] (APEC Secretariat, 2005) and forms part of the AP6 programme to which they belong, along with other major coal users – China, India and South Korea, Japan and, latterly, Canada.

CCS is seen as attractive for a number of reasons, including the ability to bring key national actors to the negotiating table by offering viable options for energy-intensive industries. Interested parties include coal producers, energy companies from the electricity and oil and gas sectors, energy-intensive industries such as aluminium, steel and cement, and key countries that are heavily dependent on coal, including China, India, the USA and Australia, and the EU with its proactive position on climate change (European Council, 2007, pp. 10–14). If ambitious goals to stabilise atmospheric concentrations at twice pre-industrial levels, which would require a 60% reduction globally by 2050, are to have any chance of being met, then it will be necessary to address the existing and planned energy infrastructure, which can last for many decades. This so-called 'carbon lock-in' (Foxon, 2002; Unruh and Carrillo-Hermosilla, 2006) is of greatest magnitude in developing countries such as China, which each year has been installing new coal-fired capacity with an electrical output of some 30–50GW (roughly equal to the total installed fossil-fired capacity in the UK). As the House of Commons Committee on Science and Technology noted in its inquiry into CCS:

It is indisputable that – in the absence of CCS – fossil fuel consumption in countries such as China and India will have a profound and potentially catastrophic impact on global atmospheric CO_2 levels, eclipsing any reductions made by the UK and others (HoC, 2006a, pp. 11–12).

From a UK perspective, CCS has risen up the agenda because of its potential at a global scale, but most especially as a result of a combination of domestic pressures. Most importantly, the UK is in the process of an energy transition driven by a shift from domestic to imported oil and gas and the planned shutdown of older coal and nuclear plants over the coming decades. This transition represents both danger and opportunity for CCS. If the nuclear and coal base were to be replaced by natural gas, as has been expected for many years, the fear is that the UK electricity sector would be overwhelmingly dominated by gas imports, increasingly drawn from Russia and North Africa. As the North Sea

[1] The Australian Prime Minister signed the instrument of ratification of the Kyoto protocol on 3 December 2007; the ratification comes into effect 90 days later.

fields near the end of their productive lives, there is also increased interest in enhanced oil recovery (EOR) using CO_2, which could serve the dual purpose of extending the life of the fields and increasing productivity by allowing tertiary recovery and simultaneously storing the CO_2 used in the EOR process. Though limited in scale compared with the overall magnitude of the CO_2 that would need to be captured from the electricity sector alone, EOR nevertheless may offer an important opportunity for the first CO_2 storage projects, for ease of permitting as much as for any major contribution to project economics.

In other cases, it is difficult to know whether the broader energy trends will encourage the development of CCS. Even accounting for the additional cost of CO_2 imposed by the EU Emission Trading Scheme (ETS), which differentially penalises coal-fired generation, the rise in natural gas prices between 2003 and 2006 made coal-fired power more attractive, leading to an overall increase in CO_2 emissions (DTI, 2007). Electric utilities will therefore need to factor in their expectations regarding coal and natural gas prices, as well as carbon prices, in future investment decisions.

If new coal plants were to be built without any provision for capture, then retrofitting the plant to add capture at a later date could be quite costly and could also affect the choice of technology. It is possible to reduce retrofit costs by anticipating the need for installing capture equipment both in terms of siting and design requirements (so-called capture-ready plant), but without clearer signals from government, firms do not yet appear ready to make the needed investments to build new plant with capture technology.

There has been a flurry of activity to improve awareness of policy makers in the UK. The Parliamentary Office of Science and Technology has published two studies on *Carbon Capture and Storage* and on *Cleaner Coal* (POST, 2005a, 2005b). In addition to the House of Commons Select Committee inquiry, there has been a Treasury consultation on the commercialisation of CCS technologies (H.M. Treasury, 2006a), and CCS has been one of the major themes of the government's major energy review (DTI, 2006), alongside such long-standing alternatives as nuclear power, renewables and efficiency. In 2003, the White Paper *Our Energy Future* (DTI, 2003) mainly provided background on the nature of the technology and on EOR but, only 3 years later, CCS has emerged as a major consideration in a national debate over the future of the UK electricity sector and the 2006 *Energy Review* was able to report on the significant activities that have been undertaken in the interim.

In this chapter, we review some of the main drivers of progress, including development of capture technologies, improvements in our understanding of the subsurface, and the economic and policy drivers. Whereas steady progress has been made in geology and engineering over the last decade, it is a combination of political and commercial forces that have turned the spotlight on CCS and moved it up the policy agenda alongside long-standing debates over nuclear power and renewables.

16.2   Carbon dioxide capture technologies

Three main approaches are currently being considered to capture a pure stream of carbon dioxide (CO_2) from power plants, generally grouped as post-combustion, pre-combustion and oxyfuel technologies, as shown in Figure 16.1. With current state-of-the-art technology, all three approaches are predicted to achieve very similar technical and economic performance for electricity production from coal, which is seen as the most immediate large-scale application in the UK electricity sector (IEA GHG, 2006). Table 16.1. provides an overview of technologies that might be considered for deployment for electricity generation in the UK.

16.2.1   Post-combustion capture

This approach keeps the power plant essentially unchanged and separates the CO_2 from the flue gases just before they are vented to the atmosphere. Retaining conventional power plant technology and

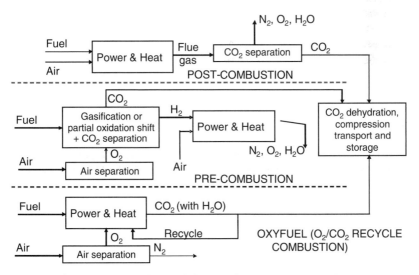

Figure 16.1. Principles of three main CO_2 capture options
Source: After Jordal, K. *et al.* (2004)

Table 16.1. *CCS technologies that might be considered for deployment for electricity generation in the UK over the next 10–20 years*

Fuel	Capture technology	Electricity generation technology	Fuel processing technology	Capture technology	New build /retrofit	Deployment and availability
Natural gas	Natural gas combined cycle (NGCC) with post-combustion capture	Combined cycle gas turbine (CCGT)	None	Post-combustion	Both	Small scale only, but similar larger capture plant in chemical industry. Clean combustion products so minimal difficulties, available to order now to at least 200MWe per absorber unit.
Natural gas	NGCC with pre-combustion capture	CCGT	Conversion to H_2 and CO_2 (reforming and shift)	Pre-combustion	Both	None, but similar fuel processing and capture plant in chemical industry. Available now.
Coal (with biomass co-firing option)	Pulverised coal (PC) with post-combustion capture	Conventional steam turbine (boiler and turbine may be upgraded before capture)	None	Post-combustion	Likely to be retrofit	Small scale only, test plants for coal combustion products just started in Europe and Japan. Near-commercial available versions up to about 100MWe on order from 2007, larger versions soon after demonstration at this scale.
Coal (optionally with	Integrated gasifier combined cycle	CCGT	Conversion to mainly H_2	(a) Shift: CO + H_2O to CO_2 + H_2	All new build, or could use	4 working IGCC plants without capture (2 in USA, 2 in Europe), others planned. Hundreds of

(biomass and/or petroleum coke)	(IGCC) with capture	and CO (gasification)	(b) Pre-combustion capture	existing CCGT	
					gasifiers + capture technology used in chemical industry. Incremental development except for new oxygen plant (ion transfer membrane – ITM). Available now.
Natural gas	Natural gas oxyfuel turbines	Steam/CO_2 turbine	None	Combustion in high-purity oxygen. Drying and cleaning only	New build	Small test plants, a number of variants, might be commercial option by 2020.
Coal (with biomass co-firing option)	Pulverised coal oxyfuel	Conventional steam turbine	None	Combustion in high-purity oxygen. Drying and cleaning only	Likely to be new build, but possibly retrofit	Base plant very widely used but significant changes for oxyfuel operation, first plant (in Saskatchewan, Canada) may be ordered in 2007.

operation methods is obviously an advantage, particularly for retrofitting existing plant. The power plant can also be operated independently of the CO_2 capture plant if required. Near-commercial post-combustion capture designs 'wash' the flue gases with a liquid solvent that absorbs CO_2 in a reversible reaction. A pure CO_2 stream is released by heating the solvent to around 120°C, using low-pressure steam taken from the power plant. However, only solvents that bind relatively strongly to CO_2 can achieve a high level of removal from a dilute, atmospheric-pressure mixture (typically 5–15% CO_2 by volume), so about 60% of the 'energy penalty' for capture in post-combustion CCS plants goes to regenerating the solvent. The CO_2 is also released at close to atmospheric pressure, so compression power is relatively high. The capture equipment is large, because it handles the full-flue gas volume at atmospheric pressure, but does not have to contain significant pressures. Flue gases from coal plants must also have virtually all the oxides of sulphur (SO_x) removed before entering the CO_2 scrubber.

Small-scale, post-combustion scrubbers are widely used to produce CO_2 for carbonated drinks, and somewhat larger units are being built to capture CO_2 from gas-fired reformers for use in urea production. But the main application for post-combustion capture systems at the scale and with the performance characteristics (e.g. oxygen tolerance, energy efficiency) suited to power plants is large-scale CO_2 emission reduction, a market that is only just emerging. As commercial interest develops and experience is gained with post-combustion systems, improvements, particularly on capital costs, are likely to follow.

16.2.2   Pre-combustion capture

Since CO_2 is a product of combustion, the term 'pre-combustion capture' at first sight seems to be an oxymoron. To produce CO_2 for capture, the carbon in the fuel must first be converted to carbon monoxide (CO) by gasification (coal) or reforming (natural gas) and the CO is then 'shifted' to CO_2 in a reaction with added steam (H_2O). Small amounts (<5%) of the CO and of the order of 50% of the added steam must remain unreacted, however, because of the balance between the rates of CO removal and formation in the reaction:

$$CO + H_2O \Leftrightarrow CO_2 + H_2$$

The CO_2 can then be separated relatively easily because the gasification and shift processes are usually run at elevated pressures, typically 30–70 atmospheres. Under these conditions the CO_2 will physically dissolve in organic liquids. CO_2 is readily released at reduced pressures, but still above atmospheric pressure, so that compression power is minimised (compared with post-combustion capture). Pre-combustion capture therefore has a much lower energy penalty for CO_2 separation and compression. These benefits must be set against energy losses in the gasification and shift process, and the energy required to produce oxygen for gasification and additional steam. The CO_2 removed from the high-pressure gases could also have been used to produce electricity by helping to drive a gas turbine. The end result is that overall coal-to-electricity efficiencies with CO_2 capture and compression for pre-combustion capture in integrated gasifier combined cycle (IGCC) plants are estimated to be similar to, or even lower than, post-combustion capture coal plants. For natural gas, pre-combustion appears less attractive (compared with post-combustion capture), principally because natural gas can already take advantage of the high efficiencies offered by combined cycle gas turbine (CCGT) technology.

Pre-combustion capture technology has already been developed at a scale for hydrogen production in the petrochemical industry, so the actual capture process involves lower risks. Coal IGCC technology is, however, still developing, and has yet to demonstrate capital cost and availability levels that can compete with the latest supercritical steam coal combustion plant. It remains to be seen whether the 'big four' actors in the IGCC world (ConocoPhillips, GE, Shell, Siemens) will be able to make gasification the mainstream power generation technology for coal, although gasification technology with CCS will almost certainly be used widely in the future for unconventional hydrocarbon fuel production and, if end-users want it as an energy vector, for hydrogen production.

16.2.3   Oxyfuel combustion

In oxyfuel combustion, the main separation step involves separating oxygen (O_2) from nitrogen in air. Much larger amounts of O_2 are required than for gasification, but large-scale oxygen production technology has been developed over a long period for use in the steel industry. Cryogenic air separation units (ASU) compress and liquefy air and then distil it into its pure constituents. Extensive thermal integration techniques have been developed to reduce energy inputs to a minimum, but energy penalties for coal oxyfuel plants with cryogenic ASUs are still predicted to be similar to those for post-combustion capture plants, even though CO_2 separation energy requirements are minimal.

To limit combustion temperatures and avoid excessive slagging in oxyfuel boilers, it is envisaged that the oxygen would be diluted with recycled combustion products (CO_2 and water vapour) to replace the nitrogen from air used in conventional combustion. This requirement may, however, be avoided in future designs, leading to moderate increases in efficiency and capital cost reductions. Greater advantages could be achieved by reductions in oxygen production costs and energy requirements, but such improvements are not straightforward, since air separation is a mature field. High-temperature membranes (ion transport membranes – ITM) are one area being researched, but these require air at elevated pressure and temperature and so may be more suitable for integration with IGCC plants than with oxyfuel boilers.

Pollutant removal in oxyfuel boilers is simplified by the smaller volume of gas that has to be processed compared with air-fired units. However flue gas desulphurisation (FGD) equipment may still be required to remove SO_x from recycle streams with high sulphur coals in order to prevent high-temperature boiler corrosion.

It appears that oxyfuel coal boiler designs can be based on conventional air-fired technology. The steam turbine generator, cooling equipment and other ancillary equipment are largely unchanged. Operating and maintenance practices may, however, require some modifications because of the greater intrinsic risks associated with oxygen use. Oxyfuel CCGT plants that use natural gas would, however, require new turbine designs to be developed, and overall plant efficiencies also appear to be relatively low; internal combustion steam/CO_2 turbine designs using liquid water recycle may be a more attractive alternative.

16.3   Economics

There are several issues that are critical to assessing the economics of carbon capture and storage technologies: the costs associated with each of the three stages (capture, transport and storage), the scale of operations at a regional and a national scale, and the availability of 'low-hanging fruit' from industrial processes with relatively pure streams of CO_2.

According to the IPCC *Special Report*, a CCS system (with good access to a geological storage site) would impose an 'energy penalty' of 10–40%, i.e. would require more energy than a plant of equivalent output without CCS, of which most is for capture and compression (IPCC, 2005). Assuming that the CO_2 would be stored securely, the net result would be an 80–90% reduction in CO_2 emissions to the atmosphere relative to a plant without CCS. Any calculation of the mitigation must specify the baseline relative to which emissions reductions are measured. Table 16.2 provides some examples of the expected avoided costs of carbon for different configurations of plant with capture and storage.

Table 16.2. *CO₂ avoidance costs for complete CCS system for electricity generation, for different combinations of reference power plants without CCS and power plants with CCS (geological and EOR)*

Type of power plant with CCS	Natural gas combined cycle reference plant (US$/tCO₂ avoided)	Pulverised coal reference plant (US$/tCO₂ avoided)
Power plant with capture and geological storage		
Natural gas combined cycle	40–90	20–60
Pulverised coal	70–270	30–70
Integrated gasification combined cycle	40–220	20–70
Power plant with capture and EOR		
Natural gas combined cycle	20–70	0–30
Pulverised coal	50–240	10–40
Integrated gasification combined cycle	20–190	0–40

Source: Based on IPCC (2005, Table SPM.4)
Note: The amount of CO₂ avoided is the difference between the emissions of the reference plant and the emissions of the power plant with CCS. Gas prices are assumed to be US$2.8–4.4/GJ, and coal prices US$1–1.5/GJ.

With current technology, CCS would be expected to raise the costs of electricity generation by 0.01–0.05 US dollars per kilowatt–hour (US$/kWh), depending on fuel, technology, location and national circumstances. EOR would reduce additional electricity production costs due to CCS by around US$0.01–0.02/kWh.

According to the IPCC *Special Report*, the differential cost of capture above and beyond the costs of a new plant will be of the order of several hundred dollars per kilowatt (e.g. IGCC without capture is estimated at US$1,169–1,565/kW and with capture US$1,414–2,270/kW) or several hundred million dollars extra for a commercial-scale plant (IPCC, 2005, p. 25).

In terms of sheer volume and relevance to the motivating goal of having a discernible effect on emissions, the most interesting source is the electric power sector, especially from coal-fired generation. Nevertheless, there are a number of industrial sectors that have received attention because they might offer some early lower-cost opportunities for capture of relatively pure streams of CO_2 generated in those industries. Processes include hydrogen and ammonia production, gas processing, as well as from the cement, steel and fertiliser sectors. Table 16.3 offers examples of some of the differences in the cost ranges for

Table 16.3. *Cost ranges for the components of a CCS system as applied to a given type of power plant or industrial source*

CCS system components	Cost range	Remarks
Capture from a coal- or gas-fired power plant	US$15–75/t$CO_2$ net captured	Net costs of captured CO_2 compared to the same plant without capture
Capture from hydrogen and ammonia production or gas processing	US$5–55/t$CO_2$ net captured	Applies to high-purity sources requiring simple drying and compression
Capture from other industrial sources	US$25–115/t$CO_2$ net captured	Range reflects use of a number of different technologies and fuels
Transportation	US$1–8/t$CO_2$ transported	Per 250 km pipeline or shipping for mass flow rates of 5 (high end) to 40 (low end) MtCO_2/year
Geological storage	US$0.5–8/t$CO_2$ net injected	Excluding potential revenues from EOR or ECBM
Geological storage: monitoring and verification	US$0.1–0.3/t$CO_2$ injected	This covers pre-injection, injection and post-injection monitoring, and depends on the regulatory requirements
Ocean storage	US$5–30/t$CO_2$ net injected	Including offshore transportation of 100–500 km, excluding monitoring and verification
Mineral carbonation	US$50–100/t$CO_2$ net mineralised	Range for the best case studied; includes additional energy use for carbonation

Source: Based on IPCC (2005, Table SPM.5)
Note: The costs of the separate components cannot simply be summed to calculate the costs of the whole CCS system in US$/$CO_2$ avoided. All numbers are representative of the costs for large-scale, new installations, with natural gas prices assumed to be US$2.8–4.4/GJ and coal prices US$1–1.5/GJ.

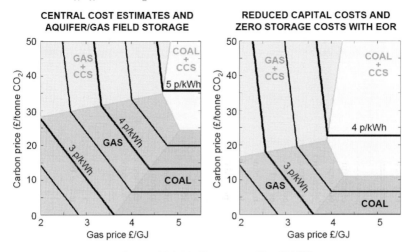

Figure 16.2. Effect of electricity price, carbon price and gas price on choice of technology
Source: Gibbins *et al.* (2006), cited in Stern (2007), p. 530

several industrial processes compared with electricity generation. The economics of CCS depends on the relationship between carbon and fossil fuel prices, and Figure 16.2 offers a sense (under a particular set of parameters) of which options will be favoured for different combinations of fuel and carbon prices.

Table 16.4 shows that almost 30% of the current UK coal-fired capacity will need to be retired over the coming decade. The EU Sulphur Directive requires that any plants that continue operating beyond 2015 will need to have been retrofitted with flue gas desulphurisation (FGD) equipment. Plants that 'opt out' from the directive will only be able to operate 20,000 hours in total from 2008–2015 and will need to close at the end of 2015. As of 2004, only 10GW had committed to FGD (DTI, 2004). From an energy security perspective, higher natural gas prices and the improved competitiveness of coal relative to gas meant that several firms such as Scottish and Southern decided to install FGD on their coal plants to achieve longer running hours up to 2015 and possibly to extend plant life beyond 2015 with the addition of selective catalytic reduction (SCR).

There remains a significant stock of coal-fired generation in the UK, but the possibility of retrofit is generally seen as uneconomic in most scenarios. Current plans (though most are still tentative) call for existing sites to be knocked down and rebuilt. For example, Kingsnorth

Table 16.4. *Status of coal-fired power stations in the UK*

Power station	Owner	MWe
Ironbridge	E.ON	972
Kingsnorth	E.ON	2,000
Didcot A	RWE npower	1,920
Tilbury	RWE npower	1,050
Cockenzie	Scottish Power	1,200
Ferrybridge (2 units)	SSE	1,000
Total Opt out		**7,975 (27%)**
Kilroot	AES	520
Eggborough	British Energy	2,000
Uskmouth	Carron Energy	393
Drax	Drax Power Limited	3,960
Cottam	EdF Energy	1,948
West Burton	EdF Energy	1,924
Ratcliffe	E.ON	2,000
Rugeley	International Power	996
Aberthaw	RWE npower	1,386
Longannet	Scottish Power	2,400
Ferrybridge (2 units)	SSE	1,000
Fiddlers Ferry	SSE	2,000
Total Opt in		**20,018 (73%)**

Source: Platts (2007)

would be rebuilt as a capture-ready plant with supercritical boiler and Tilbury would also need to rebuild its boiler; both sites would then be capable of having capture plants added. Ferrybridge could be rebuilt for oxyfuel, and so on. The existing stock of coal plants is mostly of sufficient age that capture retrofit would not be sensible. Drax is probably one of the few reasonable possibilities although, not surprisingly, its current owners have ruled out the possibility for the time being, focusing instead on co-firing the coal with 10% biomass (Webb, 2007).

Thus, by 2016, we can expect perhaps 8GW of coal capacity to be shut down as a result of the EU Sulphur Directive, along with 2.5GW of Magnox nuclear reactors and roughly 3GW of oil-fired capacity, driven by both age and environmental considerations. Thus, even assuming life-extension of the fleet of advanced gas-cooled reactors (AGRs), which would contribute an additional 6GW, and continued rapid growth of wind capacity, continued growth of over 1% per year in demand will require substantial new capacity, which will have to be either nuclear or fossil generation plus CCS if the government is also to meet its ambitious climate change targets.

16.4   CO$_2$ storage issues

According to the IPCC *Special Report*, most of the cost of CCS is expected at the capture stage, but storage also has many associated issues because: (i) available storage capacity will determine the ultimate scale of potential CCS activities; (ii) the security of the storage reservoirs will determine the reliability of CCS as a mitigation option; and (iii) it is the stage that brings CCS into direct contact with the public and hence is most crucial to public acceptability.

The CO$_2$ storage capacity of the UK could be considered a potential resource. As with many other resources, parts of it are relatively well known and can be adequately quantified, whereas other (in this case cumulatively much larger) parts are poorly quantified, poorly known, or speculative. It can be helpful to consider the UK's CO$_2$ storage potential as a resource pyramid, which has a very wide base consisting of speculative, poorly known and poorly quantified potential, and an apex consisting of well-quantified and relatively certain capacity (Figure 16.3). This resource pyramid can be divided into three parts. At the base is *theoretical* CO$_2$ storage capacity, consisting of the poorly known, poorly quantified and speculative potential. In the middle is *realistic* capacity – capacity which meets a range of geological and engineering criteria and which can be quantified with a fair degree of confidence. At the apex is *viable* capacity that meets additional criteria and can potentially be considered in terms of annual storage rates.

The theoretical storage capacity of the UK is very large because the UK Continental Shelf contains several large sedimentary basins, many of which appear to have significant potential. However, because so much

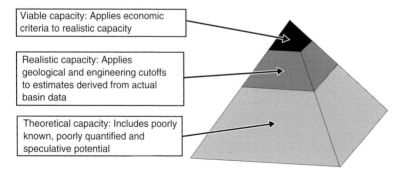

Figure 16.3. CO$_2$ storage capacity viewed as a resource pyramid
Source: After Bradshaw *et al.* (2007)

of it is poorly known, the best approach to quantifying UK CO_2 storage capacity is to incrementally upgrade fractions of the theoretical capacity into (quantified) realistic capacity, and then into viable capacity, which can best be done by careful basin-by-basin geological analysis.

The onshore area is of limited realistic CO_2 storage potential, although there are some important deep aquifers in onshore Britain. For example, the Sherwood Sandstone and Basal Permian sandstones have good porosity and permeability and are well sealed by overlying strata, and the parts of these aquifers that occur at depths >800 m have the best theoretical storage potential. But, if any of this potential is to be upgraded into realistic storage capacity, significantly sized structural or stratigraphic traps would have to be identified to contain the CO_2 in the deep areas of these reservoirs, to prevent leakage to outcrops or the contamination of the groundwater resources that are found in the shallower parts of the aquifers. The onshore oil and gas fields are individually too small to store significant amounts of CO_2, and the onshore coal seams have low permeability (evident in the lack of success in establishing coalbed methane production in the UK). Public acceptance and planning constraints are also much more likely to be an issue in the onshore area.

The oil and gas fields of the UK Continental Shelf are prime targets for CO_2 storage. Many of the gas fields in the southern North Sea are extremely well sealed and suffer little water ingress during gas production. Thus, at depletion, they contain large volumes of pore space occupied by low pressure natural gas, which appear to be highly suitable for CO_2 storage. Their total CO_2 storage capacity has been estimated at approximately 3.9 Gt (10^9 tonnes) CO_2. The gas fields in the east Irish Sea Basin may have a storage capacity of approximately 1 Gt CO_2 (Kirk, 2006). Additionally, there are several major gas/condensate fields in the northern and central North Sea. More speculatively, these may have a storage capacity of approximately 1.2 Gt CO_2. The storage capacity estimates for the UK gas fields fall into the 'realistic' category of the Bradshaw *et al.* (2007) classification, and those for the gas/condensate fields into the 'theoretical' storage capacity region.

The oil fields in the UK sector of the central and northern North Sea are mostly technically suitable for EOR using CO_2. It is considered likely that any CO_2 storage in a UK oil field would take place in conjunction with EOR, because the potential returns from the additional oil recovered are thought likely to exceed the extra costs involved. However, the costs of adapting offshore platforms and other infrastructure for EOR as opposed to pure CO_2 storage are poorly known at present. Moreover, the economics of EOR offshore are dependent on the oil price and the price of CO_2 in the EU ETS, both of which have shown volatility over the last few years. It has been estimated that approximately 1.2 Gt CO_2 could be stored in these fields as a result of economically optimised EOR (ECL Technology, 2005). If economics are ignored, and recovery processes were adapted to maximise CO_2 storage, the potential CO_2 storage resulting from EOR in the UK's offshore oil fields could be between 1.8 and 3.5 Gt (Tzimas et al., 2005). For suitable reservoirs, carbon dioxide EOR can increase recoverable reserves and improve the field's overall recovery factor by between 3% and 15%. The DTI has estimated that 950–2,250 million barrels (MMbbl) of additional oil reserves could be produced (Marsh, 2003). The estimates of storage capacity in the UK's oilfields have been made in considerable detail, and fall into the 'viable' capacity section of the resource pyramid.

The costs of storing CO_2 in the UK's offshore oil and gas fields are likely to increase significantly once the fields are abandoned, because the production wells will be plugged and the production platforms will be removed. There is therefore a window of opportunity to exploit the (progressively diminishing) CO_2 storage potential of the UK's offshore oil and gas fields that extends out to about 2030, when the major fields will have been depleted and abandoned.

Much of the aquifer storage potential of the UK Continental Shelf is poorly known and largely unquantified. However, the CO_2 storage capacity of the Bunter Sandstone Formation in the southern North Sea has been estimated to be up to approximately 14.25 Gt (Holloway et al., 2006a).

Taking into account the various components, the total quantified off-shore capacity identified above is approximately 22 Gt CO_2. The UK's total annual CO_2 emissions were approximately 561 Mt (10^6 tonnes) per annum in 2005. Given that only about half of this is from large industrial point sources, and thus amenable to capture, there appears to be adequate storage capacity available for at least the medium term. Therefore, the major issues for long-term CO_2 storage in the UK are probably uncertainties regarding security of storage, i.e. will storage sites leak, and what happens if they do?

Storage security is a site-specific question that is best considered on a case-by-case basis by a process of careful and thorough site character-isation, geological modelling, numerical modelling of CO_2 injection, risk assessment and monitoring (Holloway et al., 2006b). The potential environmental impacts of leakage and the possibilities for remediation of leaks also need to be considered.

16.5   Public acceptability

Given its stage of development, there is little public awareness of CCS technology. Opinion surveys have found that very few people in the UK have heard of CCS, although those who have do seem to know what environmental concern it addresses (Reiner, 2005). Support for CCS is mixed, although a large number have neither a positive nor a negative opinion of the technology. With additional information, particularly when conveyed by reliable sources, support for CCS does increase noticeably (Shackley *et al.*, 2005). The public most strongly supports the use of renewable energy to address global warming and as a target of future research. Offering cost and usage information results in a small shift from renewable energy towards nuclear energy and fossil fuel combustion with carbon capture and storage but, even then, renewable energy retains a strong appeal. In the UK, support for nuclear energy doubles from 9% to 18% when information is provided. Support for fossil energy with CCS increases ten-fold from 1% to 10% with information (Reiner *et al.*, 2006).

Nevertheless, as reflected in the public preferences expressed for government priorities, individual technologies and global warming strategies, the strength of public support for renewable energy as the preferred approach to addressing global warming is quite robust. Other approaches, such as CCS, will face a challenge to portray themselves in the same favourable light as renewables. Given the rather low level of public appreciation and the mixed reaction when made aware, those in positions to influence public opinion, such as environmental groups and the media, will play a large role in influencing the debate. CCS has several important attractions – it poses fewer problems for many environmental pressure groups, as it allows for a low-carbon central station power plant that is *not* nuclear power, and it is a plausible option for the rapidly growing developing world, particularly countries such as China, India and South Africa, which will be dependent upon coal in their electricity sector for many decades to come.

If the choice is posited as a zero-sum game between renewables, efficiency, nuclear and CCS, there will inevitably be strong opposition to CCS from NGOs, although not as strong or as deep as the long-standing opposition to nuclear power. If, instead, CCS is promoted as a bridging technology that does not interfere with the growth of renewables and efforts to promote energy efficiency, and particularly if the focus is on its potential role in developing countries such as China, then there is likely to be a tolerance, if not outright support, for CCS in the UK and more broadly across Europe.

The final element in determining public acceptance will be early successes (or failures) of major CCS projects. It is difficult to engage the public without real projects that make the potential a reality, and the media have tended to focus on specific, primarily storage, projects such as Sleipner and Snohvit in Norway, Gorgon in Australia, Weyburn in

Canada, and US projects such as Mountaineer, Frio Brine and Futuregen (Gough and Mander, 2006).

16.6   Deployment of CCS technologies

Unlike many other energy technologies that move from R&D to widespread deployment over the course of decades, most CCS technologies are essentially now ready to be deployed at scale. As the IPCC *Special Report* notes, each element from capture to transport to storage has already been deployed in mature markets, but what is missing is that:

There is relatively little experience in combining CO_2 capture, transport and storage into a fully integrated CCS system. The utilisation of CCS for large-scale power plants (the potential application of major interest) still remains to be implemented (IPCC, 2005, p. 7).

These two missing, but essential, elements of integration and power sector experience raise the question of who should take the role in facilitating such demonstrations, and what role government should play in encouraging such projects.

Table 16.5 reviews some of the proposals for deployment of a limited number of full-scale plants to open up the CCS option globally, including several in the UK. These projects would need to be started as soon as possible to achieve commissioning dates between 2010 and 2012, and would offer the opportunity to acquire the necessary experience to bolster utility and investor confidence for widespread deployment.

Assuming the resolution of key outstanding issues such as long-term liability and the nature of government support, then full-scale deployment could start as early as 2020, contingent upon reductions in the cost of capture, sufficient assurances for the cost of carbon, or a regulatory regime to support CCS. In the UK, such a time frame would allow for new electricity generation capacity to come on line to replace retired coal and nuclear plants.

The European Commission has called for 10–12 demonstration plants to be commissioned by 2015 (European Commission, 2007a). Based on the current activity, it would not be unreasonable to imagine perhaps ten commercial-scale plants in place by 2015 – there could be three or four in the European Union (at least one in both the UK and Germany, and perhaps others in Spain, Poland, Italy, the Netherlands and/or France), at least one each in Canada, Norway and Australia, three in the USA, and one in China.

In a similar vein, the MIT (2007) *Future of Coal* study calls for ten major global storage demonstration projects ($\sim$1 million tons CO_2) of

Table 16.5. *Global initial full-scale (>300MWe) deployment CCS projects*

Company/Project name	Fuel	Plant output/cost	Capture technology	Commissioning date*
BP DF1 Peterhead/Miller, UK	Natural gas	350MW	Autothermal reformer, pre-combustion	2010 (withdrawn by BP May 2007)
BP DF2 Carson, CA, USA	Petcoke	500MW (US$1bn)	Gasifier + shift	2011
Statoil/Shell Draugen, Norway	Natural gas	860MW	Post-combustion amine	2011
Hatfield Colliery UK	Bituminous coal	~500MW (£800m)	IGCC + pre-combustion	2011
SaskPower Saskatchewan, Canada	Lignite coal	300MW	Post-combustion or oxyfuel	2012
E.ON Lincolnshire coast, UK	Bituminous coal (+petcoke)	450MW	IGCC + pre-combustion	2012
Stanwell Queensland, Australia	Bituminous coal	N/A	IGCC + pre-combustion (Shell gasifier)	2012
RWE, Germany	Coal	450MW (€1bn)		2014
Progressive Energy/Centrica, Teesside	Coal	800MW	IGCC + pre-combustion	2010
RWE Tilbury, UK	Bituminous coal	~500 MW (£800m)	PC (supercritical retrofit) + post-combustion	2016 (with capture, SC retrofit possible earlier)

* Start date assuming that appropriate means are put in place in time by market regulators/government to allow the additional costs of CCS to be recovered.

Source: Information in the table is based on media reports, press releases and personal communication as of mid-2007 and should be regarded as indicative only

which three would be in the USA. It is unreasonable to expect coordination of projects, but such a number would allow for a diversity of approaches to develop across countries in terms of power plant technology, regulatory regimes, and storage options, and ensure greater debate and awareness of CCS in a number of countries.

16.7   UK policy considerations

There are several elements that underpin the UK policy context, including the future of oil extraction in the North Sea, the need for diversity in the electricity supply system, and ambitious government policy statements on climate change. Government action on CCS to date has included public consultations, policy statements, and some support for research and development activities, but the next critical stage involves determination of the need for, and possible form of, greater government support for commercial-scale implementation. The UK is one of the clear leaders on the international stage, as one of the most outspoken advocates for reforming international conventions to allow for the inclusion of CCS, but whether its words translate into actual industrial and regulatory leadership remains to be seen.

16.7.1   Domestic context

The first major government document in the area of CCS was the 2004 Carbon Abatement Technology (CAT) Strategy, which is focused on developing low-carbon technologies *from fossil fuels* in the power generation sector. Implementation lies with the Department of Trade and Industry's (now the Department for Business, Enterprise and Regulatory Reform) Cleaner Coal (now the Cleaner Fossil Fuels) Technology Programme. The government originally allocated £25 million to support technology demonstration, which was supplemented by an additional £10 million pledge in the 2005 *Pre-Budget Report*. The first call for proposals in September 2006 was worth £10 million and focused on the pre-commercial stage. The remaining £25 million, which is subject to a state aid review, will focus on technologies for use in existing power stations.

Although large relative to recent UK government funding of R&D in the energy sector, the funding is a small fraction of that needed for commercial-scale technologies, as seen in Section 16.3 on economics. A CO_2 price of €25 per tonne in the EU ETS would cover much of that difference and is, in any case, subject to the volatility of the ETS market. To truly incentivise new technologies, particularly for a limited number of plants, a useful model might be found in the recent US Energy Policy

Act of 2005. The Act sets aside US$800 million to fund an investment tax credit of 20% on capital that would encourage utilities to build IGCC plants by defraying the differential cost of IGCC relative to pulverised coal, and an additional US$850 million for other advanced coal and gasifier projects.

The UKs CAT strategy is not restricted to a focus on CCS; rather, major aspects include a focus on improving the efficiency of fossil fuel, particularly coal, generation. Indeed, the Treasury Consultation on Commercialisation describes CCS as 'the most radical CAT option' (H.M. Treasury, 2006a, p. 1). Another important element in the CAT strategy is co-firing coal with biomass to reduce emissions by roughly 10%. Renewables Obligation Certificates (ROCs) have been successful in providing incentives for biomass co-firing as well as onshore wind, but little else. The introduction of the EU ETS has heightened interest in a variety of low-carbon technologies, but ultimately the UK does not have a heavy burden since, as of 2007, it is one of the few EU Member States to be on course to meet its Kyoto target. Of course, the availability of low-cost options to meet near-term targets means that there is less incentive in the near term to invest in the technologies needed for more ambitious longer-term goals, such as the Government's target to reduce emissions by 60% by 2050.

R&D funding on CCS has also increased in the UK, facilitated by the launch of the Towards a Sustainable Economy (TSEC) Programme, with a £28 million budget, including funding for a UK Energy Research Centre. Carbon management is one of the broad themes being addressed by TSEC, with CCS being one of the technologies identified, resulting in the creation of a UK Carbon Capture and Storage Consortium (UKCCSC), involving researchers in engineering, geology and the social sciences (Gibbins *et al.*, 2006a). The EPSRC (Engineering and Physical Sciences Research Council) also individually supports energy innovation to encourage the development of new, longer-term options R&D, including conventional electricity generation (£2.5 million), combustion (£12 million), coal technology (£0.2 million), and oil and gas extraction (£2.8 million).

Given its possible role in extending the life of North Sea oil extraction, CCS (particularly storage) is of interest to Scotland. In August 2005, the Scottish Centre for Carbon Storage Research, based at the University of Edinburgh, was established with funding of close to £1.4 million from the Scottish Higher Education Council (SHEFC). The Centre is focused exclusively on storage, with particular emphasis on oil reservoirs (Scottish Enterprise, 2005).

Another argument in favour of CCS is that the UK possesses the necessary expertise within its existing offshore oil and gas industry, and that the oil and gas fields in the North Sea and their existing infrastructure might play a major role in CCS storage. As the CCS Inquiry noted:

The UK's geological expertise through the hydrocarbon industry and British Geological Survey is recognised to be amongst the best in the world. This expertise should be leveraged to facilitate and promote UK demonstrations of CCS and, ultimately, uptake of CCS internationally (HoC, 2006a, p. 22).

Before CCS can play a significant role in reducing carbon emissions, a number of challenging regulatory issues need to be resolved, both at home and abroad, including long-term liability. A CCS Regulatory Task Force was convened to consult with industry and other interested stakeholders in order to develop proposals on regulations that could facilitate CCS and to ensure the environmental integrity of CCS activities. A major focus has been on cost and economic feasibility.

British industry has also formed the first association bringing together all the major actors in the CCS value chain, including not just electric utilities and oil and gas companies but also equipment suppliers such as Alstom and Doosan Babcock, services companies such as Schlumberger, project management firms such as Amec, chemical companies such as BOC and Air Products, law firms and trade associations such as the British Cement Association.

The politics of CCS is also wrapped up in the wider politics of climate change, and in the UK that also means the debate over nuclear power. For example, in a pre-emptive effort to discourage the Government's embrace of nuclear new-build before the *Energy Review* announcement, the independent government-appointed Sustainable Development Commission argued that:

a sustainable energy policy would combine an aggressive suite of policies for energy efficiency and renewables, with the development of carbon capture and storage (CCS) technologies (Sustainable Development Commission, 2006, p. 13)

without the need for nuclear power.

Many environmental groups such as Green Alliance, WWF, Friends of the Earth, and even Greenpeace, have also adopted a generally positive or neutral view of CCS compared with their continued hostility towards nuclear power, although they have raised concerns about the level of government support and the potential to detract from moving towards more rapid adoption of renewable energy sources and energy efficiency (HoC, 2006b, Ev 32–36, Ev 174–179, Ev 201–202).

Consultation with many stakeholders in the 2006 *Energy Review* did relatively little to change the terms under which CCS is considered. The

British Government has a number of domestic, bilateral, EU and multilateral initiatives under way and the *Energy Review* did relatively little other than to catalogue the efforts already in progress.

One element that did receive increased attention in the 2006 *Energy Review* was the potential role of indigenous coal. The possibility of extending the life, or even expanding the role, of coal in the electricity mix is especially appealing to unions and other supporters of indigenous coal production. For example, Huw Irranca-Davies, MP, called for Welsh coal to be burnt in coal-fired power stations with CCS (BBC News, 2005). As recently as 2004, the DTI published a study of coal production prospects which showed UK coal burn declining to 7 million tonnes from 23.5 million tonnes in 2006 (DTI, 2004).

The 2006 *Energy Review* called for the creation of a 'Coal Forum', which would bring together coal-fired generators, coal producers and suppliers, power plant suppliers, unions, and others 'in order to help them to find solutions to secure the long-term generation and UK coal production' (DTI, 2006). In addition, the Clean Coal Task Group, a joint industry/union/government advisory body, has been established to advise on the creation of such a framework. The Group also calls for reform of planning procedures, such as removing existing 'presumption against' planning guidance which, they argue, 'impedes developments of new surface or deep mines' (Clean Coal Task Group, 2006).

16.7.2   EU and international context

In parallel to the domestic effort, there have also been a number of European initiatives in which the UK has played a leading role and which will impact on the UK. The most comprehensive is the recently launched European Technology Platform for Zero Emission Fossil Fuel Power Plants (ZEP), which underpins 'an EU-wide initiative which integrates *all* aspects of CO_2 capture, transport and storage – including technology, infrastructure, the environment, health and safety, legal and regulatory issues, funding mechanisms, public communication and international collaboration' (European Commission, 2007a).

There has also been EU support for research and development. Under the Fifth and Sixth Framework Programmes (2000–2009) the EU contributed more than €170 million, including support for CO_2Geonet – a major effort to coordinate geological research led by the British Geological Survey. To date, the funding has been divided roughly 55% on capture, 40% on storage, and 5% on cross-cutting activities. Funding seems set to increase even more dramatically. The Seventh Framework Programme (FP7), which was launched in 2007, sees a large increase in funding for energy research activities to €2.35 billion and CCS has been listed as one of the priorities under FP7 (European Commission, 2007b).

There has also been extensive work by British and European diplomats to try to alter the international and regional conventions governing storage of carbon dioxide under the sea bed – the London Convention and the Oslo–Paris (Ospar) Convention for the North-East Atlantic. Not surprisingly, these treaties were silent on whether storing carbon dioxide should be defined as a waste disposal, but the London Convention was amended in 2006 and considerable progress has been made in amending Ospar to allow for the storage of carbon dioxide below the seabed (Haszeldine *et al.*, 2007).

The Government has also worked to put CCS on the international agenda. During the British Presidency of the G8, climate change was one of the two major focal areas, and the G8 plan of action adopted at Gleneagles called for accelerating

the development and commercialisation of Carbon Capture and Storage technology focusing on the IEA working with the Carbon Sequestration Leadership Forum in working with industry, collaborating with developing countries, examining the capture-ready concept, looking into EOR, and working with civil society (G8, 2005).

In the hopes of encouraging the potential of CCS in developing countries, there have also been efforts to reconcile CCS with the EU ETS, as well as to accommodate CCS within the Clean Development Mechanism (CDM).

The UK has been one of the leaders in fostering international activity on CCS by signing the first Memorandum of Understanding with China on CCS and initiating the formation (and funding) of the EU–China NZEC (Near Zero Emissions Coal) Demonstration Project. The recently inaugurated UK–India Education and Research Initiative (which includes Shell and BP as two of the four founding industrial sponsors) has also identified CCS as one of the key areas for collaboration.

At the bilateral level, in late 2005, British and Norwegian Energy Ministers signed an agreement to form a North Sea Basin Task Force. A meeting between the UK Chancellor of the Exchequer and the Norwegian Prime Minister further extended cooperation by committing both countries to explore development of a commercial plant with CCS. The joint programme of work includes examining the need for a pipeline infrastructure in the North Sea, as well as developing rules for CCS within the context of the EU ETS (H.M. Treasury, 2006b)

The momentum all builds towards the decision of what support, aside from the incentive available through the EU ETS, the Government should offer to a first-of-a-kind plant and then to subsequent plants. The current plan has begun with a call for a tender for a study into the development of the transport and storage infrastructure needed in the North Sea. Insofar as the Government has an interest in the cheapest near-term CO_2 reductions, then the ETS offers a market for such reductions; but, given the relatively few levers to affect energy security or the fuel mix for electricity generation, providing limited incentives for CCS at an early stage may be an attractive proposition.

16.8   Conclusions

CCS challenges the conventional arc of development found in many other new technologies, reflecting the scales involved even in many of the first projects. It may be helpful, for example, to describe other technologies as moving through the demonstration, scaling-up and commercialisation phases; but these development phases do not easily apply in the case of CCS. The oil industry currently injects some 30 million tCO_2 into oil fields for EOR. The storage of roughly 1 million tCO_2 by Statoil in the Sleipner field in the North Sea and BP's project at In Salah in Algeria are first-of-a-kind projects, but their annual storage is significant; for example, Sleipner alone offsets 2% of Norway's total emissions (Jakobsen *et al.*, 2005).

Any one of the first announced 'demonstration' plants in the UK would, by itself, reduce emissions by a large fraction of total installed wind-power capacity in the UK. It is not the individual technology components, *per se*, that need demonstration; rather, it is the novelty of the concept and of the entire chain that requires greater scrutiny from both investors and developers, as well as from NGOs, the general public and local communities.

For carbon capture and storage technologies to become a major component in global efforts to mitigate climate change, there will need to be further advancements in geology, in engineering, and in tying the various stages in the CCS 'supply chain' together. Some potential storage sites, primarily those in the oil and gas sector, are well characterised, but more information on the subsurface is still needed and the necessity of source–sink matching will mean that some countries (and regions) will be better placed to carry out large-scale storage. On the capture side, there are some 'low-hanging fruit' available with relatively pure CO_2 streams and low separation costs, with important (but limited) appeal; but for CCS to have major impact its adoption in electricity generation, particularly coal-fired generation, will be required. Doing so will require not just testing of individual stages in the CCS chain but also experience in putting together the entire chain from source to sink.

Envisioning a significant role for CCS in reducing emissions would require a massive global infrastructure along the lines of the existing infrastructure in the oil and gas sector – not unimaginable but vast. Those who envision the end state discuss the possibility of storing many billion tonnes of CO_2 underground, with an annual flux of hundreds of millions, or even billions, of tonnes per year. This could equate to injection operations and pipeline networks of the same magnitude as those already in existence. For example, abating one Gigatonne of carbon ($\sim$3.6 Gt CO_2) per year, or roughly 20% of current global emissions, would require the injection of roughly 60 million barrels of supercritical CO_2 each day, or two-thirds of the current global petroleum production volume (Friedmann, 2006).

CCS in the UK is driven by a timely convergence of unrelated factors (Gibbons *et al.*, 2006b) Concerns over the stability of possible gas suppliers, interest in the life-extension of North Sea fields, which benefits Scottish regional development and postpones decommissioning costs, and ambitious commitments to reduce greenhouse gas emissions, all converge to make CCS attractive in the UK. Another compelling reason for the UK to demonstrate the viability of CCS is to show rapidly developing, coal-rich countries such as China and India that CCS can be an attractive option.

At the same time, governments are frustrated by the relatively weak control they can exert over electricity markets at a critical juncture in the evolution of the UK electricity sector. This timing has conspired to link CCS to the decisions that need to be taken over the future of the electric sector during the coming decade. The UK must therefore rely on other EU Member State governments to treat the issue sufficiently seriously so that the ETS will produce a price of at least €25/tCO_2.

The biggest challenge of CCS in the UK over the near term may be that its remarkably rapid ascent up the agenda makes it difficult for governments to respond to calls for significant support in a correspondingly short period of time. As indicated by the proliferation of proposals, there is no shortage of private-sector interest, but in all those cases the combination of the current high oil price and the prevailing ETS price does not warrant development of CCS without further assurances with regard to the regime that will ultimately govern it.

CCS would clearly be economic with a subsidy equivalent to that currently in place for renewables. At a time of record profits in both the oil and gas and electricity sectors, significant subsidies to major energy companies seem implausible; thus any support will probably be targeted and limited in time until the CO_2 price alone is sufficient to drive investment in CCS. Indeed, it is not simply financial support but the creation of regulatory structures and long-term mechanisms that will determine the eventual deployment of CCS technologies in the UK, the EU and globally.

References

APEC Secretariat (2005). *Carbon Dioxide Capture and Geological Sequestration Potential of the APEC Region (Phase 2)*, Report prepared by Delphi Group and Alberta Research Council. Singapore: APEC Secretariat.

BBC News (2005). MP's clean coal energy solution: unmined coal in Wales could be the answer to Britain's energy crisis, *BBC News*, 12 October.

BP (2005). BP and partners plan clean energy plant in Scotland, increasing oil recovery and reducing emissions, *BP Press Release*, 30 June. Available at: www.bp.com/genericarticle.do?categoryId=2012968&contentId=7006999

Bradshaw. J., Bachu, S., Bonijoly, D., Burruss, R., Holloway, S., Christensen, N.-P. Mathiasen, O.-M. (2007). CO_2 storage capacity estimation: issues and development of standards, *International Journal of Greenhouse Gas Control* 1, 62–68.

Clean Coal Task Group (2006). *Framework for Clean Coal in Britain*, 7 June.

Department of Trade and Industry (DTI) (2003). *Our Energy Future: Creating a Low Carbon Economy*. London: TSO.

(2004). *UK Coal Production Outlook: 2004–16*, conducted by Mott MacDonald, London: Department of Trade and Industry.

(2006). *The Energy Challenge*. London: TSO.

(2007). *Energy Trends and Quarterly Energy Prices*. Available at: www.dtistats. net/energystats/et_mar07.pdf

ECL Technology (2005). *CO_2 Flooding of UKCS Reservoirs: DTI Oil and Gas Maximising Recovery Programme*, Updated June 2005. Available at: www. og-mrp.com/dissemination/co2/co2_ogmrp_overview_update_eb250406.pdf

European Commission (2007a). *The EU Flagship Programme: the key to making CO_2 capture and storage (CCS) commercially viable by 2020*. ZEP General Assembly, Paris, 3 October.

(2007b). *Energy Research in the 7th Framework Programme*, Directorate-General for Research/Directorate Energy, Report EUR 22576, Brussels.

European Council [Council of the European Union] (2007). *Presidency Conclusions*, 7224/1/07 Rev 1, Brussels, 2 May. Available at: www.consilium. europa.eu/ueDocs/cms_Data/docs/pressData/en/ec/93135.pdf

Foxon, T.J. (2002). *Technological and Institutional 'Lock-in' as a Barrier to Sustainable Innovation*, ICCEPT Working Paper. Available at: www3.imperial. ac.uk/pls/portallive/docs/1/7294726.PDF

Friedmann, S.J. (2006). Defining an end state for CO_2 sequestration and EOR in North America, *Proceedings of the GHGT-8 Conference*, Trondheim, Norway, 19–22 June.

G8 (2005). *Gleneagles Plan of Action: Climate Change, Clean Energy and Sustainable Development*. Available at: www.fco.gov.uk/Files/kfile/Post-G8_Gleneagles_ CCChangePlanofAction.pdf

Gibbins, J., Haszeldine, S., Holloway, S., Pearce, J., Oakey, J., Reiner, D. and Turley, C. (2006a). 'Interim results from the UK Carbon Capture and Storage Consortium Project', *Proceedings of the GHGT-8 Conference*, Trondheim, Norway, 19–22 June.

Gibbins, J., Haszeldine, S., Holloway, S., Pearce, J., Oakey, J., Shackley S., and Turley, C. (2006b). Scope for future CO_2 emission reductions from electricity generation through the deployment of carbon capture and storage technologies, Ch. 40 in *Avoiding Dangerous Climate Change*, Ed. H.J. Schellnhuber. Cambridge: Cambridge University Press.

Gough, C. and Mander, S. (2006). *Carbon Dioxide Capture and Storage in the Media*, Tyndall Centre for Climate Change Research, Report Prepared for the IEA Greenhouse Gas R&D Programme.

Haszeldine, R.S., Reiner, D.M., Shackley, S., Kendall, M. (2007). Regulation for CCS beneath the UK offshore and onshore: deep geological storage and sequestration of CO_2, *Expert Workshop on Regulation of Deep Geological Sequestration of Carbon Dioxide*, Resources for the Future, Washington, DC, 15–16 March. Available at: www.irgc.org/IMG/pdf/IRGC_CCS_Haszeldine07.pdf

H.M. Treasury (2006a). *Carbon Capture and Storage: A Consultation on Barriers to Commercial Deployment*, March.

H.M. Treasury (2006b). *Infrastructure and value chain for CO_2 Transport and Storage in the North Sea: Joint Programme by the UK and Norway*, 2006 Pre-Budget Report. Available at: www.hm-treasury.gov.uk/media/E/B/pbr06_carboncapture_uknorway.pdf

Holloway, S., Karimjee, A., Akai, M., Pipatti, R. and Rypdal K. (2006). Carbon dioxide transport and storage, Ch. 5 in *2006 IPCC Guidelines for National Greenhouse Gas Inventories, Volume 2: Energy*, Eds. H.S. Eggleston, L. Buendia, K. Miwa, T. Ngara and K. Tanabe. Hayama, Japan: IGES/IPCC.

Holloway, S. Vincent, C.J., Bentham, M.S. and Kirk, K.L. (2006b). Top-down and bottom-up estimates of CO_2 storage capacity in the UK sector of the Southern North Sea Basin, *Environmental Geoscience* 13(2), 71–84.

House of Commons Science and Technology Committee (HoC) (2006a). *Meeting UK Energy and Climate Needs: The Role of Carbon Capture and Storage, Volume I*. London: Stationery Office HC 578-I. Available at: www. publications.parliament.uk/pa/cm200506/cmselect/cmsctech/578/578i.pdf

House of Commons Science and Technology Committee (HoC) (2006b). *Meeting UK Energy and Climate Needs: The Role of Carbon Capture and Storage, Volume II Oral and Written Evidence*. London: Stationery Office HC 578-II. Available at: www.publications.parliament.uk/pa/cm200506/cmselect/cmsctech/578/578ii.pdf

IEA GHG [International Energy Agency Greenhouse Gas R&D Programme] (2006). *CO_2 Capture as a Factor in Power Station Investment Decisions*, Report 2006/8, Cheltenham, UK.

IPCC [Intergovernmental Panel on Climate Change] (2005). *Special Report on Carbon Dioxide Capture and Storage*. Cambridge: Cambridge University Press.

Jakobsen, V.E., Hauge, F., Holm M., and Kristiansen, B. (2005). *Environment and Value Creation: CO_2 for EOR on the Norwegian Shelf – A Case Study*, Bellona Report, August.

Jordal K., Anhedan, H., Yan, J., Strömberg, L. (2004). Oxyfuel combustion for coal-fired power generation with CO_2 capture. In E.S. Rubin, D.W. Keith and C.F. Gilboy (eds.) *Proceedings of 7th International Conference on Greenhouse Gas Control Technologies*, vol. 1, Peer-reviewed Papers and Plenary Presentations 2004: IEA Greenhouse Gas Programme, Cheltenham, UK.

Kirk, K.L. (2006). Storing carbon dioxide in the rocks beneath the East Irish Sea, *Proceedings of the GHGT-8 Conference*, Trondheim, Norway, 19–22 June.

Marsh, G. (2003). *Carbon Dioxide Capture and Storage: A Win–Win Option? (The Economic Case)*, DTI Cleaner Fossil Fuels Programme Report R233, DTI/ Pub URN 03/812. Available at: www.berr.gov.uk/files/file18798.pdf

MIT [Massachusetts Institute of Technology] (2007). '*The Future of Coal*'. Cambridge, MA: MIT Press.

Parliamentary Office of Science and Technology (POST) (2005a). *Carbon Capture and Storage (CCS)*, POST Note Number 238, March.

Parliamentary Office of Science and Technology (POST) (2005b). *Cleaner Coal*, POST Note Number 253, December.

Platts (2007). *International Coal Report*, 1 January.

Reiner, D.M. (2005). P*ublic Attitudes towards Carbon Capture and Storage Technologies in Britain*, Written testimony submitted to the House of Commons Committee on Science and Technology (Ev 155).

Reiner, D.M., Curry, T.E., de Figueiredo, Herzog, H.J., Ansolabehere, S.D., Itaoka, K., Johnsson, F., and Odenberger, M. (2006). American exceptionalism? Similarities and differences in national attitudes towards energy policy and global warming, *Environmental Science and Technology* **40** (7), 2093–2098.

Rokke, N. (2006). CO_2 capture, transport and storage for coal, oil and gas: technology overview, Ch. 7 in *Future Electricity Technologies and Systems*, Eds. T. Jamasb, W.J. Nuttall and M.G. Pollitt. Cambridge: Cambridge University Press.

Scottish Enterprise (2005). *Carbon Capture and Storage Market Opportunities*, September.

Shackley, S., McLachlan, C. and Gough, C. (2005).s The Public perception of carbon capture and storage in the UK: results from focus groups and a survey, *Climate Policy* 4(4), 377–398.

Stern, N. (2007). *The Stern Review on the Economics of Climate Change*, Cambridge: Cambridge University Press.

Sustainable Development Commission (SDC) (2006). *SDC Submission to the DTI Energy Review, Meeting the Challenge: Energy Policy for the 21st Century*, April 2006.

Tzimas, E., Georgakaki, A., Garcia Cortes, C. and Peteves, S.D. (2005). E*nhanced Oil Recovery using Carbon Dioxide in the European Energy System*, European Commission Directorate General Joint Research Centre Report EUR 21895 EN. Petten, The Netherlands: Institute for Energy.

Unruh, G.C. and Carrillo-Hermosilla, J. (2006). Globalizing carbon lock-in, *Energy Policy* **34**(10), 1185–1197.

van der Veer, J. (2006). Vision for meeting energy needs beyond oil, *Financial Times*, 24 January.

Webb, T. (2007). There's change in the air at Drax: Europe's biggest producer of coal-fired power is out to prove that it can clean up its act, *The Independent*, 4 March.

17 Reconsidering public acceptance of renewable energy technologies: a critical review

Patrick Devine-Wright

Public acceptance is recognised as an important issue shaping the widespread implementation of renewable energy technologies and the achievement of energy policy targets. Furthermore, it is commonly assumed that 'public attitudes' need to change to make more radical scenarios about the implementation of renewable energy technologies feasible. This chapter critically summarises existing social research on the acceptance of renewable energy technologies, and provides a novel classification of personal, psychological and contextual factors that combine to shape public acceptance. It concludes by arguing the need for more systematic research on public acceptance driven by coherent theoretical frameworks drawn from psychology and other social science disciplines, explicit definitions of concepts, the use of innovative methodological tools, and a greater emphasis upon symbolic and affective aspects.

17.1 Introduction to social and psychological research

Concerns about energy security and climate change are driving significant changes in how energy, and electricity specifically, is generated, transmitted and consumed in the UK. The 2003 *Energy White Paper* contains a commitment to reduce carbon emissions by 60% by 2050, in comparison with 1990 levels, and aims for 20% of total electricity generation to be generated from renewable resources by 2020 (Department of Trade and Industry, 2003). Such targets necessitate that low-carbon technologies for generating energy, including renewable energy technologies that generate electricity from wind, sun, biomass and ocean sources, become commonplace, rather than 'alternative', as is currently the case. There are many factors that will determine the successful implementation of renewable energy technologies, one of which is widely assumed to be 'public acceptance' (e.g. Ekins, 2004), given that,

443

in the recent past, there has been widespread local opposition towards renewable energy developments, particularly wind and biomass (Toke, 2005; Upham and Shackley, 2006; Warren *et al.*, 2005). This recognition that public acceptability is a necessary condition of technology development and diffusion demands a deeper understanding of social and psychological processes, since our current level of understanding of public views about, and responses to, renewable energy technologies, the local experience of resistance and consent, and the ways in which public engagement with renewable energy technologies is constructed and practised in the UK, is both limited and restricted, excepting a few case-studies of bioenergy and onshore wind energy developments.

Empirical studies of public views about renewable energy technologies have, with a small number of exceptions, typically used a quantitative research methodology and targeted views about renewable energy generally (often through large-scale opinion polls), or views about the siting of renewable energy technologies in a particular location (typically through smaller-scale case studies). Although usually labelled as researching public 'perceptions' or 'attitudes', and using social research methodologies such as questionnaire surveys and comparative sampling techniques, few studies at either general or local level have been informed by theoretical frameworks from social science disciplines such as psychology.

Studies that have targeted general public views about renewable energy are often characterised by a market-research approach that uses descriptive rather than probabilistic statistical analyses to illustrate public beliefs and responses to specific technologies. McGowan and Sauter (2005) reviewed 33 studies of public opinion within the UK conducted since 2000, noting that 11 were commissioned by Government (e.g. DTI, 2003), 10 by industry (e.g. BWEA, BNFL), 6 by the media (e.g. BBC Newsnight) and 5 by NGOs (e.g. Greenpeace). Only one poll was commissioned by an academic organisation (MIT, see Curry *et al.*, 2005). The studies are more successful in providing one-off snapshots of public views (even if the large samples are more representative of target populations than many academic studies) than a more detailed explanation of underlying causes that may be generalised across different contexts and can help to build theory.

More generally, there is, as yet, little coherence in the literature as a whole, either in the sense of clarifying what 'public acceptance' or 'public resistance' means, or how this may relate to the unit of analysis of the research, which has included terms such as public perceptions, public opinion, public beliefs, public attitudes, public awareness, public understanding, social representations, or risk perceptions. Although there is an emerging consensus, at least amongst academics, that

NIMBYism is a deficient conceptual basis from which to explain a lack of acceptance of, or resistance to, energy technologies (Devine-Wright, 2005a; Warren *et al.*, 2005; Owens and Driffil, 2006; Wolsink, 2006), as yet there is little in the way of alternative, coherent conceptual frameworks proposed to replace the NIMBY concept and to guide social research. As a recent study concluded 'there is a need to develop a research agenda for understanding the role of subjectivity in wind energy debate' (Ellis *et al.*, 2006, p. 22). This chapter aims to help develop this research agenda by reviewing research on public awareness and understanding, and by pulling out discrete factors that the literature has indicated may shape public acceptance.

17.2   Studies of public awareness and understanding

At the general level, studies have attempted to identify levels of public understanding and awareness of different forms of energy technology and their impacts. These have produced a rather mixed set of findings, in part due to the varied nature of the questions asked. McGowan and Sauter (2005, p. 12) suggested that respondents 'tended to have only a vague idea of where energy was used but a rather better sense of the sources of energy'. Results suggest high levels of awareness that energy use is rising in the UK (e.g. Eurobarometer, 2003), that energy sources are varied and often imported into the UK (e.g. Populus, 2005), that renewable energy, particularly technologies such as solar panels, are strongly supported, both in the UK and across Europe, but that most individuals are reluctant to pay more for energy generated from renewable resources (Eurobarometer, 2006).

Although individuals are aware of different energy sources, results suggest that more in-depth understanding of these sources varies markedly, and that terms used by experts to refer to different kinds of fuels or resources are not always familiar to members of the public. For example, a study conducted by Devine-Wright (2003) found that many respondents believed 'natural gas' to be a form of renewable energy, whilst awareness of the term 'biomass' as a form of renewable energy was low. The term 'renewable energy' itself seems to be problematic – for example, only 4% of the general public and 3% of an 'informed' sample used the term 'renewable energy' in one study conducted with a representative sample (DTI *et al.*, 2003). It has been concluded that members of the public relate to specific renewable energy resources or technologies more than the general term; and wind, solar and hydro are most widely recognised (e.g. awareness by over 70% of respondents), in contrast to biomass (approximately 20% awareness) (DTI *et al.*, 2003;

MORI Social Research Institute, 2004; Curry *et al.*, 2005). Such findings have implications for the ways in which organisations and institutions engage with the public – the use of unfamiliar terms such as 'biomass' or 'renewable energy', for example, may be counterproductive.

Studies indicate that awareness and understanding also varies over the links between energy sources and climate change. Large-scale surveys of public attitudes towards the environment have noted generally low levels of awareness of the links between energy consumption and climate change, as well as a significant minority believing that technologies such as mobile phones are a major cause of climate change. In terms of energy generation, Poortinga *et al.* (2006) noted that 39% of respondents believed that nuclear power causes climate change – a finding that they note is consistent with previous studies – whilst two studies of carbon capture and storage have indicated low levels of awareness (Curry *et al.*, 2005; Shackley *et al.*, 2005).

Sources of information were probed by several research studies. These suggested that, in rural areas, local newspapers play a significant role (e.g. Braunholtz, 2003; DTI *et al.*, 2003; MORI Social Research Institute, 2004) whilst, more generally, TV is the main source of information about renewable energy mentioned by survey respondents, as well as direct experience such as having personally seen or visited wind farms. Knowledge about renewable energy sources has been shown to be higher in individuals living close to actual developments but tends to be restricted to the particular technology used in that development (DTI *et al.*, 2003).

Taken as a whole, these empirical studies suggest reasonably high levels of awareness of energy issues and sources; the 'iconic' nature of wind and solar as examples of sources of renewable energy; and low levels of familiarity with less familiar sources or technologies such as biomass, renewable energy and carbon capture.

17.3   Explaining public acceptance

Empirical studies tend to show high levels of public support for renewable energy technologies, both in the UK and across Europe (Eurobarometer, 2006). Approximately two-thirds of the UK public support further investment in renewable energy technologies, particularly wind energy, in comparison to approximately one-third support for nuclear energy, and this support has been quite stable since 2000 (McGowan and Sauter, 2005). Solar technology is the most positively regarded form of renewable energy technology, and there is evidence of polarisation of opinion around support for wind energy, with 20% of the public against it whilst 28% are strongly in favour (DTI *et al.*, 2003).

A variety of potential explanations can be identified in the literature for varying levels of public acceptance of different renewable energy technologies; however, these have rarely been analysed and categorised in detail and, in some cases, research is underdeveloped. McGowan and Sauter's review (2005) cited several personal and contextual factors explaining public views, but omitted explanations at the social–psychological level; whilst Wolsink's empirical analysis (2000) omitted contextual factors. In the following section, I provide a broader review, classifying a range of potential explanations at three levels of analysis:

- *personal* (age, gender, class, income)
- *social–psychological* (knowledge and direct experience, perceived impacts, environmental and political beliefs, place attachment)
- *contextual* (technology type and scale, institutional structure, and spatial context).

This classification builds upon environmental psychological theory (e.g. Black *et al.*, 1985; Guagnano *et al.*, 1995) in examining psychological and non-psychological influences upon environmentally significant attitudes and behaviour.

17.3.1 Personal factors

Socio-demographic characteristics such as age, gender and social class   Some regional surveys have found both higher levels of awareness and opposition towards renewable energy amongst older respondents (MORI Social Research Institute, 2003; Somerset County Council, 2004). In contrast, a national study found levels of awareness and opposition to be lower in younger and older cohorts (ages 16–24 and 65+) in comparison with middle-aged respondents (ages 35–44 and 55–64). Levels of support for nuclear energy seem to correlate with age, with older people being more supportive than young people (e.g. ICM Research, 2005; Populus, 2005). A London study of micro-scale renewables (e.g. solar PV) found that older respondents were more aware of these technologies, but less likely to install them, in comparison with younger respondents (London Renewables, 2003).

In terms of gender, existing studies have produced results showing differences between women and men, depending upon the focus of awareness: support for renewable energy generally, support for specific renewable technologies, and support for nuclear. For example, the Times/Populus survey indicated strong support by women for new renewable energy development (90%) in comparison with men (66%);

however, a national survey identified higher levels of awareness of renewables amongst men (85% vs. 67%) but lower levels of support for development in the locality (31% vs. 23%; DTI *et al.*, 2003). Women seem to support wind farms less than men do (e.g. DTI *et al.*, 2003; MORI Social Research Institute, 2003, 2004). There also seems to be a higher preference for nuclear power amongst men than women (e.g. 33% vs. 11%; ICM Research, 2005).

In terms of social class, there seems to be a positive correlation between income and class, and levels of support for both renewable energy *and* nuclear power. Separate studies suggest that individuals earning in excess of £30,000 per annum, and classified in AB social classes in comparison with DE, were more supportive of new nuclear power stations, renewable energy generally, and wind energy (e.g. MORI Social Research Institute, 2004; ICM Research, 2005).

17.3.2   Psychological factors

Degree of awareness and understanding   Although studies of public acceptance have been driven by the assumption that negative perceptions are embedded in deficits in public understanding, there is limited evidence that more informed individuals are more accepting of renewable energy technologies. Correlations between knowledge and acceptance were found in two studies (DTI *et al.*, 2003; MORI Social Research Institute, 2004); however, a third study noted that levels of support were independent of levels of awareness, high or low (London Renewables, 2003). Despite this, many organisations assume that awareness-raising will lead to more favourable attitudes, as evidenced by attempts to make the technologies more familiar to individuals through site visits, information provision and photomontages.

Political beliefs   Empirical findings suggest that political beliefs are correlated with social acceptance of different low-carbon technologies. For example, Populus (2005) indicated that 37% of individuals indicating support for the Conservative party were supportive of new nuclear power stations (in comparison with only 12% of Labour supporters and 14% of Liberal Democrat supporters) whilst being less strongly supportive of new renewable energy developments (62% as against 86% and 84%, respectively).

Perceived impacts   Many studies have investigated how individuals conceive the impacts, positive and negative, of renewable energy technologies, presuming that negative impacts equate with a lack of acceptance. Since such technologies are diverse, and since each technology captures different natural resources in different ways, the perceived impacts of technology siting vary. Public perceptions of a biomass plant may chiefly relate to the impacts of truck movements, changes in the appearance of the landscape and emitted smells (Upham and Shackley, 2006), whereas perceptions of wind energy focus more upon the perceived visual impacts of the turbines, noise levels and perceived economic impacts on residential property values and tourism (Warren et al., 2005). At a more general level, future research needs to systematise the measurement of perceived impacts, ensuring that they are captured across environmental, economic, personal and social aspects; and can vary across scales from local to national to global; and in time from now to the more distant future. Furthermore, research needs to be sensitive to how individuals make sense of ambivalent perceptions of both positive and negative perceived impacts, and how these interrelate with other factors to lead to behavioural responses.

Environmental beliefs and concern   There is some evidence that support for renewable energy technologies is motivated by levels of environmental concern. For example, Poortinga et al. (2006) identified high levels of public support for energy policy making to be driven by the goal of environmental protection. This study also indicated discriminatory levels of public support across different types of technologies designed to mitigate climate change, with 77% of a representative national sample of 1,462 individuals preferring the increased deployment of renewable energy technologies over new fossil fuel or nuclear power stations (Poortinga et al., 2006). However, findings from other studies suggest a more complex relationship between environmental concern and public acceptance of renewable energy technologies, depending upon the scale of 'environment' that is the focus of public concern, and how the various impacts of such technologies are evaluated at different scales. For example, Warren et al. (2005) noted that social conflict over proposed renewable energy technology developments such as wind farms can be characterised by action motivated by environmental concern on both sides of the conflict. Supportive individuals may be principally concerned about the impacts of climate change at the global scale, and they are opposed by individuals concerned for the environmental impacts of technologies in valued localities; a conflict characterised as 'green' on 'green'.

Place attachment   Generally, few studies of public acceptance of local developments have considered the potential significance of affective aspects of people–place or people–technology interactions. On the theme of local environments and public acceptance, the possibility that emotional attachments to places are implicated in public responses was suggested by Devine-Wright (2005a), who noted that high levels of place attachment (cf. Altman and Low, 1992) – that is, positive emotional bonds between people and valued environments – can serve to motivate both public support *and* opposition to proposed technology developments, depending upon whether the technological development is evaluated as posing a threat or an opportunity to the individual and/ or locality/community more generally. However, few studies have empirically analysed this relationship, with the exception of a Norwegian study that indicated how support for a large-scale hydro-power development was positively explained by the strength of attachment to affected areas, and that this factor was more significant than socio-demographic characteristics such as age or gender in explaining public acceptance (Vorkinn and Riese, 2001).

The relevance of the concept of 'place' has been recognised in literature on risk and wind energy conflicts. Simmons and Walker (2004, p. 91) argued that

a focus upon a sense of place enables us to develop a richer understanding of how technological activities and their associated risks can encroach upon people's feelings about where they live and compromise associated place values.

Similarly, Haggett and Smith's (2004) analysis of conflicts over wind energy concluded that

it is crucial to consider the importance of 'place', the local social and historical context of an area, and the attachment that people have to their local environment ... views are developed in the context of immediate surroundings, and any changes to this are a perceived threat to identity (Haggett and Smith, 2004, p. 5).

This suggests fruitful avenues for future research, to use the concept of place to better understand local responses to the siting of renewable energy technologies 'in place', and to specifically focus upon the affective bonds between person and environment that may influence public acceptance.

Perceived fairness of the development process and levels of trust in key actors   Several recent studies have illustrated how perceptions of fairness and levels of trust are implicated in the public acceptance of renewable energy developments. Zoellner *et al.* (2005) used a questionnaire to study the attitudes of 291 German residents towards wind energy development decision-making, drawing upon an extensive literature within the field of political science on theories of equity and justice. Their results indicate that procedural justice (i.e. the subjectively perceived fairness of a decision-making process) was significant in explaining people's negative attitudes towards wind energy, particularly concerning zoning, planning and licensing decisions. There were high levels of mistrust in political decision makers, who were considered to be in coalition with private development organisations. Similar results were found by Upham and Shackley (2006), researching public opposition to biomass plant in the UK, who found low levels of trust in key actors in the development, including the developer, local authority and regional development organisation, which in turn influenced public responses to information and assessments provided as part of the statutory planning process. The studies suggest that 'how' renewable energy technologies are sited, in addition to 'what' technologies are sited, are important factors in shaping public acceptance and responses; that pre-existing levels of mistrust in local political institutions and processes may undermine support for the siting of renewable energy technologies; and that further research is required to deepen our understanding of the interplay between general views about energy technologies and views about local siting, in part shaped by aspects of the development process.

17.3.3   Contextual factors

Technological factors: scale and type   Renewable technologies for energy generation are diverse, encompassing solar photovoltaic panels; wind turbines of different scale, design, and on- or offshore location; energy from waste plants (e.g. anaerobic digestion or incineration); biomass-fuelled plant at scales from small combined heat and power plants to large-scale power stations (e.g. combusting short rotation coppice); hydro schemes and ocean technologies (e.g. tidal and wave devices). Since each technology captures different natural resources in different ways, the environmental, economic and social impacts of each technology vary. Wind turbines have been by far the most widespread and socially contentious renewable energy technology to date and, therefore, more research has been conducted on public perceptions and attitudes to this form of renewable technology in comparison with the others.

It is possible to classify three scales of implementation of renewable energy technology:

- *micro* (at single building or household level)
- *meso* (at the local, community or town level)
- *macro* (at large-scale 'power station' level).

Since each scale of technology will present different impacts on the local economy, community and environment, public attitudes towards, and engagement with, renewable energy technologies implemented at different scales are likely to vary considerably. The majority of existing research on public attitudes has been at the macro-level, focusing upon the social impacts of larger-scale energy developments, although research at meso- and micro-scales has recently emerged (e.g. meso: Walker *et al.*, 2007; micro: London Renewables, 2003; Hub Research Consultants, 2005). In relation to the scale of wind energy development, there are consistent results suggesting that proposed wind farms that are smaller in scale are more positively accepted. Lee *et al.* (1989) referred to a 'favourability gradient' in noting a negative linear relationship between wind farm size and public support. This finding has been replicated in Denmark (AIM Research A/S, 1993), the Netherlands (Wolsink, 1989) and the Republic of Ireland (Sustainable Energy Ireland, 2003). Few studies at the micro-level have been conducted, although there is some literature from the 1980s studying the determinants of adoption of solar thermal technology (e.g. Guagnano *et al.*, 1986). A study in London identified high levels of support for solar (81%) and micro-wind (75%) (London Renewables, 2003), while a study in Wales found that 77% of respondents supported the idea of individual Welsh homes producing electricity from wind energy, and 57% reported a willingness to consider it for their own homes (NOP World Consumer, 2005).

Institutional factors: ownership structures, the distribution of benefits, and the use of participatory approaches to public engagement   Models or structures of ownership employed in renewable energy technology developments can vary widely, encompassing public/private and individual/collective dimensions; for example, ownership by public-sector institutions such as local authorities, private-sector companies, private individuals, or some mixture of each; with benefits distributed to private individuals, institutional shareholders, or in the case of cooperatives or social enterprises, a community of interest. As with issues of scale, the majority of existing research on public attitudes has been about renewable energy technologies developed by private utilities or public organisations.

It has been argued that the key to gaining local community support is to use compensation of a financial or other form to redress imbalances in the distribution of costs and benefits (Dorshimer, 1996; Toke, 2002). There is some empirical support for this argument – for example, in Denmark it has been found that people who own shares in a turbine indicate significantly more positive attitudes towards wind energy than

people with no economic interest; and that members of wind cooperatives are more willing to accept further turbines in their locality in
comparison with non-members (Andersen *et al.*, 1997, cited in Krohn
and Damborg, 1999). In Scotland, a study of public acceptance of wind
farms in the Hebrides indicated that, when income from land rental
flowed to the community under local ownership of land, levels of
acceptance rose from 28% to 39%, and levels of opposition fell from
55% to 44% (MORI Scotland, 2005). However, there is likely to be an
interaction between levels of compensation and perceptions of fairness
mentioned above. For example, a lack of trust in development institutions may result in local opposition regardless of the degree of
incentive offered.

Issues of trust and the channelling of benefits implicate the degree to
which local people are directly involved in the setting up, ownership and
management of a project. Many authors, consistent with a 'deliberative
turn' within the social sciences (Owens and Driffil, 2006), have advocated
more participatory approaches to public engagement, to at least minimise
social conflict if not to secure public acceptance (e.g. Hinshelwood, 2000;
Upreti and van der Horst, 2004; Toke, 2005; Bell *et al.*, 2005; Upham
and Shackley, 2006). There is some empirical evidence that individuals
seek to be involved in renewable energy developments. For example, a
study in Wales reported high levels of public support for wind energy
developments that were conducted 'in partnership' with local people
(88.5%), for local use of locally generated energy and profit sharing with
local people (over 80%), and for local ownership (52%) (Devine-Wright,
2005b). However, it cannot be assumed that deliberative public engagement in renewable energy developments will secure public acceptance.
In fact, it may cause the opposite, providing a means for local people to
collectively organise and communicate their concerns within an inter-
active process. Given this, it is important, as Bell *et al.* (2005, p. 28)
recognised, 'to provide policy makers with a better understanding of the
proper purpose, character and techniques of public and stakeholder
participation' in renewable energy developments.

*Spatial factors: regional and local context, spatial proximity and
NIMBYism* Some studies have noted similarities and differences
between levels of support for renewable energy technologies at national,
regional and county levels. For example, it has been shown that levels of
support in Devon (47%), and the South West region generally (61%),
varied from the national average of 55% (MORI Social Research
Institute, 2003, 2004). Another study suggested that levels of support
for wind and nuclear energy differed between respondents in the North

and South of England, with 29% of those in the South opposing wind energy in comparison with 23% in the North, and 74% of those in the South opposing nuclear energy in comparison with 83% in the North (*Guardian*, 2005).

Devine-Wright (2005a) noted a general assumption in the literature on wind energy that those living nearest to developments are likely to have the most negative attitudes. However, the empirical literature is inconclusive. Several studies suggest the opposite – that, when compared, individuals living closer to developments tend to have more positive attitudes towards them, in comparison with those living further away (Braunholtz, 2003; DTI *et al.*, 2003; Warren *et al.*, 2005). However, Hubner and Meijnders (2004) found that those living close to biomass power plants had more negative attitudes towards purchasing biomass electricity.

The search for an effect of proximity (or direct experience) on public acceptance links to one of the most common explanations for public opposition – NIMBYism. NIMBY ('not in my back yard') is a way of thinking about public acceptance of contentious land-uses, which suggests that those opposing developments are motivated by concern 'for their back yard' and, although supportive of the land use *per se*, would prefer it to be sited elsewhere. In a critical review of the literature on public attitudes towards wind energy, Devine-Wright (2005a) concluded that there was limited empirical support for the NIMBY hypothesis, given that many studies indicate higher levels of support for development in their locality in comparison to regionally or nationally (e.g. Hoepman, 1998, cited in Krohn and Damberg, 1999; Warren *et al.*, 2005). Aside from its conceptual utility, academics have been critical of the ways in which the NIMBY concept has been rhetorically applied, both by researchers and in practice. It can serve as an 'off the shelf', easy-to-use way of thinking about local opposition to renewable energy technologies that was characterised as 'lazy' by one writer, impeding understanding (Wolsink, 2006). Politically, discursive studies have revealed how the NIMBY label can be deployed by pro-development organisations in contexts of social conflict as a pejorative label used to undermine the legitimacy of opponents' views (Haggett and Smith, 2004).

In terms of empirical research, Wolsink's work (1989, 1996, 2000) reveals the complex and multidimensional nature of public views in detail. For example, in an empirical survey of three Dutch wind farm sites, Wolsink (2000) applied causal modelling techniques to examine the determinants of anti-wind-farm resistance behaviour (i.e. self-reported participation in activities such as signing a petition, writing a letter, attending a meeting, etc). Perceived visual impacts, rather than a NIMBY attitude of preferring technology to be sited elsewhere, emerged as the main factor explaining public attitudes towards a local wind farm, and resistance behaviours were directly explained by local factors rather than more general arguments in favour of wind energy (e.g. that wind energy is a 'clean' energy source).

However, this body of research leaves a number of unanswered questions that future research could explore: for example, the degree to which emotional response, perhaps linked to place attachment or identity processes (Devine-Wright and Lyons, 1997), are significant in shaping cognitive perceptions or behavioural responses, as suggested by Vorkinn and Riese (2001); and the manner in which perceptions at the individual level (e.g. those concerning perceived visual impacts) are influenced by actors such as developers, civic opposition groups, local media and local government, for example, through the media and the internet sites of proponents and opponents of renewable energy developments.

17.4 Reconsidering public acceptance of renewable energy technologies

Despite a range of studies being carried out on public attitudes towards renewable energy technologies, a genuine understanding of the dynamics of public acceptance remains elusive. One reason for this is the fact that the determinants of public acceptance are rarely considered as a whole, taking account of the multiple personal, psychological and con-textual factors described above. Another issue is the range of terms used in the literature to describe the object of study, including public or social acceptance, support, positive perceptions, beliefs or attitudes, as well as terms such as objection, resistance and opposition, which are rarely defined. This leaves it uncertain whether public acceptance is best conceived as a positive perception or evaluation, a favourable affective response, an action of a particular kind or kinds, a combination of these, or something else entirely, such as a discourse or narrative; and whether acceptance can be conceived as the absence of resistance or whether acceptance and resistance are best treated as separate social phenomena. My view is that approaches need to unbundle beliefs or attitudes from actions or behaviours, since each may be shaped by different underlying factors, and that different resistance actions, from signing petitions to forming or joining a group, need to be explored as separate but related phenomena, as has already been shown in relation to different types of environmentally significant behaviour (Stern, 2000).

Future research on public views should use more innovative methodologies and avoid attempting to identify a surfeit or deficit in public understanding, but instead probe implicit ways of thinking about energy technologies, drawing upon work by Kempton and Montgomery (1982), on 'folk' models, and the work of Moscovici (1984) on 'social representations' shaping how individuals think about, talk about and use energy technologies. An example is the work of Leggett and Finlay (2001), in which participants, sampled according to gender and profession, created collages from magazine cuttings which revealed different 'meanings' associated with energy: health and well-being, consumption, and personal energy as a metaphor for renewal.

There is also a need to better explore symbolic, affective and discursive aspects of facility siting disputes. Geographers, such as Thayer and Hansen (1988), Pasqualetti (2000) and Pasqualetti *et al.* (2002), have contributed useful discussions of the symbolic aspects of renewable energy technologies, but there is little empirical work studying either symbolic or affective aspects of renewable energy technologies, with the exception of an early study by Lee *et al.* (1989), in which 62% of a sample of 1,286 respondents associated wind turbines as a 'sign of progress', 15% with 'harking back to the past', and 16% with a combination of both. Several recent studies have employed a discursive approach to understanding public opposition to wind farms (e.g. Haggett and Smith, 2004; Ellis *et al.*, 2006), and such studies are helpful in drawing out how rhetorical and communicative aspects of the social context influence the beliefs and actions of individuals and organisations involved in siting disputes.

I would identify several implications of these studies.

- A deficit of technical understanding does not equate with an absence of personal meanings or beliefs associated with energy technologies.
- The antecedents of public views about renewable energy technologies are often complex and multifaceted, requiring systematic conceptual and methodological approaches to capture factors and how they interrelate.
- There are important symbolic, affective and discursive aspects of how individuals relate to renewable energy technologies that have been insufficiently captured in the literature thus far, but may play an important role in motivating public responses.
- Such beliefs are 'social' as much as 'personal', dynamic rather than static, in that they may be shared across a community or social network, and generated through interpersonal communication; hence

the incompleteness of an approach to public understanding based upon a more individualistic and static 'public attitudes' perspective.

- Qualitative, visual and discursive research methodologies have a useful role to play, complementing, but not replacing, more quantitative, empirical studies based upon questionnaire surveys.
- More deliberative methods of public engagement are widely cited as being necessary to address problems with public acceptance; however, there is relatively little empirical research critically examining the nature of deliberative engagement, and its impacts upon levels of public acceptance in the context of specific projects.
- There is a need for interdisciplinary research to integrate and consolidate existing research, leading to a multi-level conceptual framework integrating the many factors identified as shaping public acceptance of renewable energy technologies.

17.5 Conclusions

To conclude, instead of seeing public attitudes as an obstacle or barrier to technological progress, I would argue that we need to better understand the dynamics of public views about renewable energy technologies, particularly how they are shaped by processes of engagement in technology siting. This can be facilitated by interdisciplinary research using innovative qualitative and quantitative social research methods, with a greater emphasis on the symbolic, affective and socially constructed nature of beliefs about renewable energy technologies. As Kahn observed (2001, p. 28), there is a need to study renewable energy siting 'from different scientific disciplines and theoretical perspectives, in order to develop a more structured understanding about what characterises renewable energy siting conflicts'.

References

AIM Research A/S (1993). *Holdningsunderøgelse til vind energi*. Report prepared for the Danish Wind Turbine Manufacturers Association 1993. Copenhagen: Energy Centre Denmark.

Altman, I. and Low, S. (1992). *Place Attachment*. New York: Plenum Press.

Anderson *et al.* (1997). *Rapport om hvordan en dansk commune blev selvforsynende med ren vindenergyi og skabte ny indkomst til kommunens borgere*. Nordvestjysk Folkecenter for Vedvarende Energi.

Bell, D., Gray, T. and Haggett, C. (2005). The 'social gap' in wind farm policy siting decisions: explanations and policy responses. *Environmental Politics*, 14(4), 460–477.

Black, J.S., Stern, P.C. and Elworth, J.T. (1985). Personal and contextual influences on household energy adaptations. *Journal of Applied Social Psychology*, **70**, 3–21.

Braunholtz, S. (2003). *Public Attitudes to Windfarms: A Survey of Local Residents in Scotland.* Scottish Executive Social Research/MORI Scotland. Available at www.scotland.gov.uk/library5/environment/pawslr.pdf.

Curry, T.E., Reiner, D.M., de Figueiredo, M.A. and Herzog, H.J. (2005). *A Survey of Public Attitudes towards Energy and Environment in Great Britain.* Cambridge, MA: Massachusetts Institute of Technology (MIT) Laboratory for Energy and the Environment. Available at http://lfee.mit.edu/metadot/index.pl?id=2637&isa=Item&field_name=item_attachment_file&op=download_file

Department of Trade and Industry (2003). *Energy White Paper: Our Energy Future – Creating a Low Carbon Economy.* London: Department of Trade and Industry.

Department of Trade and Industry, Scottish Executive *et al.* (2003). *Attitudes and Knowledge of Renewable Energy amongst the General Public: Report Findings.* Available at www.berr.gov.uk/files/file15478.pdf

Devine-Wright P. (2003). A cross-national, comparative analysis of public understanding of, and attitudes towards nuclear, renewable and fossil-fuel energy sources. *Proceedings of the 3rd Conference of the EPUK (Environmental Psychology in the UK) Network: Crossing Boundaries – The Value of Interdisciplinary Research*, 160–173.

Devine-Wright, P. (2005a). Beyond NIMBYism: towards an integrated framework for understanding public perceptions of wind energy. *Wind Energy*, **8** (2), 125–139.

Devine-Wright, P. (2005b). Local aspects of renewable energy development in the UK: public beliefs and policy implications. *Local Environment*, **10**(1), 57–69.

Devine-Wright, P. and Lyons, E. (1997). Remembering pasts and representing places: the construction of national identities in Ireland. *Journal of Environmental Psychology*, **17**, 33–45.

Dorshimer, K. (1996). Siting major projects and the NIMBY phenomenon: the Decker Energy Project in Charlotte, Michigan. *Economic Development Review*, **14**(1), 60–62.

Ekins, P. (2004). Step changes for decarbonising the energy system: research needs for renewables, energy efficiency and nuclear power. *Energy Policy*, **32**, 1891–1904.

Ellis, G., Barry, J and Robinson, C. (2006). *Renewable Energy and Discourses of Objection: Towards Deliberative Policy Making. Summary of Main Research Findings.* Queen's University Belfast. ESRC grant reference: 000-22-1095.

Eurobarometer (2003). *Energy: Issues, Options and Technologies.* Eurobarometer Special Report 169, Wave 57.

Eurobarometer (2006). *Attitudes Towards Energy.* Available at http://ec.europa.eu/public_opinion/archives/ebs/ebs_247_en.pdf

Guagnano, G., Hawkes, G.R., Acredolo, C. and White, N. (1986). Innovation perception and adoption of solar heating technology. *Journal of Consumer Affairs*, **20**, 48–64.

Guagnano, G., Stern, P.C. and Dietz, T. (1995). Influences upon attitude–behavior relationships: a natural experiment with curbside recycling. *Environment and Behavior*, **27**, 699–718.

Guardian (2005). *Guardian Opinion Poll*. Prepared by ICM Research Limited.

Haggett, C. and Smith, J.L (2004). Tilting at windmills? Using discourse analysis to understand the attitude–behaviour gap in renewable energy conflicts. Paper presented at the *British Sociological Association Annual Conference*, 22–24 March, University of York.

Hinshelwood, E. (2000). Whistling in the wind: the role of communities in renewable energy development. *Network for Alternative Technology and Technology Assessment Newsletter*, **127**(Sept–Oct), 17–20.

Hoepman, N. (1998). *Foar de Wyn*. Provinsje Friesland.

Hub Research Consultants (2005). *Seeing the Light: The Impact of Microgeneration upon How we Use Energy: Qualitative Findings*. London: Sustainable Development Commission.

Hubner, G. and Meijnders, A. (2004). Public acceptance of electricity from biomass: impact of direct experience on attitudes. Paper presented at the *International Association for People-Environment Studies Biannual Conference*, Vienna, July.

ICM Research (2005). *Nuclear Power Survey*. ICM Research for BBC Newsnight. Available at www.icmresearch.co.uk/reviews/2005/BBC%20-%20 energy%20poll/bbc-energy-poll-may-2005.asp

Kahn, J. (2001). Siting conflicts in renewable energy projects in Sweden: experiences from the siting of a Biogas plant. Presented at *New Perspectives on Siting Controversy Conference*, Glumslov, Sweden.

Kempton, W. and Montgomery, L. (1982). Folk quantification of energy. *Energy: The International Journal*, 7(10), 817–828.

Krohn, S. and Damborg, S. (1999). On public attitudes to wind power. *Renewable Energy*, **16**, 954–960.

Lee, T., Wren, B. and Hickman, M. (1989). Public responses to the siting and operation of wind turbines. *Wind Engineering*, **13**, 188–195.

Leggett, M. and Finlay M. (2001). Science, story and image: a new approach to crossing the communication barrier posed by scientific jargon. *Public Understanding of Science*, **10**, 151–171.

London Renewables (2003). *Attitudes to Renewable Energy in London: Public and Stakeholder Opinion and the Scope for Progress*. London: Greater London Authority. Available at www.gcp-urcm.org/Resources/R200711290062.

McGowan, F. and Sauter, R. (2005). *Public Opinion on Energy Research: A Desk Study for the Research Councils*. Sussex Energy Group, SPRU, University of Sussex.

MORI Scotland (2005). *Hebridean Windfarm Plans*. MORI Scotland for BBC Scotland. Available at www.ipsos-mori.com/polls/2005/bbcscotland.shtml

MORI Social Research Institute (2003). *Public Attitudes Towards Renewable Energy in the South West*. MORI Social Research Institute for Regen South West.

(2004). *Attitudes Towards Renewable Energy in Devon*. MORI Social Research Institute for Regen South West.

Moscovici, S. (1984). The phenomenon of social representations. In R.M. Farr and S. Moscovici (Eds) *Social Representations*. Cambridge: Cambridge University Press.

NOP World Consumer (2005). *Wind Farms Wales*. Available at www.embracewind.com/ExecSummaryWales.pdf

Owens, S. and Driffil, L. (2006). *How to Change Attitudes and Behaviours in the Context of Energy: State of Science Review*. Paper commissioned by the Office of Science and Innovation, London.

Pasqualetti, M.J. (2000). Morality, space, and the power of wind-energy landscapes. *Geographical Review*, **90**, 381–394.

Pasqualetti, M.J, Gipe, P. and Righter, R.W. (Eds.) (2002). *Wind Power in View: Energy Landscapes in a Crowded World*. Academic Press.

Poortinga, W., Pidgeon, N. and Lorenzioni, I. (2006). *Public Perceptions of Nuclear Power, Climate Change and Energy Options in Britain: Summary of Findings of a Survey Conducted during October and November 2005*. School of Environmental Science, University of East Anglia.

Populus (2005). *Energy Balance of Power Poll*. Available at www.populus.co.uk/the-times-energy-balance-of-power-060705.html

Shackley, S., McLachlan, C. and Gough, C. (2005). The public perception of carbon capture and storage in the UK. *Climate Policy*, **4**, 377–398.

Simmons, P. and Walker, G. (2004). Living with technological risk: industrial encroachment on sense of place. In A. Boholm and R. Löfstedt (Eds) *Facility Siting: Risk, Power and Identity in Land-use Planning*. London: Earthscan, pp. 90–106.

Somerset County Council (2004). *Somerset Environment and Quality of Life Questionnaire 2004*.

Stern, P.C. (2000). Toward a coherent theory of environmentally significant behaviour. *Journal of Social Issues*, **56**(3), 407–424.

Sustainable Energy Ireland (2003). *Attitudes Towards Wind Farms and Wind Energy in Ireland*. Dublin: Sustainable Energy Ireland.

Thayer, R.L. and Hansen, H. (1988). Wind on the land: renewable energy and pastoral scenery vie for dominance in the siting of wind energy developments. *Landscape Architecture*, **78**, 69–73.

Toke, D. (2002). Wind power in UK and Denmark: can rational choice help explain different outcomes? *Environmental Politics*, **11**(4), 83–100.

Toke, D. (2005). Explaining wind power planning outcomes: some findings from a study in England and Wales. *Energy Policy*, **33**(12), 1527–1539.

Upham, P. and Shackley, S. (2006). Stakeholder opinion of a proposed 21.5MWe biomass gasifier in Winkleigh, Devon: implications for bioenergy planning and policy. *Journal of Environmental Policy and Planning*, **8**(1), 45–66.

Upreti, B. and van der Horst, M. (2004). National renewable energy policy and local opposition in the UK: the failed development of a biomass electricity plant. *Biomass and Bioenergy*, **26**, 61–69.

Vorkinn, M. and Riese H. (2001). Environmental concern in a local context: the significance of place attachment. *Environment and Behaviour*, **33**, 249–263.

Walker, G., Hunter, S., Devine-Wright, P., Evans, B., and Fay, H. (2007). Harnessing community energies: explaining and evaluating community-based localism in renewable energy policy in the UK. *Global Environmental Politics*, 7(2), 64–82.

Warren, C.R., Lumsden, C., O'Dowd, S. and Birnie, R.V. (2005). 'Green on green': public perceptions wind power in Scotland and Ireland. *Journal of Environmental Planning and Management*, **48**, 853–875.

Wolsink, M. (1989). Attitudes and expectancies about wind turbines and wind farms. *Wind Engineering*, **13**, 196–206.

Wolsink, M. (1996). Dutch wind power policy: stagnating implementation of renewables. *Energy Policy*, **24**, 1079–1088.

Wolsink, M. (2000). Wind power and the NIMBY-myth: institutional capacity and the limited significance of public support. *Renewable Energy*, **21**, 49–64.

Wolsink, M. (2006). Invalid theory impedes our understanding: a critique on the persistence of the language of NIMBY. *Transactions of the Institute of British Geographers*, NS31, 85–91.

Zoellner, J., Ittner, H. and Schweizer-Ries, P. (2005). Perceived procedural justice as a conflict factor in wind energy plants planning process. Paper presented at the *6th Biannual Conference of Environmental Psychology*, University of Ruhr, Bochum, Germany.

18 A low-carbon electricity sector for the UK: what can be done and how much will it cost?

Michael Grubb, Tooraj Jamasb and Michael G. Pollitt

The [UK *Energy White Paper* finding that] the costs of achieving the 2050 target would be negligible was not only remarkable, but also inevitably led to the conclusion that a radical objective did not need to be immediately followed through with radical policies.

Helm (2004, p. 401)

A greener, cleaner and calmer future, with safe, reliable and affordable supplies and power and energy for each and every one is attainable ... but we are nowhere near that point. The path to better things is long and tortuous.　　　　　Howell and Nakhle (2007, p. 180)

18.1　Introduction

Worldwide, power generation contributes around 41% of global CO_2 emissions, and 'business as usual' forecasts predict that its share will continue to increase to 2030 (see Chapter 1) whilst total emissions more than double. Such a trend is incompatible with all we now know about the need to avoid damaging climate change. In many ways, power generation is the most flexible energy sector, with a large array of technological options. This is particularly true in the UK where, by international standards, we have large natural wind and marine resources (see Chapter 3). If the UK cannot move towards very low-carbon electricity systems, the planet is indeed in deep trouble.

In the decade after liberalisation of its electricity system, the UK bucked the global trend, with power sector CO_2 emissions declining from around 200 $MtCO_2$ (55 MtC) in 1990 to about 150 $MtCO_2$ in 2000. However, this was largely due to the 'dash for gas' and, since then, the decline has halted. Moreover, with electricity demand continuing to increase against a backdrop of an increasingly aged fleet of baseload power plants, concerns about the security of generation gain ever greater prominence.

This concluding chapter draws together key insights to offer answers to the big questions about '*delivering* a low-carbon electricity system'.

462

The chapter first looks at the short to medium term – the prospects to 2020 – drawing upon technologies and policies that can make a significant contribution over that time scale. We then explore visions out to 2050, and then return to consider the steps that would need to be taken by 2020 to prepare for the longer term. The final section seeks to link these and discuss the wider picture and core issues underpinning the future of UK electricity.

The analysis in this book, as brought together in this concluding chapter, suggests that the trend towards a decarbonised power sector can be resumed and extended over the coming decades, while addressing concerns about the overall security of the system. In the round, it may indeed not cost much to the economy overall. But the apparent corollary suggested in the quote that heads this chapter – that this implies it should be easy – does not follow. The UK can only develop a secure, low-carbon – and efficient – electricity system if far stronger policies are adopted to deepen the economic incentives, improve both public and corporate engagement with the issues, and accelerate innovation towards that goal.

18.2   Electricity futures for the UK: prospects for 2020

18.2.1   Technical prospects

Given the conditions at the time of writing, how much could realistically change by 2020? The answer appears to be, at one level, a surprising amount for a sector that is so dependent upon long-lived investment and infrastructure. The Strathclyde scenarios (Chapter 14) set out four different views of the power system by 2020. These illustrate the scope for large changes in installed capacity of coal, CCGT, and renewables (principally wind energy). Just as important, the scenarios also span a significant range in electricity demand, from lower scenarios in which demand creeps up a little and then stabilises at around 360TWh, contrasting with those in which demand grows at roughly 1%/year, to 415TWh by 2020.

The scope of possibilities after the Energy White Paper   The range of generation capacities in the Strathclyde scenarios are broadly consistent with other detailed projections, including the Carbon Trust projections summarised in Chapter 13, and the range of scenarios modelled for the UK *Energy White Paper* (DTI, 2007a). They reflect fundamental determinants of build rates, given constraints on planning permission and rates of industrial expansion, combined with the impact of the gas price shock upon the financial and political willingness to radically expand gas power investment.

The UK *Energy White Paper* (DTI, 2007a) committed to extend the renewables obligation on a 'headroom basis' up to 20% of electricity by 2020, and banded the mechanism to support a greater diversity of investment (Chapter 13, Section 8). It also confirmed much increased investment levels in power transmission (about £4.3 billion over 2007–2012) and distribution (£5.7 billion over the period 2005–2010), in part to improve network security but also to facilitate the expansion of renewable energy. These measures make it unlikely that renewable energy capacity by 2020 will be toward the lower ends of the Strathclyde scenario ranges, though the analysis underlies the considerable uncertainty that exists about realised build rates and planning constraints. Similarly, while Neuhoff *et al.* (Chapter 6) model a much greater installed wind capacity by 2020, assuming build rate constraints of 500MW/year in each of six regions in the UK, there is currently little sign of such rapid development, given planning considerations and the temporary constraints on turbine supply. Also, the renewables obligation is capped at 20% renewables contribution (actually somewhat less, given the definitional form in the *White Paper*)[1] and, given the projected shortfall, it seems unlikely that this would be raised in time to drive even greater contributions.

The demand-side carries potentially much more uncertainty. Consistent with the seemingly inexorable trend of increasing power consumption, the Strathclyde scenarios span a slight to a significant increase in total electricity use in Great Britain by 2020. In this case, however, there is more discrepancy between the estimates of the 'probable' and the 'possible', and the 2007 *White Paper* introduced more fundamental policy changes, the impact of which is inherently harder to estimate. What will the mandatory roll-out of smart metering across business and homes, combined with the Carbon Reduction Commitment (CRC) that will place CO_2 caps on around 3,000 commercial and public sector organisations, do to their electricity use? The Carbon Trust analysis summarised in Chapter 9 estimates that a broad range of measures targeted at these sectors could save up to 50TWh by 2020, halting and maybe reversing their current rapid growth. The scope of the CRC is constrained in the first few years, but it could readily be expanded

---

[1] The *White Paper* redefined the Renewables Obligation target in terms of Certificates issued: since the 'banding' means that some less-developed sources have a multiplier, receiving more than 1 ROC per MWh generated; as explained in Chapter 13, the physical contribution would be less than 20% of physical supplies.

during the period to 2020. The analysis of the domestic sector (Chapter 8) also underlines the breadth of potential consumer responses to the information provided by smart metering in homes. Important additional opportunities and uncertainties enter through the impact of policy decisions upon both network investments and the operation of the system, discussed below.

The other big variable out to 2020 is carbon pricing. Despite the imperfections of the EU ETS discussed in Chapter 11, one unambiguous influence is upon power sector operation. As part of our studies, we have developed a relatively simple 'electricity calculator' for the UK system to facilitate rapid exploration of different combinations, and apply this to a range of circumstances around the basic capacity scenarios laid out in Chapter 14.

Emission implications of scenarios to 2020 The scenario CO_2 emissions reported in Chapter 14 assume a fixed demand and ignore carbon price effects, assuming that coal plants are correspondingly run at baseload. In contrast, Figure 18.1 applies our simplified model to explore the interaction of carbon price with electricity demand over a wide range (340–420TWh/year) for the different capacity mixes (in absolute GW installed) in the Strathclyde scenarios.[2]

One generic result is the much greater sensitivity to demand variations at the higher end of carbon prices, and *vice versa*. This is because higher carbon prices result in CCGTs operating more at baseload, with coal plants serving the additional demand. At low carbon prices, therefore, demand reductions save gas from highly efficient plants, with limited emission reductions; at high carbon prices, demand reductions back out coal power generation, with emission savings potentially twice as large. The net results present a striking range of emission possibilities:

- **Capacity mix scenario '*Strong growth*'.** This has a significant degree of both renewable energy and fossil fuel plant construction. At high demand, a move from low to high carbon price cuts emissions by about 30 $MtCO_2$, to 100 $MtCO_2$; at the lowest demand level the carbon price impact is even larger, cutting by up to 37 $MtCO_2$ to bring emissions well below 75 $MtCO_2$/year, as substantial coal capacity is not required for much of the year. The sensitivity to change in demand, in

---

[2] The dominant driver of price uncertainty is gas prices. Figure 18.1 shows results assuming a 'low' gas price scenario of 25p/therm average in 2020, with ±20% for winter/summer seasons. Figure 18.2 shows the results for a doubled gas price of 50p/therm ±20%. These are compared to UK *Energy White Paper* gas price scenarios of 21p/therm (low) to 55 p/therm (high), £2006 prices (DTI, 2007b).

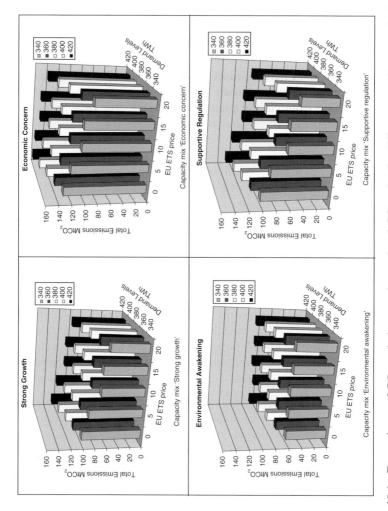

Figure 18.1. Dependence of CO$_2$ emissions on demand and CO$_2$ price for different capacity scenarios in 2020 (low gas price: 20, 25, 30p/therm variation over seasons)

absolute terms, increases slowly with the carbon price levels: the switch from 420 to 360TWh for a given carbon price saves about 20 $MtCO_2$/year with no price, rising above 25 $MtCO_2$ at higher prices.

- **Capacity mix scenario *'Economic concern'*.** This most pessimistic economic scenario is also the worst environmentally. It maintains existing plant mix with low build of renewable capacity, and the limited stock of less carbon-intensive plants make coal use relatively high in all scenarios: even the lowest-demand scenario still emits around 95 $MtCO_2$ with high carbon prices, while the high-demand case emits around 44 $MtCO_2$ more. Moreover, if demand is high, the system is stretched to capacity, and the modest reordering of operation arising from carbon price only saves around 18.3 $MtCO_2$.

- **Capacity mix scenario *'Environmental awakening'*.** This environmentally aggressive scenario maximises the build of renewable energy and largely phases out coal and nuclear. The result is a system engineered for low emissions, below 75 $MtCO_2$/year in the lower-demand cases, and around 92 $MtCO_2$ even for the highest demand level. The striking feature, however, is how the lack of coal plant makes carbon prices almost completely irrelevant to system operation – carbon emissions are basically determined by the capacity mix and have little or nothing to do with relative prices. As with *Economic concern*, the security of the system could also be problematic if demand was at the higher levels (or if there were problems with gas supply).

- **Capacity mix scenario *'Supportive regulation'*.** In striking contrast, the diverse plant mix in this scenario – with a broad mix of coal and gas complemented by a rapid build of zero-carbon sources – exhibits the greatest flexibility and responsiveness of any of the scenarios. The interaction of carbon price and demand levels is strongest of all in this scenario, because it comprises both more coal and more non-fossil sources (in this case nuclear, partly at the expense of wind). At the highest demand levels, a lack of carbon pricing allows the coal fleet to run flat out, with system emissions as high as the *Strong growth* scenario at around 130 $MtCO_2$. Dropping demand to the lowest level cuts about 27.5 $MtCO_2$ from this, but it is the combination with carbon pricing that really exerts leverage: low demand coupled with high carbon prices utilises the non-fossil and gas capacity to the full, leaving much of the coal plant unused. This more than halves the total emissions, compared with the highest combination, to well below 75 $MtCO_2$, actually fractionally below that of the *Environmental awakening* scenario, for the same demand level. This pattern is just a slightly more exaggerated version of that in the *Strong growth* scenario. Since the system does have a significant reserve capacity, it is also likely to be the most resilient to unexpected shocks (such as gas supply interruption).

This relatively simple exercise therefore demonstrates that UK power sector emissions could vary enormously just within the next 12 years. In the worst case, emissions remain roughly around the 168 MtCO$_2$ high point of 2005, when the gas price spike drove a greatly increased use of coal plant on the system. The slow growth of renewable energy in the *Economic concern* scenario only just compensates for the growth in demand (at the upper levels), while coal plants are life extended or replaced to maintain supplies.

Several other combinations lead to emissions broadly around 130 MtCO$_2$ in the absence of carbon pricing. But, even compared to this, dramatic reductions can be achieved, either by an environmentally driven engineering of the capacity to close down coal plant (*Environmental awakening*), or through the combination of enough non-fossil and gas capacity to make the system responsive to high carbon prices (*Strong growth* and *Supportive regulation*). In all these cases, emissions fall below 75 MtCO$_2$, less than half the level in 2005. It is striking that reducing emissions from UK power generation by more than 50% within 15 years, compared with the high of 2005, appears eminently feasible – and through more than one approach.

Comparative studies suggest that the model used tends to underestimate emissions in low-demand scenarios, probably because of seasonal and operational considerations not being adequately reflected in the model. The absolute numbers for the lowest emission levels in Figure 18.1 thus need to be treated with considerable caution. Nevertheless, the main insights as summarised above – including the scope for reducing emissions to less than half of 2005 levels, if the likely build-up of renewable energy is matched by lower demand and sufficiently high carbon prices – are likely to be robust against these modelling uncertainties.

Gas and emission allowance price variations   Carbon prices drive CCGT plants to operate in preference to coal. The carbon price required to achieve this depends fundamentally upon the differential between coal and gas prices. The carbon price ranges in Figure 18.1 reflect a 'low gas price' scenario, averaging 25p/therm with assumed seasonal variation of ±20%. In reality, the gas price in 2020 is highly uncertain. Although global gas resources remain abundant in total, the UK by 2020 will be largely dependent upon imports. The cost and availability of such gas will depend upon the development of remote resources, international competition for

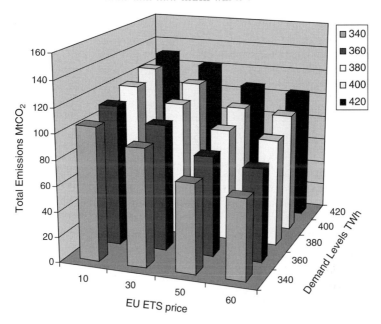

Figure 18.2. Dependence of CO_2 emissions on demand and CO_2 price for 'strong growth'/'supportive regulation' capacity mix scenarios in 2020 (high gas price: 40, 50, 60p/therm over seasons)

LNG supplies, and the pipelines to deliver cheap gas from Russian and central Asian fields.

For a given set of capacity and demand levels, the essential impact of a higher gas price is upon the carbon price required to drive the switch away from coal. To check this sensitivity, Figure 18.2 shows the most flexible of the scenarios, *Supportive regulation*, under a doubled gas price scenario (50p/therm with ±20% seasonal variation), but with coal prices kept constant. The pattern with the *Strong growth* scenario is almost identical.

This underlines the extreme interdependence of gas and EU ETS prices. At the low gas price, a CO_2 price of €20/tCO$_2$ (in Figure 18.1.) is sufficient to secure almost all the emission savings available from fuel switching. With the high gas price, CO_2 prices have to rise to around €50/tCO$_2$ to secure most of the emission savings – indeed a price of €60/tCO$_2$ is required to drive the final element of switching from coal to gas operation during the high-gas-price winter period. The influence of carbon price on emissions can be powerful – but if gas supplies are tight, the price may be considerable. We now turn to the economic issues.

18.2.2   Power system investment in low-carbon scenarios to 2020

How much might these various 2020 scenarios cost? This question has been analysed by the authors of Chapter 15. Their most fundamental conclusion is that the low-carbon scenarios require more investment. Indeed, they contrast all the Strathclyde scenarios with a *High-carbon* scenario in which electricity demand rises to 435TWh, and in which, implicitly, all supports for low-carbon investment except the EU ETS are removed. Most of the Strathclyde scenarios involve some new CCGT construction, but the *High-carbon* scenario of Chapter 15 involves 33GW of new CCGTs, in place of almost anything else. CCGTs are very cheap to build and, moreover, can be sited closer to demand centres, avoiding the need for significant investment in transmission and distribution. As a result, despite the higher electricity demand, the cumulative investment to 2020 required in this scenario is only around £15 billion.

This contrasts with the investment requirements for three of the four Strathclyde scenarios (excepting *Economic concern*) which, using technology cost data from the UK *Energy Review* (2006) are estimated to range from £34 billion to £43 billion (Chapter 15, Table 15.3) – two to three times as large.[3] Moreover, these data do not include the greater investment required in demand-side technologies. For example, the *Energy White Paper* mandates nationwide roll-out of smart metering technologies. Smart meters can reduce electricity consumption by about 2% (Devine-Wright and Devine-Wright, 2006). The cost of smart meters (with communications technology) has been variously estimated to range from £40 to £300 per unit, depending on the nature and associated IT (Sustainability First, 2007; DEFRA, personal communication). The total investment will be in billions, but most cost–benefit analyses of rolling-out smart meters indicate that this will result in net benefits (MCE, 2007). Adding the cost of demand-side investment associated with smart metering, and the transmission and distribution investment cost to facilitate distributed generation and renewables at scale, the total investment is potentially £40–50 billion out to 2020.

---

[3] Compare these estimates also to the subsidies estimated in Chapter 13, drawn in particular from the Carbon Trust analysis, required to approach the 20% renewable energy target mainly through a mix of onshore and offshore wind energy. For the mechanism that delivers the greatest capacity at least unit cost, the Carbon Trust study estimates a required total subsidy of around £15bn, when discounted to present value at the UK Gilt Rate of just 2.75% – about £40 per MWh delivered by 2020. This appears to be somewhat lower than implied by the estimates in Chapter 15, but not seriously inconsistent given the other variables at play (including the base system cost) that complicate the comparison. See also the qualification around the Energy Review (DTI, 2006) wind cost estimates in the next footnote.

On the surface, this is up to three times the investment cost of the CCGT-dominated scenario, in which case UK consumers will need to pay 10–20% higher tariffs by 2020 to fund the path towards a low-carbon economy.

The details of investment requirements implied by these scenarios are, of course, subject to uncertainty, for example, around offshore wind energy, which is a key determinant, particularly in the *Environmental awakening* scenario, and which continues to provoke strong debate.[4] The striking thing, however, is that compared with the UK's gross capital formation (around £200 billion/year at present, and rising), low-carbon electricity scenarios to 2020 cost no more than 2%, and the *additional* cost when compared to a scenario totally unconstrained by environmental or security considerations is unlikely to exceed 1%, of total UK capital investment over the period. Moreover, from a portfolio and options perspective (as discussed in Chapter 4, and by Awerbuch, 2003) such scenarios have clear benefits compared with developments which are concentrated upon fossil fuels, quite independent of climate or even innovation perspectives, because they increase the diversity of the system and reduce its cost variance in the face of fuel-price uncertainties. To this we now turn.

18.2.3   *The fossil fuels dimensions to 2020: investment, cost and risk*

The 'cheapest' CCGT-dominated, high-carbon scenario of Chapter 15 is a useful exercise because it puts into sharp relief the distinction between investment, cost and risk. The operating costs of this cheap-to-construct system are dominated by just two parameters – gas and carbon prices – which, as indicated, are likely to be very closely coupled. The corresponding risk is that the supply security of the resulting system is almost totally dependent on the availability and price of gas. Moreover,

---

[4] In particular, the underlying DTI estimates of offshore wind energy costs in the *Energy Review* (DTI, 2006) that formed the basis for the *White Paper* have been subject to serious criticism, as exceeding even the realised costs of existing offshore wind farms (UKERC, 2007 p.65). The *Energy Review* assumed a capital cost of £1,500/kW, with fixed O&M at 46p/kW/year that equates to at least 1.5p/kWh. The justification for assuming capital costs that exceed historical experience was the belief that steel and commodity price rises of recent years, and the tightness in the wind turbine market due to the global pace of expansion, will continue. The O&M costs are almost twice those of existing offshore experience, and yet the underlying documents (DTI, 2007d) indicate that almost no allowance was made for either learning or economies of scale to bring down these costs. Chapter 12 in this book discusses critically the evidence base for 'experience curves', and highlights many complexities in their interpretation in detail; but the very low learning assumptions for wind energy in the *Energy Review* (DTI, 2006) remain hard to square with the vast majority of empirical evidence, as detailed also specifically for wind energy in our previous book (see Morthurst, 2006).

such a scenario may embody some internal contradiction. The implied consumption of gas by 2020 for power generation is around double the level in 2005.[5] Such a radical increase in gas demand, if repeated across Europe, is almost bound to drive up gas prices beyond the levels assumed in the scenario.

Indeed, it is far from clear whether the infrastructure to extract and supply such huge volumes to Europe will be available in 2020, since at present the international gas industry shows little sign of making investments at the scale this would imply – partly because of the risks implied by rising geopolitical tensions. The IEA estimates that global growth of the gas industry out to 2030 on mainstream projections will require around $3.9 trillion cumulative global investment (IEA, 2006). Estimating the investment required to realise the hugely expanded supplies to Europe implicit in the high-carbon/CCGT scenarios is beyond the scope of this book – as are the consequences for gas price either of such investment or indeed of its lack. However, gas supplies at such scales would clearly require investment of many tens of billions of euros in pipeline and LNG infrastructure dedicated to European markets.

In other words, the conclusion that such a CCGT-intensive scenario minimises investment is simply a product of the line drawn between investment in the power and the gas industries, and also between domestic and international investment. Viewed from a global energy perspective, a gas-dominated future still requires massive investment. A CCGT-intensive scenario just shifts the investment needs to outside the UK power sector, enabling the UK to defer expenditure whilst others – we hope – invest.

Unfortunately, this shifts the risk in the opposite direction: the UK power sector acquires the risk that others don't invest enough or that they do so too late (leading to price spikes, as observed in 2005–2006, only perhaps worse and more prolonged), that they use our resulting dependence to extract a systematically high return on their investment – or even (*in extremis*) that, if supply is concentrated enough, dominant countries may seek to use their commanding position over UK electricity to political advantage. It also faces the risk that CCGTs prove to be not clean enough in the face of a seriously carbon-constrained world to remain the mainstay of a high-demand power system. Thus, cheaper electricity may be bought at a high price in terms of risks to both supply

[5] The 'High-carbon' scenario in Chapter 15 involves around 270TWh of gas-fired output (for either price) from major power stations, compared with 127TWh in 2006 (see Table 5.6 in DTI, 2007c): there is also quite a lot from self-generators, outside the scope of the Chapter's modelling. Thermal efficiency would rise somewhat with a large number of newer stations.

and price security and also, in the longer term, possibly to goals for deep emission reductions.[6]

Moreover, higher gas prices would, in turn, drive up carbon prices even more (to stop the system reverting to coal power), and hence electricity prices. Consequently, it is far from clear that such a low-investment-cost scenario (for UK electricity) would actually be a lower-electricity-price scenario, in a carbon-constrained world. It would more likely be a world of high profits for power generators, for the reasons set out in Chapter 15 – CCGTs, as well as renewables, would attract the 'inframarginal rent' associated with high carbon prices that bear most upon the marginal coal stations, even if allowances were auctioned.

Related issues also dominate the alternative, even higher, carbon possibilities of renewed large-scale coal investment. The operating costs would still be driven by carbon pricing and world gas prices (because of linkages to carbon prices and international fossil fuel prices). Recognising the reality of climate change and assuming that the 'new entrant' perversities in the EU ETS (Chapter 11) are corrected over time, the only defence against the future would be carbon capture and storage (CCS).

As indicated in Chapter 16, much remains uncertain about CCS. The first demonstration plants are projected to operate around 2013. Once these demonstrate the potential for success of CCS we will know more about the prospects and costs. Issues of timing and unit scale of CCS, along with associated CO_2 transport and disposal systems, will constrain the potential contribution by 2020. However, complete decarbonisation of even a single 800MW coal CCS demonstration plant would cut carbon emissions by an amount close to that from the UK's end-2006 stock of wind turbines of around 2GW.[7] Thus even a small number of large early projects could make a significant contribution to 2020 reductions.

Such retrofit would involve investment, and efficiency penalties, with some residual emissions (potentially up to half those of CCGTs). Renewing coal plant construction before demonstration plants have yielded experience about the realities of CCS technology would increase domestic investment requirements (compared with CCGT) combined with high technological, environmental and operating cost risk in the light of CO_2 restrictions. Capture-ready, coal-fired plant could be built after 2013 once demonstration plants establish the basic feasibility of CCS.

---

[6] Note that CCS could be used to strip the carbon from large-scale CCGTs – probably more easily than for coal stations – but it would be difficult for small-scale, distributed gas power generation.

[7] An 800MW coal plant with 70% load factor and 85% capture efficiency equates to about 1.6GW – the installed capacity at end 2005 – of wind at 30% load factor. The UK *Energy White Paper* commits funding for a pilot CCS plant of 300MW.

It seems less likely that the private sector will take the risk of constructing significant new coal capacity before then. Though the contribution of CCS to emission reductions by 2020 might match the modest contribution of wind energy by 2005 or so, its main promise lies beyond.

18.2.4   Current policies and the 2020 outlook

Scenarios for demand and generation to 2020 are now also set within a context of many established commitments and policy decisions. The decisions in the UK *Energy White Paper* (DTI, 2007a) on mandatory smart metering, tighter energy efficiency standards, implementation of the European Energy Performance of Buildings Directive, the Carbon Reduction Commitment, and the Zero Carbon Homes Initiative will drive substantial efforts on energy efficiency. The setting of the Renewable Energy Obligation to 20% on a 'headroom' basis, and the banding of the system, are designed to ensure that renewables investment accelerates, and that it does expand into the less established renewable technologies.

Delivering both energy efficiency and renewable energy goals in the most cost-effective manner could be significantly enhanced by greater attention to the regulatory structures that govern the 'natural monopolies' of transmission and distribution. Chapter 7 suggests a five-point policy agenda: (i) updating the RPI-X formula for price regulation; (ii) greater competitive tendering and active user engagement in the regulation of new investment; (iii) use of locational pricing signals; (iv) unbundling of distribution networks from retailing; and (v) the accelerated innovation in networks through the Innovation Funding Incentive. A move to better reflect locational costs and benefits, in particular through full nodal pricing, could be especially important in improving the economic efficiency of implementing these goals. It is hard to quantify the impacts on electricity generation and emissions, but even a 1% saving could be an important addition.[8] Locational pricing at

---

[8] Locational signals would increase prices to consumers when and where transmission and distribution (T&D) flows were straining the capacity of the system; response to such price signals would intrinsically reduce T&D costs. Moreover, with greater use of real-time pricing, consumers would face signals to reduce electricity use when generation is most expensive. If carbon pricing drives coal to the margin of generation, prices will be at their highest when demand on these coal units is highest, thus intrinsically reducing the carbon emissions associated with the system operation. This is irrespective of the impact of locational pricing upon actual total demand, which could be ambiguous. Green (2007) estimates that full nodal pricing could increase the economic efficiency of the UK power system by around 1%. To avoid any rebound effect of lower prices leading to higher energy consumption, prices would need to rise to eliminate any cost-fall-induced demand rise.

the distribution level might be very important in supporting policies for encouraging embedded microgeneration and harnessing local private (or public–private partnership) investments in low-carbon generation and demand-side management. Chapter 6 underlines the way that such locational signals would also reduce the widely disparate profits that would otherwise accrue from 'one size fits all' support mechanisms.

The *Energy White Paper* also reaffirmed the UK's commitment to strive for stronger implementation of the EU ETS post-2012. The EU ETS is already a crucial incentive to reduce the carbon intensity of power system operation. Chapter 11 discussed many of the design issues that still need to be addressed for the EU ETS also to act more effectively as an incentive for low-carbon power investments; without such reforms, the main strain for investment incentives will continue to bear upon other instruments, such as the Renewables Obligation.

All these policy directions are also buttressed by the EU Council Decisions of March 2007. The triad of '20%' targets for 2020: a 20% CO_2 reduction (unilaterally; 30% if there is a global agreement); a 20% improvement in EU energy intensity (energy to GDP); and a 20% renewable contribution to *total delivered* energy by 2020, all reinforce the basic thrust of the UK *Energy White Paper* decisions. The latter, in particular, implies up to 35% of electricity coming from renewables, as a European average, given the limitations upon renewable heat and fuel supply, and clearly implies that the UK will be under considerable pressure to increase its ambitions on renewable energy, not to fall short on them. We explore some implications further below.

All this effectively rules out scenarios with high demand that is met by new investment in CCGT or coal exclusively. In addition, the Strathclyde *Economic concern* scenario is not only economically dismal and inconsistent with these policy decisions already taken, it is also one which demonstrably fails to equip the UK for the future, from almost any perspective. It is of no great interest to energy policy to observe that, if the economy nosedives, attention may turn to other things and that established commitments, intended to help us grapple with the future, may be abandoned.

The future for UK electricity to 2020 can thus most usefully be bounded by the three remaining scenarios of *Strong growth*, *Environmental awakening* and *Supportive regulation*. The span of these scenarios – substantially increased investment in non-fossil sources coupled with greater energy efficiency – are both more likely, and more desirable, than any alternatives. The really important policy questions then are: how do the different paths sketched out prepare the UK power sector for the long-term future; what else needs to be done that cannot readily be measured in terms of delivered power, capacity and emission impacts;

and what are the corresponding implications for policy? To answer any of these questions requires us first to consider the long term, and then work backwards towards some surprising conclusions.

18.3   The long term: scenarios to mid-century

18.3.1   *Overview of mid-century, low-carbon electricity scenarios*

The previous Supergen book, *Future Electricity Technologies and Systems* (Jamasb *et al.*, 2006), focused upon the technologies potentially available to support deep mid-century emission reductions. As part of that book, the Strathclyde team corralled the key technological insights into six scenarios of the UK power system, all of which deliver deep emission reductions, but through strikingly different approaches. The extent of dependence upon nuclear, large-scale wind, biomass, varied forms of decentralised generation, coal with CCS, and CCGTs (with or without CCS) varies enormously across the different scenarios. Demand varies by a factor of more than two, and the deployment of advanced network technologies is matched so as to support a reliable and operable system across these diverse possibilities. The four 2020 scenarios summarised in Chapter 14 of this book were designed as 'stepping stones' on the pathway to these longer-term possibilities, as indicated in that chapter.

The 2050 *Economic downturn* scenario is of limited policy interest, for the same basic reason as indicated above for the 2020 *Economic concern* scenario (and the two are intrinsically linked). This leaves five scenarios for more active consideration:

- *Business as usual* and *Central direction*, which evolve from the *Supportive regulation* 2020 scenario and maintain a basic structural emphasis upon a 'classical' system structure with one-way flows from large power stations to the users.
- *Strong optimism* and *Technological restriction*, which could evolve from the *Strong growth* 2020 scenario and involve the highest levels of electricity demand, supplied through large-scale development of a wide range of options including decentralised generation in a liberalised market, but with widely varying paces of technological change between the two.
- *Green plus*, which evolves from the *Environmental awakening* 2020 scenario, with low demand growth, exclusion of nuclear power and a very strong dominance by renewable sources

Key characteristics of these scenarios are summarised in Table 18.1.

Table 18.1. *Summary of mid-century low-carbon electricity scenarios*

2050 scenario	Corresponding 2020 scenario	Electricity demand (TWh)	Renewable generation (% of total energy)	Central generation (% of total energy)	Important supply technologies (generation capacity and respective percentage of total electricity covered in parentheses)	System diversity indexes	
						Shannon** Wiener	Herfindahl*** Hirschman
Strong optimism	*Strong growth*	600	50%	10–20%	High (25–50%) Microgeneration (30–35GW, 34% of electricity), Wind (50–60GW capacity, 25% of electricity)	1.80	2,008
					Medium (10–25%) Biomass electricity generation and CHP (10–15GW, 15%) Wave and Tidal (15GW, 10%)		
					Low (1–10%) Nuclear (8–10GW, 7%), CCGT with carbon capture (10GW, 7%), Photovoltaic generation(5GW, 1–2%)		
*New diversity**	*Supportive regulation*	540	30%	50%	Medium CCGT (18–20GW, 20% of electricity), Microgeneration (15GW, 19%), Fossil fuel with CCS (12–15GW, 15%), Biomass electricity generation and CHP (10GW, 15%), Wind (20–30GW capacity, 12–15% of electrical energy)	1.74	1,432
					Low Coal (7–8GW, 7%), Nuclear (2–4GW, 5% of electricity), Wave and Tidal (6–7GW, 3% of electricity), Photovoltaic generation (4GW, 1%)		
Green plus	*Environmental awakening*	390	80%	0%	High Wind (60GW capacity, 45% of electricity), Biomass electricity generation and CHP (15GW, 25%)	1.55	2,436
					Medium Microgeneration (10GW, 19%)		
					Low Wave and Tidal (10–15GW, 8%), Photovoltaic generation (10GW, 3%)		

Table 18.1. (*cont.*)

2050 scenario	Corresponding 2020 scenario	Electricity demand (TWh)	Renewable generation (% of total energy)	Central generation (% of total energy)		Important supply technologies (generation capacity and respective percentage of total electricity covered in parentheses)	System diversity indexes	
							Shannon** Wiener	Herfindahl*** Hirschman
Technological restriction	*Strong growth*	680	40%	40–50%	High	CCGT (35–40GW, 35%)	1.65	2,250
					Medium	Wind (45–50GW, 20% of electricity), Microgeneration (20GW, 20%), Biomass electricity generation and CHP (20GW, 15–20%)		
					Low	Fossil fuel with CCS (5GW, 5%), Photovoltaic generation (3% of electricity), Wave (3G, 2%)		
Central direction	*Supportive regulation*	430	50–60%	25–30%	High	Wind (35–40GW capacity, 25% of electric)	1.88	1,592
					Medium	Fossil fuel with CCS (15GW, 20%), Microgeneration (10–15GW, 10–20%), Wave and Tidal (15GW, 15%), Biomass electricity generation and CHP (8GW, 15%)		
					Low	Nuclear (5GW, 5%), Photovoltaic generation		

* *Note: New diversity* is the name given here to the scenario previously called *Business as usual* in Elders *et al.* (2006). Its outcome has a relatively significant role for a range of the 'new' options and a lesser role for some existing ones (such as wind and nuclear). It could be interpreted as one possible result of extrapolating the current situation (no overt support for new nuclear, hesitation about big gas expansion, slow development of wind, significant but not draconian policies on energy efficiency, and some investment in new technologies both R&D and ROCs banding). However, no scenario is credibly 'business as usual' for the next four to five decades, and present policies could result in various evolutions, so the more explicit name is preferred.

**Note: Shannon-Wiener index is calculated according to $\sum_{i=1}^{I} -p_i \ln(p_i)$, where p_i is the proportion of generation represented by the ith type of generation. The minimum value taken is zero, where there is only one source of generation. The higher the value, the more diverse the system: a system with two equal components has diversity 0.69, with three this rises to 1.1. The index rises above two for a system with more than seven equal components.

***Note: Herfindahl-Hirschman index is calculated according to $\sum_{i=1}^{I} p_i^2$, where p_i is the market share assumed by the ith firm, or the proportion of generation met by one particular fuel source (expresses as a percentage). The maximum value of the index is 10,000 (in the case of a monopoly) and falls towards zero as the market moves towards a situation of perfect competition.

Along with data on demand and the contributions of different sources, Table 18.1 includes associated indices of system diversity and concentration (Grubb *et al.*, 2005). These indices are closely related but not identical. It is notable that all the low-carbon scenarios are more diverse than the default *Business as usual* 2020 and 2050 scenarios produced by the MARKAL model for the *Energy Review*. They do have interesting variations, however. *Environmental awakening*, by ruling out both nuclear and CCS, is the least diverse and most concentrated, with very heavy reliance upon wind energy (and the associated networks) providing almost half the entire supply. *Technological restriction*, with its heavy reliance on CCGT whether or not with CCS, forms the next most 'exposed' system. The most diverse – and, by implication, the most intrinsically robust against any shocks – are *Strong optimism* and *Central direction*. However, it is the two derived from the 2020 *Supportive regulation* scenario (*Central direction* and *New diversity*) that yield, by a considerable margin, the lowest concentration indices, with no individual source supplying more than 25% of demand. The general message is a positive one, implying that CO_2 constraints are unlikely to reduce diversity or increase concentration unless they are accompanied by additional environmental rejection of both CCS and nuclear. Indeed, assuming coal without CCS to be largely ruled out, the deeper CO_2 reductions to mid-century are almost certainly associated with a more diverse and secure system, less open to either market abuse or external energy security threats, than the gas-dominated alternative.

The purpose here is not to discuss which of these is more likely, more desirable, or how much they might cost – for reasons that will become all too apparent. It is rather to emphasise the technological feasibility of such diverse outcomes. We now explore further implications, including one feature that is common to all, albeit to varying degrees, namely their capital intensity.

18.3.2   2050 scenarios: key features and credibility

The scenarios were developed by the UK's leading electrical system engineers with careful consideration as to technological feasibility. The most demanding scenario, in the sense of being the most radically different from the norm, is the *Green plus*, which faces an apparently almost impossible challenge of securing 80% of its electricity from renewable sources (and renewables account for 90% of installed capacity). In contrast, *Economic downturn* and *Business as usual* are at the opposite end, in terms of their renewable energy contribution, while the other three scenarios still secure 40–60% of their electricity from renewable sources.

Given that wind energy, an intrinsically variable resource, is the UK's biggest renewable resource, the first challenge appears to be maintaining reliability.

For the mid-range scenarios with 40–60% renewable energy contribution, the issue is resolved, in part, by observing that wind energy actually only supplies about half the total renewable energy contribution in each case: the rest comprises biomass, with smaller contributions from marine, PV and others. In Chapter 5 of this book, Sinden presented an unprecedented depth of data on the geographical and temporal characteristics of the variable renewable energy resources in the UK, including exploring the extent to which geographical diversity and the complementary characteristics of the different resources combine to reduce their overall variability in aggregate.

In Chapter 6, Neuhoff *et al.* presented studies with an investment and operational planning model of the UK power system, which was adapted specifically to utilise the statistical wind energy data from Chapter 5, with the UK system divided into seven regions, including representation of the key existing transmission constraints. From this it emerges that the variability of wind energy provides no technical impediment to the UK absorbing up to 40% of its electricity from wind energy, with pretty much the existing structure of generation supplemented by some additional construction of gas-powered generation.[9] The work demonstrates that the diverse nature of the UK wind resource, combined with the existing strength of the transmission system and reserve, provided particularly through gas-powered generation, makes wind energy contributions up to 40% of supplied electricity entirely feasible from an engineering and economic perspective. The geographical distribution (which smoothes out short-term fluctuations as weather systems cross the UK), and the temporal distribution (consistently more wind energy available during the winter months when the need is greatest), facilitate the ability of the system to absorb these contributions. The exact system costs at higher reaches, including dynamic operational constraints, would certainly require further exploration, though the data on these aspects presented in Chapter 6 indicate that these operational considerations would not change the fundamental conclusions.

Chapter 6 also illustrates the economic trade-offs between transmission expansion costs on the north–south corridor to access high wind

---

[9] Under scenarios of high renewables contribution, there may be a case for open cycle gas turbines to provide back-up power. These are significantly cheaper to build, even than CCGTs, and are also more flexible in operation, though with lower efficiency. The modelling studies in Chapter 6 do not draw specific conclusions about the optimal mix, and hence the general term 'gas generation' is used here.

speeds in Scotland, and a more distributed use of wind power across the UK, with lower wind speeds and lower transmission costs.

The Strathclyde scenario *Green plus* envisages the construction of high-voltage DC cables to facilitate greater regional power flows, including linkage to a North Sea-based network that also helps to engage the regulatory capacity of Norwegian hydro-power. This, and the addition of some network regulatory capacity, in particular using power electronics with a modicum of distributed storage, underpins the wind energy contribution of 45% of UK electricity in that scenario, plus 35% of other renewables. From a resource perspective, the low demand of this scenario obviously reduces the scale of resources that have to be developed to secure such a contribution.

Indeed, most of the scenarios highlight increased attention to the demand side, which is specifically the subject of Chapters 8 and 9. This is revealed to be crucially important not just in terms of the total demand that sources must supply. In some scenarios the demand side plays a more active role in the operation of the system, which bears closer scrutiny.

Nuclear power makes an important contribution in some of the scenarios: up to 2020 new construction is unlikely, even to replace the shut-down of existing nuclear plant, but a commitment to a new generation of nuclear plant could make a contribution to lowering carbon emissions beyond 2025. On current projections, the cost of new nuclear, in the face of higher gas and CO_2 emissions prices, would seem to be favourable (see Chapter 3). However, this depends on delivered construction costs and (to a lesser extent) uranium prices, which may rise in the face of a global nuclear resurgence particulary if the technology used is relatively established with little scope for innovation and learning-by-doing. Nuclear new-build clearly has to overcome public (and perhaps investor) scepticism, green activism, and lengthy planning enquiries. Assuming that some new generation plant will be built in the UK by 2025, the relative cost and public reception of these plants will be crucial for the long-term future of nuclear in the UK electricity mix.

18.3.3 *Energy use and electricity infrastructure in buildings*

Our previous book explored electricity use in industry (Price *et al.*, 2006) and transport (Vermeyen and Belmans, 2006), but it is buildings-related uses that dominate electricity consumption, and the growth of domestic, commercial and public sector demand is widely projected to continue. The previous book's chapter on buildings (Eichhammer, 2006) presented two broad ways in which their energy use could change radically. One is through 'integrated buildings', in which thermally related loads (such as fridges and heat pumps) are managed to respond to variations on the wider power system. Buildings become a source of implicit, or in some cases explicit, storage for the wider system. Two-way metering could, moreover, facilitate the use of localised energy sources such as fuel cells and PV, selling power back to the grid. Even more radical perspectives extend similar ideas to the integration of fuel-cell cars.

The other approach is 'component buildings', which essentially become stand-alone, achieving a level of energy performance that enables their entire energy needs to be met from on-site generation. The latter, if manageable at all in northern climates for the range of possible building uses, would in practice be confined to new build. The important factor in both cases is that the *infrastructure* of the building is developed to minimise energy needs, through thermal performance, natural heat and light gain, LED lighting and heat pumps. It may also be developed to maximise on-site energy production, for example, through PV integrated into building surfaces. Such buildings offer the simplest vision of what has been termed 'infrastructure electricity' (Patterson, 2007) – electricity which becomes so integrated into the system that it may not even be measured or monitored, it just becomes a feature of infrastructure that delivers the services sought.[10] In effect, this extrapolates to buildings the properties already observed in mobile applications such as laptop computers and mobile phones, where no-one even asks what the cost of electricity is, or contemplates measuring it. The 'unit cost' of such electricity becomes a much more subtle concept if it is embodied in the infrastructure that delivers the service. If the cost of the energy-related component is small compared with the overall investment cost of the equipment, then reliability and other attributes (such as carbon footprint) may be more important to the user, and indeed services offered back to the grid (e.g. implicit storage) may also assume greater relative importance.

This forms part of Patterson's broader observation that electricity is not a fuel, it is a non-storable process.[11] It is only useful to the extent that infrastructure exists to combine its generation with its use to deliver the desired services at the appropriate time. With the focus upon these

---

[10] For most applications within buildings, low-voltage DC current is all that is required. A building DC circuit could thereby also avoid the need for transformers in every piece of equipment. Electricity becomes embodied in the building's infrastructure, whether or not supplied on-site or from a wider system – with which the building itself can be integrated.

[11] In reality, 'electricity storage' generally refers to the use of proxy stores, such as the rotational inertia in thermal power stations, the hydrostatic energy of stored water, the chemical energy of batteries, etc.

characteristics, the challenge is to maximise the service delivered for a given combined infrastructural investment in generating and using equipment. If the overall efficiency of the system is high enough, it may cease to make sense even to monitor and monetise aggregate kWh consumption at the lowest levels in the system: fixed charges based on interconnection and regulation capacities, and on net power flows at times when the system is stressed and/or using CO_2-emitting plant, may be just as relevant.

In such cases, the treatment of electricity as a commodity to be bought and sold may give way to contracts-for-services, in which companies contract to supply the final services (reliable supply of heat, light, etc.) in return for a fixed fee. Such companies would have an incentive to ensure that the building has efficient lights and appliances, automated control systems, and smart meters to manage the external interface at minimum cost and maximum benefit. Such company involvement on the demand side could also help to levelise the current discrepancy inherent in most tax systems, between supply-side investments (which are generally company investments that can be depreciated against tax) and demand-side expenditure (which in most cases involve non-deductible expenditure after tax). This offers an additional reason why demand-side investments tend to be so cost-effective when compared with supply.

Expanding the scale of the concept further brings us to the observation that low-carbon technologies tend to be more capital-intensive. This is true for both nuclear and coal with CCS, but is particularly striking for renewable energy sources.[12] This is a basic characteristic of most renewable sources: because they tap into ambient energy flows, the costs are all to do with the capital investment, not the variable costs of increasing output from a given facility. The implications for electricity prices, moreover, are intriguing: the companies need to recover the cost of capital, but the actual running costs are negligible. In competitive electricity markets, the electricity price is generally determined by the cost of operating the 'marginal' plant. In fossil-fuel-based systems, with carbon prices rising over time, the price of power is bound to rise. The price implications, if and when non-fossil sources assume a substantial fraction of energy supply, are much more subtle. Low power prices at times of high wind energy output have already been observed in some European power systems, and some countries' modelling studies find

---

[12] Indeed the UK *Energy Review* decision to present wind energy O&M costs in proportion to installed capacity, rather than output, reflects the judgement (or at least an accounting basis) that wind energy is almost 100% fixed cost with virtually no variable cost at all.

that renewable-intensive scenarios contribute to lower future power prices, returning to consumers the economic rents from carbon control that otherwise accrue to power generation.[13]

18.3.4   The economic paradox of low-carbon electricity systems

This observation is just one dimension of the economic paradoxes around low-carbon electricity systems. All the Strathclyde low-carbon scenarios imply a UK power system that is much more capital-intensive than the past dependence upon coal and gas power generation. This makes the system cost fundamentally dependent upon the assumed cost of capital.

From a market perspective, this is defined by the cost of finance that can be secured, given bank interest rates, perceived risks and financial structuring. As the technology matures and the perceived risks decline, financing costs move towards the base bank interest rates, and the terms of finance typically applied for national infrastructure projects, adjusted for continuing risks associated, for instance, with investment cycles and environmental regulatory uncertainties. This can have a radical impact on the 'cost per kWh' data for different technologies. The generation cost, far from being an intrinsic feature of the technology, turns out to be a function not so much of the technology but of the economic environment and, for public policy assessment, of political choices about the cost of capital appropriate to the investment in question.

This brings us full circle back to the topic of Chapter 2, with which this book started. This noted that the cost of climate change, in terms of the 'social cost of carbon' applicable to evaluate the external climatic costs of current emissions, turns out to be more dependent upon the assumed discount rate than almost any other parameter. The social cost of carbon is an expression of how much our society cares about the long-term future. The chapter reiterates arguments put forward in the *Stern Review* (Stern, 2006) which questions, on fundamental ethical grounds, the rationale for any significant 'social rate of time preference', implying very low discount rates.

If applied to energy investment, such low discount rates would tend to invert the relative costs of fossil and non-fossil energy sources, as compared with the costs set out in the *Energy Review* and summarised in Chapter 1, that are based on 10% discount rates. Lower rates would unambiguously tend to favour sources, such as renewable energy sources, in which the cost is all embodied in the capital investment rather than the

---

[13] See Bode (2006) and Climate Change Institute Australia (2007).

variable costs of operation. The UKERC study (UKERC, 2007) underlines the sensitivity of relative costs to this choice.

This is not to argue that the government *should* apply such low discount rates to technology choice in assessing energy options: this would
imply subsidising such energy technologies with government support (or
via consumer levies), in ways that might not be consistent across the
economy and could potentially draw finance from other projects with
higher returns. But it does throw serious doubt on the use of such
generation cost comparisons for public policy or for making assertions
about low- and high-cost paths from a macroeconomic perspective.

It is for this reason that it can become almost meaningless to debate which
of the scenarios is cheaper: the answer may be determined by the political
choice about the rate of time preference we choose to apply. The most
definitive debate of that issue is to be found in the 600 pages of the *Stern
Review*, not in the interest rate data on Bloomberg. The *Stern Review* has
made an excellent case for why public policy should use low discount rates
for setting objectives, implying that climate change is a pressing and urgent
concern: there is no ethical reason why a government should fundamentally discriminate against the welfare of future human beings.

However, to set a low-carbon economy as an objective because
governments have a responsibility to future generations, and then to cost
the resulting choices on energy sources and scenarios on the basis of a
10% discount rate, embodies a fundamental intellectual contradiction.
This tension between a public policy choice of near zero pure rate of
time preference, with low-carbon and national energy security as
objectives, and the choices of market participants to minimise investment costs and private risks whilst seeking returns often exceeding 10%/
year, has two important implications.

First, it suggests that, even ignoring the carbon externality benefit, low-
carbon electricity systems cannot be assumed to be 'higher cost' in the true
economic cost sense of the term (rather than in the observed financial cost
per kWh). They involve more up-front internal investment and probably
greater system diversity, and hence national security. To fund the investment they involve higher electricity prices, at least during the transitional
phase, but prices will be more stable (because of lower fuel dependence)
and the net impact may or may not be higher bills, depending also upon
the demand response. To put it another way: if an additional 1% of
national capital formation over the next couple of decades is all that is
required to move towards a more resilient and low-carbon electricity
system, it is probably one of the greatest economic bargains on offer.

However, the second implication is a basic dilemma for policy. An
internally consistent, efficient world would require similar rates of time

preference to be applied to both setting objectives and investment choices. Yet, even after setting a carbon price consistent with lower discount rates appropriate to public policy goals, market participants will still demand a high private rate of return and will choose to invest in faster payback, lower capital-intensity projects than implied by the use of the 'correct' social discount rate. To achieve climate change goals, either the carbon price has to be raised still higher to compensate for this, or investment time horizons need to be lengthened – which would seem to imply a public investment approach (albeit making use of private financing) where the State engages in new investments on the basis of the social discount rate.

Helm (2004, p.315) observed that

> when investment is neither a priority nor indeed needed, the higher cost of private capital matters little ... but in periods of high investment, the cost of capital becomes a key variable. Then the differential cost between Treasury finances and private debt and equity matters greatly.

Thus the need for greater investment in long-term climate change solutions exacerbates one of the most fundamental divergences between public goals and private interests. If we accept that a quasi-market system of carbon pricing aimed at stabilising CO_2 emissions at safe levels will not deliver least-cost solutions, let alone if the carbon price may be capped by political unwillingness to accept its implications, does this therefore imply a return to state direction of the technology choice and quantity of new capacity added to the system? What, overall, are the implications of such low-carbon economics for electricity policy?

18.4   Policy implications and conclusions

18.4.1   Policy foundations

Before answering the big policy questions, we need to step back and contemplate what we have learned about the nature of long-term, low-carbon electricity systems.

The analysis in Section 18.2 focused just on the options that could make substantial contributions to 2020 emission reductions. Of these, only wind energy, together with the demand-side measures, has much prospect of continuing expansion at scale in the decades thereafter. Many of the other technologies identified in the 2050 scenarios as potentially contributing to deep mid-century reductions are almost invisible in the 2020 energy scenarios. Yet action over the coming decade is likely to be essential in developing these as viable options.

Chapter 4 underlined the value of developing options. Chapter 17 discussed CCS and made the case for investment in demonstration plants. Other options abound, at various scales, including new nuclear technologies, as discussed in the previous Supergen book. Both appear in some of the long-run scenarios, but not all; either or both may appear financially attractive, in terms of cost per $MtCO_2$ abated, with sufficient combination of high carbon prices, low discount rates, low fuel prices and successful construction programmes – none of which may be taken for granted. Pretty much the same applies to the big renewable energy options, with the constraints potentially just as much to do with public opinion. Along with more radical improvements in energy efficiency, other options include greater use of higher-cost, embedded generation or, at the opposite extreme, greater use of international interconnectors to countries blessed with even greater renewable resources, for example, to Norway or even Iceland.

Thus the broad picture to emerge from the 2050 scenarios is a surprising degree of choice, combined with real uncertainty about how different options may develop, and hence a centrally important role for innovation and learning. The availability of options is important also because public preference is likely to be a significant determinant of, and constraint on, energy developments, as discussed in Chapter 16; and the role of innovation stretches well beyond just improving generating technologies, to encompass demand technologies, the wider system structure, and societal preferences about different kinds of impacts.

This is crucial to the most fundamental policy choice. If there were one single preferred technological path around which experts, government, industry and public could all rally, the case would be strengthened for direct governmental involvement to align investment choice with the consensus 'public good'. But that is not the situation at all.

Without attempting a comprehensive rehearsal of the arguments in favour of a liberalised market, it is important to be clear that the UK not only abandoned State-backed investment *à la* CEGB for good reasons; it has also had a fundamentally positive experience in absolute and relative terms, with energy market reforms in both electricity and gas (see Littlechild, 2000; Newbery 2000; Florio, 2004). The pro-market, pro-incentive-based regulation lessons from this experience must not be lost in the desire to address issues of climate change and energy security:

- All subsidy schemes and technology-specific interventions risk some forms of perverse incentives, which may include rent seeking and a lack of cost minimisation. It is important to not let climate change policy become an excuse for vested interests in particular technologies to be given inefficient subsidies which do not address the actual climate change issue at least economic cost.

- The UK's record with industrial subsidies is weak and her institutional arrangements are not well suited to the effective management of large-scale subsidy programmes. They *are* well suited to the development of sophisticated market-based instruments for addressing public policy goals. It is therefore important to recognise that, while some other countries might provide examples of successful government technology interventions (e.g. Japan), this is not the general experience in the UK.

- Market-based solutions can best respond to many of the uncertainties associated with the climate change issue. There may be technological fixes both on the demand side and supply side of the electricity industry which are as yet undeveloped, which only market incentives will uncover. This is in addition to the many uncertainties associated with the feasibility and cost-effectiveness of existing technologies (such as next-generation nuclear power or CCS): the market, ultimately, is the best arbiter for revealing the truth in the face of competing claims about the cost-competitiveness of different options.

The case for a market-based solution thus emerges as being akin to Churchill's famous defence of democracy, as 'the worst form of government except for all those others that have been tried from time to time'. The alternatives are all riddled with governmental and other failures, far more difficult to address than the mere market failures of liberalised systems. Freedom from the notion that a market-based solution necessarily corresponds to the theoretical optimum, ironically, enables a fresher look at the policy challenges of how better to align competitive energy markets with the public good.

18.4.2 *Conclusions on current policies*

The challenges of aligning competitive energy markets with the public good are indeed formidable. As Helm (2004, p. 418) observed, in electricity,

supply must instantaneously match demand; ... the assets are sunk and long-lived; the networks are natural monopolies; there are very great environmental externalities; and, critically, electricity and gas are complementary to the rest of the economy, in that failure to supply has (extremely) large costs to all economic activity. If the issue of fuel poverty and the distribution implications ... are also included, it is extraordinary that anyone could have regarded these as anything other than political industries.

Yet a major conclusion so far is that the UK does have the ability to achieve big reductions in carbon emissions from the electricity sector, both in the medium term and, more importantly, in the period out to 2050. Such reductions are technically feasible and can be achieved at a reasonable cost. Some increase in prices will be needed to fund the additional near-term investment, in both low-carbon capacity and in innovation – but not more than 20%. This is small compared with historical swings and continuing international price differentials (e.g. in the first quarter of 2007 domestic electricity prices after tax were 100% higher in Denmark than in the UK). Moreover, the aggregate cost impact is ambiguous both for energy bills (because higher prices would be offset against reduced demand) and for longer-term prices and macroeconomic welfare (because the higher investment would be in lower operating-cost sources, and would be accompanied by innovation). The UK has also developed sophisticated and effective tax and benefit systems which could be used to alleviate the welfare consequences of higher prices on the poor.

A second major conclusion, however, is that the current mix of policies in force (in 2007) will not achieve the necessary reduction in carbon emissions from the sector. Tougher policies (and higher electricity prices) will be required to do this. Indeed, a straightforward continuation of present policies seems likely to lead the UK towards higher risk in terms of price volatility, energy security, and climate change than one where a successful effort is made to meet carbon reduction targets.

A third major conclusion is that, in increasing the incentives for carbon emission reduction from the UK electricity sector, the UK needs a judicious combination of policies. The potential policy packages are numerous and their costs are likely to vary significantly in the near term. While many policies will require implicit subsidies, their costs vary, particularly in combination with other policies. Thus, reducing planning constraints on new wind farms significantly reduces the cost of carbon reductions from new wind capacity, while demand reduction may be significantly cheaper than new low-carbon generation capacity.

A fourth conclusion is that electricity sector policy must be careful to manage uncertainty and option value and facilitate successful technological innovation. The only things that we can really know about the electricity sector in the future are that much of our existing capacity is fixed in the short to medium term and, secondly, that innovations in both the supply and demand side are likely to deliver benefits if properly incentivised. This argues against simplistic policies which back one technology to the exclusion of all others, and for policies which incentivise local best responses to proper economic incentives.

Underlying all this, however, the recognition that a competitive market dominated by profit-maximising firms is not necessarily synonymous with, and need not be *expected* to lead to, a least-cost outcome, frees regulation from unrealistic expectations and presumptions. If consumers are willing to pay more for a lower-carbon, more secure, longer-term power system, this may reflect the correct social discount rate. This is something the regulatory system should facilitate and even encourage. Opposition on the grounds that it is uneconomic in the financial terms of the current liberalised market may be invalid. Thus if individuals (or local authorities) want to invest in 'expensive' PV systems and sell the surplus back to the grid, to give themselves a sense of being clean, green, independent and at the cutting edge, regulatory structures should support that freedom not oppose it. Such encouragement of local initiatives (such as local-council-led energy service companies) is consistent with a market-based approach whereby consumers are allowed to directly exercise preferences for quality attributes in production that they value. Some of the local initiatives that are already under way (e.g. in Woking) offer the prospect of substantial grass-roots contributions to carbon reduction, as well as addressing energy poverty and raising awareness of the climate change issue.[14]

Formulating future low-carbon electricity policy This long tour of the fundamental technology and economic issues around a low-carbon and secure electricity system leads us to a range of firm conclusions – together with some outstanding and fundamental uncertainties. We identify four broad principles for policy development, with eight specific policy recommendations on the way forward.

(A) Deepen structures for cost-reflective pricing and price responses through carbon and possibly diversity pricing and nodal pricing The most fundamental need is to deepen the institutional structures for cost-reflective pricing, where 'cost' includes environmental impact, diversity benefits and locational considerations, and in which consumers have the information and capacity to react to these.

Specifically, carbon pricing is the fundamental element of effective low-carbon policy. The heart of the climate change problem is the mispricing of damaging atmospheric emissions, and sensible carbon pricing is the basic starting point of any carbon reduction policy. In the short run, it is the central instrument for delivering emission reductions, as long as the UK system remains dominated by a mix of gas and coal

---

[14] See London Energy Partnership (2007).

plants. If sustained and credible in the long run, it provides the deep incentives for ongoing, deeper innovation and continuing emission reductions towards mid-century CO_2 reductions exceeding 80% in the power sector. It is also one basic element of a technology policy which supports the emergence of new and currently unknown technologies on both the supply and demand side.

However, obstacles to effective responses to such price signals also need to be addressed. Consequently we recommend:

1. ***Progressively strengthening the EU ETS***. The EU ETS strikes a balance between the realities of political economy and European-level action, on the one hand, and the ideal of simultaneous harmonised global long-term carbon pricing, on the other. It is the best available vehicle for carbon pricing in the medium term. It needs to be extended and strengthened in subsequent rounds of development and designed to give more robust signals (including greater auctioning and mechanisms to underpin a floor price) and with distinct mechanisms to frame long-term carbon price expectations (Chapter 11).

2. ***Considering technology-neutral economic incentives applied to energy security considerations***, for example, reflecting the risks inherent in over-dependency upon any one source by placing a levy in proportion to the 'concentration' of a given source in the power generation mix (Chapter 4).

3. ***Introducing nodal pricing in the UK power system to deal with congestion and losses***. Fine nodal pricing is a feasible policy option for the UK and becomes easier as time goes on. Nodal pricing reflects the costs and losses associated with transmitting and supplying power. This is particularly important when it comes to siting and accepting power from new wind farms (Chapter 7). Its implementation at the distribution level will assist with both end-use efficiency and distributed generation (Chapter 10).

Note that we place the emphasis on the need to *deepen structures* rather than defining levels, because of the uncertainties set out in Chapters 1 and 2. What matters is that private investors can see robust and credible institutional mechanisms that give conviction to future pricing. The fact of a significant future carbon price needs to be as robust as the fact of a future oil price – however uncertain the actual level of either may be.

(B) Facilitate improved information, expanded access and contractual flexibility through removing restrictions on participation, and

expanding core infrastructure investment The competitive system operates within the constraints set by licensing and contractual regulations, and the infrastructure of the physical system (Chapters 6, 8 and 9), while the ability of consumers to react to price signals depends upon the adequacy of demand-side infrastructure:

4. **Roll-out improved metering technologies across domestic homes and offices.** This will extend market-based signals to currently unreached parts of the demand side. It will assist consumers with both passive and active demand-side/low-carbon investment and behaviour. If associated with a downstream 'carbon reduction commitment' for commercial and public sectors, it will also improve their management practices in response to carbon transparency and price signals (Chapters 8 and 9).

5. **Facilitate more active individual and local community involvement in electricity demand and supply,** by removing regulatory and market impediments to individuals connecting micro-generation and to local councils innovating in the area of setting up public–private energy service companies (which can jointly address siting, demand management, energy poverty, heating and electricity supply issues at the local level). Such a policy offers the potential to harness grass-roots political concern and willingness to pay for innovation for low-carbon technologies. Thereby, consumer or local government environmental concerns can enter as a competitive force, yet with a long-term perspective that supplants State direction as the vehicle for long-term, low-discount-rate investments – and one, moreover, that can also more readily integrate supply and demand considerations (Chapters 8 and 17).

6. **Ensure funding for transmission system upgrades to facilitate generation investment,** particularly in renewable energy in Scotland and the north of England. Transmission bottlenecks between the parts of the country with the greatest natural wind and marine resources need to be improved before significant amounts of new capacity can be added to the system (Chapters 6, 7 and 10).

(C) Expand time-limited, differentiated subsidies for innovation investments through both 'push' and 'pull' mechanisms with strict convergence and exit criteria The analysis of innovation processes in energy technologies emphasises that a viable strategy for the long term must combine both R&D investment and learning-by-doing (Chapters 10, 12, 13 and 15):

7. ***Expand R&D for diverse technologies irrespective of their likely 2020 contribution.*** We need to build understanding of, and options for, carbon capture and storage, wave and tidal, and/or new generation nuclear investment at a commercial scale, starting by 2020. This recognises that deep emission reductions by mid-century can be achieved in many different ways. Such technologies need support sufficient to reach the commercial demonstration plant stage, assuming they do not prove unfeasible at earlier stages. As with carbon pricing, R&D in such technologies is a global public good (or at least has strong spillovers) and equally would benefit from wider (international) burden-sharing arrangements. Present-day decision makers do not have to make a once-and-for-all choice about the different paths. However, prioritisation of UK public sector R&D must be informed by a clear sense of where the UK can contribute most, and potentially gain the most, in the context of global efforts. Once demonstration projects have been developed, capital grants, performance-based supports and the longer-term incentive afforded by robust carbon pricing can then accelerate the take-up of those that prove to be the most commercially attractive and publicly acceptable, whether developed at home or abroad.

8. ***Use differentiated, market-based but time-limited supports for commercialisation and learning-by-doing in new low-carbon industries.*** The EU ETS is insufficient to support the scale of risk-taking involved in these processes. Mechanisms need to be predictable, take due account of the stage of development of particular technologies, and cover a sufficient range of the technologies likely to be important in the long run. Mandated performance-based supports need to differentiate according to the stage of industrial development, otherwise the most developed in any category captures the bulk of economic rents. The evidence suggests that 'feed-in tariffs' that decline over time are the most effective, and probably the most efficient, support mechanism; capital grants could also be used to differentiate support between different technologies. The UK *Energy White Paper* choice of 'banded' Renewable Obligation Certificates with an implicit floor price may also suffice, but its greater complexity and price uncertainty means that it is not the most efficient approach.

These technology policy elements are the most complex and difficult to implement. They offer the most scope for wasteful investment, and hence need to be carefully designed to focus on overcoming the market failures they are designed to address at least cost.

(D) Engage in serious and fundamental debate about the policy implications of time-inconsistency between public policy objectives and liberalised markets, separated from the innovation-related instruments We have underlined that this is a genuine and complex dichotomy, exacerbated by the long time scales of the climate change problem and the capital-intensive nature of all the low-carbon power systems that emerge from our studies. We have also explained why neither renationalisation, nor indiscriminate government subsidy, is the solution. The issue is logically distinct from the external benefits of innovation in particular technologies, and should be separated accordingly. One option is simply to accept the need for a higher carbon price than would be required if time-inconsistency did not exist, which will tend to favour higher energy efficiency as the solution relative to investment in low-carbon power sources. Capital subsidies to low-carbon technologies and long-term carbon or supply contracts (Chapter 11) – underwritten by government from electricity levies or general taxation – could contribute. Enabling more diverse participation and long-term contracting arrangements, including individuals and entities that may be happy to pay 'over the odds' for long-term benefits, offers an additional route.

The key, however, is to acknowledge that solutions exist, that they are many and varied, and that competition, pricing and public choice still need to be at the heart of how we develop solutions. Most of the great mistakes in energy policy have been driven by the assertion that there is no alternative; by a conviction of absolute need that sweeps aside public concerns. In reality, the UK has a diversity of long-run energy options; none are indispensable, even in a carbon-constrained world. Decisions taken on that basis, which engage the public in informed debate on the choices and foster competition around the best solutions, will in the long run be better and more durable decisions. By adopting policies that create the right incentives in its liberalised power system, the UK can demonstrate that low-carbon electricity futures are possible, affordable – and even desirable – to citizens and companies that engage in the challenges of building a low-carbon economy.

Acknowledgements

The authors acknowledge the very helpful comments of the other contributors to the book. However, all the comments expressed in this chapter are the responsibility of the authors of this chapter and do not necessarily represent the views of the other contributors. The authors wish to thank Alexandra Maratou for excellent research assistance.

References

Awerbuch, S. (2003). Determining the real cost: why renewable power is more cost-competitive than previously believed. *Renewable Energy World*, **6**(2), 53–61.

Bode, S. (2006). *On the Impact of Renewable Energy Support Schemes on Power Prices*. HWWI Research Paper 4–7. Hamburg, Germany: Hamburg Institute of International Economics.

Climate Change Institute Australia (2007). *Making the Switch: Australian Clean Energy Policies*. Preliminary Research Report. Climate Change Institute, Sydney, Australia.

Devine-Wright, P. and Devine Wright, H. (2006). Prospect for smart metering in the United Kingdom, in T. Jamasb, W.J. Nuttall and M.G. Pollitt (eds) *Future Electricity Technologies and Systems*. Cambridge: Cambridge University Press, 403–417.

DTI (2006). *The Energy Challenge*. Energy Review Report. London: Department of Trade and Industry. Available from: www.berr.gov.uk/files/file31890.pdf

    (2007a). *Meeting the Energy Challenge: White Paper*. London: Department of Trade and Industry. Available from: www.berr.gov.uk/files/file39387.pdf

    (2007b). *Updated Energy and Carbon Emissions Projections: The Energy White Paper*. London: Department of Trade and Industry. Available from: www.berr.gov.uk/files/file39580.pdf

    (2007c). *Digest of UK Energy Statistics (DUKES)*. London: Department of Trade and Industry. Available from: www.berr.gov.uk/energy/statistics/publications/dukes/page39771.html

    (2007d) *Impact of Banding the Renewables Obligation: Costs of Electricity Production*. London: Department of Trade and Industry. Available from: www.berr.gov.uk/files/file39038.pdf

Eichhammer, W. (2006). End-use technologies – main drivers and patterns of future demand: buildings, in T. Jamasb, W.J. Nuttall and M.G. Pollitt (eds) *Future Electricity Technologies and Systems*, Cambridge: Cambridge University Press, 333–347.

Elders, I., Ault, G., Galloway, S., McDonald, J., Kohler, J., Leach, M., Lampaditou, E. (2006). Electricity network scenarios for the United Kingdom in 2050, in T. Jamasb, W.J. Nuttall and M.G. Pollitt (eds) *Future Electricity Technologies and Systems*. Cambridge: Cambridge University Press, 24–80, 83–98, 348–375.

Florio, M. (2004). *The Great Divestiture: Evaluating the Welfare Impact of British Privatisation*. Cambridge, MA: MIT Press.

Green, R.J. (2007). Nodal pricing of electricity: how much does it cost to get it wrong? *Journal of Regulatory Economics*, **31**(2), 125–114.

Grubb, M., Butler, L., Twomey, P. (2006). Diversity and Security in UK Electricity Generation: The Influence of Low Carbon Objectives. *Energy Policy* **34**(18), 4050–4062.

Helm, D. (2004). *Energy, the State, and the Market: British Energy Policy since 1979*, 2nd edn. Oxford, UK: Oxford University Press.

Howell, D., Nakhle, C. (2007) *Out of the Energy Labyrinth: Uniting Energy and the Environment to Avert Catastrophe.* I B Tauris & Co Ltd.

IEA (2006). *World Energy Outlook.* Paris: International Energy Agency.

Jamasb, T., Nuttall, W.J., Pollitt, M.G. (eds) (2006) *Future Electricity Technologies and Systems.* Cambridge: Cambridge University Press.

Littlechild, S. (2000). *Privatization, Competition and Regulation in the British Electricity Industry, with Implications for Developing Countries.* Washington, DC: ESMAP, The World Bank.

London Energy Partnership (2007) *Making ESCOs Work: Guidance and Advice.* London: Greater London Authority.

MCE (2007). *Smart Meters.* Information Paper on the Development of an Implementation plan for the Roll-out of Smart Meters. Ministerial Council on Energy, Australia.

Morthorst, P.E. (2006). Wind power: status and perspectives, in T. Jamasb, W.J. Nuttall and M.G. Pollitt (eds) *Future Electricity Technologies and Systems.* Cambridge: Cambridge University Press, 83–98.

Newbery, D.M. (2000). *Privatization, Restructuring and Regulation of Network Utilities.* The Walras-Pareto Lectures, 1995. Cambridge, MA: MIT Press.

Patterson, W. (2007). *Keeping the Lights On: Towards Sustainable Electricity.* London: Earthscan Publications.

Price, L., Galitsky, C., Worrell, E. (2006). End-use technologies – main drivers and patterns of future demand: industry, in T. Jamasb, W.J. Nuttall and M.G. Pollitt (eds) *Future Electricity Technologies and Systems.* Cambridge: Cambridge University Press, 348–375.

Stern, N. (2006). *Stern Review: The Economics of Climate Change.* London: HM Treasury.

Sustainability First (2007). *Smart Meters in Great Britain: The Next Steps?* London: Sustainability First.

UKERC (2007). *Investment in Electricity Generation: The Role of Costs, Incentives and Risks.* UK Energy Research Council. Available from: www.ukerc.ac.uk/Downloads/PDF/06/0706_Investing_in_Power.pdf

Vermeyen, P., Belmans, R. (2006). End-use technologies – main drivers and patterns of future demand: transport, in T. Jamasb, W.J. Nuttall and M.G. Pollitt (eds) *Future Electricity Technologies and Systems.* Cambridge: Cambridge University Press, 376–402.

Index